More praise for *Women on the Edge:*

"These sparkling, eminently performable and richly annotated translations are a joy to read, and the introductions—to the volume as a whole as well as to the individual plays—a pleasure to assign! Feminist classical scholarship at its very best."

Judith P. Hallett, Professor of Classics, University of Maryland

"Finally, a translation of four Euripidean plays about women by four women critics who foreground their values and their interpretations and who offer texts that are self-aware and rooted in their social and historical contexts. Attentive to nuances and to fine detail, the translations are close to the Greek yet are presented in lively and compelling English; squarely centered on the figure of woman but very aware of the broader Greek culture that gave rise to these plays. A fine book to share with our students."

Barbara K. Gold, Professor of Classics,
Associate Dean of Faculty, Hamilton College

"*Women on the Edge* is a terrific volume. Clear, accurate translations highlight fifth-century Athens' near-compulsive concern with the relations of gender. This text will be a welcome relief for teachers of 'Women in Antiquity' courses, and should be considered by anyone who sees Greek Tragedy as something more than abstract concepts imprisoned in words on a page."

Kirk Ormand, author of *Exchange and the Maiden:*
Marriage in Sophoclean Drama

THE NEW CLASSICAL CANON

David M. Halperin, editor

Also published in the series:

Three Plays by Aristophanes: Staging Women
Jeffrey Henderson

WOMEN ON THE EDGE

Four Plays by Euripides

Alcestis *Medea* *Helen* *Iphigenia at Aulis*

translated and edited

by

Ruby Blondell

Mary-Kay Gamel

Nancy Sorkin Rabinowitz

Bella Zweig

ROUTLEDGE

New York ◆ London

Published in 1999 by

Routledge
29 West 35th Street
New York, NY 10001

Published in Great Britain by

Routledge
11 New Fetter Lane
London EC4P 4EE

Printed in the United States of America on acid-free paper.

Library of Congress Cataloging-in-Publication Data

Euripides
Women on the edge : four plays / by Euripides ; translated and edited by Ruby Blondell ... [et al.].
p. cm. — (The new classical canon)
Contents: Alcestis — Medea — Helen — Iphigenia at Aulis.
Includes bibliographical references.
ISBN 0-415-90774-8 (hb : alk. paper)
1. Euripides—Translations into English. 2. Greek drama (Tragedy)—Translations into English. 3. Helen of Troy (Greek mythology)—Drama. 4. Iphigenia (Greek mythology)—Drama. 5. Alcestis (Greek mythology)—Drama. 6. Medea (Greek mythology)—Drama. 7. Women—Mythology—Drama. I. Blondell, Ruby. II. Title. III. Series.
PA3975.A2 1998c
882'.01—dc21 98-3992
CIP

This volume is dedicated to our mothers
Hester Whitlock Blundell
Blanche Booker Gamel
Sophie Sorkin
Deborah Zweig

to the memory of BZ's grandmothers, who lived and died on the edge
Chaya Taubenfeld
Mindl Zweig

and to
David Guichard
who helped keep RB from going over the edge

Contents

Preface

The ancient Greek tragedies that have come down to us are all products of a unique historical moment in a specific place: Athens in the latter part of the fifth century BCE. Yet most nineteenth- and early-twentieth-century classical studies in Europe and the United States took an idealizing, universalizing approach to ancient texts. This approach assumed that later readers could understand the characters and situations of Athenian tragedies because of the basic, eternal truths about human nature they contained, truths which—thanks to the artistic genius of individual playwrights—transcended social and cultural differences. The texts of the plays were studied as literary documents sufficient in themselves, with little attention to the fact that they were scripts for performance in a specific cultural milieu. Studies focused on the large philosophical questions raised by tragic texts, and their aesthetic qualities, such as elegant formal structures and beautiful poetry. The surviving plays by the three Athenian dramatists were often grouped together into an entity called "Greek tragedy," both in scholarly studies and in performance.[1] Differences between the plays were regarded as results of the different sensibilities of individual playwrights and the development of the tragic form itself (often influenced by Aristotle's organic metaphor of growth/maturity/decay; *Poetics* 1449a). Little attention was focused on the context in which this form of drama was actually produced and consumed. The fact that most tragic plays feature heroic characters and mythic settings, with few obvious references to Athens, reinforced the sense that they should be understood as "classics" for all time, rather than as documents produced in a particular social, political, and artistic context. To understand these texts, readers were expected to have a broad understanding of philosophy and literature, rather than specific knowledge of Athenian history and institutions. Once the connection with the original historical, social, and performance context of the works was lost, the text was seen as the essential aspect, "a permanent written formulation distinct from, and seen as somehow possessing a timeless validity quite other than, the ephemeral process of writing, reading, enacting or experiencing the work" (Finnegan 1988: 124).

One striking aspect of the Athenian tragic drama of the fifth century BCE is the central importance of women. Of the plays that survive, only one (Sophocles' *Philoktetes*) contains no female characters at all. In Homeric epic, three centuries earlier, males are the central characters, while female figures mostly serve as the objects of the males' quest and help or hinder them in that quest. Female characters in tragedy, however, take actions and raise issues central to the plays in which they appear, sometimes in strong opposition to male characters. Women in tragedy often disrupt "normal" life by their words and actions: they speak out boldly, tell lies, cause public unrest, violate custom, defy orders, even kill. The four plays in this volume offer examples of women who support the status quo and women who oppose and disrupt it. Sometimes these are the same characters. Idealizing readings paid little attention to these issues of sexual difference and gender conflict. In so far as women were considered at all, they were regarded as neutral vessels of meaning, little different from male protagonists: Antigone's "is the pure tragedy of situation" says Kitto (1950: 117), without considering the extent to which her "situation" is determined by such factors as gender and class. Or they were perceived as an absolute Other, innately and essentially different from males: Medea is a "wild-eyed savage" who "expressed the elemental nature of woman untrammelled by Greek conventions" (Jaeger 1945: 345). Plays that focus explicitly on "women's issues" were relegated to second-class status within the corpus of tragic drama.

In the first volume of this series, Jeffrey Henderson complains that comedy has been overlooked because of its "disruptive elements . . . that threaten to complicate, if not undermine, the construction of an idealized Glory of Greece" (Henderson 1996: ix–x). Tragedy has not been overlooked, but now it is being looked over in quite a different way. During the last twenty-five years it has increasingly come to be viewed within the context of Athenian social and political institutions (see, for example, Vernant 1980, Winkler and Zeitlin 1990). And new developments in social history, cultural studies, women's studies, and critical theory have contributed to a less idealizing view of Athenian culture. Research on women's political, economic, and social position in Athens has led to greater awareness of the restrictions on their power in the public sphere. Although women are often represented in tragedy as powerful and free in their thoughts, speech, and actions, real Athenian women were apparently expected to live unseen and silent, under the control of fathers and husbands, with little political or economic power. Why, then, are female figures so prominent in tragedy? This is a paradox that must be addressed if we are to reach an adequate understanding of tragedy in its original context (we shall explore some possible explanations below, pp. 60–62).

Recent approaches have also raised our awareness of the complexities involved in representation—especially state-sponsored representation. Since all the female characters in Athenian tragedy were written and performed by men, for a notional audience of males (below, pp. 62–3), these portrayals cannot be taken as evidence for women's lives at Athens in any straightforward way. Athenian drama has increasingly come to be viewed not as a set of stable documents but as the intersection of such factors as the material conditions of production, the historical, social, and political contexts, and the audience's responses, as well as individual playwrights' visions—factors likely to produce a wide range of meanings, some of them mutually contradictory. Tragic drama's portrayals of female characters, of women's roles in domestic and public spheres, of their relationships to males, and of the various meanings associated with femaleness, are treated by many contemporary scholars as constructions with ideological causes and effects, which offer complex information about the society that produced them.

Although these plays are set in mythical times and non-Athenian locations, they contain references—both subtle and bold—to contemporary Athenian issues, institutions, and events. Audiences at the Festival of Dionysos looked for immediate, topical, ideological meanings in the plays (below, pp. 30–31, 74–6). Yet the mythic characters and settings, the poetry, songs and dances, keep the dramas from becoming simply tracts or allegories. Athenian tragedies mediate between present and past, familiar and alien. The original audience responded to them through the framework of their own culturally constructed interpretive categories. We have tried to respect that framework as far as possible, given the limitations on our knowledge and the different frameworks supplied by our own historical and cultural perspectives. Such an approach to Athenian texts, which views them as complex cultural documents, is not anachronistic and inappropriate, but reflects the spirit in which ancient audiences viewed these works.

Even during his lifetime his contemporaries thought Euripides was specially interested in issues involving women (below, pp. 80–83). This volume gives a broad sample of his plays in which women are a central concern. *Alcestis* is Euripides' earliest extant play (438 BCE), *Iphigenia at Aulis* his latest (406). (The latter will be abbreviated hereafter as *IA*.) *IA* and *Helen* offer perspectives on the Trojan War from both ends, beginning and aftermath. Each play shows women in various roles—slave, unmarried girl, devoted wife, alienated wife, mother, daughter—providing a range of evidence about the kinds of meanings and effects that the category "woman" conveyed in Athens. As our title, "Women on the Edge," suggests, the female protagonists of these plays test the boundaries—literal and conceptual—of their lives. All four plays are set at a geographic or conceptual tangent to "civilized" society (see Map). Helen is in Egypt, a land renowned for mystical knowledge. Medea is a "barbarian" from Colchis on the Black Sea, now living on the margins of Corinthian society. *Alcestis,* located in Thessaly on the northern boundaries of Greece, shows a woman crossing the boundary between life and death in both directions. Aulis, the setting of *IA,* is not physically far from Athens, but the play is balanced between land and sea, private and public responsibilities, peace and war. All four plays test the basic categories within Greek cultural ideology by which roles were defined—Greeks/barbarians, friends/enemies, free citizens/slaves, highborn/lowborn, gods/humans, males/females—and in each case the gender of the protagonist plays a crucial role in questioning those categories. These plays also test the edges of dramatic form by including comic and melodramatic elements as well as tragic seriousness and "classical" structure.

Fredric Jameson has identified the dilemma of reading objects from the past as an alternation between Identity and Difference.

> If we choose to affirm the Identity of the alien object with ourselves . . . our apparent "comprehension" of these alien texts must be haunted by the nagging suspicion that we have all the while remained locked in our own present. . . . Yet if, as the result of such hyperbolic doubt, we decide . . . to affirm the radical Difference of the alien object from ourselves, . . . we find ourselves separated by the whole density of our own culture from objects of cultures thus initially defined as Other from ourselves and thus as irremediably inaccessible. (F. Jameson 1988: 152)

Translations produced under the influence of the idealizing tradition in classical studies tend to affirm the Identity of ancient drama and smooth the rough edges of Difference. They do this by translating alien ideas into terms understandable by a twentieth-century audience and by minimizing explanatory notes, on the assumption that specific cultural details are not important to the meaning, that despite the changes in language and context the Great Ideas will nonetheless make themselves felt.

For example, Rex Warner's translation of *Medea* for *The Complete Greek Tragedies*—by far the most widely used series of translations of Greek tragedy—distorts a particular complex of ideas that is central to the understanding of cultural and gender issues in the play. Warner uses the word "love" to translate a broad range of Greek words, thus obscuring certain significant concepts and the relationships between them. He uses "love" for the Greek *phila* (871), which implies an exchange of benefits between Medea and Jason, including but not limited to erotic and emotional ties (see further below, pp. 22–4). But the word "love" is inappropriate here, threatening to reduce ethical obligations to sentimental ties. He also translates as "love" the Greek *erōs* (which refers primarily to passionate sexual desire), *gamos* (the standard Greek term for marriage), and various Greek words meaning "bed." His translation thus equates the marriage-bed with sexual "love" or *erōs,* implying that Medea is motivated simply through sexual jealousy. Warner reproduces on the interpretive level the misogynistic assumption of Greek society, embodied in Jason within the play, that women are obsessively and irrationally preoccupied with sex. In Greek culture, however, the bed is a symbol not just of sexual activity, but of the marriage bond itself. Jason's betrayal of Medea is not merely sexual, but is a violation of loyalty. Such loyalty is fundamental both to the institution of marriage, with all its social and cultural implications, and to the very possibility of human trust and cooperation. The bed thus carries potent ethical as well as sexual significance, and is the symbolic locus for the interplay of a complex of cultural issues concerning sex, gender, marriage, trust, loyalty, and betrayal. Warner's translation both obscures all this and imposes on Greek culture the inappropriate connotations of romantic love, for which there is no Greek equivalent.

The translations in this volume are intended to help readers locate these plays within their original social, cultural, and performance contexts. We cannot do this without acknowledging our own location within history, within ideology. We are all white English-speaking feminist women over the age of forty, teaching courses in ancient Greek culture at American universities. As such our outlooks have much in common. But we are also marked by cultural and intellectual differences which inform our contributions to this book. We vary in our feminisms (e.g., NSR combines psychoanalytic and structuralist approaches), our expertise (e.g., BZ has a special interest in ritual), our attitudes toward drama (e.g., M-KG is actively involved in performance) and toward translation (e.g., RB has chosen to use meter). The reader will find our various interests reflected in the introduction and notes to each play. In keeping with our commitment to pluralities of interpretation, we have not imposed a uniform style or format on the translations, which accordingly vary in such matters as their degree of literalness and consistency, and the number and specificity of stage directions. We hope this will make our readers aware of the many different kinds of interpretive decision that are involved in any translation, and make them critical readers not only of the plays, but of the process of translation itself.

Our challenge in this volume is to mediate between ancient and modern ideologies, not pretending a "value-free" understanding, but acknowledging the force of our desire—as classicists and as women—to make connections that may illuminate both the ancient texts and our own lives. We have tried to leave the edges sharp, by producing translations that preserve the alterity of language, concepts, institutions, and modes of presentation. Drawing on the rich store of scholarship on these plays, we have provided footnotes and introductions to help nonspecialist readers understand the plays more fully, focusing especially on Athenian social and cultural institutions and gender relations. Rather than offering a single reading of each play, each translator has attempted—sometimes against her own convictions—to provide various options for readers' interpretation and response. This attempt seems appropriate both to the texts' complexity, ambiguity, and interpretive possibilities, and to the range of readers we hope will use this volume.

Our focus on the topical meanings the plays may have had in their original context is not meant to imply that these are the true or only meanings, or to close out other interpretations. Instead, attention to the context of performance—a material event embodied in history—reminds us that meaning (even that which seems to us universal and timeless) is always part of a historical process. Instead of trying to achieve a "value-free" understanding of the ancient world and its texts, "we need to take into account the possibility that our contact with the past will always pass through the imaginary and through its ideologies" (Jameson 1988: 152). We believe that more careful attention to the Difference in these texts will actually allow the Identity to emerge more clearly.

In our transcription of Greek names, we have tried to steer a path between familiarity to the modern reader and our desire to defamiliarize ancient Athenian culture. Although perfect consistency is impossible, we have in general used the following criteria: Names of well-known ancient persons and places are printed in the form in which they can be found in familiar works of reference (e.g., Sophocles, Pericles, Athens). Names of ancient works have been translated. Names of mythical characters have been transliterated, but only in so far as this is consistent with the most usual modern English pronunciation (e.g., Elektra, Jason). Other Greek words have been transliterated accurately (e.g., *ekhthros*) except for commonly used technical terms (e.g., *stichomythia*). Inevitably, however, there have been some ad hoc exceptions to these general rules.

All of us have read the entire manuscript, but each of the four authors remains fully responsible for the translation, introduction, and notes to her particular play. The general introduction to the volume was prepared collectively, with each of us drafting a portion of it, but it was rewritten by Ruby Blondell and Mary-Kay Gamel. The resulting version was revised again by Ruby Blondell, with final editing by all four of us.

We thank our readers for their support and advice, especially the series editor, David M. Halperin, and the students in Ruby Blondell's Greek drama course in the fall of 1997, who made many useful suggestions for improving the general introduction.

Ruby Blondell
University of Washington
Mary-Kay Gamel
University of California, Santa Cruz
Nancy Sorkin Rabinowitz
Hamilton College
Bella Zweig
University of Arizona

INTRODUCTION

The Eastern Mediterranean and Environs

Mainland Greece

I. ATHENS AND GREEK CULTURE

Political History

The form of mass entertainment commonly known as "Greek" tragedy was not a widespread phenomenon but a peculiarly Athenian art form, closely associated with the life of a particular *polis* ("city-state") at a particular time, namely Athens in the latter part of the fifth century (500–400) BCE.[1] Many dramas from this so-called "classical" period of Athenian culture have found resonances in other times and places. But in their original form and conditions of production they are deeply rooted in Athenian history and in its social, political, and religious institutions. We know of nothing comparable in other ancient Greek states.

Athens was one of many small independent city-states scattered throughout the rocky peninsulas and islands of ancient Greece, many of them inhabited since Mycenean times (c. 1500 BCE). A city-state consisted of a fortified settlement together with the surrounding land and its inhabitants. Most city-states were centered on a defensible location to which citizens could retreat if attacked. In Athens, this central citadel was the Athenian Acropolis, a rocky outcropping at the center of the city. It is here that Euripides' plays were first performed, in a theater on the sloping side of the Acropolis hill, at the very heart of the city. The Acropolis in modern Athens is still covered with some of the most famous buildings of antiquity. The best known of these is the Parthenon—the great temple of Athena—which has become universally recognizable as a symbol of "the glory that was Greece." Few modern tourists realize, however, that this and other Greek temples were once brightly painted in complex patterns and glowing colors. The loss of these designs is an apt metaphor for the complex, colorful, cultural specificity that has been stripped away from the ancient Greeks by modern idealization of the classical world.

Each ancient Greek *polis* was a sovereign political entity. The different city-states had widely varying forms of government and there were no regular alliances among them. Citizens identified themselves closely with their own particular *polis.* Different city-states, such as Athens and Sparta, prided themselves on their own customs, politics, and general outlook. At the same time, the ancient Greeks were very much aware of themselves as a culturally distinct group. Though different regions spoke different dialects, they were all Greek speakers, as opposed to non-Greek-speaking "barbarians" (below, pp. 22–3). Myths, religion, poetry, and art all contributed to Greek self-definition by exploring what Greeks saw as distinctive about themselves. Certain pan-Hellenic ("all-Greek") cultural institutions contributed to this sense of collective Greek identity. Prominent among these were the Delphic Oracle, which was consulted by the entire Greek world, and the Olympic Games, where the various city-states vied with each other for prestige. (Delphi and Olympia are marked on the Map.)

An especially significant culturally unifying role was played by the two Homeric epics, the *Iliad* and *Odyssey.* These poems were not composed in a single Greek dialect, but in an artificial hodge-podge of dialects transcending any specific local culture. They grew out of many centuries of oral transmission, and probably reached their present form around the end of the eighth century BCE. Although they sang of Mycenaean Greek heroes from half a millennium earlier, their continuing circulation provided later Greeks with a unified view of their cultural heritage, and their versions of the heroic tales became by far the most influential. Boys whose fathers could afford to send them to school learned to recite extensive passages from Homer, and adult citizens heard the epics recited at festival competitions by professional singers known as rhapsodes. It is impossible to overestimate the importance of these poems for all kinds of Greek cultural products, including Athenian tragedy.

Until the end of the sixth century Athens was ruled by warring clans, whose wealthy aristocratic leaders controlled feudal alliances bound to them by economic and personal ties. In the Archaic period (seventh and sixth centuries BCE) many city-states underwent political revolutions, in which powerful individual aristocrats seized power with the support of the community at large, and succeeded in gaining sole rule as "tyrants." The most notable tyrant of Athens was Peisistratus, who seized power in 546. The Greek word *turannos* does not have the intrinsically negative valence of the English "tyrant," originally meaning simply "sole ruler" (compare below, p. 26). Like many other Greek "tyrants," Peisistratus was a benevolent ruler and a lavish supporter of art and poetry. He built many public monuments and reinforced religious cults and festivals. Most significantly for our purposes, he is said to have expanded the Greater Dionysia, the festival of Dionysos at which the tragedies were performed (see further below, pp. 30–33).

In 508 the last Athenian tyrant was overthrown and a limited form of democracy established. One of the most important aspects of the new system was the reorganization of the citizen body into ten groups known as "tribes," which became the primary units for political and military purposes. The term "tribe" is misleading, however, since these were not kinship groups. Each tribe was designed to cut across various social and economic groupings, thus inducing greater harmony among the various factions in the *polis.* Throughout the century that followed—in which all the surviving tragedies were produced—Athens became increasingly democratic.

Athens was not the only ancient democracy, but it was by far the most radical and influential, and it is the only one about which we have extensive information. "Democracy" literally means "rule by the *dēmos,*" i.e., by the Athenian male citizen body (women, children, slaves, and foreigners were excluded).[2] The *dēmos* wielded power through the Assembly, consisting of all free male Athenian citizens, which decided important policy matters. Every member of the *dēmos* could both speak and vote in the Assembly, making Athens a "direct" democracy, in contrast to the "representative" system of most modern democracies. The Assembly's business was prepared by the Council (the Boule), a group of five hundred citizens drawn equally from all ten tribes. Every day a different Council member presided over the Assembly. Many offices were filled not by election but by lot, giving every citizen who wished to run an equal chance of winning. Athenian citizens also served on juries, some as large as five hundred or more, which tried the numerous public and private court cases. They thus had many opportunities to participate in the processes of law and government, and were expected to serve if called upon. The democratic procedures of the Assembly and the courts also fostered the art of skilled oratorical display, of which the Athenians became connoisseurs.

Not all adult male citizens were able to participate equally in the democracy for various reasons, such as residence outside the city, or lack of money, education, or rhetorical skill. So in practice, aristocratic families continued to exert a great deal of influence. Military commanders and holders of high office came predominantly from the wealthy classes (both aristocrats and newcomers). Nevertheless, these leaders remained answerable to "the people" and were carefully scrutinized. The performance of every officeholder was subject to review after completion of his term; wealthy citizens had to work hard to gain and maintain the confidence of their fellow citizens, and they were subject to ostracism (temporary exile) for failing this trust.

During the sixth century BCE the rich, mighty Persian Empire had been gradually expanding westward (see Map). In the early fifth century, the Persians twice invaded Greek territory. Together, the two strongest Greek states—Athens, with a large fleet of ships, and Sparta, commanding a powerful land army—led the greatly outnumbered Greeks to victory over the Persians. These "Persian Wars" (490, 480–78 BCE) were a formative event in the history of Athens. For centuries afterward, writers and politicians would look back at this period as the "good old days" of Athenian valor and moral rectitude.

Euphoric at their victory over the Persians, and seeing it as proof of the superiority of themselves and their political system, the Athenians organized a Greek alliance to prevent future invasion. This alliance, known as the Delian League, was funded by tribute paid to Athens in the form of ships or money. Athens became increasingly dominant, seizing new territory and forcing its "allies" into subjection. The tribute collected was used in part to finance a major Athenian building program, which resulted in many of the great artistic and architectural monuments of fifth-century Athens, including the Parthenon. Discontent grew among other members of the Delian League, as what was nominally an alliance became *de facto* an Athenian empire. Other states, outside the alliance, also feared Athens' growing power. The only other Greek *polis* with a strong fleet was Corinth, in the northern Peloponnesus (the setting of *Medea*). Corinth controlled lucrative western trade routes to Sicily and Italy, and came into conflict with Athens several times. But the only state with the power to match Athens was Sparta, head of another alliance known as the Peloponnesian League. After various skirmishes and shifting alliances, war broke out in 431 BCE, when Sparta, with its allies, was finally persuaded by Corinth to march against Athens and its allies.

Pericles, the leading Athenian politician at the time, predicted a speedy Athenian victory. But he was wrong. The fact that Sparta's power was primarily land-based, and that of Athens depended on its navy, meant there was little opportunity for a decisive engagement. Instead, the war consisted largely of annual raids against each other's territory, which caused great suffering without leading to a conclusive outcome. The Athenians were worn down by repeated destruction of their crops, overcrowding within the city walls, depletion of their financial reserves, and a terrible plague that killed many people, including Pericles.

In 421 a fifty-year peace was declared, but war erupted again in 418. And in 415 the Athenians launched an expedition to conquer the wealthy but distant island of Sicily. The departure of this expedition was marred by acts of religious sacrilege and political scandal, and it ended in 413 in complete disaster. Most of the Athenian army were killed, and the fleet was destroyed. After this appalling débacle many

Athenian allies defected, and Sparta began building a new fleet, financed in part by the powerful Persian Empire. For their part, the Persians hoped to wrest control from Athens of Greek cities on the mainland of Asia Minor. Athens rebounded surprisingly well from this grim situation, instituting financial reforms and rebuilding its navy. An anti-democratic revolution in 411 was short-lived. The Athenians regained control of the sea, which did much to restore morale, and in 406 won a decisive victory against a superior naval force at Arginusae. The Spartans sent an embassy to Athens proposing peace, with each side to keep the territories it held, but the Athenians rejected this proposal and the war continued.

After the battle of Arginusae a storm prevented the rescue of survivors and the recovery of the bodies of the Athenian dead. This caused intense resentment at Athens, and the eight generals who were responsible were put on trial. Even though such collective trials were illegal at Athens, all the generals were condemned to death by a single vote, without being allowed to speak in their own defense. In 405 the Spartans attacked the Athenian fleet at Aegospotami near the Hellespont, the route through which crucial grain supplies reached Athens. Because the Athenians' best generals had been executed, the Spartans captured most of their ships and occupied nearby cities. When the news came of this disaster, wailing began throughout Athens,

> one man passing the word to another, so that on that night no one slept. They wept not only for the men who had been killed but far more for themselves, thinking that they would suffer the kind of fate they had imposed on the Melians, the Histiaeans, the Scionaeans, the Toronaeans, the Aeginetans, and many other Greeks. (Xenophon, *Hellenica* 2.2.3)

That fate was the slaughter of the men, the enslavement of women and children, and the razing of the city. As the chorus in *IA* imagine what lies ahead for the Trojans (788–93), at least some in the audience at Athens must have feared that the same fate was approaching themselves.

A Spartan land army marched to the walls of Athens, while a fleet entered its harbor. The Spartans were now in a position to starve the Athenians into surrender. The Athenians opened peace negotiations. Sparta's allies wanted to inflict the traditional punishment on Athens, but the Spartans demurred. Instead, Athens was forced to abandon its overseas possessions, surrender its fleet, and accept domination by Sparta. In April 404, Spartan troops began demolishing Athens' fortifications "to the music of flute girls and with great rejoicing, since they thought that day was the beginning of freedom for Greece" (Xenophon, *Hellenica*

2.2.23). The democracy was overturned by the Spartan victors and replaced with an oligarchic government of thirty Athenian aristocrats sympathetic to Sparta. But these "thirty tyrants," as they are known, ruled with horrifying brutality, and democracy was restored almost immediately, in the following year. Thereafter Athens continued as an independent democracy until 338, when it was conquered by Philip of Macedon (father of Alexander the Great) and absorbed into the Macedonian empire.

Athens' economy was originally and remained principally agricultural. But capitalization and trade gradually increased, leading to the formation of a propertied merchant class and an increase in foreign residents. These developments were promoted by Athens' fine natural harbor and rich silver mines to the south. The domestic work performed by women, especially the manufacture of fabrics, was a further crucial "hidden" aspect of the economy (below, pp. 58–9). The Athenian economy, like that of every other ancient Mediterranean society, was also dependent on slave labor. Like the founders of American democracy, the Athenians found freedom for some consistent with enslavement of others. Slaves were used for every kind of work, including domestic labor, manufacturing, and mining. Male and female slaves were routinely taken in war. Other sources included piracy and to a lesser extent home breeding (see further Garlan 1988). Most slaves, but not all, were non-Greeks from the north or east. Aristotle, an influential philosopher of the fourth century BCE, argues that "some men are by nature free, and others slaves"; the latter are inferior in intelligence, and for them, "slavery is both beneficial and just" (*Politics* 1255a). On this subject, like many others, Aristotle's views are a sophisticated development of ordinary opinion. But he also mentions thinkers who believed slavery was unnatural and unjust. Opinions also varied about whether it was appropriate to enslave fellow Greeks, as opposed to non-Greek-speaking foreigners (compare *IA* 1400–1401).

Religion

Greek religion was pragmatic. Ritual practice—such as performing the right sacrifice on the right day—was more important than theology, or faith in a canonical tradition or dogmatic set of beliefs. There were no sacred scriptures or codified articles of faith (except within private "mystery" cults, open only to initiates). Ritual formed part of a reciprocal exchange between mortals and the gods, who were believed to bestow gifts on human beings in exchange for their worship. It was important to ensure the continuing favor of the gods, since they might punish humans for failure to win their good will. Many rituals are therefore aimed at averting their displeasure.

The gods included divinities of both genders, who oversaw a wide range of areas of human life, including maturation, marriage, sexuality, fertility, material abundance, law, government, the arts, medicine, warfare and social relationships. Worship of the major pan-Hellenic Olympian deities, such as Zeus, Hera, Dionysos, Athena, Demeter, Artemis, and Apollo, predominated in public contexts, but reverence for local divinities, spirits, and semi-divine heroes was also extremely important. Any phenomenon that seemed stronger and more enduring than human beings (e.g., wind, water, sex, wine, salt) might be viewed as divine and treated accordingly.

For all its political, artistic and intellectual experimentation, Athens remained a traditional society where "everyday private life, no less than public civic life, was rhythmically regulated by all kinds of rituals, so that every moment and every stage of the Greek citizen's existence was intimately imbued with a religious dimension" (Zaidman and Pantel 1992: 27–28).[3] Such ritual practices are mentioned or enacted repeatedly in drama, including the plays in this volume, which include prayers, oaths, supplications, sacrifices, offerings, and evocation of girls' transition rites. Religious purity entailed active observance of bathing, fasting, silence, or seclusion before battle, hunting, or certain rituals, and after birth or death (hence the need for Alcestis' veiled silence after her return; see *Alcestis* 1144–46 with note). There was also a religious dimension to activities that we might not view as religious in and of themselves, such as athletic, poetic, and dramatic competitions. Major pan-Hellenic and Athenian festivals—e.g., the Eleusinian Mysteries for Demeter and Persephone, the Olympian Games for Zeus, the Athenian Panathenaea for Athena and City Dionysia for Dionysos—engaged the spiritual, athletic, and creative energies of the celebrants for personal and civic purposes.

Prayers were offered daily in the home, to the hearth goddess Hestia and other family divinities. Prayers also preceded all important activities, not only formal rituals, but the opening of the Assembly, legal trials, military endeavors, and other public events. They were also spontaneously uttered as the need arose. Such prayers both thanked and sought to propitiate the gods, reminding them of past aid and of their human devotees' past and promised offerings. Elaborated into songs, hymns in praise of the gods became an important offering by poets, by the choruses singing them, and by the community hearing them. Many choral odes in drama offer hymns of praise to particular divinities in this fashion.

Libations (poured offerings of liquids) accompanied most prayers and were important in many rituals, including rites for the dead. They were also used to seal oaths and other pacts. Treaties are therefore called *spondai,* a word that literally denotes the libations poured to seal the truce (see *IA* 60 with note; *Medea* 898 with note). Votive offerings were dedicated in gratitude to the gods for the attainment of a prayer or vow—e.g. for successful childbirth, recovery from illness, military victory, or business success—and on certain ritual occasions, such as birth, marriage, and death. These offerings might consist of clothing, clay figurines, gold tripods, statues, or even a temple. After the successful expedition of the Argonauts, Jason hangs up the prow of his ship, the Argo, as a votive offering to the goddess Hera (see *Medea* 1388 with note).

The offering of sacrifice to the gods was central to ancient Greek religion. Animal sacrifice was both a commonplace part of life and a locus of many meanings, social as well as religious.[4] It negotiated the proper relationship between human, animal, and god on a symbolic level. Recent work drawing on comparative anthropology has focused on Greek sacrifice as a complex structure that both binds and separates. Thus Vernant says,

> in a ritual that seeks to join the mortal with the immortal it consecrates the unattainable distance that henceforth separates them . . . it seats man in his proper place . . . midway between the savagery of animals who devour each other's raw flesh, and the immutable felicity of the gods who know nothing of hunger, pain and death. (1991: 280)

Human sacrifice was not part of Greek cultural practice, though like many taboo behaviors it occurs prominently in myth, where it is presented as an appalling perversion of the proper order of things (see *IA,* and *Medea* 1053–55 with note). Athenian tragedy has strong formal connections to Greek sacrifice and may even have originated from it (Burkert 1966).

Elaborate rituals sanctioned the sacrificial animal's death, which was needed for human survival and simultaneously gave honor to the gods. These rituals were governed by precise rules (see Burkert 1983: 3–7, van Straten 1995). Participants bathed, dressed in special garments, wore garlands, and moved toward the altar in procession, singing. The victim had to be a beautiful, valuable specimen, "blameless" (not damaged or worn down by work), preferably large, usually male. Special decorations such as garlands demonstrated the honor shown to it. Great care was taken to show that the victim "assented" to the sacrifice. For example, it was sprinkled with water so that it would nod or bow its head in symbolic acquiescence in its own death. Burkert (1983) and Vernant (1991: ch. 17) call these procedures a "comedy of innocence," which they believe allayed the guilt feelings of the sacrificers and enabled them to avoid retribution for the killing.

The sacrificial climax was dramatic. When the victim received its death blow the women participants raised the *ololugmos,* a piercing cry employed by women at moments of high emotion, such as victory in battle. Blood from the animal's slashed throat spilled onto the altar. The corpse was disembowelled and dismembered, the internal organs scrutinized for signs of divine approval or disapproval, and certain portions burned on the altar as a gift to the gods. The gods were said to enjoy the savory smell of the sacrifice, rising in the form of smoke from the altar. But they received only the thighbones wrapped in fat. The ritual concluded with the cooking of the slaughtered animal's meat for human consumption, and a communal feast. The meat was cut up, roasted or boiled, and shared among the participants, who usually included large numbers of fellow citizens, friends and family members. Greek sacrifice thus did not effect a wholesale destruction of the animal, or carry any suggestion of deprivation (as with the modern English word "sacrifice"). On the contrary, the occasion was more like a holiday barbecue, uniting the community and affirming their group identity as each individual shared in the emotions of the killing, the ritualization of the act, and the celebration of the feast. The death of the victim thus served the life of the community.

Burkert (1983) also argues for deep connections between sacrifice and hunting, a human activity that long predates agriculture. Like sacrifice, hunting creates a human bond by directing aggression against an appropriate object. Like sacrifice, it is an activity aimed to preserve life, yet also necessarily involves the taking of life. This paradox is enhanced by the perception that predators and prey are similar and deeply connected to one another—a perception perhaps based on the careful observation of the prey, and even identification with it, which are crucial to the success of the hunt. Rituals associated with hunting and sacrifice often seem to have as their intent the defusing of this paradox. So hunting often involves acts of atonement and reparation to the prey, just as sacrifice glorifies the victim and attempts to demonstrate its compliance. Like sacrifice, the collective aggression involved in the hunt establishes a strong connection between the group of hunters, a clear distinction between predator and prey, and a hierarchy confirming the greater importance of the predator and his right to take life. Careful rules established for the hunt ensure that death does not extinguish life and that the hunters do not suffer retribution for their violent act.

Another way in which the presence of the gods was felt in Greek life was through the institution of the oath. Oaths were of ancient origin and authority, and were used at all kinds of significant and solemn moments in an attempt to guarantee good faith. They are primarily associated with the public, male realm, for example in cementing a relationship of guest-friendship (below, p. 21). Oathbreakers were subject to divine wrath, especially from Zeus Horkios (Zeus as guardian of oaths), the ancient goddess Earth, and Helios the sun, who sees everything (compare below, pp. 160–61).

> In the institution of the oath, religion, morality, and the very organization of society appear indissolubly linked together. Its function is to guarantee that a statement is absolutely binding, whether it be a statement about something in the past or a declaration of intent for the future. In a culture without writing where there are no records to act as proof, no legal documents, this function is of unique importance. Nevertheless, in the ancient high civilizations, the written word made only slow progress against the oath and never entirely displaced it. (Burkert 1985: 250; see also Dover 1974: 248–50)

At the same time, there was a range of religious outlooks in Athens during this period. Widespread ritual practice does not signify universal belief. Ancient sources assume that the kind and degree of belief in traditional myths will vary according to gender, age, and education (Buxton 1994: 160–65). Philosophers and intellectuals criticized the nature and behavior of the traditional gods and the effectiveness of ritual. Such skepticism is strongly associated with the sophists ("experts"), a varied group of intellectuals who emerged in the fifth century BCE. The sophists traveled the Greek world selling their services as teachers of higher education. Most of them were not Athenians, but they gravitated toward Athens as the principal Greek center of culture and ideas. They taught many different kinds of subjects and had different specializations, but nearly all of them offered courses in rhetoric, the art of verbal persuasion. The flourishing democracy at Athens provided fertile ground for the teaching of rhetoric as a means to political success. Little has survived of the sophists' writings, but we know that several of them questioned traditional values and beliefs, including attitudes toward women and foreigners. They were particularly interested in the distinction between "nature" and "convention" (Greek *phusis* and *nomos*), which has important implications for such issues as the construction of gender. Many writers were influenced by the sophists, including Euripides. The philosopher Socrates, Plato's teacher and inspiration, also shared some of their interests, and is linked with both them and Euripides by Aristophanes (below, p. 68). Other evidence, especially that of Plato, suggests that in many ways Socrates was quite different from the sophists. But like them he was perceived as a threat to the status quo. Though his unconventional beliefs and behavior were tolerated for many years, in the politically charged atmosphere after the end of the Peloponnesian War he was brought to trial for "corrupting the youth" and for unconventional religious beliefs, and he was executed in 399 BCE.

Fate and Responsibility

One aspect of Greek religion is especially important for understanding Greek culture generally and tragedy in particular, namely the way in which the complex relationship between gods and mortals affects questions of human moral responsibility. This is a murky area for modern readers, not just because of specific cultural differences between the Greeks and ourselves (though these are important), but because thousands of years of interpretation have distorted some central concepts and given them wide currency in a highly misleading form.

This is, of course, a complex area, about which a great deal might be said. But certain concepts stand out as essential to a culturally sensitive reading of Athenian tragedy. One of these is the concept of fate. The English word "fate" has exerted a pernicious influence on modern readers of Greek literature. No single Greek word carries the connotations of "fate" in English. Further, the Greek words that are translated this way do not have the connotations concerning predestination and free will that have clustered around "fate" in the intervening two and a half millennia. The same applies to other words, like "doom," which may suggest predestination to the modern mind, but often translate Greek words meaning simply "disaster."

The most straightforward Greek word for "fate" is *moira*. This literally means "share" or "portion," and nearly always refers to one's "allotted share" of life, or life span, and hence to the day of one's death, or more simply, death itself (e.g., *Medea* 861, 987, 1280, *Alcestis* 523). It is only by tricking the goddesses known as the Fates, or Moirai, that Apollo is able to save Admetos from dying on his appointed day (*Alcestis* 11–12). For each of us, the day of our death is our "allotted" fate. But that does not mean we are not free to make choices about our future, or to plan and carry out our own actions. The indisputable fact that we will all die one day does not mean we are predestined to live in a certain way or cannot be held responsible for our actions. The issues of divine foreknowledge, free will, and predestination which have preoccupied Christian theology are simply not problems for most Greek thinkers and writers. And tragedy in particular places enormous emphasis on active human choice (below, pp. 17–18).

By extension, *moira* may be used for other terrible events, such as the death of close family members (e.g., *Medea* 995). Other words meaning death or disaster are also sometimes translated as "fate," in the loose sense that the word may also bear in English, whereby any disaster may be called "a terrible fate" (e.g., *Medea* 1218). Another specific word often misleadingly translated as "fate" is *tukhē*. This word, which is related to a verb meaning "hit" or "meet," is better translated as "chance" or "fortune" (whether good fortune or bad). These two meanings may seem at odds with each other, but in Greek cultural terms they are two sides of the same coin. *Tukhē,* sometimes personified as a divine force, is the cause of anything unexpected or out of one's control, whether good or bad. From a human perspective, such things seem random and unpredictable. But from a divine or a scientific perspective they are perfectly understandable and in principle predictable. An earthquake, for example, may seem like a terrifyingly random event to most human beings, but it is understandable or even inevitable when viewed as the will of the earthquake god Poseidon, or as the outcome of a geophysical process such as plate tectonics.

A key factor in the concept of *tukhē,* as with *moira,* is human ignorance. These words denote events that will happen to us, but that we cannot precisely predict or control. This ignorance is intrinsic to the human condition. When a human being can predict such things, like Medea at the end of her play (1386–88), it is a sign of superhuman status. This applies above all to death. A defining feature of humanity—*the* defining feature, in contrast to the gods—is that one day we must die. And the normal condition of humanity is ignorance of that day. According to one Greek myth, this ignorance is a blessing, bestowed upon us by Prometheus, who took away our ability to foresee our death by implanting in us blind hope (Aeschylus, *Prometheus Bound* 248–51).

Just as the role of "fate" in Greek thinking is often misconstrued, so too is the role of the gods in the everyday lives of human beings. As we have seen, ancient Greek life was pervaded at every level by divinities of many different sorts, ranging from Zeus, king of the gods, down to the local nymphs who inhabit trees and springs (above, pp. 10–11). These divinities are viewed as actively involved in human activities of all kinds. Unlike Christianity, Greek religion sees divine behavior as a cause of evil as well as good in human lives. People who suffer serious misfortunes may therefore be said to have the gods against them, or, in a common phrase, to have a bad *daimōn* ("divinity"). The word *daimōn,* when used in this way, may also be translated as "fate" (e.g., *Medea* 711, 966, 1189, 1347, *IA* 1136).

The gods often intervene in human lives by inspiring a person with specific thoughts, feelings, or attitudes. This leads to actions which may be simultaneously ascribed to human choice. Thus Helen ran off with Paris because she fell in love with him, and also because the goddess Aphrodite (who had promised her to Paris) caused her to do so. In effect, these are two different ways of describing the same event, since Aphrodite is the divine embodiment of sexual desire. This way of looking at things is sometimes called "double determination," meaning that an event is viewed as "doubly" determined or caused, i.e., simultaneously caused on both divine and human levels. Such divine interventions normally do not violate human character, but express and define it. If a god fills you with strength or lust, this is a manifestation of *your* power or desire. A crucial feature of this way of looking at the world is that in Greek thought, the fact that a god causes one do something does *not* excuse one from ultimate responsibility (though it may arouse pity or sympathy). If Helen fell in love with Paris and chose to go with him under the influence of Aphrodite, she is still responsible for that choice and may still be blamed for it. Hence Helen is portrayed in the *Iliad* as coerced by Aphrodite but still as blaming herself (below, p. 223). The converse also applies. If a divinity causes one to do something admirable, one still receives credit for that action.

By Euripides' time, these attitudes toward divine causation and responsibility were being questioned by some thinkers, especially the sophists (above, p. 14). One of the most famous sophists was Gorgias, a contemporary of Euripides, who wrote a speech in defense of Helen. He argued, among other things, that Helen was not responsible for going to Troy if she was caused to do so by a god. This kind of argument challenges the traditional world-picture of "double determination." The influence of such challenges is reflected in places in tragedy where double determination seems to be denied. Thus in *Medea,* Jason denies Medea credit for helping him, on the grounds that Aphrodite, who made her fall in love with him, was really responsible (526–28). In most periods of ancient Greek culture, however, and in most social and intellectual strata, the philosophical issues of free will and predestination did not present themselves as problems. Most importantly, arguments like that of Gorgias were not taken seriously by ordinary people. Rather, they were viewed as shocking, since they undermined the whole concept of human accountability. Even Gorgias describes his speech, in the final sentence, as a "joke" or "amusement" (*paignion*). So when Euripidean characters use such arguments, most audience members probably thought that they detracted from the characters' moral credibility and intellectual seriousness.

The issue of responsibility for action is crucial for understanding Athenian tragedy, since the plays often focus on decisive moments of human choice, which receive enormous dramatic emphasis. If humans are viewed as puppets of the gods, with no meaningful ability to choose or act freely, then much of the significance of the dramatic action is undermined. It is also important from a feminist perspective. Much feminist scholarship has been devoted to uncovering areas of female agency throughout history, even in cultures that deny women many opportunities for public action. But as Gorgias' speech in defense of Helen makes very clear, a philosophical outlook that denies human responsibility in general is also denying any agency to women in particular. Gorgias defends Helen's innocence not by arguing that she did not do what she was accused of, or that she had the right to self-determination and the free exercise of sexual choice, but by making her an entirely passive victim. He thus reinscribes philosophically the passivity that Greek gender norms prescribe as desirable for women in general. Such is the price of Helen's exculpation. It is perhaps no coincidence that Gorgias uses this strategy in "defending" a woman rather than a male offender such as Paris. (His speech in defense of Palamedes, a mythological male hero accused of treachery, employs a completely different strategy.) A similar price, which extends to both genders, is paid by modern interpreters who ascribe to tragic characters an absence of real choice.

Another common misconception about the Greek gods is that they always enforce human morality. Specifically, tragedy is often assumed to portray the divine punishment of a human being for some offense. There certainly are dramas of divine punishment (e.g., Aeschylus' *Agamemnon,* Euripides' *Hippolytos* and *Bacchants*). Yet the extension of this model to all Athenian tragedies involves a number of misunderstandings. Most importantly, the texts that have come down to us display an enormous variety of attitudes toward the gods and their relationship to human morality. One of these—but only one—is that the gods, under the leadership of Zeus, enforce a form of general justice (Greek *dikē*) in the universe. This view is memorably, if problematically, explored in Aeschylus' *Oresteia.* At other times (as in *Hippolytos* and *Bacchants*), when a god punishes a mortal it is because a specific god has been offended and exacts a personal punishment. Other gods may be indifferent or actively hostile to the punishment in question. In such cases, the gods often follow the same morality as human beings, helping their friends and harming their enemies (below, pp. 20–21). But none of these attitudes can be assumed to hold good in any text in which they are not explicitly articulated. Do the gods share human moral standards, ignore them, enforce them? All these views are presented in many different variants in surviving Greek texts. No single outlook toward the gods or their relationship to mortals can be presumed.

Further, the gods themselves are numerous and far from monolithic in their own outlooks. Though they are often referred to in convenient collective form as "the gods," this should not blind us to the fact that they can, and often do, disagree on all kinds of things. Theonoe in *Helen* refers to strife among the gods regarding the future of Helen and Menelaos (878–86). Two gods quarrel in the prologue of *Alcestis,* where Apollo also describes a dispute between himself and Zeus. Human morality is no exception to this diversity of divine opinion. The chorus and Jason assume that Medea's infanticide is abhorrent to the gods and deserving of divine punishment (*Medea* 1251–57, 1323–28, 1372–73, 1389–90, 1405–7). Yet she is saved by her grandfather Helios, the sun god. Moreover Zeus, protector of oaths and the greatest of the gods, is arguably on her side. And she gets away with murder and infanticide, never to be punished. Do any or all of the gods approve of her behavior? The final choral comment on the subject is enigmatic (1415–19). (On Euripides and religion see further below, pp. 76–7.)

The assumption that the protagonists of tragedy are punished by the gods is often associated with the so-called "tragic flaw," which supposedly causes the offense for which the hero is supposedly punished. This view of tragedy is derived from Aristotle's *Poetics,* a work that has exerted an enormous influence on the later interpretation of tragedy. But it rests on a misunderstanding of Aristotle. Aristotle does say that the downfall of the central figure of a tragedy should occur because of a "mistake" (*Poetics* 1453a). But his word for a mistake, *hamartia,* while sometimes used for moral error, is not intrinsically moral in meaning. Though it comes to mean "sin" in biblical Greek, in Classical times it most often refers simply to an intellectual mistake (related words are used, e.g., at *Medea* 498, 800, *Alcestis* 144, 709–10; compare note on *Alcestis* 144). Whether Aristotle meant to include moral faults at all is debatable. It *is* clear, however, that *hamartia* includes mistakes to which absolutely no moral blame may be attached, such as Oedipus' ignorance of who his real parents are. It is simply not true that Greek tragic "heroes" in general fall because of a moral flaw. On the other hand, the dramas would be much less interesting if the characters were perfectly good. As Aristotle also makes clear, they must be less than perfect if they are to be "like us" and hence arouse the tragic emotions of pity and fear. But this is a separate issue from the illusory "tragic flaw."

The mistaken view that Athenian tragedy is primarily about divine punishment has also led to a misunderstanding of the Greek word *hubris.* This generally refers not, as is often supposed, to an arrogant attitude toward the gods, but to status violations against one's fellow mortals. These usually take the form of specific acts of verbal or physical abuse, including assault and rape. Thus Medea uses *hubris* to refer to Jason's mistreatment of her (256, 1366), and also for his insulting language (603; compare *IA* 961 with note). In Athenian law *hubris* is a serious legal offense by one human being against another. Of course the gods do not like being treated this way any more than anyone else, and since they are more powerful than mortals, they may exact an unpleasant revenge for such insults. But when this happens (which is not very often in tragedy), they are punishing specific behavior, not a general outlook (see further Fisher 1992).

Self and Other

As the discussion of religion has already shown, many practices and concepts fundamental to an ancient Greek's worldview, such as oaths, animal sacrifice, and "fate," are alien to late-twentieth-century American ideology and behavior. Translation of such culturally specific concepts and terminology often poses serious problems. The same applies to a number of basic concepts in Greek sociocultural life and popular ethics, concepts that structured the way Greeks viewed the world and their own place in it through their orientation toward others.

Perhaps the most important of such concepts is *philia.* This is usually translated as "friendship," with the related noun *philos* as "friend" (plural *philoi*), the adjective *philos* as "dear," and the verb *philō* as "love." Since there exist no closer English equivalents, these translations are used in this book. But they remain in important ways inadequate. "Friend" in contemporary English connotes primarily someone with whom one has personal emotional ties. But the Greek concept is much more far-reaching. A *philos* was anyone to whom one owed favors or benefits, and who owed them in return. A personal emotional bond often existed between such people and was viewed as desirable, but it is not intrinsic to the concept of *philia.*

One's *philoi* thus included large numbers of those with whom one came into contact, such as political or legal allies. They also included family members, regardless of the sentiments one might feel toward them individually. In fact, the bond of "friendship" between blood-kin was one of the most central and powerful obligations in Greek culture. Marriage also created bonds of *philia,* not just between the married couple but between their families, and as such was an important way of cementing social and political ties. Although a Greek marriage ideally involved erotic attraction, this was not essential to the relationship of *philia* that it established. Unlike "love," the language of *philia* is almost never erotic in connotation. Another important related concept is that of *kharis.* This word originally meant "charm," but it came to be used for any grace or favor, whether offered or reciprocated, including sexual favors (compare e.g., *Helen* 1234). It thus also came to mean "gratitude," and was often invoked as the foundation of *philia,* including marriage (compare, e.g., *Medea* 439 with note; *Alcestis* 60 and 299 with notes).

Philia played such a fundamental ethical and social role that ancient Greek popular morality is often summarized as "helping friends and harming enemies" (see Blundell 1989: ch. 2). An enemy was someone with whom one had a relationship of mutual injury, the opposite of a *philos.* One had a right or even an obligation to reciprocate harm to such a person. There are two main words for "enemy" in

Greek. In military contexts, an enemy is a *polemios.* But a personal enemy is an *ekhthros* (a more emotional term, related to words for "hatred"). Anyone who gratuitously injures someone becomes their *ekhthros.* But the most hated enemies are usually those who were thought to be *philoi* yet violated the obligations of *philia,* especially by reciprocating harm instead of *kharis* for benefits received. Revenge for such violations is a prominent theme in many Greek texts, such as *Medea* in this volume (compare also *IA* 1171–84).

Another culturally specific type of relationship, which is also a kind of *philia,* is known as *xenia* ("guest-friendship"). It is related to the word *xenos,* which means "stranger," "foreigner," or "friend." This range of meaning seems paradoxical in English and can cause problems in translation. But in the context of Greek cultural institutions, the second meaning is logically related to the first. A *xenos* was a stranger or foreigner; once hospitality had been offered to and accepted by such a person, a bond of *xenia* was formed between host and guest. The guest thereby incurred a special obligation to reciprocate hospitality and other benefits to his erstwhile host. Strangers, hosts, and guests all fell under the protection of Zeus. One who failed to show due hospitality to a stranger in need incurred the god's wrath, as did a guest who failed to acknowledge a host's generosity or actively injured the host, as Paris did by absconding with Helen, the wife of his host Menelaos.

The historical result of *xenia* was a system that helped to organize relationships among male aristocrats (see Hermann 1987). An elite Greek male traveling away from home would expect to lodge with his guest-friends. *Xenia* rendered travel (always very dangerous) safer and more comfortable and provided a network of support throughout the Greek world. Ancient societies were largely tribal in character (i.e., based on kinship networks) and tended to exclude outsiders from citizenship, religious cults, and other positions of influence. But *xenia* gave foreigners an entrée by providing them with local sponsorship. It also cut across other forms of social and political organization, creating both some degree of independence from, and potential conflicts with, the *polis.* Like other kinds of *philia,* such relationships could be passed down over generations between families, and were quasi-institutional. *Xenia* is central to many surviving Greek texts, including Homer's *Odyssey.* In this volume it is especially prominent in *Alcestis* but also plays an important role in *Medea* and *Helen.*

One way in which both *philia* and *xenia* might be initiated was through the ritual of supplication. A person in need of refuge or assistance could seek sanctuary at an altar or other sacred place, or supplicate another person directly. To beg or "supplicate" someone formally by the beard, chin, or knees, with accompanying gestures, was a way of exerting social, moral, and religious pressure on them to grant one's request. The supplicator is debased by the gesture, since he or she is putting himself or herself at the mercy of another. If the supplication is accepted, the supplicator incurs an obligation of reciprocal loyalty toward the person who accepted it. If it is rejected, the rejector has violated an important moral and religious obligation and risks the wrath of Zeus, who protects suppliants as well as strangers. This ritual is pervasive in Athenian tragedy, including the plays in this volume.

Greek society was thus built around a complex web of reciprocal relationships, not all of which are always compatible with each other. Not surprisingly, this could lead to conflict, and it is with such conflicts of loyalties that tragedy is often concerned. As Aristotle says, the best kinds of incidents in tragedy are those that take place "in relationships of *philia*" (*Poetics* 1443b). The relationships he has in mind, as his examples make clear, are between close blood-kin, among whom obligations are strongest and emotions often most powerful. But serious and traumatic conflicts may also arise between kinship and other close ties. In this volume we have conflicts between blood-kinship and marital *philia* (*Medea*), blood-kinship and political obligation (*IA*), *xenia* and marital *philia* (*Alcestis*).

The relationship terms discussed so far may be applied to anyone, but in practice are mostly used by Greeks for fellow Greeks, whether from one's own *polis* or another. Non-Greeks may also be *philoi, xenoi,* and so on, but are collectively known as *barbaroi.* The word *barbaros* is derived from the alleged babblings of those who speak an unintelligible foreign language ("barbarbar"). It thus means not just any stranger or outsider, but specifically one whose native language is not Greek. This is the origin of our own word "barbarian," but *barbaros* has rather different connotations from "barbarian" in modern English. It does not conjure up images of brutality, primitivism, or a crude cultural and material existence. In fact, ancient, rich, and highly developed civilizations such as the Persians and the Egyptians were the most important *barbaroi* of the ancient Greek world. The Greeks were fascinated by these alien peoples, especially the Egyptians. At the same time, they shared with most human cultures a tendency to despise those who were different from themselves, and to conceptualize those Others in ways that supported their own process of self-definition and self-glorification. Non-Greeks were readily looked down upon as inferior in many ways, for example politically: Greeks were free men who ruled themselves under law, barbarians were lawless slaves ruled by kings; in their sexual behavior: Greeks were masculine, sexually restrained, in control of their women, barbarians effeminate, lustful, ruled by women; and in their general character: Greeks were rational, brave, honest, and reliable; barbarians, emotional, cowardly, deceptive and undependable. Aristotle declares that barbarians are "natural" slaves since they are inferior to Greek men in reason, and he claims that his view matches ordinary Greek attitudes (*Politics* 1252b, 1255a). *Barbaros* thus took on pejorative connotations even in ancient times and later evolved into the word "barbarian" as it is used today.

The process of Greek self-definition in contrast to the "barbarian" is exemplified throughout ancient Greek cultural products, including tragedy, and the works in this volume are no exception.[5] It is central to *Medea* (below, pp. 152–54) and also important for *Helen.* The latter is set in Egypt, a place that aroused both fascination and admiration among the ancient Greeks. This was the foreign culture most explicitly constructed by the Greeks as Other. It was represented both as an exotic source of wisdom (many early Greek wise men are said to have traveled there) and as the inversion of all things Greek. The historian Herodotus claims that the Egyptians are the opposite of the Greeks—or as he puts it, the rest of the human race—in their customs and practices. Many of his alleged examples concern gender roles: He claims that men stay home and weave, while women go out to work, and even that men squat to urinate, whereas women stand up (2.35). Euripides' *Helen* is set at the mouth of the river Nile, which was both the principal point of contact and the main highway of influence for penetrating this mysterious Other.

As a group against which the male citizen defined himself, "barbarians" were ideologically analogous to other inferior categories, especially women and nonhuman animals. It is alleged that the early Greek philosopher Thales "used to say he gave thanks to fortune for three things, 'first, that I was born a human and not a beast, next that I was born a man and not a woman, third that I was born a Greek and not a barbarian'" (Diogenes Laertius 1.33). All three of these "inferior" categories are deemed deficient in reason and often are equated with each other. Barbarians are viewed as effeminate, and both women and barbarians are frequently likened to animals (compare below, pp. 152–54). Otherness is thus a flexible concept, which shifts to suit the varying contexts for self-definition. A Greek man may define himself in opposition to female, animal, or barbarian, depending on whether he is conceptualizing himself primarily as male, human, or Greek. But in a different context, he may define himself by contrast with another group of Greek males. Thus Athenian ideology represents Athenians as superior not just to foreigners but to other Greeks as well (see especially Pericles' funeral speech in Thucydides, Book 2).

The differentiation of Self from Other is pervasive in human social organization. A closely related and equally fundamental dichotomy is that between "good" and "bad." Like most languages, ancient Greek has a wide array of evaluative terms, both positive and negative. But one pair of words is by far the most common and carries cultural associations that challenge the translator. These are the polar opposites *agathos* and *kakos* (along with their many linguistic relatives). The difficulty in translating these and many other terms is partly caused by the strong tendency in ancient Greek to pose mutually exclusive opposites, which is itself bound up with the frequent use of binary oppositions in the Greek language.

In origin, both *agathos* and *kakos* are class and status terms with strongly aristocratic associations. *Agathos* refers to a range of positive qualities attributed to the aristocratic male warrior, especially excellence at fighting, as exempified by the epic hero on the battlefield. Conversely *kakos* is associated with failure to abide by aristocratic standards of manliness, often meaning "cowardly" or "base." But these words also mean "good" and "bad" in a broader sense. As such, they are often used in a nonmoral but functional manner for any item that is good at fulfilling its predetermined cultural role (e.g., a good knife, a bad horse). Such usages are not intrinsically "moral" in a modern sense, but *agathos* and *kakos* took on increasingly moral associations, partly under the influence of ethical philosophers. They also retained aristocratic associations, which were to some extent transferred into political meanings ("aristocracy" is literally "rule by the best"). At the same time some writers, including Euripides, started to challenge the class associations of these terms and pick apart their many varied meanings within the democratic *polis.*

This complex history and set of associations makes *agathos* and *kakos* impossible to translate with any single pair of English terms. Depending on the context, *agathos* may mean "brave," "excellent," "good," "beneficial," "well-born," "noble," or even "virtuous," and *kakos* may mean "cowardly," "bad," "harmful," "low-born," "ignoble," or "evil." "Virtuous" and "evil" are dangerous terms for translating ancient Greek, since they suggest anachronistic Christian concepts of virtue and vice, based on abstract, universal moral standards. In biblical Greek they came to have these connotations, but "virtuous" is rarely appropriate for *agathos* in Euripides. "Evil," however, may at times be a useful translation for *kakos,* since it can be used quite broadly in English, and may convey a powerful sense of condemnation, as *kakos* very often does.

II. ATHENIAN TRAGEDY: A CIVIC INSTITUTION[6]

Tragedy and Athenian Democracy

The origins of tragedy are unknown.[7] But we do know that tragedies began to be performed at the Athenian festival of the Greater Dionysia toward the end of the sixth century BCE. The first named tragedian is the semi-legendary Thespis (said to have won the dramatic contest in 534 BCE), whose name gives us the word "thespian." But no tragedies from this period have survived. The development of the genre as we know it comes decades later, coinciding with the rise of Athenian democracy and the turbulent years of the Peloponnesian War. Although the overt subject-matter of these dramas comes from myth (below, pp. 44–8), they are informed by the historical conditions in which they were produced, which were marked by inter-Greek warfare, imperialism, political instability, and revolution (above, pp. 8–10).

Whatever its origins, the form and themes of tragedy are well suited to the ideology of the developing democracy. Many plays focus on the downfall or death of an aristocratic figure from the legendary age of heroes, such as Agamemnon, Oedipus, or Ajax. There is always a chorus, made up of less powerful members of the community, which invariably survives this heroic figure. As a group, they may be viewed as mediating between heroic individual and mass audience. (On the chorus see further below, pp. 38–41.) Such a form, which offered different meanings to different classes within the audience, was appropriate for a democratic civic festival (Else 1965: 66–67).

> The heroic figures . . . not only come to life before the eyes of the spectators but furthermore, through their discussions with the chorus or with one another, they become the subjects of a debate. They are, in a way, under examination before the public. . . . In the new framework of tragic interplay, then, the hero has ceased to be a model. He has become, both for himself and for others, a problem.
>
> (Vernant and Vidal-Naquet 1988: 24–25)

Or as Wiles puts it, the democratic audience "is looking at itself in relation to a different, pre-democratic world" (1997: 209).

The dramatic exploration of contemporary Athenian values in an aristocratic mythic setting often leads to a productive tension. As Vernant and Vidal-Naquet go on to argue:

> Tragedy establishes a distance between itself and the myths of the heroes that inspire it and that it transposes with great freedom. It scrutinizes them. It confronts heroic values and ancient religious representations with the new modes of thought that characterize the advent of law within the city-state. The legends of the heroes are connected with royal lineages, noble *genē* [families] that in terms of values, social practices, forms of religion, and types of human behavior, represent for the city-state the very things that it has had to condemn and reject and against which it has had to fight in order to establish itself. At the same time, however, they are what it developed from and it remains integrally linked with them.
>
> (Vernant and Vidal-Naquet 1988: 26–27)

This kind of tension in attitudes toward political authority is apparent in the shifting connotations of the word *turannos.* Historically, this word means "non-hereditary sole ruler" (above, p. 6). The myths on which most tragedies are based are concerned with royal characters located in the legendary past, long before the rise of democracy. In this context, most rulers are quite naturally autocratic kings, so the word *turannos* is not intrinsically pejorative in their case. But in democratic Athens both monarchy and a "royal" or "tyrannical" outlook, construed as uncontrolled and disrespectful of others, incurred disapproval. *Turannos* therefore became an ambiguous term, and gradually took on the negative connotations of the modern English "tyrant." The word *turannos* is thus problematic in tragedy. On the one hand, it is often used with apparent neutrality. On the other, it may hint at or explicitly convey the pejorative associations that adhered to it in democratic ideology. In *Medea,* for example, Kreon rejects a typically "tyrannical" outlook, yet he is aware that this may interfere with his role as an absolute ruler (*Medea* 348–49).

Such passages draw attention to the tensions inherent in exploring democratic Athenian concerns in an aristocratic legendary milieu. The dramatists use these "anachronisms" to explore some of the ideological tensions in their own world, not simply by "updating" myths, but by juxtaposing contemporary Athenian realities with the heroic myths towards which the Greeks looked back as their past. The complexity with which these questions are explored, and the range of variation among different plays, mean that tragedy per se cannot be construed in a simple sense either as subverting or as reinforcing the ideology of the Athenian *polis.* (For differing views on this issue see Goldhill 1987, Seaford 1994.) The politically ambiguous position of tragedy, which dramatizes an aristocratic mythological tradition but is aimed at a democratic audience, also helped to ensure the complexity of meaning that has allowed these plays to reach far beyond their original context.

Given this concern with contemporary Athenian issues, it may seem surprising that few surviving tragedies are actually set in Athens. There are exceptions (notably Aeschylus' *Eumenides*). But most plays are located in places that were hostile to Athens in Euripides' time—especially Thebes—and use myths that have little direct connection with Athens itself (see further Zeitlin 1990, Blundell 1993). In our volume the locations range from Corinth, a close but hostile city (*Medea*), to Egypt, a distant locale that for the Greeks embodied the Other (*Helen;* on Egypt see above, pp. 22–3). These alien locations may be interpreted as an "Otherwhere," a "safe" space for exploring ideological tensions that might be too threatening if dramatized in the city of Athens itself. Thus Euripides' *Hippolytos,* a tragedy potentially critical of the great Athenian hero Theseus, is set not in Athens but in nearby Troezen. At the same time, many plays acknowledge their relevance to Athens indirectly, by establishing an oblique relationship to Athens or Athenian myths. Plays like Euripides' *Medea* and *Herakles* include famous Athenian characters as visitors, creating an explicit link with Athenian mythology. Even *Helen* includes references to Athens that are entirely uncalled for by the myth it dramatizes (25, 229, 245, 1316, 1466–67). Euripides thus uses his Egyptian setting indirectly to explore the boundaries of Self and Other as an Athenian as well as a Greek.

Audience

Tragedy was a democratic form in that it was performed for a mass audience, who are often implicitly included in the drama via appeals to the citizen body within the plays (Wiles 1997: ch. 10). The theater, along with the political assembly and the law courts, was one of the main venues in which Athenians gathered in large numbers to enjoy the power of rhetorical performance. Live theater was not an elite art form but enormously popular, drawing audiences of 15,000–20,000 out of a population of about 300,000 (including men, women, children, slaves and resident aliens).[8] Women, children, foreigners, and even slaves were permitted to attend (below, p. 62). Apparently even the prisons were opened to allow inmates to attend the festival. The price of entrance for the principal dramatic festival was only two obols, a sum not out of reach of an average citizen, and at some point a fund was established to enable everyone to attend. There is no modern equivalent for Athenian dramatic performances. They combined the status of a public institution (both civic and religious), the broad popularity of a blockbuster Hollywood production, the emotional and competitive appeal of a major sporting event, and the artistic and cultural preeminence of Shakespeare.

The plays were performed in the open-air Theater of Dionysos on the southeastern slope of the Acropolis hill, at the physical and political heart of Athens. In size and shape the seating area resembled one end of a large football stadium. Most of the audience probably sat on wooden benches or the ground, on the sloping sides of the Acropolis hill above the theater, where an impressive view of the mountains and coastline of southern Attica stretched beyond the playing area. The best seats, made of carved stone, were reserved for religious figures, public benefactors, high-ranking officials, important foreign visitors, and the judges of the dramatic competition. The priest of Dionysos sat in the center of the front row, flanked by other important priests and perhaps priestesses as well. Members of the Council, young men of military age (ephebes), and other important groups had their own sections, and the rest of the citizenry may have been arranged by tribes, a fundamental form of democratic civic grouping (above, p. 7). Any foreigners, women, children, and slaves who attended were probably seated at the back and sides of the theater. The seating arrangements thus reflected a sense of civic awareness, balancing the ideology of democratic inclusiveness with marks of status and hierarchy.

Audiences arriving at the Theater of Dionysos did not anticipate watching generic examples of "Greek tragedy," but particular plays by members of the Athenian community known to them by reputation and in some cases by sight. Unfortunately, no comments by directors and actors, no production books, visual records, programs, or reviews exist for Athenian drama. The absence of such information, along with the modern focus on the written script and lack of attention to the original conditions of performance, has contributed to the "classic" status of Athenian tragic dramas and the idealizing readings which preserve that status.

The majority of the original audience was probably illiterate. The only way to find out about the plays was to attend the *proagōn* ("pre-contest"), a preliminary ceremony a few days earlier, where the authors appeared with the actors and announced the subjects of their plays. Audience members who had not attended the *proagōn* may well have heard about the play by word of mouth. But some may have been ignorant of the subject of the drama until it began. Specifics that might be found in a modern program, including background information necessary for understanding the plot, were learned from the play itself during the performance—hence the importance of the prologue or "exposition" at the beginning of each play. Further information about plot and characters was conveyed through dialogue as the play proceeded, including details of setting and behavior which would be difficult to see in such a large theater, or changing facial expressions, which could not be portrayed visually because of the rigid masks worn by all actors (below, p. 36). Dialogue also provided cues for entrances and exits (e.g., "Here comes So-and-so!" or "Go into the house!").

Performances began at dawn and lasted much of the day. References to daybreak near the beginning of some plays may allude to the actual dawn. Members of the audience who lived in the country would therefore have had to travel during the night to reach the theater, unless they came the day before and lodged with friends or family members. The text of most Athenian tragedies can be performed by a modern theatrical company in an hour and a half or less. The original speed of delivery may have been much slower, however, and music and dancing may have added considerably to the length of a show. In his comedy *Birds,* Aristophanes suggests that sitting through an entire bill of three tragedies plus a satyr play (below, pp. 34–5) was tiring; of course, as a comic poet, he had his own agenda. The spectators brought food to eat during the day, and some comic playwrights had nuts, fruit, and wine distributed in the theater. Aristotle tells us that the audience was most likely to eat when the acting was bad (*Nicomachean Ethics* 1175b12).

Once the sun rose, the size and openness of the theater were enhanced by the daylight enveloping performers and audience alike. This generated a very different and specifically more public atmosphere than the darkened theaters and artificial lighting of today. Modern theatrical conventions focus audience members' attention away from each other and promote the illusion that the drama is taking place in an independent world of its own. Athenian audience members, by contrast, would have been very conscious of each other as well as the play going on. The crowded conditions and absence of individual seats would have led to close physical contact among the audience and enhanced the transmission of shared emotion (Wiles 1997: 210; compare also Segal 1996). The theater was an extension of their world, not an escape from it.

In accordance with this highly public atmosphere, Athenian audiences did not regard the plays as antiquarian documents or "classics" whose appeal was primarily aesthetic or remote from "real life." They responded to the dramas with visceral emotion:

> The sources all depict Athenians as a demanding, unruly audience, and anything but passive in expressing approval or disapproval. The festival atmosphere did not have the polite tone of modern theater audiences. . . . The slightest awkwardness [in a tragic performance] could result in outbursts of disapproval, shouting, hissing (or whistling), clucking, heel banging, and, possibly, food throwing. Prolonged disturbances were frequently resolved only when the actors and chorus abandoned the performance, a calamity that befell even the best tragedians of the age. Crowd control appears to have necessitated a special force of theater police, called "rod holders."[9]

The closest modern analogues might be a rock concert or sporting event, rather than the contemporary theater. These powerful reactions were influenced not only by the words but by aspects of the drama that have been lost to us, such as music and performance skills. An actor who mispronounced a word meaning "calm," so that it sounded like the Greek for "weasel," was lampooned mercilessly and never allowed to forget his gaffe (Csapo and Slater 1995: 267–68).

Many anecdotes attest to the close emotional engagement of the audience. The playwright Phrynichus, for example, staged a tragedy about the capture of Miletus, a Greek city conquered by the Persians just a few years earlier. The Athenian audience was reduced to tears, Phrynichus was fined one thousand drachmas, "for reminding them of their own misfortunes," and the play was banned from future performance (Herodotus 6.21; translation in Csapo and Slater 1995: 11). Such formal restrictions on a tragic playwright's freedom of expression were rare. Athens prided itself on its *parrhēsia,* the right of any (male) citizen to speak his mind (see Csapo and Slater 1995: 165–71), and occasions on which a dramatist ran a real risk of formal censure were few. Informal criticism, however, was both immediate and vehement. All the evidence indicates that the audience scrutinized the plays carefully with regard to moral, political, and social issues, and expressed their opinions vocally. One story goes that the audience hissed in disapproval at an eloquent passage of Euripides in praise of money, "and were only quieted when the poet sprang forward and advised them to wait and see what happened to the character who uttered the sentiment" (Pickard-Cambridge 1988: 274).

Anecdotes of this kind are unreliable in detail, but convey a vehemence of emotion and a lively moralism in Athenian responses to drama which are fully consistent with our other evidence. Both popular and philosophical traditions view poetry, especially epic and drama, as having a direct moral effect on its audience through a process of emotional identification (see Blundell 1989: 12–16). This assumption lies behind the playwrights' contest in Aristophanes' *Frogs* (below, pp. 67–8, 77–8). It also underlies both the expulsion of poetry from the ideal state in Plato's *Republic* (below, p. 64) and Aristotle's attempt at an ethical defense of drama in his *Poetics.* All these texts, in their different ways, pay tribute to the enormous power of drama to move and influence its audience on many different levels.

The Festival

The close involvement of Athenian drama with public, civic, democratic life is evident in the circumstances of its production. Most of the famous tragedians' works were first produced at the Greater or City Dionysia, the principal Athenian festival for the god Dionysos.[10] This annual festival, which lasted six days, was a major civic as well as religious celebration, including processions, sacrifices, and musical and dramatic performances in different genres. It was an occasion for public festivity and civic pride, an opportunity for Athens to display to the world itself and its cultural achievements—prominent among which was drama itself.

The festival took place in the spring, when the sailing season had begun and visitors from all over the Greek world might be in town. Athens' subject-allies (above, p. 8) had to bring their tribute to Athens at this time, and this money was displayed in the theater during the festival—a striking example of the political context of Athenian drama (see further Goldhill 1987). Other ceremonies preceding the dramas included the awarding of golden crowns to public benefactors and the presentation of suits of armor to young men whose fathers had been killed in battle. All these rituals reinforced the public image of Athenian heroism, magnanimity and power, associating political, military and cultural preeminence.

Dionysos, god of the theater, was associated with song and dance, masking and shifting identities, wine and irrational frenzy, vegetation, sex, fertility, sensuality and growth. Women played an important role in his myths and his cult, in contrast to the more usual alignment of female worshipers with female divinities. Along with Aphrodite, goddess of erotic passion, he was one of the two great gods of the irrational. Like her, his influence might lead to a loosening of normal restrictions on behavior, including ecstasy and even madness. "Everyone who surrenders to this god must risk abandoning his everyday identity and becoming mad; this is both divine and wholesome" (Burkert 1985: 162). Dionysos is often accompanied in myth by bands of lecherous drunken satyrs or frenzied female worshipers called Bacchants or Maenads. As wine god he brings happiness, but he can also be very dangerous. His myths include the dismemberment of wild animals, consumption of raw flesh, kin-murder, cannibalism, and the transgression of gender boundaries.

Dionysos is a very ancient Greek divinity. His name has been found in inscriptions dating back to the Bronze Age, and well known myths recount his birth from a Greek mother. Yet he is often represented in myth as arriving in Greece as an outsider from the east. He is thus manifested as both Greek and outsider, Self and Other. This suits his identity as a god who manages various aspects of Otherness in human life. Related ambiguities are expressed in the myths surrounding his birth, which blur the lines of divine and human, male and female. In the tale most familiar to us, Zeus, king of the gods, impregnates Semele, a princess in the Greek city of Thebes. Semele asks to see her lover in his full glory, and Zeus reveals himself in the form of a thunderbolt, which incinerates her. Zeus rescues the fetus, sews it into his thigh (a part of the body with strongly homoerotic associations), and in due time gives birth to Dionysos. This male appropriation of a female reproductive role corresponds to the ventriloquizing of female voices in drama by male playwrights and actors (below, pp. 63–4).

"Thereafter Dionysos vanishes to some distant place, but again and again he will return and demand worship" (Burkert 1985: 166). This return of the god is portrayed in many myths. In most versions, he exacts a frightful revenge on those who do not acknowledge his divinity. The best known of these stories is dramatized in Euripides' *Bacchants*—the only extant tragedy in which Dionysos actually appears as a character.[11] Here the god is memorably presented as an exotic, "feminine," and deceptive "barbarian." He returns to Thebes disguised as a human, accompanied by a chorus of foreign female worshipers (the Bacchants of the title). When Pentheus the king rejects him, Dionysos causes the women of Thebes to run wild from their homes and turn to "masculine" behavior such as hunting and combat. He then lures Pentheus to his doom by playing on his desire to spy on the women, dressing him in female costume, and turning him over to the frenzied Bacchants, who tear him to pieces led by his own mother and aunts.

Such myths, including Dionysos' double birth and multiple identities as both Greek and foreigner, divine and mortal, male and female, are linked to this god's association with role-playing, gender reversal, the crossing of boundaries, masking, theater, and disguise. Under his patronage, the theater provided a religiously and culturally sanctioned (and therefore "safe") space for questioning and exploring boundaries. Along with the importance of women in rites for Dionysos, the multiple ambiguities of the god's own shifting identities may help to explain the prominence of gender issues in the Greek theater (for other explanations see below, pp. 60–62).

The arrival (or return) of Dionysos was celebrated and reenacted in procession at many of his festivals, including the Greater Dionysia. Prior to the festival, an image of the god was carried in procession to a grove outside Athens, then brought back into the city with a torchlight parade. Such reenactments

> may derive not so much from an original actual introduction of the god as from the need of the community to renew and unite itself through the imagined entry of a powerful outsider . . . This unity may moreover require the symbolic incorporation of marginal elements . . . The polis' acceptance of the supposed "outsider" god Dionysos, together perhaps with barbarian ritual practices that may have accrued to him, may also signify . . . its integration of women. (Seaford 1996: 44–5)

The image of the god was brought to the theater and remained present for the dramatic performances. On the first day of the festival there was another parade, involving various strata of Athenian society. It was led by a young unmarried woman of aristocratic family, and it included resident aliens and their daughters as well as male citizens of various ages. A group of men brought up the rear, carrying large phallic images in recognition of Dionysos' role as a god of sex and fertility. The parade involved plenty of singing and dancing and culminated in a sacrificial feast at Dionysos' shrine.

The tragedies were thus part of a festival involving many religious rituals. But it is important to emphasize they themselves were *not* rituals. Drama *used* ritual as an important part of its thematic material; drama may in some cases have been *shaped* by ritual forms; drama may possibly have *arisen* from ritual (below, p. 392, n. 7). But drama itself was *not* ritual. "The institutional religious framework for the dramatic performances remained," but "Dionysiac ritual was secularized and metamorphosed into drama" (Friedrich 1996: 272). A distinguishing feature of ritual is its precise and repetitive nature; rituals must be performed correctly each time in order to ensure the proper effect. The plays, by contrast, were each unique, enormously varied, and normally performed only once.

> Ritual . . . is more or less stereotyped. It requires unreflecting participants performing prescribed actions . . . linked to a restricted body of cult myths . . . while tragedy . . . is particularized in form and content, and requires sufficiently individuated agents capable both of making conscious ethical choices . . . and of accepting the consequences of such choices. (Friedrich 1996: 274–75)

Nor do the plays have a simple or direct relationship to religious stories. Nearly all known tragedies are concerned with the heroic legends of the epic tradition, rather than the kind of myths more commonly involved in religious cults. And Greek religion generally was not text-based (above, p. 10). The gods and their relationships to mortals are pervasive aspects of the theater, as they were of life. But religious issues are presented not as articles of faith, but rather in a way that encourages audience members to think about and discuss their meanings.

Production and Performance

Drama uses physical bodies and material objects to create meaning and involves several modes of communication at once—visual (masks, costumes, and set), aural (the sung and spoken word), musical (instrumental and vocal), spatial (the relationships of distance between actors and between them and the audience), and kinetic (the movement of actors and chorus). It exists not in abstraction but in time and space. The performance medium affects every aspect of the meaning of a dramatic script. Because there are so few records of the workings and effect of performance in Athens, and because we are accustomed to think of the text as the essence of the drama, trying to ascertain the effect of Euripides' plays in performance is very difficult. But any attempt to understand Athenian tragedy in its own context must try to do this.[12]

The plays were produced in a competition, to determine which was the finest drama and hence most worthy of the god. This kind of public contest is far from unusual in ancient Greek culture, which was highly competitive. Religious festivals often involved various kinds of contest. (The Olympic games are a prominent example.) The City Dionysia itself included a contest in dithyramb (a kind of choral song in honor of Dionysos) as well as various genres of drama. Since only three tragic playwrights were allowed to present their plays at each festival, even having one's plays produced was an honor. In keeping with the public nature of the event, the initial decision about which plays would be produced was made by a city official. How he reached his decision is uncertain, but he was a political official, not a special expert in theater. Around the middle of the fifth century BCE the state also began allocating a principal actor to each production and awarding a prize for the best actor. A wealthy citizen called the *khorēgos* ("chorus director") was appointed by lot to bear most of the production costs, including the considerable expense of training, costuming, and feeding the chorus. This extra taxation (*khorēgia,* or "chorus directorship") was a prestigious form of public service often used by wealthy citizens as an opportunity for conspicuous display.

The playwright composed his own music, choreographed the dances, directed the whole production, and originally acted as well (though there is no evidence that Euripides ever acted). The three entries competed for prizes awarded by five judges, who were carefully selected by an elaborate procedure designed to prevent undue influence and bribes. Exactly how they reached their decision we do not know, but we do know that it was made under pressure from a rambunctious crowd (above, pp. 29–30), and the judges must surely have been influenced by audience reactions. The winning playwright and *khorēgos* were publicly announced by a herald and crowned with ivy (a plant sacred to Dionysos), and had their names recorded in public on a marble monument. In Plato's *Symposium* we hear of the drunken revelry with which the poet Agathon celebrated his first victory (174a, 176ab, 212e).

Besides tragedy, the Greater Dionysia included contests in two other dramatic genres: comedy and satyr play (a kind of burlesque). These three genres shared certain features. All were written in verse. All contained music and dance as well as spoken dialogue. And all involved a chorus (discussed below, pp. 38–41) as well as individual characters. The genres were quite distinct in other ways, however, including subject matter, structure, linguistic and musical registers. Satyr play was performed in the same competition as tragedy, with the same playwrights and actors, but comedy had a separate competition. The tragic competition lasted for three days, with each poet producing three tragedies followed by one satyr play in the course of a single day. All four plays were performed by the same set of actors and chorus. In the earlier period the tragedies sometimes formed a connected trilogy, like Aeschylus' *Oresteia* (the only trilogy that survives), and even the light-hearted satyr play might be on a related theme. But Euripides and Sophocles both seem to have preferred individual, self-contained dramas.

We know much less about satyr play than either tragedy or comedy, since it was not a canonized genre in later years. The only complete surviving play of this genre is Euripides' *Cyclops,* which we owe to the chance survival of Euripides' "alphabetic" plays, an arbitrary rather than a canonized sample of his works (below, p. 85). We also have about half of Sophocles' *Trackers,* and some shorter fragments (see further Seaford 1984). Our scanty knowledge of this genre detracts from our understanding of the effect of tragedy in performance, since the satyr play was an integral part of each tragic dramatist's program. Experiencing three tragedies together, followed by a satyr play, would certainly affect our expectations, assumptions, and responses to tragedy, in all likelihood making it seem even stranger.

What we do know of satyr play indicates that it treated the same kinds of heroic stories as tragedy but burlesqued them. It was lighter in tone and had a chorus of satyrs, mythological followers of Dionysos who resembled men with animal tails and sometimes animal legs or ears. (The animal in question is usually a horse, or, mostly after Euripides' time, a goat.) Satyrs were known for their unrestrained appetites, and had the exaggerated phallus also worn in comedy. Satyr play has particular relevance to this volume of tragedies because we are told that Euripides' *Alcestis* was performed fourth in its group of plays, i.e., in the position of a satyr drama, even though it lacks many salient features of that genre (below, pp. 94, 103).

All three genres were performed in the Theater of Dionysos. In such a huge theater the playing space had to be in scale. The performance area was dominated by a large dancing floor, the *orchēstra* ("dancing area"), which was about seventy feet across. By the fourth century BCE it was circular; its precise shape in the fifth century is uncertain, but it may have been rectangular or round.[13] At the back was a wooden stage building, the *skēnē* (literally "tent" or "hut"; the origin of the English word "scene"), which served as an all-purpose set and provided a place out of sight of the audience for the players to change costumes and masks. Whether or not there was a raised stage in the fifth century is a matter of controversy. If so, it was merely a low, narrow platform in front of the stage building.[14] The *skēnē* was flanked by the *eisodoi*—two long side-entrances on either side of the *orchēstra,* used for entrances and exits that did not involve the stage building. The same *eisodos* is generally used throughout a play to represent a particular destination. In *Medea,* for example, all characters from Corinth and the royal palace would have arrived along one side entrance, while Aigeus, who is traveling from Delphi, would have entered by the other.

The setting of most plays calls for a palace or other building with functioning doors through which actors enter and exit. The *skēnē* may have been decorated in some all-purpose way, or perhaps simple set changes were made (Csapo and Slater 1995: 257–58). But the theater was so large that detailed scenery would not have been easily visible to the audience. The action takes place outside the location represented by the *skēnē.* This means that no indoor scenes are directly represented, though they are often described by characters. Occasionally, however, an interior tableau was revealed to the audience by means of a device called the *ekkuklēma.* This was a low wheeled platform, which might be rolled out of the door of the *skēnē* to reveal a scene from within. Its use to make "interior" scenes manifest on the "outside" is a good illustration of the fluidity of dramatic space in the ancient theater (Wiles 1997: 162–5).

Gods, and occasionally human characters, might also appear on the *skēnē* roof by climbing through a trapdoor from the inside or up a ladder at the back of the building. Special entrances from above used the *mēchanē,* a crane for swinging characters through the air and sometimes onto the roof. Euripides often uses this device for surprise endings and appearances by new characters, especially gods. This convention became known by the Latin phrase *deus ex machina* ("god from the machine"). The Dioskouroi in *Helen* and Medea at the end of *Medea* probably entered this way, though we cannot be completely certain in either case.

Like the entire "production team" of Athenian tragedy (producers, playwrights, dancers, musicians), all the actors in tragedy were male. This extends to the numerous female roles, all of which were played by adult men (see further below, pp. 63–4). The gender of the characters, along with such attributes as social status and age, were indicated in a formal, stylized way by costumes and masks using conventional elements. For example, heroic and divine characters were often portrayed as blond or "golden"-haired, despite the prevalence of darker skin and hair colors among Mediterranean peoples (Pickard-Cambridge 1988: 192; compare, e.g., *Medea* 834, 980, 1142, *Helen* 1224). Masks were bold in design, as they had to be in order to be visible to spectators throughout the theater. Unlike comic masks, which sometimes caricatured real individuals, tragic masks represented types, such as an old man or a young woman. In the fifth century BCE masks covered the whole head, including the ears, and had wigs attached; they were naturalistic in manner, not gaping or exaggerated like later masks, and did not amplify the actors' voices.

Costumes were lavish, with long, colorfully decorated robes, and sometimes tall boots (these lacked the platform soles of the "buskin," which came later). Props and other details added to the stage picture and helped to clarify the status of each character. A king might carry a scepter, an old man a staff, a slave-woman a pitcher, a warrior a sword. Shorn hair was a sign of mourning, garlands of festivity. More unusual props might bear special dramatic weight, such as Medea's gifts to the princess. Costumes might also reflect familiar Athenian activities, especially of a ritual nature, e.g., the black garb of a mourner, or a woman's wedding costume (both of which appear in *Alcestis*). Medea may have been dressed in exotic "barbarian" garb (below, p. 141). Euripides was mocked by the comic playwright Aristophanes for dressing his actors in rags (below, pp. 68, 75), and the shipwrecked Menelaos in *Helen* exemplifies this practice (see *Helen* 421–4). But other tragedians used such characters too (e.g., Xerxes in Aeschylus' *Persians,* and Philoktetes in Sophocles' play of that name). Their "ragged" state, often referred to by other characters, was presumably indicated somehow, but the degree of stylization or naturalism in such costumes is unknown.

The standard number of speaking actors in a tragic production in Euripides' time, apart from the chorus, was three. (*Medea* is exceptional in that it only requires two actors, though it could have been played with three.) But there were usually several nonspeaking extras playing silent parts such as guards, attendants, and children. The reasons for the restriction to three speaking actors are not known; perhaps it kept costs down, kept the competition more fairly balanced, or helped maintain a focus on the principal actor who was competing for the acting prize. In any case, this so-called "three-actor rule" explains why there are never more than three speaking characters on stage together. It also means that individual actors must regularly have played more than one role, with the same actor covering the spectrum of age, gender, and social status (Damen 1989). Sometimes a single part had to be split between two or even three actors, but this was not common. These practices were facilitated by the fact that the actors were all male, and wore not only distinctive costumes but rigid masks identifying each character clearly.

Little is known about ancient acting, but it was probably quite stylized. Performance conditions in Athens made naturalistic acting impossible, since the huge theater and the masks ruled out the use of subtle body movements or facial expressions. Cues in the texts suggest a conventional vocabulary of gesture, drawing on contemporary rituals like sacrifices, weddings, funerals, supplications, prayers, and oaths, all of which occur in the plays in this volume. Besides ritual gestures, certain types of body language would convey social, political, and moral meanings. For example, looking someone in the eye may indicate honesty or effrontery, whereas avoiding their gaze may show modesty or shame (compare, e.g., *Medea* 469–72, *IA* 320–21). The large playing space also offered many opportunities to create meaning and delineate relationships choreographically (Wiles 1997: chs. 5 and 6).

The quality and power of the actor's voice were also very important. Because of the costumes and masks, this was the primary way in which individual actors competing for the actor's prize might be identified, though gestures may have been important too. Actors playing several roles presumably differentiated them by voice as well as movement. For example, those playing female roles may have pitched their voices in a higher register. In general, actors must have delivered their lines loudly and emphatically, and used broad, clear gestures, in order to be seen and heard.

Characterization through language accords with this stylized approach to the representation of human beings. The Greek tragedians were not primarily concerned to delineate unique idiosyncratic individuals. Their dramatic characters are presented as members of social and political structures where one's gender, age, and status are essential determinants of who one is. Most characters are variations on significant types (Good Woman, Bad Woman, Good King, Old Man, Loyal Slave, etc.). Yet this lack of focus on unique personality does not mean the characters do not command our interest as compelling human figures with complex sets of moral, political, social, and emotional attitudes. Euripides in particular is famous for his interest in human psychology, especially that of women (below, pp. 74–6, 80–83).

The Chorus

A central feature of all ancient Athenian drama was the chorus (Greek *khoros*), a group who performed as a unit. In Euripides' time the tragic chorus had fifteen members. They entered early in the play—generally after the first scene—singing the *parodos* ("entry song"), which usually establishes their identity and relationship to the main actors. They normally remained in the playing area for the rest of the play, performing further songs with dancing, called *stasima* ("songs in position"), between the actors' scenes. This aspect of tragedy is unfamiliar to many modern audiences and is hard to integrate convincingly into a modern production. One unusually successful example is Lee Breuer and Bob Telson's *The Gospel at Colonus,* an American Gospel intepretation of Sophocles' tragedy *Oedipus at Colonus.* This adaptation succeeds not because of the "timelessness" of the drama, but, on the contrary, because it transposes Greek drama into an entirely different cultural idiom, and thereby renders the interplay between chorus and actors convincing in a modern setting.

The chorus was central to the place of Athenian drama in the life of the *polis.* Only Athenian citizens could belong to a chorus, and violations of this rule were severely punished. Citizens were drafted for the purpose, were punished for refusing, and might be excused military service in order to participate (Csapo and Slater 1995: 351–52). Chorus membership was thus a civic duty comparable to military service (see Winkler 1990b, who argues that the chorus were ephebes, i.e., young men of military age). Technical terms associated with theater production also indicate the essential importance of this feature of the drama. The producer was called the "chorus director," the duty of financing the production was a "chorus directorship" (above, p. 34), and the playwrights whose works were selected for production were said to have been "granted a chorus." Indeed, the most plausible hypothesis about the origin of drama is that it evolved from choral song (below, p. 392, n. 7).

The choral identity is a collective one. In contrast to the heroic individuality of the actors, the chorus members are numerous, anonymous, and undifferentiated. They have no individual names, and they speak and are addressed indiscriminately in the singular or plural. They therefore represent to a certain extent the group, showing the effects of the main actors' words and deeds on the larger human community. In a sense these performers are continuous with the audience, whose fellow citizens they are: "The chorus are simultaneously actors and onlookers within the scenic space, and fellow-citizens within the theatrical space" (Wiles 1997: 18). But whether we view them as actors or citizens, they form only one segment of the community as a whole. The scripts make clear they have a clearly defined identity, a specific gender and social status, which are important for a full understanding of the play. As citizen performers, they are free adult male Athenians. But in their dramatic persona, they represent, remarkably often, a socially marginal segment of society—women, old men, foreigners, underlings, or even slaves. They are thus far from being an embodiment of the Athenian *polis* or of "society" in the abstract. "They express, not the values of the *polis,* but far more often the experience of the excluded, the oppressed, and the vulnerable" (Gould 1996: 224).

Like the main actors, the chorus members were masked and dressed in character. Although the performers were all men, their characters are frequently (but not always) of the same sex as the central figure of the drama, with whom they tend to share a certain solidarity. The character and effect of choruses differ from one play to another, but in general choruses act as an aid and/or foil to the protagonists and offer responses to and abstract reflections on the events taking place on stage. Their "personality" is more fluid than that of the main characters, as they react to unfolding events. This fluidity is tied to their mode of performance, which was primarily song and dance, with only a few lines of spoken dialogue. Their dance movements might evoke shifts in time, space, and identity (Wiles 1997: ch. 5). Their songs often develop implications beyond the specifics of the plot, for example by reflecting on mythical parallels to the action. The lyrics are always significant for the meaning of the drama (though not always in an obvious way) and are often of the highest poetic complexity. Such profundity may at times seem inappropriate to the chorus when viewed in character, e.g., as a group of sailors or slave women. But choral lyrics give the poet a different dramatic idiom in which to explore the themes of the play. We do not know how clearly the lyrics could be heard as the chorus danced and sang, but anecdotes indicate the audience's interest in and appreciation of the words. For example, after the great Athenian military disaster in Sicily (above, p. 8), many Athenians were taken prisoner and sent to work in the Sicilian stone-quarries, but some of them were released from slavery because they could recite Euripides; other defeated Athenians, found on the battlefield, were given food and drink in exchange for singing Euripides' latest lyrics (Plutarch, *Life of Nicias* 29.2–3; quoted by Csapo and Slater 1995: 8).

We know little about the music or choreography of the choral performances, but we do know that they formed part of a rich and still living tradition.

> Every significant public and private event in Greece was celebrated by choral dances. . . . Tragedy achieves its effects by drawing upon a rich cultural vocabulary of dance forms, such as the paean [a song and dance in praise of a god], the lament, the war-dance, or the initiation dance, and it allowed the dramatic context to give those dances a changed and often inverted meaning. (Wiles 1997: 90)

The dancers' gestures certainly included a strong mimetic element, using movements from familiar activities such as battles, victory celebrations, weddings, funerals, sacrifices, religious rites, and athletic contests.

Besides varying the rhythm and tone of a play, songs mark transitions in the action and the passage of time; they also have the important technical function of providing time for actors to change masks and costumes in order to return as different characters in the next scene. We do not know how much physical contact took place between chorus and actors, or to what extent the two groups shared the *orchēstra* or the stage (if there was one). Sometimes the chorus seem to participate quite vigorously in the action, but their activity and effectiveness as a dramatic character are usually quite limited. It is usual for them to remain onstage from their entrance until the end of the play, in contrast to the comings and goings of the actors. There are occasional departures from this convention for special dramatic effect, as when the entire chorus exits as part of the funeral procession at *Alcestis*

746. They also normally remain outside the *skēnē,* and do not intervene to prevent murders or other dire events from taking place inside. Like other dramatic conventions, however, this exclusion of the chorus from the *skēnē* is occasionally violated (e.g., *Helen* 385).

Formal Elements

All genres of Athenian drama are constructed of fairly well-defined components, alternating between speech (primarily by the actors) and song/dance (primarily by the chorus). Most tragedies begin with a spoken monologue or dialogue that sets the scene and provides the audience with any necessary background information (the "exposition," in modern theater parlance). Euripides typically accomplishes his exposition through an opening monologue followed by some dialogue. This opening scene (usually called the prologue) is followed by the arrival of the chorus, which punctuates subsequent scenes with its songs. The actors' speeches in the spoken scenes range in length from the long rhetorical oration, or *rhēsis,* to *stichomythia,* a formal kind of dialogue in which the characters exchange single (or occasionally double) lines.

The alternation of actors' speech and choral song/dance is a fluid form rather than a rigid structure. The play is not formally divided into a fixed number of acts, and the choral songs are not just interludes but integral parts of the play (Wiles 1997: ch. 5). Further, both spoken and lyric elements are highly manipulable. Actors, especially in Euripides, may shift into solo lyric song and dance (a monody), which may be followed by a speech covering the same ground, as a way of giving heightened significance to a particular moment or topic (e.g., *Helen* 255–329). Monodies usually express strong emotion and are given to female characters more often than male. The actors may also interact with the chorus in a sung dialogue (a *kommos*), especially at moments of high emotion (as in the unusual *parodos* of *Helen*), or alternate their spoken lines with the lyrics of the chorus. Such passages may play the scene-dividing role of a choral ode or serve to vary the tone of a long scene. Conversely the chorus had a leader (the *koruphaios*), who not only led the dancing but exchanged a few spoken lines with the actors, serving as a mouthpiece for the chorus as a whole.

Most scenes are between two characters, sometimes with a third looking on. This contributes to the debate-like atmosphere of many scenes. Nearly all the plays, especially by Euripides, include one or more intense, semiformal debates, where two characters make long, highly rhetorical speeches on opposing sides of a central issue (e.g. *Alcestis* 614–733, *Medea* 446–622, *IA* 317–414). This kind of debate (called an *agōn,* or "contest"), along with many other long speeches, reflects the influence of contemporary rhetoric, especially the teaching of the sophists (above, p. 14). The prominence of rhetorical techniques in drama aligns the theater with other central arenas of public life in democratic Athens, in particular the law courts (*agōn* is also the word for a trial), and the Assembly, where male citizens debated and voted on public policy (above, p. 7). (On this important aspect of drama see most recently Halliwell 1997.) At the other end of the formal spectrum, *stichomythia* is often used to highlight pointed disagreements through the verbal echoes with which one character "caps" the other (e.g., *Medea* 328–29, 333–34).

Another distinctive formal element of Athenian tragedy is the so-called "messenger speech." The plots often hinge on extremely violent events, but these are rarely shown taking place onstage. The reasons for this reticence are unknown, but it cannot be adequately explained by technical limitations or a general distaste for violence. In most plays at a climactic moment an otherwise insignificant character enters to report on violent or highly dramatic events that have taken place offstage. The character is usually a humble one, but employs a grand narrative style, influenced by epic, which appeals strongly to the listeners' imagination. This use of imaginative "scene-painting" allows the playwright to introduce locations that are not presented onstage, such as wilderness or the interior of a woman's bedroom. Some plays, including *Helen* and *IA,* contain more than one such speech.

A different kind of formal resource was offered by "type-scenes," where the dramatists used variations on well-known situations. One example is the "recognition scene," a popular type-scene in which one character is disguised or unknown to another, but is gradually recognized, often by means of specific items or "tokens." The complex mutual recognition of Menelaos and Helen in *Helen* is a scene of this kind (*Helen* 541–624). Like many recognition scenes, this one makes effective use of *stichomythia,* a form well suited to the gradual revelation of new information. Another type-scene portrays supplication, a ritual that occurred in real life (above, pp. 21–2) but which is exceptionally prominent in drama. Like the shoot-out at the end of a Western, such scenes do have a connection with ordinary life, but their formality and extreme familiarity derive from their repeated appearance in well-known dramatic genres. This familiarity makes the audience alert to variations by individual playwrights for particular effects.

Both the spoken and the sung portions of Athenian drama are in verse. Greek poetry is not structured through rhyme, but depends on rhythmic patterns (meters) to create poetic form. The spoken lines of tragedy are mostly iambic trimeters, which have a regular six-beat rhythm approximating the flow of natural speech. This meter is rather like Shakespearean blank verse (iambic pentameter), except that it has six beats instead of five, and is quantitative rather than accentual. This means that, like all ancient Greek meters, it is based on the length of syllables rather than patterns of word-stress. (The latter would have been impossible in ancient Greek, since it had a tonal system of accentuation more like Chinese than English.) In rhythm the iambic trimeter roughly follows the iambic pattern short-long, i.e., a short syllable followed by a long one (equivalent to an unstressed syllable followed by a stressed one in English verse). This is by far the most frequent meter for dialogue, but other meters are occasionally used too. Most common of these is the anapest (whose basic pattern is short-short-long), a regular "marching" meter often associated with entrances or exits, or more generally with movement. Trochaic meters (long-short) are occasionally used for emotionally charged dialogue. These meters were probably chanted to musical accompaniment.

The lyric songs are composed in highly varied and elaborate meters, unique to each song. They were accompanied by music played mostly on a double-reeded wind instrument called the *aulos,* but other instruments may also have been used (compare below, pp. 472–3, n. 165). A typical choral song consists of a series of pairs of stanzas called "strophe" and "antistrophe." Each strophe has its own complex rhythmic structure, which is repeated precisely in the antistrophe. There may be several such strophic pairs, each metrically unique. They are sometimes followed by an epode—an additional single stanza with a different metrical pattern. Different types of lyric meter express different levels of excitement, and the various musical modes conveyed different moods. The actors' speeches may be highly emotional, often conveying such passions as anger through the use of grand rhetoric, but lyrics are the most frequent vehicle for the expression of intense emotions such as grief, fear, and joy. Such feelings are conveyed in a more impressionistic, less rational style than in spoken dialogue.

The linguistic style of tragedy is traditional, formal, and distinctive. The diction is elevated, including many archaic and otherwise poetic forms that were not used in ordinary life. (Comedy, by comparison, uses popular, colloquial, and flamboyant styles, including parodies of tragedy and other genres.) For the most part, socially humble characters use the same lofty diction as aristocratic characters, and foreigners do not betray their origins by the way they speak. Thus slaves like the Nurse and Paidagogos in *Medea,* and non-Greeks like Theoklymenos and Theonoe in *Helen,* speak fluent tragic Greek. (Again, there is a marked contrast with the vulgarity and caricatures of foreign dialects found in comedy.) Choral songs are highly poetic, complex in style and idiosyncratic in diction, and contain elements of a non-Athenian Greek dialect (Doric). Unfortunately, most of these effects are impossible to convey in translation. (On Euripides' diction see further below, pp. 70–71.)

When all its performance elements are considered, Athenian tragedy much more closely resembles grand opera, or non-European theatrical forms such as Japanese Kabuki, than the naturalistic drama of late-nineteenth- or early-twentieth-century Europe. In fact, when he wrote his *Orfeo,* the first surviving European opera, based on the Greek legend of Orpheus, Claudio Monteverdi was consciously attempting to recreate ancient Greek drama. Some of these aspects of tragedy may strike a modern audience as artificial, but every kind of drama relies on its own formal conventions. We tend not to notice the artificiality of our own artistic conventions (including those of film and television), because familiarity makes them seem "natural" and "realistic" to us. Just so, for the original audience of Athenian tragedy the genre's wide range of formal elements seemed "natural" enhancing rather than interfering with their ability to respond viscerally to the drama. The various elements also drew on a range of established literary traditions, such as lyric, epic, and oratory, which were familiar and satisfying to their audience. In deploying them, the dramatists provided a multifarious theatrical experience, enriched by shifting styles and perspectives.

Use of Myth

Subject matter provides one of the most striking contrasts between Athenian tragedy and comedy. Comedy was highly topical. Its plays were set in Athens itself and often represented contemporary politicians and other well-known figures, including the tragedians themselves (compare below, pp. 67–9, 77–8). The comic hero is usually an average contemporary person with certain exaggerated features. Comic characters make explicit allusions to contemporary events, often giving concrete advice about current issues and criticizing specific individuals by name. The tragic playwrights avoided this explicit topicality, setting their plays in other times and places than contemporary Athens and using myths as their primary subject matter. The main tragic characters are aristocratic, though lower status characters do appear in the chorus or in supporting roles, including slave characters who act as servants and go-betweens for their masters and mistresses.

Comedy often focuses in a highly explicit way on bodily functions, sex, and reproduction, and performances included nudity and obscenity in costume, language, and gesture. By contrast, Herakles' indulgence in and reference to bodily appetites in *Alcestis* is odd in a tragedy. Yet despite its more decorous style, tragedy is in a sense more shocking than comedy. Through the distancing medium of myth, it often deals with appalling transgressions of accepted social codes, such as incest, cannibalism, human sacrifice, and intra-familial murder. In its own way, then, tragedy addresses the same fundamental aspects of human life as comedy. Comedy makes crude jokes about food, drink, and sex, while tragedy exposes the deep anxieties surrounding these same features of mortality. Each genre in its own way explores the structural tensions built into Athenian social and cultural life.

The Athenians did not draw a sharp line between myth and history. They viewed the ancient legends as a form of history, and heroes of the past as their own tribal ancestors. This gave the old tales an immediacy for their original audience which they must inevitably lack for us. A few tragedies were actually composed around recent Greek events. We have one surviving play of this kind: Aeschylus' *Persians,* which depicts the failed Persian invasion of Greece from the invaders' point of view. Such themes did not prevail, however, perhaps because they were too close to the audience for comfort (compare Phrynichus' experience, above, pp. 29–30). Legendary "history" was more distant, more flexible, and more open to interpretation than current events. While immediate enough to engage the audience with stories of their tribal ancestors, it remained sufficiently distant to allow disturbing themes to be examined safely.

Despite its preference for legendary settings, then, Athenian tragedy was not an antiquarian art form. Although most tragedies are set in legendary times, in places other than Athens, with heroic protagonists drawn from myth, tragedy at the same time reflects and comments on the concerns of contemporary Athens. Mythic subject matter allowed for indirect allusions to contemporary events, in contrast to the explicit commentary characteristic of comedy. The tension between these perspectives was intellectually and artistically stimulating for the tragedians, who regularly used mythic stories to explore issues of pressing concern, whether social, political, or intellectual. They often achieved this by focusing on the implications of an action by one or more protagonists, with various characters discussing the ethical, religious, and political aspects from their own point of view. The playwrights were thus able to provoke reaction and discussion without taking definite stands in their own voices.

Mythological traditions were multiple and often conflicting. The gods themselves had many different aspects (sometimes contradictory), which might be highlighted or ignored, depending on the playwright's purposes. Although some elements of familiar tales were more widespread than others, and the Homeric versions were particularly well known and admired, there were no canonical versions of the traditional stories. The number and degree of variations in even the most famous myths may surprise a modern reader. This volume includes some striking examples: Helen did not necessarily elope with Paris (below, pp. 219–20, 225); Medea did not necessarily kill her children (below, p. 152); and Iphigenia was not necessarily killed by her father (*IA* 1581–1612).

The presentation of a wide variety of attitudes toward the gods, religion and myth is appropriate to an art form directed at a large and diverse audience. Many audience members may have believed literally in the myths, others may have been critical or skeptical, still others may have rejected them altogether (compare above, p. 14). Even within the city of Athens, audience members with different backgrounds, educational levels, and social positions must have had varying degrees of familiarity with different versions of the tales. This in turn depended partly on their exposure to the varied contexts in which these different versions were told, such as rituals, social events, public speeches, gossip, or works of art, as well as performances of epic and drama (compare Buxton 1994: 11, 162). We can see the importance of context by contrasting the expectations and conventions of different theatrical genres. Herakles, the great hero who became a god, is presented seriously as a mighty hero in Euripides' *Herakles,* but as a comic buffoon in Aristophanes' *Frogs.* The Herakles of *Alcestis* falls somewhere in between: He heroically conquers death, but his buffoonish appetites are undisguised.

Enormous numbers of mythic variants have been lost to us. Many of these were written in texts that have disappeared, but others must have existed only in oral versions, for example those associated with particular local rites. Diverse oral traditions preceded literacy for many centuries. Even in Euripides' time, Greece was still a society in which most of what was important was actively transmitted in oral form.[15] Typically in an oral society multiple versions of any given tale will be current, as stories change with the telling over time and in new situations and locations. Numerous variants, even apparently contradictory ones, can be accepted as part of the totality of oral tradition. This aspect of the culture includes tale-telling by socially marginal groups like slaves and women. We know, for instance, that women sang songs and told tales while weaving. But such variants have not come down to us in women's own voices, since the writers who recorded the tales were almost exclusively elite males. What influence, if any, such oral and marginal variants may have had on tragedy is unknown to us.

Not only were the myths not fixed in their incidents, they also did not have a single determinate meaning. They were connected in important ways with the rituals that pervaded Athenian life, but this was not their only function. Even when a story arose in a specific ritual or mythological context, it could be used for other purposes and evolve over time to meet changing cultural conditions. New levels of meaning might be added, which could maintain, transform, or mask older meanings. In this volume, the story of Helen's abduction is an excellent site for examining the different levels of meaning that may simultaneously coexist: in this case ritual, pan-cultural, and political (below, pp. 221–30).

The dramatists not only had a wide range of stories available to them, but themselves contributed to this range. Like their poetic predecessors and successors, they had considerable latitude in altering the myths to suit their own purposes. Some central features of legend were probably unchangeable: The Greeks always win the Trojan War, and Aristotle says that Klytemnestra must be killed by Orestes (*Poetics* 1453b). But this left a wide area in which the dramatists might transform, reorganize and reinterpret traditional mythological plots. They were also free to make up new characters (though usually minor ones), and the choice of chorus was entirely up to the dramatist (a point well emphasized by Gould 1996: 28). In some cases we see the dramatists appearing to push the limits of allowable change, or tease the audience with the possibility of radical transformations of tradition, as with the outcome of *IA* (below, pp. 296–7).

Literary traditions thus interact with oral in the (re)production and transformation of myth. The variant stories about Helen exemplify this dynamic interaction between oral and written tradition. Euripides' own divergent portrayals of Helen in different plays show both the continued vitality and diversity of traditional tales, and the uses that could be made of them by individual writers. Yet because so much written and oral material has been lost, we can rarely know for certain whether a dramatist is innovating or choosing an otherwise unknown variant. For example, it used to be widely believed by scholars that Euripides was the first playwright to make Medea murder her children, but in recent years this idea has been strongly called into question (below, p. 152).

The dramatists' creative freedom extended to characterization. Important figures usually retained key attributes or deeds from past traditions, but their characters were open to interpretation. Achilles, for example, is assumed to be the greatest of warriors in both Homer's *Iliad* and Euripides' *IA,* yet his personality is quite different in the two works; likewise the Klytemnestra of *IA* differs from that of Euripides' influential predecessor, Aeschylus. The playwrights could thus vary the portraits of mythical characters from earlier traditions or treatments. But in the very act of doing so, they were also using those traditions. Every Greek audience member would be familiar with the story of the *Iliad,* and the better educated would know the work in considerable detail. The more popular tragedies were also well known by many (below, p. 84). So when Euripides gives us a new interpretation of Achilles or Klytemnestra, he is inviting his audience to note any differences and observe them in counterpoint with previous traditions (below, pp. 311–12).

III. WOMEN IN ATHENS

Athenian Women and the Ideology of Gender

The feminism of the 1970s revived interest in the historical study of women and revitalized many areas of scholarship on the ancient world. Even after more than twenty years of research, however, discussion about the life of women in ancient Athens continues to be lively, indeed contentious. Some scholars see Athens as completely male-centered and misogynistic (e.g., Keuls 1985); others find it no more oppressive to women than other traditional societies (e.g., Lefkowitz 1986). What makes such extreme positions possible is the lack of firm evidence, difficulties in interpreting that evidence, inconsistencies between various sources, and internal ambiguities within the sources we do have. These problems are exacerbated by the fact that most of our sources are elite texts and art works produced by men, in which representations of women's lives are expressed through, and complicated by, the ideology of gender.

The different kinds of evidence for Athenian women's lives include texts (poetry, history, philosophy, courtroom speeches), the visual arts (vase painting, sculpture), and other physical remains, such as the foundations of houses. Almost no ancient Greek texts written by women have come down to us. Of the few women writers that we do have—Sappho, Erinna, and Nossis—none came from fifth-century Athens, and none wrote epic or tragedy, the most substantial public genres (see Snyder 1989). Hence there is virtually no evidence about Athenian women's lives from women's point of view. Moreover, most ancient texts do not *aim* to convey information about the social life of their time; that must be read between the lines, taking into account the genre and purpose of the text. Like other genres, tragedy represents many details of women's lives, but does so for its own purposes and in ways circumscribed by generic convention. Indeed, it is even harder than many other genres to use as evidence for actual women's lives, since most of its plots are set away from Athens and in the legendary past.

The scarcity of evidence about Athenian women is directly related to their public invisibility. Women were not permitted to participate in the civic life of the *polis:* they could not vote in the Assembly, serve on juries, testify in court, own property, or handle more than small sums of money without the consent of a man.

Throughout her life every woman remained legally a minor, under the control of a male relative known as her *kurios*—normally her father or brother until marriage, then her husband. It is sometimes suggested that women occupied a position analogous to slaves, in relationship to the free male master of the household (the *oikos*). Medea's use of the word *despotēs* ("master") suggests that the lot of women resembles that of slaves (*Medea* 233), and Aristotle says that a husband rules his wife as a master rules slaves (*Politics* 1259a). Nevertheless, there were important social and legal differences in the status of free women and slaves. For example free women were not bought or sold; a man could only have one legitimate wife, but many slaves; the relationship between husband and wife was ideally based on personal compatability and affection, whereas slaves were strictly a commodity; and a free woman in trouble could turn to her male relatives for help.

In the heroic societies portrayed by Homer, aristocratic women are subordinate to men and perform separate work, but are often consulted by their husbands on important matters and seem to have far greater freedom than they did in fifth-century Athens. Although these texts are not straightforwardly historical, they suggest that in aristocratic society women exerted more influence, since women were central to the family and the family was the basis of the aristocratic clans' power. The rise of democracy at Athens probably decreased women's political influence, since the move from aristocracy to democracy weakened family ties while strengthening civic ones. For example, large public funerals by aristocratic families celebrated and solidified clan relations. Solon, an important figure for the beginnings of democracy in early sixth-century BCE Athens, imposed restrictions on such funerals. His legislation specifically limited the dress and behavior of the women mourners as examples of conspicuous display (Plutarch, *Solon* 21; see also Alexiou 1974: 20–22; Holst-Warhaft 1992: 3, 98–103). In tragedy, Aeschylus' *Oresteia* depicts the development from monarchy to democracy as a movement from female to male power.

The growth of Athenian democracy sharpened the distinction between *oikos* and *polis* as the proper spheres of action for female and male respectively, requiring corresponding behavior and character traits. Men were destined for the military and government, women for the *oikos*.

> The contrast between public and private life in classical Athens was sharp. . . . [Public life's] locus was the open arena—assembly, market-place, law-court, gymnasium, battle-field. . . . The *oikos*, by contrast, was a closed space, architecturally functional rather than ornamental. Its relationships were hierarchic: husband-wife, parent-child, owner-slave. (Humphreys 1993: 1–2)

Men's and women's lives followed different tracks even as they went through similar stages. For example, puberty rites for males and females were parallel but separate. Both sexes cut their hair at adolescence, but in recognition of roles specific to each gender. Women's rites preceded marriage, whereas young men (ephebes), underwent a period of paramilitary training in which they did duty on the frontiers. At the festival of the Apatouria, boys born that year—but not girls—were registered in the clan (Parke 1977: 90–92; Zeitlin 1982: 141).

This sharp division between the sexes was reflected in, and enforced by, the ideology of gender, which attributed different and complementary behaviors and character traits to men and women. This can be seen at its starkest in the "table of opposites" into which Pythagorean philosophers divided the universe. The Pythagorean table associates the female with the many, unlimited, left, dark, bad; the male is associated with the one, limit, right, light, good. Such philosophical beliefs affected various aspects of people's lives, including the practice of medicine (Sissa 1992: 72–73; King 1994). Although real life was far more complex than this simple dichotomy might suggest, a male's failure to fulfill the expectations of masculinity often resulted in his being derided as female. Conversely, a strong female character who gains power at the expense of an Admetos or Jason may be viewed as violating the behavior proper to her gender (below, pp. 98, 162–6). "Masculinity" and "femininity" are polar opposites, but they define each other and cannot be understood apart from each other.

The rhetoric of ideal "masculine" conduct, even in democratic Athens, was derived to a significant degree from the norms of heroic behavior on the battlefield. The word *aretē* ("excellence"), which came to mean any kind of goodness, has the same root as the word for a man (*anēr*) and originally referred primarily to excellence in battle (compare above, p. 24). In democratic Athens it also denoted other kinds of "manliness," such as success at politics. When applied to women, it referred instead to desirable female behaviors. A character in Plato, when asked to define *aretē,* gives the conventional picture:

> If you want the excellence of a man, it's easy—the excellence of a man is to be capable of taking part in the affairs of the *polis,* and in doing so to help his friends and harm his enemies, and watch out that he does not suffer anything of that kind himself. But if you want the excellence of a woman, it's not difficult to say: she should manage the household well, preserving its contents and being obedient to her husband. (*Meno* 10e)

Chief among the motives for "manly" behavior on the Homeric battlefield are *timē* ("honor") and *kleos* ("fame" or "glory"). *Timē,* a fundamental Greek cultural concept, originally means "price" or "value." "Honor" is the value that society places upon one, or one's social status. This is typically shown through material gifts, public respect, and other visible signs. Greeks generally, and male heroes in particular, have a very acute sense of honor. *Timē* is part of the zero-sum game in which one man can achieve honor only by another's loss (compare below, p. 99). A man who feels he has been publicly dishonored is expected to redress the balance by avenging himself, which he often does in spectacular fashion. The earliest and most influential example of this is Achilles in the *Iliad.* A heroine like Medea has much in common with Achilles (below, pp. 163–4), but in accordance with the polarized ideology of gender, a woman is not permitted or expected to seek *timē* under the same conditions as men, nor is she accorded the same kind of public recognition. A woman's "price" or "value" depends on her sexual desirability and fidelity, her skill at performing household tasks, her modesty and deference to men. This renders the "heroic," "male" behavior of certain female characters in drama highly problematic.

Male heroes also strive for *kleos,* "fame" or "glory," which in epic means becoming the subject of bardic song for performing great deeds in battle. Women can gain their own *kleos,* and be praised in poetry, by fulfilling the ideals established for their gender. In tragedy, heroic women often win such praise by sacrificing themselves for men, like Iphigenia in *IA.* Conversely, for either sex to violate their respective gender ideal results in public blame. Thus Helen is aware that she and Paris will become a topic of song because of their adultery (*Iliad* 6. 356–58). In the *Odyssey* the shade of the dead Agamemnon says that, for murdering him, Klytemnestra will bring blame on all women, "even the good ones" (*Odyssey* 11.432–34).

In democratic Athens, the ideology of female invisibility creates a tension in the very concept of female *kleos,* even for virtuous women. The Athenian leader Pericles, after praising the Athenian warriors who died in battle, says to the women, "For you great reputation comes from not falling short of your assigned nature. A woman achieves *kleos* who is least talked about among men, either with blame or praise" (Thucydides 2.45). This sentiment accords with the fact that in Athens respectable women were not named in public, but spoken of as "daughter of So-and-so" or "wife of So-and-so." Yet since *kleos* by its very definition means being spoken of by others, this Athenian ideology places women in a lose-lose situation. Tragedy often brings to the fore the tension between these various ideals of female excellence and the problematic concept of female *kleos* (see e.g., below, pp. 164, 316).

The virtue most vigorously demanded of Athenian women was *sōphrosunē* (literally "sound-mindedness"). This has no single English equivalent, but ranges over self-control, self-knowledge, deference, moderation, resistance to appetite, and chastity. *Sōphrosunē* is considered desirable for men as well as women, but it is specially associated with women because of its close ties to sexual restraint and deference (compare *IA* 1158–59). Deference was to some degree required of all women in the Athenian social structure, and self-restraint was deemed harder and therefore more necessary for women than men. Many Greek texts depict women as having appetites and passions difficult for them to control, stronger than those of males, which make them irrational and often untrustworthy.

Sexual desire (*erōs*) is an especially dangerous passion because women, however politically powerless, are essential for men's production of legitimate heirs. Improper sexual behavior by women can disrupt male control over their own reproduction. Jason expresses this stereotype at its most virulent, when he claims that all women are obsessed with sex and deplores men's need of women in order to reproduce themselves (*Medea* 568–75). Accordingly, the control of female sexuality was a central factor in Athenian social organization. A seduced woman was subject to expulsion from the family and might be sold into slavery. A man caught in the act of adultery could be murdered with impunity, but merely paid a fine in the case of rape, on the ground that seduction alienates a woman from her husband and creates uncertainty about the paternity of his children (Lysias 1.32–33).

Although the primary locus of male anxiety about female agency is sex and reproduction, Greek texts frequently express more general fears about women asserting their individual will or choosing their own identity. As a force potentially threatening to their male relatives' honor, to the legitimacy of their children, to the stability of the *oikos* and the *polis,* women require constant vigilance from men. Such a system creates its own justification, but also uncertainty about its validity and perpetual anxiety about its enforcement.

So far we have stressed the polarized opposition between the sexes in ancient Athenian gender ideology. Certainly this ideology was extremely powerful in structuring and reflecting many aspects of social reality. It is important, however, to remember that ideology and actual practice are never identical. Or to put it another way, the ideological structures found in elite texts are "legislative rather than descriptive," and reflect a system rife with internal tensions (Winkler 1990a: 69). This awareness has brought us new ways of understanding the lives of real women in ancient Athens. Until recently, for example, it was common to take ideology at face value, and speak of the "seclusion" of Athenian women in their own "women's quarter." It is certainly true that the respectable wives of Athenian citizens were expected to remain in the *oikos,* to avoid speaking with men not related to them, and not to be mentioned by name in public (Schaps 1977; Sommerstein 1980). The evidence for a specific "women's quarter" is not clear, however. The houses of wealthier men seem to have been divided into men's and women's quarters, with the latter in the inner, darker regions of the house (Walker 1983). And speeches in the law courts (e.g., Lysias 1.3) indicate that males (including relatives) were expected not to enter the women's quarter. Archaeological finds, however, indicate only a demarcated men's quarter, with couches for banquets; there is no way to tell which were the women's quarters. It is possible that the entire remainder of the dwelling constituted women's space (M. Jameson 1990: 172).

The absolute ideological divisions between *polis/oikos,* male/female, inside/outside can only have been maintained (to the extent that they were) by the rich, who had slaves to perform errands outside the house. Certain texts (Lysias 1, Aristophanes' *Lysistrata*) suggest that women could easily evade restrictions on their movements (though they might be in serious trouble if they were caught doing so). In any case, seclusion from men did not mean isolation from other women. Many female activities—preparing wool, weaving, going to the fountain for water, delivering babies—were performed in the company of female relatives, neighbors, slaves, and children. Women had care of male as well as female children up to the age of seven. Less wealthy women held jobs, doing productive labor outside the household in agriculture and commerce (wood cutting, nursing, wet-nursing, jewelry-crafting, carding, spinning, weaving, constructing clothing, vase painting, and so on).

Moreover, *polis* and *oikos* were closely interlinked. The Athenian *polis* was made up of, and depended upon, individual households. Men could not participate in the *polis* without the work of women in the *oikos*—especially the work of child-bearing and child-raising. Reproduction, putatively a "private" activity, was seen as serving the city. As Vernant puts it, Athens sought "to ensure, through strict rules governing marriage, the permanence of the city itself through constant reproduction" (1980: 50). Laws regarding marriage and citizenship were adjusted to suit the needs of the *polis.* For example, in 451 BCE Pericles got a restrictive citizenship law passed because Athens was considered to be overpopulated. This law limited citizenship to men with an Athenian mother as well as an Athenian father. During the Peloponnesian War, however, enforcement of the law was apparently relaxed so that men could have legitimate, citizen children from two mates, such as a concubine as well as a wife (Diogenes Laertius 2.26). This kind of manipulation of the laws governing the family helped the *polis* to maintain the population needed for such purposes as warfare.

Athenian women also participated in certain public activities, especially of a religious nature. Ritual obligations were a proper and indeed a mandatory reason for women even of the upper classes to leave their homes. The Athenian calendar was full of religious festivals, in many of which women played central roles. These were often women-only rites for female divinities (although Dionysos was a notable exception; above, pp. 31–2). In rituals for Gaia (Mother Earth), Hestia (goddess of the hearth), Hera, Aphrodite, Athena, and others, Greek women celebrated their powers of sexuality and fertility. Festivals for Demeter (the Skira, Haloa, and Thesmophoria) were especially important. Males were excluded from these rituals, just as women were excluded from those for men.

Despite Solon's restrictions (above, p. 49), women also retained extensive responsibility for funeral rites. The ancient Greek funeral consisted of several stages: *prothesis,* in which the body was laid out, washed, and adorned; *ekphora,* the trip to the grave, usually on the third day after death; burial, followed by libations, gifts to the corpse and ritual mourning (*thrēnos, goos*); the return from the grave, and the reintegration of the survivors into the social world of the living (below, pp. 99–100; Boardman and Kurtz 1971: 71). Women participated in most of these stages, and were especially associated with the washing and mourning of the corpse. They also made later visits to the grave with offerings.

Women and Marriage: From **Parthenos** *to* **Gunē**

Like many traditional societies, Athens had a number of politico-religious rites marking stages of life for men and women (see van Gennep 1960; Turner 1977). For Athenian women these passages included that from childhood into puberty, from adolescent to adult woman, from virgin to married woman, from married woman to mother, and from life to death. A woman in Aristophanes' *Lysistrata* proudly declares that she has participated in four different transition rituals (638–47). The most important transition for women, however, was that from unmarried girl (*parthenos*) to wife and mother (*gunē*). To remain unmarried was not an available choice for women, and even among men it was extremely rare.

The goddess Artemis was especially important for women's transition rites.[16] Artemis is the daughter of Zeus and Leto, twin sister of Apollo, and a perpetual virgin. Her particular domain is the wilderness, including forests, mountains, and seacoasts. Yet she "is not wildness. She sees to it that the boundaries between the wild and the civilized are permeable in some way" (Vernant 1991: 198). As "mistress of animals," she both protects and kills wild animals. She presides over the hunt, ensuring that it is conducted with proper discipline, and fiercely punishes violations of those limits, as when she turns Aktaion into a stag to be killed by his own hunting dogs. In her capacity as *kourotrophos,* "caretaker of children," she watches over young people, bringing them safely to the threshold of adolescence, and presiding over the period of *partheneia* ("adolescence") for girls, before they make their transition to the adult states of marriage and motherhood. In Sparta, Artemis also oversees young men's transition into adulthood.

One intriguing rite of passage for girls is called the Arkteia.[17] In this ritual, which took place in Brauron and Mounichia, two different sanctuaries of Artemis near Athens, girls between five and ten years old spent a period of ritual service together in the sanctuary, away from their families. This rite was said to have been instituted as recompense for the killing of a semi-tame bear belonging to the sanctuary, after it became rough with a young girl. Spending this period in the sanctuary was called "playing the bear." We do not know all the details, but the "bears" seem to have engaged in dancing and running races (in some cases naked). Wearing a special dress is also mentioned: "When I was ten, wearing my saffron robe, I was a bear at the Brauron Festival" (*Lysistrata* 644–45).

"Playing the bear" was a ritual prior to adolescence. To the Greeks, children were by nature "wild" and *parthenoi* especially so. One word for "wife" (*damar*) is related to a word for taming animals (*damazdō*), suggesting that marriage was viewed as a form of "breaking in." To take on the "civilized" role of married woman and mother, *parthenoi* had to be "tamed" by a series of rituals. It seems likely that the "bears" performed their "wildness" in the sanctuary prior to the final "taming" of marriage. Before they were married, girls dedicated their childhood toys to Artemis. "Playing the bear" was also a gift for the goddess; perhaps "dying" like the bear was a symbolic death to honor her. Such honors were necessary because transitions were felt to be dangerous, involving as they did the death of the previous self. When a *parthenos* married she no longer belonged to Artemis, so the goddess might be angered by this defection and take revenge. Paying ritual honor to the goddess might prevent this from happening. The transition to marriage could be dangerous for males too. Admetos' fated early death (averted by Alcestis' sacrifice) is caused by his failure to sacrifice to Artemis on the occasion of his marriage (below, p. 96).

The ideal of marriage involved physical attraction and pleasure; wedding scenes on vase paintings depict beautiful brides in the company of Eros, the divine personification of sexual desire. But as in most traditional societies, the institution of marriage was aimed primarily at strengthening families and producing legitimate offspring, rather than creating an intimate personal relationship between the spouses. Marriage was a transaction between males, the bridegroom and the girl's *kurios* (usually her father). At Athens the young bride was about age fifteen, and her husband was typically twice her age. In Xenophon's *Household Management*

(*Oikonomikos*) a husband describes how he (not her mother or another woman) educated his bride in her role as wife and manager of the household. Asked what she knew before marrying him, the husband answers,

> How could she have known anything, since she came to me when she was not yet fifteen, and had lived previously under diligent supervision in order that she might see and hear as little as possible and ask the fewest possible questions? (7.5)

This passage, written from the point of view of an upper-class male, represents the ideology of marriage as a complementary union of unequals.

Marriage involved a series of ceremonies, the most important of which were the *enguē* ("betrothal") and *ekdosis* ("giving away"). At the *enguē* the bride was promised to the groom by her *kurios* with the formula, "I give this woman for the plowing of legitimate children." The two men probably sealed the contract with a handshake (Oakley and Sinos 1993: 9). Later came the *ekdosis,* or "giving away" (compare *Medea* 309, *IA* 130, 702–3; and see Leduc 1992: 274). At this ceremony the bridegroom "led" the bride in procession from her father's house to his own (see *Alcestis* 1110–11, 1115, with notes). The visual arts show the man leading the woman by her wrist. *Ekdosis* means not only "giving" but "lending:" The woman is "lent" to another family in order that it may produce heirs, but she retains her dowry and ties with her natal family, to whom she returns in case of divorce. Further celebrations took place the day after the *ekdosis.* These involved the exchange of gifts (including clothing and ornaments), sacrifice, singing, and torches carried in procession from one house to the other. Women, especially the bride's mother, played an important part in these activities and in preparing the bride for marriage (see *IA* 685–741).

Greek marriage had a number of formal and functional similarities to sacrifice (above, pp. 12–13). "Both seek to gain a propitious future through violence, loss and submission to a social order" (Foley 1985: 85). As sacrificial procedures established under what circumstances life could be taken and a living being consumed, marriage established socially sanctioned conditions for heterosexual intercourse and reproduction. Sacrifice affirmed differences between human beings (who sacrifice) and animals (who are sacrificed); marriage affirmed differences between males (who marry) and females (who are married). Sacrifice created bonds between human beings and gods by the gift of an animal; marriage created bonds between males of different households by the gift of a woman. Both involved little or no choice for the object given, although in both cases the appearance of coercion and violence was avoided.

And both involved a death—real for the animal, symbolic for the bride, as she left behind her mother, her natal family, and her former life, little knowing what awaited her (compare *Medea* 235–40). Girls are often portrayed as dreading this transition, such as in the following fragment from Sophocles' *Tereus.* (The speaker is Prokne, an Athenian princess; for her myth see below, p. 430, n. 149.)

> But now I am nothing, by myself.
> But often I have looked at women's nature in this way—
> that we are nothing. As young girls in our father's house
> we live, I think, the sweetest life of all human beings,
> for foolishness always nurtures children joyfully.
> But when we reach puberty and understanding,
> we are pushed outside and sold
> away from our paternal gods and those who gave us birth,
> some to foreign men, some to barbarians,
> some to joyless homes, some to abusive ones.
> And this, when a single night has yoked us,
> we must praise, and think we are faring well.

The idea of marriage as death for the maiden is mythically expressed in the story of Persephone, daughter of Demeter the earth goddess (Foley 1994: 104–12). Persephone was carried off against her will to marry Hades, the divine king of the underworld and of the dead. In Athenian life, a maiden's death before marriage is often represented in epitaphs as a marriage to Hades. There were also many striking similarities between funeral and marriage rituals, especially from a woman's point of view (e.g., both involve torches, processions, a veil). And the imagery of death and marriage is often intermingled in tragedy (Seaford 1987; Rehm 1994).

All this makes sense if we think of both occasions as major rites of passage, in which a woman is taken from the house of one older man (her father or other male guardian) to that of another (her husband or Hades). But the poignancy of the parallel resides in the fact that marriage, though an occasion for anxiety in the young bride, is also a time of great societal rejoicing. When marriage is replaced by death, the ritual that should lead to the incorporation of an outsider (the bride) into the *oikos,* and its renewal through reproduction, has become instead the means to destroy it by preventing its regeneration. In this volume weddings turn into funerals in *Alcestis,* in *IA,* and for Kreon's daughter in *Medea,* and a funeral becomes a wedding in *Alcestis.*

Once married, a woman was closely associated with the *oikos* of her husband. As the producer of children she was identified with the hearth, the heart of the household's continued life. Among other household cults, that of Hestia, goddess of the hearth, was especially important, since she was the emblem of the respectable wife. The Greek wife was also closely identified with the inner chamber, the *thalamos,* which was both the site of reproductive sexuality and the place where the family's wealth was guarded. The marriage bed within the *thalamos* symbolized sexual activity and fidelity, and also the bond between husband and wife which is the foundation of marriage and the family. Hence various words for "bed" are often used to signify marriage, as in Jason's complaint that women are obsessed with "the marriage-bed" (*Medea* 568–73). "The bed" for women does not simply refer to sex, however, as Jason seems to think. "Women are obsessed with 'the bed' because it is the source and site of their position in the house" (Rabinowitz 1993: 140; see also Vernant 1980: 62–66). The fact that this institutional significance is not easy to distinguish from "the bed" as a locus of sexual pleasure, shows the conceptual difficulty in Greek of distinguishing sexuality from reproduction and women's subjectivity from the female roles of wife and mother.

A married woman's double connection—to her father's and her husband's families—might create conflicting obligations. If a man died leaving a daughter but no sons, the daughter (known as an *epiklēros* or "heiress") was required to marry her nearest male relative, in order to keep the wealth within the patrilineal *oikos.* An only daughter already married at the time of her father's death could be required to divorce and remarry in such circumstances. Such tensions reveal the potentially problematic nature of marriage outside the immediate family: It brings an outsider into a new *oikos.* Thus Admetos calls his wife "a stranger, yet necessary to the household" (*Alcestis* 533). The loyalty of this outsider is frequently at issue, especially before she has borne a child. Childbirth, however, incorporates her into her husband's *oikos* by ties of blood, makes her a "woman" (*gunē*) instead of a "bride" (*numphē*), and renders her more trustworthy. A male speaker in a lawsuit reveals this attitude clearly: "When I decided to marry, and brought a wife into my house . . . I guarded her as well as possible, and paid attention, as was reasonable. But when our baby was born, I started to trust her" (Lysias 1.6).

In addition to bearing and caring for children, married women supervised the running of the household (which in wealthy families might include a large number of domestic slaves), maintained the cults of household divinities, and were responsible for many practical tasks. The most important of these was the production of clothing. Fabric was a labor-intensive and precious commodity in the ancient world, and its production included spinning, weaving, and dying. The female work of producing it was vital to the economy of the *polis* as well as the family. Its importance at Athens was symbolically displayed at the Panathenaic ("all-Athenian")

Festival in honor of Athena. This major civic event involved an elaborate procession to the Parthenon, culminating in the gift of a spectacular robe, woven and carried by female celebrants, to the city's patron goddess.

From the perspective of gender ideology, weaving was women's work par excellence. As such, it was an important symbol of "good womanhood." Yet like other attributes associated with women—such as sexual attractiveness—it might be interpreted either positively or negatively. From earliest times, weaving was connected with the use of language and came to signify the weaving of plots and snares, concealment, and deception (Bergren 1983; Bassi 1995). Woven entrapments sometimes serve virtuous purposes, as with the shroud that Penelope weaves and reweaves in the *Odyssey,* in order to deflect her suitors and remain faithful to her husband. In tragedy, however, such deceptive weavings are more often used to symbolize women's seduction, entrapment, and destruction of men. Klytemnestra in Aeschylus' *Agamemnon,* Deianeira in Sophocles' *Women of Trachis,* and Medea in this volume all use woven clothing to destroy their husbands (see Rabinowitz 1993: 143–45).

Legitimate wives and domestic slave-women were not, of course, the only women in ancient Athens. A fourth-century orator divides women into three groups: "We have courtesans for pleasure, concubines to look after the day-to-day needs of the body, and wives that we may breed legitimate children and have a trusty warden of our household possessions" (Demosthenes 59.122). Besides underlining the role of wives as housekeepers and producers of offspring, this quotation makes clear that there were other kinds of women in Athens besides the privileged class of citizens' wives, and also that men had many potential sexual partners. "Courtesans" (*hetairai*) were higher-class female prostitutes, who often performed as hired entertainers at male parties and were sometimes well educated in music and the arts. (Lower-class prostitutes were known as *pornai.*) Most prostitutes were slaves, but some managed to work their way to freedom. The word translated as "concubine" (*pallakē*) denotes a long-term mistress maintained by an Athenian citizen. Such relationships might be similar to common-law marriages, but were quite distinct from marriage proper. In most situations, a *pallakē* had little or no legal protection for herself or her children (though see above, p. 53). The quotation mentions only female sexual partners, but boys and male prostitutes were also available to men (compare *Medea* 245).

None of these sexual options was open to respectable Athenian women, either before or after marriage. Yet they were expected to tolerate their husband's mistresses, provided they were not brought into the same household, which would humiliate the legitimacy wife and threaten the social standing and economic security of herself and her children (compare *Medea* 699 with note). At the same time, female characters in drama quite often complain about male infidelity and the sexual double standard (see especially *Medea* 244–47). Concern about the position and treatment of women is also expressed in other Athenian sources, ranging from Aristophanes' plays to Plato's *Republic* (for a brief summary see Kerferd 1981: 159–62). In this, as in other respects, tragedy serves as a vehicle for the exploration of social codes and the problems they raise.

Women and Athenian Tragedy

Women may have been marginalized in Athenian public life, but in drama they often took center stage. Yet virtually all the action presented in tragedy takes place outside the house, in the public, male arena. The presence in drama of upper-class female characters engaging in public speech thus in itself transgresses Athenian gender protocols. Sometimes the presence of women outside the house receives no comment in the script. In such cases many would regard it as an accepted dramatic convention, reflecting behavior appropriate to characters in the heroic world (Easterling 1987). At other times, however, a woman's emergence from the house is strongly marked in the text (e.g., *Medea* 214, *IA* 992–96). When this happens, it is impossible to view women's presence outside as mere convention without further significance. Rather it serves to provoke questions about the ideology of gender.

Given the social and political restrictions on women in Athens, and the protocol that they not be seen, heard, or spoken of, why are female characters so important in tragedy? And why are they so often shown not conforming to Athenian ideals of proper female behavior, but defying and transgressing those norms? An early line of argument claimed that despite the testimony of other sources, the plays show that women were not in fact denigrated in ancient Athenian culture (e.g., Gomme 1925). But this argument has been rejected by many scholars (e.g., Arthur 1976; Gould 1980; Foley 1981a). More recently, it has been argued that the prominence of women in the tragedies is evidence of the power of women in myth, rather than their importance in Athenian life. This argument depends on the significance of women for the family. As Aristotle observes, most tragedies come from the histories of a few noble families and take place among close family members (*Poetics* 1453a, b). It is only to be expected, then, that women should have a prominent place in tragedy, as a result of their importance for the families central to Greek mythology. This explanation leaves questions unanswered, however. Why do so many myths focus on women and the family in the first place? Why do the tragedies of patriarchal Athens seem to select these myths rather than others? Why do some tragedies highlight, even enhance the roles of assertive women, instead of downplaying them? In the *Odyssey,* for example, Agamemnon is killed by Aigisthos (11.405–11), but in Aeschylus' *Agamemnon* his wife Klytemnestra wields the axe herself.

Psychological approaches have suggested answers to some of these questions. Taking a Freudian view, Slater sees "the combination of derogation of and preoccupation with women" (1968: 7) as the result of Athenian women's terrifying power over male children during their first seven years of life (compare above, p. 53). In myth and poetry, he argues, women are represented with the power they had over men when men were boys. Slater's psychoanalytic framework is now seen by many as anachronistic and culture-bound, yet his central insight—that the focus on women in tragedy reveals profound male anxieties about women's place in democratic Athens—remains an important one.

A related position argues that tragedy offers warnings about the dangers of women's behavior, especially when unsupervised by males (Hall 1997: 106–110). In this view the plays have little to do with the actual conditions of Athenian women's lives. Instead, the representations of female characters and gender relations are male constructions that use female figures to discuss issues of importance to men, including their anxieties about the domestic and social systems over which they preside. Case argues this view polemically, maintaining that the female roles in Greek drama "contain no information about the experience of real women. . . . Classical plays and theatrical conventions can now be regarded as allies in the project of suppressing real women and replacing them with masks of patriarchal production" (1988: 15, 7). Zeitlin argues a similar position more subtly, suggesting that "theater uses the feminine for the purposes of imagining a fuller model for the masculine self" (1996: 363). On this model, tragedy both embodies and portrays the set of cultural behaviors conventionally ascribed to women as natural and desirable, or unnatural and inappropriate. In its presentation of women it invites "the male audience to confront both their own constructions of the female and their own anxieties about the justice of the civic and family worlds over which they had claimed exclusive control" (Henderson 1996: 29).

The boundaries between male and female concerns, however, like those between *oikos* and *polis,* though sharply defined in principle, remained fluid and ambiguous both in actual practice and in the complex representations of tragedy. Yet another approach to understanding women in drama pays attention to these complexities, and suggests that Athenian tragedy as an institution, with its built-in productive tensions (between myth and history, monarchy and democracy, inside and outside, male and female), is an ideal environment for exploring these same tensions within contemporary Athenian society and ideology. In particular, issues of gender definition, behavior, and relations seem especially appropriate at a festival honoring Dionysos, who himself embodies gender ambiguity and transgression (above, pp. 31–2).

However we choose to explain the prominence of women in the genre of Athenian tragedy, the significance of the tragedies themselves for real women's lives depends crucially on whether or not women were actually present in the theater. As we have seen, Athenian tragedy was not aimed at an elite but at a large, inclusive, critical audience (above, pp. 27–30). The presence of women, however, has been much debated. Considering the many restrictions, both ideological and practical, on the public appearance of women, it would not be surprising if they were excluded from the theater, as has often been claimed. But this view rests primarily on general assumptions about the treatment of women. What little evidence we have suggests that on the contrary, some women were present, along with other marginal groups such as foreigners and even slaves (Pickard-Cambridge 1988: 263–65; Csapo and Slater 1995: 286–305). The presence of women is also supported by the evidence of comedy, which assumes that women can be influenced by the bad example of female characters in tragedy (below, pp. 80–81).

Given the ancient Greek ideology of gender, the inclusion of women in the theatrical audience may seem surprising. But although women were indeed barred from most public arenas of Athenian life, religious festivals were an important exception (above, pp. 53–4). Moreover the god in whose honor the dramas were performed was Dionysos, who, as we have seen, was the most inclusive of the gods, and one of the few male divinities in whose worship women played a conspicuous role (above, pp. 31–2). It is therefore appropriate that marginal social groups such as slaves and women should have been admitted to his festivities.

On the other hand, the plays were performed only once each (except for revivals in rural districts or later years), and clearly not all male Athenian citizens could fit into the theater, let alone all the women, children, and slaves. And many members of these latter groups were presumably unable to attend unless the male head of their household was willing to pay for them. It therefore seems likely, given the stratification of Athenian society, that socially inferior groups, including women, were present in the theater in smaller numbers than adult male citizens. In any case, whatever the exact composition of the audience, the plays are clearly aimed conventionally and primarily at adult male citizens. "The *notional* audience of drama (the executive male demos) differed by convention from the *actual* audience (the demos plus its wards and guests), so that the spectacle was at once civic/political (exclusive) and festive (inclusive)" (Henderson 1996: 17; on the *dēmos,* see above, p. 7).

Women were thus conceptually invisible, even if actually present in the audience (Henderson 1991). But this does not mean they did not pay close attention to the dramatic performances. And even those women who were not physically present may well have quizzed their husbands on what they had seen, as they did in other areas of public life. An orator warns the jurymen that they will have to explain to their wives their votes on a controversial case regarding women's status (Demosthenes 59.110–11). The comic playwright Aristophanes likewise portrays women asking their husbands how things went in the Assembly, though this time the men tell the women to shut up and mind their own domestic business (*Lysistrata* 507–21). The same range of masculine attitudes no doubt applied to questions from their wives about the theater.

There probably were some real women in the audience, then. But there were certainly none on stage. All speaking actors, members of the chorus, and presumably mute extras as well, were male, including those playing female parts. Cross-gender performance is found in many cultures, and cross-cultural comparisons (such as Garber 1992) may be helpful, provided we use them with caution. The meaning of particular theatrical practices always depends on specific cultural conditions. In Shakespeare's drama, for example, female parts were played by boys rather than adult men, often with a homoerotic subtext. Women performed in Japanese Kabuki until the seventeenth century CE, when they were replaced by boys and subsequently by adult men, since the boys, like the women, were considered too sexually provocative (Garber 1992: 245); the male actors of female roles (*onnagata*) subsequently developed a stylized art that attempted to combine "male" strength with "female" delicacy. Compared to forms of theater where cross-gender performance is the norm, late-twentieth-century drag is often transgressive in intention and/or effect and may therefore be used only with extreme caution as an analogy for Greek practice.

All of these cultural phenomena have one thing in common, however. Within each context, all male performances of female roles are constructions of "femininity" by men. As such they suggest that gender itself is not "natural" but "performative" (Butler 1990). These implications can be manipulated by self-conscious use. David Hwang's 1986 play *M. Butterfly*, for example, uses cross-gender performance to explore interlinked issues of race, gender, and imperialism. A male singer who plays female roles in the Peking Opera deceives a French diplomat into thinking he actually is a woman. He explains that males take female roles "because only a man knows how a woman is supposed to act" (Act 2, Scene 7). This "explanation" resonates on multiple levels with varying degrees of irony, suggesting that gender is as performative in life as it is in theater, that women do not always behave as they are "supposed" to do, and that male performance of female roles is a form of coercive ventriloquizing whereby men define and enforce the norms of "femininity."

Cross-gender performance thus has the potential to destablize conventional assumptions about gender roles. Greek comedy often exploits the disjunction between actor and role overtly, as when Euripides' Kinsman in *Women at the Thesmophoria* tries to "pass" as a woman and gets caught in a ridiculously inept performance of femininity. Tragedy sometimes seems to use the disjunction more obliquely, as when Medea "performs femininity" in order to win over Kreon, then assures the chorus it was only an act (*Medea* 368–72). The obvious message of this dramatic moment is one of female duplicity. More subtly, however, it suggests that the heroine's "femininity" is a consciously assumed mask to conceal her "masculine" determination. Perhaps it also hints at the male sex of the actor behind the theatrical mask (Rabinowitz 1998).

Ancient Greek sources sometimes express concern about the dangerous influence on men of dramatically portraying women. Plato's *Republic,* for example, deplores the enacting of "feminine" and "slavish" behavior such as lamentation, lust, or deception, because such enactment might affect both the actors and the audience watching them:

> We will not allow those whom we say we care about, and who must turn into good men, since they are men, to imitate a woman, young or old, abusing a man, or quarrelling with the gods and boasting because she thinks she is happy, or in the grip of misfortune and sorrows and lamentations, still less one who is sick, in love, or in labor. (395de)

Some contemporary scholars have suggested that enacting female roles may have served as a warning to men of how *not* to behave (Bassi 1995). Others argue that it may have enriched the male experience:

> Tragedy arrives at closures that generally reassert male, often paternal (or civic) structures of authority, but before that the work of the drama is to open up the masculine view of the universe . . . initiating actor and spectator into new and unsettling modes of feeling, seeing, and knowing. (Zeitlin 1996: 364)

IV. EURIPIDES

Life and Works

Euripides is one of only three ancient Athenian tragedians whose works have survived to the present. (The other two are Sophocles and Aeschylus.) The few reliable facts about his life are these: He was born between 485 and 480 BCE on the island of Salamis, an Athenian settlement near Athens. He had his first entry in the dramatic competition of the Greater Dionysia in 455. His first victory came in 441. He competed in the dramatic competition twenty-two times (that is, approximately every other year of his adult life). He therefore wrote at least eighty-eight plays (and no doubt others that were not selected for the competition).[18] He won only five first prizes, one of them posthumously, whereas Aeschylus won thirteen and Sophocles at least twenty. These playwrights also won first prizes earlier in their careers than did Euripides. He left Athens in 408 for the court of the Macedonian king Archelaus in Pella (northwest of modern Thessaloniki; see Map), and died there in 406.

Speculations, both ancient and modern, have rushed to fill in this bare outline. Euripides' leaving Athens, for example, is variously said to have resulted from his disapproval of Athens' conduct during the Peloponnesian War, disdain for democracy as a form of government, or disappointment over his failure in the dramatic competitions. The first of these hypotheses has been supported by the antiwar implications perceived in many of his works (below, pp. 78–9). The fact that his plays were frequently chosen for the competition, but rarely won, might suggest that the Athenians wanted to see his plays, but were reluctant—maybe because of the controversies they aroused—to award them first prize. But perhaps the failure of some of his plays was the result not of disapproval of their political content but of other factors, such as poor acting or cheap costumes. Even the absence of information can be used by creative biographers. There is no mention of Euripides ever holding political or religious office or serving as a soldier; hence, it is assumed, he must have disdained civic duties and been a skeptic in matters of religion. Again, his alleged religious skepticism has been supported by the evidence of the plays (below, pp. 76–7). Such inferences, however, should be treated with cautious skepticism on our own part.

Ancient sources offer some piquant details about Euripides' life. Among them: His lowborn mother made her living selling vegetables. He disliked the public, and fixed up a cave facing the sea where he did his writing (the cave has recently been "discovered" by archaeologists, but this claim should be viewed with suspicion). He was sexually betrayed by his wife, and took revenge by writing plays about women's infidelity, offending female audience members. He died by being torn apart by King Archelaus' hunting dogs. Like stories in the *National Enquirer,* these anecdotes cannot be taken for facts. All of them come from sources later than Euripides' time or are based on his works, not his life.[19] In a predominantly oral society no clear line is drawn between the playwright's personal attributes and his dramatic characters, encouraging the use of the plays to create fictitious "biography." But just as the *National Enquirer* gives insights into the culture of the United States in the late twentieth century, these ancient anecdotes about Euripides—however inaccurate—give a sense of how he and his plays were regarded by various observers. It is notable, for example, that they mention his mother, wife, and female audience. By comparison, the ancient *Lives* of Aeschylus and Sophocles include nothing about either real or fictional women.

More complete plays by Euripides have survived to our time (nineteen, including *Rhesos,* often considered not to be by Euripides) than by Aeschylus and Sophocles combined (seven each). Yet the extant plays still represent only about one-fifth of his complete output. Of those that do survive, we only have reliable production dates for a few. For the rest, metrical analysis is often used to hypothesize the order of composition (on meter see above, pp. 42–3). These statistical studies indicate that over the course of his career Euripides wrote an increasingly freer, more variable verse line.

The four plays in this volume span more than thirty years of Euripides' career. *Alcestis,* his first surviving play, was performed in 438 BCE (seventeen years after his first production, four years after his first victory). The date of *Medea* is 431, a few weeks before the Peloponnesian War broke out. Then came *Children of Herakles* (430?), *Hippolytos* (428), *Andromache* (426?), *Hekabe* (424?), *Suppliant Women* (422?), *Iphigenia among the Taurians* (416?), *Trojan Women* (415), *Herakles* (414?), and *Elektra* (413?). *Helen* was produced in 412, a year after the Athenian military expedition to Sicily ended in disaster (above, p. 8). It was followed by *Ion* (410?), *Phoenician Women* (409), *Cyclops* (a satyr play; 408?), and *Orestes* (408?). *Iphigenia at Aulis* was produced posthumously along with *Bacchants* in 406 or 405, shortly before the Peloponnesian War ended with the defeat of Athens.

It would be helpful if we could use the dates of these works to trace the author's development as an artist and thinker, or to set the works themselves in historical context. Clear paradigms of development, however, such as increasing formal experimentation, are hard to find. Late plays like *Ion, Helen,* and *Iphigenia among the Taurians* include abrupt combinations of tones and happy endings for the central characters; these plays are sometimes called "tragicomedies" or "romances." But *Alcestis,* Euripides' earliest surviving play, also has these features, making it impossible to place all the "tragicomedies" late in his career. *Bacchants* and *Iphigenia at Aulis* were produced together, yet their radical differences in theme, structure and tone show how varied was Euripides' dramaturgy even within a single set of plays.

Ancient Reactions to Euripides

In the nineteenth and early twentieth centuries, biographical criticism sought to identify authors' unique qualities and specific events in their lives which had supposedly shaped their compositions. As we have seen, such attempts are especially problematic in the case of ancient Greek writers, about whose lives we have little or no reliable information. A more recent kind of investigation focuses on audiences' or readers' reactions to an author's works, and uses this for interpretation. (This is called "reader-response theory" when a small sample of readers is involved, "reception theory" when a broader historical view is taken.) Trying to assess the public profile of Euripides and his work in Athens, and comparing ancient responses with later ones, can make us aware of the variety of possible interpretations of his works, and of the ways such readings are informed by the historical and cultural conditions of the interpreter.

Besides the anecdotes about his "life" already cited, important evidence for ancient Athenian responses to Euripides comes from his contemporary, the comic playwright Aristophanes. The tragedians were favorite targets of comic mockery. Aristophanes satirizes both Aeschylus and Euripides (though he leaves Sophocles unscathed). But Euripides was an especially popular target of both Aristophanes and other comic playwrights. In one of Aristophanes' plays a character even includes "making lewd fun of Euripides" in a list of clichés that this comedy will supposedly avoid (*Wasps* 61).

In several of Aristophanes' plays Euripides is brought on stage as a character—a reminder that the small size of Athens and the nature of its political and social institutions made prominent artists into public figures. In *Frogs* (405 BCE) "Aeschylus" and "Euripides" engage in a competition to decide who is the better playwright. The contest, judged by the god Dionysos himself, develops into a struggle between social and artistic tradition and innovation. The art of "Aeschylus" is characterized by patriotic themes, traditional piety, and impressive if lumbering and somewhat incomprehensible poetry. "Euripides," by contrast, focuses on everyday matters and takes an untraditional approach to religion. When "Aeschylus" prays to Demeter, "Euripides" invokes "private gods" such as the upper air, a quick tongue, and keen nostrils. In *Women at the Thesmophoria* (411 BCE) a woman who sells garlands used in traditional rituals complains that Euripides "has persuaded the men that gods don't exist, so that my sales are down more than 50%" (trans. Henderson 1996: 113).

As a character in Aristophanes, "Euripides" is witty, iconoclastic, and clever, but vague and finally empty. He is satirically linked with unconventional "modern" intellectuals, especially Socrates and the sophists (above, p. 14). In *Acharnians* (425) his slave says his master is "at home and yet not at home—if you understand me," explaining that "Euripides"' mind is ranging abroad while he himself is home writing. In *Frogs* "Aeschylus" and Dionysos complain that his characters talk too much (1069–73). It is this empty intellectualism that loses him the contest. At the end of the play Dionysos chooses Aeschylus as the winner, and the chorus proclaims (1491–95):

> Better not to sit at the feet
> of Sokrates and chatter,
> nor cast out of the heart
> the high serious matter
> of tragic art.
> (trans. Lattimore 1969: 90)

Aristophanes' Euripides is untraditional not only in his beliefs and attitudes but also in his dramatic technique. He boasts that he used natural conversational dialogue so that his plays would be understandable ("I staged the life of every day, the way we live"). Instead of putting only aristocratic characters onstage, he "made the drama democratic," he claims, by giving a voice to women and slaves (949–50):

> They all stepped up to speak their piece, the mistress spoke, the slave spoke too,
> the master spoke, the daughter spoke, and grandma spoke.
> (trans. Lattimore 1969: 61)

"Aeschylus" objects that "Euripides"' aristocratic characters are often shown behaving unheroically and wearing undignified costumes, and that the questioning of traditional values in "Euripides"' plays has made citizens shirk their civic duty and underlings question their superiors.

The story about Euripides' mother selling vegetables, repeated *ad nauseam* in comedy, not only undercuts the pretentiousness imputed to him but suggests that Euripides downplays noble birth and traditional values because of his own humble origin. Aristophanes also initiated the continuing critical debate about Euripides' misogyny (below, p. 80). For all his mockery, however, Aristophanes himself uses many of the same techniques and themes (including women and gender) for which he satirizes the tragic playwright. And the brilliance of his parodies shows a close—even affectionate—knowledge of Euripides' works. Another comic playwright of the period suggested their similarities by coining the expression "euripidaristophanist" (Kovacs 1994: 113).

About a century after Euripides' own time, Aristotle wrote his *Poetics,* a brief essay that has had great influence on the study of tragedy (compare above, p. 19). In discussing what makes for effective tragedy, Aristotle focuses on formal elements, especially plot structure, and prizes organic form, logic, plausibility and consistency. He criticizes Euripides more than any other playwright. For example, he complains that the title character in *IA* is inconsistent: "The Iphigenia who begs to be spared is completely different from the Iphigenia who appears later" (1454a). He criticizes as "inappropriate" an intellectual speech in the mouth of a female Euripidean character, since women should not be portrayed as too clever or courageous (1454a). He also dislikes surprising and artificial plot twists, like Aigeus' arrival at Corinth in *Medea* (1461b) and Medea's final departure in the sun-chariot (1454b). He insists that tragic characters be "between the extremes" of good and evil, hence he condemns the excessive immorality of Menelaos in Euripides' *Orestes* (1454a). But he also singles out *Iphigenia among the Taurians* for special praise (1455a).

Like many academics, Aristotle bases his criticism more on reading than on experiencing plays in performance: "The plot should be so constructed that even without seeing the play, anyone who merely hears the events unfold will shudder and feel pity" (1453b). Yet he acknowledges Euripides' power in the theater, declaring that "although Euripides manages badly in other respects . . . on the stage and in the dramatic contests . . . he is the most tragic of the poets" (1453a).

Euripides as a Playwright

Euripides' plays are so different from one another in both form and content that it is hard to make useful generalizations about his work.[20] Webster describes Euripides' dramaturgy as "bewilderingly various . . . a variety both of types of play and of incidents within the single play, a variety between plays produced at the same time and a variety between plays produced at different times" (1967: 278–96). Euripides' plays exhibit not merely variety, however, but remarkable discontinuities and contradictions on the levels of language, character, plot, and theatrical technique. Moreover these disparate elements are often juxtaposed in such a way that the contradictions draw attention to themselves.

Webster saw Euripides as experimenting primarily for artistic reasons. But the discontinuities in Euripides' plays have other effects than innovation for its own sake. Radical twentieth-century theoretician Bertolt Brecht said he wanted his plays to achieve an "alienation effect" (*Verfremdungseffekt*), a process of turning an object "from something ordinary, familiar, immediately accessible, into something peculiar, striking, and unexpected. . . . We must give up assuming that the object in question needs no explanation" (Brecht 1964: 144). In Euripides' plays discontinuities can function as alienation effects, reminding the audience that what they are watching is not a natural entity but an artifact. This in turn suggests that language, individual character, and social institutions are not natural, organic forms occurring spontaneously, but constructions located in history, influenced by ideology, and requiring interpretation.

Many different kinds of discontinuity are evident in Euripides. There is often tension between verisimilitude (literally, "similarity to truth," hence the appearance of "realism") and explicit, self-conscious artifice. The theatrical machinery is used flamboyantly, as when the *mēchanē* becomes the chariot of the Sun for Medea's escape (*Medea* 1317–1404). Dramaturgical conventions are highlighted rather than concealed. In *Frogs,* "Euripides" claims that he writes efficient prologues in which a character comes out and straightforwardly explains the background (945–47). At the beginning of *Medea,* when the Nurse laments her mistress's fortunes in front of the house, the Paidagogos calls attention to the artificiality of this prologue by asking the Nurse why she is talking to herself (49–58); she might well reply, "Because I have to provide the exposition!" When the children's cries are heard from inside Medea's house, the chorus ask whether they should go in and help (1275–76). For them to do so would violate the convention whereby the chorus does not enter the *skēnē* (above, p. 41), yet the children hear and urge them to come inside (1277).

The shape of spoken interchanges between characters is often highly formal. Debates such as those between Medea and Jason (*Medea* 465–575) or Agamemnon and Menelaos (*IA* 334–401) consist of symmetrical and self-conscious set pieces. Such rhetoric is often used ostentatiously instead of being concealed, with rhetorical "warmups" preceding speeches, as when Jason begins, "I must not be an evil orator" (522), or Klytemnestra wonders which rhetorical tack to take (*IA* 1124–26). The formality, even explicit artificiality of such speeches often contrasts with their straightforward language, the violent emotions that prompt them, and the violations of decorum that may result, as when Admetos and his father hurl insults at each other over Alcestis' dead body (*Alcestis* 629–705).

Tragedy usually employs elevated language (above, pp. 43–4). Euripides' characters often speak this way, but sometimes they use a more limited vocabulary, straightforward syntax, and colloquialisms that may be closer to the way contemporary Athenians actually spoke. In his *Rhetoric,* Aristotle praises Euripides for creating art by putting together "elements taken from the common language of everyday life" (1404b), and in *Frogs*, "Euripides" declares that "people ought to talk like people" (1058). Various other techniques also make some of the conventions of Athenian tragedy seem closer to spontaneous speech. For example, characters may interrupt each other in mid-thought (*IA* 1133), or shout down anticipated objections (*Medea* 550). *Stichomythia,* the balanced trading of lines between characters, is varied by doubling and halving the lines, and psychologically motivated by hesitation, interruption, encouragement, and the like. Paradoxically, such "naturalistic" devices can call attention to the artificiality of tragedy's formal elements, just as protestations of sincerity may call that sincerity into question (see *IA* 475–76).

Athenian tragedy does not usually characterize persons of different social ranks or ethnicities by their speech (above, p. 43). But contradictions between status and language sometimes seem exceptionally pointed in Euripides' plays. The humble foreign Nurse's prologue speech in *Medea,* for example, is a tour de force of showy, elevated language (1–45). Messenger speeches too are occasions for their speakers, who are often slaves, to use elegant diction, metaphors, and maxims (see, for example, *Helen* 1526–1618). Some of these passages are not far from the parodies of tragic language used in *Frogs.* The dissonance of this grand narrative style in the mouth of a lowly messenger may raise questions about whether such reportage can be trusted (see *IA* 1616–18). Euripides' aristocrats, on the other hand, often speak very simply, as in Admetos' "recognition" speech (*Alcestis* 935–61). The juxtaposition of these different styles is often abrupt and jarring. Similar effects may be achieved through costuming. In *Frogs,* Euripides is said to have dressed aristocratic characters in rags, in order to arouse pity (1063–4), thus reducing the grandeur of mythic figures. The presentation of highborn characters in rags, like Menelaos in *Helen,* uses the visual element of drama to raise questions about the relationship between appearance and reality—a central theme in *Helen* and other plays.

Euripides' plays also draw attention to drama's artificiality through explicit role-playing. Behavior is often assumed to be not the sincere expression of spontaneous feeling, but a conscious ploy to affect others: "Now why are your eyes filling with tears? Whose sympathy do you hope to gain?" says the Old Woman to Menelaos (*Helen* 456). Helen plays a "tragic scene," changing costume and cutting her hair, to convince Theoklymenos that she is mourning her husband's death (*Helen* 1186–1249). Herakles plays up his conventional persona—more brawn than brains—to convince Admetos to take in the veiled woman (*Alcestis* 1008–1122). The presence of onlookers in the know emphasizes the theatricality of such scenes: Helen gets to perform her love for her "dead" husband with Menelaos standing there enjoying it (*Helen* 1390–1440). Sometimes the "mask" slips during these role-playing scenes, as when Medea struggles to keep her composure while Jason embraces the children she plans to kill (*Medea* 895–931), or Agamemnon tries to keep from breaking down before Iphigenia (*IA* 640–85). The frequent references to characters' facial expressions simultaneously suggest the naturalism that theatrical masking makes impossible and direct attention beneath the mask to the character—or actor—within.

All metatheatrical devices remind the audience that they are watching a constructed artifact, not a natural creation. But they may be used in different ways. In Aeschylus' *Eumenides,* Athena calls upon the citizens of Athens (1010–13), addressing the audience in the theater and the civic body as one (Wiles 1997: 210–12). In Euripides such devices are used to point up not only the artificiality of tragedy as a medium but the constructed, performative elements in all social interaction, what Goffman (1959) calls the "presentation of self in every day life." Instead of suggesting that the theater is really the city, Euripides' metatheatrical devices suggest that the city is really a theater, a stage on which different masks, roles, and stereotypes are played against each other.

Euripides' plays, especially the later ones, employ a wide variety of metrical and musical effects. Aristotle objects that Euripides' choruses and their songs are not integrated into the action (*Poetics* 1456a), and Euripides' use of solo arias for individual characters (above, p. 41) is parodied in *Frogs* (1329–63). The length of some choral songs is unusual (for example, *IA* 164–301) as is the placement of others (for example, the first song in *Helen* does not occur until the play is almost two-thirds over). The effect of some of these techniques is very difficult to assess at this distance. Euripides' metrical and musical innovations may have made his plays seem fresh and emotionally vivid to some audience members, artificial and strained to others. Clearly, however, the different parts of the drama are not subordinated to the whole in such a way as to create an obviously integrated or smooth experience.

The same kind of variety is also evident in Euripides' plots. Aristotle condemns episodic plots, "in which the episodes do not follow one another in a probable or inevitable way," and praises those in which the events are surprising yet follow the logic of cause and effect (*Poetics* 1452a). The tragedies of Aeschylus and Sophocles generally develop in a measured way, involving a relatively limited number of closely connected events. But Euripides' plays often contain numerous events which suddenly change the direction of the plot in surprising ways. In *Helen,* for example, within just over two hundred lines Menelaos arrives in Egypt, is denied hospitality, learns that there is a second woman just like his wife Helen, meets her, rejects her, then accepts her (*Helen* 387–623). On the Greek stage exits and entrances are usually carefully prepared, but Euripides includes many surprise entrances such as those of Aigeus in *Medea,* Herakles in *Alcestis,* and the Messengers in *Helen* and *IA.* In *Helen,* Teuker seems to have wandered in from a different play and threatens to take the plot in a completely new direction, then vanishes as quickly as he came (68–163).

"The playwright cannot alter the traditional stories," says Aristotle (*Poetics* 1453b).[21] Yet Euripidean plots constantly suggest that this is not the case. These revisions of traditional material are not always subtle; often attention is drawn to the changes the playwright has made. For example, Medea's declaration that she will not "leave my sons alive to suffer outrage from my enemies" (*Medea* 1060–61) alludes to alternative stories in which others did indeed kill her children (below, p. 152). Unthinkable endings—that Iphigenia will live, for example, and the Trojan War never take place—are made to seem inevitable. But only for a while. False endings occur frequently. *Alcestis,* for example, seems to be over as the choral ode praising the heroine draws to a close (1005), when suddenly Herakles returns. The surprise ending of the *deus ex machina* (above, p. 36), concludes Euripides' plots much more frequently than those of Aeschylus or Sophocles; all four of the plays in this volume include some such device.

There are also discontinuities of tone and genre in Euripides. The idea that tragedy must always end "unhappily" has been so influential that in modern English the very word "tragedy" has come to mean anything unfortunate or sad. It is certainly true that most Greek tragic dramas include such events as death by murder or suicide. But not all of them follow this pattern. *Eumenides,* the last play of Aeschylus' *Oresteia,* concludes with the acquittal of Orestes and an extended celebration of Athens; Sophocles' *Philoktetes* portrays anguished suffering, but nobody dies, and the ending is predominantly "happy." As far as we can tell from the surviving plays, however, this "untragic" structure is most common in Euripides. In this volume, the death of Alcestis is only temporary, and the drama has an arguably happy ending. *Alcestis* was performed as the fourth play of the day, that is, in the position of a satyr play (above, p. 35), which might help to explain its comic elements. But in *Helen,* which was produced as a standard tragedy, none of the central characters dies and the play's tone is predominantly lighthearted, even comic.

Many of Euripides' plays display some of the formal characteristics of Athenian comedy, such as a wider range of diction, style, and tone, topicality, and formal experimentation than is found in the other tragedians. Few moments in the plays of Aeschylus and Sophocles seem likely to have aroused laughter (see Knox 1979: 250–74). But great variations in tone can occur in a single Euripides play, or even a single scene, as comedy follows high seriousness or vice versa. In *IA* Klytemnestra and Achilles play a hilarious comedy of errors (819–54), but the scene changes abruptly when the Old Man reveals the plot to kill Iphigenia. Scenes often have opposite meanings for different participants, as in the conversation between the servant in mourning and the drunken Herakles (*Alcestis* 773–820), or that between the innocent Iphigenia and the guilty Agamemnon (*IA* 640–85). Alternative perspectives indicate that there is more than one way to understand characters, scenes, plays, or issues, and that those ways may be equally valid. The mixing of genres suggests that genre too is a category whose characteristics are constructed rather than natural or organic. We therefore need to be cautious in making easy generalizations about what counts as "tragic," especially in the case of Euripides. We cannot even safely define a tragedy as "a play performed in the tragic competition at the Festival of Dionysos," since such a definition would include satyr plays.

As Aristotle complained (above, p. 69), there are also striking discontinuities in Euripides' use of characterization. Sophoclean characters like Antigone and Oedipus remain steadfast in the face of opposition, but Euripides' characters often change their minds and their behavior, radically and abruptly, from one moment to the next within a single play. Besides the notorious case of Iphigenia, the Medea who first comes on stage seems very different from the one screaming inside the house, and Alcestis quickly changes from delirium to cool rationality (271–80). Medea's repeated changes of intention (1021–80), like Agamemnon's during the first third of *IA,* suggest a fragmented personality whose thoughts and impulses are at war with one another. Characters' responses to the quick turns of events differ: In some cases they give up and despair, like Menelaos in *Helen,* in others they quickwittedly turn those events to their benefit, like Helen, or Medea when she takes advantage of Aigeus' surprise arrival.

The suffering of high-ranking characters like Helen and Menelaos is the stuff of all Athenian tragedy, but Euripides often shows those of marginal status—women, slaves, barbarians—behaving bravely and selflessly, like Alcestis and Iphigenia, or heroically, like Medea. The social range of his characters bears out "Euripides'" claim in *Frogs* that he "made the drama democratic" (above, p. 68). Characters such as the Watchman in Aeschylus' *Agamemnon,* the Nurse in *Libation Bearers,* and the Guard in Sophocles' *Antigone* also complement the aristocratic protagonists of those plays. But in Euripides not only do more lowborn characters, slaves, and women get to speak, they articulate their positions more consciously and explicitly *in terms of their status and gender.* Slave characters may take independent, decisive actions which affect the outcome of events. Admetos' servant reveals Alcestis' death to Herakles, and the Old Man tells Klytemnestra of Agamemnon's plot to kill

Iphigenia. The reverse is also true, when highborn characters like Agamemnon and Admetos act like cowards. Aristotle says that Sophocles portrayed people "as they ought to be" and Euripides "as they are" (*Poetics* 1460b).

Sometimes Euripides' portrayals seem to confront earlier ones deliberately; the cautious Achilles in *IA,* for example, is quite different from the impulsive protagonist of the *Iliad.* Often, however, the changes in his characterizations are matters of degree, emphasis, and perspective; the difference is that the behavior of Euripides' protagonists is depicted in close-up, examined carefully (often by the characters themselves), and made comprehensible in terms of their personal histories. The Agamemnons of the *Iliad* and of Aeschylus' *Oresteia,* for example, have some of the same qualities as the Agamemnon of *IA*—bad judgment, poor leadership—but in *IA* these qualities are depicted *from within,* with Agamemnon himself recognizing and commenting on his own behavior (e.g., 742–50). Euripides' characters also confront the mythic, sometimes fantastical, events of legend, and try to understand and respond to them in a down-to-earth way.

These methods of characterization combine to prompt the reexamination of traditional codes of values. In particular, masculine norms of heroism are reexamined in the persons of women as well as men. Heroism may consist of sacrificing oneself, like Alcestis; keeping one's cool and thinking quickly, like Helen; understanding the dreadful consequences of action and acting nonetheless, like Medea; or facing and accepting an absurd situation, like Iphigenia. As a result of these and other reversals of social expectation, standards of behavior established by custom as appropriate for certain classes and genders are brought into question. Aristocrats' wilfulness and self-indulgence are criticized in general rather than individual terms (e.g., *Medea* 119–124, *Alcestis* 551–6). Aristocrats may even envy the lowborn as a class because little is expected of them (e.g., *IA* 17–19, 446–50). And discontinuities between character and social status suggest that status, including slavery, is not the result of natural hierarchies, but imposed by custom or chance (compare above, p. 10). This destabilization of social hierarchies is further reinforced by the presentation of aristocratic characters in rags (above, pp. 37, 68).

As always with Euripides, however, the effect of such questioning is itself open to question. For example, when Medea behaves according to the standards appropriate for an aristocratic Greek male, or when Achilles prefers to use reason and argument rather than take action, what is being scrutinized—the characters, or customary standards of behavior? Overall, Euripides' portrayals of character often suggest that there is no "essential" core of personality, only responses to various stimuli, external and internal. The destabilizing of categories, especially the binary oppositions embedded in the Greek language, does not result in any simple reversals of established categories or of the hierarchy of values. For example, women, slaves, "barbarians," and other outsiders are not revealed as *essentially* different from Greek male citizens—either more or less ethical or deserving. But their *position* in the social order gives them perspectives not available to those on top.

The resulting sense of dislocation is profound, extending beyond political and social categories. Is this story true? Can anyone or anything be trusted? Are there any general truths, or only particular ones? Does truth even exist? And it extends beyond the human realm to the divine government of the cosmos. Tragedies by Aeschylus and Sophocles raise basic, unanswerable questions about the nature of the gods and their relations with human beings, but Euripides goes much further in accentuating the tensions inherent in Greek polytheism. Some of the views expressed by his characters, and by the caricature of him in *Frogs,* resemble those of the sophists and other philosophers, especially in their criticism of the traditional gods. In *Helen,* for example, Helen is skeptical about the story of her own birth from Zeus (18–21), and the priestess Theonoe voices quite peculiar religious views (1014–16).

In Euripides' plays the gods tend to be utterly capricious, pursuing their own personal agendas and demonstrating little concern for larger questions of justice or fairness, at times suddenly appearing when least expected, at other times called on, but absent and silent. Compare the appearance of Herakles as *deus ex machina* in Sophocles' *Philoketes* (1409–51) with that of the Dioskouroi in *Helen* (1519–47). The former creates a link of sympathy between the divine and human realms: Herakles, a figure dear to Philoktetes, speaks of the suffering that has been their common experience and promises him a glorious future. The appearance of the Dioskouroi instead emphasizes the gulf between human and divine. As allies of Helen and Menelaos they command rather than persuade Theoklymenos, brusquely telling him that the marriage with Helen he so desired was just not part of the divine plan. No reason is given for the human suffering that Helen, Menelaos, Theoklymenos (and, implicitly, all those involved in the Trojan War) have endured, other than the divine pecking order in which the Dioskouroi rank quite low (1660–61). Instead of revealing some pattern beneath the apparent chaos of events, this conclusion suggests that instability and divine power struggles affect the whole cosmos, as indeed the chorus have already suggested (1137–42):

> What is god? What is not god? Or what lies in between?
> Who among mortals, after searching, can claim
> they found the farthest limit to this question,

when they see the affairs of the gods
leaping about here and there and back again
in contradictory, unexpected turns of fortune?

Because of the frequency of such questioning in the mouths of Euripides' characters, he is often viewed as a religious skeptic by modern readers, as he was by his contemporaries. His unconventional attitude toward the gods is an essential part of his image in Aristophanes (above, p. 67) and may help to explain his relative unpopularity. Even though there was no standard theology in Athens (above, p. 10), religious practice was a vital aspect of civic life, and intellectuals like Socrates suffered for their unconventional beliefs (above, p. 14). But we cannot safely ascribe the views of particular dramatic characters to the playwright himself. As always in interpreting drama, each sentiment must be scrutinized in context, not taken as universal truth or the private opinion of the dramatist. In their profound questioning of religious attitudes, Euripides' plays sometimes seem to denounce traditional forms of worship, and at other times to affirm them. These varying attitudes toward the divine may be seen as a way of articulating, rather than resolving, moral disputes that take place on the human level. Each play in this volume raises large questions about the gods' existence and role in human lives, and about the value of human belief in and worship of the gods. But no simple answers are offered.

Most of the dramatic techniques discussed in this section have parallels in other Athenian tragedies. But Euripides uses them more ostentatiously and calls attention to their use more explicitly. The overall effect is to depict human beings as not in control of their environment, but controlled by external forces neither concerned nor purposeful but changeable, amoral, chaotic. In the light of twentieth-century history and physics, a view of reality as fragmented, unstable, and indifferent, of human beings as subject to forces they cannot understand or control, seems "realistic." The same may be said of Euripides' use of characterization. The insights of modern psychology make his changeable, fragmented characters seem quite "lifelike," perhaps more so than smoothly integrated ones. Thus qualities once viewed as flaws in Euripides' dramaturgy may help to explain his increasing popularity in our own time. We should remember, however, that "realism" is always an effect, and that what seems "realistic" varies greatly from one historical and artistic context to another.

The final decision in the dramatic contest in *Frogs* is made on the basis not of dramaturgy but of politics. Dionysos asks each playwright how Athens can be saved from its present military crisis (it was about to lose the Peloponnesian War). As this question clearly shows, a dramatist's reflections on contemporary events were considered an essential part of his art. Like other poets in Athenian life, the tragedians were expected in some sense to be "teachers" of the community. "Euripides" does not disagree when "Aeschylus" defines the role of the Athenian dramatist as follows (*Frogs* 1054–56):

> The little boys
> have their teachers
> to show them example, but when they grow up
> we poets must act as their preachers,
> and what we preach should be useful and good.
> (Lattimore 1969: 68)

Euripidean tragedy does not "preach" in a direct or explicit fashion, however. "Aeschylus" complains that Euripides' plays have encouraged audiences to ask questions and make distinctions instead of joining in the common cause—specifically the military cause (1025–42). But "Euripides" himself is proud of the way he encourages his audiences to think (971–79):

> I turn everything inside out
> looking for new solutions
> to the problems of today,
> always critical, giving
> suggestions for gracious living
> and they come away from seeing a play
> in a questioning mood, with "where are we at?"
> and "who's got my this?" and "who took my that?"
> (Lattimore 1969: 62)

Euripides' plays provoke these kinds of questions in a number of ways. One way is by commenting on Athenian situations and institutions through indirect topical allusions. (This might seem the opposite of an "alienation effect," but since in a mythic context such references are "anachronisms," it is in fact another kind of discontinuity.) Topical references in tragedy have different effects. In Aeschylus' *Eumenides,* for example, references to Athenian political institutions suggest that the movement from aristocracy to democracy has been one of progress toward justice and enlightenment. In Euripides' plays, such allusions are often pointed and explicit, but their effects are more ambiguous. Many passages allude to the Peloponnesian War, during which most of the surviving plays were produced (above, pp. 8–10). The legendary struggle of Greeks against Trojans offered rich parallels to the war in which Athens was engaged, and some of Euripides' Trojan War plays (especially *Trojan Women, Andromache, Hekabe, Iphigenia at Aulis*) can be read as questioning the motives for warfare and dramatizing its effects in terms of human suffering and loss. But the complex connections between historical context and dramatic texts require detailed, careful analysis (see Goff 1995; Pelling 1997). Any approach that tries to reduce the interpretive possibilities by finding a univocal "truth" in the playwright's intentions—especially when the scripts are as varied as those of Euripides—risks oversimplification. Within its specific historical context, each play allows for various, often contradictory, interpretations.

For example, Agamemnon's campaign for his appointment as general of the expedition against Troy (*IA* 337–45) is described in terms of Athenian democratic elections. Does this indicate that the generals in charge of the Peloponnesian War are, like Agamemnon, desperate and ruthless, yet doomed, or that the heroic past was not as glorious as it is often said to be? The chorus of *Medea* ask how sacred, harmonious Athens can accept a killer of children (824–49). Since the audience knows that Medea will indeed go to Athens, does this suggest that Athens' problems are the result of evil outside influences, or its own leaders' foolishness, as encoded in the naiveté of Aigeus? *Helen,* which was produced at a time of Athenian desperation, can be read as a pleasant fantasy of escape from trouble, or as a bitterly ironic argument that the cause of warfare is no more than an illusion. *IA,* produced near the end of the Peloponnesian War, can be understood as a polemic against weak leaders seeking their own gain through warfare, or as a call for renewed Athenian dedication to the cause.

In all the variety offered by these plays there is, perhaps, one constant. Impulsive action without examining possible consequences *always* leads to problems. The second messenger in Helen concludes his speech by saying, "Nothing is more useful for mortals than a prudent distrust" (1617–18). It is such a "distrust" that Euripides' plays foster among his audiences and readers. The history of scholarly readings and creative revisions of his plays shows such divergence, such fundamental disagreements about form and meaning, that those readings can serve as an indicator of the variety of responses the plays may have aroused in the diverse members of the Athenian audience—oligarchs and democrats, aristocrats and peasants, foreigners and Greeks, men and women. The education offered by Euripides' plays was not as straightforward as encouraging patriotism and military valor. But it was an education in which every citizen, including those who could not read, write, or perform, could participate.

The ancient audience members were doubtless divided in their understanding of the meanings of Euripides' plays and debated them vigorously. As we have argued throughout, the inclusive nature of the Festival of Dionysos, the variety of audience members, and the multiple viewpoints offered in the plays suggest that no single perspective, no single interpretation is irrefutably correct. The plays encourage questioning and discussion rather than assent and solidarity. Even their endings specifically avoid closure. Three of the four plays in this volume end with the chorus speaking the same five-line refrain, which says, in effect, "What a surprise!" This banal non-conclusion hands the play over to audiences—ancient and modern—to make their own meanings in their own ways.

Women in Euripides

Aristophanes depicts Euripides as particularly interested in women, and some comparative statistics bear out this claim. Thirteen of his nineteen extant plays have female protagonists; by comparison, among the seven plays of Aeschylus only one, *Agamemnon,* can be said to have a female protagonist (and even that is questionable, as the title suggests), as do two of the seven plays by Sophocles (*Elektra* and *Antigone,* though Deianeira may be considered the protagonist of *Women of Trachis*). Thematically as well, Euripides' plays seem especially concerned with questions of gender, of women's lives, of their relation to men and their role in society.

Euripides' interest in transgressive women has sometimes been seen as evidence of misogyny. Calling him "woman-hating," the chorus of Old Men in Aristophanes' *Lysistrata* agree that his hatred is justified, since women are the most shameless thing on earth (368–9). In *Women at the Thesmophoria,* Athenian women say that they are angry at Euripides for portraying them as "lover-bangers, nymphos, wine-oglers, disloyal, chattery, unwholesome, the bane of men's lives" (trans. Henderson 1996: 111). (These women do not complain that Euripides' characterizations are untrue—only that he has made it harder for them to get away with their behavior.) In *Frogs,* "Aeschylus" accuses "Euripides" of putting onstage "Phaidras and Stheneboias," stories of women who long for illicit sex. Asked by "Euripides" whether such things happen, "Aeschylus" concedes that they do, but "the poet should cover up scandal, and not let anyone see it. He shouldn't exhibit it out on the stage" (1053; trans. Lattimore 1969: 68). These portrayals of lustful women are alleged to have caused decent women to commit suicide for shame (1049–51). Such remarks, even allowing for the comic context, suggest that Euripides' women were problematic at least in part because they were seen not as part of a distant mythic world, but as reflecting contemporary Athenian realities and affecting the behavior of real women.

The main focus of criticism in Aristophanes is Euripides' representations of female violations of social norms. (Aristophanes of course ignores Euripides' "good" women, such as Alcestis and Iphigenia.) But all three major tragic playwrights show women plotting and committing violent and forbidden acts; that was expected in tragedy, and thus not a sufficient reason for Aristophanes to charge Euripides with misogyny. The problem was *how* he portrayed them. There is independent evidence that Euripides was forced to rewrite *Hippolytos* because the Athenian audience was outraged by a scene in which Phaidra, the central female character, revealed her adulterous desire for her stepson on stage, directly to him. The outrage seems to have been caused by the scene's departure from conventions of dramatic decorum, conventions that may have been felt to insulate ordinary citizens' wives from the transgressive women of tragedy.

In their representation of women, gender roles, and relations between males and females, the plays chosen for this volume feature the same kinds of discontinuities discussed above. In each of the four scripts a woman is the pivot on which the action turns, changing roles from object to subject (Medea, Helen, Iphigenia) or vice versa (Alcestis). But these women cannot be "type-cast"; they are complex, even contradictory, their motives are presented in detail, yet their actions leave many questions unanswered. Does Alcestis sacrifice herself out of wifely devotion to Admetos, dissatisfaction with him, or longing for fame? Does Jason's treatment of Medea justify her punishing him by killing their children? Does Helen's ability to deceive Theoklymenos call into question her innocence? Is Iphigenia's self-sacrifice an example of glorious patriotism, fantastic delusion, or both?

Euripides' female characters are represented as speaking from women's point of view. Though erratic, they are psychologically plausible human beings; even Iphigenia's change of heart, criticized by Aristotle, is comprehensible in terms of her relationship to Agamemnon, Klytemnestra, and Achilles. Women's social status as inferior to males, their use as objects traded between males, the restrictions on their sexuality and social interactions and on their freedom to speak their minds, the social and sexual double standard, their lack of control over their children's destinies—all these are depicted in detail. And these conditions are not assumed to be correct or taken for granted as the status quo; they are examined by female characters, their injustice is criticized, and they are sometimes violated or rejected. Other playwrights also represent women's point of view; Deianeira's eloquent lament about the difficulties of being the wife of Herakles is a case in point (*Women of Trachis* 1–48; compare also the fragment of *Tereus* quoted above, p. 57). But in Euripides, women's complaints are frequent enough to constitute a central theme of his surviving works.

Besides overt critiques of women's lot, the ideals established for them as devoted daughters, wives, and mothers come into question when Helen, Alcestis, Klytemnestra, Iphigenia, even Medea fulfill those ideals with ironic results. Conventional gender roles are destabilized when men behave in a cowardly fashion, worry about others' opinion, are gullible and impulsive, while women are physically and morally courageous, unconcerned with social custom, intelligent, capable of careful planning and execution, and willing to die for what they believe in. Medea suggests that warfare takes less courage than childbirth (*Medea* 250–51). In *Helen,* Menelaos is ready to give up at the first setback; it is Helen's intelligence that saves them both. Males' understanding, especially their understanding of women and their own relationships to them, seems very limited. Admetos does not know what Alcestis means to him until after she is gone; Jason does not understand his children's real value to him until they are dead. Theoklymenos is entranced by Helen's presentation of herself as a loving wife. Jason never suspects Medea's duplicity; Kreon does but gives in anyway. Klytemnestra does not deceive Agamemnon; she tells him in so many words that she will take revenge on him for killing Iphigenia (1171–84), but he still does not understand or believe her. In some cases men and women even use language differently. For example, the word "bed" means both "sex" and "marriage" (above, p. 58), but Jason focuses on its sexual connotations, while Medea uses it emphatically for the marriage bond.

The gender of the choruses also affects the meaning of the plays. The male chorus in *Alcestis* feel more sorrow for Admetos than for Alcestis. The female chorus of *IA* admire the beauty as well as the exploits of the male heroes they see (164–301). The female chorus of *Medea* respond to Medea's calculated self-presentation as a downtrodden woman with a promise to keep her plans secret and a resounding "feminist" song (410–30). The female chorus in *Helen,* though slaves, risk their lives to stop Theoklymenos from killing his sister.

These dramas are not feminist tracts. Euripides' women can be violent, foolish, unjust. They can use rhetoric and deception to manipulate others and themselves. They can cause as much havoc and damage as male protagonists. What they cannot be is disregarded or eliminated, no matter how much Jason and company wish this could happen (*Medea* 573–75). Nor is there any simple or consistent portrayal, as in some Greek texts, of males and females as different by nature, with males as rational and civilized, women as wild, emotional creatures. Jason's attempts to reassert such stereotypes at the end of *Medea* ring hollow (1329–45). The detailed, psychologically compelling portraits of Medea and Klytemnestra suggest that criminal actions are motivated by particular historical and social circumstances, not simply by innate evil.

The dramaturgical techniques of Euripides discussed above—variety, abrupt change, mixtures of tones, metatheatricality—present an intrinsically theatrical view of human "nature." In keeping with this view, masculinity and femininity are portrayed not as fixed attributes bestowed by "nature" as part of an integrated, stable personality, but as behaviors that can be performed by different actors. We know little about the techniques male actors in the Theater of Dionysos used to perform female roles, but the metatheatricality of the dramas certainly offered opportunities for explicit, self-conscious play with the performance conventions for portraying gender. Medea and Helen "perform femininity" in order to deceive unwitting males (*Medea* 869–975, *Helen* 1184–1249). Iphigenia is transformed from a shy bride into a hero whose physical and moral courage inspires Achilles. Medea's debate with herself (1021–80) can be seen as a choice between "masculine" and "feminine" courses of action, and the actor might have used different acting styles to represent this wavering. Such moments destabilize gender categories and suggest that they are "performative" rather than "essential" off stage as well as on (Rabinowitz 1998; compare Butler 1990).

The discontinuities of Euripidean drama not only separate and set into conflict items traditionally connected, such as *oikos* and *gamos* (household and marriage), but suggest continuities between those not traditionally connected, such as *oikos* and *polis*. "Aren't I allowed to be head of my own household?" yells Agamemnon (*IA* 331). All these plays show that *oikos* and *polis,* domestic and state and international affairs, cannot be as easily disentangled as ideology might suggest. Just as women are defined by their relationships with fathers, sons, and husbands, so too men are defined by their dealings with mothers, daughters, and wives, which in turn affect their conduct as warriors, leaders, friends. Recurrent references to the social context suggest the crucial effect of social structures on the behavior of men and women alike. Resemblances to contemporary Athenian institutions and recognizable social situations bring these critiques and actions out of the mythic world and close to home. Aristophanes was surely not the only one to see the implications of these plays for gender and other social issues.

V. THE "AFTERLIFE" OF EURIPIDES

Survival and Canonization

The book you are now holding in your hands arrived there by a circuitous route. Athenian tragedies were originally composed for a single performance at the

Festival of Dionysos, two and a half thousand years ago—some two thousand years before the invention of printing. The fact that any have survived into the late twentieth century is therefore remarkable. The story of these scripts' transmission shows three factors at work: materiality, ideology, and chance.

Of the hundreds of plays written by Aeschylus, Sophocles, Euripides and many other Athenian tragedians, only thirty-three survive complete. Few Athenians were literate, and even fewer owned books (that is, texts written on rolls of papyrus). (Euripides supposedly possessed a library; even if this story is untrue, it is another sign that he was regarded as different from most Athenians, and specifically as more intellectual.) Athenian drama of the fifth century BCE was almost certainly composed in writing, but orally rehearsed and performed for a mostly nonliterate audience. With regard to composition, audience, and transmission, then, these plays represent a transitional stage between Homeric epics, which were orally composed and delivered, and literature designed for private reading (Havelock 1982: 261–312). Most of Euripides' audience would have known the *Iliad* and the *Odyssey* from hearing them performed (above, p. 6). These poems, orally composed and transmitted, were the "encyclopedia" of Greek culture (Havelock 1967: 61–86). Non-literates have prodigious memories, and much of Athenian tragedy assumes that the audience knows the Homeric epics well. In the first few years after their production, the dramas too were kept alive in the memories and on the lips of those who saw them. Many jokes in Aristophanes' comedies depend on the audience remembering details of tragedies presented in earlier years, and Athenians captured after the Sicilian disaster won their freedom by teaching their captors selections of Euripides' poetry (above, p. 40).

During the fourth century BCE, as literacy increased and political conditions changed, Athenian drama's connections to the immediate political and historical context weakened, while attention to its aesthetic aspects and its distinctive features as an art form increased. It is at this time that Aristotle's *Poetics* was written. New plays continued to be produced, but Aeschylus, Sophocles, and Euripides were designated as the three great masters of tragedy. In the fourth century selected plays of these masters were taught as part of the school curriculum. Revivals were staged, the playwrights' statues were erected in the Theater of Dionysos, and authorized editions of their plays were produced to keep actors from distorting the work of the masters by interpolations. This historical and ideological process—what we would now call "canon formation"—continued during the next century. Institutional libraries proliferated in Greek cities, the most monumental of which was at Alexandria in Egypt. At this time scholars working to classify and interpret earlier literature identified certain authors as "the included." Works by "included" authors had a much better chance of survival, since the scholarly commentaries made them easier to study and more likely to be available to be recopied.

Among the surviving fifth-century Athenian dramas are seven plays each by Aeschylus and Sophocles. These, apparently chosen for school editions and transmitted with their Alexandrian commentaries, survive in a number of manuscripts. A similar selection from Euripides' complete works includes ten tragedies, probably in chronological order, among them *Alcestis* and *Medea.* These were presumably the "canonized" plays of Euripides. In addition, another nine plays were preserved arranged alphabetically by title. Among these plays were *Helen* and *Iphigenia at Aulis,* as well as *Cyclops,* the only complete surviving satyr play (above, pp. 34–5). These nine plays exist in fewer manuscripts, so their texts are far less certain, and they have no ancient scholarly commentaries.

The survival of a greater number of plays by Euripides than either Sophocles or Aeschylus is said to demonstrate his popularity after his death. But it also shows how subject to chance was the survival of all ancient works, especially non-canonized ones. The accident of survival of the "alphabetic" plays, which probably came from one volume of a "complete Euripides," gives us a rare opportunity to examine a sample of dramas selected by criteria other than deliberate choice. On the other hand, the inclusion of *Rhesos* among the ten "official" plays is something of an embarrassment, since most modern critics find it mechanical and uninspired. The ideology of "the included" means that anything by the masters must be superior. The solution: *Rhesos* is declared not to have been written by Euripides at all, but to have been included accidentally among his ten "official" plays. But even if this play really is not by Euripides, the ancient scholars who transmitted it did not object to including it among the canonized sample of his plays. Such indications that the ancient canon was different from our own should warn us against universalizing judgments of taste or value.

Textual Criticism

A new approach to ancient texts began in late-fifteenth-century Italy and spread throughout Europe. Whereas medieval readers assumed a continuity between past and present, readers of the "Renaissance" (named for the "re-birth" of ancient Greek and Roman texts and artworks) began to see the ancient world as a separate entity quite different from their own times. Textual scholars developed new methods for distinguishing between different manuscript copies of ancient works and for establishing correct editions; these methods were further refined in the eighteenth and nineteenth centuries. In the case of dramatic scripts, theatrical production offers special dangers for the integrity of the text, since actors and producers often change the words of the play in order to create effective performances. Textual critics aim for scientific accuracy, trying to recover the original text by discerning the author's intentions beneath the mistakes and additions. Since most textual critics approach dramatic texts as if they were intended to be read, not experienced in performance, repetitions and other features appropriate to performance are often eliminated.

Much textual criticism attempts to lift the text out of history, where it may suffer change, into timeless transcendence. "The critical edition . . . embodies an illusion about its own historicity (or lack thereof). According to this view of itself, the critical text is reproduced with a minimum of interference by contemporary concerns on the one hand, and a maximum of attention to the historically removed materials on the other;" so textual critics are not encouraged to "reflect upon the contemporary motivating factors which operate in their work" (McGann 1983: 94). But these editions are not in fact outside history. Textual criticism required study "with as full a sympathetic consciousness of the social context as it was possible to gain: because authors, their works, and their texts were not isolated phenomena. All were part of a continuing process, a changing and sometimes even a developing history of human events and purposes" (McGann 1983: 118–19). Like canon formation, then, textual criticism is affected by artistic and ideological presuppositions, including assumptions about status, gender, and other aspects of social relations.

Here is an example from one of the plays in this volume. The Oxford Classical Texts are the most influential and widely used texts of ancient authors in the world; these are the standard editions used by most British and American scholars and students. James Diggle, the distinguished editor of the current Oxford Classical Text edition of Euripides, is critical of the exchange between Agamemnon and Klytemnestra at *IA* 716–31. In this scene, Klytemnestra is asking her husband about the details of the wedding celebration for their daughter Iphigenia, which puts Agamemnon on the spot, since he has made no plans for a wedding. Klytemnestra asks Agamemnon where she is to hold the feast for the women. Diggle comments,

> The location of the marriage feast may, in normal circumstances, be a legitimate preoccupation for the mother of the bride. Here, the space which is devoted to the matter is surprising. . . . "Where shall I set the marriage feast for the women?" is not poignant. Who, in any case, are these women whom she wishes to enter-

> tain? The chorus of girls from Calchis? The young women who have accompanied her from Argos? If Klytemnestra's question is surprising, Agamemnon's reply is astounding. . . . The whole line is in blatant contradiction to 731–35, where Agamemnon orders Klytemnestra home to Argos with the statement that the camp is no place for women. (1994b: 499–500)

Diggle ends by arguing for the deletion of nine lines of this conversation. His excision helps to create a more streamlined exchange, which conveys "essential information by a swift and logical series of questions and answers" (1994b: 497). But the "essential information" communicated by theatrical dialogue includes details of character and relationship as well as plot, and these are not always "logical." What is being conveyed in this scene is Agamemnon's and Klytemnestra's relationship, which will be forever changed when she discovers his plan for Iphigenia. Diggle seems to see this scene from Agamemnon's point of view, as his phrase "in normal circumstances" shows. For Klytemnestra, who does not yet know Agamemnon's plan, these *are* normal circumstances, and she is trying to maintain social decorum despite the strangeness of a wedding in an army camp; only Agamemnon knows how abnormal the circumstances really are. Cutting these lines would eliminate her thinly veiled sarcasm and his blunders, bullying, and lies. It would also undermine the connection made here between family life and public affairs, and change the shape of the scene by reducing the buildup of tension. Overall, Diggle's suggested excision ignores the effect of these lines in performance, and serves to make the scene conform to post-classical assumptions about "classical" clarity, consistency, and form.

The Artistic Legacy

Roman writers were greatly influenced by Greek literature, and various Roman authors wrote plays in Latin based on Athenian dramas. Of these the most important was Seneca (first century CE), whose tragedies exerted a strong influence on Shakespeare and his contemporaries. Throughout the sixteenth century in Europe, Greek works became more accessible, usually through translations into Latin and the vernacular languages. (It was not until the eighteenth century that Greek art, institutions, and texts in the original language began to be widely known and admired.)

Even in translation, ancient Greek texts sparked a sense of new discovery in Renaissance readers. Combined with their respect for the authority conferred by age, this led to the creation of new artistic works based on classical models.

Translations, versions, imitations, and creations inspired by Athenian drama have been produced steadily ever since. From the fifteenth through the twentieth centuries, Euripides' plays have been the models for countless major works in many different media. The tragedies in this volume have inspired plays such as Racine's *Iphigénie en Aulide* (1674), poems such as Robert Browning's *Balaustion's Adventure* (1871), dance pieces such as Martha Graham's *Cave of the Heart* (1946) and *Alcestis* (1960), operas such as Richard Strauss's *Die Ägyptische Helena* (1924), and films such as Jules Dassin's *A Dream of Passion* (1978).

Some authors intend their versions to be faithful to their ancient sources, others do not much care (artists are generally far less interested in "authenticity" than are scholars). In any case, these works too are affected by their historical and ideological circumstances, as well as by culture-bound presuppositions about the "classics" and the bounds of acceptable taste. In the case of Euripides' works, such presuppositions often soften the hard edges. The formal variety, the complex characterization, the irony and humor are often reduced, the social and political implications become less subversive. In Gluck's opera *Alceste* (1776), Alcestis offers her life for Admetos' without his knowledge; when he finds out, he is horrified and seeks to die with her; Herakles does not get drunk or deceive Admetos, and saves Alcestis before she dies; at the end Apollo makes an appearance, to praise Admetos' and Alcestis' love. Michael Cacoyannis begins his film *Iphigenia* (1976) with a forty-minute prologue that depicts the army, eager to get to Troy, being inflamed by Odysseus (the army in effect takes the role of Euripides' chorus of female tourists); because of the accidental death of a sacred stag, Kalchas hates Agamemnon and seeks to revenge himself on the king by means of a false prophecy. The overall effect is to arouse sympathy for Agamemnon and suggest that he really has no choice in sacrificing his daughter. H. D.'s long poem *Helen in Egypt* is an explicit "defence, explanation or apology" (Doolittle 1961: 1) of Helen (totally different from that of Gorgias; above, p. 17); all the events of the Trojan War are seen from Helen's perspective in a dreamlike meditation, and she achieves a kind of universal, godlike understanding.

At the end of Tony Harrison's *Medea: A Sex-War Opera* (1985), the female chorus sing *Medea* 410–30 in the original Greek, as one of them addresses the audience in English:

> Did you know that what you hear
> is from Euripides' *Medea*
> of 431
> that's 431 BC!

> The breaking of male monopoly
> has just begun!
>
> These words from a women's chorus
> at least 2000 years before us
> weren't much heeded,
> but since what they sang then
> should still be listened to by men
> a translation's needed . . .
> (T. Harrison 1985: 447)

A translation is always needed. Translations vary widely and serve many different purposes. Literal or poetic translations into another language, stagings of a dramatic script, visual representations, films, critical editions—all are translations. None is a value-free transmission of Great Ideas; all are material processes located in history which transform what they translate. The translations in this volume are no exception. We hope that our readers will use them to open a critical and culturally informed dialogue with an extraordinary playwright.

ALCESTIS

Translated and with an Introduction by

Nancy Sorkin Rabinowitz

I. INTRODUCTION

Alcestis must be crucial in any consideration of gender or women's roles in classical Athens, for its main character is used to establish a model for female behavior. She is repeatedly called the "best of women"; moreover, her excellence is based on her willingness to give up her life so that her husband can live. As such an exemplar, she establishes that pattern as a criterion for excellence in womanhood. In part as a result of its deployment of this theme, the play also puts into question ideological assumptions about the relative strengths and virtues of men and women.[1]

The structure and plot are deceptively simple. The Olympian god Apollo, son of Zeus and Leto, most closely associated with prophecy, song, and light, opens the play; he speaks a prologue directly to the audience, informing us about the past and preparing us for the action. He tells us that he was once a servant to the mortal Admetos and that in gratitude for the good treatment he received, he won Admetos the chance to avoid his fated premature death, if he could find someone to take his place. Although even Admetos' parents refused his request, his wife Alcestis agreed. The action proper begins with a confrontation between Apollo and Death; Apollo tries and fails to convince Death not to take Alcestis. He then flees the scene, because the underworld deities were a source of pollution to the Olympians. After a servant describes her private farewells, Alcestis enters to take her leave of Admetos and her children; she asks one thing of Admetos: that he not remarry. He agrees and vows eternal mourning. Soon, however, his friend Herakles[2] arrives on his way to perform one of his labors, and despite his grief, Admetos welcomes him, keeping him ignorant as to who has died. In the next scene, Admetos engages in battle with his father, Pheres, insulting him for not being willing to die in his place; Pheres insults him in turn. Then, all exit to bury Alcestis.

When Herakles discovers who has really died, he rushes off to retrieve Alcestis from Death; he returns to offer her as a gift to Admetos, but pretends she is merely a prize he has won in a contest. The play ends with a protracted scene between Herakles and Admetos, in which the latter, attempting to be faithful to Alcestis' dying wish, resists accepting the strange woman who, unbeknownst to him, is his wife. She stands, silent, covered, and unrecognizable, while Herakles convinces Admetos to welcome this "strange" woman into his home. He finally takes her with his own hand, and only then finds out who she is. Thus the play has an apparently happy ending.

What is the genre of this play? At the City Dionysia (above, p. 34), *Alcestis* was presented fourth after three tragedies, the position typically reserved for a satyr play; as a result, the play's genre has been discussed at least since the time when the *hypothesis* (a brief prose introduction to the plays in the library at Alexandria) was added. The author of the paragraph remarks that "the play has a change of fortune rather of the comic kind. . . . The drama is of the satyric kind in that it turns to joy and pleasure at the end, contrary to the tragic kind." Subsequent generations of scholars have puzzled over its form, calling it variously an anti-tragedy, a pro-satyr drama, or a tragicomedy.[3] *Alcestis* is not an actual satyr play, i.e., it did not have a chorus of satyrs, but it is possible, nonetheless, that the placement of the play resulted from and had an effect on its form or plot (see below).

The Myth

This play depends on two separate story lines, one primarily involving Apollo and Admetos, the other Admetos and Alcestis, each with parallels to fairy tales (Conacher 1967: 327–39).[4] Euripides has tied the two together in a manner which seems to have been unique. In the extended version of the first story, Apollo begets Asklepios on the maiden, Coronis, who later betrays him with her cousin; Apollo then kills Coronis and rescues their child (see Pindar *Pythian* 3). Asklepios goes on to become a great healer, but when he dares to bring mortals back to life, Zeus kills him with the thunderbolt. The killing of Asklepios reestablishes the finality of death for mortals and thus defines the difference between mortal and immortal (see lines 112–31, 455–59, 962–90, and on Asklepios 122–29, 988–99).

Enraged at Zeus for killing his son, Apollo retaliates by attacking the Cyclopes, makers of the thunderbolt; he pays for his insubordination by having to serve Admetos as herdsman—as a god he cannot die, but he must be punished. Comparison with other myths indicates that Apollo's servitude to Admetos is a symbolic form of death. The story of Apollo and Admetos, then, is imbricated in material that stresses the gods' power over human life and death; more particularly, Zeus asserts his hegemony in this area. The conflict between Asklepios/Apollo and Zeus/Cyclopes is also about father-son rivalry; the fact that it centers on the thunderbolt, sign of Zeus' authority, relates that rivalry to the son's desire for phallic power. Not only does the son want to destroy the father's weapon, as a male he arrogates to himself the biological power of women to give life. In this arena, too, Apollo is less successful than his father Zeus. Zeus blasted his mistress, the Theban princess Semele, with the thunderbolt and carried Dionysos to term (above, pp. 31–2); Apollo similarly rescues Asklepios from Coronis. But Dionysos lives, while Asklepios does not.

This masculine Olympic contest over life and death leaves its traces in the presence of Death in the play, although the character in the play is not a lofty abstraction but is more like a fairy-tale "ogre." In many fairy tales, the hero must conquer monsters to win a bride, even from death. King Pelias had, like other fathers/kings, set up a contest to determine who would marry his daughter Alcestis. While Apollo was in service to Admetos, he helped him yoke the requisite lion and boar to win her hand in marriage. Typically, when the fairy-tale hero enters a contest for the princess, he also becomes heir to the king and gains wealth and rule, but in the case of Pelias, Alcestis is the only gift.

It is significant that Admetos always has some god or hero to help him; while that is true of Perseus, Theseus, and Odysseus, too, Jason and Admetos are alike in their inadequacy. The story of Alcestis and Admetos is further related to that of Jason and Medea through Alcestis' father Pelias, the uncle who usurped Jason's kingdom and sent him after the Golden Fleece (below, p. 150); when Medea cuts up and boils Jason's uncle, Alcestis is the virtuous and sage daughter who does not participate. The two stories are also structurally similar. The Golden Fleece is an object Jason needs—with Medea's aid, Jason yokes the beasts and wins the Fleece. While Medea helps Jason win the Fleece, Alcestis is herself the prize, won with Apollo's aid.

In the fairy-tale analogues, the wife follows Death to save her husband, but no one wins out over death itself. The fact that Alcestis comes back to life may be related to her status as a prize in the first place. In Louis Gernet's theory of sacred objects (1981: 92), the appropriate object for sacrifice is a valued object; these objects often descend to the underworld and rise from it. The prize in a contest, Alcestis is suitable for (self) sacrifice as well as for return from the underworld. Objectification gives her a kind of glory.

Because of the scarcity of pre-Euripidean evidence, it is difficult to tell just what was Euripides' invention and what was in the tradition handed down to him.

Homer mentions the servitude of Apollo, and names Alcestis and Admetos as parents of Eumelos but not much more (*Iliad* 2. 763–66, 713–15); Hesiod's *Catalogue of Women* tells only the Apollo section of the story; two fragments of an earlier tragedy by Phrynicus, also called *Alcestis,* allude to a wrestling match and the figure of Death, but there are no further details. Euripides may well have added Herakles as the hero to save Alcestis; his presence may follow from the playwright's emphasis on the comic elements and on the character of Admetos (Conacher 1988: 34, nn. 14, 15; cf. Lattimore 1955: 2).

Later versions of the myth give coherent (but perhaps rationalizing) narratives that answer the questions left unanswered in these early references. We hear that because Admetos failed to sacrifice to the goddess Artemis, snakes were in the marriage chamber, snakes that either required or foretold his early death (see Apollodorus, *Library* 1.9.15). Some of these versions reveal more fully the great strength of Alcestis, who is after all the only mortal woman to make the journey to the underworld *and return.* According to Plato (*Symposium* 179 b–d), the gods of the underworld (Hades and Persephone) respected Alcestis so much that they freed her; in Apollodorus, it is Persephone alone who does so. This story of the return to the upper world stresses Alcestis' relationships to other females and her status as a Persephone figure; sexuality and death are linked. Persephone was abducted by Hades and resides in his realm as his bride; because of the circumstances surrounding the wedding, Alcestis' marriage entails her death (see below, lines 261, 746, with notes). Moreover, the name Admetos bears a striking similarity to Adamastos, meaning the unconquerable one, also a name for Hades. As was mentioned above, in myth servitude symbolically represents death, and the Apollo legend is embedded in the struggle for control over life and death; if he thus serves a character who is a form of Death, the connection to the Asklepios story would be more apparent.[5]

By the time of Aristophanes at least, a popular drinking song was named after Admetos, which connects his name with cowardice ("Learn the story of Admetos, my companion, love the good, keep away from the cowards, knowing that there is little grace from cowards"). While the song does not refer to the events of the play, Admetos' cowardice is dramatically significant; it is particularly apparent in his argument with Pheres and in his regrets after burying Alcestis. Both myth and play raise doubts about Admetos' manliness; both also suggest a form of power for Alcestis. Women did not have overt or political power in fifth-century Athens, as the general introduction explains (above, pp. 48–49), but there were spiritual and ritual avenues to influence. In some late Italian vases, for instance, Alcestis is represented as a figure in male initiation rites, which would seem to refer to her potency in having negotiated the journey to the underworld and back. Such an implication of female power remains a subterranean thread in *Alcestis.* Admetos and his parents are afraid to die, while Alcestis is brave in the face of death; she dies in public and makes a significant contribution to Admetos' education, which is one of the themes of the play. While such a power, and used for men at that, may not correspond to late-twentieth-century norms or feminist ideals, it must nonetheless be taken seriously in the ancient Greek context.

The figure of Alcestis played a paradigmatic role in following periods. She is remembered by Phaedrus in Plato's *Symposium* (179b–d) for her love (*erōs*) of her husband, a love that surpassed his parents' devotion (*philia*), and in respect for which she became one of the very few mortals to be released by the gods of the underworld. Geoffrey Chaucer too makes use of Alcestis. Like Euripides, Chaucer was taken to task for maligning women; to make amends he has Alcestis accompany the Goddess of Love in the prologue to the *Legend of Good Women,* his palinode recanting the malicious lies he was reputed to have told about women. Praising Alcestis' faithful love, he hopes to make up for *Troilus and Criseyde* and *The Romance of the Rose.* We can see the continuing force of such self-sacrificing virtue in the faithful, uncomplaining, and noble Queen in Shakespeare's *Winter's Tale;* Hermione, who was presumed to be dead, appears as a likeness to herself, and is turned into a statue in a sanctuary before being restored to her husband.

Cultural Context

Despite its significance in later periods, *Alcestis* is dependent on its historical context for meaning; because of its prominent dependence on myth and ritual, as well as its deployment of culturally specific values, it is especially revealing about the relationship between gender ideology and other cultural institutions (above, pp. 48–60). In lauding the character of Alcestis, Euripides' play performs important cultural work; it defines one ancient Greek model of female excellence, one that is based on a woman's first being married, then having children and being willing to die for her husband. Given the debate about the virtues of Admetos (Burnett 1965, 1971; Rabinowitz 1993; Segal 1993), there is a question as to whether Euripides is enforcing or challenging gender roles. As the drinking song (discussed above) makes clear, at least in one tradition, Admetos is antiheroic. Alcestis is praised.

Euripides' *Alcestis* is his earliest extant play (438 BCE), written before the outbreak of the Peloponnesian War, but after Athens had undertaken and won the nine-month siege of the island of Samos (439 BCE) (Plutarch, *Pericles* 8, 9; Thucydides 1.4.118). One can see in the play a concern with heroism analogous to that which appears to have been articulated in Pericles' Funeral Oration celebrating those who died defending the city at Samos. The fragmentary remains of that speech (Plutarch, *Pericles* 8) indicate that there he spelled out a model of male excellence:

> Again, Stesimbrotus says that, in his funeral oration over those who had fallen in the Samian War, he declared that they had become immortal, like the gods; "the gods themselves," he said, "we cannot see, but from the honors which they received, and the blessings which they bestow, we conclude that they are immortal." So it was, he said with those who had given their lives for their country.

As Loraux argues, the funeral oration was a mode of creating the community: "But the community turned the honor paid to its most valorous men to its own account, since in doing so it expressed its cohesion and greatness, solemnly attested in the face of the universe" (1986: 20; see also 40–42). In order to move from aristocracy to democracy, rule by individual great men to rule by the people, Pericles used the funeral oration; by praising famous men he praises Athens, both in the snippets reported to us about Samos and in the more famous speech given in its entirety by Thucydides (2.6.35–47). Pericles lauds death for patriotic motives and distinguishes it from cowardice (2.6.44); he then turns to the male survivors (sons and brothers) and the envy they will feel for the dead. He mentions the female survivors at the end of his speech, not to comfort them but to identify their form of excellence:

> if I must say anything on the subject of female excellence to those of you who will now be in widowhood, it will be all comprised in this brief exhortation. Great will be your glory in not falling short of your natural character; and greatest will be hers who is least talked of among the men whether for good or for bad. (2.6.46; compare above, pp. 50–51)

The glorification of masculine virtue is explicitly contrasted to the silence appropriate for and as women's virtue.

Alcestis may simultaneously reinforce and subvert this value system. On the one hand, it supports Athenian social goals by defining female excellence as dying to save men and the family, that is, as an equivalent to men's death for the city. By praising Alcestis for sacrificing herself, it creates the motivation for other women to see such a path as worthwhile because it is a route to good reputation and fame (*kleos*) (Rabinowitz 1993). While this praise may then seem to contribute to the continued suppression of women, as glory granted to a woman, it also counters the suppression of women, since such glory is usually granted only to men. Given the Periclean position and the general cultural silence about women, female fame is hard-won, even oxymoronic (compare above, p. 51).[6]

In the context of the zero-sum game of Athenian male competition (Gouldner 1965: 45–55; Winkler 1990a: 46–54), Alcestis' heroism may be won at the expense of Admetos' glory. At least according to Pheres (696) and Admetos' own imaginary enemies (955–56) Admetos appears to have chosen life with shame; the battle with death traditionally fought by the husband in folk tale is instead fought by the god and Herakles on his behalf. Thus, Alcestis' courage undermines Admetos' claims to masculine strength and may even unsettle codes of gendered behavior (compare below, pp. 162–4). In her silent return, she may be paradigmatic of the model Periclean wife, yet she has been forceful earlier in the play. Her silence may be equally forceful and threatening.

Specific cultural practices are significant in this play, for it makes extensive use of ritual elements. The first half of the action takes place before Alcestis dies and culminates in her death (on the stages of the funeral see above, p. 54). In ancient Greek culture, there was a well-worked-out semiotics of mourning, and much of the poetry and plot of *Alcestis* depend on the widely known identifying signs of death: Greek mourners cut their hair short, tore their clothes, scratched their faces. As a result, Herakles was able to interpret Admetos' face and his shorn hair (751, 826–27). He knew that someone had died but was not sure who. Moreover, both pain and pleasure have their appropriate musical expression; songs of mourning should be kept separate from songs of pleasure or drinking, as Herakles and Admetos (549–50) and then the Servant (760) make explicit. Admetos remembers the pleasant songs of marriage (918, 922) when he returns to his empty house. In the course of the play, the two forms problematically intermingle (specifically when Herakles gets drunk and starts to sing while the servants are forced to keep their expressions of grief private).

Funerals, like initiation and marriage, may be considered as rites of passage (Turner 1977; van Gennep 1960); the particular forms differ, but they share a general structure that facilitates the transition of the individual from one stage to another. Funerals work not only by moving the deceased from the realm of the living to that of the dead, but by effecting the reconciliation of the survivors to life. In *Alcestis* the preparation of the body for burial is described, and the "carrying out" is ordered. In an uncharacteristic moment for tragedy, her death occurs onstage, but the funeral ritual is interrupted before the reintegration of Admetos into the realm of the living can take place. When he returns from the grave site, Admetos makes a long speech expressing his reluctance to reenter the house because it reminds him of his happy marriage to Alcestis; the contrast is too much for him. He also thinks about how miserable his life will be without her. Thus, the ritual of reintegration is not complete.

The staging emphasizes the break between the two parts of the play. It is highly unusual to witness death onstage in tragedy, and it is unusual to have a completely empty playing area (when the actors leave, the chorus usually stay behind and sings a choral ode). As a consequence of Alcestis' dying onstage the stage also empties, because the chorus leave to participate in the burial. Each part is marked by a ritual, for what the funeral leaves unresolved is brought to conclusion by the representation of marriage (compare above, pp. 56–7; Segal 1993: ch. 3 and 4). When, in the final scene, Herakles insists on placing Alcestis in Admetos' hands (1113–15), he uses words reminiscent of the betrothal, which typically took place between the man in charge of a woman (her *kurios*) and her husband-to-be (Foley 1985: 88; Arrowsmith 1975: 117). Moreover, Alcestis is veiled as the bride would have been. This veiling and her silence mark her liminality; she is in between two worlds and must remain silent for three days. Thus, the ending of the play is full of signs of irresolution.

Alcestis is a "most excellent" woman because she is the ideal wife, devoted to her husband and his household. This emphasis marks a problem inherent in exogamy: The wife essential to the family is not of the family by blood. Admetos is able to confuse Herakles with puns not only because the Greek word for woman also meant wife (*gunē*), but also because the ceremony of marriage integrated the wife, an outsider, into the husband's family (above, pp. 57–8). So, for instance, when Herakles asks who has died, Admetos does not exactly lie, but he does not exactly tell the truth when he says she was "a woman" and "an outsider" (531, 533).

Modern ideas about love and marriage may lead readers to infer that Alcestis dies because she is "in love with" her husband, but that would not have been necessarily or even probably the case in ancient Greece where erotic desire (*erōs*) is a force to be feared (see for example *Medea* 627–28) and marriages were arranged between fifteen-year-old girls and much older men. Alcestis exhibits a form of *philia* that is primarily centered on the family. A. M. Dale (1954: xxvii) assumes that she is in love with her husband and jealous of a rival, and thus that her passionate tears cohere with her somewhat frosty demand that he not remarry. Alcestis, however, may shed tears as she approaches her marriage bed because she recognizes that it is her marriage that has killed her (178–79); her calm when facing Admetos indicates that her primary commitment is to the family, in particular her children. This commitment is further verified by her association with Hestia (162), goddess of the hearth (above, pp. 57–8) because as a loyal wife she is identified with the hearth of her husband and the wealth and well-being of his household.

Alcestis emphasizes marriage ritual as an operation between men, where one man gives and another receives; it is thus embedded in the system of hospitality, one of the play's most important themes. Favor or gift (*kharis*) and hospitality play off against one another from the beginning: Death won't do Apollo the favor (60) of releasing Alcestis; because he, like Pheres, demands his just deserts, he will not incur any obligation for like favors from Apollo (70).[7] The ancient ritual and reciprocal practice of hospitality made it possible for men to distinguish between friend and enemy. This code, like other rituals, protected men outside their own realm by providing allies against an unfriendly world. Significantly, hospitality is the characteristic virtue of Admetos: To repay him for his graciousness as host, Apollo gained him the original reprieve from the Fates. Moreover, the second salvation is also based on hospitality, for in the prologue Apollo predicts the advent of Herakles, saying that he will be entertained by Admetos; we assume that he saves Alcestis as a result (68). Not only is hospitality Admetos' dominant character trait, but he adheres to an extreme standard, welcoming Herakles as a guest even though he is in mourning (and in opposition to the chorus' advice, 551–52). The text highlights the conflict between duties owed to wife and those owed to a guest, which do not always comfortably coexist. In particular, Herakles acts like the rowdy he is in legend, and thus creates revelry in the house when Admetos has just promised Alcestis that he will have no singing. The servants, loyal to Alcestis, resent having to restrain their grief in order to act appropriately before the master's guest (761–64). When Herakles returns and insists that Admetos accept "the strange woman" from his hand, he chides Admetos (1008–10) and claims that he is a good guest (1119–20).

In general, Euripides' use of Herakles to rescue Alcestis emphasizes the element of exchange in the myth because it establishes a crucial male-male dynamic at each end of the story (Apollo/Admetos = Herakles/Admetos). As male bonds were preferred to mourning for the female dead in the first scene between Admetos and Herakles, so male obligations to men supersede fidelity itself in the end. In both moments where Admetos may be said to betray Alcestis, he does so in the interests of male friendship. Significantly, then, each of Admetos' failures to honor his oath to Alcestis are the other face of his virtue of hospitality.[8]

Alcestis, of course, owes her life to the same obligation of hospitality, since Herakles goes to the underworld to retrieve her in recognition of Admetos' hospitality, not for Alcestis herself (842, 854–57). Herakles tells a very revealing lie to account for his having this strange woman, one which underlines the exchange aspect of the transaction; he claims to have won her in a contest. She is his trophy "thrown in with the livestock" (1032), and he presents her as such to Admetos. Moreover, the latter accepts the woman from Herakles, not out of overwhelming desire for her, but out of desire not to anger Herakles (1054). If he accepts her, he affirms Herakles' quality as a guest: "Keep her and you will say that the son of Zeus is a noble guest" (1119–20). Thus, in this reading, the relationship of hospitality does integrate Alcestis back into the family, but the dominant enacted relationship is not between man and wife, but between the two men. Alcestis is a veiled and silent presence.[9]

Within the play, Alcestis is promised two commemorative songs, one at the festival of the Karneia, the other at Athens (445–52). We do not know what role Alcestis played at the Karneia, a ritual where, as Calame (1997: 202–5, especially 203) points out, there were not even female choruses. The Karneia was a festival of Apollo, which marked the integration of young men into the adult life of soldiers; it was a markedly male homosocial ritual. The homosocial ties of initiation are explicitly homoerotic in late variants of the Apollo-Admetos story where we see traces of a sexual relationship between god and king. The poet Callimachus reports that Apollo was burning with love for Admetos and served him out of desire not as punishment. Perhaps Alcestis is honored at the festival because Apollo facilitated Admetos' marriage to Alcestis at the end of his period of homoerotic involvement with Admetos.[10] On the other hand, if initiation ceremonies represent a transformation from one phase to another for the adolescent male, then Alcestis may be present as someone who made the journey to the dead *and came back.* In Plato's version, Persephone recognized and rewarded Alcestis' sacrifice; at the Karneia, Alcestis might have had a heroic celebration.

Interpretive Issues

As will be even clearer in the notes, there is much ambiguity surrounding this play. For instance, how sympathetic are we meant to be to either Admetos or Alcestis? Why does Admetos accept her sacrifice in the first place? An important theme of the play is "late learning" (see notes on lines 145, 940). What does Admetos learn? Does it warrant his final reward? If Admetos' recognition is that life is not worth saving at any cost, why is he saved again? Alcestis, of course, knew all along what Admetos needs to learn; she suffers nonetheless. Admetos is privileged to learn this lesson without suffering for very long because Alcestis' generous gift (299) is matched by the boon of Herakles (1074).

In discussions of the play's genre, critics often refer to the comic or joking spirit of the ending. Why does Euripides not simply restore Alcestis to life? In some interpretations the scene presents a test to Admetos, which he either fails or passes depending on the critic's point of view; in others, it is just a good-hearted joke, with Herakles getting back at Admetos for having deceived him. In either case, the scene puts Admetos and Herakles in prolonged contact, while the woman is only an onlooker and cannot interfere. Her silence is enforced. The pleasure is theirs. As enacted, Alcestis drops out to facilitate the interaction between the men. In each conversation, Alcestis is necessary, but she is neither the one who gives nor the one who receives. Is this a happy ending?

Alcestis should be at her most powerful when she returns from Hades; the ritual interpretation of her silence suggests that she is taboo, and taboos generally exist as a hedge around danger (Douglas 1978: ch. 9). But precisely what is the danger? On one level, it is the danger of pollution from death: Alcestis is threatening because she is liminal, between life and death. Does she retain this power, or is the woman—full of a dangerous wildness, because connected with death—domesticated? What will Alcestis say after she completes the ritual silence enjoined on her?

In translating the play, I have tried to be attentive to repetitions of a word in Greek by repeating it in the English; because of the many different words for wife in Greek, I have tried to find appropriate synonyms in English; the footnotes highlight some of these points. It is a literal translation, for the most part, and where possible, I have matched the lines of the English to those of the Greek, although the translation is in prose. The translation is based on the Oxford Classical Text editions of Gilbert Murray (1902) and J. Diggle (1984); I depend heavily on the commentary of A. M. Dale (1954). Where I have accepted these editors' emendations or excisions, it is marked in the text with [ ]. I have kept stage directions to a minimum, since they are not present in the Greek text; they would, of course, be essential for performance; this no doubt represents my bias toward the literary.

As is always the case in completing a project that has been in process for a long time, there are many individuals to thank. My co-conspirators read and commented on every word in this introduction and translation. Their help was invaluable; of course, the errors are my own. My colleagues in Classics, Barbara Gold, Shelley Haley, Carl Rubino, provided valuable counsel. Non-classicists also read this and made important contributions; I want to thank Carole Bellini-Sharp, Patricia Cholakian, Michael Rabinowitz, and Peter J. Rabinowitz for their thoughtful reading and advice.

II. THE PLAY

Characters

APOLLO
DEATH
CHORUS of citizens
Alcestis' SERVANT
ALCESTIS, Queen of Pherai
ADMETOS, King of Pherai
CHILDREN of Alcestis and Admetos
HERAKLES
PHERES, father of Admetos
SERVANT of Admetos

[*The scene is set outside the house of Admetos, King of Pherai.*]

APOLLO:[1] Oh, house[2] of Admetos, where I patiently
accepted servants' board though I am a god.[3]
Zeus was responsible, for he killed my son
Asklepios, hurling a flaming bolt at his chest.
Enraged at this, I slew the Cyclopes,
artificers of Zeus' fire; and my father made me serve
this mortal man as penalty for these deeds.[4]
Arriving in this land, I herded cattle for my host,[5]
and I have safeguarded his household until this very day.
I encountered a deeply honorable[6] man in the son of Pheres;
honoring him, I protected him from dying
by tricking the Fates: the goddesses accepted[7]
Admetos' escape from immediate death,
if he would furnish another corpse to those below.
When he had approached and tried all his loved ones,[8]
even his aged father and the mother who bore him,
he found no one except his wife[9] who was willing
to die for him and look on the light no more;
she is within, carried in his arms,
her spirit breaking from her body; for on this very day
it is fated that she will die and pass from this life.

I, lest some pollution touch me in this house,
leave the roof over these well-loved halls.[10]
I already see Death himself nearby,
the sacrificial priest of the dead, who is about to lead her
down into the house of Hades; he has arrived on the stroke
to keep watch over this day on which she must die.

[*Enter Death.*]

DEATH: Aha!
Why are you here in these halls? Why are you
loitering here, Phoibos,[11] to wrong those below,
trespassing on our honors and putting a stop to them?[12]
Wasn't it enough that you interfered with the fated death of Admetos,
tripping up the Fates
with your tricky devices?[13] Now, armed with bow in hand,
you again keep watch over this woman,
she who has undertaken to free her husband
by dying in his place, the daughter of Pelias.

APOLLO: Be brave; I have only justice and trusty words for you.

DEATH: What is the bow for, if you intend justice?[14]

APOLLO: It is in my nature ever to carry these things.[15]

DEATH: Yes, *and* to help this household beyond what is just.

APOLLO: I am weighed down by the troubles of this dear man.

DEATH: And would you rob me of this second corpse, too?

APOLLO: But I did not take the first one by force.

DEATH: Then how does he come to be on the earth and not below?

APOLLO: He exchanged places with his wedded wife, for whom you come now.[16]

DEATH: I will indeed lead her below the earth, to the underworld.

Apollo: Take her, and go; for I know I could never persuade you.

Death: To kill those whom it is necessary? That we are assigned to do.

Apollo: No, to defer death for those who are about to die.[17]

Death: I understand what you say *and* what you want.

Apollo: Is there then any way that Alcestis might reach old age?

Death: No there is not; taking delight in my honors seems good to me too.

Apollo: You won't get any more than one soul in any case.

Death: When the young die, I gain a greater prize.[18]

Apollo: If she dies as an old woman, she will be buried more lavishly.

Death: You set up a law weighted toward "the haves," Phoibos!

Apollo: What did you say? I never noticed that you were so clever before.[19]

Death: Those who could afford it would pay to die old.

Apollo: So you are not willing to do me this favor?[20]

Death: Not at all. You know my ways well.

Apollo: Indeed, hateful to mortals and loathsome to the gods.[21]

Death: You cannot have everything, including what is not allotted to you.

Apollo: Even so, you will stop, even though you are exceedingly fierce;
Such a man will come to the house of Pheres—
sent by Eurystheus for a team of horses
from the wintry lands of Thrace—[22]
having been a guest in the house of Admetos,
by force he will take this woman from you.[23]

You will get no return favor from us,
but all the same you will do it, and you will be hated by me.

[*Exit Apollo.*]

DEATH: If you had spoken longer, you would have gained nothing more;
this woman will descend into the house of Hades.[24]
I approach her, to begin the sacrifice with this sword,[25]
for whoever is dedicated to the gods below the earth,
this strong sword consecrates their hair.

[*Exit Death.*]

[*Enter the Chorus singing.*][26]

CHORUS:[27] —Why is it so still in front of these halls?
Why is the house of Admetos silent?
—No one of the household is nearby
to tell us whether the Queen is gone
and we must mourn, or whether the daughter of Pelias yet lives
and looks on the light,
Alcestis—who is considered by me and all others
to have been the best wife possible
to her husband.[28]

—Does anyone hear groaning, or *Strophe A*
the beating of hands on breasts under this roof,
or a lament, as if it were all over?[29]
—Not at all, nor does any of the servants
stand about the gates.
If only from the waves of destruction,
O Healer Apollo, you would appear.
—If she were gone, it would not be so quiet!
—The corpse is not already
gone from the household.[30]
—How do you know that? I am not so confident. What emboldens you?

—How could Admetos make such a desolate burial
for such a cherished wife?[31]

—Before the gates I see no *Antistrophe A*
lustral spring water as is the custom
at the gates of the departed.
—Nor is there a lock of shorn hair before the doors,
such as is usually let fall in grief
for the corpse
nor do the young women's hands beat their breasts.
—And yet this is the appointed day . . .
—Why do you say that?
—On which it is necessary for her to go beneath the
earth.
—You have touched my soul, you have touched my
heart.
—When the good are worn away to death, it is fitting
that those long considered
loyal should grieve.

But there is no place on earth *Strophe B*
to which one can make a voyage,
neither to Lycia
nor to the unwatered
plain of Ammon[32]
in order to free this sufferer's
soul. For the apportioned fate[33]
draws near. I know of no sheep-sacrificing altar
of the gods to which I can make my way.

Only if he, the son of Phoibos Apollo, *Antistrophe B*
still had eyes to look on the light,
then might she come, leaving behind
the shadowy seats and gates of Hades.
For he raised up the vanquished,
until the Zeus-thrown bolt
of fiery thunder took him.[34]
Now what hope of life for her can I hold onto?

All the rituals have been completed by the kings;
the altars of all the gods flow with
the full measure of blood sacrifices;
and yet there is no cure at all for these troubles.[35]

CHORUS: But look, here comes one of the servants from the house
in tears; will I perhaps get some news?

[*Enter Alcestis' servant.*]

Grieving is understandable if something has befallen
your masters;[36] but I would like to know
whether the woman still draws breath
or has already perished.

SERVANT: You could say that she is both living and dead.[37]

CHORUS: How could the same person both die and see the light?

SERVANT: Her head is already dropping down, and her spirit breaks from her body.

CHORUS: Oh the poor wretched man, such a fine man to lose such a fine woman.[38]

SERVANT: Not yet does the master understand this, not until he suffers it.[39]

CHORUS: Is there no hope that her life may be saved?

SERVANT: No, for the fated day bears down hard.

CHORUS: The appropriate funeral offerings are being made for her, are they not?

SERVANT: And the finery in which her husband will bury her is ready.[40]

CHORUS: Let her know that she dies now with glory,
by far the best woman under the sun.[41]

SERVANT: How not the best? Who would deny it?
What must she be like, the woman who surpasses her?[42]

How could any woman show more honor
to her husband than by being willing to die for him?
These are things the whole city knows;
but you will be amazed at what she has done in the
house.[43]
When she recognized that the appointed day
had come, she washed her white skin with river water,
and taking the clothing and finery from their houses of
cedar
she dressed herself most fittingly,
and standing before the altar of Hestia, she prayed:[44]
"Mistress, since I am going beneath the earth,
I fall before you for the last time, and I beg you
to care for my orphaned children: to my son
join a loving wife, to my daughter, a noble husband;[45]
do not let my children die unseasonably early,
as I who bore them am dying, but let them be blessed
to fill out a joyous life in their fatherland."
She approached all the altars of Admetos' house
and she prayed as she placed wreaths around them,
cutting off a sprig from the myrtle branches,
without crying or groaning, nor did the coming
evil alter the natural loveliness of her skin.
But later, in her chamber, she fell on her marriage bed,
then she wept and spoke thus:
"Oh marriage bed, where I gave up my girlish
maidenhood for this man, on whose account I am now
dying,
farewell; I do not hate you; you destroyed me
alone; shrinking from betraying you and my husband,
I die. Some other woman will possess you,
no more virtuous than I, but perhaps luckier."[46]
Falling forward, she kissed the bed, drenching the whole
bedstead
with a flood welling up from her eyes.
When she had sated herself with her many tears,
she walked, head drooping forward, tearing herself away
from the bedstead,

and many times having left the chamber, she turned back
and threw herself on the couch again.
Her children cried, hanging from their mother's robes;
taking them in her arms, she
embraced them one after the other as one about to die.
All the servants under the roof cried
in pity for their mistress. She stretched her right hand
to each one—no one was so low[47]
that she did not speak to him and allow herself to be addressed in return.
Such are the troubles in the household of Admetos.
Dying he would have been destroyed, but in escaping death he has
an aching pain of the sort that he will never forget.

CHORUS: Surely Admetos is groaning over these troubles,
since he is to be deprived of such a noble wife?

SERVANT: He cries indeed, holding his dear bedmate in his arms,
and he begs her not to abandon him, demanding the impossible.[48]
For she is already fading and withering away in her illness.
Fainting, a wretched weight on his arm,
breathing only a very little,
all the same, she wishes to look on the rays of the sun
[since never again, but now is the last time
she will look on the bright circle of the sun].[49]
But I will go and announce that you are here;
for not everyone thinks so well of the rulers
as to stand by them with good will in their troubles,
but you are an old friend to my masters.

[*Exit Servant into the house.*]

CHORUS:[50] —Oh Zeus, what way out or what deliverance from their misfortune *Strophe A*
is there for our rulers?
—Aiaii,[51]
will someone come? Should we cut our hair,
must we cover ourselves even now

in the apparel of black robes?
—It is clear, friends, clear, but all the same
let us pray to the gods;
for the power of the gods is very great.
—Oh Lord Apollo, the Healer,
discover some way out of these troubles for Admetos.
—Contrive a way; contrive a way; for once before
you discovered a way out; now again
be our deliverance from death,
stop bloody Hades.

—Woe. . . .[52] *Antistrophe A*
Oh son of Pheres, how you have suffered,
deprived of your wedded wife.[53]
—Aiai. These things call for the knife
and more, for putting one's neck in a
noose hung from the heavens.
For he will look on his dear—no his dearest—
wife dead
on this very day.
—Look, look,
she and her husband are coming out of the house.

[*Enter Alcestis, children, and Admetos.*]

—Cry out and groan, Pheraian
land, for the best
woman wastes away in illness
to the underworld regions of Hades.

CHORUS: Never will I say that marriage cheers
more than it hurts,
judging from earlier experience
and observing the fortunes of my king,
who, having lost his most excellent mate,[54]
will live a life which is no life for his remaining time.

ALCESTIS:[55] Helios and light of day *Strophe A*
and heavenly eddies of fast moving clouds

ADMETOS: That sun sees you and me, both suffering wretchedly,[56]
having done nothing to the gods for which you should die.

ALCESTIS: Earth and roofed chambers *Antistrophe A*
and the bridal couch in my fatherland, Iolchos.

ADMETOS: Lift yourself up, poor sufferer, do not abandon me;
pray to the powerful gods to have pity.

ALCESTIS: I see the double-oared skiff in the lake; *Strophe B*
Charon, the ferryman of the dead,
has his hand on the pole and
is calling me already: "What are you waiting for?
Hurry up; you are causing a delay!" Thus urgently does
he hurry me along.[57]

ADMETOS: Oh me, you have named the voyage bitter to me.
Ill-starred, how we suffer.

ALCESTIS: Someone is leading me, leading me away; *Antistrophe B*
someone is leading me—don't you see—
into the courtyard of the dead,
a winged Hades looking out from under dark
eyebrows.[58]
What are you doing? Release me. What a
road I, most miserable of women, am setting out on.

ADMETOS: Pitiful for your loved ones, and most of all for me
and the children, who share this grief with me.

ALCESTIS: Let me go, let me go now. *Epode*
Let me lie down, I have no strength in my legs;
Hades is near.
Shadowy night creeps over my eyes.
Children, children, no longer, truly
no longer do you have a mother.
Be of good cheer, my children, and look on the
light.[59]

ADMETOS: Oh me, I hear this painful word,
even worse than any death to me.

Do not, do not abandon me, by the gods
and by the children you make orphans,
but bear up, be strong.
With you gone, I would be no more;
we live or die in you;[60]
for so greatly do we revere your love.[61]

ALCESTIS:[62] Admetos, you see how things stand with me;
I want to tell you what I wish before I die.
I—because I put you before my own life and
arranged for you to continue to look on the light—
I am dying; it was possible for me not to die for you,
but to take any Thessalian husband I wanted,
and to dwell in the blessed house of a ruler.[63]
I did not wish to live torn away from you
with orphaned children, and I did not begrudge you
my youth, which I delighted in.
And yet he who sired you and she who bore you
abandoned you;[64]
they had reached that stage of life when they could have
died nobly, nobly saved their child and died with glory.
For you were their only son, and there was no hope
that they could raise other children if you died.
You and I could have lived our remaining time together,
and you would not be alone mourning your wedded wife
and caring for your orphaned children. But
one of the gods has arranged things thus.
So be it. You now should remember the favor you owe
me;[65]
I demand nothing of equal worth—
for there is nothing more valuable than a life—
only justice, as you will agree, for you love these children
no less than I, if indeed you are in your right mind.[66]
Set them up as rulers in my house,
and never re-marry, never give the children a stepmother,
an inferior woman who, in jealous rivalry,[67]
might lift her hand against your children and mine.
Never do this, this is what I demand of you.

For the successor is an enemy to the children
of the earlier marriage, no softer than an echidna.[68]
The boy child has his father as a strong tower
[whom he can turn to and be addressed by in turn],[69]
but you, my child, how well will you pass your maidenhood?
How will you find this new yokemate of your father's?
May she not spread some shameful rumor about you
at the peak of your youth and spoil your marriage!
For you will not have a mother to lead you at your wedding
nor to give you courage in childbirth, child,
when nothing is more cheering than a mother.[70]
It is necessary for me to die; and this evil comes not tomorrow
nor the next day nor in a month,
but as of now I am no more.
Farewell and be of good cheer. You, my husband,
can boast of having had the best wife,
and you, my children, that you were born of such a mother.

CHORUS: Be brave; I am not afraid to speak for this man;
he will do these things, if he does not stray from his right mind.[71]

ADMETOS: It will be as you ask, it will, don't worry; just as I
held you in life, so in death you alone
will be called my wife, and no one but you,
no Thessalian bride, will call this man husband.
For there is no woman with a more noble father
nor more outstanding in beauty,
and I have enough children; I pray to the gods I may get
full benefit from them, since we do not benefit from you.[72]
I will bear my grief at your loss not just for a year,
but for as long as my life lasts, wife,
loathing the one who bore me, and hating
my father; for they were dear to me in words but not deeds.[73]

But you gave up what is most dear
and saved my life. Why would I not groan aloud at
losing such a yokemate as you?
I will leave off revelry and the company of my drinking partners,
the wreaths and song which used to fill my house.
Never never more will I touch the lyre
nor lift up my heart to wail to a Libyan
pipe, for you have taken all delight from my life.[74]
Thanks to the clever skill of an artist, a form
resembling yours will be stretched out in the bed;
I will fall upon it, and enfolding it in my arms
while calling your name, I will seem to cradle my dear wife
in my arms even though I don't really hold her;
A frigid delight, I realize, but all the same,
I would thus lessen the burden on my spirit.[75] Wandering through
my dreams, you will cheer me up; it is sweet
to see our loved ones even in the night, for however long they stay near.
If only the tongue and limbs of Orpheus were mine,[76]
so that I could charm Demeter's daughter or that one's husband
with my songs and take you from Hades,[77]
I would go down there, and neither Pluto's hound
nor Charon, the conductor of the dead, with his oar
would stop me until I had set your life up again in the light.
But at least await me there whenever I die
and make ready a house so that you can live together with me.
I will command them to place me in the very same cedar coffin
as you, stretched out side by
side with you; for when I have died
I do not wish to be separated from you, the only one loyal to me.

CHORUS: And as friend to friend, I too will share
your painful grief for her; for she is indeed worthy of it.

ALCESTIS: Oh children, you yourselves have heard
your father say that he will never marry another
woman to set over you or dishonor me.

ADMETOS: And I say it again, and I will bring these things to pass.

ALCESTIS: On these conditions, receive these children from my hand.

ADMETOS: I receive them, a dear gift from your dear hand.

ALCESTIS: You will now be the mother to these children instead of me.

ADMETOS: Great is the necessity, since they are deprived of you.

ALCESTIS: Oh children, when I should live, I go below instead.

ADMETOS: Oh me, what will I do alone without you?

ALCESTIS: Time will soften your suffering; the dead are nothing.

ADMETOS: Take me with you, by the gods, take me below.[78]

ALCESTIS: I am sufficient, dying for you.

ADMETOS: Oh my unlucky star,[79] what a yokemate you deprive me of.

ALCESTIS: Even now my eye is shadowed over and weighed down.

ADMETOS: Then I am destroyed, if you will really leave me, wife.

ALCESTIS: You must speak to me as to one who is no longer.

ADMETOS: Hold up your head, do not leave these children of yours.

ALCESTIS: Not at all willingly, but still, I say farewell, my children.

ADMETOS: Look on them, look.

ALCESTIS: I am no more.

ADMETOS: What are you doing? Are you abandoning us?

ALCESTIS: Farewell.

[*Alcestis dies.*][80]

ADMETOS: Wretched me, I am destroyed.

CHORUS: She is gone, the wife of Admetos is no more.

BOY [*Singing*]:[81] Oh my ill fortune. Mama has gone *Strophe*
below; she is no longer
under the sun, father.[82]
Abandoning us, the poor sufferer
has made me an orphan for the rest of my life.
Look, look at her eyes and hands limp at her sides.
Hear me, listen, mother, I implore you.
It is me, me, mother,
your little bird, who is calling you
and falling on your lips.[83]

ADMETOS: She neither hears nor sees; thus are we, I
and you two, struck a heavy blow.

BOY [*Singing*]: I am young, father, and left to go on *Antistrophe*
alone without my dear mother;
what harsh travails
I undergo . . .
and you my maiden sister
you suffer with me. . . . O father,
in vain did you take a bride, in vain,
for you did not reach the fullness of age with her,
since she died before you; with you gone,
mother, the household is completely destroyed.[84]

CHORUS: Admetos, it is necessary to bear this blow;
for you are neither the first nor the last of mortals
to lose a noble wife; understand that
everyone is obliged to die.

ADMETOS: I know it well, this trouble did not
swoop down suddenly; knowing it I have long been distressed.
But, since I will arrange for the carrying out of the body,
stand by and while you wait shout out

a libationless paian to the god below.[85]
I bid you Thessalians over whom I rule
to share in my grief for this woman
by cutting your hair and putting on black robes;
cut the horses' manes on their necks with an iron knife,
both those yoked by fours and those in single harness.
Let there be no flute playing in the city nor strumming
on the lyre
for twelve full moons.
For I will never bury another body
more dear to me nor better than this one; she is worthy
of honor from me, since she alone would die instead of me.

[*Admetos, children, and servants exit into the house, carrying Alcestis.*]

CHORUS: Oh daughter of Pelias, *Strophe A*
fare well as you make your home
in the sunless household of Hades.
Let Hades the dark-haired god
and the old one
who plies oar and rudder,
the conductor of the dead, let him know,
that he brings by far, by far the best woman
across the lake of Acheron on his two-oared craft.[86]

Often musicians *Antistrophe A*
will sing of you, glorifying you both to the
seven-stringed
mountain lyre[87] and in hymns without the lyre,
in Sparta when the circling
season of the Karneian month comes around,[88]
and the moon is high
all night long,
as well as in rich and blessed Athens.
In dying you have left behind such a song
to the singers of melodies.

Would that it were in me, *Strophe B*
that I had the power to send you
into the light, from the chambers of Hades

and from the streams of Kokytos,
by rowing on the underworld rivers.[89]
For you alone, dearest of women,
dared to exchange your husband's life from Hades
for your own. Lightly
may the earth weigh on you, woman. If
your husband should choose any new marriage,[90]
then he would
be most loathsome to me and to your children.

Antistrophe B

His mother was not willing
to hide her body under earth for her son,
nor was his old father. . .
they bore him but did not dare to save him,
harsh even though they had gray hair.[91]
Whereas you, in your flowering
youth, went to your death, dying early for this young
man.
I wish that I might find
such a loving wedded wife; for
in life this is a rare portion; then may she
remain with me painlessly
through life.

[*Enter Herakles.*]

HERAKLES: Strangers,[92] villagers in the land of Pheres,
will I find Admetos at home?

CHORUS: The child of Pheres is in the house, Herakles.
But tell us what business brings you to the land of
Thessaly,
approaching the city of Pherai.

HERAKLES: I am performing a labor for Eurystheus of Tiryns.[93]

CHORUS: And where are you going? To what wandering course are
you yoked?

HERAKLES: I am after the four-horsed chariot of Thracian Diomedes.

CHORUS: How will you be able to get that? or do you not know about your host.

HERAKLES: I know nothing; I have never before been to the land of the Bistonians.

CHORUS: It is impossible for you to master those horses without a battle.

HERAKLES: But neither is it possible for me to refuse these labors.

CHORUS: Then, having killed him you will return, or dying you will remain there.

HERAKLES: This is not the first such contest I will enter.

CHORUS: What profit do you get if you conquer the master of these horses?

HERAKLES: I will lead the horses back to the lord of Tiryns.

CHORUS: It will not be easy to put the bit between their jaws.

HERAKLES: If only they don't breathe fire from their nostrils.

CHORUS: But they cut men to pieces with their quick jaws.

HERAKLES: You speak of wild beasts and their fodder, not of horses.

CHORUS: You will see their stalls running with blood.

HERAKLES: The one who raised them, who does he claim as his father?

CHORUS: Ares, lord of the gilded Thracian shield.

HERAKLES: You describe a labor that fits my destiny;
for my way is ever rugged and steep.
If it is fated for me to join battle
with the children of Ares—first Lykaon,
then Kyknos—now I embark on this third
contest, a contest with the master and the horses.[94]
But no one will ever see the offspring of Alkmene
running away from the enemy's arms.

[*Enter Admetos from within.*]

CHORUS: And here is the man himself, the ruler of this land, Admetos, coming out of the house.

ADMETOS: Good day, child of Zeus and the blood of Perseus.[95]

HERAKLES: Good day to you, too, Admetos, lord of Thessaly.

ADMETOS: I wish it were; I know you mean well.

HERAKLES: What is the matter that you cut your hair in grief?

ADMETOS: On this very day I am about to bury a body.

HERAKLES: May the god keep such suffering from your children.

ADMETOS: The children I have fathered are alive within the house.

HERAKLES: At least your father is old, if he indeed has gone.

ADMETOS: That one is still alive, as is she who bore me, Herakles.

HERAKLES: It is not your wife Alcestis who has died, is it?

ADMETOS: I have a double story to tell about her.

HERAKLES: Did you say whether she has died or is still living?

ADMETOS: She both is and is no longer, I ache to say.

HERAKLES: I know nothing more from this, for your words are unintelligible.

ADMETOS: Do you not know the fate decreed for her?

HERAKLES: I know that she has undertaken to die for you.

ADMETOS: How therefore can she still be living, if she has agreed to this?

HERAKLES: Do not lament your wife ahead of time, but put it off until later.

ADMETOS: The one who is about to die is dead, and thus is no longer.

HERAKLES: Existence and nonexistence are usually considered separate.

Admetos: You judge it one way, Herakles, I in another.

Herakles: Well then, why are you lamenting? Which one of your family has died?

Admetos: A woman; we were just referring to a woman, weren't we?[96]

Herakles: An outsider or one who is related?

Admetos: An outsider, but one who was necessary to the house.[97]

Herakles: How did she happen to end her life in your household?

Admetos: When her father died, she was left here as an orphan.

Herakles: What a pity.
I wish I had not found you in such painful straits.

Admetos: What do you propose to do with that string of words?

Herakles: I will make my way to the hearth of some other host.

Admetos: It is not possible, lord, may it never come to such an evil![98]

Herakles: A guest coming is a burden to those who are in pain.

Admetos: The dead are dead; go into the house.

Herakles: It is shameful for the guest to be dining alongside those who lament.

Admetos: The guest quarters where we will lead you are set well apart.

Herakles: Let me go, and I will owe you an inestimable favor.[99]

Admetos: You simply cannot go to another man's hearth.
You there, lead him inside and open up distant guest quarters
so he will be out of sight; tell those in the house[100]
to put out plenty of food; tightly close the
doors between the halls; it is not fitting for the guests who are dining
to hear the groaning nor be in any pain.[101]

[*Exit Herakles and servants.*]

CHORUS: What are you doing? With such misfortune right on top of you,
Admetos, do you dare to be receiving guests? Are you a fool?

ADMETOS: But if my friend had gone away, driven from my house and city, would you have approved of that?
Surely not, since my misfortune would have been
no less, and I would have been inhospitable as well.
And this evil would have been added to the other evils,
that my house would be known as one that rejected its guests.
I myself find him a most excellent guest-friend
whenever I go to the thirsty land of Argos.

CHORUS: How then could you hide your present misfortune when
the man who has come is as dear to you as you say this one is?[102]

ADMETOS: He would not have been willing to go in the house
if he knew the extent of my suffering.
I know that doing this does not seem sane to some,
and they won't approve of me, but my halls know not
how to deny or dishonor guests.

[*Exit Admetos.*]

CHORUS: Oh house ever hospitable and free, like this man, *Strophe A*
even Pythian Apollo of the lyre[103]
considered you worthy to inhabit
and endured herding sheep
in your domains;
across the sloping hillsides
he piped pastoral marriage songs
to the flocks.[104]

Spotted lynxes joined the flock charmed by the songs, *Antistrophe A*

and leaving the grove of Othrys,
a tawny band of lions came;[105]
A dappled fawn danced
to your lyre, Apollo,
crossing the towering pines
moving with a light foot
and rejoicing in the cheerful song.

Thus flocks most abundant *Strophe B*
grace the hearth you inhabit beside the
beautifully flowing Boibian lake.[106] He sets
the borders to his ploughed fields and flatlands
in the west around the dusky
stable of the sun, at the sky over Molossus,
in the east he rules up to the harborless headland
of Mt. Pelion by the Aegean Sea.[107]

And now opening up his house *Antistrophe B*
he receives his guest with his eyes still moist
as he cries over the corpse of his dear mate
who has just died in this house; for noble birth
gets carried away when it comes to showing respect.[108]
Amongst the well-born there is all manner of wisdom.
I am amazed;[109]
in my soul sits the confidence that
a god-fearing man will do well.

[*Enter Admetos, with servants carrying Alcestis and her funerary offerings.*]

ADMETOS: Men of Pherai who kindly accompany me,
the corpse is all prepared; the servants
carry it aloft toward the tomb and pyre;[110]
you address the dead, as is customary,
as she makes her last journey.

CHORUS: Now look, I see your father coming as fast as his old feet can carry him,
and his servants are bringing finery for your wedded wife,
pleasing gifts for those below.

[*Enter Pheres and attendants.*]

PHERES:[111] I have come to commiserate with you in your troubles, my child;
for no one will deny that you have lost a noble and
virtuous woman.[112] But it is necessary
to bear even such unbearable events as these.
Receive this fine raiment and send it beneath the earth.
For it is fitting that the body of this woman be honored,
the one who died to save your life, my child,
and would not render me childless nor allow me
to fade away in a grief-stricken old age deprived of you,
and who made life more glorious for all women,
having dared to do this noble deed.
Oh you who saved this man, and raised up
those who were fallen, farewell, and in the house of Hades
may it go well for you. I say such marriages are
profitable for mortals, otherwise it is not worth marrying.

ADMETOS: You didn't come to this funeral at *my* behest,
nor do I count you in the company of my friends.
She will never put on this finery of yours;
she has no need of anything from you to be buried in.
The time for you to sympathize with me was when I faced destruction.
You kept out of harm's way then, an old man letting another
younger person die, and now you would cry over the corpse?
Surely you were not truly father of *this* body of mine,
nor did she, who says she bore me and is called
mother, give birth to me; rather, born from some slave's blood,
I was secretly put to the breast of your wife.[113]
Being put to the test you showed who you are,
and I do not consider myself to be your natural child.[114]
Surely you surpass everyone in your lack of spirit,
you, so old and at the end of your life,
had neither the will nor the courage to die

for your son, but rather you let
this woman from outside the family do it, she who
alone justly counts as mother and father to me.
And yet this could have been a fine contest for you to
enter,
dying for your child, since only a very short time
remained for you to live in any case.
[And then both this woman and I would have lived out
the time remaining to us,
and I would not be left alone to bemoan my misfortunes.][115]
And you have experienced whatever good fortune a man
may experience,
as a youth, you were the ruler,
you had a child and heir to your house in me,
so you were not dying without children, not about
to leave your house an orphan for others to tear apart.
Nor can you say that since I dishonored your old age,
you abandoned me to die, I who behaved most respectfully
toward you; in exchange for all I did,
you and she who bore me make me this favor.[116]
So do not delay begetting other children
who will tend you in your old age and, when you are dead,
prepare your body and carry out the corpse.[117]
For I will not bury you with this hand of mine;
as far as you are concerned, I am dead indeed; if having
found another savior,
I still look on the light, I count
myself child of that one and dear nurse of her old age.[118]
Vainly do the old say they wish to die,
cursing old age and the length of life;
when death comes near, no one wishes
to die, and old age no longer seems burdensome to them.

CHORUS: Stop! the present misfortune is enough;
child, you should not provoke your father's temper.

PHERES: Child, why do you bluster thus, as if you were insulting
and driving away
some Lydian or Phrygian slave bought with your silver?

Do you not know that I am a free Thessalian man,
nobly born from a Thessalian father?[119]
You are too insulting, and you will not get away with
hurling childish words against me and shooting off your mouth.
I gave you life and brought you up
as master of this household. I am not obliged to die for you;
for this was not a custom that I inherited from my father,
that fathers should die for their children, nor is it the custom anywhere in Greece.
You were born either lucky or unlucky on your own;
what was due to you from us, you have.
You rule over many, and I will leave you extensive lands
—the same things I received from my father.
How have I wronged you? What have I taken from you?
Don't you die on behalf of this man [*pointing to himself*], and I won't die for you.
You rejoice in looking on the light; do you think your father doesn't?
Truly I reckon that the time spent beneath the earth is long,
the time to live is short, but sweet all the same.
You shamelessly fought not to die,
and you live on exceeding your allotted fortune
by having killed that woman; then you talk about of my lack of
spirit, you lowest of the low, weaker than the woman
who died for you, such a fine youth?
Cleverly indeed you have discovered a way never to die,
if you will always persuade your present
wife to die on your behalf; and you would blame your family
for not being willing to do these things, when you are so base?
Be quiet! Consider, if you love your own
life, everyone else also loves life; if you insult us,
you will hear many insults in return, and they won't be lies.

CHORUS: More ill will has been spoken now even than before.
Stop speaking ill of your son, old man.

ADMETOS: Let him speak, since I have already spoken; if it pains you to hear the truth, you shouldn't have failed me.

PHERES: By dying for you, I would have made an even greater mistake.[120]

ADMETOS: Is it the same for a young man and an old one to die?

PHERES: One life, not two, we are obliged to live.[121]

ADMETOS: May you live a longer time than Zeus!

PHERES: Do you curse your parents though you have suffered nothing unjust from them?[122]

ADMETOS: I recognize that you are in love with long life.

PHERES: But aren't you carrying out this corpse in place of yourself?

ADMETOS: Signs of your lack of spirit, you base coward.

PHERES: She did not die for us; you cannot say this.

ADMETOS: What!
I hope you will need me some day!

PHERES: Marry many women, so that more may die.

ADMETOS: This blame is yours, for you were not willing to die.

PHERES: Dear is this divine light, dear indeed.

ADMETOS: Your spirit is cowardly, not manly.

PHERES: Holding this corpse in your arms you cannot mock an old man.

ADMETOS: You will die with ill fame, whenever you do die.

PHERES: It won't bother me to be spoken ill of when I am dead.

ADMETOS: Woe, woe, the prodigious shamelessness of age.[123]

PHERES: This woman was not shameless; you found one who was brainless!

ADMETOS: Go away and let me bury the dead.

PHERES: I am going. You will bury her, her very own murderer,
but you will still have to give satisfaction to her relatives.
For surely her brother Akastos is no man,
if he does not avenge the blood of his sister.

ADMETOS: Get out of here, you and that woman who lives with you,
grow old without children, as you deserve,
even though your child is still alive;
for you will no longer live here under this roof;
if it were fitting for me to have heralds banish you
from your paternal hearth, I would do it.

[*Exit Pheres.*]

For us—since this immediate trouble must be borne—
let us go, so that we may place this corpse on the pyre.

CHORUS: Oh, oh! How steadfast[124] you were in your courage!
Oh noble and most excellent woman,
farewell; may underworld Hermes
and Hades receive you with good will.[125] If there is
any profit for the good in the netherworld, may you share
in it as you attend the bride of Hades.[126]

[*Exeunt all.*][127]

[*Enter a servant, from within.*]

SERVANT: Many guests from all over the world
have I seen come to Admetos' house,
and I have served them dinner, too; but never
have I received a worse guest than this one at our hearth.
First of all, seeing that my master was grieving
he had the audacity to cross the threshold and come in.
Then he did not, with restraint,[128] accept
the hospitality provided, understanding the situation;

rather, if we didn't bring something, he prodded us to
get it.
Taking the drinking cup wreathed in ivy[129] in his hand
he drank the wine of the black mother grape unmixed,[130]
until the fire of the wine came over him and warmed him;
then he crowned his head with branches of myrtle,
while croaking out his cacophony; there were two strains
to hear—
on the one hand, he sang, showing no respect for
Admetos'
troubles, and on the other, we servants were crying for
our
mistress; we could not show a moist eye to the guest,
for Admetos had ordained it thus.
And now I entertain this guest-friend at our hearth,
this outrageous thief or highwayman, and
she has gone from the house, and I could not follow
nor stretch out my hand, nor lament my
mistress, who was to me and all the servants
a mother; she saved us from countless troubles,
softening her husband's temper. Don't I justly
hate this guest who has arrived here in our troubles?

[*Enter Herakles from within.*]

HERAKLES: You there, why do you look so solemn and thoughtful?
It is not right for a servant to glower at a guest
but rather, he should receive him with an easygoing
temper.
But you, seeing your master's companion arrive,
receive him with hateful and scowling visage,
in your concern over some stranger's suffering.[131]
Come here, so that you may become a little wiser.
Don't you know that this is the nature of mortal affairs?
I think not; for how would you? But listen to me.
Death is a debt all humans must pay,
and no mortal can know
if he will live through the next day;
it is unclear which way luck will go,

and it can't be taught or grasped by any craft.
Therefore, having heard and learned from me,
cheer up, have a drink, reckon your life
by the day, leave the rest to luck.
And honor Kupris, who is by far the sweetest of the gods
to mortals;[132] for she is a kindly god.
Let everything else go and trust in what I say
—if indeed I seem to you to speak rightly.
And I think I do. Setting aside your excessive suffering
and throwing your misfortune overboard,
why not wreathe your head and have a drink with us?
I am sure that a stroke from the wine cup
will cut you loose from this glowering and furrowed turn of mind.[133]
Mortals must think mortal thoughts,
Since for all who are solemn and scowling,
if you accept my judgment,
life is not truly life but a catastrophe.

SERVANT: We know these things; but what we suffer now
is not worthy of revelry and laughter.

HERAKLES: But the woman who died was a stranger; don't grieve
too much; for the masters of the house still live.

SERVANT: How do they "live"? Don't you know the troubles of this house?

HERAKLES: If your master didn't tell me a lie.

SERVANT: That one is far, far too good a host.

HERAKLES: Should I not be treated well just because of some outsider's corpse?

SERVANT: Very much the outsider indeed![134]

HERAKLES: Surely there not some blow he did not tell me about?

SERVANT: Go now with good cheer; our masters' troubles are our concern.

HERAKLES: This kind of talk does not come from a stranger's suffering.

SERVANT: In that case I would not have been irked watching your revelry.

HERAKLES: But then have I suffered terribly at the hands of my host?

SERVANT: You did not come at a propitious time to be received in this house.
[We were grieving; didn't you see our black
robed attire and cropped hair?

HERAKLES: Who then has died?][135]
Not one of the children or the aged father surely?

SERVANT: The wife of Admetos has perished, friend.

HERAKLES: What are you saying? And in those circumstances he still made me his guest?

SERVANT: Yes, for he had too much respect for you to turn you away from his house.[136]

HERAKLES: Oh poor wretch, what a helpmeet you have lost!

SERVANT: We are all destroyed, not her alone.

HERAKLES: I did notice his eyes full of tears, and
his face and shorn hair; but he convinced me
by saying that he bore a stranger's funeral offerings to the tomb.[137]
In violation of my feelings, I crossed the threshold
and drank in the house of this hospitable man,
who was suffering so. And then I revelled,
covering my head with these wreaths? But you did not tell me
the extent of the trouble besetting the house.
Where is he burying her? Where will I find him?

SERVANT: Along the road which takes you straight to Larissa,
on the outskirts of the city, you will see a carved tombstone.

[*Exit Servant.*]

Herakles: Oh my heart and hand, daring and suffering so much,
reveal now what sort of a child Tirynthian
Alkmene of Elektryon bore to Zeus.[138]
I must save the woman who has just died,
Alcestis, and set her up once more in this house,
as a favor for Admetos.[139]
Going now I will watch for that black-robed lord of corpses,
Death; I expect to find him
drinking the sacrificial blood near the tomb.
If I catch him as I rush out from my hiding place,
I will encircle him with my arms,
and there is no one who could drag him away,
chest heaving, before he yields the woman to me.
If I should miss my prey, if he doesn't come
for the clotted blood, I will go below
into the sunless house of Kore[140] and her Lord;
I will demand her and I do believe I will lead
Alcestis back up and put her in the hands of my host,
who received me into his house and did not drive me away,
even though he was struck a heavy blow.
He hid it because he is noble and had respect for me.[141]
Is any Thessalian more hospitable than this man,
or any household in all Greece? He will never say that being
noble he did a good deed for an ignoble man.

[*Exit Herakles.*]

[*Enter Admetos.*]

Admetos: Oh hateful
entrances, hateful sight of these deserted
halls![142] Oh me! Woe is me.
Where can I go? Where stand? What can I say? What not?
How might I perish?
Surely my mother bore me with a very heavy fate.
I envy the dead, I am in love with them,
I wish with all my heart to inhabit their houses.

I rejoice neither in seeing the rays of sun
nor in setting foot on the earth;
what a hostage Death has robbed me of
and given to Hades.[143]

CHORUS: Go on, go on. Go into the depths of the house. *Strophe A*

(ADMETOS: Woe!)

What you have suffered merits wailing.

(ADMETOS: Oh, oh)

You have gone through painful labor, I know it well.

(ADMETOS: Woe, woe)[144]

You don't help the one who is below.

(ADMETOS: Oh me, oh me)

Never to look directly on the face of your beloved
mate
is bitter indeed.

ADMETOS: You mentioned what has been eating away at my heart;
for what greater evil is there for any man than to lose
a faithful mate? Would that I had never married
nor lived with her in this house.
I envy those mortals who are unmarried and childless.
To suffer for one life is
enough of a burden;
children's illnesses and nuptial
couches plundered by death
are unbearable to behold; if only one could live childless
and unmarried for all time.

CHORUS: Fortune, fortune so difficult to wrestle *Antistrophe A*
with, arrives.

(ADMETOS: Oh, oh)

You can set no limit to suffering.

(ADMETOS: Oh, oh)

Heavy to bear, but all the same . . .

(ADMETOS: Woe, woe)

you must bear them; you are not the first one who has lost[145]

(ADMETOS: Oh me, me)

a wife; other catastrophes appear and press down on other mortals.

ADMETOS: Oh what great grief and suffering for the loved ones
beneath the earth!
Why did you prevent me from throwing myself
into the hollow tomb so that I could lie dead
with her, who was by far the best of women?
Instead of one, Hades would have had the two
most loyal souls crossing over
the underworld lake together.

CHORUS: There was once someone *Strophe B*
in my family, whose son perished in the house,
cause enough for a threnody,
and this was the only child; but all the same
he bore the trouble well enough, even though he was childless,
already slipping toward gray hair
and advanced in years.

ADMETOS: Oh frame of this house, how shall I go inside?[146]
How shall I live here when my fortune has fallen so?[147]
Oh me! Much has intervened:
then, I walked in with pine torches from Mt. Pelion
and marriage songs,
holding my dear wife's hand,
and a band of echoing revellers followed
blessing the one who has just died and me,
saying that we were well-born, a pair

from noble stock on both sides;
now a funeral lament contends with the marriage songs
and instead of white robes, black clothes
usher me within
to the desolate couch my marriage bed has become.[148]

CHORUS: In fair fortune, *Antistrophe B*
this heartache has come upon you, inexperienced
in suffering, but you saved
your own life and soul.
Your wife has died, she left behind the bonds of
affection.[149]
What is new in this? Many men
has death cut loose
from their wedded wives.

ADMETOS:[150] Friends, I consider my wife's fate more fortunate
than my own, even if it does not seem so;
for no more heartache will catch hold of her,
but rather with glory she has ended many struggles.[151]
I, who was not supposed to live, exceeding what was
allotted,
will lead a painful life; I have just learned this.[152]
How will I bear to enter the house?
Who will I address, who will address me in turn,
that I might take delight in going in? Where will I turn?
Desolation within will drive me out,
whenever I look on the empty bed of my wife
and the empty seat on which she used to sit, the
dirty floors under my roof, and the children
falling about my knees calling for their mother, and the
servants, too,
grieve that they have lost such a mistress from the house.
Thus it is throughout the house; but outside,
Thessalian marriages and gatherings of women
will drive me back in again; for I could not bear
looking on the age-mates of my wedded wife.
And whoever hates me will say this when he meets me:

"Look at him living shamefully, he who could not bear to
die;
lacking spirit, he gave up instead the one he married,[153]
and escaped Hades; does he seem to be a man then?
He loathes those who bore him, but he himself was not
willing
to die." Such a reputation among the lowborn
will I have. What's the gain in my living, friends,
ill-spoken of and faring ill?[154]

CHORUS: I flew high in the air *Strophe A*
and through music,[155]
catching at many doctrines
I have found nothing stronger than Necessity,
no drug
in the Thracian tablets,
which the voice of Orpheus wrote down,[156]
nor such drugs as Phoebus gave to the Asklepiads,
cutting them as a cure
for long suffering mortals.[157]

To Necessity alone there is no altar *Antistrophe A*
that one can approach, nor any image,
nor does she listen to sacrifices.[158]
Oh Goddess, may you never
come against me with greater force
than you have already in this life.
For even if Zeus should nod assent
he accomplishes his will only with you.[159]
You tame even Chalybian iron with your force,
nor do you show any respect for sheer will.[160]

And you that this goddess' hands have *Strophe B*
seized with inescapable bonds,
bear up; for groaning will not keep above ground
those who have faded away below.
Even the shadowy children of the gods
fade away in death.[161]
Dear was she when she was among us,

dear she will be even though dead,
for the most noble bedmate of all
did you yoke to your couch.

Let her tomb not be counted as the mound *Antistrophe B*
of one of the departed;
rather, let it be honored
as the gods are, a place of reverence for travelers.
And someone climbing up the sloping
path will speak thus:
"This woman once died for her husband,
Now she is a blessed spirit;
Hail, oh mistress, may you grant us good."
Such are the speeches which will greet her.[162]

And now, it would seem that the offspring of Alkmene
wends his way to your hearth, Admetos.

[*Enter Herakles with a closely swathed woman.*][163]

HERAKLES: A man should speak freely to his dear friend,[164]
Admetos, not silently keep reproaches in his heart.
I thought I was worthy to be enlisted as a friend
who would stand by you in your troubles;
you did not tell me that the corpse laid out was
your wife, but instead made me a guest in your house
as if your concern was for the suffering of some stranger.
So I crowned my head and poured libations to the gods
in your household of misfortune.
And I blame you, I truly do, that I went through this;
but I surely do not want to hurt you in your suffering.
I will tell you why I have turned around and come back;
take this woman here and keep her safe for me,
until I come back with the Thracian horses,
having killed the Bistonian tyrant.
If, however, it should turn out badly for me (and I hope
not for I would like to get home),
I give you this woman to serve in your house.
With a great effort did she come into my hands;

for I came upon some people holding a general contest,
a worthy labor for athletes,
from which I carried her off as a victory prize.
For those who won the smaller events there were
horses, for those who won in the greater events,
boxing and wrestling, there was a herd of cattle;
this woman went along with them; happening on them,
it seemed a shame to let slide the glorious prize.[165]
But, as I said, you must care for the woman;
for I come bringing something not stolen, but won with
labor; and perhaps in time you will approve.

ADMETOS: It was not at all to dishonor you or to put you in a false position
that I concealed the wretched fate of my wife.
But it would only have added grief to grief
if you had set off to the house of another host;
it was enough for me to bemoan my own trouble.
As for the woman, if at all possible, I beg you, lord,
ask some other Thessalian, one who has not suffered what I have,
to safeguard her. For you have many
guest-friends amongst the Pheraians; do not make me remember my troubles.
Seeing her in the house, I would not be able to remain
dry-eyed; do not add this illness to the illness I already suffer;
I am sufficiently weighed down by catastrophe.
And where in the house would one keep such a young woman?
Young she is, as is clear from her clothing and finery.[166]
Will she then live under the same roof with men?
And how will she remain untouched, wandering back and forth
among young men? It is no easy thing to restrain youth,
Herakles; I am thinking of you.
Or, shall I lead her into my dead wife's chamber and keep her there?

And how shall I bring this woman to the couch of that
one?
I fear double blame, from the people—
lest someone charge me with betraying my helpmeet
by falling on the bed of another young woman—
and the deceased—who is worthy of my reverence;
I must think ahead. You, woman,
whoever you are, know that you have the same size and
shape as Alcestis
and you resemble her in form.
Oh me! By the gods, take this woman out of my sight,
do not attack one already overcome.
For looking on this woman I seem to see my wife;
she stirs up my heart, and from these eyes
streams burst forth. Oh wretched me,
now I get the full flavor of my bitter suffering.[167]

CHORUS: I cannot speak well of this turn of fortune;
but it is necessary, whoever a man is, to endure the gift of
a god.[168]

HERAKLES: If only I had enough power to bring your
wife back into the light from the underworld domains
and to
accomplish this favor for you.

ADMETOS: I know well that you would be willing. But where does this
get us? It is not possible for the dead to come into the light.

HERAKLES: Do not overdo it but bear it properly.

ADMETOS: It is easier to give advice than to be patient when you have
suffered.

HERAKLES: What would you gain from moaning and groaning forever?

ADMETOS: I know that myself, but some desire leads me on.[169]

HERAKLES: Loving the dead leads to tears.

ADMETOS: It has destroyed me even more than I can say.[170]

HERAKLES: You have lost a noble woman; who can deny it?

ADMETOS: As a result, this man can no longer enjoy life.

HERAKLES: Time will soften your suffering, now it is still in its youth.[171]

ADMETOS: You can speak of time, if you mean time to die.

HERAKLES: A woman and a new marriage will end your longing.

ADMETOS: Be quiet! What a thing to say! I would not have thought it.

HERAKLES: Why then? Will you never marry but keep your widower's bed?

ADMETOS: There is no woman who will share a couch with this man.

HERAKLES: How do you expect that this will benefit the deceased?

ADMETOS: It is right for her to be honored even where she is.

HERAKLES: I approve, I approve, but nonetheless you gain a name for stupidity.

ADMETOS: Just so you never again call this man bridegroom.

HERAKLES: I approved of you for being a faithful husband to your mate.

ADMETOS: May I die if I abandon that one even though she is no longer.

HERAKLES: Receive this one now into your noble home.[172]

ADMETOS: No, I beseech you by Zeus who sired you.

HERAKLES: You make a mistake if you do not do this.

ADMETOS: And doing it I will eat my heart out with suffering.

HERAKLES: Trust me; this favor will soon turn out to be useful.

ADMETOS: Oh dear. I wish that you had never won her at that contest!

HERAKLES: All the same, you will share in my winnings.

ADMETOS: You have spoken well; but let the woman go away.

HERAKLES: She will go if it is necesary; first look to see if it is.

ADMETOS: It is necessary, unless you will be really angry with me.

HERAKLES: It is because I know something that I am so eager.

ADMETOS: You win now; but what you do does not give me any pleasure.

HERAKLES: But there will come a time when you will approve; only trust me.

ADMETOS: Bring her in, if she must be received in my house.

HERAKLES: I would not give this woman over to your servants.

ADMETOS: You yourself lead her into the house, if you wish.[173]

HERAKLES: Into your own hands will I place her.

ADMETOS: I would rather not touch her; but she can go into the house.

HERAKLES: I trust in your right hand alone.

ADMETOS: Lord, you force me to do what I do not want to do.

HERAKLES: Be brave and stretch out your hand and touch this guest.

ADMETOS: And I stretch it forth, as if to decapitate the Gorgon.[174]

HERAKLES: You have her?

ADMETOS: Yes, I have her.

HERAKLES: Keep her now and you will say that
the son of Zeus was a noble guest.
Look on her, to see if she does not seem to resemble
your wife. Being fortunate, leave off your grieving.

[*He lifts her veil.*]

ADMETOS: Oh gods, what shall I say—this unhoped for miracle—
am I looking on my wife, truly my own wife,
or does some teasing charm from the gods confound me?

HERAKLES: Not at all; you look on your wedded wife.

ADMETOS: See if this is not some phantasm of the underworld.

HERAKLES: You did not make a conjurer your guest.[175]

ADMETOS: But am I looking on my wedded wife, whom I buried?

HERAKLES: Know it well; I am not surprised that you marvel at your
luck.

ADMETOS: Should I touch and speak to her, as to my living wife?

HERAKLES: Speak to her; you have everything that you wanted.

ADMETOS: Oh visage and form of the dearest woman,
I have you beyond all hope, for I never thought to see you.

HERAKLES: You have her; may there be no jealousy from the gods.[176]

ADMETOS: Oh noble child of greatest Zeus,
may you be happy and may the father who gave you life
keep you safe; for you alone set me right.
How did you send her back into the light from below?

HERAKLES: By joining battle with the one in charge of the spirits.

ADMETOS: Where do you say you had this contest with Death?

HERAKLES: From my ambush by the tomb itself, I snatched her with
these hands.

ADMETOS: Why does my wife stand there without speaking?

HERAKLES: It is not yet lawful for you to hear her speak,
not until she is purified from the gods below
and third day dawns.[177]
But lead her within now; be just
in the future, Admetos, and treat your guests with
reverence.

Farewell; for I must go and carry out the labor
assigned me for the tyrant son of Sthenelos.

ADMETOS: Remain with us and share our hearth.

HERAKLES: Some other time; now I must press on.

ADMETOS: Well then, may you have good luck, and complete the homeward trip.

[*Exit Herakles.*]

I command the citizens of the whole region
to set up choruses in honor of these fortunate events
and to invoke the gods by making
the altars redolent with bull-sacrifices.
Now we are transformed into a better way of life
than before; for I will not deny that I am fortunate.

CHORUS: Many are the shapes of the spirits, and
the gods ordain many things beyond our hopes;
things that seem likely don't come to pass,
and the god finds a way for things that are unlikely.
Thus has this affair come out.[178]

MEDEA

Translated and with an Introduction by

Ruby Blondell

I. INTRODUCTION

Medea and Athens

At *Medea* 824–65 the chorus sing of an idealized Athens, home of Harmony and the Muses, goddesses of poetry and song; here Aphrodite, goddess of beauty and sexual desire, makes passionate desire (*erōs*) sit down by the side of wisdom, or "cleverness," and engender human excellence. The chorus wonder how this sacred place can possibly give shelter to a woman who has murdered her own children—a woman, we may add, who embodies the power of Aphrodite, *erōs* and "cleverness" at their most terrifying.[1] In mythology, Athens would do just that, with near-disastrous consequences: Medea tried to poison Theseus, the greatest Athenian hero, son and heir of Aigeus, king of Athens. In classical Athens, this event was memorialized in ritual. But the problem embodied in Medea cannot be confined to ritual or myth. Euripides' drama concerns the position and treatment of women and outsiders in Athenian life and ideology in his own day. On a metatheatrical level, the chorus are asking how Athens, in light of its own most cherished values, can incorporate the story of this murderess into the civic body by and for whom the play was first performed.

The year was 431 BCE (*Medea* is Euripides' second surviving play, after *Alcestis*). Athens was at the height of its power and prestige. But this was also the year of the outbreak of the Peloponnesian War, which was to bring decline and demoralization over the next quarter century. That war was imminent: The Spartans had just attacked Plataea, an Athenian ally, and the Athenian citizen army was mobilizing. There was also acute hostility between Athens and Corinth, where this play is set.[2] It was a time of anxiety, distraction, and fervid activity, of patriotic enthusiasm and military pride. Such was the atmosphere in which the chorus sang lyrically of the greatness and beauty of Athens, and in which Medea declared that she would rather "stand three times behind/a shield in war than give birth to one child" (250–51).

These words offer a startling challenge to contemporary Athenian assumptions about gender roles. Along with other military language used by Medea (e.g., 263–66, 1242–44), they also raise questions about the value of violence and warfare, which played such a huge role in Greek life and literature. Like Medea herself, the Peloponnesian War would destroy many children of the rising generation. But the extended bloodshed of that war was yet to come, and whether or not the play questions male military values, it did not find favor with the Athenian audience. It came third out of three in the tragic competition. Sophocles won second prize, and first was Euphorion (one of Aeschylus' sons), perhaps with a revival of some of his father's plays.

The Myth

Euripides' drama is the first detailed account we have of the Corinthian portion of Medea's story, and has exerted a powerful influence on later representations in art and literature.[3] We know from ancient references that there were earlier versions (including one by Aeschylus), but none of them survives. The myth of the Argonauts and the Golden Fleece, however, which forms the background to the drama, was certainly familiar to Euripides' audience: Jason's ship, the Argo, is described in the *Odyssey* as "known to all" (12.69–70), and an ode by Pindar that predates this drama tells the tale in considerable detail (*Pythian* 4). Euripides himself had shown an early interest in the story: one of his first plays, produced in 455 BCE but now lost, concerned Medea's murder of Pelias (below, p. 151).

The Golden Fleece belonged to Aietes, king of Colchis, a non-Greek region at the eastern end of the Black Sea (see map). It was a treasured possession, guarded by an unsleeping dragon. The Greek hero Jason was sent to fetch the Fleece by his wicked uncle Pelias, who had killed Jason's father Aison and usurped the throne of Iolcus. When Jason, the rightful heir, arrived to claim the throne, Pelias sent him for the Fleece, hoping that the long and dangerous journey would destroy him. Jason sailed to Colchis with the Argonauts (his comrades on the ship Argo), who included many famous heroes, such as Herakles, Kastor, and Pollux.[4] Aietes agreed to give up the Fleece if Jason could yoke his team of brazen-hoofed fire-breathing oxen, plow and sow a field with dragon's teeth, then defeat the armed men who would spring up from those teeth. Jason did so with the aid of the Colchian princess Medea, who had fallen in love with him.[5]

Medea, the daughter of Aietes and a nymph named Iduia ("she who knows"), is a disturbing mythological figure. Her own name suggests Greek words for "cunning" or "full of plans" (compare lines 401–2, with p. 422, n. 68), but also evokes a word for genitalia, as well as the name of the Medes or Persians—the greatest foreign enemy of the Greeks in Euripides' lifetime (above, p. 8). In some stories she actually becomes the ancestor of the Medes, via a son named Medeus. She is noted above all for her sinister magic powers. This is just what one would expect from her family background. She was not only a grand-daughter of Helios the sun-god (father of Aietes, and a god closely associated with magic), but niece of Circe (Aietes' sister) and dimly related to the goddess Hekate.[6] Medea, Circe, and Hekate are the three most notorious witches in Greek mythology.

In Greek culture magic can be positive or negative, but we hear much more about the latter variety. Destructive magic is strongly associated with women, sexual enchantment and female song (a sub-theme of Euripides' play; see especially 415–30). Circe, for example, is an eroticized witch who sings as she weaves, an expert in magic drugs who bestializes and emasculates the men she ensnares (*Odyssey* 10.133–574).[7] These ancient figures are not culturally identical to the witches persecuted in medieval Europe or early modern America, who belong to a specifically Christian context. For example, Greek "witches" are not devil-worshipers, but women with magical powers for good or ill. (There is no concept of the devil in ancient Greek religion.) But there are certain points of continuity, above all in the persistence with which male anxiety conceptualizes female agency and sexual autonomy as an exertion of demonic power.

Medea used her magic arts to help Jason carry out Aietes' "impossible" exploits, kill the dragon and abscond with the Fleece, her furious father in hot pursuit. In the course of their flight she killed her only brother, Apsyrtos.[8] After Medea and Jason delivered the fleece to Pelias, she used her magic arts to convince Pelias' daughters to kill him too. She cut up an old ram, then restored it to youth by boiling it in a cauldron with magic herbs (a popular scene on Greek vase paintings). She then convinced the daughters of Pelias to do the same to him, but omitted the herbs so that he remained dead.[9] Similarly in our play she uses a combination of magic and persuasive speech to destroy the king through his own daughter and crush Jason through his sons.[10]

The couple then took refuge in Corinth, where Euripides' drama is set. When the play opens, Medea has just discovered that Jason has secretly married the daughter of Kreon, king of Corinth.[11] Moreover, the king, out of fear of retaliation, has decided to exile her with her two young sons. Enraged by this betrayal she devises and enacts a horrible revenge. First she arranges a refuge for herself with

Aigeus, king of Athens. Then she uses poisonous drugs to kill the princess, causing the king's death as well. Finally she kills with her own hand the two sons she bore to Jason. At the end of the play she escapes punishment by fleeing to Athens in a dragon-drawn chariot given to her by her grandfather, the sun-god Helios.

This precise sequence of dramatic events could not have been predicted by Euripides' audience. It is true that Medea's track record was not a good one. But there are also favorable stories about her, since like most magical figures she is ambiguous in her powers. In some stories she is involved in the foundation of cities—normally a positive role.[12] The nurse alludes to her assistance in saving Corinth from a famine and claims she was a model wife to Jason (11–15). Her powers will enable Aigeus to produce offspring. The lyric tradition prior to Euripides speaks of her marriage to Achilles in Elysium, and a later story makes her instrumental in reviving her father's kingdom (Visser 1986: 164 n. 54). In other stories prior to Euripides she attempted to make her children immortal (see further below). In any case, the Greek dramatists enjoyed considerable liberty in adapting traditional characters and stories (above, pp. 45–8). So the audience, though aware of some of the myths about Medea, would not have known in detail how Euripides would handle this material.

In particular, they *may* not have known that she would kill her sons. We know of several other traditions about the children's death. One suggests that Medea killed them accidentally in the temple of Hera Akraia while trying to render them immortal, and was banished by Jason for this reason. Another tells us that the Corinthians (or women of Corinth) killed Medea's seven sons and seven daughters in that temple, out of hostility to her barbarian ways. Yet another says that she killed Kreon then fled the vengeance of his family, leaving her children in the temple for Jason to protect (compare 1301–5); Kreon's family killed them there (compare 1303–5), then spread the rumor that she had murdered them herself. From these accounts it is a short but very significant step to Euripides' version, where she kills them purposefully out of revenge for Jason's betrayal. Some scholars think this was an innovation by Euripides, but opinion has recently inclined against this view (see Michelini 1989; Johnston 1997b). In any case the infanticide is crucial to the play, and the poet carefully builds suspense toward this shocking climax.

Medea as Other

Medea was probably in origin a Greek figure, from northern Greece or Corinth (Hall 1989: 35). But ethnicity is fluid in myth, and Euripides' Medea is not Greek, but a foreigner or "barbarian," from the distant land of Colchis.[13] It seems that he was the first to "barbarize" Medea in this way (Hall 1996: 344). The geographical gulf that separates Greek from "barbarian" is emphasized in the Nurse's opening words, where she speaks of the passage of the Argo through the Symplegades or Clashing Rocks, which marked the entrance to the Black Sea (compare also 1263–64). The playwright has thus developed a core attribute of Medea's mythological persona—her status as outsider—by locating her origins at the far (and hazy) limits of the Greek world.[14]

A famous passage from the historian Herodotus tells us that the people of Colchis were "black-skinned and woolly-haired," and resembled the Egyptians, from whom he thought they were descended (2.104).[15] The precise historical relationship between these peoples is much disputed by modern scholars, but the Colchians were evidently known to be a dark-skinned race, historically as well as mythologically. Black skin was a clear marker of non-Greek origin, and some "barbarians" in tragedy may even have appeared in dark-skinned masks (Hall 1989: 139–43). But there is no sign that Euripides' Medea was one of these, and her children are light-haired (1142; compare above, p. 36). (Contrast the attention drawn to the blackness of the Danaids in Aeschylus' *Suppliants.* See Snowden 1970: 157; Hall 1989: 139.) But Medea probably did appear in exotic "barbarian" costume. All our vase paintings of her in such dress post-date Euripides' play, and it seems likely that it was his presentation of her as a "barbarian" that influenced these portrayals.[16]

As a "barbarian" female witch, Medea is located at the very margins of Greek society. Jason points out that she was raised without the benefits of Greek "civilization" (536–38), and later claims that no Greek woman would have behaved as she has done (1339; but see below, p. 430, n. 149). There is heavy dramatic irony here, since he has himself violated the Greek ethical norms of trust and honesty in his treatment of her (see further below, p. 161). But the ancient Greeks, like most peoples, projected their own culturally undesirable qualities onto outsiders. Many such "barbarian" attributes are reflected in Medea: unrestrained emotion (especially extreme displays of grief and anger); lust, sensuality, and transgression of normative Greek gender roles; bestiality;[17] wealth, especially gold (a motif of this play, starting with the Golden Fleece); luxurious clothing (like Medea's gifts to the princess); brutal violence and lawlessness; untrustworthiness, duplicity, and expertise with magic drugs.

Many of these attributes are characteristic weapons of the powerless. Not coincidentally, many of the same stereotypes were attached to (Greek) women, since the barbarian and the female were the primary categories of Other through which the adult Greek male defined himself (above, p. 23). Chief among these negative female stereotypes are duplicity, emotionalism, and lustfulness. So a barbarian woman like Medea was doubly damned. The only way she could sink any lower on the ideological scale would be as an old slave-woman, like her own nurse.[18] In addition, she violates in the most drastic way the positive ideals and desirable stereotypes of Greek womanhood—sexual restraint, deference first to one's father and then to one's husband, and devotion to one's children.

Euripides' Medea, then, the barbarian, female, witch, and murderer of her own children, is the quintessential transgressive outsider. Picture her as an orientalized drag queen in a red and black kimono, with vivid make-up, tattoos, nipple- and nose-rings, and long black leather boots, and holding a whip. Such was the image offered to the audience in the 1992 production by Greek Active, a Seattle theater group specializing in drag performances of classic dramas.[19] It is a remarkable testament to Euripides' drama that its emotional power survived and even throve on the camp theatricals of Greek Active, from slapstick and explicit SM sex-play to a disco chorus of drag queens lip-synching "Don't leave me this way," and "I will survive." But this extraordinary production was not just further evidence of the perennial fascination of the play, or a way of putting a new spin on an old favorite. Rather, it was a brilliant cultural "translation," in that it effectively transposed into a contemporary American idiom the threat of Medea as the ultimate Other. In our own culture, who could be more marginal or shockingly transgressive than a drag queen who combines orientalized exoticism with the frisson of nipple-rings and leather?[20]

Like Euripides' barbarian witch, such a figure challenges the most sacred mainstream conventions and assumptions concerning sex, gender, and social roles.[21] Homosexuals today are commonly suspected and accused of behavior destructive to these conventions (e.g., recruitment of children, leading to extinction of the "traditional" family). Medea's transgression likewise strikes at the heart of the patriarchal family, which was the primary unit of Greek society, and at the carefully constructed and maintained gender roles on which that society depended. Above all, she stirs the primal male fear that women may depart from their "proper" role as bearers and nurturers of men's children (above, pp. 55–6). The primary locus of this male anxiety about female agency is sex and reproduction. In an "inappropriately" erotic woman (i.e., just about any erotically active woman except a faithful and contented wife and mother), female power is often conceptualized as witchcraft.[22] It is no accident that the witches of Greek myth tend to be destructive mothers and hostile toward children in general (Parry 1992: 120).

The threat posed by Medea is underscored by repeated references to the house, home or household (*domos* or *oikos*), which lies at the heart of Greek culture.[23] This threat is not only personal but structural, extending to the loftiest embodiments of patriarchal rule. Medea does not just kill her own children and wipe out Jason's family line. She also kills the king himself, and the daughter who would have borne him heirs,[24] just as she earlier killed King Pelias and before that wiped out her royal father's line by murdering her only brother, Apsyrtos, and her own children. A more benevolent side of Medea is shown in her promise to ensure offspring for Aigeus, king of Athens, by means of her magic. But this too shows her awesome female power to control men, and the perpetuation of their line and name, by controlling their fertility. As the Athenian audience knew well, Aigeus and his son Theseus would have a narrow escape from her deadly charms.

Medea and Marriage

As part of the ideology that both supports and assuages this patriarchal fear, the Greek construction of gender (like our own) posits mother-love as the most powerful "natural" emotional bond. In a typical example, the orator Isaeus describes the maternal bond as "the closest by nature."[25] Despite the conflicting feelings aroused by the fact that Jason is her children's father (36, 113–14), Medea clearly embodies this affection (see 1021–80, esp. 1069–75). It is crucial to recognize that Euripides does not portray her as a cold or uncaring mother, but an intensely loving one, even after she has killed them (1397). In this respect, as in her preoccupation with marriage, Medea is not the bloody, passionate, and transgressive barbarian sorceress of myth, but a stereotypical Greek woman. Euripides draws on the former persona when it suits him, but also gives Medea aspects of a normative Athenian wife and mother.

A helpful way to consider this apparent dissonance is through Sourvinou-Inwood's terminology, borrowed from cinema, of "zooming" and "distancing" (1997: 254–62). Medea's character is constructed through various conceptual schemata, such as "good woman," "normal woman," and "bad woman." These are the cultural models or parameters through which ancient audience members made sense of their theatrical experience. Euripides, like other dramatists, employs various poetic and dramatic techniques to activate ("zooming") or subvert ("distancing") these schemata in accordance with his own purposes.

> This vacillation between Medea as a representative of the woman's condition in marriage and Medea as the ultimate Other (and as the embodiment of woman as the Other)—the outsider, the monster, the creature of uncontrollable and

> destructive passions—corresponds to the vacillation of the world of the play between a familiar domestic world and a mythic realm of nightmarish possibilities. (Segal 1996: 31)

Some critics construe these varying aspects of Medea as a radical incoherence in her character, others as a complexity corresponding to that of actual human motives and behavior. Since we interpret the behavior of real people through the same schemata that we bring to drama, these modes of interpretation are not necessarily incompatible.

One way to read the play is as an attempt to address the disturbing question of what could make a devoted wife and mother murder the children she loves so much. The question is one that exerts a continuing fascination. Toni Morrison's *Beloved* is a contemporary fictional approach to the same subject, and the media handling of Susan Smith's murder of her children in 1994 bears witness both to the deep-seated fears that the idea of maternal infanticide still provokes, and the potentially mythic status of such a tale in our own time.[26] Nowadays, such status is conferred primarily by media representations. The fact that news stories and popular accounts explicitly likened Susan Smith to Medea (e.g., Peyser 1995: 161), bears witness to the ways in which we still use Medea to read our world. Conversely, it is only from the perspective of our own world that we can read Medea. Thus Jules Dassin's 1978 film, *A Dream of Passion,* uses a contemporary setting to explore the relationship between Medea and real mothers who kill their children.

One might expect any representation of a woman who kills her own children to be unequivocally negative. But Euripides (like Morrison) goes beyond such easy judgments to explore the cultural, material and psychological circumstances that might make a person behave in such a way, and even to stir sympathy for his heroine. In doing so he is in accord with an interesting countercurrent in Greek literature, xenophobic and misogynistic as it so often is. The Other—whether foreigner, enemy, or woman—is often portrayed with remarkable sympathy (e.g., the Trojans in the *Iliad,* the Persians in Aeschylus' play of that name, and Kassandra in Aeschylus' *Agamemnon*).

Euripides starts his play by gaining sympathy for Medea, who is represented in the prologue as a desperate women maltreated by a contemptible man. Her famous opening speech gives us a much fuller picture of a female perspective, with its forceful and sustained complaint about the wretched lot of women in general, and specifically in marriage (230–51). This is not the only surviving complaint about the position and treatment of women in classical Athens. (The closest parallel is the fragment of Sophocles quoted above, p. 57). But with its long and specific account of the perils of marriage for a woman and the sexual double standard, it is unique in surviving classical literature for its insight into the position of women and sympathy for their lot.

In simple plot terms, this speech is designed to win over a chorus of conventional Greek women by identifing the speaker with her audience as a woman burdened by an oppressive and unjust institution. But it goes far beyond what is necessary for that limited dramatic purpose, clearly suggesting that Medea's behavior is in part the outcome of her plight as a woman in a patriarchal culture. We can only speculate as to the effect it may have had on an ancient Greek audience, either at the moment of utterance (when the audience does not yet know the crimes Medea will commit), or in retrospect, when the play can be interpreted as a whole. The internal audience—the chorus of Corinthian women—responds sympathetically, but this is not a sure guide to the responses of men—or women—in the Athenian theatrical audience. A wide range of possible interpretive strategies and responses was available to them, as it is to us.

One possibility is to read the speech as a bold "feminist" statement on Euripides' part, to be heard independently of its overall context. Such an approach would be compatible with the common practice among ancient authors of quoting drama for one's own purposes without regard for context. Yet the speech may look entirely different if dramatic context *is* taken into account. It may, for example, be taken to suggest that any woman critical of the prevailing social structure, is a (potential) murderer.[27] On the other hand, maybe a murderous monster is the only culturally "safe" vehicle for the articulation of such views, enabling Euripides to voice a radical or woman-identified position without being too closely associated with it. It might even be the only conceivable such vehicle, in the sense that within the cultural parameters of classical Athens, female discontent might be equated by definition with murderous witchcraft. Even in this case, however, such monstrous figures might serve a useful purpose for articulating socially unpalatable critiques. Nor does Medea's monstrous behavior at the end of the play necessarily erase the sympathy aroused earlier (Barlow 1995). Broadening the context in a different way, the speech might suggest that male mistreatment of women—or more specifically, male violations of the ethical norms of loyalty and friendship—will provoke women to protest against, and even destroy, the status quo. A rather different methodology suggests that the "feminist" message is simply erased by the fact that the speech is written, performed, and directed toward men. "The feminist reader might conclude that women need not relate to these roles or even attempt to identify with them," since they are "properly played as drag roles" (Case 1988: 15; see further above, pp. 60–64).

Of course, these interpretive strategies are not all mutually exclusive, and ancient audience members, like modern critics, doubtless varied greatly both in their immediate responses and in their subsequent reflections. It is particularly interesting to speculate on the reactions of any women who were present in the audience (above, pp. 62–3), and of how their presence may in turn have affected the responses of the men. A further complication is introduced by the predominant tendency in Greek literary theory to view audiences as directly influenced in their feelings and behavior by dramatic characters, via the mechanism of emotional identification (above, pp. 29–30). Is Medea so monstrous that she is impossible to identify with? Is she a (dangerously) sympathetic role model for women? Is she a warning to men and women alike? We can only speculate as to ancient reactions. But clearly Medea's speech does not necessarily make this a "feminist" play in any simple sense. The emotions and judgments aroused by the drama are complex, and they shift kaleidoscopically as it develops.

However we interpret this speech and its impact, one function it clearly fulfills is to give us a powerful picture of the centrality and significance of marriage in ancient Greek women's lives. Like every other character in the play, Medea assumes that sex and/or marriage, often referred to as "the bed" (above, p. 58), are the central concerns of a woman's life (compare 263–66, 1367–68). Her great speech tells us why. In a perverse and mythic way, Medea is an extreme embodiment of what marriage meant for a Greek girl.[28] In a sense, every bride was a stranger in a strange land. And every married woman was dependent on her husband (compare 228 and below, p. 420, n. 51). But Medea's situation is exaggerated because she is from a place far beyond the boundaries of the Greek world and has cut herself off, by terrible crimes, from her paternal home. She is therefore far more radically separated from her natal family than a Greek woman married within her own city-state, who might return to her paternal home in certain circumstances, such as divorce or widowhood (compare 252–8). And now Medea is to be banished even from her adopted home. Exile, especially in a tribal society like that of ancient Greece, is a terrible fate even for an independent man (as many passages in Greek texts attest), let alone for a single woman with young children (compare especially *Medea* 645–53). Medea's situation thus takes the Greek woman's lot to a nightmarish extreme. If she is the patriarchal male's nightmare, Jason is the dependent woman's.

On the other hand, Medea did not exactly walk down the aisle in white. (For the Greek cultural equivalent, see above, p. 56.) Her "marriage" to Jason was an elopement lacking all the proper elements of an Athenian marriage, from the formal betrothal when the bride's father (or other empowered male) promised her to the groom, to the procession in which the bridegroom "led" her from her father's house to his own (Jason uses this verb at 1331), to the further family celebrations that took place the next day. These ceremonies involved the exchange of gifts (including clothing and golden ornaments), sacrifice, singing, and torches carried in procession from one house to the other—all of which play a role in the imagery of Euripides' play, but were *not* involved in Medea's union with Jason. Despite her implicit claim to marital status in her opening speech, her position is more like that of a *pallakē* at Athens, a concubine or common-law wife, who might be a foreigner cohabiting with an Athenian citizen and had little or no legal protection for herself or her children (above, p. 59).

Moreover, in an Athenian marriage, the woman had little say in the matter, whereas Medea's union with Jason was her own choice. She, not her father, chose her husband, "bought" him with her stolen "dowry" (the Golden Fleece), and entered an alliance of *xenia* ("guest-friendship") with him (see 1392 with note).[29] She speaks misleadingly when she uses passive verbs of her "abduction" by Jason (255–56).[30] In contrast to the passive princess of many tales, she accepted her future husband as a suppliant (496–98), and actively saved him from disaster more than once (476–82). She omits to mention, when bewailing her lack of natal family, that she cut these kinship ties herself—quite literally in the case of her brother (257–58). In the course of the drama she disposes of ancestral patrilineal gifts in her own right: the finery she sends the princess was "a gift from Helios, my father's father, to his heirs" (954–55). She cements an alliance of guest-friendship with Aigeus, which removes any pressing economic need for a husband (compare 514–16, 616–18).[31] She makes independent plans for the future, and when she decides to leave, does so under her own power, thus violating the expectation that a married woman's place is fixed at her husband's hearth, the literal and symbolic center of the household (above, pp. 57–8).

Medea represents the threat posed by female subjectivity and independent will, especially the active exercise of women's erotic desire. Her elopement was prompted by the overwhelming power of the goddess Aphrodite, i.e., by sexual passion. Aphrodite and her son Eros often appear in wedding scenes in art and literature, showing that sexual attraction was viewed as a necessary, or at least a desirable, condition of a successful marriage (compare 627–44). But the institution of marriage exists in large part to domesticate the awesome power of these divinities, especially over women (whom Greek ideology viewed as less able than men to resist sexual desire), and to render it safe and productive of legitimate offspring only. A "marriage" blessed only by Eros and Aphrodite (compare 527–31), as opposed to the primary gods of marriage such as Hera, is perverted and uncontrolled, and might seem doomed to disaster from the start.

There is in fact no mention in the play of any wedding rite of any kind between Jason and Medea. (One's little brother is not the usual sacrificial victim on these occasions.) In contrast to Jason's match with the king's daughter, their union is rarely referred to as a marriage (*gamos*).[32] But this does *not* mean Medea's sense of betrayal is unjustified. This is myth, not history, so the formal marriage procedures of Euripides' own day are not literally applicable. Besides, significant elements of Athenian marriage *are* present, especially the fact that Jason and Medea have lived together publicly in a household and produced children. Jason's language at 1330–31 evokes an Athenian wedding, and other characters besides Medea refer to him as her *posis,* a word normally used for a lawful husband.

Even supposing the marriage is acknowledged, however, one might question whether a husband in Euripides' Athens would feel obliged to consult his wife before divorcing her. Such arrangements would be made not with the woman herself but with her *kurios* (her father or another empowered male). But the validity of Medea's point is shown by the fact that Jason feels the need to answer it (588–90; so Gill 1996: 163, n. 245). More important, perhaps, is the fact that Medea is in effect her own *kurios* (below, p. 161). In any case, all the other characters, including Aigeus, view Jason's behavior as disgraceful. Neither Kreon nor even Jason tries to argue either that he was not really married to Medea, or that a husband has the right to divorce his wife behind her back. As Gill drily puts it, "the claim that one has remarried (in secret) for the sake of one's previous wife and children (549–67) seems abnormal by virtually any standard" (loc. cit.). Medea's marriage is a perverted one by Athenian standards, but her claim against Jason is legitimate.

Oaths and the Aigeus Scene

Quite apart from the question of their marriage, the fact that Medea helped Jason in response to his supplication places him under a reciprocal obligation of loyalty to her (496–98). This obligation was acknowledged and sealed by a formal oath, in which they both pledged their right hands (see e.g., 21–23). Since no one challenges this, not even Jason, we may take it as given. In fifth-century BCE Athens, such an oath was not part of the marriage ritual—the contract was between the bride's father and the groom (compare Klytemnestra and Achilles at *IA* 831–6). But formal pacts of friendship between *men* were often sealed with an oath and the ritual clasping of right hands. Medea seems to view the matter this way when she accuses Jason of violating the relationship of *xenia* (1392), a formal friendship that might be sealed with oaths and the clasping of hands (above, pp. 21–2). The bride's father and the bridegroom probably also sealed the contract of betrothal with a handshake (above, p. 50). Medea thus places herself in two masculine roles: that of an equal participant in a formal relationship of *philia,* and that of her own *kurios,* the man empowered to give his daughter to another man in marriage.

Jason's oath to Medea places him under a powerful moral and religious obligation to abide by his word (above, pp. 13–14). Moreover, the principal gods of oaths include Medea's own grandfather, Helios the sun god, along with Zeus and the ancient goddess Earth (compare 149, 746, 752–53, 1251, and, e.g., *Iliad* 19.258–60). Oath-breaking was viewed as "twin to kin-murder" (Burnett 1973: 13), and the customary imprecation against a transgressor "is that utter destruction . . . should befall the oath-breaker and his line" (Burkert 1985: 251; compare 253 and see Rickert 1987: 109–13). This does *not* mean the offended party is morally or legally justified in carrying out such a penalty in person, rather than leaving it to the gods, even if, like Medea, they have no legal recourse. Yet this is exactly the punishment that Medea brings upon the head of Jason, using that same right hand whose pledge he violated—a connection emphasized throughout the play (22, 496, 898, 1070, 1365; see further Flory 1978). Since Jason has broken the male side of the marital bargain by abandoning her, she retaliates by breaking the female side through killing their children. Aigeus, by contrast, will beget children as a result of keeping his oath.

The enormous significance and binding power of oaths is brought out through the Aigeus scene, which culminates, at the exact center of the play (709), in a formal supplication resulting in a solemn oath of protection. This dramatic reenactment shows us how Jason's oath to Medea should be envisaged. Besides the connection with supplication (709–10), note both the invocation of Earth and Sun (746, 752) and Aigeus' acceptance of the customary punishment for transgression (754–5). Unsurprisingly, Athenians are usually portrayed in Athenian tragedy as models of virtue, and Athens itself as a sanctuary for people in distress.[33] Euripides' audience would know that in keeping with Athenian ideals, Aigeus did keep the oath he swore to Medea. His oath binds him to protect even a child-murderer, just as Jason's oath bound him to Medea despite her bloody deeds. Aigeus stands for, and abides by, the Greek values of justice and law in which Jason takes such pride (536–38). This time, Medea's trust in a Greek man will not be misplaced (compare 800–1).[34] But the audience would also know the mythological consequences of Aigeus' oath—that Medea would attempt to murder Theseus, Aigeus' son and heir. It is Aigeus' straightforward, simple, even naive adherence to Athenian moral and religious ideals which guarantees the arrival of Medea in Athens, and thus forces the Athenians to confront the transgressive attitudes and behavior that she embodies.

The Aigeus scene has often been criticized as artificial, ever since Aristotle (*Poetics* 1461b21). Aigeus turns up unexpectedly, and all too conveniently for Medea's purposes. But it serves an important role in the dramatic economy of the play. Besides enacting and highlighting the binding power of an oath, and providing an external (and Athenian) judgment that Jason is in the wrong, Aigeus brings out the fundamental importance of (male) children to a Greek man, especially a king. Sons not only provide support for their parents' old age (compare 1032–35, 1396), but bestow a kind of immortality through the perpetuation of a man's family name, his property and line. A woman, by contrast, is viewed as a passive conduit of male fertility, passing on her husband's name and property to his (male) heirs.[35] However much she may love her sons, she does not have the same *kind* of stake in children as their father does.[36] It is only after Medea's encounter with Aigeus that she declares her intention to kill her children (contrast the indirection of 375). She rightly sees that only the death of Jason's sons *and* his new bride, who might bear other sons (compare 804–5), will make him suffer just as he has hurt her, not only by stripping him of family and friends, but by striking at the heart of his social status and gender identity through the destruction of his entire house (compare 114, 139, 794).

Medea as Hero

Medea's reliance on the oath underlines the fact that in important ways she is not *merely* a stereotypical barbarian female. Rather, Euripides uses her to problematize such simple dichotomies as male/female, Greek/barbarian, human/animal, and divine/human. As we have seen, she plays a "masculine" role in arranging her own marriage. Aristotle calls barbarians "natural slaves" (above, pp. 22–3), but Medea is certainly not servile. Nor is she effeminate or cowardly. On the contrary, she displays many stereotypically Greek male attributes, such as courage, intelligence,[37] decisiveness, resourcefulness, power, independence, and the ability to conceive and carry out a plan effectively. In these qualities she surpasses every male character in the play.

Medea the "barbarian" is also skilled in the use of language and persuasion in which Greeks—especially Athenians—took great cultural pride.[38] The controlled, "masculine," "Hellenic" character of her opening speech in the public domain contrasts with the lyric emotional outbursts that we have heard from within, which tend to be coded as "female" and "barbarian" (Hall 1989: 130–31). With her first sentence, "I have come out of the house," she moves out of the space culturally defined as female, and steps forward in a masculine gesture to justify herself in public to the female "jury" of the chorus. Her argument in the next sentence, that one who secluded himself or herself would be considered either proud or lazy, is much more easily applicable to a man than a woman in Greek culture. This is especially true of democratic Athens, where all male citizens were expected to participate in public life while women were largely secluded (above, pp. 48–54). A few lines later Medea alludes to herself with the word "man" (*anēr;* see below, p. 419, n. 39). She will continue to use the language of male experience throughout the play, especially imagery of warfare and sailing.

Above all, Medea is "clever" or "wise" (*sophos*). This is the fundamental source of her power and independence (compare especially 677), and Jason claims it has brought her glory among the Greeks (539–40; compare 11–12). But this is not an unproblematic claim (compare above, p. 51). The words *sophos* and *sophia* (translated "clever" and "cleverness" respectively) connote skill and sophistication, and less frequently, wisdom of a moral kind. But they can also refer to reprehensible cleverness, especially that which is used to trick or deceive. "Cleverness" may thus be viewed with suspicion even in men (compare 285, 292–305, 319–20, 1224–47).[39] In women, whether good or bad (Penelope or Klytemnestra), it nearly always takes the form of deviousness, often linked with sexual licentiousness (see e.g., Euripides, *Hippolytos* 640–44). This kind of cunning, negatively coded, is also a "barbarian" attribute.

A distinctive feature of Medea's complex relationship to gender stereotypes is the way in which her "feminine" deviousness takes the form of performing a "femininity" that she belies by her behavior (compare 368–9). In particular she deprecates her own sex, as women portrayed by men often do in Greek texts (263–64, 407–9; compare the chorus at 1081–84 and Iphigenia's famous line at *IA* 1394). Medea uses such deprecation to manipulate Jason, exploiting his conventional gender expectations in order to dupe and destroy him (869–93, 908–13, 922–28).

Another factor further complicates these ideological categories. Euripides has portrayed Medea as a heroine in the tradition of the heroic male warrior. In particular, she bears a striking resemblance to Homer's Achilles, the greatest warrior hero of the *Iliad.* She resembles him especially in her passionate angry spirit, her pitilessness, and her pursuit of revenge and glory.[40] The Nurse's opening monologue, epic in style, recalls many details of Achilles' grief at the death of his friend Patroklos: Medea does not eat (24; compare *Iliad* 19.205–14); she lies prostrate on the ground (27–28; compare *Iliad* 18.26–27); the nurse fears she will kill herself (38; compare 1444–47, *Iliad* 18.32–24). The Nurse also suggests she is somehow inhuman, by likening her to a rock or the sea, as Patroklos famously does Achilles (28; compare 1279 and *Iliad* 16.34–35). Like Achilles, Medea displays both subhuman behavior and superhuman powers connected with divine ancestry, in particular an extraordinary—though limited—prophetic knowledge of the future (1386–8; compare *Iliad* 9.410-16). Like Achilles, she debates with her passionate spirit (her *thumos*) what she should do (1042–63; compare *Iliad* 9.644–48). Like Achilles she refuses to be bought off with material compensation (616–18; compare *Iliad* 9.378–87). And like Achilles, she is willing to give vengeance priority over the well-being of her dearest *philoi*—her children (compare *Iliad* 18.79–82). (On *philia* or "friendship" see above, pp. 20–22.)

Like Achilles, Ajax, and many other great male heroes (especially in Sophocles), Medea has an overwhelmingly powerful sense of honor (see e.g. 20, 26, 33). She reacts to dishonor with an equally powerful sense of disgrace, consuming anger at a friend's ingratitude, and a passionate desire for extreme revenge at any price, including her own life (392–93). Like them she alienates herself even from innocent friends (36, 187–90), is deaf to persuasion (853–55), a dangerous enemy (45), and destructive to her friends as well as her enemies (94–95). The moral code she purports to live by, to seek "glorious renown" by helping her friends and harming her enemies (807–10; compare 765–66), is that of Greek culture generally (above, p. 20), but she expresses it in ways strongly evocative of male heroism. *Kleos*—"glory," "fame," or "renown"—is a prominent goal of the warrior hero in the *Iliad,* and runs directly contrary to the notorious remark of the Athenian leader Pericles, that a good woman should have the least possible *kleos* among men, whether for good or for bad.[41] When Medea does finally kill her children, she does so out of a desire to avoid mockery from her enemies (797, 1049–50, 1354–56, 1362)—a typically male heroic motive—and uses a sword, the manly weapon par excellence (1244, 1324–6). For the earlier murders, she contemplates using fire or the sword, but rejects open violence for the more "feminine" (i.e., devious) method of poisoned clothing, again in order to avoid mockery from her enemies (376–85, 404–5; compare 391–94).[42] Euripides thus associates Medea and her deed of violence with male as well as female stereotypes.

The *Iliad* was the most influential of Greek literary works, and Achilles, its hero, was enormously admired. We might therefore expect Medea's heroic qualities to meet with approval from a Greek audience. But her gender complicates this issue. Certainly it can be a compliment to call even a "good" woman "manly" for her intelligence or courage.[43] And women in drama often display such "manly" qualities. But in tragedy this usually leads to disaster—most notably in the case of Klytemnestra, Aeschylus' "woman with a heart of manly counsel" (*Agamemnon* 11). This is because women's power over men is located within the family. So when the violent, vengeful nature typical of the heroic male is unleashed in the person of a woman, it leads to acts of appalling violence against intimate family members, rather than outsiders, who may be slaughtered with relative impunity. Men in myth do also kill their children (Agamemnon and Herakles are two examples). But the domestic sphere is not the sole locus of their power. As a woman, then, Medea is caught in a double bind: If she is to crush her husband as he has crushed her, she must strike within this female realm. But by doing so, she also destroys her "essential" femininity (herself as mother), in the service of "masculine" revenge, and earns the horrified condemnation of her community.

Medea embodies this female predicament at its most extreme. But in a sense, all women in Greek drama are trapped in a double bind when faced with a situation demanding decisive action. Just as a female character cannot enter the stage without challenging her idealized gender role, which requires her to remain in the house (above, p. 60), so too no woman can be portrayed taking decisive public action without being to some extent masculinized (above, p. 51). Even a character like Sophocles' Antigone, whose behavior is clearly right in the eyes of the gods and beneficial to the *polis* as well as the family, is played off against her conventionally feminine sister (*Antigone* 61–62), and poses a severe threat to the masculinity of Kreon, the king whom she defies (*Antigone* 484–85, 525, 577–79, 678–80, 746, 756). It is far from clear how a Greek audience would have responded to her, let alone the murderous Medea. These assertive heroines are an obvious expression of male anxiety about any woman who transgresses her approved gender role. But the consequences may also be viewed as a critique of a system that allows women no other form of self-assertion, or even a critique of male values per se.

In accordance with the polarized gender ideology of ancient Athens, the appropriate counterpart to the masculinized woman of tragedy is the feminized man. This is made explicit in Aeschylus' *Agamemnon,* where Aigisthos, Klytemnestra's lover who stays home from the Trojan War, is addressed as "woman" by the chorus (1625–27). But it applies more subtly to Jason as well. By actively saving him and arranging their marriage (480–85), Medea cast him in a subordinate and "feminine" role complementary to her own "masculine" one. She continues to do so within the play, e.g., by sending him inside the house (623–24, with note). His second marriage is more conventional (below, p. 413, n. 32), yet even here he takes the "female" role by relocating to his bride's ancestral home.[44] Jason's behavior also displays many of the negative stereotypes associated with women and barbarians in general and Medea in particular. She accuses him of being motivated by sexual lust (623–24), just as he does her, each of them ignoring the other's avowed motives (compare 555–75). And his injustice, violence and duplicity clearly violate the Greek ideals that he himself affirms (536–38).[45] His death, appropriately, will be an unheroic and emasculating one (see 1386–88, with note). Jason and Medea are thus perversely united not only by their similar behavior, but by their distortions of ideal gender and cultural roles: he the barbarous feminized Greek, and she the masculine Hellenic barbarian.

These distortions are constructed as complementary, shifting along with the power dynamic between the two characters as the drama unfolds. The role reversal becomes complete, and theatrically manifest, in the final scene. Medea is now in complete control, while Jason occupies an inferior "feminine" position, reduced to the female activity of mourning for dead kin (compare Segal 1996: 39–40). He is as helpless and wretched as Medea was at the outset. This reversal is underlined by the linguistic texture of the play. Jason's language for his predicament at the end of the drama echoes Medea's for hers at its beginning.[46] One verbal echo is particularly striking. When the Chorus question her resolve to kill her children, Medea replies that she must do it, because this is what will "bite" Jason "to the quick" (817). By the end of the play, she has succeeded in this goal (1370), in revenge for the way her husband "bit" her earlier (110). The wording clarifies Medea's motive: It is the age-old justice of the *talio,* of repayment in kind.

In the final scene Jason even displays Medea's "maternal" values, including tender expressions of physical affection (1403, 1411–12; compare 1069–75), lamentation at the sufferings of parenthood (1349–50, 1413–14; compare 1024–37, 1090–1115), and use of the word "dearest" (*philtata*) for his children (1397; compare 795, 1071, 1247). Medea sends him back once more to the house, the female realm, to attend to the funeral of his dead wife, and he accepts her command (1394–95). In his final words (1403–4), Jason voices the futile wish that he had never begotten these children, echoing the Nurse's futile wish which opened the play. He now fully shares Medea's regrets about the past. She has reached her goal of reducing him to the state she herself was in at the start of the drama, by depriving him of everything that is important to him, as he destroyed everything that mattered to her (compare 228, 1074).

Medea ex machina

There is one last way in which Medea transgresses the limits of her cultural role. She challenges not only the categories "man/woman," and "Greek/barbarian," but even "divine/mortal." In the most ancient traditions, she was a goddess, subsequently demoted to mortal status like some other early female divinities (such as Pandora and also Helen, on whom see below, pp. 221–3). At the beginning of

Euripides' version she is a hurt woman, evidently human. She is inside the house (where a woman should be), present to the audience only through her inarticulate offstage cries of torment and the anxious description of the Nurse. Her magic powers and superhuman qualities are only gradually revealed. It is not until the end that she emerges in her dragon-chariot as godlike, awesome in her power and the brutality of her revenge. This final appearance combines chthonic imagery (snakes) with sky imagery (wings), to create a demonic inversion not only of the earth- and sky-gods invoked in oaths, but also of the pure, sacred, land and sky of Athens, praised in the ode with which we began.

This virtual apotheosis is prepared for by Medea's emerging use of magic, which is hinted at early in the play (e.g., by references to the death of Pelias, such as 9–10), and reaches a climax in the messenger speech (compare esp. 1207–8). But it is ultimately achieved by theatrical means. When Medea makes her final entrance, she is either on or above the roof of the stage building, in the dragon-chariot provided by her divine grandfather, Helios the sun god (below, p. 430, n. 151). This is a theatrical space normally reserved for divinities. Euripides in particular likes to introduce gods this way at the end of his plays (above, p. 36), and Medea fulfills exactly this role. She appears aloft, interrupts the action below, justifies her revenge on the grounds that she has been dishonored, arranges for the burial of the dead, predicts the future, gives orders to the mortals below (who are helpless against her), establishes a cult, and announces her own departure and destination—all functions of the Euripidean *deus ex machina.*[47] Her tone is also like that of a god—she conveys a fixity of will, finality and ruthlessness that have seemed to some to signify a loss of her humanity (e.g., Cunningham 1954: 158–59).

This does *not* mean Medea is now exempt from moral judgment. Even gods may be judged and found wanting by mortals, especially in Euripides (compare above, pp. 76–7). What mortals *cannot* do is control the gods in any way. When Medea appears on the roof she is untouchable by the now pathetic Jason, with whom Medea's apotheosis encourages the mortal audience to identify. She belongs now to a different realm of being. She also belongs to a different cultural and aesthetic realm. The magic chariot is an irruption of the fantastic, which detaches the stage action from the mundane world of the audience and reminds them that Medea is, after all, no mere woman but a female figure of mythic proportions. But what does it mean that Medea has symbolically entered this other realm? Jason failed to live up to the Greek ideals for which he is such a hypocritical spokesman, and by doing so unleashed a power beyond his or anyone's control. This power is always there, simmering away, in a patriarchal culture that treats women as outsiders yet requires them for its own perpetuation.

The Greek Active production of *Medea* ended with a final brilliant touch. Instead of the dragon chariot, Medea appeared on a bank of video screens. When Jason voiced his outrage, she replied, "You can't touch me—I'm on video!" This is an apt modern analogue for the gulf that divides us mortals from the world of the gods. They exist in a different realm of being, from which they can manipulate and control us, but we cannot touch them. Medea's dangerous mythic autonomy and power continues to be exerted (and controlled) through public representation, whether in the theater or on the screen.

Note on the Translation

I have attempted to translate the iambic portions of the play into English iambic hexameters, much like blank verse but with six feet instead of five (on the Greek meters see above, pp. 42–3). I have allowed myself some of the liberties of blank verse, e.g., replacing an iamb (short-long) with an occasional trochee (long-short) or spondee (long-long), substituting a choriamb (short-short-long-long) for two iambs, or inserting an extra unstressed syllable in the middle or at the end of a line. In the latter case the extra syllable may be followed by a pause or punctuation, or run on (with enjambment) to serve as the first syllable of the next line. This play also has quite extensive passages of anapests (short-short-long, with many substitutions allowed), which have been printed in italics in the translation. I have tried to render these into English that roughly approximates the Greek meter, using stress rather than quantity. In accordance with the natural stress patterns of English, many of the feet are trochees (long-short) where Greek would have spondees (long-long). I have translated the lyric portions with short lines, that are often intended to be rhythmic but make no attempt at any systematic meter. These have been indented in the text. Where the Greek line division leads to an irregular number of lines, I have regularized the number of lines in the translation to make the marginal numbers correspond exactly to the lines of the text.

My attempts to use verse form (I would not call it poetry) have inevitably led to some slight departures from the Greek. Nevertheless, I have tried to be as literal as possible, even though this causes awkwardness in places. I have also tried to be consistent in my translation of specific words, especially those with particular thematic significance. E.g., I have translated *sophos* as "clever" throughout—even though this sometimes sounds rather odd in English—in order not to disguise its thematic importance. I have also tried not to erase the Otherness of the text and culture (e.g., I have translated metaphors more rather than less literally).

I have followed Diggle's Oxford Classical Text with a few exceptions. One feature of this text is the large number of lines and passages judged spurious by the editor, usually for linguistic reasons or because they are thought not to fit their context. Such passages are bracketed by Diggle in the Greek text, but I have not judged it useful for the purposes of this translation to retain his brackets.

This work was supported in part by sabbatical leave from the University of Washington, which is hereby gratefully acknowledged. It is also a pleasure to thank the many friends, colleagues, and students who have read the translation and introduction at various stages and offered their suggestions. Besides my colleagues in this volume, and the series editor, David Halperin, I would especially like to thank Roo Borson, Christopher Dale, David Guichard, Stephen Hinds, Kirk Ormand, and Michael Halleran, who as always did his best to keep me honest.

II. THE PLAY

Characters

Medea's childhood NURSE (an aged female slave)
PAIDAGOGOS (an aged male slave attending the children)
MEDEA, a princess from Colchis, Jason's first wife
CHORUS of fifteen Corinthian women
KREON, king of Corinth
JASON of Iolcus, recently married to Kreon's daughter
AIGEUS, king of Athens
MESSENGER, from within the palace (a slave)
TWO YOUNG BOY CHILDREN of Medea and Jason
Guards and attendants of Jason, Kreon, and Aigeus

Setting: Outside the house of Medea and Jason in Corinth. The scene shows the façade of the house, which has a central door. One of the two eisodoi *(side-entrances) represents the way to the rest of Corinth, including the royal palace, the other the road out of Corinth.*

[*Enter Medea's Nurse from inside the house. She addresses the audience in iambic trimeters, the meter of dialogue (above, pp. 42–3.)*]

NURSE: If only the Argo's hollow hull had never flown
to the land of Colchis, through the dark-blue Clashing
Rocks.[1]

If only the pine had never fallen in the glades
of Pelion,[2] cut down to furnish oars for hands
of men most excellent—the men who went to fetch
the Golden Fleece for Pelias.[3] For then my mistress,
Medea, never would have sailed for Iolcus' towers,
heart-struck with passionate desire for Jason,[4] or
persuaded Pelias' daughters into killing their
own father and be dwelling here in Corinth with
her husband and her children,[5] bringing pleasure by
this exile to the citizens whose land she reached,[6]
and benefiting Jason with compliance in
all things—indeed, this is the greatest safeguard, when
a wife does not stand separate from her husband's side.[7]
  But now all's enmity; the dearest ties of friendship
have grown sick.[8] Jason's betrayed his own sons and
my mistress, sleeping in a royal marriage-bed
with Kreon's daughter (he's the ruler of this land).[9]
Wretched Medea, cast into dishonor,[10] cries
aloud, "The oaths he swore!", invokes the greatest of
all pledges, his right hand, and calls upon the gods
to witness what repayment she has got from him.[11]
She lies there without eating, gives her body up
to grief, melting away all of her time with tears,
since she first heard of this injustice from her husband.
She doesn't raise her eyes, or lift her face up from
the ground; and when friends try to offer her advice,
she hears them no more than some rock or surging sea,
except perhaps to turn away her milk-white neck,[12]
and moan to herself, crying out for her dear father,
the land and house that she betrayed to run away
with Jason—he who now has so dishonored her.[13]
She has found out, poor wretch, from this disaster, just
how much it means to leave behind one's native land.
She loathes her children; seeing them brings her no joy.
I fear her—fear she's planning something unexpected.
Her mind is harsh; she won't put up with being treated
badly; I know her, and dread that she may go
into the house, in silence, to the marriage-bed,

and thrust a sharpened sword into the liver of
the bride,[14] or kill the king and his new son-in-law,
and then bring down some worse disaster on herself.[15]
She's awe-inspiring;[16] one who earns her enmity
won't easily survive to sing the victory-song.[17]

[*Enter Paidagogos from the house, with Medea and Jason's two sons.*][18]

Here come the children, finished with their game of hoops.
They are not thinking of their mother's evil lot—
a mind so young does not tend to experience grief.[19]

PAIDAGOGOS: Ancient possession of my mistress's household,
why do you stand here all alone before the gates,
loudly bewailing evil tidings to yourself?
How could Medea want you to leave her all alone?

NURSE: Old man attending Jason's children, when a master's
lot falls badly, it is likewise a disaster
for a worthwhile slave, a blow that strikes the heart.[20]
So my own grief had grown to such intensity
that I was gripped by a desire to come outside
and tell my mistress's fortune to the earth and sky.[21]

PAIDAGOGOS: What? Has the poor wretch not yet ceased from lamentation?

NURSE: I envy you; her torment's barely under way.[22]

PAIDAGOGOS: The fool—if it's allowed to speak of masters so.
She doesn't know yet of the latest evil news.

NURSE: What is it, old man? Don't begrudge me what you've heard.

PAIDAGOGOS: Nothing. In fact I now regret what I just said.

NURSE: I beg you by your beard, tell me, your fellow-slave.[23]
I will keep silent on these matters, if I must.

PAIDAGOGOS: I'd gone down to the place where old men sit and play
at backgammon, beside the sacred fountain of
Peirene, and I heard—without seeming to hear—

some man declare that Kreon, ruler of the land,
is going to drive these children from Corinthian soil;
their mother too. I don't know if this story's
clearly true; I only wish that it may not be so.

NURSE: Even if Jason's quarreled with their mother, will
he stand by while his children suffer in this way?

PAIDAGOGOS: New family ties have taken over from the old;[24]
that man is not a friend toward this house of ours.

NURSE: We are destroyed, then, if we have to take on board
new evils now, before we finish bailing out the old.

PAIDAGOGOS: Stay calm and silent. Don't say anything. It's not
the moment for our mistress to be told this news.

NURSE: Oh children! Do you hear what your own father is
to you? May he not perish—he's my master still—
but he is guilty of bad treatment of his friends.

PAIDAGOGOS: What mortal isn't? Have you only just found out
that everyone is more his own friend than his neighbor's,
[some people justly, other men for profit's sake?][25]
So for a marriage-bed this father slights his sons.

NURSE: Children, go in, into the house. All will be well.
And you, keep them apart as much as possible.
Don't take them near their mother while she's in despair.
I've sometimes seen her eye them like a glaring bull,
as if she wants to act; she will not cease from rage,
I know, until she's crushed someone. Oh may it be
an enemy she acts against, and not a friend!

[*The meter shifts to anapests, a regular chanted rhythm (above, p. 38), as the Nurse reacts to the lamentations of Medea, heard from within the house.*]

MEDEA: [*within*] *Oh oh!*
I'm so unhappy, so miserable in my troubles!
Oh how I'm suffering! How may I perish?

NURSE: *It's just as I said, dear children. Your mother*
stirs up her heart; she stirs up her rage.
Hurry now quickly, into the house!
Do not approach where she may see you.
Do not go near her but be on guard for her
savage temper, the loathsome nature
of your mother's wilful mind.
Be gone now inside, as quick as you can,
for the storm-cloud of grief's just starting to gather.
Soon she will set it ablaze, her heart more
fiery still. What deed will her spirit perform,
swollen within her, not to be thwarted,
bitten by evils right to the quick?

[*Exit Paidagogos with children. A scream of anguish is heard from inside the house.*]

MEDEA: [*within*] *How I have suffered—poor wretch!—suffered*
hurt that is worthy of vast lamentation.
May you perish along with your father, accursed
sons of a loathsome mother! Death to the whole house!

[*The Nurse cries out in horror.*]

NURSE: *Oh you poor, you wretched woman!*
How can your children share in their father's
wickedness? Why hate them? Poor children!
How I'm tortured with fear that you may suffer.
Royalty's temper is awesome in spirit;
rarely submissive, used to commanding;
they don't abandon anger with ease.
Better for us that we be accustomed to
living with others on equal terms;
I'd rather be humble and reach old age.
Best for mortals is moderation—it
conquers by far in name and in practice.
What goes beyond is unable to bring
mortals opportunity; when a divinity
has become angry that house is paid
with greater doom.[26]

[*The Chorus enters along the side-entrance leading from the city, singing and dancing to their entry song* (parodos). *This takes the unusual form of a lyric dialogue between chorus and Nurse. It consists of an introductory passage of lyrics and anapests (131–47), followed by a strophic pair (148–58, 173–83) interspersed with anapests (159–72, 184–204), and a closing lyric passage (205–13).*][27]

CHORUS: I heard her voice, I heard her cry,
the unhappy woman of Colchis.
Is she still not calm? Old woman, speak.
From within my two-doored hall
I heard the sound of lamentation.[28]
I take no pleasure, woman,
in this household's grief,
for we are mingled together in friendship.

NURSE: *There's no such household; it's disappeared.*
He lies in a royal marriage-bed,
while my mistress dissolves her life in tears,
in her bridal chamber, her mind not soothed
in the slightest by warming words of friends.

[*Another scream is heard.*]

MEDEA: [*within*] *May heavenly fire strike me through the head!*
Why go on living? What does it profit me?

[*She wails in lamentation.*]

Life is loathsome! Let me leave it!
Let me free myself in death![29]

CHORUS: Do you hear, oh Zeus and Earth and light,[30] *Strophe*
how she sings out her agony,
unhappy bride?
what is this passionate desire, you fool,
for the bed none dares approach?[31]
Will you hasten the outcome of death?
Don't pray for such a thing!
If your husband reveres a new marriage-bed,
don't be provoked at him;
Zeus will plead the justice of your cause.

Don't waste away, lamenting your bedmate to
excess.

MEDEA: [*within*] *Oh mighty Themis and great lady Artemis,*[32]
see how I'm treated, athough I bound him with
mighty oaths, my accursed husband!
If only one day I may see him crushed
into pieces, his bride too, along with their palace,
for daring to do this injustice to me,
when I did none to them first.
Oh my father! Oh city![33] *I left you,*
shamefully killing my brother to do so!

NURSE: *Do you hear what she's saying? She's crying aloud*
to Themis, who listens to prayers, and Zeus,
who's worshiped by mortals as steward of oaths.
There is no way that my mistress will ever
cease from her rage for some trivial cause.

CHORUS: If only she would come into our sight, *Antistrophe*
and accept the sound of the words we speak.
Perhaps she might then put aside
the anger lying heavy on her heart,
her mind's fierce temper.
I'm eager to support my friends.[34]
Go, bring her here outside the house;
tell her she'll find friendship here.
Be quick, before she does
some evil to those within;
the torrent of her grief is surging mightily.

NURSE: *I'll do that. I fear I shall not succeed*
in persuading my mistress, but still I'll give
you this further favor of my own toil;
yet when anyone tries to approach her
offering words, she turns on her servant like
some wild bull, she glares like a lioness
who's given birth. You'd be right if you said
that the mortals of old were clumsy, not clever.[35]
It was they who invented songs for feasts,

songs for banquets and dining together,
giving delightful sounds to our life;
but no mortal invented a way that
music and intricate song could banish
loathsome pain; it is this that makes
death and dread fortune bring down a house.[36]
It would profit mortals to heal such things
with song; why raise up a cry in vain
at feasts that are laden with food?
Feasting itself will give satisfaction,
bringing to mortals its own delight.

[*Exit Nurse, into the house.*]

CHORUS: I heard the mourning sound of lamentation.
She sends forth painful, piercing cries of grief
against her evil-wedded husband, traitor to her bed.
She's been unjustly treated, and she calls upon
the goddess Themis, child of Zeus, guardian of oaths,
who carried her away to Greece,[37]
over the sea by night,
through the salty Bosporus,
gate of the boundless Black Sea.

[*The chorus stops singing. Medea enters from the house and speaks to the Chorus in iambic trimeters.*]

MEDEA: Women of Corinth, I have come out of the house
to forestall criticism.[38] Many folk, I know,
are proud, some in seclusion from the public eye,
and others out of doors; still other people take
a quiet path, and gain a lazy reputation.
For there's no justice in the eyes of humankind—
before they clearly learn the insides of a man,[39]
they loathe on sight, although they've suffered no injustice.
A foreigner especially must adopt the city's
ways; nor do I praise a willful native who
offends his fellow-citizens through boorishness.

As for myself, this unexpected blow has crashed
down on my head, destroyed my spirit. I am crushed.
I've lost my joy in life. My friends, I long to die.
For he on whom my all depended, my own husband,
turned out—how well I know!—the evilest of men.
Of all those beings capable of life and thought,
we women are most miserable of living things.
First we must buy ourselves a husband, at great cost,[40]
and thus acquire a master over our own bodies—
a second evil still more grievous than the first.[41]
The greatest ordeal here is whether we will get
a worthwhile or a bad one;[42] for departure harms
a woman's reputation,[43] and she can't refuse
a husband.[44] Then she comes to new customs and ways,
and must divine prophetically—not having learned
at home—what kind of bed-mate she'll be dealing
with.[45]
If we succeed in working all this out, and if
our husband bears in peace the yoke of living with us,[46]
our life is enviable; if not, we must die.[47]
But when a man is burdened by the company
within, he goes outside to ease his heart's distress
[by turning to a friend or someone his own age];[48]
we, by necessity, must look to one alone.
They say there is no danger in the life we lead,
staying at home while they do battle with the spear.
How wrongheaded they are! I'd rather stand three times
behind a shield in war than give birth to one child![49]
Of course, your situation's not the same as mine.
you have this city and your father's house,
the benefits of life and friends' companionship,
while I'm alone and citiless, the victim of
my husband's outrage, seized from a barbarian land.[50]
I have no mother, no brother, no relative
to offer me safe anchorage from this disaster.[51]
Therefore I'll ask you to assist me just this far—
if I discover some device, some path, to make
my husband pay the just price of his evil deeds,

[along with his new bride, and with her father too][52]
keep silent.[53] Elsewhere womankind is full of fear,
a coward both in self-defense and at the sight
of steel; but when she meets injustice in the marriage-
bed, no mind exists that is more bloodthirsty.

CHORUS: I'll do that. Justly will you pay your husband back,
Medea. I am not surprised that you are grieved
by your misfortune.
But here's Kreon, this land's lord,
coming to bring the latest news about his plans.

[*Enter Kreon,*[54] *with attendants, along the side-entrance leading from the royal palace.*]

KREON: You there! You with the scowling face and heart enraged
against your husband—you, Medea! I order you
to leave this land, an exile, taking with you both
your children. No delays! I shall enforce these words
myself. I won't return back home again until
I've cast you out beyond the limits of this land.

[*Medea screams with distress.*]

MEDEA: Ah, wretched as I am, I'm utterly destroyed!
My enemies have spread their sail before the wind;
there is no place to land and save myself from doom.
But I will ask, though I've been treated badly: for
what reason, Kreon, do you send me from the land?

KREON: No need to wear a cloak of words: I am afraid
you'll do my daughter some irrevocable harm.
Many considerations lead me to this fear:
by nature you are clever, skilled in evil arts;[55]
you are in pain, bereft now of a husband's bed;
I hear you're threatening—so they report to me—
to act against the bride, her father, and the groom.
I'd rather guard against this now than suffer it.
Better for me to earn your enmity today,
woman, than soften now and later mourn for it.

[*Medea gives a cry of despair.*]

MEDEA: It's not the first time, Kreon. Often in the past
my reputation's injured me and done great harm.
A man of prudent nature shouldn't educate
his children to be cleverer than other folk.
Besides the idleness this causes, they will gain
hostile resentment from their fellow-citizens.
For if you offer fools new kinds of cleverness,
you'll seem by nature useless, not clever at all.
And if the city thinks you better than those folk
who seem sophisticated, they'll be pained at you.
Such is the fortune I've experienced myself:
Because I'm clever, there are some who are resentful,
to some I'm quietist,[56] to some the opposite,
others dislike me. But I'm not so very clever.
So you're afraid of me—that you may suffer something
jarring?[57] Do not dread me, Kreon. I'm in no
position to transgress against a man—a king!
You've done me no injustice. You just gave away
your daughter as your heart directed.[58] It's my husband
I detest. You merely acted sensibly.[59]
I don't resent it if things turn out well for you;
Good luck to you![60] Enjoy your marriage! Just let me
live in this land. I've been unjustly treated, but
I shall stay silent, conquered by superior strength.

KREON: Your words are soft to hear, but I still shudder with
the fear you're planning something evil in your mind.
In fact I trust you less now than I did before.
It's easier to guard against a woman—or
a man—of fierce heart than a clever, silent one.
Get out, as fast as possible! Not one word more!
It's settled. You've no scheme that will enable you
to stay here with us in hostility to me.

MEDEA: I beg you by your knees! Your newly-married child![61]

KREON: Your words are wasted; you will not persuade me, ever.

MEDEA: You'll drive me out, without respect for suppliant
prayers?

KREON: Yes. My own household is a dearer friend than you.

MEDEA: My fatherland, how strongly I recall you now!

KREON: I love my own land most of all—except my child.

MEDEA: *Ah, ah!* What evil comes from passionate desires!

KREON: Depending on the fortune that accompanies them.

MEDEA: Oh Zeus, do not forget who caused these evils here!

KREON: You fool, get moving! Free me from my troubles now.

MEDEA: I've got my troubles too; I don't need any more.

KREON: All right. I'll have my servants throw you out by force.

MEDEA: No no! Don't do that, Kreon, I'm beseeching you!

[*She clings to his knees and hand in a ritual gesture of supplication.*]

KREON: It seems, woman, that you are going to pester me.

MEDEA: I'll go. I'm supplicating you for something else.

KREON: Why force me once again by clinging to my hand?[62]

MEDEA: Let me stay here, I beg you, just for this one day,
to finish thinking out a plan for exile, and
arrange my children's future, since their father does
not see fit to devise provision for his sons.
Pity them! You're a father too, with your own child—
it's reasonable that you should feel good will for them.
I am not thinking of my own exile; I weep
for them, that they're involved in this disaster too.

KREON: My natural temper's far from that of royalty;
yet by respecting others I've spoiled many things.[63]
This time as well I see I'm making a mistake—
but your request is granted, woman. Yet I say
to you that if the next torch of the sun-god sees
you and your sons within the limits of this land,
then you shall die. These words of mine will not
prove false.

So if you need to stay, stay just for this one day;
that's not enough to do the awful things I fear.

[*Exit Kreon, down the side-entrance leading to the city of Corinth.*]

[*The Chorus cry out in sorrow.*]

CHORUS: *Ah, ah! I am wretched in your miseries!*
Unhappy woman!
Where on earth will you turn? To what foreign land?
What house or land will you find to save
you from harm? Indeed some god has launched
you out on a surging sea of evils,
Medea, a sea unnavigable.

MEDEA: Who can deny that evils lie on every side?
But things aren't yet so bad; do not think that they are.
Ordeals are still to come for the new bride and groom,
and trouble—no small trouble!—for their relatives.
Do you think I ever would have fawned upon that man,
if not to gain some profit or advance some scheme?
I would not have addressed him, or touched him with my
two hands. But he is so far gone in foolishness
that though he could defeat my plans by exile, he's
permitted me to stay one day—a day in which
I shall make corpses of three enemies of mine:
the father, and the girl, and him, my husband, too.
There are so many paths of death for them that I
could tread, my friends, I don't know which to try out first.[64]
Shall I set fire to the couple's bridal home?
Or go inside, in silence, to the marriage bed,
and stab them to the liver with a sharpened sword?
But there's one obstacle to that. If I get caught
while entering the house or acting out my scheme,
I'll die, providing laughter for my enemies.
No, the straight road is best, where we are cleverest
by nature:[65] I'll use poison to dispose of them.
All right. They're dead. What city will receive me then?
What foreigner will offer me security,

grant me a safe house and protection for my person?[66]
No one. So I shall wait a little longer here,
and if some tower of safety does appear for me,
I'll go about this bloody deed with silent guile;
but if intractable disaster drives me forth,
I'll grasp the sword myself, though I shall die for it,
and kill them, following the daring, valiant path.
For by my mistress Hekate, whom I revere
above all other gods, she whom I choose as my
accomplice, dwelling in the recess of my hearth,[67]
not one of them shall grieve my heart and then rejoice!
I'll make their marriage bitter and lamentable,
bitter their new ties and my exile from this land.
Come now! Spare none of all the strategems you know,
Medea.[68] Weave your plans, concoct your crafty schemes.
Move toward this awful thing. Your spirit's brave ordeal
is now. See how you're treated? You must not incur
laughter from Jason's Sisyphean marriage-bond.[69]
Your father's noble; your grandfather's Helios;[70]
you have the knowledge. And besides, we're women, so
our nature's most intractable for doing good,
most clever at constructing evil of all kinds.

[*The Chorus sing and dance their first* stasimon, *or "song in position."*]

CHORUS: Streams of sacred rivers are flowing uphill; *Strophe A*
all things are twisted backward, even justice;
it is men whose plans are full of guile;[71]
pledges made in the name of the gods
no longer stand secure.
The stories that they tell
will twist my life around,
bestow on it a glorious reputation.
Honor is coming to the female race![72]
No longer will malicious stories
hold women in their grasp.

Muses of singers born of old *Antistrophe A*
will cease from singing songs

that say I can't be trusted.[73]
Phoibos,[74] lord of music,
did not grant my understanding
the lyre's inspired song,
or I'd have made a song ring out
in answer to the race of men.[75]
Time's long passing has much to tell
of their lot as well as ours.

But you, Medea, you sailed away *Strophe B*
from your father's house,
heart mad with frenzy,
threading through the sea's twin rocks,[76]
and now you dwell on foreign soil.
Poor wretch, you've lost your marriage-bed,
your bed's unmanned, and you yourself
are driven in dishonor from the land.[77]

The graceful favor of oaths has fled,[78] *Antistrophe B*
respect for others stays no more in mighty Greece—
it has flown into bright air.[79]
You have no father's house, unhappy one,
to offer anchorage from your toils;
another queen rules in your marriage-bed,
another is the mistress of your house.

[*Enter Jason, along the side entrance leading from the royal palace.*]

JASON: It's not the first time. I have often seen how savage
anger is an evil that's intractable.
You could have kept this land and house, if only you
had lightly borne the plans of the more powerful;
but your own foolish words have caused your banishment.
It's all the same to me—I don't care if you say
unceasingly that I'm the evilest of men.
But as for what you've said against the royal house—
regard your punishment by exile as all profit.[80]
I kept on trying to dispel the anger in
King Kreon's raging heart; I wanted you to stay.

But you stuck to your folly, to your evil words
about the royal house; this caused your banishment.
Yet even so, I'm not one to reject my friends;
I've come here, woman, with your best interests in mind,
to keep you—with the boys—from being destitute
or needy in your banishment. Exile is dogged
by many evils. And however much you loathe
me, I could never think an evil thought of you.

MEDEA: Unutterably evil man!—my tongue can't speak
more evil words than these for your unmanliness.
You've come to me? You've come, most greatly hated
enemy of gods, myself and the whole human race?
This conduct is not boldness or brave daring, to
do evil to your friends then look them in the face.
No, it's the greatest of all human sicknesses,
shamelessness! Yet I'm also glad that you have come.
For speaking evil words to you will lighten my
own spirit, while you, hearing them, will suffer pain.
I shall begin my speech where everything began.
I saved you, as the Greeks know well—all those who came
and sailed with you in that same ship, the Argonauts—
when you were sent to master the fire-breathing bulls
by yoking them, and then to sow the field of death.
I killed the snake that wrapped its many coils around
the Golden Fleece and kept it safe unsleepingly,
and by this means I held up safety's light for you.
Then I myself betrayed my father and my house
and came to Iolcus, Pelias' land, with you, impelled
less by my cleverness than the impulse of my heart.
I caused King Pelias an excruciating death
at his own children's hands, and ruined his whole house.
And you, most evil of all men, were treated thus
and then betrayed me, gaining a new marriage-bed,
though children had been born. If you were childless still,
your passion for this marriage-bed could be excused.[81]

But as it is, the trust that's pledged in oaths has gone.
I don't know if you think those old gods have retired,
or think new rules apply to mortals nowadays,
since you know very well you broke your oath to me.
This poor right hand of mine, which you so often
grasped,
these knees as well! It was in vain that we were touched
by such an evil man, and cheated of our hopes.[82]
I'll share my thoughts with you as if you were a friend.
Of course I don't expect that you will treat me well;
but still, my questions will show up your shame still
more.
Where can I turn now? To my father's house? But I
betrayed it and my fatherland to go with you.
To Pelias' wretched daughters? They'd give me a fine
reception, at the house where I killed Pelias.
That's how things stand. I am at enmity with friends
at home, and I've made enemies of those I should
not have done evil to—just to do you a favor.
And in return, how blessèd you've made me among
Greek women! What a wondrous husband I have got,
and what a trusty one—wretch that I am!—if I
am to be cast out into exile from this land,
bereft of friends, a woman all alone with just
her children. Fine reproach for a new-married man—
your children and the one who saved you wandering
as beggars! Zeus, why did you furnish humans with
clear evidence for gold, to tell if it is fake,
but place no natural stamp upon the body of
a man, by which we could pick out the evil ones?[83]

CHORUS: The anger that's provoked when friends engage in strife
with friends is awful, and it's difficult to cure.

JASON: I must not be an evil orator, it seems,[84]
but like a worthy steersman on a ship I must
reef up my sail, and run with narrow canvas to
escape the painful lashings, woman, of your tongue.
You build up to excess the favors that you did;

I do believe that Kypris was the only one
of gods and mortals who brought safety to my voyage.[85]
You have a subtle mind—but it would give offense
to tell the tale in words, how Eros forced you with
his arrows inescapable to save my life.
I won't tell that in too much detail—where you did
bring benefit to me, things haven't turned out too badly
But in return for saving me like that, you gained
more than you gave, as I shall now proceed to show.
   First, you now dwell in the land of Greece, instead of on
barbarian soil; you know of justice; you know how
to use laws rather than indulge in violence.
Moreover, all the Greeks have heard that you are clever,
which brings you reputation; if you lived at earth's
remotest boundaries, there'd be no word of you.
Myself, I wouldn't want gold in my house, or skill
to sing a song more beautifully than Orpheus,[86]
unless my fortune were conspicuous to all.
   Well, so much for the story of my troubles—it
was you who challenged me to this contest of words.[87]
And as for your reproaches at my marriage with
the princess, I shall prove that I have been in this,
first, clever, second, sensible, and thirdly a
great friend to you and to my children.

[*Medea starts to protest.*]

Quiet now!
   When I moved from the land of Iolcus and came here,
dogged by intractable disasters of all kinds,
what lucky find could I have made more fortunate
than this: an exiled man to marry a king's child?
I did not do it—as you fret—from hatred for
your bed, or stricken with desire for a new bride,
or wishing to compete by fathering new sons.
Our children are enough—no criticism there.
I did it, first and foremost, that we might live well

and not in need—I realized that everyone
flees from the path of an impoverished friend; also
to give my children nurture worthy of my house,
sow brothers for the children that I have from you,[88]
and then combine the families, bind them into one,
to make me happy. Why do *you* need further sons?
But it would profit *me* to help the children I
have now by siring new ones. Is that plan so bad?
You would agree, but for the marriage-bed which frets
at you. You're so far gone, you women, that if things
in bed go right, you think that you have everything;
but if disaster strikes you in the marriage-bed,
you treat the finest and most beautiful of things
as acts of war. Better if mortals could get children
elsewhere, and the race of females not exist;[89]
then there'd be nothing bad at all for human beings.[90]

CHORUS: Jason, you have adorned these words of yours with skill.
But even if it's rash to say so, I still think
that in betraying your own wife you were unjust.

MEDEA: In many ways, no doubt, I'm not like other mortals.
To me, an unjust man who also has a natural
way with words deserves the greatest punishment.
He boasts at dressing up injustice with his tongue
and dares all crimes; but he is not so very clever.
Like you. Spare me your specious posturing, your
awesome
way with words; one word of mine will flatten you:
if you weren't evil, you should have persuaded me
before the marriage, not stayed silent to your friends.[91]

JASON: And I suppose you'd be a humble servant to
my words, if I had told you of the marriage—you
who still can't bear to rid your heart of mighty rage.

MEDEA: It was not that. No, a barbarian marriage-bed
began to tarnish your good name as you grew old.

JASON: You can be sure it was not for a woman that

I took the royal marriage-bed that I have now;
but, as I said before, I wished to keep you safe,
and to beget blood-brothers for the sons I have—
children of royalty, a bulwark for my house.

MEDEA: May I not have a happy life that gives me pain,
nor a prosperity that frets my mind and heart!

JASON: Know how to change your wish, and you'll seem cleverer:
that worthwhile things may never seem like painful ones,
and in good fortune not to think your fortune's bad.

MEDEA: Insult me, for you have a refuge; whereas I
am going into exile from this land, alone.

JASON: You chose this for yourself; cast blame on no one else.

MEDEA: How so? Did I betray you? Did I take a wife?[92]

JASON: You hurled unholy curses at the royal house.

MEDEA: I did! And I'm a curse upon your house as well.

JASON: I won't dispute this matter with you anymore.
But if you wish to get the children or yourself
material assistance for your exile, speak.
I am prepared to give with an unstinting hand,
and introduce you to my foreign friends, who'll treat
you well. If you reject this, woman, you're a fool;
you'll gain a better profit if you cease from anger.

MEDEA: I won't make use of your friends' hospitality!
I won't accept a thing from you! Don't offer it!
Gifts from an evil man can bring no benefit.

JASON: All right. I call divinities to witness that
I wish to serve you and the children in all ways;
but good things do not please you; in your wilfulness
you push away your friends; this will increase your grief.

MEDEA: Be gone! No doubt you're overcome with longing for
your new-tamed girl. You linger here outside too long.[93]
Go play the bridegroom! But the gods are with me
when
I say you may have made a marriage to be mourned.

[*Exit Jason, along the side-entrance leading to the royal palace. Medea remains onstage while the Chorus sing the second* stasimon.]

CHORUS: Passionate desires, coming in excess, *Strophe A*
don't give men good name or excellence;
but if Kypris comes enough—
not more—no other goddess is
so gracious in her favors.[94]
Oh mistress, never loose at me
barbs from your golden bow,
your arrows inescapable,
anointed with desire.

May it cherish me, sensible restraint,[95] *Antistrophe A*
most beautiful gift of the gods;
may she never strike me, awesome Kypris,
with contentious anger or quarrels insatiable,
driving the stricken heart
to yearn for another's bed;
may she be a shrewd judge
of women's marriage-beds,
revering beds unwarlike.

Oh fatherland, oh home! *Strophe B*
May I never lose my city,
living a life intractable,
a life unnavigable,
most pitiful of griefs.
Before that may death tame me,
death, ending my days;
no toil surpasses this:
to be bereft of one's paternal land.

I've seen this for myself: *Antistrophe B*
the tale I have to tell

does not come from another.
You've suffered most awful sufferings, Medea,
but no city pities you, no friend.
May that man perish, joyless, unavenged,
who does not honor friends,
unlocking a clear, transparent mind.
He'll be no friend of mine.

[*Enter Aigeus, king of Athens, along the side entrance representing the road from outside Corinth.*][96]

AIGEUS: Medea, greetings! No one knows a prelude that's
more beautiful than this, when speaking to a friend.

MEDEA: Greetings to you Aigeus, clever Pandion's son;
where have you come from that you travel to this land?

AIGEUS: I've just come from Apollo's ancient oracle.[97]

MEDEA: Why travel to earth's navel-stone inspired with song?

AIGEUS: To find out how the seed of children may be mine.

MEDEA: Oh gods! Are you still childless so far on in life?

AIGEUS: Childless, by fortune sent from some divinity.

MEDEA: Have you a wife, or is that bed unknown to you?

AIGEUS: I do not lack the yoke that is the marriage-bed.

MEDEA: What then did Phoibos say to you regarding children?

AIGEUS: Dark words, too clever for a man to understand.

MEDEA: Is it permitted that I know the god's response?

AIGEUS: Of course. In fact it needs a clever mind like yours.

MEDEA: What is it? Speak, if it's permitted that I hear.

AIGEUS: I must not loose the wineskin's dangling foot until . . .

MEDEA: Until you do what, or until you reach what land?

AIGEUS: Until I come once more to my paternal hearth.[98]

MEDEA: And for what purpose did you voyage to *this* land?

AIGEUS: There is a man called Pittheus, lord of Troezen's soil.[99]

MEDEA: The son of Pelops; a most reverent man, they say.

AIGEUS: I wish to share with him Apollo's prophecy.

MEDEA: Yes, he's a clever man and practiced in such things.

AIGEUS: To me he is the dearest of my spear-friends too.[100]

MEDEA: Good fortune to you. May you get all you desire.

AIGEUS: But why this downcast eye, this pale and wasted skin?

MEDEA: My husband is most evil of all men to me.

AIGEUS: What? Tell me clearly, what's the cause of your despair?

MEDEA: Jason's unjust to me, though I've done him no harm.

AIGEUS: What has he done? Tell me more clearly what occurred.

MEDEA: A woman over me is mistress in his house.

AIGEUS: No! Has he really dared this shamefullest of deeds?

MEDEA: Know well he has. We, once his friends, are now dishonored.[101]

AIGEUS: Was it from passion, or from hatred of your bed?

MEDEA: A mighty passion; he's unfaithful to his friends.

AIGEUS: Forget him, if he is as evil as you say.[102]

MEDEA: His passion was to tie his family to the king's.

AIGEUS: Who is the father of the bride? Come, tell me more!

MEDEA: Kreon, the present king of this Corinthian land.

AIGEUS: Woman, your sense of pain is quite excusable.

MEDEA: I'm done for! And I'm being driven from the land.

AIGEUS: By whom? You're speaking of a further evil now.

MEDEA: Kreon is driving me, an exile, from this land.

AIGEUS: And Jason lets him? That's another thing I cannot praise.

MEDEA: He speaks against it, but endures it valiantly.

[*She clings to Aigeus' knees and touches his chin in a ritual gesture of supplication.*]

But I beseech you, by this beard and by your knees,
Aigeus, I implore you as a suppliant,
to pity me, yes, pity this ill-fated one!
Do not stand by and see me banished all alone;
accept me in your country, at your house and hearth.
So may the gods fulfill your passionate desire
for children; so too may you die a prosperous man.
You don't know what a lucky find you have in me:
I'll end your childlessness and make you capable
of sowing fertile seed. I know of drugs for this.

AIGEUS: For many reasons I am eager to bestow
this favor on you, woman; firstly for the gods,
then for the birth of children that you promise me—
as far as that's concerned I am entirely lost.
Here's my position: reach my land, and I shall try
to welcome you in justice as a foreign friend.
There's only one condition that I stipulate:
I do not want to take you with me from this land.
If you can reach my house yourself, you may stay there
in safety; I won't give you up to anyone.
But you yourself must first set foot beyond this land.
I don't want to be held to blame by foreign friends.[103]

MEDEA: So be it. But a trusty pledge of this would give
me everything I want from you—all would be well.

AIGEUS: Do you not trust me? What is it that's troubling you?

MEDEA: I trust you. But the house of Pelias and Kreon

are my enemies. If they should try
to take me from your land, you will not let them—if
you're yoked with oaths. If you just promise verbally,
not swearing by the gods, you might befriend them,
might
believe their overtures; my side is weak, while theirs
prospers with all the riches of a royal house.

AIGEUS: You demonstrate great forethought in the words you speak,
and if an oath seems best to you, I won't refuse.
Indeed, this makes my own position more secure—
it gives me an excuse to show your enemies—
and also makes your lot more settled. Name your gods.

MEDEA: Swear by the plain of Earth, and Helios the sun—
my father's father—and the whole race of the gods . . .

AIGEUS: That I shall do or not do what? Tell me the terms.

MEDEA: That you yourself will never cast me from your land,
or give me up of your free will while you still live,
if any of my enemies should come for me.

AIGEUS: I swear by Earth and the bright light of Helios,
and all the gods, to stand by what you stipulate.

MEDEA: All right. What may you suffer if you break this oath?

AIGEUS: May that which comes to impious mortals fall on me.[104]

MEDEA: Go on your way rejoicing, for now all is well.
As fast as possible I'll reach your city, when
I've done what I shall do, and got the things I want.

CHORUS: *May lord Hermes, escort of travelers,*[105]
take you home, and may you accomplish
that which you long for and think of so eagerly,
since you have shown us, King Aigeus
that you're indeed a noble man.

[*Exit Aigeus along the side-entrance by which he entered. Medea addresses the Chorus.*]

MEDEA: Oh Zeus! Oh Justice, child of Zeus! Oh Helios' light!
Now, friends, shall I be glorious in victory
over my enemies—I've started down that road.
Now I can hope my enemies will justly pay
the price, since that man has appeared; he'll serve me as
a harbor, just where I was weakest in my plans.
I'll tie the anchor-cable of my boat to him,
by going to Athena's town and citadel.
And now the time has come to tell you *all* my plans.
Receive my words without expecting pleasure from
them.
I'll send one of my house-slaves to seek Jason out,
and beg him to come here to me, into my sight.
When he arrives, I'll speak soft words to him, saying
that I've decided he is right, and all is well.
I'll say the marriage he has made with royalty—
betraying *me!*—is beneficial and well planned.
But I shall also beg him that my sons may stay.
I shall not really leave them in this hostile land
where they may suffer outrage from my enemies;
but using them I'll kill with guile the king's own child.
I'll send them bearing in their hands gifts for the bride
to beg that they may not be exiled from this land—
a fine delicate robe, a wreath of beaten gold;
and if she takes this finery and puts it on,
she'll die an evil death, and so will anyone
who touches her—with such drugs I'll anoint the gifts.
But that's enough about that portion of my plan.
I groan now at the deed that I must perpetrate
next after that. For I shall kill the children—my
own children! There is no one who can rescue them.
Then, after devastating Jason's house, I'll leave
this land, an exile from my dearest children's blood,
one who has dared a most unholy deed, my friends;
for laughter from an enemy can't be endured.[106]
So be it. What does living profit me? I have
no fatherland, no house, no refuge from my evils.
That's when I made my big mistake—when I first left

my father's house, persuaded by a Greek man's words—
a man who'll justly pay the price, with the gods' help.
He'll never see the children that he got from me
alive again; nor will he ever get a child
from his new-yoked bride, since that evil girl must by
necessity die evilly, killed by my drugs.
Let no one think me insignificant and weak
or quiet-tempered; I am just the opposite—
harsh to my enemies, and well-disposed to friends;
this is the life that wins most glorious renown.[107]

CHORUS: Since you have shared these words with us, and I both wish
to help you and support the cause of human law
and custom, I prohibit you from doing this!

MEDEA: Impossible! But such words are excusable
from you, who've not been badly treated, as I have.

CHORUS: But woman, will you dare to kill the seed you bore?

MEDEA: Yes! *This* is what will bite my husband to the quick.

CHORUS: And make *you* the most miserable of women too!

MEDEA: So be it. You will never talk me out of this.[108]

[*She calls to the Nurse, who reenters from the house.*]

Come now, be gone at once; bring Jason here to me.
You are the one I use for tasks requiring trust.
Do not tell any part of my resolve, if you
are loyal to your masters, and a woman born.

[*The Nurse exits by the side entrance leading to the royal palace.*[109] *The Chorus sing and dance the third* stasimon.]

CHORUS: The children of Erechtheus *Strophe A*
prosper from ancient times,
children of blessed gods,[110]
born from a sacred, unravaged land,[111]
feeding on a cleverness

that is most glorious,[112]
ever stepping lightly through bright air
that gleams most brilliantly;
it's here, they say, that once
the nine pure Muses of Pieria
gave blond-haired Harmony her birth.

Beside the stream of Cephisus *Antistrophe A*
flowing in beauty,[113]
Kypris paused to draw water,
so they say;
over the temperate land she breathed
sweet-blowing breezes' breath;
ever binding around her hair
wreaths of roses, fragrant-flowered,
she sent passionate desires
to sit at the side of Cleverness,
accomplices in every kind of excellence.

How can this city of sacred rivers, *Strophe B*
this land escorting friends in safety,
hold you dwelling in its midst,
you the child-murderer, you the unholy?
Think of it—to strike into your children!
Think of the bloodshed you're planning!
No! Don't do it!
By your knees we supplicate,
we beg you by all means possible:
don't shed your children's blood!

Where will you find the boldness *Antistrophe B*
of mind or hand or heart,
the awful daring to kill them, your own sons?
How will you ever be able,
looking at them, your children,
to seal their bloody fate without a tear?
When they fall suppliant for their lives,
you will not have the power,

your raging heart will not endure,
to dye your hands in their blood.

[*Enter Jason, along the side entrance leading from the royal palace.*]

JASON: I've come at your command. Although you're hostile, you
won't fail to get this much—I'll listen to your words.
What favor, woman, do you want from me this time?

MEDEA: Jason, I beg you to excuse me for the words
I spoke before. It's only reasonable for you
to tolerate my anger—we've been friends so long.
I've talked things over with myself, scolding myself:[114]
Oh willful woman, why am I in such a mad
and hostile frenzy at the ones who plan things well?
Why make myself an enemy to this land's king
and to my husband? He's just doing what is best
for me, by marrying a royal princess and
begetting brothers for my children. Why not rid
my heart of rage? What has come over me? The gods
are kind to me. Don't I have children? Don't I know
that I'm an exile from the land, and short of friends?
These thoughts made me perceive how great was my
imprudence, and how vain the rage that filled my heart.
So now I praise you and I think you're sensible
to add this family tie. It's I who am the fool.
I should have helped you make these plans. I should have helped
fulfill them, and then stood beside the marriage-bed
to tend your bride with pleasure, like a relative.[115]
But we are what we are, we women—I won't say
we're evil, but in evil you should not resemble
us, or pay back childishness with childishness.
So I give way, admitting my wrongheadedness
at that time; now I've planned things in a better way.
Oh children, children! Leave the house and come to me!

[*Enter the children with the Paidagogos from Medea's house.*]

Come out! Embrace your father. Speak to him along
with me. Join with your mother in abandoning
the enmity we felt before toward our friends.
We've poured libations, made a truce;[116] our rage has
gone.
Take hold of his right hand.

[*Medea cries out in anguish.*]

I cannot help but think
about some hidden evil that the future holds.[117]
My children, will your lives be long? Will you still reach
your dear arms out to me as you are doing now?
Poor wretch, how quick to tears I am! How full of fear!
At last I have made up my quarrel with your father,
but now I've wet your tender faces with my tears.

CHORUS: A dewy tear has sprung up in my eyes as well.
Oh may the present evil not grow any worse!

JASON: I praise these words, woman; yet I don't criticize
your previous words. It's normal for the female race
to rage when husbands smuggle a new marriage in.
But now your heart has come round to a better view;
with time, you've realized which plan it is that wins—
the action of a woman who is sensible.
And you, my sons, your father's taken thought for you,
and, with the gods' help, guaranteed your safety too.[118]
I think some day you will be leaders in this land
of Corinth, side by side with brothers still unborn.
Grow up! Your father will take care of all the rest,
along with any god who's well-disposed to us.
I want to see you nurtured into fine young men,
who'll keep the upper hand over my enemies.

[*Medea turns aside and weeps.*]

But you, why do you wet your eyes with dewy tears?
Why do you turn your pale white cheek away from me?
Why do you not accept these words of mine with joy?

MEDEA: It's nothing. I was thinking of our children here.

JASON: Take heart! I shall make sure that they are cared for well.

MEDEA: I'll do that. I will not distrust your words. But by
her nature woman is a tearful, female thing.

JASON: Why do you mourn these children so excessively?

MEDEA: I gave them birth. And when you prayed that they might
live,
pity consumed me, as I wondered if they would.
But as for what you came here to discuss with me,
part has been said, and now I shall explain the rest.
The king's decided to expel me from the land.
I realize this course is best for me as well—
to dwell out of your way, and of the way of those
who rule the land; for I'm thought hostile to their house.
So I am going from this land to exile, but,
so that our children may be nurtured by your hand,
beg Kreon that *they* not be exiled from this land.

JASON: I don't know if I can persuade him—I must try.

MEDEA: Command your wife, then, to beseech her father not
to send our children forth to exile from this land.

JASON: I will indeed. What's more, I think I shall persuade
her, if she is indeed a woman like the rest.

MEDEA: I too shall share this trouble with you. I shall send
her gifts that are more beautiful by far, I know,
than any other treasure now in human hands—
a fine delicate robe, a wreath of beaten gold.
Our sons will bear the gifts. Quick as you can, let one
of my attendants bring the finery to me.

[*Exit an attendant, into the house.*]

Then she'll be happy in ten thousand ways, not one;
she'll have a man most excellent—yourself—to share

her bed, and also gain this finery, a gift
from Helios, my father's father, to his heirs.

[*The attendant returns with a casket containing the gifts.*]

Boys, take these wedding gifts into your hands,[119] then bear
them in and give them to the blessèd royal bride;[120]
she'll be accepting gifts that can't be criticized.

JASON: You fool, why let these things leave your own hands?
Do you think the royal house is short of splendid robes,
or short of gold? Keep them. Don't give these things away.
For if my wife thinks I'm worth anything at all,
she'll value me far more than money, I know well.

MEDEA: Don't stop me! They say gifts persuade even the gods;[121]
for mortals, gold is stronger than ten thousand words.
It's she who's blessed by fate, the gods now raise her up,
she's young and royal. As for me, I'd give a life
to buy my children back from exile—not just gold.
Come, children! Go inside that wealthy house; go to
your father's new wife, now my mistress. Supplicate
and beg her that you not be exiled from the land.
Give her this finery. And—here's the crucial point—
she must accept these gifts herself with her own hands.
Go quickly now! May you do well, and bring your mother
that good news for which she passionately longs.

[*Exit Jason and the children with the Paidagogos along the side entrance leading to the royal palace. The Chorus sing the fourth and last* stasimon.]

CHORUS: Now there is no more hope for the children's lives. *Strophe A*
No more! Now they are walking to bloody death.
The bride will accept the band of gold,
accept her doom, unhappy one.
Around her blond hair she will place
with her own hands the finery of Hades.

The grace of the gifts, their immortal gleam, *Antistrophe A*
these will persuade her to adorn herself
with the robe and the gold-wrought crown.
She will dress as a bride of the dead.
She will fall into the snare
of her fated death, unhappy one.
She will never escape her doom.

You too, you wretch, you evil-wedded man, *Strophe B*
tied by marriage to royalty—
although you do not know it,
you're bringing on your sons
destruction of their life,
on your wife a loathsome death.
Unhappy one, oblivious of your fate!

I mourn for your grief too, *Antistrophe B*
oh wretched mother of children,
sons you'll slaughter bloodily,
for a bride and her marriage-bed.
Your husband lives with another bed-mate;
your bed he has lawlessly left.

[*Enter the children with the Paidagogos along the side entrance leading from the palace.*]

PAIDAGOGOS: Mistress, the exile of these children is revoked!
The royal bride accepted into her own hands
your gifts with joy. She is at peace now with your sons.

[*The Paidagogos pauses for Medea to respond.*]

What?
Why stand there devastated, when your fortune's good?
Why do you turn your pale white cheek away from me?
Why do you not accept these words of mine with joy?

[*Medea gives a scream of anguish.*]

This sound is not harmonious with the news I bring.

[*Medea screams again.*]

PAIDAGOGOS: Could I be bringing news unknowingly of some
misfortune? Was I wrong to think my news was good?

MEDEA: You brought the news you brought. I do not criticize
you.

PAIDAGOGOS: Then why cast down your eyes and pour forth floods
of tears?

MEDEA: I do it by necessity, old man. The gods
and I in my wrongheadedness devised it so.

PAIDAGOGOS: Take heart! One day your sons will bring you home
again.

MEDEA: Before that I'll send others home, wretch that I am.[122]

PAIDAGOGOS: You're not the first to have her sons unyoked from her.
We're mortal, so disaster must be lightly borne.

MEDEA: I'll do that. As for you, go back inside the house
and pay attention to the children's daily needs.

[*Exit Paidagogos into Medea's house, leaving the children with her.*][123]

Oh children, children! You still have a city and
a house where you will always live, bereft of your
own mother, leaving me behind in misery.
But I must go in exile to another land,
before I benefit from you or see you happy,
before I can arrange your splendid weddings, tend
your bath and marriage-bed, hold up the wedding-
torch.[124]
A sorry wretch am I, through my own willfulness.
In vain, my children, did I raise and nurture you;
in vain I toiled and troubles tortured me to shreds,[125]
enduring cruel labor-pains to give you birth.
Unhappy woman that I am, I had high hopes
for you, that one day you would tend me in old age,
that when I died your hands would dress me for the
grave—

an enviable thing for human beings. But
that's perished now, sweet thought; I'll live bereft of
  you
the rest of my poor life—a life of grief and pain.
And you, you'll no more look upon your mother with
those dear eyes, after leaving for a different kind
of life.

[*She gives a cry of lamentation.*]

My sons, why are you gazing at me with
those eyes? Why smile at me this final laughing smile?

[*She screams in anguish.*]

Aiai! What shall I do? Women, my heart for this
deed disappears when I catch sight of my sons' shining
eyes. I cannot do it! Farewell to the plans
I made before! I'll take my sons away from here.
Why should I do this evil to them, just to bring
their father pain, when doing so will gain me twice
the evil for myself? I won't! Farewell, my plans!
  But what's come over me? Do I want to incur
laughter for leaving enemies unpunished? No!
This must be dared. What cowardice it was in me,
to let those soft words even come into my mind!
Be gone, my sons, into the house. If anyone
is not permitted to attend my sacrifice,
that is his own concern.[126] I won't let this hand fail!

[*She lets forth a cry of anguish.*]

  Ah no, my raging heart! Don't carry out this deed!
Leave them alone, you wretched thing! Spare your sons'
  lives!
If they are living there with me they'll bring you joy.[127]
  But no! By Hades' vengeful demons down below![128]
There's no way this can be—that I should leave my sons
alive to suffer outrage from my enemies.
In any case, it's necessary that they die;

and since they must, I'll kill them—I who gave them
life.[129]
In any case, it's done. There will be no escape.
The crown's already on her head, and in the robe
the royal bride is perishing—I know it well.
Now shall I take a road most unendurable,
and send my sons on one still harder to endure.
And so I wish to speak to them. My children, give
oh give your mother your right hand to clasp and kiss!
Oh dearest hand, and dearest of all lips to me,
and dearest form and noble faces of my sons!
May you be happy, both of you—not here, but there.
What we had here your father took. Oh sweet embrace!
Oh soft skin of my children! Oh most pleasing breath!
Be gone, be gone! I am no longer capable
of looking at you, now that evil conquers me.
I understand the evil I'm about to do,
and yet my raging heart is stronger than my plans—
the heart which causes mortal kind the greatest evils.[130]

[*Exit the children into Medea's house, for the last time. The Chorus now chant an anapestic interlude.*]

CHORUS: *Often before this have I delved into*
subtler words and arrived at contests
greater than those that the female race
should seek out.
But we too have a muse who associates
with us to bring forth cleverness—not all
(you might perhaps find one among many),
but just a few of the race of women
have indeed been blessed by a muse.[131]
And I say that those among mortals who
have no experience in being parents of
children have better fortune than those who
have given birth. Through lack of experience
of whether children are something pleasant or
painful for mortals—because they have none—
childless people are spared many toils.

As for those who have in their houses the
sweetness of offspring, these I see
ground down by cares their whole life long.
First they are anxious to nurture their children
well, and to leave them a livelihood.
Further, it is not clear if their toil is for
worthless children or worthwhile ones.
Finally, I shall tell you the ultimate
evil of all, for all of us mortals:
suppose that they've found enough to live on,
and that the children's bodies have grown up,
and that the children are worthwhile—
still, if a divinity brings it about,
off death goes to the house of Hades,
carrying with him the bodies of children.
So where is the profit to us, if the gods
in addition to our other troubles inflict
on mortals this most grievous of pains,
for the sake of children?[132]

MEDEA: My friends, I have been straining in anticipation,
waiting for quite some time to learn how fortune will
turn out in there. Now I see one of Jason's serving-
men approaching us. His agitated breath
shows clearly that he's bringing us some evil news.

[*Enter Messenger, along the side entrance leading from the royal palace.*][133]

MESSENGER: Oh you who carried out this awful lawless deed,
Medea, flee! Flee into exile, whether in
a sea-carriage or chariot that treads on land.[134]

MEDEA: What have I done, that I deserve an exile's flight?

MESSENGER: She's dead, the royal princess, just now, dead—both she
and Kreon who begot her—poisoned by your drugs.

MEDEA: You tell a tale most beautiful! Henceforth I shall
count you among my benefactors and my friends.

MESSENGER: What, woman? Are you in your right mind, or in some

mad frenzy? You've done outrage to the royal hearth,
yet you enjoy the story and are not afraid?

MEDEA: I could provide an answer in reply to what
you say. But do not rush, my friend. Tell me your tale.
How did they die? You'll give me twice as much delight
if it was an appalling, truly evil death.

MESSENGER: When your two sons, your pair of offspring, and their father
first arrived and came into the bridal house,
we slaves—those troubled by your evil lot—were pleased.
At once our ears were full of talk that you and your
husband had put aside your quarrel and made peace.
One of us kissed the children's hands, another their
blond heads;[135] myself, I was so greatly pleased that I
accompanied the children to the women's rooms.[136]
Our mistress—that's to say the one we now admire
as queen instead of you—before she saw your sons,
that pair of yokemates, kept her eyes fixed eagerly
on Jason. Then she drew a veil before her eyes
and turned away her white cheek,[137] in disgust at the
arrival of the children. But your husband kept
on trying to dispel the young girl's angry rage
by saying this: "Now don't be hostile to my friends!
Cease from the rage that fills your heart, and turn your head
back here. Think of your husband's friends as your friends too.
Accept the gifts, and ask your father to rescind
the children's exile, as a favor just for me!"
And when she saw the finery, she yielded and
praised everything her husband said. And then, before
your children and their father were far from the house,
she took up the embroidered robe and put it on;
she placed the crown of gold around her curling locks,
took a bright mirror and arranged her hair, smiling
and laughing at her body's lifeless image there.[138]

And then she got up from her chair, and walked about
the chamber, stepping lightly with her milk-white foot,
rejoicing greatly in the gifts, time and again
stretching her leg out straight and seeing how it looked.
  But what came next—that was an awful thing to see.
Her color changed; she staggered sideways back again,
trembling in all her limbs, and scarcely reached the chair
before collapsing there instead of on the floor.
An old female attendant, no doubt thinking that
it was a fit from Pan, or from some other god,
raised up a ritual cry of joy.[139] But then she saw
white foam spew from the girl's mouth, saw her eyes
  twist out
of sight inside their sockets, blood drained from her skin.
Then she sent forth a mighty cry of lamentation,
instead of joy. At once one woman rushed to the
girl's father's house, another to the newly-wedded
husband, to tell him of the disaster to his bride.
The whole house rang with the quick thud of racing feet.
  The time that it would take a speedy runner to
race over a two-hundred-yard limb of a course
and reach the limit,[140] that's how long she lay there with
her eyes closed, silent. Then she gave an awful moan
and woke, poor wretch. A double torment was at war
with her: the golden wreath that lay around her head
emitted an amazing stream of all-devouring
fire; the delicate robe, the gift your children brought,
fed hungrily on her white flesh, ill-fated girl.
  She stood up from the chair, ablaze with fire, and fled,
shaking her hair, her head, this way and that, as she
attempted to throw off the crown; but the gold kept
a tight grip on its bonds, and when she shook her head
the fire just blazed up twice as brilliantly. At last
she fell down, conquered by disaster, to the ground.
No one besides a parent could have recognized
the princess then: the normal state of her eyes showed
no more, nor did the natural beauty of her face,
blood dripped down from her head, all mixed with fire,

the flesh flowed from her bones like tears of sap oozing
from pine-wood, eaten by the poison's unseen jaws—
an awful thing to see. All of us feared to touch
the corpse—her fortune taught its lesson all too well.
But her poor father didn't know of the disaster.
Arriving suddenly within the house, he fell
upon the corpse. He groaned, folded his arms around
her, kissing her, and said, "Unhappy daughter, what
divinity's destroyed you so dishonorably?
Who has deprived me of you—me, an old man near
the grave? Alas, my child, if only I might share
your death!" When he'd ceased mourning and lamenting, then
the old man wished to raise his agèd body up,
but that delicate robe adhered to him, the way
that ivy clings to shoots of laurel. Awful was
their wrestling match. He tried to raise his knee, but she
would not let go. And if he pulled away by force,
she ripped the agèd flesh away from his old bones.
At last the life of that ill-fated man was quenched;
his spirit fled—evil had gained the upper hand.
They lie there, corpses, an old father and his child
together, a misfortune crying out for tears.
As for your lot, I'll speak not of it; you yourself
will find out that such deeds bring their own punishment.[141]
It's not the first time—I have often thought that mortal
matters are but shadows. I'd make bold to say
that clever folk among us mortals only seem
to be so; those concerned with words and arguments
are guilty of the greatest kind of foolishness.
There's not one mortal man who's blessed with happiness;
if wealth flows in, one man may be more fortunate
than others, but he will not have real happiness.

[*Exit Messenger, along the side entrance leading to the royal palace.*]

CHORUS: It seems that some divinity has justly fixed
on Jason many evil sufferings this day.
And you, poor wretched child of Kreon, how we pity
you for suffering this disaster; just because
of Jason's marriage you have gone to Hades' house.

MEDEA: My friends, I have decided what to do. As quickly
as I can, I'll kill my children and depart
this land. I shall not dally and give up my sons
for some more hostile hand to slaughter bloodily.[142]
In any case they must die, by necessity,
and since they must, I'll kill them—I who gave them life.
Come, heart, put on your armor![143] Why do I delay
to do this awful, evil, necessary deed?
Come now, my wretched, daring hand, take up the sword!
Take it, approach the starting-post of lifelong pain.
Do not be cowardly; do not think of your sons—
that they're your dearest ones, that you gave birth to them.
Forget your children this short day. Then later mourn;
for even if you kill them, they're by nature dear.
As for myself, I am a woman of misfortune.

[*Exit Medea, into her house.*[144] *The Chorus sings an agitated lyric song punctuated by a few trimeters (1273–74, 1277–78, 1284–85, 1288–89), the first four of which come from the children offstage.*]

CHORUS: Oh Earth! All-shining beam of Helios! *Strophe A*
Look down, look on this deadly woman,
before she strikes with murderous hand
her children, spilling her own blood.
They sprang from your golden race;
it is fearful for blood of a god
to fall on the ground at the hands of men.
Oh god-born light, prevent her! Stop her!
Take from the house this wretch, this Fury,
bold, bloody and inspired by demons of revenge.[145]

In vain you toiled for your children, *Antistrophe A*
in vain bore beloved offspring,
leaving the dark-blue crags of the Clashing Rocks,
that inlet least hospitable to foreigners.
Wretch, why does rage fall on you, heavy on the
mind,
and bloodshed follow violent bloodshed?[146]
Kindred bloodstains on the earth
are harsh to mortals;
grief falls on a house from the gods,
in harmony with those who kill their own.

[*A child's scream is heard from inside the house.*]

CHORUS: Did you hear the children, hear their cry? *Strophe B*
Oh bold, oh wretched woman of evil fortune!

1ST CHILD: [*from within, with another scream*] What shall I do? How can I flee my mother's hand?

2ND CHILD: [*within*] I do not know, my dearest brother. We're destroyed!

CHORUS: Shall I enter the house? I think I should
protect the children from bloodshed.

1ST CHILD: [*within*] Yes, by the gods, protect us! We have need of it![147]

2ND CHILD: [*within*] How close we are now to the hunting net of swords![148]

CHORUS: Wretch, you must be rock or iron,
to inflict this fate with your own hand,
to kill the crop of children that you bore.

I've heard of one woman in the past, just *Antistrophe B*
one,
who laid hands on her own dear children,
Ino, in frenzied madness from the gods, after
the wife of Zeus sent her forth wandering from
home.[149]
She fell, poor wretch, into the salt sea

for the impious bloodshed of her children;
she stretched her foot beyond the edge of the sea-cliff
and perished, sharing in the death of her two sons.
What awful thing is now impossible?
Oh women's marriage-bed, full of troubles,
how many evils you have done to mortals!

[*Enter Jason, with attendants, along the side entrance leading from the palace.*]

JASON: You women standing by this dwelling-place, is she
who carried out these awful deeds—Medea—still
inside the house, or has she fled away to exile?
She must conceal herself beneath the earth, or lift
her body up on wings into the bright air's depths,[150]
if she is not to pay the price of justice to
the royal house. Does she believe that she can kill
the rulers of the land and flee this house unpunished?
But I am thinking less of her than of my sons.
Those she did evil to will do the same to her,
so I have come to save my children's lives, lest they
be hurt by members of the royal family,
in vengeance for their mother's bloody, impious deed.

CHORUS: Poor wretch. You don't know, Jason, how far gone you are
in evils, otherwise you wouldn't voice these words.

JASON: What is it? I suppose she wants to kill me too?

CHORUS: Your sons are dead, destroyed by their own mother's hand.

[*Jason gives a scream of horror.*]

JASON: No! What is this you're saying, woman? You've destroyed me!

CHORUS: You can be sure your children are alive no more.

JASON: Where did she kill them? Outside or within the house?

CHORUS: Open the gates; you'll see your children's bloody death.

JASON: Push back the bars, attendants, quickly as you can.
Release the bolts, that I may see this double evil—
the children dead—and make her justly pay the price.

[*Enter Medea, on or above the roof of her house, in a chariot drawn by winged serpents.*[151] *She has with her the bodies of the children. Jason beats violently at the door, which is barred on the inside.*]

MEDEA: Why shake the gates and try to lever them apart,
seeking these corpses and myself who did the deed?
Cease from your trouble! If you need me, speak—if you
so wish—but you will never touch us with your hands;[152]
such is the chariot that Helios, my father's
father gave me to keep hostile hands at bay.

JASON: You loathsome thing! Most hateful woman! Greatest
enemy of gods, myself, and the whole human race,
who dared to thrust a sword into the sons you bore
yourself, making me childless and destroying me!
How can you look upon the sun and earth when you
have done this thing, have dared this deed most
impious?[153]
May you perish! I'm no fool now. I was a fool
back then, when I led you from your barbarian home
to a Greek household[154]—you great thing of evil, who
betrayed your father and the land that nurtured you.
The gods have crushed me with your demon of
revenge,[155]
for killing your own brother at the hearth before
you boarded my ship Argo, beautiful of prow.[156]
That's how you started. Then, when you became the
bride
of this man here before you,[157] and bore children to
me, you destroyed them merely for a marriage-bed.
There's no Greek woman who'd have dared this deed;
yet I
thought fit to marry you instead of one of them—
a hostile, hateful, and destructive marriage to
a lioness, not a woman, in your nature even

savager than Scylla of Tyrrhenia.[158]
I couldn't bite you to the quick, not with ten thousand
such reproaches—you're so brazen in your nature.
Get out of here, you shameful, bloodstained child-killer!
All that remains for me is to lament my fate.
I'll never benefit from my new marriage-bed,
never be able to address, in life, the sons
that I begot and nurtured—I have lost them now.[159]

MEDEA: I would have made a lengthy answer to your speech,
but for the fact that father Zeus already knows
how you were treated by me and what deeds you did.
You were not going to bring dishonor to my marriage-
bed and live on in delight, laughing at me,
you or your princess; nor was Kreon, who proposed
your marriage, going to cast me from this land and get
away with it. Call me a lioness if you wish
[and Scylla, who inhabits the Tyrrhenian plain[160]]—
I've struck you to the heart, just as I had to do.

JASON: But it's your pain as well. You share these evils too.

MEDEA: Of course. But if you cannot laugh, grief profits me.[161]

JASON: My children, what an evil mother gave you birth!

MEDEA: My sons, how your own father's sickness has destroyed
you![162]

JASON: At least they weren't destroyed by this right hand of
mine.[163]

MEDEA: No, by the outrage of your new-tamed marriage-tie.[164]

JASON: And you saw fit to kill them for a marriage-bed?

MEDEA: You think a woman finds this torment trivial?

JASON: Yes, if she's sensible; but all's evil to you.

MEDEA: They live no longer—this will bite you to the quick!

JASON: They live—alas!—as vengeful demons on your head.

MEDEA: The gods know who it was began this agony.

JASON: The gods know, then, that it was your repulsive mind.

MEDEA: Keep hating me! I hate your bitter voice as well.

JASON: And I yours. But departure's easy to arrange.

MEDEA: How so? What shall I do? I long for this as well.

JASON: These corpses—let me bury them and weep for them.[165]

MEDEA: No! I shall bury them with my own hands. I'll take
them to the shrine of Hera Akraia;[166] that way
no hostile person can do outrage to them by
the desecration of their tomb. And in this land
of Sisyphos I'll found a sacred festival
with rites in payment for this impious deed of blood.
And I myself shall travel to Erechtheus' land,
to live together with Aigeus, Pandion's son.[167]
But you, you'll die an evil death that fits an evil
man, your head struck by a remnant of the Argo,
seeing a bitter outcome to our marriage-bond.[168]

JASON: *May the children's Fury destroy you,*[169]
and bloody Justice!

MEDEA: *Who hears you? What god or divinity?—*
false to your oaths and deceiver of foreign friends.[170]

[*Jason gives a cry of anguish.*]

JASON: *You vile woman, destroyer of children!*

MEDEA: *Go to your house now and bury your new wife.*

JASON: *I am going, bereft of my children.*

MEDEA: *You are not yet mourning; just wait till you're old!*

JASON: *Dearest sons!*

MEDEA: *To their mother, not you.*

JASON: *But you killed them.*

MEDEA: *To agonize you!*

JASON: *Oh! How I long to embrace the beloved*
face of my children, wretch that I am!

MEDEA: *Now you address them. Now you embrace them.*
Then you rejected them.

JASON: *In the name of the gods,*
let me touch my sons' soft skin!

MEDEA: *That cannot be. Your words are hurled in vain.*

JASON: *Zeus, do you hear how I'm driven away,*
how I'm treated by her, this vile, this bloodstained,
child-killing lioness?
But as far as I'm able, as far as I can,
I mourn and I call on the gods,
I call on divinities to bear witness:
you have killed my children, nor will you let
my two hands touch them or bury the corpses.
If only I had never begotten them
rather than see them destroyed by you.[171]

[*Exit Medea, in her chariot.*]

CHORUS: *Zeus is the steward of much on Olympus;*
gods accomplish much that is unforeseen;
things that seem certain are not fulfilled;
god finds a path for the unexpected.
That is how this affair turned out.[172]

HELEN

Translated and with an Introduction by

Bella Zweig

I. INTRODUCTION

"Helena, which was the dream, / which was the veil of Cytheraea?"

H. D., *Helen in Egypt.*[1]

Helen in Euripides' play, produced in 412 BCE, poses questions of identity similar to this one that Achilles asks in H. D.'s modern epic poem *Helen in Egypt.* For the ancient play questions many aspects of the mythological tradition connected to the figure Helen and to the social arenas they shape. While these questions prompt new perspectives in various areas—mythological, historical, dramatic—they particularly foreground attention to the construction of gender identity, how both women's and men's identities are constructed against ideal notions for each: beauty for women, heroic, martial valor for men. Through its central character, Helen, the play brings up issues of beauty, erotic desire, and women's identity, suggesting views about women's identity in many ways distinct from those shown in *Alcestis* or *Medea,* or many of Euripides' other plays. *Helen* spotlights the challenges faced by the most beautiful woman in the world, asking questions still relevant in contemporary construction of female gender identity: What does the ideal of beauty mean for actual women's lives; how can one woman embody it; how is this imposed cultural ideal used by the larger cultural ideology? In the play, Helen's character, her words and actions, speak both for the particular social formation of woman's identity as well as for the placement of female identity within the general thematic issues affecting the larger community.

The story of Euripides' play *Helen* may surprise modern readers, who are probably more familiar with the story of Helen of Troy, "the face that launched a thousand ships" (Marlowe), the woman whose beauty led her to be the cause of a ten-year war between Greece and Troy. But Euripides dramatizes the story of a

Helen who spent the war years not in Troy but in Egypt, under the care of King Proteus, while the Trojan War was fought over a phantom image of her. In the action of the play Helen uses the tomb of the now dead King Proteus as a refuge to avoid marriage with his son, the new king, Theoklymenos. Her Spartan husband Menelaos, one of the two Greek commanders in the war against Troy, arrives, shipwrecked, believing the phantom he brings from Troy is the "real" Helen. The result is an elaborate recognition-and-reunion scene, the disclosure of the phantom Helen, and a plotline that tends more to romance than to tragedy (Burnett 1960, 1971). Helen and Menelaos devise a successful escape plan, obtaining the support of the king's sister, Theonoe, holy prophet and seer: On the pretense of Menelaos' death and Helen's obligation to perform the necessary funeral rites at sea, they deceive the king into providing them a getaway ship. In a possibly "tragic" turn that unabashedly evokes the heroism of the Trojan War, and which, like epic poetry, is eloquently reported by messenger speech, the Greeks victoriously battle against the ship's crew of Egyptian sailors. The final epiphany of the savior gods the Dioskouroi ("Sons of Zeus"), Helen's brothers, brings to an end Theoklymenos' anger and seals Helen's triumphant return home to Sparta with her husband Menelaos.

Helen was produced in the wake of the Sicilian disaster and the devastating losses Athens had suffered after almost twenty years of intense warfare with Sparta (above p. 8). Euripides' staging a story with a glamorized Spartan heroine who returns home to a gloriously portrayed Sparta must have had a shocking impact upon a late fifth-century Athenian audience. Aristophanes' biting anti-war comedy with a strong central female character, *Lysistrata,* was produced in the following year. The historical moment of production calls for placing its meaning securely in its historical and cultural setting: Why at this time does Euripides choose as his central character Helen, a heroine from Sparta, Athens' enemy, and a figure whose mythology depicts the illusory value of war? Other Euripidean plays both before and after this one present the character Helen as a vain and culpable embodiment of beauty—*Hekabe, Trojan Women, Orestes.* But this Helen agonizes over the war being fought for her name, an event deemed by all an action of the gods, while she, blameless, has been removed far from the war's arena. The questions that emerge throughout the innovative dramatic action reveal multiple levels of concern: epistemological, the nature of being and appearances, illusion and reality; social, the value of culturally maintained icons, such as notions of female beauty and male martial virtue; and dramatic, by resisting conventional expectations of tragic plot and tone. Helen, the mythological figure deemed to be the cause of war because of her beauty, is also the character who poses most of the play's challenging questions.

However odd this version of events may appear to a modern audience, Euripides in fact drew upon diverse ancient portrayals of Helen that presented complex images of her: On the one hand as a major goddess in Sparta, she was associated both with adolescent girls' transition rites and with marriage. She embodied, therefore, a dual ritual nature, representing two highly charged yet distinctive moments in a woman's life. In contrast, the pan-Hellenic stories portray a mortal Helen; yet they too depict enigmatic dualities about her: Was she or was she not the cause of the Trojan War; was she abducted or seduced, a willing or unwilling follower of Paris; should she be blamed or exonerated for her actions? She serves as a cultural icon of beauty and ideal womanhood; at the same time, these ritual and poetic dualities create a web of ambiguities that hovers over her (Bergren 1983). Fashioning his protagonist from this rich background, Euripides creates a dynamic Spartan heroine who self-critically explores the meaning of these multiple dualities, and who voices fundamental questions of war, identity, and existence, issues critical to the Athenian polis on the brink of defeat barely two generations since its rapid rise to Greek hegemony after their victory over the Persians.

I. Background

Poetic

The quality of doubleness characterizes the many portrayals of Helen in the ancient tradition. From the outset she was both divine and mortal, having mortal parents, Leda and Tyndareos, and immortal: while some traditions name the goddess Nemesis ("Apportionment," "Punishment") as Helen's mother, most favor the story of Zeus' rape of Leda in the form of a swan (see lines 17–21). She then laid two eggs, producing (an immortal) Helen, her mortal sister Klytemnestra, and her twin brothers, Kastor and Polydeukes (also known as Pollux), the Dioskouroi, who shared immortality between them. Helen shares with other mythological offspring of Zeus and a mortal mother, who are mostly male, the ambivalent status of embodying divine qualities while at the same time being subject to the demands of human mortality and ethical standards; the Chorus comment upon this tension in the play (1143–47; see also the struggles waged by Herakles in Sophocles' *Women of Trachis* and Euripides' *Herakles*). While these varying versions of her birth were familiar parts of Helen's story, evident from the casual allusions to them throughout Greek literature, and while they reveal the pervasive ambiguity surrounding Helen, they were not themselves the principal interest of Helen's story, but helped to fill in its background.

Helen's role in the Trojan War cycle weaves together different groups of stories. Fundamental to these is the Judgment of Paris, a popular subject in Greek poetry and art as early as the seventh century BCE. Eris ("Strife") entered a feast of the gods and ignited a rivalry over their beauty among the three goddesses Hera, Athena, and Aphrodite.[2] At Zeus' behest, they chose as the judge of their contention the most beautiful man, Paris, who, even though the son of Priam, and himself a Trojan prince, was idyllically herding sheep on the slopes of Mount Ida. Each goddess offered Paris a bribe: Hera political dominion and Athena military victory. Aphrodite offered him the most beautiful woman in the world, Helen, unconcerned that the mortal woman was already married to Menelaos (*Helen* prologue 23–30; compare *Trojan Women* 919–33). And so Paris chose Aphrodite: he seduced and abducted Helen; the Greeks besieged Troy for ten years for her sake; in the end they devastated the ancient city, while Helen, captured by Menelaos, returned to rule at her home in Sparta, as portrayed in the *Odyssey* Book 4.

While these events pull Helen into the pan-Hellenic accounts emerging from the Ionian coast of eastern Greece, her story retains a strong Spartan component. Typical of the marriage stories of wealthy, beautiful, and potentially powerful women in ancient mythological and historical tales, Helen was courted by a vast number of young men, including most of the Greek heroes who went to Troy. Menelaos, whose brother Agamemnon wooed Helen on his behalf, won not by any feats of skill or daring, but because he brought the most booty. To avoid hostilities among the suitors, Helen's father Tyndareos had them all swear to unite to recapture Helen if in the future anyone were to kidnap her—a highly foresighted oath given the subsequent events. Paris' abduction of Helen activates the oath. The Greek heroes gather under Agamemnon's command to fight the Trojans for Helen's return, and by this action the two storylines merge.

Finding precedent in some earlier poetry, Athenian drama cast these core events of the ancient stories in strongly condemnatory tones.[3] In his *Oresteia,* produced in 458 BCE, Aeschylus vehemently denounces Helen for being the cause of much bloodshed: the *Agamemnon*'s Chorus vividly imagine her like an adorable lion cub, vainly raised as a pet in the house only to wreak murderous destruction once it has grown (727–76). Moreover, their wordplay on Helen's name, the first two syllables of which, *hele-,* match the stem of a word meaning "destroy"—"ship-destroying, man-destroying, city-destroying"—embeds this destructiveness as inherent in her nature (689–90). Aeschylus' virulent vilification of Helen accords well with the gendered program of the *Oresteia,* and its purposeful dismissal of women's (and goddesses') spheres of action while validating patriarchal codes in both human and divine societies (Zeitlin 1978). The immense influence of this trilogy must have firmly implanted the image of a blameworthy Helen into fifth-century Athenian minds, one that Euripides reinforces in many of his other plays, dating both before and after *Helen: Hekabe, Orestes,* and *Iphigeneia at Aulis.* In the *Trojan Women,* produced just three years before *Helen,* the queen of conquered Troy, Hekabe, condemns as immoral Helen's beauty and her ability to use it to attain her own ends. Nevertheless, the play shows Helen using her power successfully to keep Menelaos from killing her. In the version of events he presents in *Helen,* therefore, Euripides challenges the predominantly negative Athenian dramatic portrayals, ones to which he himself had contributed, and which must have compounded the impact created by the play's historical timing.

And yet, startling as it may have been in its own day and to many today, Euripides' *Helen* had more in common with a wider tradition about Helen than the one presented in Athenian drama. This tradition presented Helen from various perspectives, and it began with the most influential early poet, Homer, whose versions of stories were often treated as canonical in the Greek tradition. At the same time that the Homeric poems present Helen as the cause of the war and the trophy to be awarded to the victor, in the polyphonic manner of Homeric poetry, her character is presented as having agency for her own actions and as speaking in her own voice (Martin 1989). Both Homeric poems endow her with traces of her divine origin and present her as highly skilled in weaving and poetic creation, while the *Odyssey* also depicts her with uncanny powers and the knowledge of painkilling drugs she learned in Egypt (Bergren 1979, 1981; Clader 1976). The *Iliad*'s portrayals, in particular, raise interesting questions of human responsibility for one's actions and the role of the gods (above p. 17): Helen as mortal character attempts to assert her own will, fighting against the role that Aphrodite has imposed upon her, that of being the human embodiment of divine beauty and erotic desire. In her rejection of her role she is much like Achilles, who struggles in a different way against his imposed "destiny" (see Reckford 1964 for an exploration of some of the similarities between the two; on "destiny" see above pp. 15–17). While Helen reviles herself for her actions, others lay blame elsewhere: The Trojan elders want to hold her responsible, but ultimately blame the gods who created the situation, hence deflecting direct censure of her (*Iliad* 3.154–165). Helen herself sees a higher purpose for their actions as material for poetic creation, the honor of the song outlasting, and perhaps balancing, the moral condemnation of human judgments (*Iliad* 6.356–58). Finally, the *Odyssey* depicts a queen in command of her home, insightful, skilled at drugs and storytelling; A gracious hostess to her guests, the final image shows her giving a spectacular weaving of hers as a parting gift to Odysseus' son (15.271–89). Despite Menelaos' veiled critique of Helen's actions in

Troy (4.104–8), the lasting impression of the Homeric poems shows her as self-confident and in command and exonerates her from moral culpability (see Juffras 1993; Austin 1994).

In a few very brief scenes, Homer portrays a figure of Helen possessing many facets. The basic storyline of her abduction by Paris which results in the Trojan War is a given in the Homeric poems, as is the perception of her as a possession, Menelaos' prize that was stolen, that is now being fought over, and that will go to the victor in the war. Rather than limiting his portrayal to Helen's material value, which might well represent an ancient Greek woman's status in the patriarchal economic, legal, and kinship systems, the poet explores various levels of complexity in Helen as a human character, features that diverge from the abduction story that drives the epic plot. Thus, if Homer establishes the canonical version of Helen's story on the one hand, he seems at the same time to be setting the lead for challenging the very version he is passing on.[4]

While much of Athenian drama demonized Helen, cursing her for the very status imposed on her by patriarchal ideology, the questions raised by the Homeric portrayals—the degree of Helen's agency and her moral culpability for her actions—attracted the attention of other poets and writers. A striking early version, which shows its awareness of both Homer and the basic epic account, is that of a seventh-century West Greek, the Sicilian poet Stesichorus. In lines that have come down to us as quoted by Plato (*Phaedrus* 243a), Stesichorus openly rejects the story of Helen as cause of the Trojan War:

> That story is not true.
> You never embarked on the well-fitted ships.
> You never arrived at the towers of Troy.
> (Stesichorus, fr. 192 Page)

That morality is the basis of this recantation, well known in antiquity as the so-called "palinode" ("the song re-sung"), is made evident by Socrates' next remarks. He adds that once Stesichorus was struck blind for composing a song that like Homer's blamed Helen for causing the war; but the poet realized his error and upon recanting, regained his sight.[5] On one level this apocryphal story, like other tales of mortals offending deities, evokes a Helen with divine status (see further below), who, thoroughly goddess-like, wields the power to harm or heal at her pleasure. But for the mortal character Helen, at issue is her culpability for her actions. Stesichorus absolves Helen, by singing instead of the *eidōlon,* the phantom over which Greeks and Trojans fought, and of Helen's sojourn in Egypt under the protection of King Proteus until Menelaos retrieves her on his way back from Troy—the core elements of Euripides' play. Although ancient writers credited Stesichorus with creating idiosyncratic versions of traditional stories, many, nevertheless, followed his versions. Ironically, in the process of his recantation, Stesichorus, too, acknowledges and passes on the very version of Helen's story he appears to be challenging (Bassi 1993).

But Stesichorus was writing within a tradition that was already familiar and greeted with relish alternate versions of traditional tales. Both the stories of the *eidōlon* and of Helen's stay in Egypt are known from other early sources: the former possibly in Hesiod (fr. 358, M–W); and the latter, as we have already seen, in Homer; and in a different corroborating source, the fifth-century cultural anthropologist and historian, Herodotus, whose works were known in Athens. In his *Histories,* Herodotus gives extensive details about Helen's sojourn in Egypt that he claims to have learned from Egyptian priests (*Histories* 2.112–20). While Herodotus stresses the moral dimensions of Helen's story, he does so through the lens of the male exchange values she represents: the Egyptian King Proteus' outrage at Paris' violation of his Greek host's *xenia* ("hospitality"; see above p. 21) by seducing his wife and escaping with her and the household wealth; and Proteus' righteous guarding of Menelaos' possessions, including Helen, until the Spartan king will come for them. In another moral twist, Menelaos also violates his Egyptian host's hospitality by sacrificing two Egyptian children in order to receive favorable winds, forcing him to flee Egypt by way of Libya. This provided Euripides with the key elements for the closing action of his play. Herodotus is concerned to show the independently attested validity of this story of Helen's presence in Egypt, not Troy, during the Trojan War, providing dual proofs: Morally, the Trojans would surely not have allowed their men, their homes, and their city to be destroyed so that Paris might sleep with Helen; and poetically, by invoking Homer, claiming that several Homeric passages show that the epic poet knew the story of Helen in Egypt but chose to suppress it for the purposes of his epic storytelling.

While the fragments of Stesichorus' verse seek to absolve Helen of any moral censure, and Herodotus' *Histories* emphasize the moral dimension of Helen's story as refracted through the networks of relationships among men, one aspect of the Homeric portrayal of Helen is not evident in them—that of her agency for her actions. It is, however, important to the one ancient Greek female poet whose extant poetry describes Helen, Sappho, a seventh-century poet from the eastern Greek island of Lesbos, whose distinctive female lyric (and possibly ritual) perspective had immense influence on the later Greek and Roman poetic traditions. In using Helen's story to illustrate that the power of erotic desire is greater than that of battle epic (fr. 16), Sappho depicts Helen as willingly accompanying Paris, and shows, like Homer, a Helen who acts of her own volition.[6] Since she acts under a greater power, that of Aphrodite, erotic desire, the deity most honored by Sappho's poetry, Helen also appears blameless for her action in Sappho's verse.

Finally, in the decade or so before Euripides' play, these issues of Helen's agency and her moral culpability receive a sophistic twist in the *Encomium of Helen* by the Sicilian orator Gorgias, who created a stir when he came to Athens as ambassador in 427. Gorgias was a well-known sophist (above, p. 14) and the subject of a dialogue by Plato. His work was probably known to many in Euripides' audience. In his rhetorical defense of her actions, Gorgias exonerates Helen for yielding to the power of erotic desire, which seductively acts on the mind like a drug. Although Gorgias' defense absolves Helen, unlike Homer's or Sappho's poetry, it does so by denying her agency. Gorgias exploits what Homer and other poets strove against—using the figure of Helen reductively for her symbolic value only. By reducing her to a figure in a rhetorical exercise, Gorgias' defense robs Helen of the complexity portrayed in the earlier poetry. At the same time, this sophistic defense may have provided the model for the self-defense speech Helen delivers in Euripides' *Trojan Women* (914–65) in 415.

The predominant image of Helen in all these works outside of Athenian drama is of a complex, powerful figure with a commanding presence: one who is for varying reasons not held accountable for the Trojan War; who may have safely and chastely sat out the war in Egypt; or who may have voluntarily left with Paris, an action that might be understood and even praised, as it appears to be in Sappho's fragment. Most treat Helen sympathetically rather than hostilely, presenting her as blameless for her actions. The currency of these "alternate" versions of Helen's story in fifth-century Athens means that however unfamiliar they may be to a contemporary audience, they were well known, popular story lines in antiquity, as available to ancient poets as the Helen at Troy story more familiar today. Hence, however much Euripides' play may have stood out when compared to the images of Helen prevalent in fifth-century Athenian drama, it actually accords with the generally positive, or at worst ambivalent, image of Helen presented in most of the literary tradition. In fact, it is very likely the immense influence of Athenian drama upon later writers that established the negative, judgmental portrayal of a destructive, blameworthy Helen as the canonical one for subsequent generations. Euripides himself, in the years just prior to *Helen,* and despite his vilification of her elsewhere, prepares for this play's presentation of Helen's story: The powerful portrayal of the superbly self-confident Helen of the *Trojan Women* may be seen as an early hint. But in their epiphany at the end of Euripides' *Elektra,* which may have been produced only a year before *Helen,* the Dioskouroi assert Helen's blamelessness, stating that she was with Proteus in Egypt and that Zeus fashioned an image of her for men to die over (*Elektra* 1280–83). Euripides thereby creatively announced the plot of his upcoming play.

Rituals and Myths

Since the stories about Helen predominantly known in the Western literary tradition feature her as a mortal character, the fact that she was a goddess of major significance in Sparta often provokes great surprise. Yet awareness of her ritual role is as important as knowing the broader literary tradition for understanding Euripides' play. From the stories Euripides fashions the dramatic action and basic meaning, while his references to Helen's ritual dimensions, in ways that imply his audience's familiarity with them, furnish critical elements of Helen's character and of the play's themes (see notes to the play). Although worship of Helen is known from various parts of the ancient Greek world, Sparta, her mythological home, seems to have been her ritual center, and she may have held the same importance for the Spartans that Athena held for Athenians. Helen's primary ritual associations were with two highly significant ritual stages for women: adolescent girls' rites of transition into adulthood and marriage. Since Helen's own origins are associated with vegetation—her name probably derives from a water reed (compare the modern Greek *heleneion* for the healing plant comfrey), and she was widely worshiped as Helena Dendritis, "Tree (Goddess)"—her oversight of these periods in a woman's life would be regarded as an extension of her nurturant care of growing plants.[7] Euripides embeds Helen's dual ritual associations into his play, representing Helen first as the marriageable *parthenos,*[8] and, after her reunion with Menelaos, as the married bride.

In contrast to young women in Athens, whose adolescent transition rites were much attenuated and coincided with a marriage arranged shortly after menarche, young Spartan women of the aristocratic class enjoyed an extended *partheneia* ("adolescence") that may have lasted till age eighteen, and which culminated in major rites of entry into adulthood in Spartan society, recognized independently of their marital status. Spartan girls marked this period of *partheneia* together through the choral song and dance that formed the basis of their educational system, rehearsing in particular the choral pieces they would perform at the public Spartan festivals that celebrated this transition. Euripides draws upon Sparta's renown for its vital choral and ritual life in creating the play's contextual environment, as when the Chorus envisage the delight of these Spartan rites in their final, celebratory ode (1465–75). In this passage and elsewhere, rites for Athena in Sparta are also evoked, no doubt serving political purposes as well, to show the importance of Athens' own goddess in supposedly enemy territory.

Alkman's *Partheneion* ("Maidens' Song"), which may have been composed for such a festival in honor of Helen (Calame 1997), illustrates the themes important at this stage of life, and the playful and exuberant competition among the young women. The song, divided between two half choruses which occasionally unite, describes the qualities of excellence the girls display as they vie with one another in running races, in singing, and especially in beauty. Beauty, encapsulated in physical attractiveness, crystallizes the blossoming of those qualities that make up a mature, adult, sexually potent, and capable woman. Helen, as a divinity, embodies all these qualities—she is most beautiful, most nubile, most charming, and sexiest; through her rituals she bestows these qualities on young women, qualities important as they move into the next stage, that of marriage.[9] Euripides unmistakably evokes Helen's ritual associations in the very first line of the play, through his adjective *kalli-parthenoi* ("beautiful maidens") to describe the Nile, and through repeated use of the word *parthenos* in the first ten lines (see play and notes).

Although we might find it strange that one deity would be associated with these two apparently distinctive stages in a woman's life, *parthenos* and bride, the connection was a meaningful one in ancient Greek belief, and was expressed also in certain rituals for Hera and for Demeter and Persephone together. Helen bridges these two stages through her beauty, in the fullness of what that concept means for each: for the adolescent, the coming to fruition of her nubile potential, and for the newly married woman, the active expression of her sexuality (*Helen* 1400). Yes, beauty does mean sex. In contrast to the mixed messages contemporary Western society puts out about sexuality, especially women's sexuality, whose beauty pageants pretend to ignore the sexual elements in a body-obsessed competition, the ancient rites provided a different approach. Through ritual the highly charged sensations of budding and first sexuality, of erotic desire and its important role in sexuality, are sanctified, allowed expression, and placed into their culturally appropriate niches. As a goddess Helen represents, and bestows, Beauty, the visible emblem of erotic desire: its potential in maturing adolescent women; its fulfillment in the new bride and married woman.

Since ritual acknowledges these deep feelings, channeling their energy into socially acceptable behavior, it is perhaps from this perspective that we should consider another element of Helen's stories and perhaps ritual role, abduction and rape. The motif of rape characterizes many stories of young women's transitions from *partheneia* into adulthood and marriage, as in the rape of Persephone. Although many (though not all) rape stories accompanied adolescent transition rites, there is no evidence that actual rape occurred in the girls' rites (though it may have been a part of some of the adolescent boys' transition rites).[10] But mock capture may have occurred, as in the rites for the Spartan Leukippides ("Daughters of Leukippos ['White Horse']"), which were possibly connected to those for Helen. The Leukippides were two sisters, whose story tells of their abduction by their cousins, the Dioskouroi, on their wedding day, and whose rites in Sparta may have entailed a capture scenario (see lines 1466–67; Calame 1997). To be sure, from a social perspective, the rape narratives reflected social conditions and the institutionalization of violent acts against women (Arthur 1973; Keuls 1985). Myths, however, operate on many levels; in particular, the myths associated with ritual carry symbolic meanings that may differ considerably from social interpretations. Ritually, the mythic rape narratives must have held some meaning for the young women experiencing this major rite of transition, no doubt symbolizing on one level the violent wrenching entailed in the adolescent's passage from one stage to another and the changes consequent to this passage (Zeitlin 1986; Dobson 1992).

Although the defining element of Helen's stories is abduction, her abduction narratives suggest meanings different from these (Juffras 1993). Before her abduction by Paris, Helen was kidnapped at age seven, or ten, by the Athenian hero Theseus and his companion Peirithous. While the ages given for her abduction reflect those of girls' puberty rites, any ritual connection remains obscure. It would be noteworthy if this story had this ritual association, for then Helen would be in the unique position of overseeing three significant female ritual stages. The story, however, which concludes with Helen's divine twin brothers, the Dioskouroi, rescuing her untouched, reveals affinities with widespread Indo-European narrative motifs of the twin savior gods who come to the rescue of their endangered sister (Lindsay 1974).

Varying even more from other narratives is Helen's later abduction by Paris, which is distinguished both from her childhood kidnapping and from other abduction tales by the fact of her already adult, married status when Paris takes her. At this point her story explodes with numerous variations: Paris steals her as a possession, or abducts her; or he seduces her, or she willingly elopes with him. The abduction/seduction/elopement serves as a model for other stories about Helen, such as Menelaos abducting her from the Egyptian king, or stories about other female characters, such as Briseis in the *Iliad.* From this point she is also renowned for her many husbands: Menelaos, Paris, and after his death, briefly, the Trojan Deiphobos. Once again it is unknown what connection, if any, these stories may have had with Helen's ritual oversight of married women. But erotic desire is clearly a prerogative of married women and celebrated by them in rituals to Aphrodite, with whom Helen is most intimately connected, to other goddesses, and to some gods, notably Dionysos (see the Chorus' second *stasimon,* 1347–52). Thematically, the attributes characteristic of the ritual Helen underline the story portrayals which take on their own dynamics and new meanings as they are regenerated in the oral and literary traditions. However much the mortal character in these stories must deal with human concerns of volition, agency, and culpability, Helen's power continues to be that of the Spartan goddess of beauty, whose sexual potency is regarded as an extremely valuable prize, whose divine qualities are deemed worth fighting for, and who is victorious at the end.

II. The Play

In the dramatic action and structure of *Helen* Euripides makes allusion to, transforms, and plays around with all these aspects of the tradition connected with Helen to produce one of the most intellectual and innovative of all his plays, frequently examined by scholars as a play of ideas (Burnett 1960; Arrowsmith 1963; Segal 1971; Wolff 1973). The play, and in particular the character Helen, raises philosophical, yet also timely questions about appearance and reality, the basis for knowing anything, identity, the value of cultural ideals such as beauty or heroism, and of warfare. None of these themes is treated simply. Recently, scholars have been especially interested in issues of Helen's agency and her role in perpetrating these levels of illusion (Downing 1990; Goldhill 1993; Holmberg 1995).

The setting in Egypt is established in the first line, and the play variously displays an awareness of the otherness of this locale. Well documented from Minoan and Mycenaean times (second millennium BCE) through the fifth century and beyond, contact between Greece and Egypt is evident in numerous areas of human endeavor: trade, military alliances, warfare, settlements, artistic exchange, and other cultural influences. On the one hand, the Greek view of Egypt places it with other foreign lands in the category of "barbarian" (above pp. 22–23), so that Egyptians are little distinguished from the Taurians in Euripides' *Iphigenia Among the Taurians* just a few years before, both treated with stock attributes as despotic, boorish, unmanly, and generally inferior to brave, free, aristocratic Greek men. The depiction of Theoklymenos in *Helen* exemplifies this stock negative treatment. However, in the Greek imagination, Egypt is also a land of mystery and wisdom. All Greek wise men were said to have studied there. In the *Odyssey* Proteus is a shape-shifting god of wisdom and Helen learned her knowledge from the Egyptian priestess Polydamna (*Odyssey* 4.227–29, 351–570); and Herodotus, as we have seen, trusts in the validity of the Helen story he heard from Egyptian priests. In the play, the character Theonoe and the memory of the former king, Proteus, both represented as pious, upright individuals, illustrate this admiring view of Egypt.

One final association of Egypt is with death, which may derive from some Greek awareness of Egypt's elaborated culture of the dead, through its pyramids, mummifying, and elaborate funerary rites. Conceptually, this notion of a land of death contains deep meaning, as death too is regarded as a place of wisdom where epic heroes or heroines must journey to gain the knowledge important for human understanding, as illustrated in the tales of Gilgamesh, Odysseus, and Persephone. This association with death further enables Helen's story to be allied with Persephone's, as Helen's sojourn in Egypt may then appear analogous to Persephone's in Hades (see Juffras 1993: 46). The setting in Egypt, then, reflects a dual vision of Egypt as embracing both negative and positive dimensions of foreignness, the former through stock comments about "barbarians," but the latter reflecting an extensive, contact-based tradition of admiration for Egypt. Altogether, the setting in Egypt brings into relief the dualities and ambiguities already associated with Helen in the mythological tradition and that Euripides will further explore in the play.

This chord of ambivalence characterizes the play's treatment of the dramatic themes. From the outset Helen questions her identity and the validity of the mythological stories about her, and she bemoans her misfortune in having her name and image used as a cause for war, while she herself was safely, and chastely, living in Egypt. Unhappy with her situation, Helen asks questions that tie into philosophical concerns about the nature of reality and the ability of humans to distinguish between reality and illusion. The drama stages these abstract questions through the comedies of error characterizing Menelaos' exchange with the Gatekeeper, in which he cannot believe what he hears (470–500), and the recognition scene, where he refuses to believe what is literally before his eyes, since he trusts only in the phantom Helen he has brought from Troy (557–93). These dramatic renderings of philosophical musings seem to conclude in favor of the "real" in the celebratory songs of the reunion scene. At the same time, the character Helen exhibits great concern for appearances—how she looks, the sight of her husband in rags, how his actions appeared to others; and she is the one to conceive the illusive scenario of their escape plan. Since this dramatic action appears to favor illusion, the question arises of the relation between the two movements: Are they to be taken together, two sides of the coin of human existence; is one a comment upon the other; or is Euripides playfully exposing his own technology of the drama, by staging scenarios of appearances as the principal dramatic action of his play?

The dramatic use of the *eidōlon* and the value of warfare are also presented ambivalently. The ruse of the phantom Helen caused much destruction and grief; once she is unmasked, she acknowledges she was created as a pretext for men to go to war (608–15). This ultimate exposure is perceived as beneficial, both for Helen's position and for mortals' understanding of their situation. The value of illusion, however, is not entirely discounted, for the play then shows Helen and Menelaos achieving their goal by an elaborate ruse of a "phantom" ("dead") Menelaos, which also causes much destruction, until it is unveiled by the Dioskouroi at the end of the play as serving a beneficial purpose for Helen's situation and for mortal understanding. The value of warfare is treated analogously: Though the deaths in the Trojan War are repeatedly decried, and the Chorus even express a rare pacifist view (1151–60), Menelaos and Helen avidly urge the Greeks on to battle the Egyptian sailors, rallying them to remember they are Greeks, the conquerors of Troy, and their victorious battle enables them to escape (1591–1612; see Segal 1971). The very feature that is condemned from one perspective, when it appears harmful, is nevertheless exploited fully when its use appears advantageous. If a question of moral judgment enters here, it is a highly personal, self-serving one; any claim to an abstract moral condemnation of deceitful ruses or warfare cannot hold up to the successful use of these activities in the dramatic action of the play.

Adding another enigmatic facet to these complex dualities is the treatment of the nature of deity and the significance of belief in the divine. Various passages affirm a deep belief in the gods, and Helen's ritual aspects are evoked throughout the play, showing their importance to the Chorus, the characters, and to the play's meaning. The entire second *stasimon* reverently evokes the rites of worship for Demeter and the Great Mother; but the last stanza suggests a tension between Helen's rites and those for Demeter in which Helen apparently favors her own beauty over the Great Mother's rites (1353–68; see notes). While the play affirms ritual aspects of the goddess Helen, it also depicts its mortal protagonist as self-centered and vain, and apparently lacking the spiritual dimensions of her divine namesake.

In addition, the character Theonoe, the Egyptian prophetess, brings in new levels of complexity. After disclosing the disappearance of the *eidōlon,* the first Messenger, Menelaos' old servant, a low-status character of a kind that often presents commonsense views in Euripides' plays, rejects the value of prophets and prophecies. But the play has already shown the respect paid by all to Theonoe and the validity of her prophecies. Represented as living in a state of ritualized purity, expressing in her actions the piety she proclaims in her words, she describes a theological outlook that may reflect Greek perceptions of Egyptian beliefs, but that oddly resembles contemporary philosophical discussions on the nature of the physical world (865–72, 1014–16). Though the play emphasizes the Egyptianness, the foreignness of Theonoe's spiritual character, it also shows her attuned to the councils of the Greek gods, able to prophesy unerringly for them, and able to affect the outcome of events among them by her decision (878–93, 1005–27). This is a rare privilege for a human being, since humans are usually presented as having to endure whatever the gods may dispense, whether they wish to or not, as we have seen in Homer's presentation of Helen in *Iliad* 3. Despite Theonoe's purity and truthfulness in reporting the intent of the gods, she too participates in the deceit, in illusion, in order to enable Helen to clear her name and to return home with Menelaos.

The questions of illusion and reality—how they can be distinguished; their values in human lives—imbue every theme of the play, casting each in dual forms, calling each theme up for reflection, and leaving modern readers (and perhaps ancient audience members) uncertain as to Euripides' meaning. Interestingly, the two issues connected with Helen that the tradition presents most ambiguously—her culpability and her agency—are treated most forthrightly by Euripides. From its setting to its action to the final exculpatory stamp by the Dioskouroi, the play completely absolves Helen of culpability; its plot is driven by the need of its mortal heroine to erase the moral blot from her name. Similarly, though faced with adverse circumstances, Helen repeatedly takes action on her own behalf: setting up her bedroom at the tomb for sanctuary, leading Menelaos through the steps towards their recognition, supplicating Theonoe, carrying out the escape plan she conceived, and actively spurring the Greeks on to battle so they may make their way home to Sparta. Yet even these dramatic assertions of Helen's innocence and independent agency are rendered questionable, as Helen's eagerness to clear her name results in actions that, though not adulterous, appear morally weak. In this regard, Helen might appear like Medea, whose independent ability to act appears as a danger rather than a strength of women.

The highly original structure of this play, which has the basic formal structure of Athenian tragedy and was produced as a tragedy at the City Dionysia, but which plays as a tragic parody rather than a conventional tragedy, adds to this ambience of ambivalencies where one is never entirely sure how to take any particular dramatic moment. As we have seen, and as is typical for Athenian tragedy (above, pp. 45–8), Euripides draws his basic material from the mythological tradition, but the particular storyline was probably his own invention. Refining a dramatic experimentation begun in the *Ion* and *Iphigenia Among the Taurians,* Euripides combines several plot motifs with ironic and even comical twists that carry the action: sanctuary, recognition, supplication, plan-escape-and-rescue schemes (Burnett 1971). He also incorporates other rare elements: two messenger speeches, a choral exit mid-play (see above p. 91 for a similar feature in *Alcestis*), and a unique choral ode structure. Ironically, working in tandem with this inventive structuring, is a thrust toward reinscribing the principal action motifs connected with the Trojan War: Helen is once again the cause of abduction, or attempted abduction, which leads ultimately to the Greeks' victory in bloody battle to win her possession. Despite the shifting plot turns, and the possible tragedy of the final reported battle, the Chorus celebrate and the Dioskouroi approve Helen and Menelaos' successful escape and return home. In this way, Euripides continues the movement seen in Homer and Stesichorus, of passing on the basic, traditional Helen of Troy story at the same time that he appears to be presenting an entirely different version of the tale.

Finally, *Helen*'s unusual choral structure also contributes to the play's original effect. After their *parodos* ("entry song," 167–251), distinctive in that it is actually a *kommos* or lyric dialogue that spotlights Helen and thus reduces their choral role, the Chorus do not sing their standard *stasima* ("songs in position") until the last third of the play (for these terms, see above p. 34). Thus, except for a short choral interlude at lines 515–27, for most of the play the Chorus are silent, not singing or dancing, while the Chorus leader has minimal interaction with the characters. This is a highly unusual limitation on choral participation in the drama, which might well contribute to the play's meaning: What perception of the characters' actions is the play presenting if it finds these actions do not need or merit traditional choral comment? Conversely, what meaning may attach to the play's presentation of the action in the last third, where the three *stasima* follow one another in rapid succession (1108–64, 1302–68 and 1451–1511), all three reflecting traditional choral themes in conventional structures? It is certainly possible to regard the ending as a conservative turn, recalling the kinds of odes, plots, and structures that fulfill expectations of tragic form and action. If so, the question still remains of how this complex dramatic structuring affects the meaning of the play.

This combination of unusual plot and choral structures contributes yet other levels of ambiguous nuance to this play, whose genre, themes, and meaning defy easy interpretation. As with the other plays in this volume, questions posed earlier still hover unanswered. Helen's questioning of her own identity and mythological background at the beginning of the play seems of little consequence in the successful escape action. The play's wiping clean the slate of her moral position, by representing Helen as a chaste, faithful, devoted married woman—might this also have been the cause for amusement in the audience?—does not thereby diminish her cultural value as icon of beauty. Although the scarlet stain of adultery has been cleared from her reputation, she in other ways dramatizes how a woman who is the living embodiment of the female ideal of beauty would act—her boudoir at the tomb, her concern with appearances, her reported role at the end as Beauty Queen who urges men on to war. For the purpose of her escape scheme, Helen feigns mourning, part of which entails cutting her hair and scratching her face; Theoklymenos remarks upon these visible signs of mourning Helen displays, omitting, however, the face scratches (1186–89). The feigned mourning enables Helen to make her beautiful face uglier, as she claims earlier she wishes she could do (262–63). Knowing whether this change was portrayed by mask or gesture, or whether Helen really de-beautifies her face or only puts forth token gestures in that direction as part of her dramatic feint, would aid in understanding the play's treatment of beauty and Helen's relationship with it.

What finally, is the impression this play leaves on its audience? Clearly that differs for different members of the ancient as well as modern audience. Comments relating to contemporary historical events seem evident: the questionable practice of war, even as men inevitably continue to engage in it; presenting, in tune with philolakonic ("Spartan-friendly") circles in Athens, a positive view of Sparta, its ritual culture, deities, and heroines, particularly as grounds for overcoming their hostilities. Through this tragicomedy of illusions, Euripides seems to be presenting a concerned message about the possibility of reconciliation. And the instrument of this reconciliation is the figure of divine Helen, whose representations of women's rituals, women's transitions, and female qualities, whose connection with rites of other deities, particularly Athena, are shown as vital, core elements of the community, which enable it to thrive. The same figure, cast in mortal guise, can, because of her divine powers, be the cause of fighting. Yet she is eternally successful, always returning home, not culpable, to reign, transcending the very mortal, and moral, havoc she appears to cause.

In the end, what seems to remain most puzzling is how we are meant to understand the value of beauty. Helen the goddess, divine representation of beauty and erotic desire, retains her power, the reverence of her worship. But Helen the mortal embodiment of beauty appears mostly vain and self-absorbed; and to conform to changing human moral standards, her eroticism is all but ignored, though its presence is palpable beneath the surface and may be stressed in actual performance. Nevertheless, being Helen she wins out in the end, the final image of her sailing triumphantly home to Sparta. As with all the other paradoxes he presents in this play, Euripides does not serve up a conveniently pat moral evaluation. But, as befits a dramatist rather than a philosopher, he presents a dramatic picture that requires the audience to reflect upon the ideas staged. He shows the actions of mortal characters and the cultural ideals they hold valuable to be problematic. In contrast to this troubling area of human existence, Euripides accentuates the reverence for the divine Helen, the value of her worship and that of other female deities, and the significance of women's rituals. As these are the only aspects presented unambiguously in the play, by showing the importance of these female arenas in the life of the community, Euripides appears to be suggesting them as starting points to recover from decades of pointless war and enmity. In this play, though war is still in the background, for a momentary change, it is Beauty in all its meaning that prevails.

III. Helen in Later Literature

"We all know the story of Helen of Troy," H. D. begins her epic (Doolittle 1961). This is the image of Helen preeminent in the Western tradition, perpetuated as we have seen in Athenian drama, on through Roman literature and popularly down through numerous cinematic treatments in our own time. Even so, poets have continued to challenge this image, Chaucer, like Stesichorus, presented both the destructive Helen of Troy and a Helen who proudly proclaims, "I am myn owene woman, wel at ese" (Troilus and Criseyde 2.108). Goethe cast her as the promising image heralding the dawn of a new world (Faust). The female imagist poet H. D. explored what Helen represents for women's identity not only in her monumental epic poem, but throughout her poetic corpus, and the contemporary lesbian poet Judy Grahn poetically explores the impact of Helen as a cultural icon of Beauty imposed on women's lives (*Queen of Wands*).[11] These poets have continued to imagine the figure Helen with the positive, complex dimensions apparent in much of the ancient literature.

The play has had a different kind of impact. Within a few years it provided a major scene for comedic parody in Aristophanes' *Women at the Thesmophoria* (see line note). *Helen* is often grouped with the other experimental plays Euripides produced in the 410s, such as *Ion* and *Iphigenia Among the Taurians.* With their often comic, non-tragic undertones and the positive outcome of their plots, these plays acquired the designation "romantic comedies," so-called from the later drama whose plots they inspired: from the "New Comedy" of the fourth-century Greek playwright Menander, to the Roman comic playwrights Plautus and Terence, and finally to the European comedies of Shakespeare, Corneille, Molière down to Neil Simon in our own time.

IV. Manuscripts, Translations, and This Edition

The manuscript tradition for this play has many problems, including many passages in a highly fragmentary state. I have noted occasional problems in the commentary when pertinent for the meaning. Besides the Oxford Classical Text of Euripides' plays by Diggle, I have used primarily two annotated Greek editions as my basic text for this translation, Dale 1967 and Kannicht 1969, incorporating their or other suggested emendations for a more coherent translation. I have tried to capture both the literal and connotative meanings of the Greek, and to reflect to some extent the rhythm of the dramatic presentation.

Finally, a note on reading: It is easy to approach ancient Greek drama with an air of solemnity and treat the plays as uniformly serious. I believe this approach is a mistake in regard to *Helen*. From the opening scene Euripides' use of parody, humor, and satire is evident, and I have no doubt that certain scenes would have evoked hearty laughter from the audience. The comedy of the plot does not, of course, diminish the seriousness of the issues Euripides seems to be exploring.

This translation was supported by a 1992 University of Arizona (UA) Small Grants Program Award and by a UA Women's Studies Advisory Council (WOSAC) Faculty Research Grant, summer 1994. I also wish to acknowledge the help of the following individuals: David Halperin, for enthusiastically including this unusual play and his sensitive direction for the whole volume; Norman Austin, for our many conversations about Helen and for encouraging my line of interpretation; and especially my co-translators in this volume for their careful readings and tireless efforts in producing a quality text, and for their personal support and camaraderie. Finally, besides my mother I wanted to include my grandmothers in the dedication to this volume, women whose lives were severely traumatized by the Holocaust: One was killed in the camps, the other, uprooted and relocated; women who lived and died on the edge.

II. THE PLAY

Characters

HELEN, Queen of Sparta, married to Menelaos
TEUKER, a Greek soldier
CHORUS of captive Spartan women

MENELAOS, husband of Helen, king of Sparta[1]
OLD WOMAN, doorkeeper at the palace
FIRST MESSENGER, Menelaos' servant, his slave and old comrade in arms
THEONOE, priestess, prophet, sister of Theoklymenos
THEOKLYMENOS, King of Egypt
SECOND MESSENGER, Theoklymenos' servant
DIOSKOUROI, Kastor and Polydeukes, Helen's brothers

Scene: Egypt, near the mouth of the Nile, before the palace of King Theoklymenos. The time is seven years after the Trojan War and not long after the death of King Proteus, Theoklymenos' father. Proteus' tomb, where Helen has taken sanctuary,[2] is a visible scene marker, and may be set near the right side entrance (see above p. 31), which leads to the country; the left one leads to the sea. Helen speaks the opening monologue to the audience.

HELEN: Here flow the beautiful-maiden streams of the Nile,[3]
which waters the lands, the plain of Egypt,
from melting white snow instead of heavenly rain.
Proteus ruled this land while he was alive,
King of Egypt, but living on his island home, Pharos.
He married Psamathe, one of the sea maidens,
after she had broken off her marriage to Aiakos.
She bore two children for this house,
a boy Theoklymenos, named for his father's reverence to the gods
during his lifetime,[4] and a noble maiden,
called Eido while a child, her mother's joyous pride.[5]
But when she reached the prime of her youth, the age for marriage,
they named her Theonoe, for she has divine understanding,
knowing all things that are and all that will be,
powers she got from her mother's father Nereus.[6]
But my homeland is not unknown either,
Sparta, and my father was Tyndareos.
One account claims that Zeus flew to my mother
Leda in the shape of a swan,
that he got her into bed by deceit, claiming he was fleeing an eagle

in his pursuit—if that's a reliable account.
But I'm called Helen. Let me tell you the evils I have endured:
Three goddesses, arguing over their beauty,
came to Alexander in his cave on Mount Ida:[7]
Hera, Kypris, and Zeus' maiden daughter,[8]
wanting a decision to their contention over beauty.
By offering my beauty in marriage as a lure to Alexander
—if you can call beautiful whatever brings misery—
Kypris won. So Paris left his herds on Mount Ida
and came to Sparta expecting to marry me.[9]
Meanwhile, Hera, upset that she didn't defeat the goddesses,
blew my marriage to Alexander away into thin air,
by giving to the son of King Priam, not me,
but a living, breathing image looking just like me
she had made out of the air. So he thinks that he has me—
an empty thought!—he doesn't. Then Zeus
devised other evils to add to these.
For he brought war to the land of the Greeks
and to the unfortunate Trojans in order to lighten
Mother Earth's load from an abundance of human beings,
and in order to make Achilles famous as the greatest hero of Greece.[10]
And yet I was not the cause of the Trojan War,
a prize for Greek spears, but my name was.[11]
For Zeus did not forget me. But Hermes took me up[12]
in folds of ether, hiding me in a cloud,
and he set me down here, at the home of Proteus,
whom he considered the most honest of all men,
so that I might keep my marriage to Menelaos unharmed.
So I am here. But my miserable husband
raised an army and sailed on a hunt to the towers of Troy
to avenge my abduction.
Many souls have died because of me by the
streams of the Scamander. And I must put up with all of this.
People curse me, believing I betrayed my husband

and that I ignited this great war for the Greeks.
Then why am I still living? Because I heard this promise from the god
Hermes, that I would again live in the famous plain
of Sparta with my husband; that he would know
I never went to Troy, and that I was never unfaithful with anyone.
While Proteus still looked on the light of the sun,
my marriage was safe. But now that he's dead
and buried in the dark of the earth, his son hunts to marry me!
Still respecting my husband from before,
and still trying to preserve my marriage to him,
I cling to this tomb of Proteus as a suppliant,
so that, even though I bear a name of ill repute throughout Greece,
my body at least will not incur any shame here.

[*Enter Teuker from the left side entrance leading to the shore.*[13] *He does not at first see Helen.*]

TEUKER: Who rules over this fortified palace?
For it looks like a house worthy of Ploutos,[14]
with its regal enclosure and well-fitted stones.
Hey!
Oh gods! What do I see?!! I see the most hated,
deadly image of that woman, she who destroyed me
and all the Greeks. May the gods spit you away,
for looking so much like Helen! If I weren't a stranger
standing on foreign soil, using my sure-hitting arrows,
death would have been your reward for looking like the daughter of Zeus.

HELEN: What's this, you wretch, whoever you are?
Why do you turn away from me and hate me for her misfortunes?

TEUKER: I made a mistake. I let my anger get the best of me.
For all Greece detests the daughter of Zeus.
Pardon me, Lady, for what I just said.

HELEN: Who are you? Where do you come from to travel to this land?

TEUKER: I'm a Greek, ma'am, one of those wretched Greeks.

HELEN: Then it's no wonder you hate Helen.
But, who are you and from where? Whose son should we call you?

TEUKER: My name is Teuker; the father who bore me was Telamon,
and the fatherland that raised me was Salamis.[15]

HELEN: And what brought you to this valley of the Nile?

TEUKER: I've been driven out in exile from my fatherland.

HELEN: Oh, you are miserable! Who drove you out from your fatherland?

TEUKER: Telamon, the one who begot me! The one who should be the closest to me.

HELEN: But why? This exile brings you misfortune.

TEUKER: When my brother Ajax died at Troy he also destroyed me.

HELEN: How? Surely you didn't take his life with your own sword?

TEUKER: He killed himself, hurling himself on his sword.

HELEN: Was he mad? What person in his right mind could bear to do such a thing?

TEUKER: Have you heard of a certain Achilles, Peleus' son?

HELEN: Yes. He came once as Helen's suitor, or so I've heard.

TEUKER: His death started the warriors arguing over his arms.

HELEN: How does this lead to Ajax's death?

TEUKER: When someone else got the arms, he took his life.

HELEN: And now you suffer the pains of his agony?

TEUKER: Yes, since I didn't die together with him.

HELEN: So did you go, stranger, to the famous city of Troy?

TEUKER: I helped to sack it, then destroyed myself as well.

HELEN: Has it already been torched and burned to the ground?

TEUKER: So that there's not even a clear trace of a wall left.

HELEN: Oh, poor Helen! Because of you the Trojans have been destroyed!

TEUKER: And plenty of Greeks too! Great evils were done.

HELEN: How long since the city was destroyed?

TEUKER: Almost seven harvests have come and gone.

HELEN: And how long were you at Troy before that?

TEUKER: Many moons passed, ten years in all.

HELEN: So, did you capture the Spartan woman?

TEUKER: Menelaos got her and dragged her off by the hair.

HELEN: Did you yourself see the poor woman, or are you speaking from hearsay?

TEUKER: I saw her with my own eyes, no less than I'm seeing you now.

HELEN: Did you ever think it was an image from the gods?

TEUKER: Mention another story, no more about her.

HELEN: Well, do you think the image is so infallible?

TEUKER: I'm telling you, I myself saw her with my own eyes . . . and "my mind saw" too.[16]

HELEN: So, is Menelaos home already with his wife?

TEUKER: He's not in Argos, nor by the streams of the Eurotas in Sparta.

HELEN: Oh no! [*Recovering from her cry*] What terrible news, how terrible for those whom it affects.

TEUKER: Rumor has it he's disappeared with his wife.

HELEN: Didn't all the Greeks sail back together?

TEUKER: They did, but a storm scattered everyone all over the place.[17]

HELEN: Where in that broad sea did this happen?

TEUKER: Right in the middle when they were crossing the Aegean Sea.

HELEN: And since that time no one knows of Menelaos' homecoming?

TEUKER: No one. Throughout Greece he's said to be dead.

HELEN: [*Aside*] Oh, I'm destroyed. [*To Teuker*] And what of Thestios' daughter?

TEUKER: You mean Leda? They say she too is dead and gone.

HELEN: You don't mean that Helen's shameful reputation killed her?

TEUKER: So they say. Being noble, she wound a noose around her neck.

HELEN: And Tyndareos' sons, are they still living?[18]

TEUKER: Two stories are going around. They're said to be both dead and not dead.

HELEN: Which is more likely? [*Aside*] Oh, I'm wretched with sorrows.

TEUKER: The one that says they've become gods, turned into stars.

HELEN: This one sounds good. What's the other one?

TEUKER: That on account of their sister's death they breathed their last in life.
But enough of these stories. I don't need to be lamenting twice.

The reason I came to this royal palace
is to consult with the prophetess Theonoe.
Would you be my sponsor, so I may learn from the oracle[19]
how I can best guide my ship's wings with a favoring wind
to the island of Cyprus. Apollo prophesied
I would settle there, and give my new home
the island name of Salamis, in honor of my fatherland.

HELEN: Sail, stranger. The course will show itself to you. But you must leave this land.
Escape before the son of Proteus who rules this land
sees you!—He's away right now,
following his hounds on a bloody wild beast hunt.—
For he kills any Greek stranger he captures.[20]
Don't try to find out why he does this,
and I won't say. For what good would it do you?

TEUKER: You've spoken well, Lady. May the gods
grant you good rewards in return!
Though you look just like Helen physically, your heart and mind
are not alike, but completely different.
May she be wickedly destroyed and may she never reach Eurotas' streams.
But you, Lady, may *you* be fortunate always!

[*Exit Teuker*]

HELEN: For my great sorrows I begin a deep lamentation.
What kind of wail can I sing? Which Muse do I implore
with tears, or with dirges, or with my sorrowful moans?
Aiai!

Strophe A

Oh, you young feathered women[21]
maiden daughters of Earth,
Sirens, if only you would come
to hear my grief, bringing your Libyan[22]
flute or panpipes or lyres, your tears
joined with my mournful plaints—
Pain with pain, dirge with dirge.

If only Persephone would send
her deathly songs to harmonize with my laments;
in gratitude, with tears, I would sing
  the dirge for the dead
in her halls of night.

[*The Chorus enter.*]

CHORUS: Near the deep-blue sea *Antistrophe A*
on spirals of green grass
by the young shoots of reeds
  I was drying my purple robes
in the golden rays of the sun
  when I heard her cry out a painful wail,
  a loud lament, a sad lyreless song,
such as some nymph in grievous pain might cry out,
like a Naiad in the mountains under a rocky cave
letting loose her mournful strain in flight,
  as she cries out with sharp screams
against rape by Pan.[23]

HELEN: Oh, oh! *Strophe B*
Spoils of barbarian oars,
Daughters of Greece,
  a Greek sailor came,
he came bringing tears upon tears for me.
Troy lies in ruins,
  destroyed by fire,
because of me, the killer of many,
because of my name that has caused so much grief.
Leda chose death,
  hanging herself
out of shame at my disgrace.
My husband, wandering over many seas,
  is lost, gone.
And Kastor and his brother,
the twin-born glory of their fatherland,
  are vanished, vanished.
They have left the horse-thundering plain,

the training fields by the reeds of the Eurotas
  where young men work out.

CHORUS: *Aiai! Aiai!* *Antistrophe B*
What grievous fortune,
the lot in life you have received, Lady![24]
  an unlivable life
is what you drew, you drew, when Zeus, flashing
  through the sky
with wings of a snow-white swan,
  begot you on your mother!
What evils have you not suffered?
What miseries have you not endured?
First, your mother is dead,
Then, Zeus' own twin sons
  no longer enjoy a blessed life.
You do not look upon your fatherland,
while rumor spreads throughout the cities
  giving you up, my queen, to barbarian beds.
Your husband has lost his life
in the sea's salt waves
and you will never again bless your father's halls
  or the Bronze Temple.[25]

HELEN: Bah! Who was it, was it a Trojan *Epode*
or someone from the land of Greece
who cut the pine that brought
  tears to Troy?[26]
From that wood the son of Priam
rigged together the deadly barque
and sailed with a foreign oar
  to my hearth,
intending to possess my cursed beauty,
intending to marry me!
and with him came the deceitful killer of many,
  Kypris,
who brought death to both Greeks and Trojans.
Oh, misfortunes I've had to endure!
Then Zeus's beloved,

the object of his embrace,
holy Hera, of the golden throne,
sent the swift-footed son of Maia.[27]
As I was gathering fresh rose petals in my dress
to take to Bronze-Templed Athena,
he snatched me up through the air,
to this unfortunate land,
and he created strife, bitter strife
between the Greeks and Trojans.
All the while my name
endures a false reputation
by the streams of the Simois.

CHORUS: You have your sorrows, I know. But you'd be better off
if you bore the constraints of life more lightly.[28]

HELEN: Dear women, what fate am I yoked to?
Did my mother bear me to be a monster for humankind?
For neither a Greek nor barbarian woman
gives birth to the white shell of young birds,
in which they say Leda bore me from Zeus.
For my life and all its events have been monstrous,
some because of Hera, some due to my beauty.
I wish I could have been wiped clean, like a statue, and painted again,[29]
getting an uglier face instead of my beautiful one.
The Greeks would then forget the evil fortunes I now have;
and they would hold better thoughts of me,
just as they now cling to the bad ones.
When someone has their sights set on one lucky chance,
and they are deprived of it by the gods, it's hard, but it must be borne.
But I'm enveloped by many disasters.
First of all, I've received this ill repute though I'm innocent.
And this is far worse than if it were true,
to be heaped with crimes that aren't even one's own.
Then, the gods took me from my fatherland and resettled me

among barbarian peoples. Deprived of my family and loved ones,
I've been made into a slave, though I was born free.
But everyone among these barbarians is a slave, except for one man.
And now, the sole anchor which held my fortunes,
that my husband would one day come and release me from these evils,
no longer holds, since he has died.
My mother is dead and I killed her.
The accusation is unjust, yet the injustice is mine.
My daughter, my own delight and the pride of our house,
is turning grey unmarried, without a man.
And my brothers, the ones they call Dioskouroi, sons of Zeus,
no longer live. Filled with all these misfortunes
I've already died in my sufferings, though I'm living still.
And this is the worst: even if I did reach my homeland,
I'd be barred from the doors—for people think
I'm the Helen Menelaos sought in Troy.
If my husband still lived, we would recognize each other
by signs known only by us.[30]
But this can no longer be, nor could he still be alive.
Why then do I still live? What chance do I have left?
Shall I choose marriage as an escape from my troubles
and live with this barbarian man, sitting at his rich table?
Whenever a hateful husband lives with a woman,
even her body becomes hateful.
It's best to die. How can I die in a noble way?[31]
Hanging, dangling from on high is ugly;
even the slaves think it's unseemly.
Killing oneself by sword has something fine and noble;
but the opportune time for exchanging this life is short.[32]
This is the depth of disasters I've come to;
their beauty brings good fortune to other women,
but this same beauty has destroyed me.

CHORUS: Helen, that stranger who came, whoever he is,
don't believe that everything he said was true.

HELEN: But he clearly stated that my husband was dead.

CHORUS: Many things that appear true turn out to be lies.

HELEN: And the opposite, many are shown to be true.

CHORUS: You tend to misfortune, instead of considering the good that's possible.

HELEN: Fear wraps around me; it's thrown me into a state of dread.

CHORUS: In that case, how much good will do you have inside the palace?

HELEN: Everyone's friendly to me except for the hunter of marriage.

CHORUS: Do you know what you should do? Leave your seat by this tomb . . .

HELEN: What kind of story, what kind of advice are you leading up to?

CHORUS: Go into the palace, ask Theonoe, daughter of the sea Nereid,
she who knows all things,
inquire whether your husband still lives or
whether he's left this life. Once you know better about
your situation, you can have joy or grief.
But before knowing anything for sure, why would you rather
give into pains? Trust me.
Leave this tomb and consult the girl
from whom you will learn all things. Since you have someone
in these halls who can tell you the truth, why look further?
And I'll willingly go into the palace with you
to learn the maiden's prophecies together with you.
For a woman must suffer together with a woman.[33]

HELEN: Friends, I accept your advice.[34]
Go, enter the palace,

find out within the house
what trials await me.

CHORUS: You call me, and I willingly come.

HELEN: Oh sad day!
Miserable as I am, what further
tale, and cause for grief will I hear?

CHORUS: Don't prophesy pains, dear one,
don't latch onto weeping in advance.

HELEN: What has happened to my poor husband?
Does he see the sunlight,
the sun's four-horse chariot
and the paths of the stars?
Or has he gotten his earthly lot,
among the dead under ground?

CHORUS: Put better hope
into the future, which has yet to come.

HELEN: I call upon you, I swear by you,
fresh Eurotas with your marshy reeds,
if this rumor is true that my husband is dead
—and what in this is not clear?—
I will stretch a deadly noose
around my neck
or, with a quick thrust of cold steel,
I will drive the murderous sword
through my flesh, with throat-streaming slaughter,
becoming a sacrifice to the three goddesses,
and to the son of Priam who used to honor them
with his pipe song while herding his sheep.

CHORUS: I pray these evils be turned aside elsewhere,
and that you may enjoy good fortune.

HELEN: Oh, wretched Troy, the pains you suffered!
You were destroyed by a deed that was never
committed.

My gifts from Kypris gave birth to much blood
and to many tears—adding pains to pains,
tears to tears, and sufferings upon sufferings.
Mothers lost their children,
and maidens cut their hair in mourning
for brothers, corpses by the Trojan streams of the Scamander.
Greece too has cried out,
screamed and wailed,
she has beat her hands against her head,
with her nails she has wet her soft-skinned cheek
with streams of blood.[35]
Oh, blessed Kallisto, maiden once in Arcadia, you who
went away from Zeus' bed on four legs,[36]
How much better was your lot than my mother's,
for you exchanged your burden of griefs
for the shape of a bear
with shaggy limbs and a fierce look.
Blessed too was the daughter of Merops the Titan's son,
whom Artemis drove out of her girls' choral band, turning her
into a deer with golden horns, on account of her beauty.
But my body destroyed the towers of Troy,
destroyed the wretched Greeks.

[*Exeunt Helen and the Chorus into the palace. Enter Menelaos, shipwrecked, in rags, wrapped in a tattered sail.*][37]

MENELAOS: Oh Pelops, you who once rivaled Oinomaos[38]
in that famous four-horse chariot-race in Pisa,
if only you had given up your life then,
when you had trustingly become a banquet for the gods,
before you ever engendered my father Atreus,
who from his marriage to Aerope produced
Agamemnon and me, Menelaos, that famous pair.
For I believe—and I don't mean to boast—that we

launched the greatest naval military force against Troy,
commanding our armies not as a tyrant by force,
but ruling over the young men of Greece who served willingly.[39]
And we can count up those who have died
and those who gratefully escaped the dangers of the sea,
bringing back home with them the names of the dead.
But I have had to endure wandering over the waves of the grey sea
ever since we destroyed the towers of Troy.[40]
Though I long to return to my fatherland,
it seems the gods don't think I'm worthy of a homecoming.
I've sailed to every desolate, inhospitable landing-site of Libya.[41]
Whenever I approach my fatherland,
the winds drive me away again; never once has a favoring wind
filled my sails so that I could return home.
  And now, a miserable shipwreck, my companions lost,
I have been cast out onto this land, our ship shattered
against the rocks into countless bits of wreckage.
Only the keel remains of the skillfully worked ship
on which by an unexpected stroke of fortune, I managed to save myself
together with Helen, whom I dragged out from Troy.[42]
And now, I do not know the name of this land nor
what people are here. I was ashamed to go among people
and ask, concealing my misfortune
from shame at my shabbiness. When a man
of high class suffers evils, he is worse off from the unfamiliar experience
than someone who has been unfortunate for a long time.
Need is wearing me out, for we've no food
nor clothing for our bodies, as one can infer
from these remnants of the ship's sails which I've thrown around myself.
The sea seized the robes and the splendid,

shining garments I used to own.
But I have hidden my wife, the cause of all my troubles,
deep within a cave,
ordering my surviving friends to guard her.
I have come alone, seeking for my friends there,
if I might somehow find a way to get food.
When I saw this palace surrounded by smoothed-stone walls
and impressive gates of some wealthy man,
I approached. There's always the hope that seamen will get something
from wealthy homes; for those without any livelihood
couldn't give anything even if they wanted to.

[*Menelaos approaches the palace doors and knocks.*]

Hello! Is there a porter who can come out of the house
and announce the news of my misfortunes to those within?

[*An Old Woman gatekeeper enters from the house, irritable and short-tempered.*][43]

OLD WOMAN: Who's at the gates? Won't you leave this house
and quit standing by the courtyard gates,
bothering our masters? Otherwise you'll be killed,
since you're a Greek. Greeks are not welcome here.

MENELAOS: All right, all right, old woman, your words are well said.
I'll concede the point and obey you. But leave off the anger.

WOMAN: Go away. For it's my duty, stranger, to keep
any Greek from entering these halls. [*She shoves him.*][44]

MENELAOS: Hey! Keep your hands off me and quit pushing me.

WOMAN: You're not listening to what I'm telling you. It's your own fault.

MENELAOS: Just go in and tell your masters that . . .

WOMAN: I think your story will mean bad luck for the messenger.

MENELAOS: I come here as a shipwrecked foreigner, a protected class.[45]

WOMAN: Then go to another house instead of this one.

MENELAOS: No. I'm going in. And you, follow my orders.

WOMAN: You sure are offensive. You'll be thrown out by force.

MENELAOS: Alas! Where is my famous army now?

WOMAN: Well, maybe you were someone great over there, but here you aren't.

MENELAOS: Oh, gods! I don't deserve these insults!

WOMAN: Now why are your eyes filling with tears? Whose sympathy do you hope to gain?

MENELAOS: Just thinking of former, more fortunate times.

WOMAN: Well, go away then and give your tears to your friends.

MENELAOS: What land is this? Whose royal palace is this?

WOMAN: This is Proteus' home. The land is Egypt.

MENELAOS: Egypt? Oh, miserable me, where have I sailed to?

WOMAN: Why are you so critical of the pride of the Nile?

MENELAOS: I am not criticizing this place. I'm bemoaning my own fortunes.

WOMAN: Many people are badly off. You're not the only one.

MENELAOS: Well, then, your king, whatever his name is, is he at home?

WOMAN: This is his tomb. His son rules the land now.

MENELAOS: Where is he then? Is he at home or away?

WOMAN: He's not here. And he's completely belligerent to Greeks.[46]

MENELAOS: What reason does he have that I get to enjoy this benefit?

WOMAN: Helen, Zeus' daughter, is here in this house.

MENELAOS: What did you say? What story are you telling me? Repeat it to me.

WOMAN: The child of Tyndareos, who used to live in Sparta.

MENELAOS: Where did she come from? [*Aside*] What's the meaning of all this?

WOMAN: She came here from Sparta.

MENELAOS: When? [*Aside*] Surely my wife couldn't have been stolen from the cave!

WOMAN: Before the Greeks ever went to Troy, stranger.
But leave this house. For right now the situation in the house
is turning the whole palace into an uproar.
You've come at a very bad time. If the master
catches you, death will be your hospitality.
As for me, I like Greeks. My harsh words
earlier were out of fear of my master.

[*The Old Woman returns into the palace.*]

MENELAOS: What can I say? What can I possibly say?
The miseries I hear of now overwhelm former ones.
If I brought my wife here whom I captured
from Troy and who is being guarded in the cave,
then another woman lives in this palace
who has the same name as my wife.
But she also called her a child of Zeus.
Could a man living by the banks of the Nile
have the name of Zeus? There's only the one Zeus in heaven.
And where else in the world is there a Sparta except
where the streams of the Eurotas with its beautiful reeds flow?
Plainly, Tyndareos is a well-known name.
Is there another land named Sparta or Troy?
I certainly don't know what to say.
For it seems that many men on this great earth
can have the same name—as can women and cities.
There shouldn't be anything surprising in that.

So I won't run off because of a servant's threats.
For surely no barbarian is so uncivilized in his heart
that when he hears my name he won't give me some food.[47]
For the burning of Troy is well known, and so am I who
lit the fires,
Menelaos, not unknown anywhere in the whole world!
I'll wait for the ruler of the palace.
I need to be on guard for two possibilities. If he's savage,
I'll hide myself and return to the shipwreck.
But if he shows any softness, I'll ask him for
the supplies we need in the present circumstances.
This is the worst of all the sufferings I've been through—
even though I'm a king I've got to beg other rulers
for basic necessities. But I'm forced to do it.
For, it's a wise saying, not one that I made up,
that nothing is stronger than dire necessity.

[*Reenter Chorus and Helen from the palace, at first unaware of Menelaos' presence. The Chorus sing a short song before the meter returns to the trimeters of dialogue with Helen's speech.*]

CHORUS: I heard what the young prophetess
has clearly announced in the royal palace,
that Menelaos is not at all dead,
hidden in the black
darkness of the earth.
But still alive he's being worn out
on the salty sea waves
unable to reach harbor in his fatherland.
Wretched from this wanderer's life,
bereft of friends and loved ones,
he has touched shore on all kinds of land
on his sea journey
since he left Troy.

HELEN: I come to take my place again by this tomb,
hearing welcome words from Theonoe,
who knows all things truly.
She says that my husband is alive and sees the light of day.

A wanderer, he has sailed over countless passages
and has become seasoned in his wanderings here and there.
Whenever he reaches the end of his trials, he will come here.
But there's one thing she didn't say, whether he'll be safe when he comes.
I refrained from asking about this more clearly,
I was so happy when she told me he was alive.
She did say that he was somewhere close to this land
and that he was shipwrecked with a few companions.
Oh my, when will you come? How I long for you to come!

[*Helen proceeds to the tomb when she sees Menelaos, whom she does not at first recognize. For the next few lines, Helen is racing for the tomb while Menelaos tries to intercept her.*]

Help! Who's this? It must be some scheme
of that ungodly son of Proteus, stalking me!
I'll have to kick a leg like a racing filly, or the god's Bacchant,[48]
back to that tomb. He looks fierce,
as if he's hunting me as his prey.[49]

MENELAOS: [*Blocking her.*] Why this terrible rush to the tomb?
This reaching out for its base or those smoke-blackened posts?
Wait! Why are you fleeing? From the moment you showed yourself,
you have struck me dumb with amazement!

HELEN: I'm being abused, women! This man's keeping me
from reaching the tomb, and once he's captured me,
he'll hand me over to that tyrant whose marriage offers I have been avoiding.

MENELAOS: I am no kidnapper, and I am not the servant of any evildoers!

HELEN: But you're wearing an ugly garment on your body![50]

MENELAOS: Stand still! Please stop this running. Don't be afraid!

HELEN: I'll stand still, now that I've finally reached this tomb!

MENELAOS: Who *are* you? Whose face, Lady, am I looking at?

HELEN: But who are *you?* For I'm gripped by the same question.

MENELAOS: I have never seen a more remarkable likeness!

HELEN: Oh gods! For surely it's the work of the gods to recognize one's loved ones!

MENELAOS: Are you a Hellenic woman or native to this land?

HELEN: Hellenic! But I want to know your country too.

MENELAOS: So like Helen! You look so much like her, Lady.[51]

HELEN: And to me you look just like Menelaos. I don't know what to say.

MENELAOS: You have correctly recognized that most ill-fortuned man.

HELEN: Oh, come here at last to your wife's arms!

MENELAOS: What do you mean, "wife"? Don't touch my robes!

HELEN: The wife that Tyndareos, my father, once gave to you!

MENELAOS: Oh, light-bearing Hekate, send me kindlier visions![52]

HELEN: I'm not some nightly phantom sent by the Goddess of the Crossroads!

MENELAOS: Well, I'm certainly not the husband of two women!

HELEN: And just what other wife are you the master of?[53]

MENELAOS: She whom the caverns conceal! Whom I won back from the Trojans!

HELEN: You have no other wife besides me!

MENELAOS: My mind seems clear; are my eyes failing me?[54]

HELEN: When you look at me, don't you believe you are seeing your wife?

MENELAOS: Your body looks like hers, but clearly it's deceiving me.

HELEN: Look at me! What else do you need? Who is wiser than you?

MENELAOS: Well, I can't deny that you look like her.

HELEN: Who can instruct you better than your own eyes?

MENELAOS: That's just where the problem lies, since I already have a wife.

HELEN: But I never went to the Trojan land; it was an image of me.

MENELAOS: And just who fabricates living bodies?

HELEN: Ether. A handiwork of the gods, your "wife" is made of air.

MENELAOS: And which one of the gods made her? This is too much to be believed!

HELEN: Hera, as a substitute, so Paris couldn't have me.

MENELAOS: What's this? You were here, and in Troy, at the same time?

HELEN: A name can be anywhere; it's the person who cannot.

MENELAOS Just leave me alone. I came here with more than enough pain.[55]

HELEN: Will you leave me? And then go after your phantom wife?

MENELAOS: I wish you well, since you look so much like Helen.

HELEN: I am doomed. First I have you, and then I lose you, my husband.

MENELAOS: The weight of the pains I suffered in Troy are far more convincing than you.

HELEN: Oh, woe is me! Can anyone be more wretched than me?
Those dearest to me are abandoning me!
I shall never return to Greece, or see my fatherland again!

[*Enter First Messenger, Menelaos' servant.*]

1ST MESSENGER: Menelaos, I've been wandering all over this
barbarian land searching for you.
The companions you left behind sent me.

MENELAOS: What happened? Have you been robbed by some of these barbarians?

1ST MESSENGER: It's incredible! Words don't begin to describe it.

MENELAOS: Just tell me, since you're so eagerly bringing some news.

1ST MESSENGER: I'll tell you this: all the thousands of pains you suffered were in vain.

MENELAOS: You're chanting old dirges filled with sorrow—What news are you bringing?

1ST MESSENGER: Your wife's gone, poof! caught up into valleys
of thin air, hidden in the sky!
She left that sacred cave where we were guarding her.
But first she said this: "Oh, you miserable Trojans,
and all you Hellenes too, because of Hera's schemes,
you all died by the banks of the Scamander because of me,
thinking that Paris had Helen when he did not.
But as for me, since I have stayed for the time allotted,
I am going back to my father sky.
And all the terrible rumors the wretched daughter of Tyndareos
heard about herself, she wasn't even guilty!"
Oh, greetings, daughter of Leda. So you were here!
I just reported that you rose up into the depths of the stars,
and I didn't even know you could sprout wings!
Well, I won't let you mock us again.
You gave your husband and his allies
their fill of troubles in Troy.

MENELAOS: Then it's true. Everything she said,
it all fits together.—Oh, longed-for day,
that has given you back into my arms again!

[*Helen sings.*]

HELEN: Oh, Menelaos, my dearest husband, it's been such a long, long time,[56]
But now we have this perfect joy!
Dear friends, I'm delighted to have my beloved husband back again,
My arms embrace him, so dear to me after this long cycle
of the light-bearing sun.

MENELAOS: And I embrace you. I have many tales to tell of what's happened in this time,
that I don't know where to begin first.[57]

HELEN: I'm overjoyed! Like a bird rustling its wings,
the hairs on my head stand tall while my tears flow.[58]
What a joy to throw my arms around your body, oh, my husband!

MENELAOS: Oh, dearest sight, I have no fault to find,
for I'm holding my own wife, the daughter of Zeus and Leda . . .

HELEN: My brothers, the white-horse twins, blessed me long ago
when they sang the wedding songs
beneath my marriage torches.

MENELAOS: But the god who stole you away from my house
is driving us to a different fortune,
better than the one we now have.

HELEN: A lucky misfortune brought you and me back together again
after a long time, my husband. May I only be able to enjoy my fortune!

MENELAOS: May you enjoy it indeed! I join you in the same prayer.
For one member of a pair cannot be happy while the other one's miserable.

HELEN: Dear friends, dear friends,
I will no longer grieve and lament the past.
I have, I have my husband, the one I have been waiting for,
waiting so many years for him to come from Troy.

MENELAOS: You have me, just as I have you. I have passed through thousands of days
till I finally understood, and with great pains, the schemes of the goddess Hera.

HELEN: I weep for joy. My tears are filled with happiness, not with pain.

MENELAOS: What can I say? Who of mortals could ever have hoped for this?

HELEN: I hold you unexpectedly against my breast.

MENELAOS: And I hold you, when I thought you had gone to the city
by Mount Ida, to the unhappy towers of Troy.
By the gods, how did you leave my house?

HELEN: Oh no, you are stepping into a bitter beginning.
You are inquiring into a bitter tale.[59]

MENELAOS: Tell me; I've got to hear it. All things are a gift from the divinities.

HELEN: I spit the story away, such a tale I have to bring out!

MENELAOS: In any case, tell it. You know it's sweet to hear of hardships.

HELEN: I did not enter the marriage-bed of the barbarian youth,
I was not carried away by his winged oars,
nor by a lust winging for an illicit love.[60]

MENELAOS: What spirit, what fate tore you away from your fatherland?

HELEN: The son of Zeus, my husband, of Zeus and Maia,
brought me to the Nile.

MENELAOS: Amazing! Who sent him? What a strange tale!

HELEN: I've cried and cried, always wetting my eyelids
with my tears. Zeus' wife destroyed me.

MENELAOS: Hera? Why would she want to harm us?

HELEN: Oh, my terrible fate. The baths and springs
where the goddesses bathed, made their beauty bright,
where the judgment was held.

MENELAOS: What in this judgment caused Hera to beset you with evils?

HELEN: So she could rob Paris of . . .

MENELAOS: Of what? Speak![61]

HELEN: . . . me. Kypris had promised me to him.

MENELAOS: Oh, cruel goddess!

HELEN: A cruel, cruel goddess who brought me thus to Egypt!

MENELAOS: And she gave him the phantom as a substitute, you say?

HELEN: Oh, the sufferings, the sufferings within your halls, mother!
Oh me!

MENELAOS: What do you mean?

HELEN: My mother is dead. Because of me my mother hung herself,
a noose around her neck, the shame of my improper union.

MENELAOS: Oh no! And what of our daughter, Hermione? Is she still living?

HELEN: Unmarried, childless, my husband, she consumes herself grieving
for my marriage that is no marriage.

MENELAOS: Oh, Paris, you completely destroyed my whole house!

HELEN: But you thereby destroyed yourself too and thousands of bronze-armed Greeks.
A god cast me, ill-fated and cursed, out of my fatherland,
away from my city and away from you,
when I left my home and marriage-bed,
but not for a shameless marriage.

CHORUS: If your future is blessed with good fortune,
that will compensate for the events of the past.[62]

1ST MESSENGER: Menelaos, let me share your joy, which I too can perceive,
though I don't clearly understand it.[63]

MENELAOS: Of course, old man, you too must share in these tales.

1ST MESSENGER: Isn't this the woman who presided over our trials at Troy?

MENELAOS: She is not the one. We were duped by the gods;
we had only the withering image of a cloud in our hands.

1ST MESSENGER: What are you saying?
That all our sufferings were merely over a cloud?

MENELAOS: This is Hera's doing, and the strife of the three goddesses.

1ST MESSENGER: So this woman here is your real wife?

MENELAOS: She is. Take my word on it.

1ST MESSENGER: My daughter, what intricate beings the gods are,
hard to interpret. They turn things all around and upside down,
yet ingeniously make everything turn out fine. One man toils,

striving to achieve; another doesn't strive and nevertheless comes to a bad end,
having no guarantee of permanent good luck.
For instance, you and your husband have had your share of sufferings,
you because of the tales, and he from his eagerness for the spear.
For all his efforts he gained nothing. But now he has got
the greatest good fortune, and the blessings just come on their own.
And you did not shame your aged father and the Dioskouroi
since you didn't do the things told about you.
I recall your wedding day,
remembering the torches I carried as I ran along
by your four-horse chariot, which carried you,
a bride, away from your blessed home with your husband.[64]
For whoever does not revere his masters' affairs, both rejoicing
together with them and grieving with them in their sufferings, is no good.[65]
And even though I was born a slave,
I want to be counted among those noble slaves
whose minds are free even if they are not.
Better this than the double misfortunes of
having to obey everyone around because you're a slave,
and having an evil mind to boot.

MENELAOS: Come now, old man, you fought through many battles
with the shield, laboring hard with me.
So share now in my good fortune.
Go and report to the friends we left behind
how you found things here and our present good fortune.
Tell them to wait on the shore for the outcome
of the trials I'm sure still await me.
And then, if we can somehow steal her away from this land,
they must be alert so that we can join forces,
and, if possible, escape from these barbarians.

1ST MESSENGER: I will do it, my lord. But, you know, I see now
how foolish and full of lies the claims of prophets are.
There is just no sense at all in watching the burning flame
or listening to the cries of birds. And it's silly to think
that birds can help human beings.[66]
Not once did Kalchas, watching his friends,
ever say or point out to the army that they were dying for a cloud.
Neither did Helenos, whose city was destroyed for nothing.
You might say, "But that wasn't god's will."
Why then consult prophets? We should sacrifice to the gods,
asking them for blessings, and leave prophecies alone.
For they were invented as a bait for making a living,
But no one ever got rich by idly hanging around oracles.
The best prophet is common sense and good judgment.

[*Exit First Messenger.*]

CHORUS: I agree with the old man about prophets.
If you have the gods for friends,
you have the best prophet in the house.

HELEN: All right, up to now, things have gone well.
Even though there's no advantage in knowing,
nevertheless, my poor wretch, I want to know how you survived Troy.
For loved ones want to learn about the sufferings of those dear to them.

MENELAOS: You ask much of me with your one brief question.
How can I tell you of the shipwrecks in the Aegean Sea,
the false beacon fires Nauplios lit in Euboia,[67]
or the places we journeyed to: Crete, the cities of Libya,
and Perseus' lookout rock? For if I were to give you your fill
of these stories, I would suffer twice: feeling terrible pains
in telling it, suffering again what I already went through.

HELEN: Your answer is better than my question.
Tell me one thing then, leaving everything else to the side. How long
have you been wasting away, wandering over the salty back of the sea?

MENELAOS: Add to the ten years I spent at Troy
another seven circles of years.

HELEN: Oh, poor wretch! What a long time!
You were saved from there only to come here for sacrifice.

MENELAOS: What are you saying? What do you mean? You're destroying me, woman.

HELEN: Flee, leave this land as quickly as you can.
The man whose palace this is will have you killed.

MENELAOS: What have I done to merit this misfortune?

HELEN: Your unexpected arrival stands in the way of my wedding.

MENELAOS: You mean someone here wants to marry my wife?

HELEN: Yes, and he's tried to assault me. The things I've had to endure!

MENELAOS: A powerful individual or a ruler of this land?

HELEN: The one who rules this land, the son of Proteus.

MENELAOS: Now I understand the gatekeeper's riddles.

HELEN: What barbarian gates have you been standing at?

MENELAOS: These, and I was driven away from here just like a beggar.

HELEN: Surely you weren't begging for food? Oh, miserable me!

MENELAOS: That's what it was, though I didn't call it that.

HELEN: Then you know everything, it seems, about my wedding.

MENELAOS: I know. But I don't know if you have avoided his bed.

HELEN: Know that I've preserved your marriage-bed for you untouched.

MENELAOS: What guarantee do I have of this? For how sweet, if you're telling the truth!

HELEN: Do you see my wretched seat at this tomb?

MENELAOS: I see a straw mattress, poor thing. What's it for?

HELEN: I'm seeking sanctuary here from his marriage-bed.

MENELAOS: Are there no altars here, or is this a barbarian custom?

HELEN: It's saved me just like a sanctuary of the gods.

MENELAOS: Does that mean you can't sail back home with me?

HELEN: A sword, not my bed, waits for you.

MENELAOS: Then I would be the most miserable of mortals!

HELEN: Don't be ashamed, just flee this land.

MENELAOS: And leave you? I destroyed Troy for your sake!

HELEN: Better that than for my marriage to kill you.

MENELAOS: Cowardly advice, unworthy of Troy.

HELEN: Well, if you're planning to kill the king, you can't.

MENELAOS: Why, is his skin impervious to iron?

HELEN: You will see. Attempting the impossible is not a sign of intelligence.

MENELAOS: So, am I to quietly hold my hands out for binding?

HELEN: You're stuck. We need some scheme.

MENELAOS: It's sweeter to die taking action than doing nothing.

HELEN: There's only one hope that might save us.

MENELAOS: What? Bribery? Daring? Or by words?

Helen: If only the king doesn't find out that you've come.

Menelaos: Who will tell him? He won't know who I am.

Helen: He has an ally inside equal to the gods.

Menelaos: Does an oracular voice sit deep within the house?

Helen: No, but his sister does. Her name is Theonoe.

Menelaos: Quite an oracular name. Tell me what she does.

Helen: She knows everything. She will tell her brother you are here.

Menelaos: Then I'm dead, since there's no way for me to hide.

Helen: Perhaps we can persuade her with supplication.

Menelaos: To do what? What hope are you leading me to?

Helen: Not to tell her brother that you are in this land.

Menelaos: Once we persuade her, would we be able to escape from this land?

Helen: With her help, easily, but not secretly.

Menelaos: This is your task. A woman should approach a woman.

Helen: You can be sure my arms will cling to her knees in supplication.[68]

Menelaos: But what if she won't accept our words?

Helen: You will die; and wretched me, I shall be married by force.

Menelaos: You traitor! You're just using force as an excuse.

Helen: But I solemnly swore, by your head, . . .

Menelaos: What? To die? Never to change your marriage-bed?

Helen: To die by the same sword as you; I will lie next to you.

Menelaos: Swear to it by clasping my right hand.[69]

HELEN: I take it: I will leave this light on the day that you die.

MENELAOS: And I take yours: if I am robbed of you, I will end my life.

HELEN: How then should we die and receive honor for our deaths?

MENELAOS: I will kill you on the ledge of this tomb, and then kill myself.
But first, I have a great struggle to wage
over your marriage. Let the one who wants it come!
For I won't bring dishonor to my fame won at Troy,
nor will I return to Greece to receive abuse:
I am the one who robbed Thetis of Achilles;
I witnessed the suicide of Ajax, Telamon's son,
and I watched as Nestor, son of Neleus, became childless.[70]
Won't I think dying for my wife to be worth doing?
Of course I will! For if the gods are wise,
they wrap the brave man killed in battle by his enemies
lightly with earth in his grave,
but they toss the cowardly out on a hard-earth reef.[71]

CHORUS: Oh, gods, may the descendants of Tantalos finally find
blessedness and a release from their sufferings.

HELEN: Oh, I am wretched! The luck I have!
Menelaos, it's all over for us.
The prophet Theonoe is coming out of the palace;
the house creaks as the door-latches are loosened.
Flee! But what good is fleeing? Whether she's here or somewhere else,
she knows you've come here. Oh, so wretched, I'm destroyed.
You survived Troy, were saved from one barbarian land,
only to fall upon another barbarian sword here.

[*Theonoe enters from the palace, with servants bearing torches and incense burners.*]

THEONOE: You, carrying the torches' flame, lead the way before me,
purify the recesses of the air, a sacred rite,
so that I may draw the pure breath of heaven.

And you, if anyone has desecrated this path,
stepping on it with an unclean foot, strike the torch upon the ground before me,
treating it with the purifying flame, so I may pass through.
When you have rendered my service to the gods,
take the fire back to the palace hearth.
Helen, what of my oracles? How are they holding up?
Your husband Menelaos stands here visible before you,
bereft of ships and of the phantom image of you.
Oh, wretched man, the pains you have escaped to come here
and not know whether you will return home or remain here.
For an assembly of the gods is in strife concerning you
meeting beside Zeus on this very day.
Hera, who used to be ill-disposed toward you before,
is now favorable and wants to bring you back safely to your fatherland,
together with Helen, so that Hellas may learn that Alexander's marriage,
a gift from Kypris, was a false marriage with no bride.
But Kypris wants to wipe out your homecoming,
so it will not be proved that she bought the prize of
beauty with an unprofitable marriage to Helen.
The outcome rests with me, whether to destroy you as Kypris wants,
by telling my brother that you are here,
or whether to stand with Hera and save your life,
by hiding it from him, though he ordered me
to tell him if by chance your journey home brought you to this land.[72]
[*To her attendants*] One of you go and tell my brother
that this man is here so that my own safety is assured.

HELEN: Oh, maiden. As a suppliant I fall before you and embrace your knees,[73]
humbly I kneel and implore you,
for myself and for this man, whom I barely got back

and am now on the point of seeing him die.
Please don't tell your brother that this most beloved
husband of mine
has come back into my arms.
Save us, I beg you. Don't ever betray
your own sense of reverence for your brother's sake,
purchasing dishonest and unjust gratitude.
Abhorring force, god orders
all people not to acquire their possessions by theft.
[Leave the wealthy man alone even if he is unjust.][74]
For the sky is shared by all mortals,
as is the earth, on whom we must fill up our homes with
possessions,
without stealing by force and keeping someone else's
goods.[75]
For me it was both a blessing and a misery
when Hermes gave me to your father to keep safe for my
husband
who is here now and wishes to get me back.
If he's dead, how could he get me back? And how could
your father return the living to the dead?
Consider well the commands of the god and those of
your father:
would the god and your dead father
want to return another's belongings or not?
I think so. You should not give more weight
to a rash brother than to your noble father.
If you, as a prophet and believer in the gods,
destroy your father's good deed
in order to preserve your unjust brother's cause,
then it is shameful that you know all things divine,
the present and the future, but not know what's right![76]
Save me, wretched as I am, from these misfortunes
I'm engulfed in.
Grant me this extra grace of fortune.
There is no mortal alive who doesn't hate Helen.
Throughout Hellas the talk is that I betrayed my husband,
living in the gold-laden palaces of the Trojans.

But if I get back to Greece and ever step foot again in Sparta,
people will see and hear that they were destroyed by the crafts of the gods,
that I never did betray my loved ones,
and they will restore my good name once again.
I will arrange for the marriage of my daughter, whom no one wants to marry now,
and I will finally leave this bitter life of begging
to enjoy my own possessions in my own home.
If this man had died at Troy, the pyre would have consumed him,
and even though he was far away, I would have shown my love for him with my tears.
Am I now to have him snatched away from me when he's alive and safe?
No, maiden. But I beseech you again:
grant me this favor and thus emulate the ways
of your just father. For children of a good father
acquire the finest reputation if they live up to
the same good character as their parents.

CHORUS: The words you presented here are pitiful,
and you too are to be pitied. But I long to hear
what Menelaos will say in order to save his life.

MENELAOS: I cannot bring myself to fall down to your knees
and wet my eyes with tears. Such cowardice would bring
the greatest disgrace to our Trojan exploits.
And yet they say that even noble men
shed tears in times of disaster.[77]
I will not choose this form of nobility, if it is nobility,
and choose manly courage instead.
If you think it is best to save a foreign man
rightly seeking to get his wife back,
then give her back and save us both. If you do not agree,
this will not be the first of my frequent miseries;
you, however, will be shown to be a wicked woman.
But I'll say what I consider right and worthy of me,

and what will most touch your heart as well,
right here by your father's tomb.

[*Menelaos turns toward Proteus' tomb.*][78]

Oh old man, you who inhabit this marble tomb,
I present you my demand: give me my wife back,
whom Zeus sent here for you to keep safe.
I know that you will never return her to me, since you are dead,
but surely your daughter will not think it right that her father,
who is beneath the earth, and who once enjoyed the greatest renown,
be invoked to hear reproaches. For she is now empowered to act.[79]
Oh Hades of the underworld, I call on you too as an ally.
You received many bodies fallen by my sword
for Helen's sake. You have your payment.
Either return those dead alive again,
or else compel Theonoe to show herself even more righteous
than her pious father, by giving my wife back to me.

[*Menelaos turns back to Theonoe.*]

But if you and your brother rob me of my wife,
I will tell you what she omitted from her words.
You should know, maiden, that we are bound by an oath:
first, I'll meet your brother in battle,
where, in brief, either he or I must die.
But if he will not step forward to engage me bravely,
and intends to trap the two of us with starvation while we are suppliants at this tomb,
I have decided to kill her and then
thrust this two-edged sword into my own heart
here on the ledge of this tomb, where the streams of blood
will drip down the grave. Corpses, the two of us will lie
side by side on the marble tomb,
an eternal torment for you, and reproach for your father.[80]

For neither your brother nor anyone else
will marry Helen. But I will take her away with me;
if not back home, then to death.
Why am I doing this? Resorting to tears the female way
I would have been pitiful rather than a man of action.
Kill us, if that seems best to you. You will not kill our glory.
Far better though if you are persuaded by my words;
you will act justly and I will get my wife.

Chorus: It's up to you, oh young one, to arbitrate their words.[81]
Judge it so the outcome is pleasing to all of us here.

Theonoe: I am by nature a pious person, and so I want to be.
Because of my self-respect, I would not sully
my father's reputation, nor do a favor for my brother
that will bring me a dishonorable reputation.
A great sanctuary of Justice resides in my nature
which I got from my grandfather Nereus,
and I will try to preserve it, Menelaos.
So I cast the same vote as Hera,
since she wants to help you. May Kypris
be merciful to me, but we have never been in accord.
I intend to remain a maiden forever.[82]
That reproach you made to my father at the tomb,
the same words reproach me too. I would have acted unjustly
if I did not give her back. For were my father alive,
he would surely have given you back to each other.[83]
All people can expect retribution for their actions
among both the living and the dead. The mind
of the dead, even though they are no longer living,
retains a deathless awareness once it reaches the deathless ether.[84]
Therefore, to keep my recommendation brief, I will keep silent
concerning your request as suppliants, nor will I ever
become a collaborator with my brother in his folly.
For I am acting for his good even if I do not seem to be,[85]

if instead of impious I make my brother reverent.
But you yourselves must find some escape.[86]
I will stand out of the way, not interfere, and I will keep silent.
Begin with the gods: pray to Kypris
to allow you to return to your fatherland.
And pray to Hera to maintain her present good will
to you and to your husband, which will guarantee your safety home.
And you, my dead father, as long as I have the strength,
you will never become known as impious rather than pious.

[*Exit Theonoe into the palace.*]

CHORUS: The unrighteous have never fared well;
our hopes for safety rest on our acting rightly.

HELEN: Menelaos, we are safe as far as the maiden is concerned.
At this point you've got to propose your ideas
so we can devise a common escape plan.

MENELAOS: Listen, then. You've lived under this roof for a long time
and have grown familiar with the king's attendants.

HELEN: Why are you saying this? For you bring the hope
that you will do something beneficial for the two of us.

MENELAOS: Could you persuade someone in charge
of the four-horse chariots to give us one?

HELEN: I could persuade one of them. But how can we escape
not knowing our way around the plains of this barbarian land?

MENELAOS: You're right, that's not workable. How about this: what if I hide myself
in the palace and kill the king with this two-edged sword?

HELEN: His sister would not put up with it and keep silent
knowing you were about to kill her brother.

MENELAOS: But we don't even have a boat to escape in
and save ourselves. For the sea took the one we had.

HELEN: Listen, if a woman too may speak a clever word.[87]
Are you willing to be called dead in a story, even though you're not dead?[88]

MENELAOS: That might bring bad luck. But if there's anything to be gained, say it.
I'm prepared to have it said I am dead, even though I am not dead.

HELEN: Indeed, I will mourn you as women do,
with cut hair and dirges, before the impious king.

MENELAOS: But how can this be a remedy for our safety?
For it is already an old story.

HELEN: I will say that you died at sea, and ask the ruler of this land
to let me perform your burial rites over an empty grave.

MENELAOS: Suppose he agrees. Without a ship,
how can we save ourselves by this empty funeral?

HELEN: I shall command him to give me a ship, from which I can send down
adornments for your burial into the embrace of the sea.

MENELAOS: Now that's well said! Except for one thing—if he orders you
to perform the funerary rites on land, then your pretext comes to nothing.

HELEN: But I'll say that it's not the custom in Greece
to bury on land those who have died at sea.

MENELAOS: You've straightened that out. Then I will sail with you
on the same boat and help you send down the burial ornaments.

HELEN: Of course, you must be there, together with
your sailors who escaped the shipwreck.

MENELAOS: Once I get a ship at anchor,
my men, armed with swords, will stand in battle-ready order.

HELEN: It's up to you to execute everything. May we only have
favorable winds in our sail and a swift ship!

MENELAOS: So it will be, for the gods will put an end to my troubles.
But how will you say you found out that I was dead?

HELEN: From you. Say that you alone survived when you
were sailing with Atreus' son and that you saw him die.

MENELAOS: Indeed, and these tattered rags I've thrown around my body
will testify to the shipwreck.

HELEN: It did come in handy, though the loss of your clothes seemed unfortunate then.
That wretched occurrence might turn out to be a blessing.

MENELAOS: Should I go into the palace with you now,
or should I sit here quietly by the tomb?

HELEN: Wait here. For if he does anything outrageous to you,
this tomb and your own sword can save you.
I will go into the palace and cut my hair;
I'll exchange my white clothes for black,
and I'll draw my nails across my cheeks bloodying the skin.[89]
For the contest is great, and I can see the balance tipping two ways:
either I must die, if I'm caught carrying out my scheme,
or I'll save you and go home to my fatherland.
Oh, Lady, you who lie in Zeus' marriage-bed,
Hera, we are two pitiful human beings; grant us refreshing relief from our pains,
we beseech you, throwing our arms up to heaven
where you dwell within the intricate pattern of the stars.
And you, who won the prize of beauty at the cost of my marriage,

Kypris, daughter of Dione, do not destroy me.
The outrageous treatment which you inflicted on me
before was enough
when you presented my name—but not my body—to
barbarians.
Let me die, if you want to kill me,
in my fatherland. Why this insatiable desire for evils,
for devising passions, tricks, deceitful schemes,
and love charms that are deadly to the home?
If only you were moderate, for in other ways you are the
sweetest of the gods
to humankind. I do not deny it.[90]

[*Exit Helen into the palace.*]

Chorus:[91] You, deep within your leafy nests, *Strophe A*
who perch singing in your song chambers
I call out to you! Oh, sweetest singing
most melodious bird, weeping nightingale,[92]
Come, your tawny,
shimmering throat trilling,
join your voice to my lament,
as I sing of Helen's sorrowful trials
and the tearful pains of the Trojans
beneath Greek spears,
when he sped over the roaring expanse of the sea
with his barbarian oar—
the one who came, came bringing you from Sparta,
oh Helen, a bride baneful to the sons of Priam—
Paris, the deadly bridegroom,
escorted by Aphrodite.

Many Achaians breathed out their life from *Antistrophe A*
spears
and hurled stones, and now inhabit miserable
Hades,
their wretched wives have cut their hair,[93]
their homes lie brideless.
Many more Achaians went down at Nauplios'
hands,[94]

who rowed out alone and lit the fiery beacon
on Euboea's sea-girt coast,
dashing them on the Kapherian rocks
and outcroppings in the Aegean Sea
by flashing his treacherous star.
Inhospitable loomed the cliffs of Malea, when
Menelaos rushed,
blown by storm winds, far from his fatherland,
bringing on his ships the reward of a barbarian
booty
—not a reward, but strife, for the Greeks—
with the sacred image made by Hera.

What is god? What is not god? Or what lies in between?[95] *Strophe B*
Who among mortals, after searching, can claim
they found the farthest limit to this question,
when they see the affairs of the gods
leaping about here and there and back again
in contradictory, unexpected turns of fortune?
You, Helen, were born the daughter of Zeus,
for winged your father conceived
you in Leda's womb.
And yet throughout Hellas you have been
proclaimed
disloyal, faithless, unjust, and godless.
I don't think I have ever found
any story about the gods that is current
among mortals to be true.

Senseless are you who win your honor in war *Antistrophe B*
by the sharp point of the mighty spear,
foolishlessly trying
to end the pains of mortals!
For if a contest of blood will decide the issue,
strife will never depart from the cities of
humankind.

By bloody strife they won for their lot bed-chambers
in the Trojan earth,
when they could have settled with words
their rivalry over you, Helen.[96]
But now, some are gone below to Hades,
and like a lightning flash from Zeus, flames have
rushed upon the walls,
while you bear pains upon pains,
sufferings added to wretched sufferings.

[*Enter Theoklymenos from hunting, with attendants, via the right side entrance leading to the country.*]

THEOKLYMENOS: Greetings, oh tomb of my father! For I buried you
here by the gateway, Proteus, so I can address you,
and whenever I go in or out of the palace,
I, Theoklymenos, your son, greet you, father.
You, servants, take the dogs and hunting nets
inside the royal palace.
I have often reproached myself,
for I am failing to punish the wicked with death.
I have just learned that a Greek has openly
come ashore and has escaped the guards:
he must be a spy or on the hunt, aiming to steal
Helen. He's dead as soon as he's caught.
Hey now!
So I find out that everything's already been done.
For Tyndareos' child has left her seat at the tomb empty
and has already sailed away from land.
Hey, attendants, loosen the bolts, let the horses
out of their stalls, and bring out the chariots.
Not for lack of effort will the wife I aim to get
secretly escape from this land.

[*Enter Helen from the palace.*]

Wait! For I see that she is still here
in the palace. She has not fled.
You, woman! Why have you changed
from your white clothes and put on black?

Why have you put the iron blade to your head and cut off your noble hair,
and why are you weeping, wetting your cheeks with fresh tears?
Are you upset, overwhelmed by night-time dreams,
or have you heard some report from home
that's breaking your heart with grief?

HELEN: Oh, master—for at this point I already call you by this name—
I am dead. My hopes are gone and I no longer exist.

THEOKLYMENOS: What misfortune are you in? What happened?

HELEN: My Menelaos—oh, how can I say it?—has died.

THEOKLYMENOS: I do not rejoice at all at your words, though it means my good fortune.
How do you know? Did Theonoe tell you?

HELEN: She told me, and so did someone who was present when he died.

THEOKLYMENOS: Has someone come who can give a clear report of these things?

HELEN: Someone has come. May he only go there where I want him to go!

THEOKLYMENOS: Who is he? Where is he? I want to understand this clearer!

HELEN: This man who's sitting cowering at the tomb.

THEOKLYMENOS: Apollo, but he's a sight in his hideous rags![97]

HELEN: Alas, I think my husband must look like this.[98]

THEOKLYMENOS: Who is this man and where did he come from to reach this land?

HELEN: A Hellene, one of the Greeks who sailed with my husband.

THEOKLYMENOS: How does he say Menelaos died?

HELEN: In the most pitiful way, drowned in the wet waves of the sea.

THEOKLYMENOS: In what barbarian waters was he sailing?[99]

HELEN: He was cast out on the rocky, harborless coast of Libya.

THEOKLYMENOS: How come this man wasn't killed if he was sailing on the same ship?

HELEN: Sometimes the lowborn are more fortunate than the noble.

THEOKLYMENOS: Where did he leave the shipwreck when he came here?

HELEN: Where I wish he had died, and not Menelaos.

THEOKLYMENOS: Menelaos is dead. But what kind of boat did this man come in?

HELEN: Sailors chanced upon him and picked him up, he says.

THEOKLYMENOS: Where is that evil that was sent to Troy instead of you?

HELEN: You mean the image made of a cloud? It has gone into the ether.

THEOKLYMENOS: Oh, Priam and Trojan land, you were destroyed in vain!

HELEN: I too shared this disaster with the children of Priam.

THEOKLYMENOS: Did he leave your husband unburied or did he cover him with earth?

HELEN: Unburied. Oh, the evils I have to endure![100]

THEOKLYMENOS: Is this the reason you cut the locks of your golden hair?

HELEN: He is still dear to me, wherever he is.

THEOKLYMENOS: Are you really weeping for this misfortune?

HELEN: No doubt it's easy to deceive your sister?

THEOKLYMENOS: No, of course not. So, are you still making this tomb your home?

HELEN: Why do you mock me? Won't you leave the dead alone?

THEOKLYMENOS: As long as you are faithful to your husband, you'll be avoiding me.

HELEN: Not any longer. Go ahead, begin my marriage rites.

THEOKLYMENOS: It has been a long time in coming, but I'm happy nevertheless.

HELEN: Do you know what we should do? Let's forget the past.

THEOKLYMENOS: On what terms? For one favor should be given in exchange for another.

HELEN: Let's make peace and be reconciled.

THEOKLYMENOS: I let go my quarrel with you. Let it fly away.

HELEN: [*Kneeling*] Now I beg you by your knees, if you truly care for me . . .[101]

THEOKLYMENOS: What do you seek, reaching out to me like a suppliant?

HELEN: I want to perform the funeral rites for my dead husband.

THEOKLYMENOS: What's this? Is there a tomb for the missing? Will you bury a shade?

HELEN: It's a Greek custom, when someone dies at sea . . .

THEOKLYMENOS: To do what? Pelops' descendants are wise in these matters.

HELEN: To perform the burial rites in empty robes.

THEOKLYMENOS: Bury him then. Erect a mound on my land wherever you wish.

HELEN: That's not how we bury those lost at sea.

THEOKLYMENOS: How then? I am not familiar with Greek customs.

HELEN: We take all that's needed for the dead out to sea.

THEOKLYMENOS: What shall I provide you then for your dead?

HELEN: This man knows; I'm inexperienced in these things since up to now I have been fortunate.

THEOKLYMENOS: Oh, stranger, you have brought me welcome news.

MENELAOS: Well, it's not welcome for me or for the dead man.

THEOKLYMENOS: How do you bury those who died at sea?

MENELAOS: Each one according to his own means.

THEOKLYMENOS: For Helen's sake, make it as wealthy as you want.

MENELAOS: We first offer a blood sacrifice to those below the earth.

THEOKLYMENOS: Of what animal? Tell me and I'll obey.

MENELAOS: You decide. Whatever you give will be fine.

THEOKLYMENOS: Among us barbarians, the custom is a horse or a bull.

MENELAOS: As long as what you give is in no way ignoble.

THEOKLYMENOS: We do not lack for good offerings in our rich herds.

MENELAOS: And a decorated bier is carried out without a body.

THEOKLYMENOS: It shall be done. What else does custom require be supplied?

MENELAOS: Bronze weapons, for he loved spears of war.

THEOKLYMENOS: What we shall give will be worthy of the descendants of Pelops.

MENELAOS: In addition, whatever fine produce the earth brings forth.

THEOKLYMENOS: What then? Do you drop it into the waves in some way?

MENELAOS: We need a ship and men who know how to row.

THEOKLYMENOS: How far from land should the ship be?

MENELAOS: So that the splash of the oars can barely be seen from shore.

THEOKLYMENOS: Why? Is there some reason Hellas respectfully fulfills this rite?

MENELAOS: So that the waves don't wash the pollution back on land.

THEOKLYMENOS: You will have a swift Phoenician ship.

MENELAOS: That would be good, and pleasing to Menelaos.

THEOKLYMENOS: Can't you perform these rites on your own, without Helen?

MENELAOS: This is a task for the mother, or wife, or children.

THEOKLYMENOS: So it is Helen's duty, from what you say, to perform the burial rites for her husband.

MENELAOS: Out of reverence, we do not rob the dead of their due rites.

THEOKLYMENOS: All right then, let her go. My role is to nurture my wife's piety.
Go into the palace and select out the adornments for the corpse,
and I will not send you away from this land with empty hands
since you are doing this kindness for Helen. Because of the good news
you brought me, you will get clothing
in exchange for your rags and food so you can go to your fatherland,
since I see you are in a bad way.
And you, poor dear, do not waste yourself away
on endless grieving. Menelaos has met his fate,
nor will laments bring the dead to life again.

MENELAOS: [*To Helen*] This is your task, young lady. You must love
the husband who is present, and let go the one no longer living.
This is best for you in these circumstances.
If I come safely to Greece,
I will put a stop to the former slander against you,

if you become the kind of wife you should be to your husband.

HELEN: I will do it. My husband will have no cause to complain of me.
You will be close by and will know for yourself.
But, poor man, go in and bathe
and change your clothes. I will not put off
taking good care of you. For you will be more favorably inclined
to do what's necessary for my dearest Menelaos
if I do what you deserve.

[*All three exit into the palace.*]

CHORUS: Once the Mountain Mother[102] *Strophe A*
of the gods rushed on frantic, running legs
through woody groves,
through rivers and surging streams,
and through the deep-roaring waves of the sea,
longing for her missing daughter,
whose sacred name must not be spoken.[103]
Her clattering cymbals
raised a piercing din
as the goddess yoked her lion-team
to her chariot in search of her daughter
who was snatched away from
the circle-dances of the maidens.
Running with her on lightning-swift feet
came first Artemis with her bow,
then she with the grim Gorgon eye,
fully armed and brandishing her spear.[104]
But Zeus, observing clearly from his heavenly seats,
determined another outcome.

When the Mother ceased from the pains *Antistrophe A*
of her frenzied, far-ranging wanderings,
her all-out quest for her daughter seized by deceit,
she had reached the snow-covered peaks of Mount Ida,

home of the mountain nymphs,
and threw herself in her grief
beneath a snow-deep rocky thicket.
For mortals, she withered the plains of the earth,
allowed no fruit to ripen in the fields,
and she destroyed the people's young.
For the flocks, she sent forth no fresh shoots,
food of curling leaves.
Life had left the cities.
The altars of the gods received no blood sacrifices,
no unburnt cake-offerings of barley, honey, and oil.
She dried up the dewy springs,
stopped their flow of gleaming-white waters,
in vengeful grief for her child.

Strophe B

When she brought to an end feasts
for both gods and mortals,
Zeus spoke, trying to soothe the Mother's raging temper,
"Come, holy Graces,
and you too, Muses,
go and drive away her griefs,
Deo, in a rage over her maiden daughter,
with your trilling songs, hymns, and choral dances."[105]
Then first, the most beautiful of the blessed gods,
Kypris, took the bronze cymbals with their earthy voice
and the hide-covered drums.
The goddess Demeter laughed,
taking the deep-toned flute
in her hands,
delighting in its music.[106]

Antistrophe B

Neither right nor holy was[107]
that fire you burned in your chambers,
and you have incurred the wrath
of the Great Mother, my child, by not honoring

the goddess' sacrificial offerings.
Her rites have great power:
wearing the dappled fawnskin dress,
the green of the ivy wound around
  the sacred fennel stalk,
the shaking, whirling circle dance
  of the bull-roarer high in the air,
with a Bacchant's hair free for Bromios,
and the women's all-night dance rituals for the goddess,
  when the moon gleams beautifully down
over their threshing floor.[108]
But you have depended only on beauty.

[*Enter Helen from the palace.*]

HELEN: Oh, friends, we were fortunate with everything inside the palace.
Proteus' daughter helped to conceal my husband's presence here,
never telling her brother, though he questioned her in detail.
She told him he was dead, gone beneath the earth,
that he no longer sees the sun's rays, all as a favor to me.
My husband has seized upon the most beautiful good fortune.
For that armament that he was supposed to drop into the sea,
he's wearing it, his strong left arm through the shield-strap,
holding the spear in his right hand,
as if he were helping to fulfill his service for the dead.
So he's conveniently armed, dressed for battle,
as if he will set up trophies over thousands of barbarians
he will kill with his hand, once we embark on the oared ship.[109]
I changed his clothing; instead of that shipwrecked cloth,
I outfitted him, and I gave him a bath
at long last in fresh stream water.[110]

But the king is coming out of the palace, thinking he holds
a ready-made marriage to me in his hands.
I'll keep quiet. I consider you our friends in this,
and ask you too to guard your tongue.[111] If we're able
to save ourselves, we'll rescue you too one day.

[*Enter Theoklymenos from the palace, followed by Menelaos and the king's servants carrying the offerings for the sea burial.*]

THEOKLYMENOS: Men, go out in order, as our guest has arranged,
taking the sea's funeral offerings.
But you, Helen,—don't take what I'm saying in the wrong way—
listen to me and stay here. You'll perform the same rites
for your husband whether you are there or not.
For I am afraid that an overpowering desire
will persuade you to hurl your body into the sea's waves,
struck by memories of your former husband.
For even though he is not here, still you mourn him too much.

HELEN: Oh, my new husband, I am bound to honor
my first marriage-bed and my young bride's sexuality.
Because I love my husband,
I wish I could die with him. But since he is dead,
what good would it do him if I died too?
Let me go myself to give the burial gifts to the dead.
Then may the gods grant you all that I wish for you,
and to your guest here for helping out in this task.
For your kindness to Menelaos and to me,
you will have me as the kind of wife you should have in your home.
For this is certainly leading to good fortune.
So order someone to give us the ship on which we will take
these offerings, so I may fully enjoy the gift you are giving.

THEOKLYMENOS: You, go and give them a fifty-oared
Sidonian ship with rowers.

HELEN: Since this man is overseeing the funeral, will he be in charge of the ship?

THEOKLYMENOS: Of course. My sailors must obey him.

HELEN: Command them again, so they will clearly know it's from you.

THEOKLYMENOS: I'll command them a second and a third time, too, if it pleases you.

HELEN: Blessings on you, and on my plans too!

THEOKLYMENOS: Now don't melt your cheeks away with too much weeping.

HELEN: This day will show you my gratitude.

THEOKLYMENOS: The dead are nothing; don't waste your efforts.[112]

HELEN: I'm speaking of matters that concern us both here and there.

THEOKLYMENOS: In me you will have a husband no worse than Menelaos.

HELEN: I find no fault with you. I only need some good fortune.

THEOKLYMENOS: That is in your power, as long as you are well-disposed to me.

HELEN: I do not now need to learn how to cherish my loved ones.

THEOKLYMENOS: Would you like me to accompany you and direct the voyage myself?

HELEN: No, don't. Do not slave for your slaves, my lord.

THEOKLYMENOS: All right then. I'll forego these Greek rites.
My home is unpolluted,
for Menelaos did not breathe out his spirit here.
Someone go and tell my subject kings to bring

wedding gifts to my house. Let this whole land
ring out with blessed wedding songs,
celebrating Helen's and my happy marriage.
And you, oh stranger, go and give these offerings
for Helen's former husband into the sea's embrace.
Then hurry back to the palace with my wife
and join me in our wedding feast.
You may then return home or stay here and prosper.

[*Exit Theoklymenos into the palace.*]

MENELAOS: Oh, Zeus, you are called father and wise god.
Look at us and release us from our evils.
As we drag our misfortunes up a steep hill,
reach out your hand to us. If you just touch us with your fingertips,
we will reach the good fortune we want to have.
Enough of the pains that we suffered before!
I have often called upon you, gods, to hear both good things
and painful. But I cannot always be having bad luck,
and I need to walk upright. Just show me one act of grace
and you'll make me fortunate forever.

CHORUS: Oh, swift Phoenician ship from Sidon, *Strophe A*
mother of the oar's beat
dear to the surging waves,
dance leader of the beautifully dancing
dolphins, whenever
the sea is calm with gentle breezes,
and the grey-green daughter of the Sea,
Galaneia, speaks:[113]
"Spread open the sails,
and give them over to the sea winds.
Take up your pinewood oars,
oh sailors, sailors,
and bring Helen to good harbor
on the shores by Perseus' home."[114]

Antistrophe A

There, Helen, you will see
the maiden daughters of Leukippos by the swelling river;
or you might join again in the choral dances
before the temple of Pallas
or in the festivals for Hyakinthos
that last through the kindly night—[115]
competing in the discus throw,
Phoibos killed him
with the whirled disk.[116]
The son of Zeus decreed a day of sacrifices
for the Spartan land to honor the youth.
And the calf you left at home,
your child Hermione,
no pine torches have ever been lit for her wedding.

Strophe B

Oh, to be winging through the air,
like flocks of cranes
flying over Libya,
who left behind winter storms
following the trumpet sound
of their eldest,
the shrill cry of their leader as he flies over the waterless plains
and the fruit-bearing fields of the earth.
Oh, you long-necked, winged birds,
partners in the clouds' races,
fly beneath the Pleiades and
Orion standing in the middle of the night sky,
and sitting upon the banks of the Eurotas
announce the news
that Menelaos has taken the city of Troy
and that he is coming home.

Antistrophe B

Come swiftly through the air
on your speeding horses
under the whirlings of the bright stars,
sons of Tyndareos,
who dwell in the sky,

come, saviors of Helen,
go out upon the grey-green swell
of the deep, the dark-blue waves
and the grey foam of the sea,
and send the sailors
favorable winds from Zeus.
Push the false report of a barbarian marriage-bed
away from your sister,
which she got as a punishment
for the strife on Mount Ida,
though she never went to the land of Troy,
to the towers of Phoibos.[117]

[*Enter the Second Messenger, a servant of Theoklymenos, from the direction of the sea, and shortly after, Theoklymenos from the palace.*][118]

2ND MESSENGER: Oh, lord, I've found out the worst news for your house,
you'll hear about these strange new ills from me right away.

THEOKLYMENOS: What is it?

2ND MESSENGER: Work on finding another woman to marry.
For Helen has left the land.

THEOKLYMENOS: Did she sprout wings or walk away by foot?

2ND MESSENGER: Menelaos has sailed away with her.
He's the same one who came reporting his own death.

THEOKLYMENOS: Oh, this is terrible news. What ship took her away
from this land? Your story is unbelievable!

2ND MESSENGER: So you may know in a few words, she took off on the one
you yourself gave the stranger, and taking your own sailors along.

THEOKLYMENOS: How? I'm eager to know. For it's beyond belief
that a single arm could overrun
so many sailors as you had set off with.

2ND MESSENGER: When she left this royal palace,
Zeus' daughter was escorted to the sea.

She stepped forward daintily, and with great cunning she grieved
for her husband who was right there and not dead.
When we reached your shipyards,
we hauled down a brand-new, Sidonian ship
with fifty oars and rowing benches,
and we performed our jobs in order.
One raised the mast, others got their oars ready;
another set up the white sails,
while the rudders were lowered by their guiding-ropes.
While we were engaged in all this work, observing this,
some Greek men who had sailed with Menelaos
approached us on the shore dressed in shipwrecked clothing,
fine-looking men, but filthy to look at.
Seeing them here, Atreus' son
addressed them with cunning pity for our benefit.
"Oh, wretched men, was it a Greek ship
you came on? How did you wreck it?
But help us bury the dead son of Atreus, even though he's not here,
Helen here, Tyndareos' daughter, is giving him an empty burial."
Shedding some false actor's tears,
they came on board ship with the sea-gifts for
Menelaos. We were suspicious
and were talking among ourselves about the number
of extra passengers. But we kept quiet,
obeying your orders. For you gave the command
that the stranger be in charge of the ship, thus bringing all this on.
Since they were light, we easily loaded
the rest of the offerings on board, but the bull balked,
refusing to set foot upon the steep gangplank.[119]
Instead he bellowed out loud, rolled his eyes in a circle,
arched his back, and looked askance at his horns
to keep anyone from touching him. Helen's husband
commanded, "Hey, you destroyers of the city of Troy,

hoist that bull on your strong
young shoulders the Greek way
and hurl him into the prow; with drawn sword
you will force him to be our sacrifice for the dead man."
Following his orders, his men raised up the bull,
carried it and set it down in the ship.
And Menelaos stroked its neck and forehead
and persuaded it to go into the hold.
  Finally, when everything was aboard ship,
with her dainty feet Helen climbed up every rung of the ladder
and she sat down in the middle of the quarter deck,
while the one reported to be dead, Menelaos, sat next to her.
The rest of the Greeks sat equally along the right and left sides of the ship,
arranged one man by the next with their swords
hidden under their cloaks, while the waves were filled
with our shout as we responded to the boatswain's calls.
  When we had gone out not too far away from land,
but not too close either, our steersman asked,
"Oh, stranger, do we still sail further, or is this good enough?
For you're in command of the ship."
And he answered, "Far enough for me." Then he took his sword in his right hand
and proceeded to the prow standing ready to sacrifice the bull.
And with no mention of anyone dead,
he cut the bull's throat and prayed: "Oh, you who inhabit the deep,
Poseidon, god of the sea, and holy daughters of Nereus,
rescue me and my wife and bring us
unharmed to the coast of Nauplia," and the streams of blood
spurted with good omen for the stranger into the sea.
Then one of us said, "This trip is a trick.
Let's sail back. You, command the rowers to the right

and you, turn the rudder." From where he stood after killing the bull,
the son of Atreus called out to his fighting men,
"What are you waiting for, oh flower of the land of Greece?
Slaughter and kill these barbarians, and throw them off the ship
into the sea." Then the boatswain
shouted out to your sailors to resist,
"Come on, grab the end of a spar,
break up the seats, and wrench the oars from their pins,
make the heads of these hostile strangers run with blood."
Everyone sprang up, some with the ship's planks
in their hands, others with swords.
The ship ran with blood, while Helen cheered
them on from the stern: "Where is your Trojan glory?
Prove it against these barbarians!" In the heat of battle,
some men fell, others stood, and you could see
the dead lying around. Menelaos was in armor,
and wherever he saw his companions in trouble,
that's where he attacked, his sword in his right hand,
so that we jumped ship and the benches
were cleared of your sailors. Then he approached the helmsman
and told him to set the barque straight for Greece.
They raised the sail and favoring winds arrived.
And so, they're gone from this land. I escaped death
by lowering myself into the water by the anchor.
A fisherman picked me up half dead
and brought me to shore
so I could give you this message. Nothing is more useful
for mortals than a prudent distrust.

[*Exit Messenger.*]

CHORUS: I never would have believed, my lord, that Menelaos could have been here
without you or me knowing it, as he just was.

THEOKLYMENOS: Oh, my miserable self, I've been snared by women's designs.
My marriage has fled from me, and if that ship could be caught by pursuit,
I would exert myself and quickly seize the foreign guests.
As it is, I'll punish the sister who betrayed me,
who saw that Menelaos was in the palace and didn't tell me.
Well, she'll never deceive another man with her prophecies!

CHORUS:[120] Oh, you, oh—where are you heading—oh, my master—to what murderous act?

THEOKLYMENOS: Where the right commands me. Stand out of my way.

CHORUS: I won't let go of your robes. You're rushing into a terrible evil.

THEOKLYMENOS: Are you going to rule the master, you who are a slave?

CHORUS: I'm thinking of your good.

THEOKLYMENOS: Not mine, you're not; if you don't let me

CHORUS: No, we won't let you.

THEOKLYMENOS: . . . kill my evil sister . . .

CHORUS: Just the opposite, she's the most reverent.

THEOKLYMENOS: . . . who betrayed me . . .

CHORUS: Then it was a fine betrayal, since she acted rightly.

THEOKLYMENOS: . . . by giving my wife to another.

CHORUS: to the one who has more right than you.

THEOKLYMENOS: Who has a right to my things?

CHORUS: The one who received her from her father.

THEOKLYMENOS: But fortune gave her to me.

CHORUS: And necessity took her away.

THEOKLYMENOS: You have no right to judge me!

CHORUS: Only if I have something better to say.

THEOKLYMENOS: Then I'm being ruled, not the one with power!

CHORUS: Yes, to do the right and holy thing, not the unjust.

THEOKLYMENOS: You long to die I think.

CHORUS: Kill me. But you won't kill
your sister as long as I can do something about it. But kill me, since for noble slaves
to die for their masters brings the most glorious name.[121]

[*Enter Dioskouroi, from above.*]

DIOSKOUROI: Restrain your anger, for you do not rightly bear it against her,
Theoklymenos, lord of this land. We, the twins,
the Dioskouroi, call you; Leda gave birth to us
and to Helen, the one who has just fled your palace.
You rage over a marriage not meant to be,
nor does the daughter of the Nereid goddess,
your sister Theonoe, wrong you, when she honors
the ways of the gods and the just commands of her father.
It was necessary for Helen to live
in your palace until the present time,
but once Troy's foundations were uprooted,
the reason she had lent her name to the gods, it was no longer needed.
She must be reunited in her own marriage,

to return home and live together with her husband.
Keep your dark sword away from your sister
and realize that she acted wisely in this.
We would have rescued our sister a long time before now,
once Zeus had made us gods,
but we were less powerful than destiny
and the gods, who determined that this is how things would be.[122]
These things I say to you, and to my sister I say,
sail with your husband, you will have favoring winds.
We, your twin savior brothers,
will ride along over the sea and bring you home.
And when you reach the end of your life's course,
you will be called a goddess and will share
with us in the libations we receive from people
at the hospitality feasts of the Xenia.[123] For thus does Zeus will it.
And where Maia's child made the first stop
along your journey through the air, after he had lifted you off from Sparta,
stealing you away so Paris could not marry you
—I mean that island stretched out like a watchguard along the Attic coast—
"Helen" it will be called from now on by mortals,
because it received you after your abduction from home.[124]
And for the wandering Menelaos, the gods
have decreed that he should live on the Isle of the Blessed.
For the gods do not hate the well-born,
who have more trials than the countless many.

THEOKLYMENOS: Oh, sons of Leda and Zeus, I'll let go
my earlier quarrels over your sister,
and I will no longer try to kill my sister.
Let Helen go home, if so the gods decree.
Know that you are born of the same blood
as the best and most virtuous sister.
Go, rejoicing in Helen's most noble character,
which is not found in many women.

[*Exeunt Theoklymenos and Dioskouroi.*]

CHORUS: Divine beings take many shapes,
and the gods accomplish many things beyond our expectations:
what we thought is not fulfilled,
but god finds a way for what no one considered.
So ends this story.[125]

IPHIGENIA AT AULIS

Translated and with an Introduction by

Mary-Kay Gamel

I. INTRODUCTION

a wicked pleasure
hangs over war
the voluptuousness of blood
like a red storm-sail over a black man-of-war.
Your feelings blossom in the surging of the blood.
The blood surges through your body
and through their bodies
like torrents tumbling together in a snow-thaw,
like a long-postponed night of love
but this night more passionate
and more furious
the blood bubbling in our hearts like fire

—Charles L. Mee, Jr., *The Bacchae*

Near the end of *Iphigenia at Aulis,* Iphigenia has offered herself as a sacrificial victim in order that the Greek expedition against Troy can proceed. The actor playing Iphigenia goes offstage toward the Greek camp, where the sacrifice is to take place, while the Chorus sing her praises. The play seems to be over. Suddenly a messenger arrives from the Greek camp. He describes how, at the moment the knife struck, Iphigenia vanished and a deer lay on the altar. The Greek leaders and the messenger himself interpret this as a sign of divine favor toward Iphigenia, Agamemnon, and the Greek war effort, and the Chorus rejoice at the news. Only Iphigenia's mother, Klytemnestra, remains doubtful, suspecting that this whole story is a lie (1615–18).

The reactions of the characters onstage to the events they have just been through suggest the radically different ways this play can be interpreted. *IA* raises questions about the value of an individual life, and under what circumstances that life can be taken. Is the play's central event, the sacrifice of Iphigenia, a pointless waste, or a sad necessity? Is the war for which she is willing to die a just cause, or a petty quarrel between individuals? Is her decision to offer herself an act of heroic patriotism? Acceptance of the inevitable? A sign of delusion, even madness?

As Iphigenia announces her decision to sacrifice herself, she invokes several hierarchies of value important to Greek ideology. Human beings must obey the will of the gods (1395–96). The community is more important than the individual (1386). Greeks must prevail over barbarians (1400) as free men do over slaves (1401), and males are more valuable than females (1394). Death in defense of these values is glorious and brings everlasting fame (1398–99). These issues, and the social, political, and religious institutions that underlay them, were being hotly debated in the tense atmosphere in which *IA* was first produced in 406 or 405 BCE. The Peloponnesian War had been going on for twenty-five years, and was soon to end with the defeat of Athens (above, pp. 8–9). For *IA* and the other plays produced with it (including *Bacchants*) the judges awarded Euripides the first prize in the dramatic competition. It was only the fifth first prize of his fifty-year career as a playwright. But he knew nothing about it. Before the play was produced he had died in Macedonia, far from Athens.

I. Iphigenia in Story, Cult, and Ritual

I. The myth of Iphigenia. The events at Aulis are part of a much larger story (*muthos* in Greek, from which comes the word "myth"), of which there were many accounts. Some of these versions have survived as literary texts (epic and tragedy), others we know only by report, and no doubt there were oral traditions as well. In addition, scenes from this story were painted on Greek pottery, and Iphigenia was an important figure in certain religious cults. The Athenian audience was probably quite familiar with this story, and characters in the play allude to various events in it. But it has many variants, and we cannot know which ones members of the audience would have known.

The principal events of the larger story: At the wedding of the goddess Thetis and the mortal Peleus, the goddess Strife (*Eris*) threw a golden apple with the words "for the most beautiful" among the wedding guests. Three goddesses reached for it—Hera, Athena, and Aphrodite. Unable to resolve the dispute, they appeared to a handsome young man herding his flocks near Troy, a city near the entrance to the Hellespont in Asia Minor (see map). This was Paris, son of Priam, king of Troy. He was a shepherd because his mother Hekabe, while pregnant with him, had dreamed that she carried a firebrand in her womb. So his father, King Priam, had the newborn infant taken to nearby Mount Ida and left to die. This was a way to avoid the pollution involved in actually killing a blood relative, but like Oedipus, Moses, and other legendary heroes he was saved from premature death. When the goddesses appeared to Paris, each promised him a gift if he chose her as most beautiful. Hera offered political power and Athena wisdom, but Aphrodite promised him the most beautiful woman in the world as his wife—Helen of Sparta, wife of Menelaos. Paris chose Aphrodite, went to Sparta, and Helen and he sailed back to Troy (where he had now been recognized as the king's son). A force from all over Greece was organized under the leadership of Agamemnon, Menelaos' older brother, in order to take revenge on the Trojans. They gathered near Aulis, a town on the shore of Boeotia looking across to Chalkis in Euboea (see map). But the fleet was prevented from sailing by unfavorable weather. A seer named Kalkhas announced that if the expedition were to proceed the goddess Artemis required the sacrifice of Iphigenia, eldest daughter of Agamemnon and Klytemnestra.

Euripides' play begins at the point when Agamemnon has summoned his daughter from home under the pretext that she is to marry Achilles, a prince who is part of the Greek force, famous in the *Iliad* as the mightiest Greek warrior. After impediments caused by Agamemnon's doubts and the resistance of Klytemnestra, Achilles, and Iphigenia, the sacrifice takes place, and at the end of the play the army is preparing to leave for Troy. The *Iliad, Odyssey,* and other sources recount how after ten years of war the Greeks captured and destroyed Troy. Meanwhile Klytemnestra took as a lover his cousin Aigisthos, who hated Agamemnon as a result of an ancestral feud. Agamemnon returned home to Argos and was killed by Klytemnestra and Aigisthos. Later Orestes, Agamemnon, and Klytemnestra's only son, avenged his father's death by killing his mother and Aigisthos.

II. War and sacrifice. Sacrifices (above, pp. 12–13) were performed at important transitions both public and private, such as marriages, funerals, the swearing of oaths, and the making of treaties. In warfare, sacrifices were performed before departure, before crossing borders including rivers and the sea, and immediately before battle. Warfare shares many characteristics of the hunt: aggression directed at an Other, the need for bonding and cooperation among the warriors, the danger that death will spread beyond acceptable limits. The sacrifice before battle was sometimes called the "preamble" (*proteleia*) to combat; the only definite historical example of such a sacrifice was made to Artemis (M. Jameson 1991: 209–12), and may reflect her care for young males making the transition from adolescence to manhood (above, pp. 54–5). As *parthenoi* become *gunai* ready for marriage, young men (*neoi*) become men (*andres*) when they are ready to engage in warfare (Vernant 1991: 244–57). For all warriors the aggression involved in warfare, like that of the hunt, needs rules, clear distinctions, and calm on the part of the warriors. Otherwise it can easily become disordered, so that warriors fail to discriminate between comrades and enemies, flee in confusion, or engage in wild butchery (Hanson 1989: 185–93). Sacrifice, which provided a calm, ordered form for violence, offered a model for the warriors' conduct on the battlefield: "men at the threshold of hand-to-hand combat sought unusual ritual remedies in an effort to cope with extraordinary psychological strain, and with the threat to their lives" (Henrichs 1980: 216).

There is virtually no *historical* evidence for the practice of human sacrifice in Greece (M. Jameson 1991: 213–17). There are a number of Greek *stories,* however, in which a human maiden dies. This death, almost always associated with warfare, is often voluntary self-sacrifice (Burkert 1983: 65; Larson 1995: 101–10).[1] War requires warriors to leave home, abandoning the claims of the *oikos* and family life, production and reproduction. They must engage in the destruction of life, which may take their lives as well. The sacrifice of a virgin, then, can symbolize the renunciation of marriage, sexual activity, and reproduction which the warriors are making. As a victim of the *proteleia* before war, a *parthenos* represents in a more extreme form the vulnerability of the young warriors, drawing attention to the magnitude of the transition they are making. A marriageable maiden is also a potential source of conflict, as the story about the rivalry between males caused by the desirable maiden Helen shows (*IA* 51–57). In that case the suitors' oath turned their rivalry into solidarity (*IA* 58–65); similarly, a sacrifice that eliminates such a source of conflict can unite the band of warriors.

III. IA *as* proteleia, *initiation, marriage. IA* draws upon important elements of the Greek socio-religious system described above. The occasion is the opening of war. The war cannot proceed without the *proteleia* of a victim to Artemis. The community desires the war. The sacrificial *parthenos* causes numerous conflicts between members of the army which threaten to undermine the war effort. Once the sacrifice is determined, however, the last man to oppose it, Achilles, takes his place among the warriors, speaking for the army as a whole (1572–76). After the sacrifice Kalkhas urges the army to act as one (1598–1601). The completion of the sacrifice is the beginning of the war (1624).

The process leading up to the sacrifice is depicted as a rite of passage whereby Iphigenia is transformed from child to adult. (On rites of passage and Artemis, see above, pp. 54–5.) She first enters as a shy girl, who has to be urged to play her proper role in public ceremonies (613–16, 627–30), who wants to run inside when

Achilles appears (1340–42). To her Agamemnon is just "Daddy"; all she understands about his public responsibilities as king and leader of the army is that they keep him from her and make him sad (644–63). When she first learns of her father's plan to sacrifice her, Iphigenia pleads with him to spare her, calling the reason for the expedition a private matter, "the marriage of Helen and Paris" which doesn't concern her (1236–37). She prefers to live, even as a coward, than to die nobly (1252)—an explicit rejection of the code of conduct established for aristocratic males.[2] But when she offers herself for sacrifice (1368–1401) she speaks so differently that Aristotle criticized Euripides for the inconsistency of her character (*Poetics* 1454a). No longer is she a child who belongs to a family, a private individual focused on emotional connections. Now she speaks as an adult, a member of the citizen body, a Greek who shares the concerns of other Greeks. Instead of thinking of herself, she focuses on others—Achilles, other members of the army, all Greeks. Now she sees the cause of the war not as a private matter, but as theft of a Greek woman by a barbarian (1380–82), a public issue, an offense to the fatherland which will be repeated by unless the perpetrators are punished as they deserve (1380–82).

The actual sacrifice includes all the formal requirements for a sacrificial rite. The victim designated by the goddess is unblemished and special. She is garlanded (1477–78, 1512, 1567), accompanied by a procession to the altar (1462–63), sprinkled with water (1479, 1513), honored in song (1510–20), the object of public admiration (1561–62). By both words and actions she shows that she offers herself willingly (1397, 1555, 1559–60). The victim receives the death blow (1582) and blood spills on the altar (1587, 1589). The sacrifice is successful: The Greeks are granted their request to go to Troy (1596–97), while the victim is said to receive divine favor (1596), even apotheosis (1622).

Euripides' drama emphasizes the similarities between Iphigenia's sacrifice and marriage. The word *proteleia* can also mean "the sacrifice before marriage" (433, 718, 1310). Iphigenia is brought to the camp thinking she will be married to Achilles, and the procession that brings her includes her mother in the traditional role of *numphagōgos* ("bringer of the bride," 610), but her father has the right to give her away. Both rites include garlands (436, 905–06), 1477–78, 1512), music (437–39, 1036–48, 1467–68), fire (732, 1470–71, 1601–2), and feasting (720, 722–23, 1049–53). Iphigenia's bridegroom is not a mortal man, but either the personification of Death (461) or Greece (1396). The marriage will be productive; its "children" will be the destruction of Troy (1399).

Iphigenia seems to fulfill the paradigm of an ideal Greek woman, one who knows what is expected of her and does it. Accepting her lesser importance, she bows to her father's will, refusing to blame him for her death (1456), rejecting her mother's attempts to save her, to accompany her to the altar, even to mourn for her (1437–47), and attempting to calm her mother's anger at her husband (1454). She depicts herself as "good woman" who chooses to support males and their values, who keeps men alive, against "bad woman" Helen who chooses to undermine male values and gets men killed (1393, 1417–19). Iphigenia's action resolves the crisis in terms of character (Agamemnon changes from anguished, indecisive father to resolute leader), plot (the stalled expedition gets under way), and meaning (individual, domestic needs marked as feminine yield to the masculine requirements of the state). Finally, the story of the miraculous substitution indicates divine favor for Iphigenia and the expedition. The salvation reported by the messenger seems to be Iphigenia's reward for her virtuous action. As members of the Athenian audience would have known, in various locations Iphigenia received cult honors as a heroine, even a goddess (Lyons 1997: 137–57). The miracle is also a reassurance that Iphigenia's death was only symbolic after all: Instead of dying, she only "played the bear" (see above, p. 55). On the narrative level, the possibility of a radical variation (Iphigenia is saved by Agamemnon or Achilles; the war does not take place) yields to the traditional conclusion of the story (she is sacrificed; the war proceeds). Viewed in this way, the ending of this play may suggest that underneath the chaotic surface of events, deep patterns of action are moving towards the proper conclusion, guided by higher powers even without the human participants' participation or understanding.

The ending of this play, then, seems to resolve all tensions—artistic, sociocultural, and religious—in favor of traditional values. This conclusion can be evaluated positively, with Iphigenia a savior who restores the social order and reestablishes proper contact with the gods through a "politics of love" (Foley 1985: 91, 102). The only character onstage at the finale who refuses to accept this resolution, Klytemnestra, may appear to be a woman for whom only domestic affairs matter, whose vision remains narrow (like Iphigenia's at first), who cannot see the issues from a civic or cosmic point of view. Her lack of understanding will result in unnecessary death for Agamemnon and herself, and unnecessary suffering for Orestes. Alternatively, the conclusion of the play can be read negatively, with Iphigenia persuaded into willingly serving the traditional (though "outworn") ideals of a masculine order that keeps her and other women subordinated and manipulated in male struggles for power (Rabinowitz 1993: 38–54). Still another alternative is to see the ending not as resolving but maintaining these tensions, provoking the audience to thought and discussion (see above, pp. 77–80).

II. Euripides' IA *as a Text*

The kind of structural analysis used in the preceding section considers individual documents in terms of large patterns, focusing particularly on the movement from conflict to resolution. Such a movement has been seen as basic to mythical thought, which "always progresses from the awareness of oppositions towards their resolution. . . . The purpose of myth is to provide a logical model capable of overcoming a contradiction" (Lévi-Strauss 1963 [1967]: 221, 226). Such a *structural* approach is not concerned with *particular* moments in texts, or with *contradictions* within the text including discontinuities of various sorts, or with their *effect* in their immediate (historical, performative) context. Similarly, ritual can be seen as aiming to minimize and to regularize uncertainties, contradictions, and discontinuities, to organize into clear categories, to encourage participants to act without thinking. But tragedy is not ritual (above, p. 33). Tragedy draws on traditional stories (*muthoi*) but presents them to an audience in a *particular* form, in a special location, at a specific moment in time. And tragedy does not necessarily resolve contradictions. In *IA* the clear categories invoked by Iphigenia become blurred and their ranking becomes questioned.

1. Gods and human beings. Artemis has not made an *absolute* demand for Iphigenia's life. Instead, as often with Greek prophecies and oracles, a *choice* is involved: *If* the expedition to Troy is abandoned, Iphigenia can be saved. This puts the burden on Agamemnon in his double role as father and leader of the expedition. He must choose between his role as leader of the Greeks and his role as head of his family, between his public responsibilities and the obligations of *philia* (see above, pp. 20–22). This is the kind of ethical and emotional conflict Aristotle describes as arousing the responses proper to tragedy, pity and fear (Poetics 1453b). In Aeschylus' play *Agamemnon,* produced in 458 and probably reperformed within ten years of *IA*, Kalkhas' announcement that Artemis is angry at Agamemnon and Menelaos is quoted at length (126–55). Aeschylus' Agamemnon makes a conscious choice that the sacrifice is the lesser of two evils (211–17, alluded to at *IA* 1257–58):

> Which of these choices is without dreadful consequences?
> How can I become a deserter,
> abandon the alliance?
> Rage for sacrifice to stop the winds,
> for a maiden's blood,

with tremendous rage they desire it . . .
it is right! May this go well.

In *Kypria,* a poem in the "Epic Cycle" composed after the Homeric poems to fill in the gaps left in Homeric accounts of the Trojan War, reasons are given for the goddess's demand. There, after the army had gathered at Aulis, Agamemnon offended Artemis by killing a deer (perhaps a sacred deer) and boasting that he was a better hunter than the goddess. In still another version of the story Agamemnon vowed to sacrifice to Artemis the most beautiful thing born in the year Iphigenia was born, but failed to keep his vow (*Iphigenia Among the Taurians* 20–24).

In both these versions Artemis' blocking of the voyage is presented as punishment for Agamemnon. In *IA* there is no mention of any offense against Artemis; this focuses attention directly on the *human* participants' motives and actions as they respond to the question whether the war is worth this sacrifice. Little attention is paid to the religious dimension of the problem. Agamemnon implies that Kalkhas is manipulating the unfavorable weather conditions to his advantage (88–92). Even the Old Man inserts "so Kalkhas says" when revealing Agamemnon's plans to Klytemnestra (879). Agamemnon frequently refers to the sacrifice not with ritual terms such as *thuein* ("ritually slaughter") but with secular terms for "murder" (364, 396, 463, 512). Even when urging Agamemnon to go through with the sacrifice (334–75) Menelaos makes no reference to obeying the goddess's commands.

Artemis and the gods shift in their meanings according to the intention of the speaker. Agamemnon declares the suitors' oath invalid even though it was taken in the gods' name, and even insists that the gods agree with him (394–95). He, Menelaos, and Achilles all express contempt for prophets and their prophecies (520–21, 955–58). The Old Man calls the sacrifice "a dreadful deed" (887), and even after Iphigenia dedicates herself to Artemis the Chorus directly criticize the goddess as "sick" (1403). The first time Agamemnon invokes the decrees of the goddess is when he tells Iphigenia he has no choice (1268). And it is only once she has decided to die that Iphigenia sees herself as selected by Artemis (1395–96), praises the goddess (1480–83), and insists that others join in the praise (1467–68, 1491–92). But no one directly suggests that either the goddess or her demand is a fiction, or dismisses them as unimportant. Nor is the goddess's demand necessarily inexplicable and cruel: "there is a kind of sane justice in making the leaders take one more look at the perversion of public and private that the war demands" (Luschnig 1988: 113).

2. Household and state affairs. IA draws upon the strong distinction in Athenian ideology between *to koinon,* (literally "what is shared") and *to oikeion,* "household affairs" (above, pp. 49–50). Warfare seems especially far from domestic life, since it takes males away from home, women, children, and domestic life, joining nonrelated men in dedication to a common cause. Agamemnon and Klytemnestra both refer to the separation between public and private when he tries to get her out of the army camp (731) and when she insists on her right to rule the home (740–41).

But private, domestic issues have led to this war. It is the result of an individual man's being publicly shamed by his wife (77–79). The army includes warriors from many Greek states, but those warriors are present because they wanted that same woman. Agamemnon leads the expedition as older brother (hence head of the family) of the shamed man (84–85). For the first three-quarters of the play only Menelaos suggests that there is a public issue involved, and he does so by insisting that Greece shares his shame (370–72, 410). So long as Agamemnon puts his concern for his family (*philoi*) ahead of his duties as commander of the expedition, he sees his brother's true motive as personal—to get Helen back (386), and calls the Greeks "stupid" for wanting to pursue the war (394). Only much later, when trying to convince Iphigenia, does he declare that the war is in the interest of all of Greece (1273). Private need becomes public cause.

The male head of household moved between the private and public realms, fulfilling his public duties while protecting his property and *philoi.* But when Agamemnon uses Iphigenia to advance his military aims, he confuses the two realms. His *oikos* literally arrives onstage when Klytemnestra moves into his tent with their children. Agamemnon still tries to maintain control, saying it's inappropriate for his wife to be mixed up in a crowd of soldiers (735). But he does not behave as a *philos* (family member) toward Iphigenia and Klytemnestra, but as an *ekhthros* (personal enemy), even a *polemios* (military enemy). When she discovers Agamemnon's plan to kill Iphigenia, Klytemnestra turns to a man outside the family for help—just as she will later turn to Aigisthos. The mixing of the two realms in this play suggests their interdependency in Athenian life (see above, p. 53). It also shows that Agamemnon's roles as general and as head of *oikos* and army affect each other, and his performance of these roles is similarly incompetent.

3. Greeks and barbarians. Greeks characterized as "barbarian" a variety of characteristics and behaviors on the margins of what they considered civilized (see above, pp. 22–3 and 153–4). In *IA* the "barbarian" Paris is characterized in directly opposite ways. He is introduced as decadent—rich, overdressed, luxury-loving, effeminate, lustful (73–75)—but two lines later he is a country hick going back to his "cowbarns" (77) where he "tunelessly tootles" on his rustic panpipe (574–79). More striking in this play are the instances in which Greeks behave in ways considered typically barbarian. The Greek army is violent, out of control, lawless, driven by lust (808, 1265). Agamemnon is unstable, changes his mind constantly, attempts to deceive Menelaos, Klytemnestra, and Iphigenia, frequently gives in to tears, at times seems on the verge of madness.[3] Scared of the army (1012), he is only nominally its leader, instead is ruled by it (514). Most strikingly, in taking Klytemnestra from her first husband, Agamemnon has done what Paris did—only worse, because he killed the man and their child (1148–52; Luschnig 1988: 117). The oath Helen's suitors took obliged them to punish anyone who stole her, "Greek or barbarian" (65), so if Paris had been Greek the army would now be preparing to attack a Greek city (Luschnig 1988: 39). Within two lines Agamemnon speaks of barbarians stealing Greek wives (1266), and Greeks invading Argos and killing Iphigenia, Klytemnestra, and his other daughters (1267–68). Neither Menelaos nor Agamemnon can control their wives (383, 739–45). The result of the insistence that Greeks must not have their women taken from them by barbarians (1275) may be that they themselves must kill those women.

Yet the practice of human sacrifice is the ultimate sign of barbarism (Hall 1989: 145–48). In Euripides' *Iphigenia Among the Taurians,* produced some ten years before *IA,* Iphigenia has been rescued from the altar and is living among a barbarian people who practice human sacrifice (to Artemis!). This practice is repeatedly denigrated by the Greek characters, and at play's end an image of the goddess is transferred to Greece, where Artemis will be honored with a rite *imitating* human sacrifice (*IT* 1446–61). In *IA* the Chorus sing that the sacrifice of Iphigenia by Greeks means that there is no longer *any* civilized place on earth where self-restraint, law, and religion rule (1089–97).

4. Free people and slaves. To Iphigenia the most important difference between Greeks and barbarians is that Greeks are free (1400–1). Yet the characters in this play are under various yokes. Some are constrained by accepted standards of behavior, as when Agamemnon says that aristocrats are slaves to their public dignity (450) and Achilles worries what others will think (998–1001). Some are subject to others' authority, as Klytemnestra and Iphigenia are to Agamemnon. Klytemnestra is willing to humiliate herself by supplicating (899), even enslaving herself (1033) to Achilles to get him to help her. Agamemnon especially is enslaved by his own needs, fantasies, and fears; he sees himself without power of choice, as others make demands on him which he thinks he has no power to refuse. In the very process of declaring that Greece must be free Agamemnon calls himself the slave of Greece (1269–75).

Paradoxically, the only actual slave in the play is free enough to tell Agamemnon to stop whining (28–33), to denounce Agamemnon's plan to murder his daughter both to him and others (133–35, 887), to fight with Menelaos for the letter

(302–16), and to take the dangerous action of betraying Agamemnon's secret to Klytemnestra (855–95). And the one who talks the most about freedom is Iphigenia, who does not get to choose whether to live or to die, but only whether she will die voluntarily or involuntarily.

5. Males and females. These issues coalesce in the contrasting figures of Helen and Iphigenia. Helen is the "bad woman" *par excellence.* She was free—free to choose first a husband, then a lover. By leaving her home she became a public issue, causing the mobilization of a community of warriors. By choosing a barbarian she impugned the superiority of Greeks. So every effort must be expended to get Helen back where she belongs—at home, under Greek male control. But whether Helen left willingly, out of love for Paris, or was kidnapped by him, remains uncertain; both versions are mentioned by different characters (voluntary departure, lust, 75, 271–72, 585, 1168, 1204, 1253, 1316; Paris responsible: 180, 467, 663, 1382), and Aphrodite's involvement also makes the lines of responsibility unclear (on "double determination" see above, pp. 16–17). Sometimes supremely desirable (386), often hateful (1169), even pitiable (781–83), Helen is a phantom, a verbal construct, an object of longing or aggression which changes according to the viewer's perspective (as Euripides' *Helen* makes so clear). Helen's phantom status redirects attention back to the need that drives this war—the lust of the suitors (392), the "strange lust" (808), "some kind of Aphrodite" (1265) propelling the army. The army is the former suitors, driven by lust to violence now as they were before. Significantly, the object of the suitors' violence is left unnamed: "whoever didn't get the girl said he would kill" (54)—the successful suitor? Tyndareos? Helen?

The supreme proof that Iphigenia is a "good woman" is her acceptance of her father's will. Euripides *may* have been the first author to make Iphigenia a willing victim; Aeschylus and Sophocles both wrote plays called *Iphigenia,* which do not survive. In Aeschylus' *Agamemnon,* Iphigenia's tears and pleas are ignored, she is gagged so that she cannot curse her father, stripped of her clothes, and lifted over the altar "like a baby goat" as she searches the crowd with her eyes, silently begging for mercy (228–47). This is how Euripides' Agamemnon too imagines the scene of his daughter's sacrifice (*IA* 462–66); instead she accedes to her father's will. Yet in the process Iphigenia claims a masculine role. Respectable women, especially unmarried girls, were expected to remain inside the house, far from the public gaze (993), and Perikles says "the greatest glory of a woman is to be least talked about by men, whether they are praising you or criticizing you" (Thucydides 2.45.2). Achilles wants to marry Iphigenia and take her to his house (1405–6, 1410–14), but she is now "something shared (*koinon*) with all the Greeks" (1386). She glories in the attention focused on her (1375–76, 1378), embraces the masculine code of conduct she previously rejected (1252), seeks a public reputation for heroism (*kleos* 1375–76, 1383–84) and expects her fame to last far into the future (1398–99). She commands the destruction of Troy (1398) and calls herself the destroyer of the enemy (1475–76). Altogether she is acting like an adult male warrior, claiming the glory that that will belong to Agamemnon and Achilles as the sackers of Troy. The contradiction between Iphigenia's previous behavior and her behavior now is striking, as Aristotle noted, and would have been even more so in performance, as the actor wearing the costume and mask of *parthenos* spoke these bold words. It is as if in this rite of passage Iphigenia has not made the transition from *parthenos* to *gunē,* but from female to male.[4]

Iphigenia's decision to offer herself is further highlighted by the contrast with Achilles' behavior. As the central character in the *Iliad,* Achilles would have been well known to the audience. When he first appears, however, he is very different from the impulsive warrior of the Homeric poem. Despite what he says about his "uncomplicated character" (927), he is concerned about social propriety (821–34), prides himself on his good education (926–27), and checks his impulse to take action so that he can think things through (919–25). He carefully weighs alternatives in terms of his own self-interest, growing indignant at slights to himself (936–41, 962–69), concerned to avoid scandal or blame (944–47, 998–1001) and trying to figure out exactly how much to do (933–34) to enhance his good name and public image (1019–23). What really offends Achilles is Agamemnon's using his name in order to get Iphigenia to Aulis; the larger questions involved are never mentioned.

The result of Achilles' careful thinking is to advise Klytemnestra to beg Agamemnon for Iphigenia's life, while he stays carefully out of the whole thing (1015–18, 1023). Achilles' words (especially 1019–21, 1409, 1415, 1424–30) reflect the vocabulary, reasoning, and rhetoric characteristic of the sophists (above, pp. 14). Although later he does prepare to battle the Greeks to defend Iphigenia, she easily convinces him to let her die (1415–23). He still thinks her decision is "thoughtless," his final advice to her is "keep thinking" (1424–30), but he takes a lead role in her sacrifice (1568–76). Iphigenia is physically more courageous, a more persuasive speaker, better able to act on her intentions, more public-spirited—in sum, more masculine, more like the Achilles of the *Iliad*—than is this Achilles.

Like Iphigenia, Klytemnestra is portrayed as stronger and braver than the males she deals with. Her goals are traditional female ones, however. Klytemnestra in *IA* is not an outsider like Medea who has chosen her own way, but a woman whose life resembles that of a typical Greek woman: Her father decided whom she would marry (1155–56); she bore children; she worked to fulfill the expectations of a good wife—chastity, good household management, support of her husband (1157–61).[5] Her first scene with Agamemnon (685–741), which portrays a husband and wife discussing a domestic issue, is very unusual in Athenian drama. Although Agamemnon as head of the *oikos* has the power to decide the issue of a daughter's marriage, Klytemnestra negotiates carefully to make sure that the bridegroom is appropriate, and defies her husband when he violates custom (740–41). Like Medea (see *Medea* 13–15), Klytemnestra is portrayed as a resourceful woman who supports the status quo in gender relations until the males in charge change the rules. As she begins to imagine taking revenge on Agamemnon (1171–82), Klytemnestra does not just threaten him, but begs him to keep her from turning from "good woman" into "bad woman" (1183–84). Like Medea, Klytemnestra turns her talents to destruction only when the system she has upheld betrays her.

Euripides' portrait of Klytemnestra, like those of Iphigenia and Achilles, is quite different from other versions that we know. In the *Odyssey* the story of Klytemnestra's infidelity and Agamemnon's murder serves as an important narrative counterpoint to the story of Odysseus' return to his household and his faithful wife Penelope. In Homer's version it is Aigisthos who sets out to murder Agamemnon; he seduces Klytemnestra in order to get her as an ally. There is no mention of Iphigenia. The only motive given for Klytemnestra's betrayal is her own evil nature: "there's nothing more deadly, more shameless, than a woman who conceives acts like this in her mind" (11.427–28). At the end of the poem Agamemnon predicts that there will be different stories about these two women—the faithful Penelope will get a glorious song of praise, but for Klytemnestra "there will be a song full of hatred, and she will bring a bad reputation on women, even the good ones" (24.200–2). In Aeschylus' *Agamemnon,* Klytemnestra herself murders Agamemnon in revenge for Iphigenia's death, but she is depicted as the agent of the curse which is punishing Agamemnon's family (see *Agamemnon* 146–55, 1468–88). *IA* takes us back in mythic time before Aeschylus' version, showing how Klytemnestra's plan to murder her husband develops. Here Klytemnestra's act can be understood as the result neither of her innate wickedness, nor of an ancient curse using her as agent, but as a psychologically comprehensible consequence of her history with Agamemnon, his behavior as head of the *oikos,* and his violations of *philia.*

6. *"I wish all wars would vanish" (658).* Raising questions about the values for which this particular war is fought raises questions about war itself, and about the role of war in Greek culture. What happens at Aulis makes the *Iliad*—the Greek poem of war—possible, and various aspects of *IA*—plot, character, language—recall the Homeric poem.[6] The strongest echoes of Homer come in the Chorus' opening song (164–302). This song is so exceptionally long that its last third

(253–302) has been considered inauthentic. But it is based on long descriptions in the *Iliad* of the forces mustered for the war (2.494–877 and 3.161–244), and athletic contests between the Greeks (23.262–897). The Chorus celebrate the warriors and ships they have come to see, ending with a patriotic flourish (296–300). This enthusiasm can be seen as an appropriate response to this impressive sight, especially given the scenes of indecision and division which precede and follow this song: "the epic tone of the ode creates a strong counterpressure for a return to past myth and a more glorious world than that of the *stasis*-ridden army" (Foley 1985: 79).

Yet this celebration of military might is voiced not by male warriors, as in the *Iliad,* but by young women. Given all the stress in *IA* on the army as a force driving the action, it is significant that Euripides created a chorus of female outsiders rather than a chorus of soldiers.[7] Like other female choruses in tragedy, the women from Chalkis seem to have more freedom of movement than respectable Athenian women did. Tourists eager for sightseeing (164–79), they focus only on glittering appearance and dashing movement. References in the song to their gender (174, 187, 234) may suggest that such enthusiasm is naive and emotional, characteristic of those who don't know the reality of war. Also, the warriors are not fighting, but playing at sports and games (197–98).

As the plan to sacrifice Iphigenia develops, however, the Chorus' enthusiasm for warfare changes to awareness of the suffering that will result, especially for the Trojan women—including Helen!—brutalized by the "civilized" Greeks (774–93). They express increasing horror at the prospect of the sacrifice (1080–97) and address Agamemnon directly, urging him to save his daughter (1209–10). Although they praise Iphigenia's nobility in offering herself for sacrifice, they condemn the circumstances that have brought this about (1402–3). Iphigenia moves from lack of understanding of war to support for it and the hierarchized categories it will defend. By contrast, the Chorus cross the barriers—spatial, intellectual, and emotional—that separate classes, the genders, city-states, even Greeks and barbarians, and end by finding the war horrible, not glorious.

As the Athenian audience knew, Troy did fall, but many of Iphigenia's other desires in her final speeches were not fulfilled, or only in a form she did not intend (Sorum 1992: 540–42). She declares a single man more valuable than a thousand women (1394), but for the sake of a single woman thousands of men will die (1389)—including Achilles, whom she hopes to save by her action (1392–93). Klytemnestra does mourn for her and continues to hate her husband (1437–55). Agamemnon will conquer Troy and come home (1557–58) only to be killed by his wife. Orestes will "come to the aid of kinfolk" (1452) by violating *philia* in killing

Klytemnestra. Even though she dies willingly, Iphigenia's words "Make the sacrifice! Eradicate Troy!" (1398) are still a curse. Sacrificial ritual is supposed to contain death, but here death spills and runs over. The Furies were virgins, like Artemis and Athena, and Iphigenia becomes a kind of Fury, spreading violence against children caused by lust and greed—the curse on the house of Atreus—to all of Greece. The eradication of Troy means the sacrifice of the next generation *on both sides:* Iphigenia's "wedding with Greece" will produce dead children, both Trojan and Greek (1399). Her combination of masculine and feminine qualities in this speech lets her stand for all those involved in the war, male and female, Greek and Trojan, warriors and victims. Ironically, she gives herself an epithet used by Aeschylus (*Agamemnon* 689–90), who puns on Helen's name by calling her *heleptolis,* "destroyer of the city" (1476). Twice the question is asked "What do Iphigenia and Helen have to do with one another?" (494, 1236). One answer that Euripides' ambiguous dramatization of the story allows us to provide is that "good woman" and "bad woman," "barbarian" Troy and "civilized" Greece, free man and slave, private and public have become indistinguishable.

As a "prequel" to the *Iliad* and to *Agamemnon, IA* asks the audience to rethink the events of the epic in terms of those of the drama and to reconsider events made to seem inevitable by their canonical status. As a sequel, *Helen* offers a similar change of perspective on the *Iliad.* In *IA* there are many suggestions, on the level of plot, character, and dialogue, that despite the pressure—the massed army, the literary tradition, the ritual patterns—the war is *not* inevitable. Agamemnon thinks the sacrifice is necessitated by the army's desire to get to Troy (512–37). Yet when Menelaos sees Agamemnon weep he changes his mind about the sacrifice (477–84), and Klytemnestra implies that the army would support her when she calls them "rowdy, ready for crime, but good and useful, whenever they want to be" (914–15). The soldiers respond happily to the idea of a wedding (430–34) and both Menelaos and Achilles report that the men are ready to leave Aulis, to pursue their normal lives as husbands, fathers, and sons (353, 805–18) just as in the *Iliad* Achilles threatens to abandon warfare for domestic life (9.394–429). So the scene between Achilles and Klytemnestra (819–52) is not just momentary comic relief. It suggests an alternative plot, the plot of comedy, which ends in marriage—perhaps even a good marriage, given Achilles' uncustomary "proposal" to Iphigenia (1404–13).

The choral song (1036–97) brings the themes of male lust, female victimization, military values, and prophecy together. Here the Chorus contrast Iphigenia's marriage to Death with the wedding of Peleus and Thetis, where the Centaurs predicted that Thetis would bear a glorious son (1065–75). As usual the Chorus enjoy the idea of a spectacle full of well-dressed celebrities, but there are dark shadows on the edge of this bright scene. Despite Agamemnon's assertion (703), Thetis was not a willing bride; with Zeus' help Peleus violently subdued her. The child of this marriage, Achilles, will get his beautiful golden armor (1072) by losing his best friend, and achieve his glory by brutally destroying Troy; in the *Iliad,* the poem that celebrates him, neither he nor his parents have a single happy moment. The "inspired song of Apollo" (1064) has left out a few details.

However real the possibility of change raised in *IA,* that possibility gradually vanishes as characters and events become fixed into their usual configuration, and the play ends with the traditional values of Athenian ideology still in place. This return to the familiar can be seen as comforting, at least for those to whom "the thought that Achilles' brilliance is to be expended in protecting Iphigenia from his own army, and not on the battlefield of Troy, is at the very least discomforting" (Foley 1985: 97). Or it can seem "suffocating" (Luschnig 1988: 78). In any case, tradition has worked to close down choices and alternatives in political, social, and artistic terms. *IA* shows that traditions are not fixed in stone by divine fiat, but created by human need. It suggests that even the Homeric poems, those inspired songs of Apollo, are particular versions concocted and performed by fallible humans for their own reasons. At the exact midpoint of the play the Chorus wonder whether the story of Helen's divine origin is true, or the result of "stories in poets' writing tablets" that "have brought to human beings these lies which do us no good" (798–800). Whether traditions are true or false, however, they have consequences in real life.

III. Euripides' Iphigenia at Aulis *in Performance*

The preceding section has been a reading of the text of *IA,* that is, the words of the play printed on paper, a process that makes it possible to identify themes, structural patterns, internal connections, and references to other texts. But the audience in the Theater of Dionysos did not read this play. They experienced it in performance, as a combination of visual, aural, and other sensory stimuli. Performance uses more than words: As Iphigenia says, Orestes can plead even without being able to speak (1244). The meaning of *IA* in performance would have been affected by a variety of factors.

1. Physicalization. The idea of sacrifice focuses on the body of the actor playing Iphigenia. When there are references to dragging off, knives, a slashed throat, spilling blood, a body is there, available to experience those things. The Athenian audience had seen sacrificial animals die; many had seen violent death in war, and knew how it looked, felt, and smelled (this may have been one reason why playwrights rarely put deaths onstage). Vernant calls the sacrifice before battle "an offering that sums up everything the clash of battle conceals in the way of unjust violence and savage brutality" (Vernant 1991: 256). An actor's physical vulnerability makes even reported violence more vivid.

2. Set. The spareness of the playing space in the Theater of Dionysos focused strong attention on the stage-building (*skēnē;* above, pp. 35–6). In most tragedies, including the other three plays in this volume, that stage-building stands for the solid *oikos* of some major character. Here it is Agamemnon's temporary quarters. When Klytemnestra arrives with children and lots of baggage and moves into the "tent," the combination of public and private is literalized. Another intriguing possibility concerns the *thumelē,* the stone in the center of the orchestra, used in many plays to represent an altar and/or a tomb (Wiles 1997). This is probably the place where Helen hides at the beginning of *Helen.* The double nature of this stone can be read as validating Iphigenia's statement that she will have no tomb, since the altar will be her monument (1444). The onstage *thumelē* cannot serve as the altar where Iphigenia is sacrificed, since this occurs offstage and the actor playing Iphigenia must go offstage to return as the Messenger. But as visually the most powerful spot in the theater it would have been the focus of attention much of the time. If the Messenger's speech involved miming of the offstage sacrifice, it could have served as the altar in this mini-drama (see below, p. 324).

3. Lighting. IA was apparently the first play of Euripides' entry in the competition to be performed, and, like a number of other Athenian tragedies, it begins shortly before dawn. The actors playing Agamemnon and the Old Man may have gestured or referred to the actual sky in their discussion of the stars (6–7).[8]

4. Costume. Klytemnestra says she put Iphigenia's bridal wreath on the girl (905). This may be metaphorical, but if Iphigenia is actually wearing a wreath at her first entrance, the marriage/sacrifice connection would be established visually. The transformation of Agamemnon in the course of the play might also be symbolized by a costume change, from more casual clothes at the beginning to full military gear in his last entrance as he prepares to leave for Troy (1621–26).[9]

5. Music and dance. The loss of these elements creates the greatest difficulty in understanding the effect of Athenian tragedy in performance. (Translating the songs into prose, as in this volume, exacerbates this loss.) Greek poetry was divided into different rhythms, Greek music into different modes and genres, all with specific emotional connotations (above, pp. 42–3). *IA* is full of opportunities for powerful effects created by poetry, music, and dance, which amplify the play's themes. The song describing Peleus' and Thetis' wedding (1036–79), for example, might be joyful, then turn dark as the Chorus sing of Iphigenia's sacrifice (1080–97); in that case the tight parallelism of the strophe-antistrophe structure (like that of the parallel marriage/sacrifice) would be maintained rhythmically but disturbed musically. The change in music from Iphigenia's lament (1283–1335) to the joyful hymn of praise to Artemis (1475–1531) would have been striking.

6. Gesture. Supplication was one of the "type-scenes" that occurred frequently in tragedy (above, pp. 21–22, 42). Suppliants knelt or prostrated themselves, demonstrating their helplessness and utter dependence on the person supplicated. In this play acts of supplication such as Klytemnestra to Achilles and Iphigenia to Agamemnon show the subordination of women to men. "Barbarians" also prostrated themselves, so the connection women/slaves/barbarians was established visually.

7. Gender. It is not known what acting conventions Athenian actors used to convey gender difference. Comparison with other theatrical traditions, such as Japanese Kabuki drama, in which males perform female roles suggests that a complex system of gender signification may have been employed.[10] If it was, Iphigenia's assumption of masculine characteristics could have been physicalized by a change in the acting from female to male. The implications of cross-gender performance in Athenian drama are much debated; Iphigenia's masculinization in her speech of dedication can be seen either as demonstrating that only a male (playwright, actor) knows how a woman is supposed to act, as acknowledging that Athenian drama has nothing to do with women (above, p. 61), as critiquing male values—or as all of these. At the very least the same actor's playing both male and female roles suggests that gender is performative, not natural (see Butler 1990).

8. Role division. The three-actor rule meant that an actor would play several characters in a single performance. There is no direct evidence that the ancient audience paid attention to who was playing which role. But a prize was given for the best actor; in order to determine who this was, judges (and no doubt audience members too) would have noted which actor played which role. In the case of *IA,* the role division is as follows: One actor played Agamemnon and Achilles, another Menelaos and Klytemnestra, the third the Old Man, the Messenger, and Iphigenia. This arrangement underlines the similarities between Agamemnon and Achilles and their final reconciliation, between Menelaos as a weak opponent of Agamemnon and Klytemnestra as a strong one, between Iphigenia and other marginal characters (Damen 1989).

9. Surprises. Athenian tragedies are usually rather stately in plot development, with carefully prepared exits and entrances. Like other plays by Euripides (above, pp. 72–3), *IA* contains a number of surprises which not only change the direction of the plot but require characters to "improvise." For example, even though his letter to Klytemnestra has been intercepted, the Messenger's sudden appearance announcing the arrival of his wife and daughter catches Agamemnon by surprise. Klytemnestra asks "Did you come to this decision by careful thought?" (1194), and his awkward improvisation indicates that he has not thought through the consequences of his decision. Like Medea with Aigeus, Klytemnestra displays superior skills of improvisation as she supplicates Achilles for help, changing her tactics as she gets a sense of him (977–95).

10. Offstage and onstage. IA is full of references to characters who have a strong influence on the behavior of onstage characters but never appear, among them Helen, Kalkhas, Odysseus, the army, and Artemis. Their nonappearance emphasizes their existence in the characters' minds as verbal constructs, projections of the needs and fears of those who invoke them. In this play "offstage" is associated with words, the expected, tradition, the past, inevitability, "onstage" with actions, surprise, unpredictability, the present, the possibility of change.

11. Audience as character. The Theater of Dionysos was very different from the proscenium theater of the nineteenth and twentieth centures, with its audience in rows in the dark looking at a light stage. The Greek theater's round playing-space almost surrounded by the audience created quite a different dynamic, one in which the audience would have been very aware of itself. The audience was outside the playing area, yet it had a strong influence on it (especially given the non-passivity of Athenian audiences; above, pp. 29–30). In *IA,* the audience often seems to be in the position of the army, as when Menelaos asks who is forcing Agamemnon to kill Iphigenia, and the king answers "The whole Greek army gathered together" (514), or when Iphigenia says "All of Greece is looking at me now!" (1378). These lines and others give ample opportunity for metatheatrical gestures toward the audience on the part of the actors, or the parallel may have remained implicit.[11] The audience of tragedy is also comparable to the army in its expectations that the plot will go in the traditional direction, ending in violence and death, and those expectations can close down the comic alternatives. Yet in the actual audience there was undoubtedly a range of responses—perhaps including vocal ones—to the issues raised in *IA.*

12. Metatheatricality. References within *IA* to the theater and performance remind the audience that they are watching a constructed artifact. *Skēnē* is the word used for Agamemnon's "tent" (12); it also means "stage building," so the theatricality of this play is established in the first scene. The letter Agamemnon writes and rewrites (34–41, 98–110) is the script of the play: Will it be a tragedy or a comedy, with a happy ending? Iphigenia's speech declaring her intention to die (1368–1401) also has a metatheatrical dimension. The actor "upstages" Klytemnestra and Achilles by interrupting their scene and focusing attention on himself, glorying in the gaze of "all of Greece" in the audience (1378), validating Iphigenia's role as protagonist of the play.

In their first song, the Chorus looking at the dashing heroes and beautiful ships seem like an audience focusing only on spectacle, not meaning. They begin to question the war and its cost, but then are convinced again by the Messenger's speech reporting Iphigenia's salvation (1540–1612). They are easily distracted by spectacle: when Klytemnestra and Iphigenia enter they have just been singing about the disastrous consequences of Paris and Helen's love (573–89), but immediately become a group of fans applauding the celebrities (590–97). Though the Messenger says he's rattled (1541–42) he presents the sacrifice in the form of a very tight mini-drama. Like other messenger speeches, it may well have been performed mimetically, with the Messenger acting out what he describes. In this "play within the play" all the participants play their parts correctly and in character: Agamemnon still unable to face the consequences of his action (1547–50), Iphigenia calm and brave 1552–60, Achilles taking over the role of leader (1568–76), the onlookers feeling both admiration and sorrow (1561–62, 1580–81). Then the miracle turns grief to joy, and Kalkhas delivers the "message" (1591–1601), which the Chorus dutifully repeat (1627–29). With its perfect coherence between form and meaning, this mini-drama fulfills Aristotle's prescriptions for decorum and organic form. But it is not a Euripidean play.

The miraculous salvation was part of the myth of Iphigenia as early as *Kypria,* and there are foreshadowings of the miracle in *IA* (1507–9, 1521–22). Yet the messenger speech lacks the visual confirmation and emotional impact of drama (Zeitlin 1994: 157–71). Its performance by a single character may suggest that the Messenger is performing a script written by Agamemnon. In other Euripidean dramas, a *deus ex machina* often appears at this point to lay out the meaning of the events from a divine perspective (above, p. 36).[12] But Artemis does not appear in *IA.* As a result, Klytemnestra's suggestion that the messenger speech is a trick, or even that the miraculous subsitution is a performance arranged to convince the whole army, is never disproved. This does not mean that the messenger speech is *clearly* a lie. Just like the rest of the play, this is a performed script, one of those "stories in poets' writing tablets" (798) which may be true or false. The question of belief is handed over to the audience.

IV. *Iphigenia in Athens*

Like almost all extant Athenian tragedies, *IA* was performed in the context of war—not a war between Greeks and non-Greeks, like the Persian Wars of 490 and

480–78, but a war between the two most powerful Greek states and their allies (above, pp. 8–9). Since we do not know the exact date when *IA* was produced at Athens, it is impossible to determine the precise historical situation at that moment. That members of the audience would have seen connections between the situation depicted in the play and their own, however, seems more than likely.[13] The references to different city-states involved in both sides of the Peloponnesian War, and "anachronisms" reflecting contemporary Athenian life, such as Agamemnon's "campaign" for the generalship (337–45) and Achilles' sophistic arguments, invite these connections.

Many passages in Thucydides' history of the war read like footnotes to *IA*. As the war begins, he writes

> Zeal is always at its height at the commencement of an undertaking; and on this particular occasion the Peloponnesus and Athens were both full of young men whose inexperience made them eager to take up arms, while the rest of Hellas stood straining with excitement at the conflict of its leading cities. Everywhere predictions were being recited and oracles being chanted. (2.8)

As tensions increase within a *polis* under the pressure of war, he says

> Family relations became a weaker connection than party membership, since party members were ready to go to the extreme. . . . Revenge was more important than self-preservation. . . . The cause of all these evils was the lust for power arising from greed and ambition. . . . Neither side had any use for conscientious motives; more interest was shown in those who could produce attractive arguments to justify some disgraceful action. (3.82)

At the funeral of the Athenians who died in the first year of war he has Perikles say

> They gave Athens their lives, and won praises that never grow old, the most splendid of graves—not that in which their bodies are laid, but the one where their glory remains eternal in men's minds, always there on appropriate occasions to arouse others to speech or to action. . . . For heroes have the whole earth for their memorial. . . . Make up your minds that happiness depends on being free, and freedom depends on being courageous. (2.43)

Parents who have lost their children are encouraged by Perikles to produce more, since

> they will be a help to the city, filling the empty places and assuring her security. And it is impossible for a man to put forward fair and honest views about our affairs if he does not have children whose lives may be at stake. (2.44)

Perikles' policies had led to this war. Like Agamemnon, his policies cost him one of his children: His son (also named Perikles) was one of the generals executed after the battle of Arginousai.

Setting *IA* in its historical context does not resolve the question of how the play should be interpreted. It can be read as encouraging the Athenians to make peace and end the bloodshed:

> Euripides was saying to the Athenians . . . "What slavery could be so terrible as the things this war is forcing you to do? . . . Like Iphigenia you are willing to sacrifice yourselves, or like Agamemnon to sacrifice your children, in order to fight a war you cannot win." (Dimock 1978: 20)

But it can also be construed as encouraging the Athenians to make any sacrifice in order to win the war: "a stirring trumpet-call . . . 'Defence of freedom . . . of the home . . . of the Greek way of life . . .' so eloquently do Agamemnon and Iphigenia plead this theme, so enthusiastically does the Chorus develop it, that the spectators too . . . must surely have responded to it" (Conacher 1967: 264). Moreover, the Greeks in *IA* are not necessarily to be identified only with the Athenians. In Thucydides, representatives of Corinth urge the allies of Sparta to declare war on Athens:

> Defeat will mean nothing but total slavery. . . . Some of us are already suffering from aggression, and the rest are certain to suffer in the same way. . . . That dictator city has been set up in Greece to dominate all alike. . . . Let us therefore go forward against it and destroy it, and let us win future security for ourselves and freedom for the Greeks who are now enslaved! (Thucydides 1.124)

Finally, all the references to decadent/uncivilized "barbarians" can be read as referring to the Persian Empire, which was very much a player in the Peloponnesian War, mostly on the side of Sparta. Agamemnon's attacks on "barbarians" can be understood not as an appeal to the Athenians to renew their efforts to defeat the Spartans and their allies, but as a call to Greek states to forget their differences and join in a Panhellenic crusade against the Persians, as they had done many years before. At the Olympic Games of 408, Gorgias, a prominent sophist, gave a speech urging the Greeks to do just that. The power that gained most from the Peloponnesian War was in fact the Persian Empire.

The many discontinuities in *IA,* the variety of perspectives it offers, and the questions it raises about perception, judgment, values, and traditions in individual, ideological, and artistic terms, make any definitive judgment of its meaning (either in its original context or later) impossible. *IA* gives ample support for regarding Iphigenia's sacrifice as a noble action, as an absurd waste, or as a noble action wasted on an absurd cause. But the play's discontinuities do not encourage audiences to abandon all hope of meaning. *IA* fits Aristophanes' description of Euripides' drama as encouraging the audience to ask basic questions not only about the issues it raises but about the process of interpretation itself. "The play insists that we cannot interpret it without our own desire entering in. The play makes us aware, in a way meant to be disturbing, of the intrusiveness of our wants into our interpretation" (Mathews 1994: 13). To use Iphigenia to satisfy desire for definitive meaning, for closure, is to sacrifice her again for another cause.

V. Note on the Translation

The text of this play has been the subject of considerable controversy for more than two hundred years. Problems in meter, citations of this play by other authors which do not appear in existing manuscripts, and apparent illogicalities and inconsistencies have prompted editors to make extensive revisions and rearrangements. The beginning (lines 1–163) and especially the ending (lines 1510–1629) have been especially suspected and subject to revision.[14] My policy has been to make no excisions, but to assume that the whole script is Euripidean, even the finale, and to stick as closely as possible to the manuscripts. I have used primarily Diggle's and Günther's editions, but have also consulted those of England, Murray, Jouan, and Stockert, as well as Page 1934. This is a prose translation, fairly literal, not intended for the stage; it follows the diction and word order of the original closely, with little attempt to evoke the poetic effects of the original. The stage directions are my additions, based on my own experience in the modern production of Athenian drama.

Many people helped me with this project. In addition to my collaborators on this volume, I am very grateful to Lisa Morris, Gary Mathews, Sharon James, Nona Olivia, Leslie Cahoon, Michael Warren, and Mark Edwards for various kinds of advice and support. Tom Vogler gave all kinds of support, intellectual, moral, and emotional. My understanding of Athenian drama has been greatly influenced by translating, producing, directing, and working as dramaturg on various productions of ancient drama over the last thirteen years, and in the process I learned invaluable lessons from Christopher Grabowski, Tim Earle, George Chastain, Dale

Robinson, Phil Collins, Andrew Doe, Bonnie Reese, Sommer Ulrickson, Robby MacLean, John Maloney, Greg Fritsch, Tyffyne Stuart, and Ralph Denzer. My understanding of *Iphigenia at Aulis* was shaped by a production of the Don Taylor translation at the University of California, Santa Cruz in May 1991, a production deeply affected by the recent Gulf War. Sam Halpern (Agamemnon), Jennifer Chan (Iphigenia), Anna Stearns (Klytemnestra), Jennifer Wheat (dramaturg), and especially director Paul Graf created a powerful, moving experience with this extraordinary play.

II. THE PLAY

Characters

AGAMEMNON, king of Argos, leader of the Greek expedition against Troy
OLD MAN, slave in Agamemnon's and Klytemnestra's household[1]
CHORUS of women from Chalkis
MENELAOS, king of Sparta, Agamemnon's younger brother, husband of Helen
MESSENGER, slave of Klytemnestra
KLYTEMNESTRA, wife of Agamemnon
IPHIGENIA, eldest daughter of Agamemnon and Klytemnestra
ACHILLES, prince of Phthia, member of the Trojan expedition

*Scene: The scene-building represents Agamemnon's temporary dwelling (called both "tent" and "house") in the Greek army encampment at Aulis. One of the side entrances (*eisodoi*) leads to the Greek army camp, the other toward Argos.*[2] *The opening interchange informs the audience of the location, the time of day, and the season of the year, as well as the identity of the speakers.*

[*Enter Agamemnon from his tent, holding a writing-tablet.*]

AGAMEMNON: Old man, come out here in front of the house.[3]

OLD MAN: I'm coming. What new plan are you working on,
Lord Agamemnon?

AGAMEMNON: Hurry!

OLD MAN: I am hurrying.
My old age doesn't sleep.
My eyes are sharp.

AGAMEMNON: What's that star sailing along there?[4]

OLD MAN: That's Sirius, near the seven Pleiades,
still sparkling in mid-heaven.

AGAMEMNON: Well, anyway there's no sound of either birds or sea.
Silence, without wind,
encloses this place near the straits of Euripos.[5]

OLD MAN: Why are you dashing around outside your tent,
Lord Agamemnon?
It's still quiet here at Aulis.
The guards of the camp aren't stirring.
Let's go inside.

AGAMEMNON: I envy you, old man.
I envy any man who leads an unendangered life—
unknown, unfamous.
Those who live among honors I envy much less.[6]

OLD MAN: What? Why, that's where life's glory is.

AGAMEMNON: That "glory" is slippery.
And ambition's sweet,
but on closer inspection, painful.
Sometimes something sent by the gods goes astray
and turns your life upside down.[7]
Other times men's ideas—various, hard to satisfy—
tear you to pieces.

OLD MAN: I don't like to hear this from a nobleman.
Atreus didn't breed you
for nothing but pleasure, Agamemnon.
You have to have both happiness and pain:
you were born mortal, and even if you don't like it,
that's what the gods decided, and it stands.
You light your lamp,
and write a letter—
the one you're holding in your hand right now.[8]
You write some words, then scratch them out.
You seal it, then unseal it again,

and throw the tablet on the ground,
pouring out great tears.
You give every sign of going mad.
What are you struggling with?
What's going on with you, my king?
Bring out the story and share it with me.
You'll be telling a good trustworthy man.
Back then Tyndareos gave me to your wife—
part of the dowry,
a faithful attendant to the bride.[9]

AGAMEMNON:[10] Leda gave birth to three daughters:
Phoebe, Klytemnestra (my wife), and Helen—
she was the one the richest
young men in Greece came seeking in marriage.[11]
Terrible threats were arising, and envy of one another;
whoever didn't get the girl said he would kill.
For Helen's father Tyndareos, whether he gave away his
   daughter or not
there seemed no way out of the situation—
no good way for him to grasp what he'd been handed.[12]
Then this idea came to him:
join the suitors' hands, make them swear
   an oath with one another,
and with libations and burnt offerings[13]
solemnly vow to join in defending whatever man should
   get Tyndareos' daughter:
if someone should take her out
of her home and deprive the legal husband of his wife,
they'd make war on him and dig his city up by the roots,
whether it were Greek or foreign, by force of arms.[14]
Once they'd taken the oath, and somehow old man
Tyndareos had caught them in his tight plan,
he gives his daughter the choice: take one of the suitors,
go wherever the winds of Aphrodite might take her.
She chose—how I wish she'd never gotten him!—
   Menelaos.[15]
And then, from the East, *he* came,

the one who judged the goddesses (or so the story has it[16])
to Sparta, blooming in his fancy getup,
sparkling with gold—Oriental pansy![17]
He lusted after Helen, she after him.
Since Menelaos was away, *he* snatched her up,
went back to the cowbarns of his native land.[18]
   Stung by his lot,
Menelaos gallops around Greece, reminding everyone of
   Tyndareos' ancient oath:
"now is the time for all good men
to come to the aid of the wronged!"
At once the Greeks seized their armor,
and raced, spear in hand, decked out in their ships,
and shields, and many horses and chariots, here
to the city of Aulis beside the narrow straits.
And they chose me as leader, because of Menelaos,
as his brother.[19] If only some other man
had gotten this honor instead of me!
The army's gathered and ready, and here we sit
at Aulis, without wind. And Kalkhas the seer,
making use of the standstill, said
to sacrifice my daughter Iphigenia to Artemis,
the local goddess, and the launch would happen,
and the Trojans' destruction—if we sacrificed her.
If we didn't, none of this would happen.[20]
When I heard this oracle, I ordered Talthybios the herald
to make a loud, clear announcement
   and send the whole army away.
I had no intention of murdering my own daughter.[21]
But my brother, utilizing every argument,
   convinced me to do
this terrible thing. In the folds of a tablet I wrote,[22]
I sent my wife instructions to send my daughter here,
in order (I said) that she might marry Achilles.[23]
I magnified Achilles' virtues,
and said that he refused to sail
unless he'd sent a wife from our house
   to his home in Phthia.[24]

I used these lies on my wife, concocting a fake marriage
in exchange for my daughter.
The only Greeks who know the truth
are Kalkhas, Odysseus, and Menelaos. But then I realized
how wrong this was! I made it right,
took back my word, wrote it over again, in *this* tablet,
the one, old man, you saw me tying and untying
in the darkness of the night.
Now go, get going! Take this letter to Argos.
I'll tell you what the tablet hides in its folds,
every word I wrote.[25]
You're faithful to my wife and to my house.
"Offspring of Leda, I send to you,
in addition to my previous letter . . ."[26]

OLD MAN: Go on! Tell me, so the words I say
can confirm what you write!

AGAMEMNON: "Do not send your offspring
to the wing-shaped bay of Euboea,
to peaceful Aulis.
We will celebrate the child's
wedding feast another time."

OLD MAN: But what about Achilles, deprived of his wedding?
Won't he be furious at you and your wife?
That's dangerous. Tell me what you're saying.

AGAMEMNON: Only Achilles' name is involved, not the man himself.[27]
He knows nothing about this marriage—
not what we're going to do, or that I promised
to deliver my child into his arms, in the marriage-bed.

OLD MAN: You've dared to do something terrible,
Lord Agamemnon.
By calling your daughter the bride of the goddess's son
you've brought her to the Greeks
to be slaughtered?[28]

AGAMEMNON: Oh God! I was out of my mind! Aaaah!

Now I'm falling into disaster!
Go! Row with your feet!
Don't give in to old age!

OLD MAN: I'm hurrying, my lord.

AGAMEMNON: Don't sit down by a spring in the woods!
Don't be enchanted by sleep!

OLD MAN: Don't say such a thing![29]

AGAMEMNON: Whenever you come to a fork in the road,
look carefully. Make sure it doesn't get by you,
rolling on swift wheels,
the carriage bringing my child here to the Greek ships.

OLD MAN: I'll make sure.

AGAMEMNON: Even if you meet her with her escort enroute
just outside the gates,[30] turn her,
grab the horses' bridles, send them back
to the sacred city built by the Cyclopes.[31]

OLD MAN: If I give this message, how can your daughter
possibly believe me? or your wife?

AGAMEMNON: Take good care of the seal
which is on the letter you carry. Now go!
The shining dawn,
the horse-drawn chariot
of Helios, is already brightening.

[*hands him the letter*]

Here's your task.

[*Exit the Old Man by the side entrance going toward Argos.*]

No one among human beings is fortunate
or blessed right to the end.
No one yet born has avoided pain.[32]

[*Enter Chorus from the side entrance leading toward the army camp.*[33]]

Strophe A

CHORUS: I've left my own city,
Chalkis, home of that famous spring
close to the sea—Arethusa![34]
I rowed across the narrow Euripus,
landed and walked
along the sandy shore of Aulis,
close to the sea,
so I might see the army of the Greeks,
and the seafaring ships
of the famous, godlike heroes
(the ones, our husbands say,
highborn Agamemnon
and red-haired Menelaos
are taking to Troy
on those thousand swift ships
after Helen).
Paris the cowherd took her
from the lush banks of the Eurotas
as Aphrodite's gift to him, after
she held the beauty contest
with Hera and Athena.[35]

Antistrophe A

I ran through the grove of Artemis
where many sacrifices are held,
blushing like a girl,
because I'm embarrassed
by how much I want to see the shields,
the tents full of armor,
the throng of horses.
I saw the two Ajaxes sitting together,
one Oileus' son, the other Telamon's,
the star of Salamis,
and Protesilaos,
with Palamedes (Poseidon's grandson!)
playing checkers, enjoying the many
intricate shapes of the game,[36]
and Diomedes, happily involved
in throwing the discus

with Meriones—
Ares' descendant, no ordinary man,
also the son of Laertes, Odysseus,
who's left his island's mountains,
and with him Nireus, handsomest of the Greeks.

Non-Strophic Interlude

The one whose lightly running feet
go fast as wind—Achilles,
son of Thetis,
Chiron's pupil[37]—I saw him,
racing along the sand,
fully armed,
competing on foot
against a four-horse chariot,
pushing, really trying to win!
The chariot driver, Eumelos,
Pheres' grandson, shouted,
and I saw him lash
his beautiful horses;
their bridles were all worked with gold!
The two center horses—dapple greys
with white manes—were yoked to the chariot,
while those on the outside (pintos with reddish
manes),
harnessed with only a trace-line,
confronted the turns in the course.[38]
Right beside them
the son of Peleus ran,
armor and all,
keeping even with the chariot rail,
close to the whistling wheels.

Strophe B

Then I came to the multitude of ships,
an indescribable sight! It was
a greedy pleasure to fill
my woman's eyes with looking![39]
The Myrmidons from Phthia
were holding the right wing of the fleet
with fifty speedy ships.[40]

Golden statues, the sea-goddess daughters
of Nereus, stood high
on their sterns—the badge
of Achilles' war force.

Antistrophe B

The ships from Argos,
equal in number, were anchored nearby;
their leaders were the son of Mekisteos,
grandson of Talaos,
and Sthenelos, son of Kapaneus.
Leading sixty
ships in a row from Attica,
the son of Theseus waited, his emblem
the goddess Athena in her chariot
drawn by winged horses,
a symbol of good luck to sailors.[41]

Strophe C

I saw the sea-going force
from Boeotia, fifty ships
each adorned with an effigy:
theirs was Kadmos,
holding a golden dragon
on the stern of every one.[42]
Leitos (a man born from the earth)
commanded this army of ships.
From the land of Phocis . . .[43]
and from Locris, leading an equal number,
was the son of Oileus, who'd left
the glorious city of Thronion.

Antistrophe C

From Mycenae, the city built by the
Cyclopes,
the son of Atreus sent a throng of sailors
crowding a hundred ships.
With him was the leader Adrastos,
a friend at his friend's side,
so Greece could take action
because of a woman who left her home
to marry a barbarian.[44]

And from Pylos I saw the son
of Gerenian Nestor . . .[45]
saw the emblem on his prow,
his neighbor the river-god, bull-footed Alpheus.

Epode

The ships of the Ainians were twelve;
Lord Gouneus
was their commander.
Near them, the leaders of Elis
(the whole army called them "Epeians");
Eurytos commanded them.
Next came the fleet of the Taphians,
with their white oars, led by Meges,
Phyleus' son,
who'd left the islands
of Echina, which sailors won't approach.

Ajax,
born in Salamis,
led the right wing toward
those stationed nearest on the left,
weaving together the ends of the line
with his twelve very agile ships.
That's what they told me,
and I saw that army of sailors.
If someone brings barbarian scows
against a fleet like this,
they won't get home again!
So powerful was the naval expedition
I saw there, just as I heard at home.[46]
I keep safe the memory
of that army called together.

[*Enter Menelaos and the Old Man from the side entrance going toward Argos, arguing. Menelaos holds Agamemnon's letter.*]

Old Man: Menelaos, you're doing something terrible. You should not commit such an outrage![47]

Menelaos: Back off! You're too faithful to your master.

OLD MAN: This insult you've given me is really praise.

MENELAOS: You'd bawl if you do what's not right for you to do.

OLD MAN: It was wrong for you to open the letter I was carrying.

MENELAOS: It was wrong for you to carry something that would harm all Greeks.

OLD MAN: Debate that with others. Just hand this letter over to me.

MENELAOS: I won't let it go!

OLD MAN: And I won't give up!

MENELAOS: Soon I'll beat your head bloody with my staff![48]

OLD MAN: Dying for a master is an honorable death.

MENELAOS: Let go! You talk too much for a slave.

OLD MAN: [*calling out*] Lord Agamemnon, we are being wronged! This man here
has grabbed your letter out of my hands by force,
and refuses to deal justly.

[*Enter Agamemnon from his tent.*]

AGAMEMNON: Hey!
What's this shouting, these unruly words in front of the door?[49]

MENELAOS: My words, not his, take precedence.

AGAMEMNON: Why have you come into conflict with this man, Menelaos, and used force?

MENELAOS: Look at me, so I can begin this discussion.

AGAMEMNON: Surely you're not suggesting that I don't dare look at you? I'm the son of Atreus![50]

MENELAOS: Do you see this letter, which conveys a coward's message?

AGAMEMNON: I see it. First of all, let go of it.

MENELAOS: Oh, no! Not till I've shown all the Greeks what's written here.

Agamemnon: So you broke the seal? You learned what you have no right to know?

Menelaos: Yes, I opened up what you were secretly concocting, to cause you pain.

Agamemnon: How did you get hold of it? Gods! You have no shame!

Menelaos: I was watching out to see if your daughter would come from Argos to the army camp.

Agamemnon: Why should you spy on my affairs? Isn't that shameless?

Menelaos: Because I felt the urge. I'm not your slave.

Agamemnon: Is that not an outrage?! Aren't I allowed to be head of my own household?

Menelaos: No, because your plans are crooked: now one way, now another, soon a third.

Agamemnon: That line sounds fine, but it's a lie. A smart mouth is an attribute all cowards want.

Menelaos: A fickle heart, one your friends can't depend on, is an unworthy thing to have.[51]
I want to cross-examine you. Don't you get angry
and reject the truth, and I won't go too far either.[52]
You know very well, when you were hoping to lead the Greeks against Troy, you avoided
any appearance of wanting the command, but in your heart you longed for it.
How humble you were—shaking everyone's hand,
keeping your doors open to any one of the public who wanted in.
You invited everyone to talk to you (even those who weren't interested),
trying by your conduct to buy public honors from the masses.[53]
Then, once you'd gotten the command, you changed your style.
You were no longer a friend to those you formerly loved;

your door was shut, you made yourself quite scarce.
But it's not right for a *good* man to change his behavior
once he's achieved success. That's when he should be the most dependable for his friends—
when he's doing well, so he can do them good.[54]
That's the first charge I bring against you, since that's the first time I found you at fault.
Later, once you and the whole Greek army arrived at Aulis,
you were a nothing, knocked flat by what the gods handed you: you didn't have a wind that was good for sailing.
The Greeks started talking about disbanding the fleet, so as not to waste time in Aulis.
What an unhappy face you had then! what confusion!
if you weren't going to be able to lead the thousand ships,
and fill with arms the plain before Priam's city!
You summoned me: "What should I do? How can I find a way out?"
—so you wouldn't lose your power, be deprived of your precious fame.
Then when Kalkhas told you to sacrifice your daughter as an offering
to Artemis, so the Greeks would be able to sail, you were delighted.
You gladly promised to sacrifice your child.
You sent for her willingly, not under duress—you can't say that.
You wrote to your wife to send your child here, saying, as a coverup, she was going to marry Achilles.
And then you did an about-face: you got caught substituting another letter
saying you weren't willing any longer to be your daughter's murderer.[55] Oh, right!
This is the same sky that heard you make that promise.[56]
Thousands of men have done this exact same thing:
they work so hard to achieve success, then once they've got it they back off, like cowards.
Sometimes it's the fault of the people's stupid judgment, other times

the leaders themselves are incapable of ruling the city.[57]
It's poor Greece I'm sorry for most of all.
She's trying to do something noble, but she'll have to let
barbarians—those nobodies!—laugh at us on account of you and your little girl.
I'd never appoint a man my country's leader, or general of the army, just because there's need.
The commander-in-chief of a state has to have *brains.*
Any man can lead, if he happens to have good sense.

CHORUS: It's awful when arguments happen between brothers—
fights, even, once they've fallen into strife.[58]

AGAMEMNON: I want to speak harshly to you, but appropriately. I'll be brief.
I won't go too far and act toward you completely without respect, but behave moderately,
as a brother should.[59] A good man prefers to maintain respect.
Tell me, why are you puffing up so terribly? Why are your eyes all red with blood?[60]
Who's doing you wrong? What do you want? Are you longing for a *faithful* wife?
I wouldn't be able to provide you with that, since you couldn't control the wife you had.
Why should I pay the penalty for your mistakes? I didn't make them.
Or is it my public honors which gnaw at you? No—
discarding all rationality, all morality, you just want
to get that beautiful woman back in your arms.[61] The bad pleasures of a worthless man!
As for me, if my earlier intention was wrong, and I changed my mind for a better plan,
am I insane? Aren't you the crazy one? You got rid of a trashy wife.
The gods granted you that good fortune, but you want her back!
Helen's suitors swore the oath Tyndareos proposed because they were out of their minds with lust.

Hope really is a god, I think; hope is what made this
expedition happen—not you, or your authority!
Well, *you* take the men. *You* lead them. They're ready—
because they're stupid. But the gods
aren't stupid; they can tell when oaths have been set up
deceitfully, and sworn under duress.[62]
I will not kill my children. It would be unjust
for your affairs to turn out well, for you to get revenge for
your faithless bedmate,
while I'll be worn out every night, every day, with tears,
because I committed unjust crimes against my child.
There—my words to you have been brief, clear, and to the
point.
Even if you persist in your immoral views,
I will conduct my own affairs in the right way.

CHORUS: These words are different from those spoken before,
but you are right to spare your child.

MENELAOS: God! Poor me! I've got no one on my side![63]

AGAMEMNON: You would have, if you didn't want to destroy those on
your side.

MENELAOS: How will you prove you are really my brother?

AGAMEMNON: I want to be sensible together with you, not share your
sickness.

MENELAOS: Family members ought to share each other's sufferings.

AGAMEMNON: Call on me when you're helping me, not when you're
trying to hurt me.

MENELAOS: Isn't it right for you to share these trials with Greece?

AGAMEMNON: Greece, including you, is sick; some god's the cause.

MENELAOS: Go on, strut with your sceptre, while betraying your
brother.
I'll turn to other methods,
other allies—[64]

[*Enter Messenger from the side entrance leading toward Argos.*]

MESSENGER: Lord of all the Greeks!
Agamemnon! I've come, bringing your daughter,
the one you called Iphigenia when you were home,
Her mother's accompanying her, your Klytemnestra in person,
and the child Orestes. You'll be delighted
to see them, since you've been away from home for so long.[65]
They've made a long journey, so they're refreshing
themselves beside a bubbling spring, cooling the women's feet.
The mares too—we turned them loose
in a grassy meadow, so they could graze.[66]
And I've come running ahead, so you could get ready.
The army knows already—the rumor
went through it quickly—that your daughter's come.
The whole crowd is running out to get a look,
so they can see your daughter.
Those whom fortune blesses are famous,
stared at by everyone. They're saying,
"Is it a wedding? What's going on?
Has Lord Agamemnon been missing his daughter,
so he sent for her?" You might have heard this too:
"They're performing the ritual done before marriage,
consecrating the girl to Artemis, goddess of Aulis. But who's the bridegroom?"
Now, come on! Prepare the baskets of sacred barley,
put a garland on your head![67] You too, Lord Menelaos,
start practicing the wedding song,
let the flute resound through the house, and the beat of feet dancing!
This turns out to be Iphigenia's happy day!

AGAMEMNON: Thank you. Enough. Now go inside the house.
As for the rest, whatever happens, all will be well.[68]

[*Exit Messenger into Agamemnon's tent.*]

Oh God! Poor me, what shall I say?
Where shall I begin?[69]
What an unavoidable trap I've fallen into![70]
Some god, much smarter than all my smart plans, has caught me!
Being lowborn has something of value.
They are allowed to shed tears easily,
say anything at all. But for someone who's nobly born
such things are crude. *We* have dignity to rule our lives,
so we're the slaves of the masses.
I'm ashamed to shed tears—
but just as ashamed if I don't weep,
faced with such a catastrophe.[71]
Well, then . . . what shall I say to my wife?
How will I receive her? What sort of expression will I throw together?[72]
Her coming uninvited, on top of the problems
I have already, has destroyed me! And yet . . .
it's understandable that she'd come along,
to see her daughter married, to give her all the sweetest things . . .[73]
and so she'll find me out as the criminal I am.
And then the poor girl . . . Girl?
Soon she'll be a bride—of Death, that is!
How I pity her! I know she'll plead with me,
"Will you kill me, Daddy? Then I hope you yourself
get a wedding like this one, you and whoever you love!"[74]
Orestes will be there too. He can't talk yet.
He'll cry . . . meaningless cries, but I'll know what they mean.
Aaaaah! Paris, son of King Priam, when he married Helen,[75]
destroyed me! He's the one who did all these things to me.

CHORUS: I feel very sorry too—as much as is right for a foreign woman
to grieve for a king's disaster.

MENELAOS: Brother, let me touch your right hand.

AGAMEMNON: Here. The power is yours. I'm shattered.[76]

MENELAOS: I swear by Pelops, who is called my father's father,
and yours as well, and by our father Atreus,
that I'm going to speak to you straight, and from my heart,
nothing calculated, but just what I am thinking.[77]
When I saw those tears falling from your eyes,
I felt sorrow for you, and I too wept for you.
So I take back all my previous arguments.
I'm not your enemy. Now I stand with you.
I urge you not to kill your child, not to put
my interests ahead of your own. It's not right
for you to be in agony while my life is sweet,
for your children to die while mine are still alive.
What do I want, after all? If it's a wife I'm eager for,
couldn't I have any one I choose? But should I choose
Helen,
destroy my brother, the last person in the world I should
hurt,
trade good for bad?[78] I was impulsive, adolescent.
Looking more closely at the matter, I have seen
what sort of thing it is to kill a child.
Besides, pity for your poor daughter came over me.
I remembered I'm the *uncle* of the one who's going
to be sacrificed—because of my marriage.
What do your daughter and Helen have to do with each
other?[79]
Disband the army! Send them away from Aulis!
My brother, stop bathing your eyes in tears,
which make me weep too.
If you have something to gain from these oracles
about the girl, leave me out of it; I give my share to you.[80]
I've made a move away from my dreadful words.
What's happened to me makes perfect sense: I've changed
out of love for my brother, born
from the same parents as I.
This is the behavior of no wicked man:
always follow the most noble course.

CHORUS: You've spoken noble words, worthy of Tantalos,
son of Zeus; you don't disgrace your ancestors.[81]

AGAMEMNON: Menelaos, I appreciate how you've put forth arguments
as I never expected, in a way worthy of you.
Discord often arises between brothers over love affairs,
or the family estate. I spit out
such family feuding poisonous to both.
But I've reached such a point of inevitability
I have to shed my daughter's blood—to murder her.

MENELAOS: What? Who will force you to slaughter your own child?

AGAMEMNON: The whole Greek army gathered together.[82]

MENELAOS: No! Not if you send her back to Argos.

AGAMEMNON: I might get away with it at first, but not later.

MENELAOS: What do you mean? There's no need to fear the masses.

AGAMEMNON: Kalkhas will tell the army about the prophecy.

MENELAOS: No, not if he dies first. That's easily done.

AGAMEMNON: Whole worthless breed of priests, consumed with self-interest!

MENELAOS: Absolutely good for nothing!

AGAMEMNON: Something else just occurred to me. Aren't you afraid?

MENELAOS: Unless you tell me, how can I figure it out?

AGAMEMNON: The spawn of Sisyphos—he knows the whole story![83]

MENELAOS: There's nothing Odysseus can do to hurt you and me.

AGAMEMNON: He's innately crafty, and in with the masses.

MENELAOS: Yes, consumed by desire for public honors—an evil and dangerous thing.

AGAMEMNON: Can't you see him standing in the midst of the Greek army?[84]

He'll tell all the prophecies Kalkhas spelled out,
how I promised to make the sacrifice to Artemis,
and then went back on my word! Once he has the army
in the palm of his hand, won't he order the Greeks to kill you and me,
then slaughter the girl? Even if I should escape to Argos,
they'll come and grab the land, dig it up by the roots,
even the stones of the walls built by the Giants!
Those are the sufferings I'm going through. Poor me—
thanks to the gods I've got no way out of this situation!
Do one thing for me, Menelaos: as you go among the troops
make sure that Klytemnestra doesn't learn of this
till I get hold of my child and send her to Hades,
so I can carry out this ugly deed with as few tears as possible.
As for you, foreign women, you keep quiet.[85]

[*Exit Agamemnon into his tent, Menelaos by the side-entrance leading to the Greek camp.*[86]]

CHORUS: Happy are those who get their share *Strophe A*
of Aphrodite[87]
in just the right measure—
under control, none of those stings
that drive you mad,
when that blond boy Eros
aims his bow that delivers two gifts:
one brings a lifetime of joy,
the other complete disaster.
That's the one, most beautiful Aphrodite,
I try to keep out of the room in which I sleep.
I pray for just the right measure of your favor,
acceptable pleasure.
I want my share of desire,
but more than that let me fend off.

People are different by nature. *Antistrophe A*
They behave differently too. But

proper conduct, real nobility, is always obvious.
Education is another important guide
to excellence.[88]
It's a wise thing to feel shame
and it gives exquisite pleasure, too, to use one's intellect
to choose the right course,
since a good reputation
brings undying fame to a mortal's life.
To hunt after excellence is a great thing.
For women excellence means chastity;
for men, a kind of personal harmony
which, multiplied,
makes a great city greater.

Epode

Paris, you went back where you grew up
beside the gleaming heifers,
a cowherd on Mount Ida,
tootling tunelessly on your reed-pipe—
a barbarous imitation
of Olympos' Phrygian melodies![89]
The cows were grazing, full of milk,
when the contest between the goddesses waited for you
and sent you off to Greece. 581
Before Helen's palace
of ivory you stood,
looking her in the eyes,
and you stirred desire in her,
and with desire were lifted up yourself.
So strife leads Greece to strife,[90]
with men and ships,
toward the high towers of Troy.

[*Klytemnestra and Iphigenia enter in a horse-drawn wagon from the side entrance leading to Argos.*][91]

CHORUS: Hurrah! Hurrah! The great are greatly fortunate!
Look at Iphigenia,

the king's daughter,
my mistress, and Klytemnestra, daughter of Tyndareos.
Just as they have flowered from great families,
they have come here for a great destiny.[92]
The rich and powerful are gods indeed to those people
who are not so fortunate.
Women born and raised at Chalkis, let's stand here.
Let's welcome the queen down from her carriage
to the ground without slipping,
with gentle hands and concerned spirits,
so that the new arrival,
the famous child of Agamemnon,
feels no fear.
To these foreign women from Argos
let us foreign women offer no fright or uproar.

KLYTEMNESTRA: I take this as a good omen,
your warm welcome and kind words.
I too have some hope that I'm coming here
conducting a bride to a good marriage.[93]
Now take the things I've brought, a dowry for my
daughter,
out of the wagon, and take them carefully into the
house.[94]
You too, child, leave the horse-drawn wagon.
Put down your delicate, faltering foot.
And you, young women, take her in your arms,
bring her out of the wagon. Someone,
give me a hand too, as a support, so I can get down
from the carriage gracefully. Some of you,
stand in front of the yoked horse-team—
horses spook so easily, they don't listen to reason.
Receive this boychild, too, Agamemnon's offspring,
Orestes.[95] He doesn't talk yet. Baby,
are you sleeping? Tired out by the wagon's jolting?
Wake up to a happy day—your sister's wedding!
The son of a noble man, himself a fine fellow,
whose mother's the daughter of the sea-god Nereus,

is going to marry her! Take your place here next to me,
beside your mother, Iphigenia! Stand near me,
show these foreign ladies what a lucky woman I am,
and address your dear father from here.[96]

IPHIGENIA: Mother, running ahead of you—don't be angry—
I have to throw my arms around Father.
I want to run to you, Daddy,
and throw my arms around you after such a long time.
I need to see your face. Don't be angry.

KLYTEMNESTRA: [*to Agamemnon*] Lord Agamemnon, whom I reverence as no other,
we have come, obedient to your commands.
[*to Iphigenia*] Well, child, you have to. Of all the children I have
you've always loved your father the best.

IPHIGENIA: Father, I'm so happy to see you after such a long time!

AGAMEMNON: And your father you. What you say is true for both of us.

IPHIGENIA: Greetings! You did the right thing by bringing me here, Daddy.

AGAMEMNON: I don't know how to say that, and not say it, child.[97]

IPHIGENIA: Why . . . you don't look relaxed and happy, when you look at me.

AGAMEMNON: Many things weigh on a man who's a king and a general.

IPHIGENIA: Be with me now. Don't focus on your responsibilities.

AGAMEMNON: I am with you now, completely, and nowhere else.

IPHIGENIA: All right then, put away that frown and give me a smile![98]

AGAMEMNON: Look! I'm as happy as I can be when I see you, my child.

IPHIGENIA: And that's why tears are seeping out of your eyes?

AGAMEMNON: A long parting is coming quickly upon us.

Iphigenia: I don't understand what you're saying, dearest Father. I don't understand.

Agamemnon: You speak so sensibly you make me cry even more.

Iphigenia: Then I'll talk nonsense, if I can make you happy.

Agamemnon: Oh God! I don't have the strength to keep silent! Thank you.[99]

Iphigenia: Stay at home, Daddy, with your children.

Agamemnon: I want to. But I can't have what I want; that's why I'm in pain.

Iphigenia: I wish all wars would vanish, Menelaos' troubles too!

Agamemnon: They will kill others first, those things that have already killed me.

Iphigenia: What a long time you've been away in the bay of Aulis!

Agamemnon: Even now it's holding on to me, so the army can't set out.

Iphigenia: Where do they say those Trojans live, Daddy?

Agamemnon: Where I wish he didn't live, Paris the son of Priam.

Iphigenia: You're setting out on a long journey, leaving me behind?

Agamemnon: You'll arrive, my daughter, at the same place as your father.[100]

Iphigenia: Well . . .[101]
I wish it was all right for you to make this journey with me.

Agamemnon: You'll have a voyage that will make you remember your father.

Iphigenia: Will I set out with Mother, or sail alone?

Agamemnon: Alone, left alone by your father and your mother.

Iphigenia: You don't mean you're sending me to another home, Father?

AGAMEMNON: That's enough now. It's not proper for young girls to know such things.[102]

IPHIGENIA: Hurry home from the Trojans, for my sake, Daddy,
after you fix up everything over there.

AGAMEMNON: First I have to make a certain sacrifice here.

IPHIGENIA: Of course! It's necessary to keep sacred observance with holy rites.

AGAMEMNON: You will be there. You'll stand near the basins.

IPHIGENIA: Will I lead the dances around the altar, Daddy?

AGAMEMNON: I envy you, more than myself, for your ignorance.
Go on inside the house. It's wrong for girls
to be seen in public.[103] But give me a kiss, and your right hand,
since you're going to live too long apart from your father.
[*embraces her*] Oh, your body, your cheeks, your golden hair,[104]
what a torment the city of Troy, and Helen too,
have turned into for us. I'll say no more!
Sudden tears come to my eyes when I touch you.
Go into the house.

[*Exit Iphigenia into Agamemnon's tent. Agamemnon turns to Klytemnestra.*]

As for you,
daughter of Leda,[105] I beg your pardon for this, if I
became too overwhelmed with sorrow, since I am going to give my daughter away to Achilles.
Departures are happy, of course, but nevertheless
they hurt the parents, when a father, after spending much labor
to bring up his daughter carefully, hands her over to another house.[106]

KLYTEMNESTRA: I'm not so insensitive. These events will make me suffer too—
be sure of it—when the time comes when I lead

my daughter forth with the wedding songs. So I don't blame you.
But habit, and the passage of time, will soften the pain.
Now—I know the name of the man to whom you've promised the child,
but I wish to know what family he's from, and his country.[107]

AGAMEMNON: Aigina was born daughter to Asopos.[108]

KLYTEMNESTRA: Which god or mortal man married her?

AGAMEMNON: Zeus. She bore Aiakos, king of Oenone.

KLYTEMNESTRA: Which child of Aiakos inherited his house?

AGAMEMNON: Peleus. Peleus married the daughter of Nereus.

KLYTEMNESTRA: Did the god give her? Or did Peleus steal her, in defiance of the gods?[109]

AGAMEMNON: Zeus made the match, and her guardian gave her up.

KLYTEMNESTRA: Where did he marry her? Amidst the swelling billows?

AGAMEMNON: Where Chiron lives, in the sacred foothills of Mount Pelion.

KLYTEMNESTRA: Where they say the race of Centaurs make their home?

AGAMEMNON: There the gods celebrated Peleus' wedding.

KLYTEMNESTRA: Did Thetis or his father raise Achilles?

AGAMEMNON: Chiron did, so he wouldn't learn the habits of evil men.

KLYTEMNESTRA: Hmmm![110]
The one who raised him was wise, the one who arranged it even wiser.

AGAMEMNON: That's the sort of man who will be your child's husband.

KLYTEMNESTRA: No faults there. In what Greek city does he live?

AGAMEMNON: Near the river Apidanos, in the mountains of Phthia.

KLYTEMNESTRA: That's where he will take your daughter and mine?

AGAMEMNON: That will be his decision, the one who has acquired her.[111]

KLYTEMNESTRA: Well, may they both prosper. On what day will he marry her?

AGAMEMNON: Whenever comes the full moon bringing good luck.

KLYTEMNESTRA: Have you already slaughtered the preliminary sacrifices to the goddess?[112]

AGAMEMNON: I am about to. That's just what we're involved in now.

KLYTEMNESTRA: Then afterwards you'll hold the wedding feast?[113]

AGAMEMNON: After sacrificing the sacrifices which I must sacrifice to the gods.

KLYTEMNESTRA: Where will I hold the party for the women?

AGAMEMNON: Here, near the Argives' well-sterned oars.[114]

KLYTEMNESTRA: Fine—as it has to be. May it turn out well nevertheless!

AGAMEMNON: You know what to do, woman! Obey me!

KLYTEMNESTRA: By doing what? I've become accustomed to obeying you.

AGAMEMNON: I, right here, where the bridegroom is, will—

KLYTEMNESTRA: [*interrupting*] Without her mother? How will you do the things which *I* must do?

AGAMEMNON: I will give away your daughter, together with the Greeks.

KLYTEMNESTRA: And where must I be during this time?

AGAMEMNON: Go back to Argos and take care of your daughters.[115]

KLYTEMNESTRA: Leaving the child? Who will hold the wedding torch?[116]

AGAMEMNON: I will provide the light which is appropriate for the couple.

KLYTEMNESTRA: That's not our custom! Do you think these things are so unimportant?[117]

Agamemnon: It's not appropriate for you to be mixed up with a crowd of soldiers.

Klytemnestra: It's appropriate for me to give away my children. I bore them.

Agamemnon: It's not appropriate for girls to be at home alone.

Klytemnestra: They are well guarded in the maidens' quarters.

Agamemnon: Obey!

Klytemnestra: By the goddess who is mistress of Argos![118]
You go take charge of the public matters. I, inside the house,
will take care of what's necessary for girls getting married!

[*Exit Klytemnestra into Agamemnon's tent.*]

Agamemnon: Damn! Trying to send my wife out of my sight,
I took my shot and missed what I hoped to hit.
I act so smart, devising tricks
on those who are closest to me, and get defeated every time.
Nevertheless, together with Kalkhas the seer
I'm going to arrange that event dear to the goddess,
not fortunate for me, and a burden for Greece.
A smart man needs to nurture in his house
a good, trustworthy wife—or none at all.

[*Exit Agamemnon out the side entrance leading to the army camp.*][119]

Chorus: They really will go to the Simois River[120] *Strophe*
and its eddies which run silver,
the gathered army of the Greeks,
in their ships, with arms,
to Troy
and the plain of Apollo,[121]
where, I have heard, Kassandra
tosses her blond hair
decorated with garlands of fresh laurel
whenever the unavoidable prophecies of the god
blow into her.[122]

Antistrophe

The Trojans will take their stand on the bastions,
all around the walls,
whenever Ares who carries a bronze shield,[123]
by rowing the well-sterned oars,
approaches on the sea
the channels of the Simois,
seeking to convey Helen
(sister of the twin sons of Zeus in the sky)[124]
away from Priam
to Greek land,
by means of the spears and shields
of the Greeks who endure many blows.

Epode

After he encircles the city of the Trojans
with bloody war around its stone towers,
after he wrenches heads back
to cut their throats,
after he destroys the city completely,
he will drag out the screaming girls
and the wife of Priam.
Helen too, the daughter of Zeus,
has been yanked out, weeping hard
after abandoning her husband.
Not to me! Not to my children's children
may this prospect ever come,
such as what will happen
to the wealthy Lydian and Phrygian wives.[125]
They will stand beside their looms
whispering to one another:
"Which man will root me out
like a flower, seizing me by my beautiful hair?
after he has flattened the defenses
of my fatherland, wept for, destroyed!"
Because of you, daughter of the long-necked swan—
whether the story's true
that Leda met with a flying bird
when Zeus changed his shape—

or if, instead, stories in poets' writing-tablets
have brought to human beings
these lies which do us no good.[126]

[*Enter Achilles from the side entrance leading to the Greek camp. He approaches Agamemnon's tent. Finding no attendants about, he addresses the Chorus and/or the audience.*]

ACHILLES: Where's the general of the Greeks gathered here?
Which of the servants is going to announce
that the son of Peleus, Achilles, is at his door, looking for him?[127]
We're not all alike, those waiting here by Euripos.
Some of us, not yet yoked into marriage,
have left our homes empty, and are sitting around idle
here on the beach. Others have bedfellows,
but no children.[128] What a strange lust for this expedition
has fallen on Greece—not without the gods' involvement!
Well, I must discuss my own situation;
if someone else wants to, he can speak for himself about his.
After leaving Pharsalia and Peleus, do I wait around,
contented with these weak breezes of Euripos,
holding my Myrmidons in check? They're always pressing me:
"Achilles, why are we waiting? How much more time
is it necessary for us to measure out
till the expedition against Troy?
Do something, if you're going to do anything! Or else lead the army home!
Don't wait around for the procrastinations of the two sons of Atreus!"

[*Enter Klytemnestra from Agamemnon's tent.*][129]

KLYTEMNESTRA: Child of the goddess daughter of Nereus,[130] from inside
I heard your words, and came out in front of the house.

ACHILLES: Goddess of Propriety![131] Who is this I see,
a woman possessing a beautiful appearance?

KLYTEMNESTRA: No wonder you don't recognize me, since you've never
met me. But I admire your respect for self-restraint.[132]

ACHILLES: Who are you? Why have you come to this gathering of Greeks,
a woman among men defended by shields?[133]

KLYTEMNESTRA: I am the child of Leda, Klytemnestra by name.
My husband is Lord Agamemnon.

ACHILLES: You've said well, and concisely, the appropriate things.
But it's shameful for me to be exchanging words with a woman.

[*Achilles starts to leave.*]

KLYTEMNESTRA: Wait! Why are you running away? Join your right hand
to mine—the beginning of a happy marriage![134]

ACHILLES: What are you saying? I—to you—my hand? I'd couldn't face
Agamemnon, if I touched what's not right for me to touch.

KLYTEMNESTRA: It's completely proper, since you're going to marry
my child, son of the sea-goddess daughter of Nereus!

ACHILLES: What marriage are you talking about? Speechlessness grips me, woman.
Unless you're out of your mind and making up this amazing speech . . .

KLYTEMNESTRA: It's completely normal for people to feel embarrassed
when they meet their new relatives, especially when discussing marriage.

ACHILLES: I've never asked to marry your daughter, woman,
and no proposal of marriage has ever come to me from the sons of Atreus.

KLYTEMNESTRA: Then what could have happened? For your part, go ahead, be amazed at my words!
What comes from you is also amazing to me.

ACHILLES: Consider—it's in both our interests to consider this situation.
We can't both be deceived by words—can we?

KLYTEMNESTRA: Has some terrible trick been played on me? I'm trying to arrange
a nonexistent marriage, it seems. I'm so ashamed!

ACHILLES: Perhaps someone has decided to insult both you and me.
Forget about this matter. Take it lightly.

KLYTEMNESTRA: Goodbye. I can't even meet your eyes any longer.[135]
I've been made to seem a liar, though I don't deserve it.

ACHILLES: Goodbye to you too from me. I'm going
inside this house to try and find your husband.

[*The Old Man opens the door of the tent.*]

OLD MAN: Foreigner, descendant of Aiakos, wait! Yes, I'm addressing you,
child born from a goddess, and you too, daughter of Leda![136]

ACHILLES: Who's that who's opened the door and is calling out? How panic-stricken he sounds!

OLD MAN: A slave. I'm not proud of it. My lot doesn't let me.

ACHILLES: Whose slave? Not mine. My affairs are quite separate from Agamemnon's.

OLD MAN: That woman's, the one in front of the house. Her father Tyndareos gave me to her.

ACHILLES: All right, I've stopped short. Speak if you must. Tell me why you've detained me.

OLD MAN: Are you two standing all by yourselves out there near the door?

ACHILLES: Come out of the royal house so you can speak to us alone.

OLD MAN: Fortune, and my forethought, save the ones I want to save![137]

ACHILLES: His words will reveal the future, no doubt. He's got some pretensions![138]

KLYTEMNESTRA: Don't wait for an oath, if you need to say something to me![139]

OLD MAN: You know me, then—that I've always been devoted to you and your children?

KLYTEMNESTRA: I know that you've served my house for a long time.

OLD MAN: And that Lord Agamemnon got me as part of your dowry.

KLYTEMNESTRA: You came to Argos with me. You've always been mine.

OLD MAN: That's right. And I am devoted to you, but less to your husband.

KLYTEMNESTRA: Unveil to me now the words you wish to speak.

OLD MAN: Your child—her father—the one who sowed her—intends to kill her with his own hand—

KLYTEMNESTRA: What?! I spit out your words, old man! You're out of your mind!

OLD MAN: Bloodying the poor girl's white neck with a knife!

KLYTEMNESTRA: I'm in torture! Has my husband gone mad, then?

OLD MAN: He's in his right mind, except where you and your child are concerned. There he's not thinking straight.

KLYTEMNESTRA: For what reason? Which of the evil spirits is driving him?[140]

OLD MAN: A decree from the gods, so Kalkhas says, so the army can set off—

KLYTEMNESTRA: Where? Poor me! Poor girl, whom her father's going to kill!

OLD MAN: Toward the city of Dardanos,[141] so Menelaos can get Helen back.

KLYTEMNESTRA: So the homecoming of Helen has doomed Iphigenia?

OLD MAN: You've got the whole thing. Her father is going to sacrifice your child to Artemis.

KLYTEMNESTRA: The marriage offered a pretext to get me to come here from home . . .

OLD MAN: So you'd bring your daughter gladly, marrying her to Achilles.

KLYTEMNESTRA: My daughter, you have journeyed to your death—you and your mother both.

OLD MAN: The suffering you're both undergoing deserves pity. Agamemnon has dared to undertake a dreadful deed.

KLYTEMNESTRA: It's all over for me. I'm lost! I can't keep the tears from my eyes any longer.

OLD MAN: Being torn from children is painful. Go ahead and weep.

KLYTEMNESTRA: You—these plans, old man, how do you say you learned them?

OLD MAN: I was on my way bringing you a second letter.

KLYTEMNESTRA: Cancelling the order to send the child to her death? Or repeating it?

OLD MAN: Telling you not to send her. At that moment your husband was in his right mind.

KLYTEMNESTRA: Then if you were carrying this letter, why didn't you deliver it to me?

OLD MAN: Menelaos—the cause of all these disasters—stole it from me.

KLYTEMNESTRA: Child of Nereus' daughter, son of Peleus, do you hear these things?

ACHILLES: I hear that you are in trouble, and I don't take my part in this lightly.

KLYTEMNESTRA: They've tricked my child with marriage to you, and they're going to kill her!

ACHILLES: I too find fault with your husband, and that's no simple matter.

KLYTEMNESTRA: I will not be ashamed to fall at your feet,[142]
a mortal born of a goddess. Why should I try to look dignified now?
Is there anything I should care about more than my child?
Help, child of the goddess!—both my misfortune, and the girl
who's called your wife—a lie, certainly, but nevertheless
I put on her bridal wreath and brought her here thinking she was to be married,
but really I transported her to slaughter. Blame will fall on you, too,
because you didn't help her: even if you didn't marry her,
you were called the poor girl's very own husband.[143]
For the sake of your manly beard, of your right hand, of your mother—
I won't say of your name, since that has destroyed me, but because of that name you ought to save me!
I have no altar to flee to, other than your knees.[144]
No one on my side smiles at me here. You hear what Agamemnon plans,
savage, stopping at nothing. I've come, as you see, a woman
into an army ready to sail, rowdy, eager for crime,
but good and useful, whenever they want to be. If you have the courage
to stretch your hand out over me, we're saved. If not, we can't be saved.

CHORUS: Having children is strange; it's like a powerful drug.
Suffering for their children is something shared by all.[145]

ACHILLES: My lofty spirit is impelled onward!
It knows how to feel distress when things go badly,

and also how to be happy when they're swelling high—
both within measure, though.
Among human beings such men as this are accounted
to live their whole lives through in accord with thought.[146]
There are times when it's pleasant not to think too much,
others when it's useful to use thought.
Since I was raised by the very righteous Chiron,
I learned to have an uncomplicated character.
The two sons of Atreus—if they're thinking straight,
I'll obey them, but when they're not I won't obey.
Both here in Aulis and at Troy I'll demonstrate a free man's spirit,
doing my part with my spear to honor Ares the wargod.
As for you, who have endured cruelty from your closest kin,
insofar as it's possible for a young man,
cloaking you in just the right amount of pity, I will arrange things,
and your young girl will not be slaughtered by her father,
since she's been called my woman.[147] I will not offer your husband
my person to use in weaving his conspiracies!
My name—even if it did not wield the knife—
will be the murderer of your child. The cause
is your husband, but my body will no longer be guiltless
if because of me, and "marriage" to me, she dies,
that maiden who's experienced awful, unbearable things,
dishonored in such an amazingly unworthy way!
I'd be the biggest coward among the Greeks!
I would be nothing! Menelaos would be ranked among real men,
and I as sprung not from Peleus, but from an evil spirit,[148]
if my name becomes a murderer for your husband.
In the name of Nereus, nurtured in the wet billows,
progenitor of Thetis, who bore me,
Agamemnon will not lay a hand on your daughter,
not even stretch the tip of his finger toward her robe!
Or else Sipylos, that barbarian frontier

from which the family tree of the two generals comes,[149]
will be a civilized place, and my own country Phthia will never be mentioned again.
Kalkhas the prophet will get busy with his basins
and bitter barley-grains[150]—but what kind of man is a prophet?
Even when he gets lucky he tells a few true things along with a lot of lies;
when he doesn't get lucky, he leaves.
This declaration hasn't been made so I can marry your daughter (thousands of girls are seeking my bed)
but because Agamemnon has shamefully abused me.[151]
He should have *asked* me for my name
as a snare for the child. Klytemnestra was convinced
to give her daughter to *me,* rather than anyone else, as a husband.[152]
I would have given my name to the Greeks, if the trip to Troy
was endangered because of that.[153] I wouldn't have refused
to help the common cause, along with those I set out with.
But as things are I'm nothing, and the generals find it easy
to treat me well at some times, not at others.
My sword will soon find out, the sword
which I will anoint with bloodstains even before we go to Troy,
if anyone tries to take your daughter away from me!
Don't be upset! I have appeared to you as a god, a very great one. I'm not—but I will be![154]

CHORUS: Child of Peleus, you have spoken words worthy of yourself
and of the sea-divinity, an august goddess.

KLYTEMNESTRA: Well . . .[155]
How am I to praise you correctly, neither going too far
nor saying too little, so that I lose your favor?
Noble men, hearing themselves praised, sometimes dislike
those who praise them, if they praise too much.
I'm ashamed to put forth appeals for sympathy

when my suffering is mine alone; you are not sick with my disease.
Yet it looks good when a worthy man aids
a person in trouble despite being outside the family.
Take pity on us! What we've suffered deserves pity!
At first, thinking I'd have you for my son-in-law,
I grasped at an empty dream. But still,
it might be an omen for your marriage in the future—
my daughter, dead, something which you are obliged to prevent.[156]
Yet you spoke well at the beginning, well at the end, too;[157]
if you have the will, my child will be saved.
Do you want her to embrace your knees as a suppliant?
An unmarried girl should not do that, but if you like,
she'll come, gazing at you with modesty, yet frankly.[158]
If I can achieve the same effect on you without her here—

ACHILLES: Let her stay inside. Respectable things receive respect.

KLYTEMNESTRA: Nevertheless, there are limits to propriety.[159]

ACHILLES: Don't you bring out your child into my sight,
and let's not leave ourselves open to criticism, woman, from those who don't understand.
An army crowded together, far from home with nothing to do,
loves scandal and nasty gossip.
Whether you two kneel to me or don't kneel makes no difference.
Only one challenge exists for me now, the greatest:
to save you both from disaster!
So listen, and believe one thing: that I won't lie.
If I tell lies and trick you, let me die! Let me not die if I save the girl.[160]

KLYTEMNESTRA: May you receive perpetual benefit for helping the unfortunate!

ACHILLES: Now listen, so the matter may turn out well.

KLYTEMNESTRA: What have you decided? Of course I must listen to you.

ACHILLES: Let's appeal to the father again, to reach a better decision.

KLYTEMNESTRA: The man's a coward! He's too scared of the army!

ACHILLES: But arguments can wrestle down arguments.

KLYTEMNESTRA: That's a cold hope. But what must I do? Tell me.

ACHILLES: First, kneel to him and beg him not to kill children.
If he goes contrary to you, you must come back to me.
If the asking persuades him, there would be no need
for me to make a move, since this brings your salvation.
And I'll look better in the eyes of my ally,[161]
and the army couldn't criticize me, if I work things out
by using reasoning instead of force.
So, with everything arranged properly, this situation would turn out
with you as well as your family members pleased, with no involvement on my part.

KLYTEMNESTRA: With what self-restraint you have spoken![162] I must do what you think best.
But if I don't accomplish what I hope I will,
where will I see you after that? Where can I go,
desperate to find your strong arm to protect us from disaster?

ACHILLES: I'll be on the lookout for you, where I should look out.
Don't let anyone see you going all upset
through the throng of Greeks. Don't bring disgrace
on your forefathers' house. Tyndareos does not deserve
to be spoken of disrespectfully; he's a great man in Greece.[163]

KLYTEMNESTRA: Yes. You be the leader. I must be your slave.
If the gods exist, you—a man who behaves justly—
will find good fortune. If not, why bother about anything?[164]

[*Exit Achilles out the side-entrance leading to the Greek camp, Klytemnestra into Agamemnon's tent.*]

Chorus: What an outcry that wedding song set up, *Strophe*
accompanied by the Libyan flute,
the kithara which loves dancing,
and the pipe made of reeds![165]
when the Muses with their beautiful hair
came up Mount Pelion,[166]
stamping their feet shod in golden sandals
on the earth at the banquet of the gods
for the wedding of Peleus,
honoring Thetis and the son of Aiakos
with melodious sounds
in the mountains of the Centaurs
throughout the forests of Pelion.
And the Trojan Ganymede, grandson of Dardanos,
the darling pride of Zeus' bed,[167]
was pouring nectar
out of the mixing-bowls
into hollow cups of gold.
And on the shining white sand
twirling in circles
the fifty daughters of Nereus[168]
were dancing for the wedding.

With their pine-tree spears and their heads *Antistrophe*
crowned with grass
the troop of Centaurs came riding
to the feast of the gods
and the mixing-bowls full of Bacchus.[169]
And they gave a great shout: "Daughter of Nereus!
Chiron the seer,
who knows the inspired song of Apollo,
has spoken: you will bear a child,
a great beacon to Thessaly,
who will go
with his Myrmidons[170]
armed with spears and shields

to Troy and burn to the ground
the famous land of Priam,
with his body fitted out with golden armor,
the work of Hephaistos—
gifts from his mother, Thetis,
the goddess who gave birth to him!"
Back then, the gods made
a happy marriage,
the wedding of the eldest of Nereus' daughters
and Peleus.

Epode

But on your head, Iphigenia, on the beautiful
locks of your hair,
the Greeks will set a garland
—as they do on a virgin heifer with dappled skin
coming from the rocky mountain caves—
before they bloody your human throat,
you, who were not brought up to the sound
of whistles and the shepherds' reed pipe,
but close by your mother's side,
to be dressed as a bride for the sons of Inachos![171]
Where does the mask of propriety
or that of excellence
have any force,
since what is unholy now holds sway,
excellence is disregarded
and left behind by human beings,
lawlessness rules over law,
and humans don't join in trying
to keep the gods from punishing them?[172]

[*Enter Klytemnestra from the tent.*][173]

KLYTEMNESTRA: I've come out of the house anticipating my husband
who went out and left the house a long time ago.
My unhappy child is in tears,
breaking into many different kinds of laments,
since she's heard about the death her father is planning
for her.

But I was mentioning the very one who's now approaching,
yes, Agamemnon, the one who'll be found guilty at once
of plotting unholy deeds against his own children.

[*Enter Agamemnon from the side entrance leading to the Greek camp.*]

Agamemnon: Offspring of Leda, how fortunate that I've found you
outside the house, so I can discuss with you, without the maiden,
matters which are not appropriate for girls about to be married.[174]

Klytemnestra: What is it, this matter you're taking the perfect occasion to discuss?

Agamemnon: Send the child out in front of her father's house.
The basins are all decorated and ready,
the barley's ready for hands to sprinkle on the purifying fire,
the calves too, which before a marriage must fall for the goddess,
snorting out streams of black blood for Artemis.

Klytemnestra: You speak well, in words at least, but as for your actions,
I don't know how I could use words to speak well of them.

[*calling toward Agamemnon's tent*]

Daughter, come outside! You know in detail
what your father plans to do. And bring Orestes too,
your brother; wrap him in your dress, child.[175]

[*Enter Iphigenia with Orestes.*]

Look, here she is, obedient to your authority.
In everything else I will speak for her and for myself.

Agamemnon: Child, why are you crying? And you're not looking happily at me anymore,
with your eyes cast down and holding your dress in front of them.

KLYTEMNESTRA: Ughhh![176]
What beginning can I find for your crimes against me?
I can start at any point—
the latest events, the middle, anywhere!

AGAMEMNON: What is it? How you've all come together against me,
with your distress and upset eyes.

KLYTEMNESTRA: Husband, answer like a well-born man what I'm going to ask you.

AGAMEMNON: There's no need for orders. I want you to ask me.

KLYTEMNESTRA: The child, yours and mine—do you intend to kill her?

AGAMEMNON: Ah!
You've said something dreadful! You've got no right to be imagining such things—

KLYTEMNESTRA: [*interrupting*] Shut up!
Again—answer that first question for me.

AGAMEMNON: If you were to ask an appropriate question, you'd get an appropriate answer.

KLYTEMNESTRA: I'm not asking anything else. Don't you tell me anything else.

AGAMEMNON: Goddess of Fate! and Chance! and the spirit which drives me![177]

KLYTEMNESTRA: And me and this girl, too. One spirit, three people cursed.

AGAMEMNON: What wrong's been done to you?—

KLYTEMNESTRA: You ask *me* that?
This man seems to have sense, but really he makes no sense.

AGAMEMNON: I'm done for! My secrets have been betrayed.

KLYTEMNESTRA: I know everything. I've learned what you are planning to do to me.

Moaning and groaning, even keeping silence, both are signs that you confess.
Don't go to the trouble of making a long speech.

Agamemnon: Look—I'm keeping quiet. Why should I add to this disaster
by brazenly attempting to tell lies?

Klytemnestra: Then listen. I'm going to take the veil off my words.
No longer will I use hints and double meanings.[178]
In the first place (so that I may shame you with this first)
you married me against my will and took me by force,
after killing my first husband, Tantalos.[179]
My tiny baby you ripped violently from my breasts
and you smashed him on the ground.
My brothers, the twin sons of Zeus,
glittering on their horses, made war on you,
but my aged father Tyndareos saved you,
when you begged him for help, and you got your marriage to me back.[180]
Once I had reconciled myself to you, you will admit
that concerning you and your household I was a flawless wife,
controlled as far as sex was concerned,[181] always trying to increase your estate,
so that you were happy when you came home,
and seemed a fortunate man when you went out.
For a man it's a rare hunt to capture such a consort,
not so rare to have a worthless woman.
After three daughters, I bore you a son, this child here,
and one of these children you will arrogantly steal from me.
And if someone should ask you for what reason you will kill her,
speak! What will you say? Do I have to speak for you?
So that Menelaos can have Helen. A fine answer,
to give children as payment for a bad woman!
We will be buying the most hateful thing in exchange for the very dearest!

Go ahead, but if you go off to war and leave me behind
in the house,
and you are over there, during your long absence
what sort of feelings do you think I will have
in that house,
when I see the chairs she used to sit in empty,
and her bedroom empty, and I sit alone,
in tears, always singing this lament:
"He killed you, my child, the father who sired you,
killed you with his own hand, not someone else, not some
other hand,
leaving behind such a reward to his family."
When all it takes is a tiny excuse
for the children—the ones that are left—and I
to welcome you with the welcome by which you ought
to be welcomed.
Don't, in the gods' name! Don't make me become
wicked toward you![182] And don't you become wicked
yourself!
Well, then . . .[183]
You'll sacrifice the child. Then what prayers will you offer?
What blessing will you ask for yourself as you slit your
daughter's throat?
An evil homecoming, since you wickedly set out from
home?
Is it right for me to pray for some blessing on you?
Should we assume that the gods aren't paying attention,
if we're going to be friendly toward murderers?
When you come back to Argos, will you fall on your
children?
You have no right. Which of your children will look at you,
if you choose and kill one of them?
Did you come to this decision by careful thought,
or is waving your sceptre and leading the army the only
thing that matters to you?
The right speech to make to the Greeks was this:
"Achaeans, do you wish to sail to the land of the Trojans?
Hold a lottery for whose child must die."

That would have been the just thing, not to provide your child
to the Greeks as a chosen victim.
Or let Menelaos kill his daughter Hermione in front of her mother.
This is his affair. But as things stand,
I, who stayed faithful to my marriage-bed, will lose my child,
while the one who betrayed hers will take
her coddled little daughter back to Sparta, and live happily.
Reject my claims, if what I've said was wrong.
But if I've spoken well, don't kill
your child and mine! Then you'll be thinking straight.

CHORUS: Be persuaded! It's a good thing to join together in saving a child,
Agamemnon.[184] No human being will contradict these words.

IPHIGENIA:[185] If I had Orpheus' way with words, Father,
to persuade by singing, so that rocks would come to me,
and by my words I could charm whomever I wanted,
that's what I would have done.[186] But as things are,
as my wise sayings I will offer only my tears, since I might have some effect with them.
As the suppliant's olive-branch,[187] I wrap my body
around your knees, the body which this woman bore to you.
Don't kill me before my time! It's sweet to look upon the light.
Don't force me to look at the things beneath the earth.
I first called you "Father," you first called me "child."
I was the first who sat upon your knees,
gave you sweet kisses, and got them in return.
This was what you said then: "Will I see you, daughter,
in the house of your fortunate husband,
living and thriving in a way that's worthy of me?"
This was my answer as I touched your beard
which I'm grasping now with my hand:

"What about me seeing you? Will I welcome you as an old man
with the sweet hospitality of my house, Daddy,
paying back the work of nurturing you gave while raising me?"
I still hold the memory of those conversations,
but you've forgotten them, and you want to kill me.
No! I beg you, in the name of Pelops, and your father Atreus,[188]
and Mother here, who endured pain when giving birth to me
and is now undergoing this second labor pain.[189]
What do I have to do with the marriage of Helen and Paris?
How does that result in my destruction, Daddy?
Look at me, give me a glance and a kiss,
so that if I die I'll have this at least, a memory of you,
if you aren't persuaded by my words.
Brother, you're very small to come to the aid of your dear ones,[190]
but weep with me nevertheless, entreat our father
not to kill your sister. Some sort of understanding of awful things
is inherent even in little babies who don't speak.
Look, he's pleading with you although he's silent,
Father. Value me, take pity on my life!
Yes, by your beard we beg you, two of your kin,
one still a baby bird, the other grown.
Cutting this whole speech short, I will win with one word:
this light is the sweetest thing for humans to see,
the things down below are nothing. Someone who prays to die
is mad. Living badly is better than dying well.[191]

CHORUS: Oh, reckless Helen, because of you and your marriage
a great struggle has come for the sons of Atreus and their children.

Agamemnon: I'm aware of what's worthy of pity and what is not,
and I love my children. Otherwise I'd be mad.
Taking this awful step fills me with horror, wife,
but not to take it is horrifying too. *I have to do it.*
See, both of you, how huge is this army, fenced in with ships,
how many chiefs of the Greeks in their bronze armor,
for whom there'll be no voyage to Troy's towers,
who won't get to overturn its famous foundations,
if I don't sacrifice you as the seer Kalkhas says.
Some kind of Aphrodite[192] has driven the Greek army mad
to sail as quickly as possible to the barbarians' land,
and put an end to their thefts of Greek wives.
These men will kill my daughters in Argos
and both of you, and me, if I reject the decrees of the goddess.[193]
It isn't Menelaos who's enslaved me, child.
I haven't come around to what he wants.
It's Greece for which I must sacrifice you,
whether I want to or not. We are all less important than this.
Greece must be free, and so much as it is in you
and me for her to be free, so much we must do,
and not, since we are Greeks, have our wives
taken from us by force, by barbarians.

[*Exit Agamemnon toward the army camp.*]

Klytemnestra: Oh my child, oh foreign women,
I can't bear the pain of your death.[194]
Your father hands you over to Hades, and runs away.

Iphigenia: I lament for myself, Mother. The same melody of misfortune
has fallen to both of us.
No more for me the light,
this brightness of the sun.

[*She sings*][195] Oh. . . .
Snow-whipped grove of the Trojans,
mountains of Ida
where once Priam cast that tender little baby[196]
robbed from his mother
and consigned to death—
Paris, who was called "the one from Ida"
in the city of Troy.
I wish he had never
settled that herdsman,
Alexander, "the Defender,"[197]
nurtured among the cows,
by the shining water
where lie the springs of the Nymphs,
the meadow blossoming with tender green shoots,
with flowers of hyacinth and roses
for goddesses to cull.
That is where Athena once came,
and Hera, and wily Aphrodite,
and Zeus' messenger Hermes—
Aphrodite proud of the desire she arouses,
Athena of her spear,
Hera the wife of Zeus
of her royal marriage—
they came to a hateful conflict,
a judgment on their beauty.
Artemis has established, maidens,
a preliminary sacrifice for the voyage to Troy
which brings a famous name to the Greeks,
but to me, death. Mother! Mother!
The father who sired me
has betrayed me in my suffering and gone away.
Suffering, I look upon
that hateful, hateful Helen
and I am slaughtered, I die
by the unholy murder-strokes
of an unholy father.
I wish Aulis had never welcomed

into this harbor
the ships with their bronze beaks,
and the oars that will take them to Troy.
Zeus should not have blown
contrary winds on the Euripos,
soothing the breeze now for some men's sails,
now for others,
so they are delighted,
but for others there's pain, and harsh necessity:
some must set forth, some must land, some must wait.
The human race works so hard,
and suffers so much,
and still it always must find an evil fate.
Oh, oh!!!! . . . the daughter of Tyndareos has brought
great pain, great misery on the Greeks.

Chorus: I pity you for this awful disaster you are going through, something you should never have experienced.

Iphigenia: Mother who gave birth to me, I see a crowd of men near by.

Klytemnestra: It's the son of the goddess, Achilles, for whom you came here.

Iphigenia: Women, open up the house for me, so I can hide myself.

Klytemnestra: Why are you running away, child?

Iphigenia: I'm ashamed to see Achilles.

Klytemnestra: Why?

Iphigenia: This marriage that turned out wrong brings shame upon me.

Klytemnestra: After what's happened, you're not in a position to worry about manners!
Stay here! If we have any power, it doesn't come from dignity!

[*Enter Achilles.*]

ACHILLES: Unhappy woman, daughter of Leda—

KLYTEMNESTRA: You speak no lie.

ACHILLES: Terrible shouts among the Greeks—

KLYTEMNESTRA: Shouting what? Tell me!

ACHILLES: —about your child—

KLYTEMNESTRA: You've spoken bad, ominous words.

ACHILLES: —that she must be killed!

KLYTEMNESTRA: And no-one says no?

ACHILLES: Into the uproar I myself came close—

KLYTEMNESTRA: What, stranger?

ACHILLES: to being stoned to death!

KLYTEMNESTRA: Why, for wanting to save my daughter?

ACHILLES: Exactly that.

KLYTEMNESTRA: Who had the courage to touch your body?

ACHILLES: All the Greeks!

KLYTEMNESTRA: Wasn't the Myrmidon army by your side?

ACHILLES: As the first rank—of enemies!

KLYTEMNESTRA: Then we are lost, child.

ACHILLES: They called me a slave to my wife!

KLYTEMNESTRA: And what did you answer?

ACHILLES: Not to kill my future bride!

KLYTEMNESTRA: That's right!

ACHILLES: Whose father promised her to me!

Klytemnestra: And brought her here from Argos!

Achilles: But I was defeated by their bellowing.

Klytemnestra: The masses are an evil to be feared.

Achilles: I'll defend you nevertheless!

Klytemnestra: One man fighting many?

Achilles: Do you see these men carrying my armor?

Klytemnestra: May your courage be rewarded!

Achilles: I will be rewarded.

Klytemnestra: My child won't be slaughtered?

Achilles: Not if I can help it.

Klytemnestra: Will someone come to take my daughter?

Achilles: Thousands. Odysseus will lead them.

Klytemnestra: The offspring of Sisyphos![198]

Achilles: That very one.

Klytemnestra: On his own initiative? Or commanded by the army?

Achilles: Chosen, but willing!

Klytemnestra: A wicked choice, to commit murder!

Achilles: But I'll hold him back!

Klytemnestra: Won't he seize her and drag her off against her will?

Achilles: Yes, by her golden hair!

Klytemnestra: What should I do then?

Achilles: Hold on to your daughter!

Klytemnestra: For that reason she won't be killed?

Achilles: That's what it will come to.[199]

IPHIGENIA: [*interrupting*] Listen to my words, Mother![200]
I see you raging against your husband, but it's useless.
It's not easy for us to bear what can't be borne.
It is right to thank this stranger for his good intentions.[201]
But even you must see this: he must not be attacked by the army.
We would gain nothing, while he'd meet with disaster.
Listen, Mother, what sorts of things have come to me as I've been thinking.
Death has been decreed—for me and by me.
I want to carry out this same act
in a glorious way, casting all lowborn behavior aside.
Look at it this way with me, Mother, see how well I reason:
All of Greece, great Greece, is looking at me now![202]
In me lies the setting forth of the ships, the ruin of the Trojans,
and women, in the future, even if barbarians try something,
never again to allow them to rob those happy women from Greece,
once they have paid for the theft of Helen, whom Paris stole.[203]
I will fend off all these things by dying, and my glorious fame,
as the woman who made Greece free, will become blest.
Also, I should not love my life too much.
You bore me as something shared with all Greeks, not just for yourself.
Now thousands of men have armed themselves with shields,
thousands grasp their oars, since our fatherland has been wronged;
they will boldly take action against the enemy, and die for Greece.
Will my single life hold back all this?
How is that just? Would I have a single argument to make against it?

Let me move to other points. This man must not go into
battle with all the Greeks for a woman's sake, or die.
It's more important for one single man
to look upon the light than a thousand women.[204]
If Artemis wishes to take my body,
will I, a mortal, stand in the way of a goddess?
No! Impossible! I give my body to Greece.
Make the sacrifice! Eradicate Troy! For a long time to come
that will be my monument, my children, my marriage, my fame![205]
It's proper for Greeks to rule barbarians, Mother, not barbarians Greeks,
because they are slaves, but Greeks are free!

CHORUS: Your intention, young girl, is noble.
But what is happening here, and the goddess, are sick.

ACHILLES: Daughter of Agamemnon, some one of the gods
was intending to make me happy, if I were to gain marriage to you.
I compete with you for Greece, and with Greece for you.
You have spoken well, worthy of your fatherland,
abandoning the idea of fighting
with the gods who rule over you,
you figured out what was both noble and necessary.
So greater desire to marry you comes over me,
now that I see your true nature. You are noble.
But look: I want to help you out
and take you to my house. I am upset—let Thetis know this—
if I am not to save you by going to battle the Greeks.[206]
Think carefully. Death is a bad, terrible thing.

IPHIGENIA: I speak these words without fear or hope of anything.
Helen, Tyndareos' daughter, because of her body
is strong enough to establish war and death for men.
Don't you, stranger, die on my behalf, or kill anyone.
Let me save Greece, if I am able to.[207]

ACHILLES: Brave spirit! I have nothing more to say in answer,
since this course seems right to you. Your thought
is noble. Why shouldn't someone speak the truth?
Nevertheless, you might still, perhaps, change your mind about this.
So you can understand the things I've said,
I will go now and place my arms near the altar,
so as not to let it happen, but keep you from dying.
You will take me up on my words, perhaps,
when you see the knife close to your throat.
I won't allow you to die because of your own thoughtlessness.
I will go now, with these arms of mine, to the goddess's altar,
and there I'll watch carefully for your arrival.

[*Exit Achilles toward the army camp.*]

IPHIGENIA: Mother, why are you silent, drenching your eyes with tears?

KLYTEMNESTRA: I have a dreadful reason to feel anguish in my heart.

IPHIGENIA: Stop it! Don't make me a coward. Let me convince you about this.

KLYTEMNESTRA: Speak. You will get whatever you want from me, child.

IPHIGENIA: Don't cut off a lock of your hair.
Don't wrap black garments around your body.[208]

KLYTEMNESTRA: Why did you say this, child? After I've lost you?

IPHIGENIA: You won't! I have been saved, and you'll be famous because of me.

KLYTEMNESTRA: How's that? I should not mourn for your death?

IPHIGENIA: Not at all, since no burial mound will be heaped over me.

KLYTEMNESTRA: What? No tomb? That's our custom for the dead.

IPHIGENIA: The altar of the goddess, Zeus' daughter, is my monument.[209]

Klytemnestra: My child, I will obey you. You speak so well.

Iphigenia: As a fortunate woman, one doing service to Greece!

Klytemnestra: What shall I tell your sisters?

Iphigenia: Don't put black clothes on them either.

Klytemnestra: May I say to the girls some kind word from you?

Iphigenia: Just "goodbye." And bring up Orestes here for me, to be a man.

Klytemnestra: Kiss him. You're looking at him for the last time.

Iphigenia: [*to Orestes*] My dearest, as much as you could you came to the aid of your kinfolk.[210]

Klytemnestra: Is there anything you'd like me to do back in Argos?

Iphigenia: Don't hate my father, your husband.

Klytemnestra: Because of you that man deserves to undergo awful trials.

Iphigenia: For the sake of the Greek land, unwillingly, he destroyed me.

Klytemnestra: Yes, by deception, like a lowborn man, unworthy of his father Atreus.

Iphigenia: Who will conduct me before I'm dragged off by the hair?[211]

Klytemnestra: I, with you—

Iphigenia: Not you! What you say is wrong.

Klytemnestra: Holding onto your robe—

Iphigenia: Mother, obey me.
Stay here. That's better for you and me both.
Let one of my father's servants here escort me
to the grove of Artemis, where I will be slaughtered.

Klytemnestra: Oh child, are you really going?

IPHIGENIA: And I will never, never come back again.

KLYTEMNESTRA: Abandoning your mother?

IPHIGENIA: Yes, as you see. It's not what you deserve.

KLYTEMNESTRA: Stop! Don't leave me!

IPHIGENIA: I won't allow you to shed tears.
[*to the Chorus*] You, young women, because of my fate
sing a hymn of praise to Zeus' daughter Artemis.
Let ritual silence go among the Greeks.[212]
Let someone provide the baskets, let the flame
be kindled with the sacred barley-grains,
let my father circle the altar to the right.[213]
I am coming,
the woman who will give the Greeks victory and
salvation.

[*sings*] Lead me on, the destroyer
of Troy and the Trojans.[214]
Bring me garlands, place them on my head.
Here is my hair for you to crown.
Bring spring water from basins too.[215]
Dancing, circle around the temple, around the altar
of Artemis,
powerful Lady Artemis,
the blessed one.
With my own blood, if it must be,
and my sacrifice
I will wash away the prophecies.[216]
Oh Mother, dear mother,
no tears of ours
will we give you;
it isn't proper at a sacred rite.
Young women,
sing with me to Artemis,
whose temple stands opposite Chalkis,
where the armed force grows mad with waiting
because of my name

here in this narrow anchoring place at Aulis.
Farewell,
mother earth Pelasgia
and Mycenae which nourished me![217]

CHORUS: [*sings*] You call on the city of Perseus,
the work of the Cyclopes' hands?

IPHIGENIA: You brought me up to be a light for Greece.[218]
I do not reject dying.

CHORUS: Your glory will never leave you.

IPHIGENIA: Farewell, torch-bearing day,
light of Zeus,
I will inhabit
another time, another place, another life.
Farewell from me, sweet light of the sun.

[*Exit Iphigenia along the side entrance leading to the Greek camp, Klytemnestra and Orestes into the tent.*]

CHORUS: [*sings*] Oh look
at the destroyer of Troy and the Trojans,
as she goes, putting on garlands
and spring water from basins,
dying at the altar
of the goddess who rules her life,
her beautiful neck slashed and streaming with drops of blood.
Fountains of lovely dew
and basins held by your father
wait for you, and the Greek army too,
longing to go toward the city of Troy.
But we will call on Artemis, the daughter of Zeus,
a strong goddess, for a fortunate outcome.[219]
Oh Lady, Lady,
pleased by this human sacrifice,
send the army of the Greeks
to the land of the Trojans

and the treacherous city of Troy
and grant that Agamemnon,
by force of arms, place on Greece the most glorious garland,
and encircle his own head
with fame which will always be remembered.[220]

[*Enter Messenger from the side-entrance leading to the army camp.*][221]

MESSENGER: Child of Tyndareos! Klytemnestra! Come out
of the house, so you can hear my words!

[*Enter Klytemnestra, with Orestes, from the tent.*]

KLYTEMNESTRA: Hearing your cry, I've come here,
frightened, unhappy, driven mad with fear.
Surely you haven't come bringing some other disaster
to add to the present one?

MESSENGER: No—about your child
I want to tell you marvelous, strange things.

KLYTEMNESTRA: Don't delay then. Speak as quickly as you can.

MESSENGER: Dear mistress, you will learn everything clearly.
I'll start from the beginning, unless my mixed-up thoughts
confuse my tongue as I speak.
When we came to the grove of Artemis,
daughter of Zeus, and the meadows full of flowers
where the Greek army had gathered,
leading your child, at once the crowd of Greeks
gathered around. When Lord Agamemnon saw the girl
walking into the grove toward slaughter
he groaned, and turning his head away
he shed tears, holding his cloak in front of his eyes.
She took her place next to her father
and spoke: "Father, I am here for you,
and on behalf of my fatherland
and of the whole land of Greece,

I give my body willingly for them to take and sacrifice
at the altar of the goddess, if that is the prophecy.
For my part, may you all fare well, may you get victory by arms
and come back to your native land.
Therefore, let none of the Greeks take hold of me;
I will offer my neck silently, and with good cheer."
That is what she said. Every one who heard her was struck
by the courage and the manliness of the maiden.
Standing in their midst, Talthybios (whose function this was)
enjoined silence, ritual silence, upon the army.
With his hand Kalkhas the seer placed in a golden basket
a sharp knife which he had drawn from its sheath,
and he put a garland on the girl.
The son of Peleus took the basket and the water,
circled the altar of the goddess holding them,[222]
and spoke: "Child of Zeus, killer of animals,
you who turn your lamp as a light during the night,
receive this sacrifice which we offer you as a gift,
the army of the Greeks together with Lord Agamemnon,
the unstained blood from the neck of a beautiful maiden,
and grant an easy sailing for the ships,
and let us uproot Troy's citadel with our armed force."
The sons of Atreus and the whole army stood looking at the ground.
The priest grasped the knife, spoke a prayer,
and looked at the throat to see where he would strike.
And pain, no small pain, came into my heart,
as I stood with my head bowed.[223] Suddenly there was an incredible sight!
Every single person could clearly hear the sound of the blow,
but no one saw where the girl fell to the ground.
The priest cried out, the whole army echoed him,
seeing an unexpected sign from some god
which one can't believe even if clearly seen.

A deer lay on the ground, gasping its life out,
very large, very beautiful to look at,
whose blood was raining all over the goddess's altar.
And—what do you think?—at that point Kalkhas said joyfully
"Leaders of this army of Greeks united,
do you see this sacrifice, which the goddess
has placed on the altar? A deer which ranges the mountains!
She prefers this to the girl,
so as not to stain her altar with noble blood!
She has received this with pleasure, and grants to us
a voyage with fair winds, and a landing at Troy!
Therefore let every sailor lift up his courage
and dash for his ship. This very day we must go,
leaving the hollow bay of Aulis
to cross the Aegean swells!" Once the sacrifice
had been completely consumed by Hephaistos' fire,[224]
he prayed for a favorable outcome, that the army might come back safe.
And Agamemnon sent me to say these things to you,
and tell what fate from the gods he meets with,
and that he's got undying fame throughout Greece.[225]
I was there, and I speak as one who saw the event:
your child has obviously flown away to the gods.
Put away your grief, lay aside your anger at your husband.
To human beings, what the gods do is unexpected.
They save the ones they love. This day
has seen your daughter both dead and alive.

CHORUS: I'm so happy, hearing what the messenger says!
He says your daughter is alive and living among the gods!

KLYTEMNESTRA: My child, which of the gods stole you away?
How can I speak to you? How can I not say
that this story was fabricated
to make me leave off my painful grief? But it won't work.

[*Enter Agamemnon from the side entrance leading to the army camp.*]

CHORUS: Here comes Lord Agamemnon,
with the same story to tell to you.

AGAMEMNON: Wife, we may let ourselves be happy on account of our daughter:
she really does have fellowship with the gods.
It's your duty to take this young calf[226]
and go home. You see the army's ready to sail.
Goodbye. My greeting to you when I return from Troy
is a long way off. I hope things go well with you.[227]

[*Exit Agamemnon by the side entrance leading to the army camp.*]

CHORUS: Go happily, son of Atreus, to the Trojan land,
and come back happy,
bringing to us very splendid spoils from Troy!

Notes

Preface

1. Both translators and theater companies have combined plays by different dramatists in order to create a "unified" story line about particular characters and events. E.g. John Barton and Kenneth Cavander combined ten plays by the three playwrights into a three-part piece called *The Greeks,* which was performed by the Royal Shakespeare Company in 1979 (Barton and Cavander 1981); in 1992 Garland Wright presented Euripides' *Iphigenia at Aulis,* Aeschylus' *Agamemnon,* and Sophocles' *Elektra* as a trilogy at the Guthrie Theater in Minneapolis (see Bly 1996: 1–62).

Introduction

1. For an accessible, illustrated history of Greece see Ehrenberg 1968.
2. For a basic introduction to the Athenian democracy see Stockton 1990. For a sophisticated analysis of its workings see Ober 1989.
3. For a full discussion see Zaidman and Pantel 1992: ch. 4, Burkert 1985.
4. Burkert 1983 (esp. 1–82) offers an evolutionary, cross-cultural analysis of Greek sacrifice. Vernant 1991: 290–302 provides an excellent short overview, Guepin 1968 a survey of ritual elements in Athenian tragedy, Girard 1977 a more ambitious theory. Foley 1985: 17–64 gives an excellent summary and critique of approaches to sacrifice in Greek culture and in tragedy and detailed readings of four of Euripides' plays, including *IA.* Cf. also Burkert 1985, Detienne and Vernant 1989, and Zaidman and Pantel 1992. In June 1982, on the island of Lesbos, a Greek family was observed by BZ ritually slaughtering their lamb on an ancient altar for Aphrodite before taking it home to cook.
5. For a full discussion of the role of barbarians in tragedy, see Hall 1989. See also duBois 1982.

6. The ancient evidence for most topics covered in this section may be found in Pickard-Cambridge 1988 and Csapo and Slater 1995. For a useful recent discussion of theater and production see Rehm 1992: Part I.

7. The word "tragedy" literally means "goat-song," but its significance is uncertain. Tragedy may have developed out of the dithyramb, a choral song in honor of Dionysos. In his *Poetics,* Aristotle associates tragedy with satyrs, and at the Athenian dramatic festivals performances of tragedy were followed by plays involving satyrs (see pp. 34–5). Others have argued that tragedy arose from sacrificial ritual (Burkert 1966; compare pp. 12–13). Another speculative hypothesis connects tragic drama to funeral laments (Else 1965: 75).

8. Csapo and Slater 1995: 286. There is no secure evidence for the population of Athens, so these numbers are far from certain. But Athens was a very small city by modern standards.

9. Csapo and Slater 1995: 290 (with reference numbers omitted). Most of the evidence for audience response comes from comedy, or from the fourth century BCE or later, but a few anecdotes concern fifth-century tragedy.

10. The name indicates its location and importance as compared to "lesser" or "rural" festivals. Dramas were also performed at other festivals of Dionysos. The most important of these was the Lenaea in January, which lasted four days. For details see Pickard-Cambridge 1988; Csapo and Slater 1995: 103–38.

11. *Bacchants* was produced posthumously, together with *IA* (see p. 66). Dionysos also appears in Aristophanes' comedy *Frogs* (see p. 67), where we see his comic person as a cowardly, lecherous buffoon.

12. For various examples of "performance criticism" of Athenian tragedy see Taplin 1977, 1978; Walton 1980; Arnott 1989; van Erp Taalman Kip 1990; Wiles 1997.

13. The idea that the *orchēstra* was round has recently been strongly defended by Wiles 1997: ch. 3. He also defends the traditional notion that there was some kind of altar at the center.

14. Against a raised stage see Wiles 1997: ch. 3. But for convenience it is usual in discussing Greek drama to use the word "stage" to refer to the entire performance area, and we have followed that practice in this book.

15. The level of literacy in fifth-century BCE Athens is much debated. Literacy was on the increase, and there is evidence that at least some women could read, but the possession of books was still a subject for comic humor (e.g., Aristophanes, *Frogs* 1114). Two recent discussions are Harris 1989 and Thomas 1992.

16. Vernant 1991: 195–206 offers an excellent overview of Artemis' various features; see also King 1983. On Iphigenia and Artemis see Lloyd-Jones 1983; Lyons 1997: 137–68.

17. For a full account see Sourvinou-Inwood 1988; see also Vernant 1991: 217–19; Demand 1994: 107–114; Dowden 1989: 9–47.

18. Webster 1967 surveys all the known plays including those now lost. Collard, Cropp and Lee 1995 provide the major fragments with translations, useful introductions, and annotations. On the transmission of Euripides' plays see pp. 85–7.

19. The ancient sources are provided in both Greek and English by Kovacs 1994. Stevens 1956 and Lefkowitz 1981: 88–104 discuss the biographical evidence and its interpretation.

20. For a succinct summary of nineteenth- and twentieth-century critical responses to Euripides, see Michelini 1987: 3–51.

21. The surviving plays show that this was true only to a quite limited extent (see pp. 44–8). As always, Aristotle should be used only with great caution as a guide to the drama of the preceding century.

Alcestis: Introduction

1. This introduction is in part based on material in Rabinowitz 1993.

2. Herakles was one of the great Greek heroes. Zeus promised that whichever of his sons was born first would rule over Tiryns. At the instigation of Hera, who was jealous at the birth of a son to Zeus and Alkmene, Alkmene's labor was delayed. Eurystheus was born first and usurped the lands intended for Herakles and set him to performing the twelve labors which are virtually synonomous with his name in mythology. The eighth labor was to capture the horses of Diomedes, king of Thrace.

3. Dale suggests that the addition of Herakles is a result of the form, which she calls "pro-satyric," meaning in place of the satyr play (1954: xx). Of course, Aristotle in the *Poetics* did not discount the possible happy ending from tragedy, and the *Oresteia,* as well as several of Euripides' other plays (*Ion, Helen, Iphigenia Among the Taurians*) end with a change of fortune from bad to good.

4. There are many fairy-tale motifs to the legend: wrestling with death, rescuing a woman from death, a man finding a replacement for himself with death, the battle of hostile (Death, the Fates, Pheres) and friendly forces (Apollo, Herakles), with good winning out. The ancient sources are Hesiod, fragments 59–60 (West); Apollodorus, *Library* 3.10.3–4, 1.9.15; Plutarch, *Lovers* 761e.

5. There are other Euripidean heroines who are sacrificed; these tend to be maidens and are modeled on Persephone's virginity (see introductions to *Iphigenia in Aulis* and *Helen*). These heroines are in some sense sisters of Alcestis and share an ideology of self-sacrifice (Burnett 1971: 23–27).

   On Admetos and Hades, see Foley 1985: 87–88; compare Conacher 1967, who is dismissive of this connection.

6. This debate resonates with the recent debates within women's studies between varieties of feminism. How much strength readers see in Alcestis, how much value they

see in that form of strength, how much subversion they see in the praise she wins will depend to some extent on what they think about current women's strengths and goals.

7. Burnett (1971) argues extensively for the similarity of Death and Pheres, lining Admetos up with Apollo on the basis of his hospitality. Herakles is a better analogue for the god, however, since he doubles for him in rescuing Alcestis. Death perhaps should be played as a member of a lower class compared to the noble Apollo, who can have the generosity of spirit that the Greeks associated with aristocracy.
8. Burnett 1965: 251–53 finds the mixture part of the "drama of death and its reversal." Compare Gregory 1979: 265.
9. Rabinowitz 1993; cf. Segal 1993: 81–82, who emphasizes the irresolution and ambiguities.
10. On initiation, see Sergent 1986: 103–7. This is his interpretation of the Karneia, corroborating that of Calame.

Alcestis: The Play

1. The prologue, 1–76, is a good representative of a common Euripidean strategy: A god appears and gives both background and a hint of what is to come (compare above, p. 41). In this case, Apollo sketches in the background of preceding events in the legend as well as the solution that the hero Herakles will provide.
2. The words for house, *domos* and *oikos,* occur frequently in the text. I have tried to distinguish between them in English, using "house" and "household" respectively, but it is not always possible to make the distinction. Either term can refer to the family or lineage (as in House of Atreus) as well as to the physical place. Slaves were considered part of the household (*oikos*).
3. The notion of a lesser god suffering or accepting punishment at the hands of Zeus is central to Greek polytheism, but Apollo's service to a mortal is unusual; it is a weakened form of the death visited on Asklepios in the same struggle (above, pp. 94–5). He is reputed to have been the lover of Admetos.
4. Punishment here is *apoina* in Greek, which has the sense of ransom. The gods are not free, but are subject to Necessity; Zeus can make Apollo do his bidding.

   The Cyclopes were huge one-eyed beings from the earlier generation of gods; hurled to the underworld by Ouranos, they were freed by Zeus so that they could aid him in his struggle against Kronos and the Titans. In payment, they gave him the thunderbolt.
5. With these words, Euripides initiates the hospitality theme. The word for host, *xenos* (8), refers to Admestos' role in the system of guest-friendship, *xenia.* See above, p. 21, and pp. 101–2.

When Apollo says "I safeguarded" (*esōizon*) the house, he introduces the question of salvation, also thematic to the play.

6. The word *hosios* used here of both Admetos and Apollo literally means pure or holy; its usage here is peculiar in that humanity's holiness depends primarily on maintaining a proper relationship to the gods, and gods are not generally described in that language at all. Here it gives a measure of equality to Apollo and Admetos.

7. Euripides links Apollo's submission to his father to this action by the Fates by using the same word (*ainesai, ēinesan* 2 and 12), which means to accept or approve. In the prologue, we get a brief picture of the complicated relationships among divinities.

   Aeschylus refers to this deception of the Fates in *Eumenides* (713ff.); Apollo apparently got them drunk. See also the speech of Death, 32–34.

8. *Philoi* are those bound by ties of affection or solidarity, including family and other members of the household, as well as allies (above, pp. 20–22).

9. The word here is *gunē,* meaning both mature woman and wife. See above, p. 52. While *anēr* can mean man or husband, the ambiguity is not so thoroughgoing as in the case of woman and wife.

10. The separation between the Olympians and Death is similarly marked in Euripides' *Hippolytos* (1437ff.), where Apollo's sister Artemis abandons her devoted follower Hippolytos when he is on the point of death; in the opening to Aeschylus' *Eumenides,* Apollo reviles the Furies for their underworld associations.

    Death here is distinct from Hades, Lord of the Dead, and Charon (254), the keeper of the ferry to the underworld. This monstrous figuration of Death is from folklore and suggests the satyr-drama qualities of the text. He typically appears with his brother Sleep, as in *Iliad* 14. 231.

11. Phoibos, "the bright one," is a name for Apollo, directly related to his quality of light.

12. On *timē,* see above, pp. 50–51. Gods received honor from mortals in the form of worship, offerings, sacrifices; mortals received honor from other mortals; compare line 53.

13. A reference to the way in which Apollo gained the reprieve for Admetos, 11–14 (see above, n. 7).

14. The play here is on word (*logos*) and deed (*ergon,* not translated), a pair frequently contrasted in Greek rhetoric (see 339 and above, p. 23).

15. From birth Apollo was associated with bow and lyre; see the *Homeric Hymn to Apollo* for the legends surrounding them.

16. I have translated *damar* "wedded wife" to mark the distance from *gunē* (woman/wife); unfortunately there is no word in English that would also suggest the root of *damar* in *damadzō* meaning to tame. The maiden was imagined as like a wild horse, tamed and trained to the yoke in marriage; the eternal virgins, Athena and Artemis,

as well as the Amazons, present a threat to the institution of marriage (compare n. 45). See above, pp. 54–5.

17. Defer is a translation of an emendation; the manuscript has "*embalein,*" which would mean "throw upon." If you read with the manuscript, Apollo might be saying Death is assigned to cast death on those who are delaying (Admetos' parents in this case); I have translated with the emendation. Apollo wants to persuade Death to delay killing those who are on the point of death (Alcestis).

18. The system sketched in refers to the immortal plane—Zeus dispensed the offices or honors (*timē,* see 30, 53) to the lesser gods when he took power. Death is also like Achilles and other heroes in the *Iliad* for whom prizes or loot signify honor. See above, pp. 50–51.

19. The word here, *sophos,* means wise, but in the second half of the fifth century could have a negative edge to it; Apollo is surprised to find him a clever speaker. On the sophists, see above, p. 14.

20. The debate between Apollo and Death reveals their two different views of the world: Apollo believes in *kharis,* reciprocal favor or grace but freely given, while Death believes in getting exactly what is due him (compare 70; see also *Medea* 439, with note, and above, p. 20). Alcestis and Herakles also give favors. Alcestis says she has given Admetos a favor he cannot repay (299–301); Herakles takes after Apollo and returns a favor with a favor (compare 544, 1101).

21. The word "hateful" (*ekhthros*) is also active, implying that Death hates mortals, as well.

22. See above, pp. 93–4, 393, n. 2.

23. Here Apollo alludes to the arrival of Herakles and his rescue of Alcestis but without mentioning his name. Herakles and his labors were well known, and the Greek audience would have understood immediately who was meant.

    The hospitality motif is reinforced, for Herakles will save Alcestis as a favor to Admetos in return for his having entertained him (*xenōtheis*). Compare 8 with note.

24. Hades, one of the twelve Olympian deities, is the god of the underworld; the nether regions are separated from the upper world by the River Styx, over which Charon ferries the dead. Alcestis later refers to the lake, the marshy Acheron, which she must cross (253–55, 443).

25. The verb *katarkhesthai* (used here) was the technical word for performing preliminary sacrifices, and particularly for cutting off a lock of hair from the sacrificial animal's head with a sword (Burkert 1985: 56).

    Death is thus cast as the sacrificial priest. See Dale 1954: 58, on these lines, for the suggestion that Euripides supplies all these details because this role was unusual, but in tragedy in general murder is often portrayed as sacrifice. In Aeschylus's *Oresteia,* Clytemnestra imagines herself performing a sacrifice when she kills Agamemnon. In

Iphigenia at Aulis, for example, murder and sacrifice are conflated because Agamemnon fears murdering his daughter, but she is demanded as a sacrifice (e.g., 396, 481, 718, n. 117). See also Medea's consideration of killing her children (1055, with n. 126).

The animals in an animal sacrifice would have their hair cut; in the case of natural death, mourners cut their own hair (215) and offer hair (101). Here we have a depiction of Alcestis as an offering.

26. See general introduction (pp. 38–41) on the choral songs in tragedy, distinction between *parodos* and *stasimon,* and the stanzaic form.

27. This is a chorus of men of the city; there is some dispute in the manuscripts as to how the lines were distributed between the whole chorus and half choruses; the hemi-choruses seem to differ in the extent of their fear or confidence. Where it is clear that there was a division, the change from one half chorus to the other is marked with dashes.

28. The motif of "Alcestis the best of women" is sounded here for the first time; her self-sacrifice receives continual praise (for instance 150–55). See above, pp. 93, 97–9.

29. Because of its uncertainty, the Chorus lists the external signs by which a Greek would know that a house was in mourning. The mourners cut their hair short, tear their clothes, beat their breasts (in the Greek text, we have hands beating, with the breast implied; I have supplied it in the English), and scratch their faces; thus Herakles was able to interpret the meaning behind Admetos' face and his shorn hair (751, 826–27).

The funeral as a semiotic system reinforces the social order; there are cries appropriate to the funeral mood, and songs appropriate for times of rejoicing. Later on, Herakles and Admetos (549–50), then the Servant (760), mention the necessity for keeping songs separate according to mood. See above, pp. 48, 90.

30. Conacher 1988, following Diggle 1984, prints this as one line; in the manuscripts, there are two separate lines. The Chorus is trying to figure out what has happened: the silence would be replaced by mourning if she were dead, unless she had already been taken from the house. They cannot believe the latter because the Queen would have a more extensive funeral (96).

31. Some texts note a gap at 96 to account for metrical irregularities with the antistrophe. See Dale 1954: 60–61.

32. The plain of Ammon indicates the shrine of Zeus in Egypt, who was identified with the Egyptian god Amon-Re. Lycia was a shrine of Apollo in Asia Minor. Lycian Apollo and Zeus in Egypt are both geographically distant deities, signifying the remoteness of help.

33. The Fates were supposed to spin and cut the thread of one's fate; here the word *apotomos* (translated as "apportioned") literally means cut off.

34. The Chorus refers to Asklepios, whose death was mentioned in the prologue; now we find out that Zeus punished him for bringing the dead back to life, and in that way breaking the boundary between mortal and immortal (see above, pp. 94–5). The text at the beginning of this passage is difficult to construe; in his edition, Diggle 1984 substitutes a feminine singular for the masculine (121), thus making Alcestis not Asklepios the subject of the verb.

35. Diggle and others would delete these lines; Dale 1954: 64 does not agree that they are spurious. The word *kakos* has a wide range of meanings, from coward, in the epics, to evil; anything or person who is "bad" can be *kakos* (see above, p. 24; see also lines 194, 196, 199, 211, etc.)

36. The word *despotēs* here (and again at 145, 212 for instance) implies both a master/slave relation and dominion over the household. Therefore, although the word used for the male and female servants in the cast of characters does not denote a slave, it seems likely that both servants were slaves. The Greek word used of the female servant (*therapaina*) is the feminine of *therapōn,* which can also mean companion at arms and even associate of the gods.

37. Admetos employs similar logic in his interaction with Herakles (519–27).

38. The word translated as "lose" is *hamartanein,* which also means to fail or to miss the mark in archery (compare above, p. 19). Here the word choice could be related to the question of Admetos' character: Did he make a mistake in accepting her sacrifice? The same word is used in the interchange between Pheres and Admetos (709–10), and later (1099) between Herakles and Admetos.

39. As the Chorus predicts, Admetos' reaction undergoes modification; in fact, he exemplifies the tragic theme of "too late learning," that is, he has to suffer the loss of Alcestis to understand what he has given up; compare 940 and note.

40. The word *kosmos,* ornament or adornment, is part of the larger group of words signifying order. The word as used here conjures up not only the robe for the laying out of the dead, but also the objects that would have been buried with Alcestis, such as jewelry and a funerary urn. Robes also would have made appropriate wedding gifts, as well as constituting part of the bride's dowry, compare *Medea,* note on 957. This similarity of adornment may derive from or lead to the cultural connection between death and marriage for women.

41. On the contradiction of fame or glory for women, see above, p. 51. For the theme in this play, see also 292, 938.

    The word for woman here is *gunē* and is situated at that ambiguous site of woman/wife, allowing for wordplay in the text.

42. This line causes difficulty, leading some to change the manuscript reading and others to mark it as corrupt. It could refer either to Alcestis or to some nameless woman who could not possibly surpass her. In any case, it suggests that what marks excellence in a woman is her willingness to die for her husband.

43. This contrast depends on the contrast of city/house (*polis/oikos*); typically a respectable woman would not be known in the city (see above, pp. 51–3). There is another anomaly here in that these preparations would ordinarily be made for the deceased by another woman of the house.

44. Hestia was a maiden daughter of Zeus to whom the hearth was sacred; see also above, pp. 9, 92; *Medea* 397 and note.

45. Here Euripides does not use the ambiguous words which also mean man and woman but the specific terms *alokhos* and *posis*. The verb is *suzeugnumi,* meaning to yoke together. The image of yoking is more often used of the young woman but sometimes, as here, also of the groom (compare n. 16, *Medea* 242).

46. The probability of Admetos' remarriage is accepted here; compare *Medea* 311 with note.

The word *sōphron* can mean chaste, modest, temperate; for women it most often has the connotation of chastity (above, pp. 51–2).

47. Here we have the word *kakos* connoting low birth (compare 196, 199 where it connotes suffering or ill fortune).

48. Admetos is quoted here as using the word that Alcestis has just used; he calls her death betrayal or abandonment, while she saw dying for him as refusing to betray him (180). He will use the word again later (250, 275). His fear of abandonment, typical of the lamenting widower, is ironic in the current circumstances.

49. Lines 207–8 are the same as *Hekabe* 411–12; they add little here and are considered by some editors to be an intrusion from a marginal note of the parallel.

50. This brief choral song is divided between hemi-choruses until the last stanza. See Dale 1954: 67–68 for discussion and characterization of the moods of prayer and doubt.

51. The Greek text supplies sounds of grieving, lamenting, such as *aiai,* or *papai.*

52. It is assumed that there is a gap in the text here because of the lack of metrical responsion with the strophe, although the sense is acceptable.

53. The Greek word *epraxas* can mean either suffer or do, depending on whether it is taken as intransitive or transitive; thus, the line could constitute a reproach to Admetos for what he has done or could indicate sympathy for what he has undergone. The theme of Admetos' suffering is highlighted in these speeches.

54. Again, the word for "lost" might blame Admetos for that loss or might portray him as having suffered a loss.

55. Alcestis sings here in metrical stanzas.

56. Throughout Admetos focuses on his own suffering; it reaches ludicrous proportions when, using conventions of mourning, he accuses Alcestis of abandoning him (250, 275).

57. Charon is the traditional ferryman who meets the dead and carries them across the river Styx to the underworld; for more geography of the underworld, see note 24 on 73; see also 443 with n. 86.

58. In the first scene Apollo struggled with a personified Death, often winged in the iconography. Moreover, typically Thanatos, and not Hades, accompanied the dead to the underworld (Hermes was another *psykhopompos,* conductor of souls, compare n. 125). We can assume either that Euripides uses them interchangeably, or that here Hades is not the god so much as the region he represents.

Typically a bridegroom is said to "lead" (*agein*) the bride; here Alcestis is shown going from one house to another, from the house of her husband to the house of Death; the implication is that Death is a form of marriage, or marriage a form of death. On the Bride of Hades see 746 n. 126; above, pp. 57, 96; *IA* esp. 666–67, 1080–81.

59. The word *khairein* means both "be of good cheer" and "farewell." Throughout the play, characters pun on the double meaning. Here Alcestis is saying good-bye to her children as well as commenting on their good fortune, in that they outlive her.

60. The plural here may denote only Admetos or may include him and the children. If he is dead anyway, then Admetos' entire effort in securing a substitute with Death and Alcestis' sacrifice are in vain.

61. This line is difficult to interpret. Is it that he can't live without her because he so respects her love for him, or because of his own love for her? He may be acknowledging what she sacrifices because of her feeling of *philia* for him.

62. The text returns to dialogue from the lyrics of her vision of death; Admetos' anapests provide a bridge to this section.

63. This line indicates that the marriage pattern imagined is that of heroic times—in the *Odyssey,* for instance, Penelope was courted by the suitors because the Ithacan throne went with her hand—not classical Athenian practice, in which she would have gone back to her father's house and been remarried from there.

64. *Prodidōmi,* first used by Alcestis to indicate that she would not abandon her marriage vows (180), then by Admetos to ask Alcestis not to abandon him (250, 275), is now used of the parents (290).

65. See line 60 n. 19, 544 n. 98, and above, p. 101.

66. The idiom, "to be in one's right mind," implies both sanity and rectitude, or the lack thereof; compare 327.

67. Compare 1135 for the gods' jealousy.

68. Alcestis draws on the stereotype of the wicked stepmother; Euripides sketches in other aspects of the paradigm in *Ion* and *Medea.* This stereotype might have arisen from actual economic and social conditions, in particular the fact that an Athenian woman was dependent on the power of her male children to care for her. Thus she

might not have been happy to have to share her husband's wealth with his children from a former marriage.

It is interesting to note that Alcestis now speaks of her house (304), whereas before the emphasis has been on the house as that of Admetos.

The echidna is a kind of viper, dreaded and mythologized in Hesiod's *Theogony,* and personified in Aeschylus' *Oresteia,* where Klytemnestra is called both echidna and Skylla.

69. This line is bracketed by some editors to indicate that it should be deleted because it repeats 195 where Alcestis speaks to the servants.

70. While the father of the bride arranged the marriage, the mother was instrumental in dressing the bride and participating in the bridal procession (compare *IA* 732, n. 116; with respect to male children, see *Medea* 1026–27). The central role of women in wedding preparation is clear in Attic vase painting.

71. The Chorus implies that it would be a mistake if Admetos did not grant Alcestis' wish; see 144 with note on the word *hamartanein,* 303 for Alcestis' view of what constitutes a "right mind."

72. Admetos here rehearses the reasons for remarrying, a better woman or more children; he then renounces them (compare *Medea* 555–58, 591–97). Children are a gain for the parents, in particular because they care for them in old age, but that expectation is overturned in this play (especially in the contest between Pheres and Admetos).

73. The opposition of words and deeds was thematic in fifth-century discourse (see above, 39, 51); for instance, Sophocles' Orestes is willing to be reported dead in words, as is Menelaus in *Helen,* because it is not true in fact; compare *IA* 128. The antithesis is roughly equivalent to that between appearance and reality.

Admetos begins reviling his parents here; these points will be made more explicitly and at greater length in his shouting match with his father (614–740). Since one of the greatest obligations of a Greek son was to his parents, this behavior undermines his own claims to virtue. See above, pp. 96, 98.

74. Libya was the source of a lotus tree that was used in the production of these pipes, generally and incorrectly called flutes.

Admetos starts off to make ordinary promises of mourning to show his respect for Alcestis. When he says he will mourn forever, his excessive grief makes it seem that his life is worse than Alcestis' death, thus defeating the purpose of her death, compare 246 and n. 56 (Gregory 1979).

75. There may be a reference here to the Protesilaus story, in which Laodameia kept a representation of her dead husband in her room (Dale 1954: 79, citing Wilamowitz); Euripides wrote a play on that theme called *Protesilaos.* There are no necrophiliac implications in that story, however.

The device of the statue is viewed alternatively as a delicate promise (Burnett 1971), absurd (Bradley 1980), or ludicrous (Beye 1959); for lengthy considerations see O'Higgins 1993; Segal 1993; Rabinowitz 1993.

76. The physical body parts stand for the words and music of Orpheus.

77. Orpheus was famous in antiquity as the singer who could charm the animals; after his wife Eurydice died, he used his voice to convince Persephone (daughter of Demeter) and Hades to let her follow him to the upper world. The bargain they struck required that he not look at his wife until they were safely on earth; he turned back and she returned to Hades. It is Herakles who is the successful Orpheus (850–56); not only does Admetos not rescue Alcestis, but he is prevented from looking at her in the end by the thick covering over her.

Hades was guarded by Cerberus, hound of Pluto, another name for the god of the underworld.

78. Admetos uses the same word that Alcestis used earlier when she saw Hades coming to take her away (259); what he and she resisted, he now desires. The stress on the verb *agein* may be a suggestion of marriage ritual, see 259, n. 58, but it is the groom who takes the bride by the wrist, as we see at 1112–13 where Herakles insists that Admetos lead Alcestis inside.

79. The Greek word here is *daimōn,* which may refer to a god or a spirit controlling an individual's life; in combinations, it can mean good or ill fortune.

80. It was a convention of Greek tragedy that death took place offstage (compare to Aeschylus' *Agamemnon* and *Libation Bearers,* Sophocles' *Oedipus the King, Oedipus at Colonus, Women of Trachis,* Euripides' *Medea, Bacchants, Hekabe,* etc.). Nicole Loraux (1987: 28–29) calls Alcestis' death "glorious"; it defies the strictly feminine tradition of death as well as the tragic tradition. See above, pp. 97–9 on the anomaly.

81. This monody (lines sung by a single character) has severe textual problems; the main difficulty is that the strophe is longer than the antistrophe, but it is not clear where the lacuna should be placed. Children speaking or singing in tragedy are rare (but see *Andromache* 504–36, *Medea* 1270); their more frequent presence in Euripides may be part of his tendency to heighten pathos in the drama.

82. The word here is *pais,* generic child but also boy; it is Admetos' son who speaks, as is clear from his use of pronouns and his reference to his sister (410). The word he uses for mother is very colloquial, in keeping with his youth, although the rest of the speech is more conventional in its expression of grief.

83. The text is almost certainly corrupt at this point; Dale 1954: 84–85 discusses the suggestions; the antistrophe is shorter than the strophe, but the sense is complete as it stands. Editors have hypothesized a gap at 410 to account for the metrical inconsistencies.

84. Here is the crucial irony: Alcestis has died for the good of the house of Admetos, to which she was devoted, but her death brings destruction to the household.

85. The gods of the underworld did not receive libations (sacrificial drink offerings, see above, pp. 11–12); they were also not celebrated with the paian, a joyful song appropriate, for instance, to Healer Apollo (compare 92). It is possible that what is meant here is that the paian for Alcestis is sung as a way of contesting the power of these libationless deities (see Dale 1954: 87: "I am inclined to think that Admetus means in effect to sing a paean of Alcestis which will be a kind of *challenge, echoing upon* the ears of the god who is so deaf to this form of human approach.").

86. In her speech at 252–57, Alcestis connects Charon and Hades; they are intertwined again in this passage.

87. The god Hermes made the first lyre out of a tortoise shell (*khelus*) that he found on the mountains (as opposed to the sea tortoise); tortoise then became a word for lyre (*Homeric Hymn to Hermes,* 33).

88. It is not clear what is meant by the association of Alcestis with the Karneia, a festival of Apollo, which marked the integration of young men into the adult life of soldiers (Calame 1997: 202). The allusion may be evidence that the Alcestis part of the story has a connection to Apollo (Conacher 1967: 331). See above, p. 102, for the possibility that she was heroized at the festival.

89. Because of a lack of responsion with the antistrophe, some editors would delete here, or hypothesize a gap in the text at 468; see Dale 1954: 91–92.

90. The Greek here is simply the word for bed (*lekhos*), frequently used to stand for marriage (compare *Medea* 19 with note), and related to one word for wife (*alokhos*).

91. *Skhetlios* is one of those words (like *tolmaō* and *tlaō*) with a wide range of meanings: here it refers to the harsh parents, but at 741 it refers to the steadfast Alcestis, and at 824 to the suffering Admetos; it can mean patient, wretched, or harsh.

92. *Xenos* here might also be translated "friend," to emphasize the relationship between Herakles and his guest-friend Admetos (on the concept of guest-friendship, see above, p. 21). Since the Chorus immediately recognizes him, we can assume that Herakles bears the marks that characterized him: a club, and animal skins.

93. Compare Apollo's oblique reference to Herakles and his labors (65–67 with note) and the introduction.

94. Lykaon and Kyknos were obscure sons of Ares, the god of war. The battle with Lykaon is mentioned only here; Kyknos robbed travelers on their way to Delphi until killed by Herakles according to Hesiod (*Shield* 327ff.) and Apollodorus (*Library* 2.5.11 and 2.7.7).

95. Herakles was descended from Perseus, who was Alkmene's grandfather; to make matters more complicated, Perseus was also a son of Zeus.

96. By not using Alcestis' name and using the word *gunē,* which could mean woman or wife, Admetos is able to tell the truth and deceive Herakles simultaneously. The

word for "refer to" here is *memnēmetha,* which while it can mean "mention" always also means "remember."

97. Since the bride was not a blood relation, she was an outsider (*othneios*); the word Euripides chooses for Admetos' reply is *anankaia,* which means "necessary" as well as related, and thus Admetos again deceives while telling the truth. See also above, p. 58.

98. The value of *xenia* or hospitality is here set against the obligations owed to the dead. Having promised to mourn for the rest of his life, Admetos now admits this honored guest, whose entertainment will require singing and banqueting. He hopes to be able to separate the two sets of demands spatially in different quarters of the house, but as we see later, the servants provide a pivotal connection between the two places and the two songs. On hospitality, see above, pp. 21–2, 101–102. Admetos takes hospitality to an extreme (compare 551–52, 1008–10).

99. Another use of the word *kharis,* compare 70, 299.

100. The Greek word, *ephestios,* repeats the word for hearth that has been so prominent in the exchange; it literally means "at the hearth."

101. See above, p. 99, on the unsuitability of mixing these different songs.

102. While the previous discourse has been on the nature of *xenia,* the exchange-governed code of hospitality, the Chorus's remark indicates that something more is owed to the friend who is bound to him by ties of friendship (*philia*). At 567 and 569 (*xenous* and *poluxeinos*) the text returns to the language of hospitality.

103. The epithet Pythian refers to Apollo's shrine at Delphi, north of Athens, where his priestess, the Pythia, gave prophetic oracles.

104. The Chorus refers here to the servitude of Apollo (compare 1–9 with notes). For a general discussion of the myth, see above, pp. 143–7.

105. Othrys is a mountain range in Thessaly. This ode sketches in the geographical features of Admetos' realm, which underline how fortunate he has been. In addition, Thessaly was often viewed as magical by the Athenians (see Jones 1968: 58); the animals are charmed by the god's music. The Thessalian setting may be part of the fairy-tale aspect of the play, which is dominated by bargaining and fighting with death; but it would also have the effect of distancing Admetos and Alcestis from the audience by making the characters so decidedly *not* Athenian.

106. The Boibian Lake was to the north of Pherai.

107. These lines vaguely identify the western (Molossus) and eastern (Aegean) limits of Admetos' realm. There are problems of text and interpretation, particularly as to the "sky of Molossus" and what precisely are the relationships between Admetos and the Aegean, but the point of this passage is clear: the extent of Admetos' wealth and land, thus bolstering Pheres' later claim (686–88) to have done right by his son by leaving him a vast realm.

108. The idea of being carried away is most often negative, but *aidōs* is a positive value, meaning respect, modesty, shame (601–2) (on two forms of *aidōs* see *Hippolytos* 385–87; compare *IA* 821–22, 900, 997). Does this notion of excess indicate a contrast indicated between hospitality and *aidōs?* Does Admetos' high value on hospitality lead him to be excessive? Here again, the Chorus is ambivalent in their judgment on Admetos, withholding complete approval.

    The passage continues on the same ambivalent note: the aristocrats (literally "the good") have wisdom, so the commoners simply marvel at them and trust that they will do what is right (or that things will turn out well for them, 604–5).

109. This line, if punctuated differently, could read "All things are possible for good men; I admire their wisdom."

110. Gifts would have been brought to the dead, as gravestones depict; 608 cannot refer to an actual funeral pyre since Herakles will rescue Alcestis, and since Admetos imagines his own burial beside her. Dale 1954: 103 cites parallel passages where the pyre suggests the burial mound.

111. The scene between Pheres and Admetos is one of the most debated in the play; it is enacted like a typical contest (*agōn*) in a Euripidean drama (above, pp. 41–2), and consequently critics expect there to be a winner and a loser. Pheres comes to support his bereaved son and behaves appropriately (if disingenuously) until provoked. Admetos definitely shows a shocking disregard for the normative obligations due to parents (Golden 1990: 101–4); moreover, the insults he hurls at Pheres about his cowardice are true of himself. Perhaps we are meant to see that father and son are perfectly matched in character.

112. "Virtuous" here is *sōphrōn,* compare 182.

113. For a free-born Greek man to prefer the fantasy that he was born of a slave is so incredible that editors have tinkered with these lines; if the passage is taken as authentic, the sentiment reveals the extent of Admetos' inner disturbance and alienation. Murray, followed by Dale 1954, inserts question marks at the ends of these sentences. Comparably outrageous by contemporary Athenian standards is his disowning of his own father, a legal device normally used by a father against a son.

114. "Put to the test" (*elenkhon,* 640) is from the same root as "tried" (*elenxas,* 15); Admetos tested his parents and found them wanting in loyalty.

115. This is bracketed in the editions because it repeats lines 295–96; the practice of deleting repetitions shows the editors' tendency to think only of reading and not of performance, where repetition might be helpful.

    Admetos' point is based on certain cultural norms: one, the value of children and the expectation that children should outlive their parents; two, the desire for honor won in contests. Pheres defies these norms.

116. Euripides again raises the question of what favors and what obligations individuals and family members owe one another (compare Apollo/Death, 70; Admetos/Alcestis, 299).

117. These statements are extreme rejections of Athenian codes of behavior; children were expected to outlive their parents and provide the appropriate burial (compare *Medea* 1032–33).

118. This again reveals Admetos' illogic; it is because he has found a savior in Alcestis that he will not have occasion to bury her.

119. The underlying distinction in these lines is between the barbarian and the Greek, between the slave and the free; in this case Thessalian stands for Greek, in contrast with these Eastern peoples, and Greek stands for free (compare above, p. 22).

120. The word here, *hamartanein,* is the same word used at 709 as well as above, 144.

121. *Psukhē* (life) means the breath, life, spirit, and self in different contexts. In Homer, the soul leaves the body of dead warriors. It means different things in this play. For instance, Alcestis' spirit is breaking from her body when she dies (143); Admetos accuses his father of cowardice, using the word *apsukhia* (642).

122. Zeus' name suggests the word "to live," (*zēn*). In strict stichomythia, Pheres would be responding to Admetos; therefore, line 713 must be a wish. The exaggeration may be taken to mean its opposite in a sarcastic fashion.

123. The heroic code of behavior is explicitly denied with Pheres' casual attitude to reputation; Alcestis' concern for glorious reputation is more typical of the heroic male. Compare Jason's carelessness about reputation and Medea's heroic values (451–52, 797, 810), as well as the debate in *IA* (250–52, 1375–76). See above, pp. 50–51.

124. The word again is *skhletlios* (see 470 with note). The Chorus may be thinking of Alcestis as suffering because of her bravery, or as unflinching in the face of the consequences of her boldness.

125. This is the Hermes who conducts the traveler to his/her final resting place in Hades.

126. The bride of Hades is Persephone, daughter of the goddess Demeter and abducted by Hades. According to Plato (*Symposium* 179 b–d), Persephone valued Alcestis' love of her husband and therefore released her from the underworld (see above, p. 88). A woman who died young was sometimes referred to as a bride of Hades; that motif is suggested by the numerous references in the play to the house of Hades. Alcestis goes from one *kurios* (person in charge) to another, like an Athenian bride (compare 259 n. 58, 382 n. 78). On marriage and death, see also above, pp. 56–7, 96.

127. It is very unusual in Greek tragedy for the entire stage to be empty; the chorus usually remains onstage between episodes. The effect is that the Servant makes a direct address to the audience. The burial gives way to the new wedding.

128. The Greek here is *sōphronōs* a word with a range of meanings, but having to do with self-control; for women, it often connotes chastity (see above, pp. 51–2).

129. The ivy plant was sacred to Dionysos, the god of the vine, and garlands wreath the god on vase paintings; very large cups were decorated with ivy.

130. The grape is the "mother" of the wine because it is its origin. The Greeks typically mixed their wine with water to minimize drunkenness; Herakles' taking his wine unmixed is a sign of his rowdiness and lack of *sōphrosunē.*

131. Herakles calls the trouble "*thuraios,*" which literally means out of doors; while Admetos fooled Herakles by pretending that it was some outsider woman who had died, Herakles makes her even more remote from the family.

132. Kupris is another name for Aphrodite, who was closely connected with the island Cyprus.

133. "Throwing overboard," "stroke," and "cut loose" are attempts to render the Greek nautical metaphor into English; Herakles imagines them plying the oars of drink and setting out from the harbor of grief as a result.

134. Herakles says *othneios,* meaning that the deceased is not of the family; the manuscripts have the Servant say either *thuraios,* which has the sense of outsider, or *oikeios,* of the house. Since Herakles does not yet get the point, the Servant can't give a direct clue. *Thuraios* could refer to the fact that the corpse is already out of doors as well to Herakles' own use of the word at 805. All of these puns and misunderstandings derive from the wife's outsider status in the home of her husband (see 532–33, with n. 97 and above, p. 57).

135. These lines disturb the *stichomythia* and exhibit other irregularities that make it likely that they are added; one of the manuscripts indicates an interpolation of three lines, which would include 820, meaning that a response from Herakles is missing.

136. The verb form of *aidōs* (822) here returns us to the earlier question of whether Admetos' respect for his guest was excessive (601).

137. In Greek, *kēdos* means grief or care, funeral ritual or the dead; it can also mean a connection by marriage.

138. Herakles names himself by giving his lineage—he was the son of Alkmene, daughter of Elektryon in Tiryns, and Zeus.

139. Here it is explicit that the return of Alcestis is part of the theme of favor and gift, which began with Apollo's request of Death (60, 70), continued in Alcestis' request of Admetos (299) and in the quarrel between Pheres and Admetos (660).

140. Kore is another name for Persephone; it means maiden and thus relates the goddess to the life stage of all young, unmarried women. The "Lord" is Hades.

141. At this point the word *aidōs* recurs, marking the reward Admetos gains for having shown respect for his guest.

142. After marching in to anapests, Chorus and actor sing a kommos (above, p. 41); Admetos' cries punctuate the lines of the Chorus.

Admetos has a terrible problem in reentering the halls so closely associated with Alcestis (see her farewell to her bed and chamber, 163–88). He personifies the house and identifies its passageways and face with hers; his fear of the inner chambers is sexual, as is made clear by the fact that he remembers and contrasts this entry with the entry on their wedding day. The word for entry could mean intercourse itself in Greek.

143. The notion of hostage here is unclear; it could mean that Hades now has a hostage which will ensure that Admetos will come after her, or that she was only lent to Admetos since she had long ago promised to die for him (compare 13–15, 49) and has been living and dead (compare 141–42, 521) since then.

144. The recesses of the house (872) are associated with the womb, and the word for pain used here can also refer to birth pains (see Loraux 1995: 32). There is much that feminizes Admetos in the play; he will be mother and father to the children (377) and occupies a womanly position in his mourning. Being antiheroic and femininized were not unproblematic for the Athenian male given its masculinist ideology (see above, p. 50); however, it may be the price of Admetos' gaining knowledge (on male femininity see Zeitlin 1985 [rpt. in Zeitlin 1996], Loraux 1995).

145. Another word with passive and active meanings. The active meaning is to destroy, passive is to lose; the question is obviously one of interpretation. How responsible is Admetos for his own suffering?

146. This line is all but untranslatable; *skhēma* means the figure or shape of a person, as well as character, appearance. Admetos fears what the house stands for, as at 861–62.

147. See 384 on *daimōn;* his personal luck has taken a downswing.

148. On 96 the Chorus speculates that Alcestis has not been buried because the scene is too "desolate"; the wedding bed is now like the grave.

149. The phrase can either mean she left behind a legacy of affection, or that she abandoned affection. Compare the ambiguity around *philia* at 279.

150. Admetos returns to iambics from anapests (compare Alcestis' recovery and change of meter at 280).

151. The theme of fame, *eukleia,* started in 150 with the assurance that Alcestis was dying with glory; Pheres renounced glory (292); now Admetos realizes that Alcestis has won good reputation.

152. Late learning is a common theme in tragedy. In most tragedies, however, the learning takes place only after final and irrevocable violence (for instance Euripides' *Hippolytos, Bacchants,* and Sophocles' *Oedipus the King, Antigone*). Compare 145 with note. In the *Poetics,* Aristotle discusses the different kinds of discovery appropriate to tragedy at length (11.4–9, 14.12–20, 16.1–12); sometimes the recognition comes before the fatal action (as in *Ion* and *Iphigenia Among the Taurians*), sometimes only after (most notably in the case of Oedipus in *Oedipus the King*).

153. The imagined antagonist repeats the words that Admetos and Pheres had bandied about; he now hears in his head the voices that his father had predicted he would.

154. *Prassein* (to do or suffer) if taken in the active here would indicate that Admetos knows that he has made a mistake; taken in the passive it indicates that he is still focused on his suffering.

155. The traditional scholarly quest for what the historical Euripides thought often found him here, and took this to be a reference to Euripides' own study of astronomy. The Chorus here speaks for itself and intones one of the themes of the play: the place of Necessity. Death is the underlying necessity for mortals, the defining condition of the mortal as opposed to the immortal, but death is what Admetos managed to escape. The play does not fully resolve the question of necessity, since Admetos and Alcestis both escape death, but for how long (Gregory: 1991)?

156. Orpheus, named before (357) as a singer, was also the source of a religion whose writings were inscribed on tablets and saved at the temple of Dionysos in Thrace; reincarnation was a central belief of the cult (at 357 Admetos alluded to Orpheus' journey to the underworld). Orphic lore is explicitly linked here with the healing practices of Asklepios, whose death was the remote cause of the action of the play (4, 122–24).

157. The metaphor of cutting a cure comes from the herbalist's practice of cutting plants to make drugs to work against disease; thus the Greek word (*antitemnein*) literally means to cut against.

158. See the earlier choral ode where the Chorus points out the impossibility of cure for death (119–21); they think that there is no hope from sacrifice, but of course Herakles is able to save Alcestis.

159. This is related to the notion that even the sons of the gods, like Sarpedon in the *Iliad,* have to die since Zeus rules within the laws of necessity.

160. The Chalybians were a mining community in the south of the Black Sea; their products were legendary for their hardness.

161. This phrase was taken by an ancient commentator to refer to the bastard children of the gods, born of mortal women; at the same time, it can mean shadowy, as in "amongst the shades" or inhabitants of the underworld.

162. Here it seems as if Alcestis will be celebrated with a hero cult. There is a notable contrast between the speeches that meet her and the speeches that Admetos imagines hearing.

163. There are no stage directions in the Greek manuscripts; the hypothesis, brief summaries placed before the plays in the Alexandrian collections, says merely that "Herakles hid the woman in garments" and then "when Admetos was unwilling he unveiled her." The garments must have included a veil; the references to unveiling and the gestures in the end of the play allude to the marriage ceremony.

164. Herakles, like the Chorus (562), makes a distinction between a friend and a guest-friend; here the word is *philos* not *xenos.*

165. Herakles entered a contest; the prize is a profit to him; this deceit makes up part of the profit/loss motif that runs through the play: Will Death give up his prize, did Admetos get to profit from his wife, will he profit from his children? Obviously in the first scene between Apollo and Death, it overlaps with the *kharis* motif, for Apollo threatens Death, saying he will lose his prize and not get any gratitude for it. We can see similar overlap between the favor that Alcestis does Admetos, and the fact that Admetos and the children don't get to profit from the long life of their wife/mother. See above, pp. 101–102.

166. The phrasing here repeats line 161, *esthēs* and *kosmos* mark Alcestis' propriety and that of this "new" young woman; on *kosmos,* see n. 40.

167. Admetos has moved another stage in recognition; he had earlier said "I have just learned" indicating intellectual understanding (*arti manthanō* 940), now he has a visceral experience of loss (*arti . . . geuomai*), sharpened by the presence of the "substitute."

168. I have translated the line as the manuscripts have it, *hostis,* which would mean that any man, "whoever he is," must bear the fate which the gods bestow. Diggle (1987) in his edition accepts an emendation to a feminine, *hētis.* The feminine pronoun would suggest that Admetos should accept the woman, whoever she is.

169. Admetos here uses the word for sexual desire, *erōs;* he wants to mourn, but the erotic connotation fits in with the sexual subtext of Herakles' offer, which is the reason for Admetos' conflict about accepting the "new woman."

170. There is no explicit subject in this line; it probably refers to the previous line. It can nonetheless mean either that Alcestis kills him, that loving her kills him, or that her death kills him; in any case it is ironic, since of course she died in order to save his life.

171. Herakles repeats the sentiments that Alcestis had expressed earlier (381).

172. This abrupt shift suggests to some critics that Admetos has now passed his test by having denied the woman entry and that Herakles therefore rewards him. Herakles, however, continues the deceit, making it likely that Admetos accepts the woman on line 1108 before he knows who she is.

173. *eisage,* a form of the verb *agein,* refers to the bridal aspect of this exchange, compare 259, 382, 746; see above, pp. 56, 100.

At 1115, Herakles insists on a gesture that is reminiscent of the ancient wedding ceremony, seen often on vases, where the groom takes the bride in his hand. The veiling of Alcestis, necessary for the plot, also comes from wedding imagery. They will start a new life over again; white robes will replace the black ones of mourning, reversing his fears expressed at lines 915–25. Compare the significance of the right hand in giving and receiving oaths (above, pp. 160–61) and Medea's power in not having been given by one man to another.

174. Admetos feels like Perseus killing the Gorgon, whose glance had the power to turn men to stone; Athena had helped Perseus by providing him with a mirror so that he did not have to face his adversary. Alcestis' veil may serve the same purpose.

175. Hermes, who leads the dead to the underworld, is legitimately a leader of souls (*psykhagōgos*); Herakles here disclaims the negative associations of a mortal assuming the power of necromancy (*psukhagōgon*).

176. The gods felt jealousy (*phthonos*) at overweening pride or excessive good fortune and might arrange a consequent fall; this problematic is a motif of tragedy (compare above, p. 18). The word highlights the potential danger of the good luck that has attended Admetos from the beginning. Compare 306 for Alcestis' fears of the rival's jealousy.

177. The pollution attaching to death is here supposed to attach to Alcestis on her return from the land of the dead; the third day after death was traditionally the day of burial, ending the period of marginality by completely breaking the connection to life. In this scene, the third day will mark the end of a different sort of marginal period by reintegrating Alcestis into the family. Her silence has of course been endlessly interpreted, since the significance given by Herakles can refer only to the fairy-tale realm where the dead can come back to life.

178. These closing lines with some minor variations also end *Helen, Medea, Andromache,* and *Bacchants.* Given the differences in effect of these very different plays, these endings cannot be taken seriously as conclusions. See notes to *Helen* and *Medea.*

Medea: Introduction

1. Medea is not only a victim of Aphrodite, but is assimilated to her in various ways. See Boedeker 1997: 140–42. On Medea's "cleverness" see below, p. 163.
2. Corinth was an ally of Sparta, and had already been involved in incidents which would precipitate the war (above, p. 8).
3. For some recent examples see Johnston 1997a; McDonald 1997.
4. The latter two are Helen's brothers, also known as the *Dioskouroi* ("sons of Zeus"). They appear at the end of Euripides' *Helen.*
5. These events were the subject of a lost play by Sophocles. The fullest account of Jason's adventures known to us is Apollonius of Rhodes' epic poem, the *Argonautica,* written long after Euripides in the third century BCE.
6. On magic and Medea as witch see further Parry 1992. Circe and Hekate are both goddesses, and Medea was originally divine herself (below, p. 153). On Hekate see notes on *Medea* 397 and *Helen* 569 (below, p. 392 and 411).
7. For the connection between sex and drugs compare below, p. 226.
8. See lines 1334–5 with note. The age of Apsyrtos varies in different accounts, but in early versions of the myth he was probably a young boy. This creates a telling connection with Medea's later child-murders.

9. The only daughter of Pelias who protested was Alcestis, heroine of Euripides' play of that name (above, p. 95).

10. Magic and language are closely allied in Greek thought. Magic often depends on the correct wording of incantations or spells, and the power of language is sometimes viewed as dangerously "magical" in its ability to persuade. See further Romilly 1975. On women and language see Bergren 1983.

11. In Euripides' play the princess remains nameless. (Compare the normal Athenian practice of referring to a respectable woman not by her name but as So-and-so's daughter or wife: above, p. 51.) Later sources call her Glauke or Kreousa, which are generic names for a noble woman, meaning "Bright" and "Queen" respectively.

12. On the other hand, this is usually a function of men, and Medea's role is an ambivalent one here too (Krevans 1997).

13. On "barbarians" see above, pp. 21–22. The discussion which follows is much indebted to Hall 1989.

14. On Medea as outsider see Graf 1997: 38 (a useful introduction to the myths surrounding Medea). Other core features are her connections with Aphrodite and with magic (id., 30–31).

15. Already in Pindar the Colchians have black faces (*Pythian* 4.212). On the Egyptians see above, p. 22.

16. The evidence is discussed thoroughly by Sourvinou-Inwood 1997, who argues that Medea dons barbarian dress only in her final appearance.

17. Medea is likened to several monsters and wild beasts, especially a lioness (92, 188–90, 1340–43, 1358, 1406). Note the connection of animal imagery with the rejection of human language and persuasion at 187–89. Compare also 103, and the dragon-chariot in which Medea disappears. She is further dehumanized by comparisons with inanimate powers and substances, such as stone, ocean, iron (29, 1279, and fire (a pervasive image for her power, connected with Helios the sun-god).

18. Note that slavery was the role in which many Athenians were most familiar with foreign women.

19. Medea was played by Mark Mitchell. The show was directed by Keenan Hollahan (Dan Savage). It is reviewed by Sue-Ellen Case in *Theater Journal* 1993. For some other contemporary uses of Medea as outsider see McDonald 1997.

20. Drag theater and film have become quite fashionable at the time of writing (1995), but Mitchell's Medea was a far more threatening figure than the femme drag queens of such productions as *Paris Is Burning, Priscilla Queen of the Desert, The Crying Game,* or *Wigstock.* On theatrical cross-dressing and drag see further above, pp. 63–4.

21. I use the word "sacred" advisedly. Greek authors tend to view gender roles as "natural" and sanctioned by the gods (see esp. Xenophon, *Household Management* vii.16–30).

22. The three main types of Greek witch are the young seductress, the unfaithful or unhappy wife, and the old hag (Parry 1992: 91–3). These correspond neatly to the three main stages of a Greek woman's life: maiden, wife, and old (i.e., post-menopausal) woman.

23. E.g. 32, 114, 139, 445, 483, 487, 502, 505, 608, 1299, 1300, 1330, 1331. On the Greek household see above, pp. 53, 55–6.

24. Lines 916–17 imply that Kreon has no sons or other heirs who would take priority over his daughter's children.

25. Isaeus 11.17. Men are also assumed to love their children by nature, but women have the edge. For further examples see Blundell 1989: 40–41.

26. On this abiding "myth of our time" see Warner 1994: ch. 1, "Monstrous Mothers." Susan Smith drowned her children in a lake, inside a car, in Union, South Carolina. She was characterized in the mass media as an intensely loving mother.

27. The most famous Greek parallel is Klytemnestra in Aeschylus' *Agamemnon,* an assertive woman who kills her husband and complains about the sexual double standard (1412–21).

28. It is characteristic of mythology to express social and cultural realities in an extreme or perverted form. On marriage see further above, pp. 54–60.

29. *Xenia* operated almost exclusively between elite males (Hermann 1987: 34–5; above, p. 18). An Athenian woman might engage in small financial transactions, but she could not make her own contracts. Note that Medea's relationship of *xenia* with Aegeus also became a quasi-marriage (see below, p. 432, n. 167).

30. Contrast the Nurse's active verbs at 7–15. At 801 Medea views herself as having been passively "persuaded," but uses active verbs for her own "mistake" in abandoning her home.

31. Her use of this aristocratic male preserve enables her to dispense with support from Jason (compare 613), just as it gave Greek men some independence from the *polis,* especially in exile (Hermann 1987: 7–8).

32. Exceptions are 1341, 1388 (but note that *gamos* can also be used simply for sexual union). Jason's new wedding is represented as conventional in its form and aims (compare 288, 309–10). Yet Medea symbolically renders it a perverted ritual, culminating in the princess's marriage to death (compare 886–88, 956–58, 978–85, 1136–1221, and see further Rehm 1994: ch. 7; for the equation of marriage with death generally see above, pp. 56–7, and below, p. 418, n. 31).

33. The Greek idiom for "preaching to the converted" is "praising Athens to Athenians." For virtuous Athenians in tragedy see especially Sophocles' *Oedipus at Colonus,* Euripides' *Herakles* and *Suppliant Women.* The character of Theseus in Euripides' *Hippolytos* is more ambiguous, but the play is not set in Athens itself.

34. The chorus of Corinthian women also keep their word to Medea (given at 267), though they seem regret it later (850–65).

35. Compare the role of the *epiklēros* or heiress in Athenian law (above, p. 52). The idea is sometimes expressed (notoriously in Aeschylus' *Eumenides*) that the woman is a mere incubator for the man's seed. This is just one among several ancient speculations about the contribution of the two sexes to reproduction, but most theories did give women an inferior role.

36. This applies primarily to boy children, but in the absence of male heirs a girl might become the conduit of the family property, as with Kreon's daughter.

37. Aristotle specifically says that women in drama should not have these two attributes, as they are not "fitting" to the female (*Poetics* 1454a23–5; compare above, p. 69).

38. Like most foreigners in tragedy, she uses standard tragic Greek, and her language is not marked in any way as foreign. (For the full picture, which is slightly more complex, see Hall 1989: 117–21.) This is also true of most "low" characters like the Paidagogos and Nurse.

39. This negative kind of cleverness was often attributed to the contemporary intellectuals known as "sophists," with whom Euripides was associated (above, p. 14).

40. The nurse uses the word *kholos* for her wrath (94), a word sometimes used for Achilles' anger in the *Iliad* (e.g., 1.283, 18.108). Medea's words at 1080 also suggest the wrath theme of the *Iliad* (Kovacs 1993: 62–63). For an ethical comparison of Achilles and Medea see Gill 1996: 154–74. A striking difference is that Achilles is re-humanized at the end of the *Iliad,* when he shows mercy to his enemy's father, whereas Medea is progressively de-humanized. The other hero she most closely resembles is Sophocles' Ajax. See further Knox 1977; Bongie 1977; Rehm 1989.

41. Thucydides 2.45.2, quoted above, p. 46. The most acceptable way for legendary women to seek *kleos* is by sacrificing themselves for men, as both Alcestis and Iphigenia do (compare *Alcestis* 623–24, *IA* 1375–76). See also below, p. 418, n. 29.

42. She ends up using all three methods, since her poison burns the princess and Kreon like fire (1185–94). Fire is marked as feminine (Buxton 1982: 224, n. 28), like the gift of woven clothing, which signifies duplicity (see above, p. 59). Medea's gift of clothing may be an innovation by Euripides (Page 1938: xxvi).

43. E.g., Xenophon, *Household Management* 10.1, Sophocles, *Elektra* 982–83, Euripides, *Elektra* 1204–6; compare also Sophocles, *Oedipus at Colonus* 337–56.

44. This pattern, which is the opposite of the norm in Euripides' Athens, is not an uncommon one for the wandering heroes of mythology. But it takes on particular resonance in a play as concerned as this one is with proper marital roles and behavior.

45. Note also his interest in gold, especially his pursuit of the "barbarian" Golden Fleece. His attitude toward life is a narrowly calculative or mercantile one (e.g., 559–67, 959–63).

46. Compare 1323–24 with 465–68; 1331 and 1363 with 228–29, 465, 498, 690; 1405–6 with 160, 208, 404, also 1353; 1409–10 with 159–61; 1349–50 with 1029. Note especially the verb "driven away" (1405), which echoes Medea's predicament even though it is not immediately relevant to Jason's (compare 71, 326, 392, 438, 704).

47. See further Knox 1977: 303–6, and compare the speech of the Dioskouroi at *Helen* 1642–79. Hatzichronoglou 1993 notes that Medea particularly resembles Dionysos in Euripides' *Bacchants,* another "effeminate barbarian" who disrupts gender norms (above, pp. 31–2).

Medea: The Play

1. The Symplegades or "Clashing Rocks," guarding the entrance to the Black Sea at the Bosporus (see map), were thought to crash together, crushing ships between them. They symbolize the outer limits of the "civilized" (Greek) world, beyond which the Argo traveled to reach Colchis at the eastern end of the Black Sea. On the mythological background, see above, pp. 150–52.

   The ancient Greeks were seafaring people, and Athens in Euripides' time was the major naval power of the Greek world. Sea and sailing imagery is common in Greek texts generally (e.g., *Alcestis* 794–98), but it is especially notable in this play (e.g., 78–79, 278–79, 361–63, 443, 523–25, 770). The metaphor of flying for sailing is often found, with the boat's sails (or oars) viewed as wings (e.g., *Helen* 147, 667). Traditionally, the Argo was the first ship, and in many Greek sources the invention of seafaring is regarded as a transgression of human boundaries and a token of moral decline (compare Hesiod, *Works and Days* 236–37, 618–94; also *Helen* 229–32).

   The Nurse's opening speech has an epic grandeur of style. Compare the elevated, tragic diction of the Paidagogos at line 49. Greek tragedy makes little attempt to give lower-class characters or foreigners a more realistic way of speaking.

2. Pelion is a tall, wooded mountain in Thessaly near Iolcus.

3. Gold is another important theme of the play. It has both divine and barbarian associations, as well as suggesting issues of economic value and exchange.

4. "Passionate desire" translates the Greek *erōs* (from which "erotic" is derived). I have used "heart" here and elsewhere to translate *thumos,* a Greek concept with no English equivalent. *Thumos* is the seat of powerful and often aggressive emotions, such as anger and desire. Unlike the English "heart," it does not suggest sentimental affection, so I have often linked it with the word "rage" in the translation. Euripides also uses the physical heart (Greek *kardia*) for the seat of the emotions (99, 245, 433, 590, 857, 1042, 1242, 1360).

5. The play uses two main words for a child of either gender. I have translated both

words variously as "child," "son," "daughter," "boy," or "girl," for convenience and to reflect the variation in the Greek.

6. Medea used her magic powers to end a famine at Corinth.

7. In Greek, as in many languages, the most common words for "husband" and "wife" are simply the words for "man" and "woman" respectively. This should be borne in mind throughout. On Medea's marital status see above, pp. 158–60. The sentiment expressed by the Nurse is a conventional one, but it does *not* mean that Jason is morally justifed in treating Medea any way he wishes (above p. 160).

8. The sickness metaphor is a common one in Greek for moral, social, and political ills (compare 471, 1364), and suggests that such relationships are organic or "natural." Greek popular ethics was based on the principle of helping friends (especially family members) and harming enemies (above, pp. 20–21). To mistreat friends is a serious offence, and strikes at the heart of the social and moral order. Note that "friend" and "dear" are the same word in Greek (*philos*), and the words for "enmity" and "hatred" are related.

9. On the princess's name, see above, p. 412, n. 11. On the marriage-bed see above, p. 52. Part of the conflict between Jason and Medea is that he tends to view her concern for "the bed" more in sexual terms, and she more in terms of contractual loyalty.

10. On the important concept of honor (*timē*) see above, pp. 50–51, 164.

11. For the significance of this oath, the right hand, and the contractual relationship between Jason and Medea, see above, pp. 160–61.

12. Paleness is associated with women, who did not go out into the sun, at least if their husbands could afford to keep them inside. It also suggests vulnerability or suffering (compare 689, 923, 1006, 1148, 1164, 1174, 1189).

13. The Greek words *oikos* and *domos* are translated as "house" or "household," according to context. This important concept includes the physical house, the family members (whether living, dead, or as yet unborn), the entire household, and the family property.

14. The Greeks often use the liver, as well as the heart (above, n. 4), to signify the biological seat of life and/or the emotions.

15. Diggle 1984 and some other editors believe lines 38–43 were written not by Euripides but by an interpolator. One reason for suspicion is that lines 40–41 reappear at 379–80, where they fit the context better.

16. I use "awe-inspiring" or "awesome" (119, 584, 638) to translate *deinos,* an adjective that can connote fear, wonder, admiration, and/or skill.

17. Literally, the song "of beautiful victory" (*kallinikos*), a word associated with male athletic victories and with the great hero Herakles. Medea uses it of herself at 765. On the competitive imagery of the play see further below, p. 429, n. 140.

18. A *paidagōgos* was a kind of male nanny, a slave who cared for boys in well-off families. This scene, between two slaves, is exceptional in extant Greek tragedy, and adumbrates the gender conflict which will be a principal theme of the play.

19. "Evil" translates *kakos,* a very common Greek word which can be used for any kind of harm or "badness" (above, pp. 20–21). The ambiguities of this word often cannot be disentangled. To bring out its frequency and thematic range, I have mostly translated it as "evil," even though this sometimes sounds a little archaic or strange. Occasionally, however, I have used "bad" (39, 54, 84, 236, 280, 533, 567, 575, 815, 1120), "harm(ful)" (283, 293, 361), "coward(ly)" (264, 1051, 1246), or "wrong" (250, 892, 1014).

20. This time "heart" translates *phrenes,* a word with both intellectual and emotional connotations, which I have generally translated as "mind" (occasionally "mind and heart"). Such loyalty is often expressed by slaves in Greek literature (especially in Euripides: compare 83, 822–23, 1137–38, *Alcestis* 138–39, *IA* 45–47, 312, *Helen* 726–33, 1640–41), almost none of which was written by anyone who had actually lived as a slave.

21. "Fortune" translates the Greek *tukhē,* which means anything that happens to one which is unexpected or out of one's control, whether good or bad (above, p. 13). In the latter case, I have sometimes translated it "misfortune." Compare 198, 268, 302, 331, 544, 671, 1010, 1117, 1203.

    The Nurse's explanation has an articificial air, as if Euripides were drawing attention to the theatrical convention of an opening expository monologue (compare below, pp. 429–30, n. 147 and above, pp. 69–70). But it may have been customary to air misfortunes outside, in the purifying sun and air, as a way of counteracting fear or bad luck (compare 1327–8). Note that the Nurse invokes both earth and sky, the two major realms of the gods, also represented by Helios and Earth, two of the principal gods invoked in oaths (above, p. 159).

22. The Nurse envies the Paidagogos for his ignorance of the true state of affairs. Such envy of an innocent lack of awareness is not uncommon in Greek texts (compare, e.g., Sophocles Frag. 583, quoted above, p. 57).

23. On the ritual of supplication see above, pp. 21–2, and compare *IA* 336–37, 709–10, 900.

24. The Greek here for family ties (*kēdeumata*) ironically suggests funerals as well as marriage, since both were important family obligations (related words are used at 367, 400, 700, 885, 888, 990). Compare *Alcestis,* p. 407, n. 137.

25. Most editors judge this line to be spurious, in part because it is irrelevant to the Paidagogos' point.

26. The Nurse invokes the traditional Greek view that excessive prosperity brings ruin from the gods, often because such prosperity leads to outrageous behavior for which one is divinely punished. Such sentiments are appropriate to the Nurse, who is not

only a humble character herself, but has witnessed first hand the excessive behavior of royalty. In the event, however, Medea herself will be the angry "divinity" who "repays" Jason's house with doom.

27. For the meanings of these technical terms, and an explanation of the structure of Greek tragedy, see above, pp. 38–9, 41–4.

28. The precise meaning of the unique adjective translated as "two-doored" is uncertain. It could mean that the chorus heard Medea through the back door of their houses. It *might* also mean "standing by my door." In either case, it provides a minimal explanation as to why they have ventured out of the house (compare above, p. 60).

29. Suicide threats are part of the heroic persona going back to Achilles (compare, e.g., *Helen* 353–59; for Achilles see above, p. 164). Male heroes rarely carry out such threats (Ajax is the major exception), but noble women in tragedy frequently do (e.g., Sophocles' Antigone, Deianeira, and Jocasta). This is often represented as the most honorable course for a maltreated woman. In our volume, both Alcestis and Iphigenia are honored for choosing death as a "solution" to their problems. Medea's words here raise the expectation that she will take a similar course (compare 227, 243).

30. Zeus is king of the gods and guardian of hosts, guests, the family, oaths, and justice. Earth is the most ancient goddess, and mother of all. "Light" suggests the sun-god Helios, who is also Medea's grandfather. It is customary to call these three gods to witness oaths (above, pp. 13–14).

31. This is the "bed" of death, which resembles sleep and is often linked with marriage. Women who die as virgins are "married" to Hades, the divine lord of the underworld and of the dead. For the mingling of the imagery of death and marriage compare, e.g., 976–88 and above, pp. 56–7. In this passage the "singing" of the "bride" and the word translated as "outcome" (*teleutē*) both suggest the culmination of some kind of ritual (compare 1388).

32. Themis is the divine personification of abstract law or justice. Artemis is goddess of hunting, wild creatures, and young girls, and, strongly associated with women's lives, especially virginity and childbirth (above, pp. 54–5).

33. The "city" or "city-state" (*polis*) is the primary political unit of classical Greek society, embracing not just an urban settlement but the surrounding lands and villages (above, pp. 5–6).

34. The Chorus are friendly toward Medea, but not affectionate. This is the closest they come to calling her their "friend" (*philos*) (compare also 138, 180). Elsewhere she addresses them as "friends," but they call her simply "woman."

35. On *sophos* and *sophia* see above, p. 163. For consistency I have used "clever" for *sophos* throughout this translation. It is tempting to use "wisdom" in places were *sophia* is clearly positive (e.g., 828 and 844). But it is important to remain aware that this is the same word that is used for Medea's "cleverness," in order not to obscure

the questions that the drama raises about the nature of "true" cleverness and/or wisdom. The question "What is *sophia?*" is explored elsewhere in Euripides (explicitly at *Bacchants* 877).

36. This is at variance with the more commonly stated view that music and song can indeed alleviate sorrow (see especially Hesiod, *Theogony* 98–103, and compare *Helen* 1337–52 with note). This passage introduces the play's exploration of what poetry, including tragedy, is *for* (see especially 410–30).

37. Themis (above, n. 32) is said to have "taken" Medea to Greece because she went there relying on Jason's oaths.

38. On Medea's emergence from the house and its "masculine" character see above pp. 162–3 and compare p. 60. Wiles suggests that Medea's entrance recapitulates her transition from Colchis to Greece, with the *skēnē* doors corresponding to the Clashing Rocks, and the *orchēstra* representing the sea (1997: 121–22).

39. "Insides" translates *splankhna,* which means "the innards, the general collection of heart, liver, lungs, gallbladder, and attendant blood vessels" (Padel 1992: 13). This is a seat of strong emotion and is associated with prophecy, animals, darkness, and the womb.

    Ancient Greek has different words for "human being" (*anthrōpos*) and "man" (*anēr*). Yet it is widely assumed that the male is the normative standard for humanity, so the word "man" may be used in a statement about human beings generally, as here.

40. This refers to the custom of giving a dowry with the bride. In Athens it would be the bride's father who provided the dowry, whereas Medea herself "bought" Jason with the Golden Fleece (above, p. 159).

41. By using the word "master" (*despotēs*), Medea likens the lot of women to that of slaves (compare *Helen* 572). Elsewhere in Greek thought we can also see this homology between women and slaves, especially in relation to the free male master of the household. But there were also fundamental differences in their status (above, p. 49).

42. In Euripides' Athens a woman was entitled to divorce her husband, but this is rarely attested, no doubt in part because a woman was not permitted to go to court on her own behalf, but needed a man to make her case. The word "ordeal" (*agōn*) has a competitive coloring (compare above, p. 42). In this context it evokes mythological competitions between men to win women as their wives.

43. The word translated as "departure" (*apallagē*) is not the usual word for divorce. It can also mean "release" or "escape," and foreshadows Medea's extraordinary departure at the end of the play (compare the verbal echo in line 1375).

44. The last point is ambiguous between "refuse to have a husband at all," "refuse the husband who is given to her," and "refuse to have sex with her husband"—a good example of the conceptual interdependence between women's sexuality and their status as wives.

45. This applies most obviously to a foreign woman, like Medea. But when any woman married, she left her natal household, whose "customs" she was familiar with, and had to adapt to her husband's household.

46. Medea uses the language of breaking in and yoking animals, more often used by men for the sexual and/or marital "taming" of women (compare 624, 1366, and above, pp. 54–5). The yoking image may be used of both marriage partners (compare 673, *Alcestis* 166, 921, 994). It primarily indicates subordination; it may also suggest the teamwork of a yoked pair of animals, but even a team of horses would have a leading member (the trace-horse).

47. This is a rhetorical exaggeration, emphasizing women's total dependence on men for their well-being. It also continues Medea's earlier hints at suicide (see lines 145–47 with note). The early epic poet Hesiod makes similar remarks about men's predicament with regard to their wives (*Works and Days* 702–5).

48. This implies that a man can seek sexual satisfaction outside the home, as he could in classical Athens with prostitutes of either sex. (The bracketed line is probably a moralistic later interpolation designed to neutralize these sexual implications.) This does *not* mean, however, that a man could take a second wife, or bring a mistress to live in his marital home (above, p. 59).

49. This is the most famous instance (and exceptional in an Athenian democratic context) of the homology in Greek culture between childbirth and fighting. These were the leading causes of unnatural death for women and men respectively, and were often viewed as the corresponding male and female contributions to the *polis.* Medea's preference displays a masculine persona (compare above, pp. 164–5), but at the same time offers a challenge to male values by suggesting that the quintessentially female act of childbirth is more "heroic" than the defining male act of risking one's life in battle.

50. On the word "barbarian" see above, pp. 22–23. "Outrage" here translates the Greek *hubris* (also at 1366; at 603 it is translated "insult"). This usually refers *not,* as is often said, to an arrogant attitude toward the gods, but to specific acts of verbal or physical abuse, including assault and rape (as at *Helen* 785). See further above, pp. 18–19).

51. This recalls the famous words of Andromache to Hektor in the *Iliad:* "I have no father or lady mother. . . . Hektor, you are my my father and lady mother/and my brother, as well as my flourishing husband" (*Iliad* 6.413, 429–30). The crucial difference is that Andromache has lost her relatives through warfare, Medea through her own criminal behavior.

52. This line does not fit the context well (compare 267), and was probably added by a later hand to fit in with Medea's eventual revenge.

53. The constant presence of the Chorus means that Medea must extract this promise of silence from them. Note that they do not go back on their promise (given at 267), although they seem to regret it later (850–65).

54. Note that this is not the same character as the Kreon of Sophocles' "Theban plays" (*Antigone, Oedipus the King, Oedipus at Colonus*). It is a generic name for a king, meaning simply "ruler" (compare above, p. 412, n. 11).

55. The word translated "skilled" (*idris*) evokes the name of Medea's mother Idyia ("she who knows"). See further above, p. 151.

56. This word has political connotations, suggesting disengagement from public life. Compare 808, and related words at 81, 217, 550.

57. This is in origin a musical metaphor, literally meaning "out of tune," but extended to mean "wrong" or "bad."

58. The Greek verb "gave away" is the usual one for this aspect of a formal marriage (above p. 56). Contrast the transgressive "marriage" between Jason and Medea (above, p. 159).

59. I have used "sensible" throughout for the Greek *sōphrōn.* This refers to the virtue of *sōphrosunē,* which literally means "sound-mindedness," and ranges over self-control, self-knowledge, moderation and deference. See further above, pp. 51–2.

60. Medea switches here to plural forms, so that the "you" addressed in 310–11 could implicitly include Jason as well as the king, though it might also be a poetic plural.

61. Kreon and Medea move here into *stichomythia,* a kind of formal dialogue in which two characters speak alternating lines. On supplication, and the ritual gesture of touching the knees, see above, pp. 21–2. It is not clear whether Medea actually falls at the king's knees here, or whether her appeal remains verbal until 336. I have adopted the latter interpretation, since it is plausible that the physical gesture, which gives the supplication its full ritual force, should precipitate Kreon's final breakdown (compare line 339).

62. Kreon is not speaking of physical force, but of the moral and religious force of supplication.

63. Kreon is claiming that, unlike most kings, he does in fact respect the moral claims of others (compare above, p. 26).

64. On Medea's range of methods see above, p. 164.

65. This is probably a poetic plural ("we" for "I"), but may also suggest "we women" (compare 407–9).

66. Medea is using the official language of interstate law, as well as guest-friendship (*xenia*). For the latter compare 613, 616, 687, 723–4, 730, 1392, and see above, p. 21.

67. Hekate is an underworld goddess, goddess of night, darkness, the moon and crossroads, of magic and demons, of childbirth and nurture (see further above, p. 151). The hearth is the center of the household, the women's realm, and as such is the proper location for the shrine to divinities protecting the household, especially Hestia,

goddess of the hearth (above, pp. 57–8), and Zeus in his capacity as protector of the hearth and family. Hekate, by contrast, is a goddess of the outside (in Euripides' time, her shrines stood *outside* the gates of private houses and the city). Medea violates sacred female space by killing first her brother (at the hearth: 1334) and then her children (inside the house: 1053–5). She also violates the royal hearth by killing the king and princess (1130). She then abandons the hearth in each instance.

68. The language here plays on the connection of Medea's name with Greek words for "cunning" or "full of plans" (above, p. 151).

69. Sisyphos was the founder of Corinth, but his name was also a by-word for treachery. He offended the gods (specifically Hera, goddess of marriage) and ended up in the underworld, eternally rolling a boulder up a hill. In one story he was actually married to Medea.

70. Medea speaks like a man in invoking her patrilineal male ancestors. The language of 393–4 and 403 and the concern with mockery also sound a note of male heroism (see further above, p. 164).

71. This is a reversal of the traditional stereotyping of women as deceivers. The reversal of sex roles is accompanied by other reversals of the natural and moral order. But the idea of heroic female honor and glory is problematic in a culture in which women are most respected when least visible (above, p. 51).

72. Greek texts often speak of men and women as belonging to different species or races (compare 428, 574, 909, 1084, 1088).

73. The Muses are goddesses of music and poetry, invoked notably in epic, and these lines are epic in diction (Garner 1990: 94–5). There is a strong tradition of misogyny from the beginnings of Greek literature, notably in Hesiod's accounts of the myth of Pandora, who brought evil to the human race (*Theogony* 570–613; *Works and Days* 53–105).

74. Phoibos is a common title for Apollo, god of archery, prophecy, music, and light (compare 667–8). It literally means "bright."

75. There were in fact female poets in ancient Greece (above, p. 43). But they played a very minor role in comparison with male poets, and none of them (to our knowledge) engaged in the large-scale public genres of tragedy or epic. We have no evidence of any Athenian women writers of any kind before the third century BCE (Snyder 1989: 39–40).

76. The "twin rocks" are the Symplegades or "Clashing Rocks" (see above, line 2 with note).

77. The word "dishonor" has political connotations in Athens, referring to a citizen's loss of civil rights. It is used again at 696.

78. "Graceful favor" translates *kharis.* This untranslatable word is used for reciprocal favors but also connotes charm, joy, and grace (for its range compare 186, 227, 508, 526, 630–31, 659, 720, 982, 1155). See further above, p. 20.

79. These words evoke the famous lines of Hesiod in which the decline of human society from the Golden Age to the present will culminate in the departure of Aidos and Nemesis (Respect and Retribution) from the earth to Olympus, home of the gods (*Works and Days* 197–201).

80. I.e. she is lucky to get away with exile rather than execution.

81. Since the primary purpose of marriage was the production of legitimate children for the perpetuation of a man's *oikos* (above, pp. 55–6), childlessness would naturally be an acceptable reason for him to divorce his wife.

82. Medea is referring to the ritual gestures of supplication. Jason does not deny that he supplicated Medea in this manner, or that she did what he asked. He is therefore bound to her by a reciprocal obligation.

83. Gold was tested by rubbing it on a touchstone, on which real gold would leave a particular color. Greek authors, especially Euripides, often express this desire for a clear test of a person's honesty and loyalty (compare below, line 659–62, also Euripides' *Hippolytos* 925–31, *Herakles* 655–72, *Elektra* 367–79). This concern is part of a larger theme that pervades Greek writings, and has a special relevance to theater, namely the contrast between appearance and reality.

84. This could also mean "I must prove that I am not by nature bad."

85. Kypris is a title for Aphrodite, who had a famous shrine in Cyprus. Eros (line 531) is her son. These are the two principal divinities of sexual desire. Traditionally in Greek thought, the fact that a god causes one to do something does not excuse one from responsibility (above, pp. 16–17).

86. Orpheus was a hero famed for his skill at singing to the lyre and for his devotion to his wife Eurydike, whom he tried to bring back from the dead (compare *Alcestis* 357–62; *IA* 1211–13). This devotion makes him an ironic parallel for Jason. He was also one of the Argonauts who sailed with Jason to get the Golden Fleece.

87. This alludes metatheatrically to the *agōn,* the central quasi-formal rhetorical debate that is a notable feature of Euripidean drama (above, pp. 41–2 and 70).

88. The agricultural metaphor recalls the Athenian marriage ritual (above, p. 56). Jason's fantasy of "one big happy family" is implausible, since the children of two different mothers would usually be at loggerheads, and the new wife would feel threatened by the old wife's children (compare 1147–9 and *Alcestis* 304–10).

89. The Greek word for "female" (*thēlus,* also used at 909, 928, 1083) is etymologically related to suckling. It comes to mean "female" in general, with connotations of fertility, softness, and weakness.

90. This is a standard theme of Greek misogyny, going back to the Pandora story in Hesiod, which posits a carefree world of men existing before the creation of the first woman (*Theogony* 507–616, *Works and Days* 47–105).

91. The principle that one should not go behind a friend's back, but convince him by open persuasion, is a standard feature of Greek *philia* (see Blundell 1989: 36–7 and compare above, p. 20).

92. The translation reflects the fact that Medea uses a verb form normally confined to men.

93. By sending Jason into the house (the female realm), and assuming that he is overcome by erotic desire, Medea establishes a reversal of both status and gender roles between herself and Jason (compare 1394, and above, p. 161). The imperative "be gone" (623) is used elsewhere only to subordinates: Medea to the Nurse (820); the Nurse to the children (105); and Medea to her children (1053, 1076). Compare also the way Sophocles' Kreon speaks of Antigone and her sister: "Take them inside . . . from now on they must be women and not roam loose" (*Antigone* 577–9).

94. Kypris = Aphrodite (above, n. 85).

95. "Sensible restraint" is *sōphrosunē* (above, p. 421, n. 59 and pp. 51–2).

96. On this surprise entrance see above, p. 155.

97. This refers to Delphi, the most famous and prestigious of the ancient oracles (see Map). People traveled from all over the Greek world to consult it on public and personal matters. The navel-stone (*omphalos,* 668) was a sacred stone at the oracle, thought to mark the center ("navel") of the earth. The oracle's response is a "song" (668) because it was given in verse (Apollo is god of poetry and music as well as prophecy and light).

98. Wineskins were leather containers that retained the approximate shape of the animal they were made from, and thus had a "foot" from which the wine could be poured. Aigeus' oracle seems quite easy to interpret, and one may wonder why Medea does not use her vaunted cleverness to solve it on the spot. But according to legend, Aigeus *did* stop off on the way home, at Troezen, where he "loosed the wine-skin's foot" and begot Theseus, the greatest Athenian hero. If Medea had successfully interpreted the oracle for him here, this well-known lapse on his part would be hard to explain.

99. Corinth is not on the way from Delphi to Athens, but it is on the way to Troezen (see previous note, and map).

100. A "spear-friend" is a *xenos* (above, p. 21) whose friendship is based on military alliance.

101. Again, this may be a poetic plural, but it points to the effect of Jason's behavior on his children as well as Medea herself.

102. At this point, Aigeus is reacting as if Jason is involved with another woman in a way which, while humiliating, does not threaten Medea's economic security. It is only when she mentions a formal tie to the royal family (700) that he starts to take the situation seriously (compare above, p. 49).

103. Aigeus is referring diplomatically to his good relations with the Corinthians, which he does not wish to sully. At the same time, his words pointedly raise the dramatic question of just how Medea—a woman alone—is to escape from Corinth at the end of the play. (I have followed the usual order of lines in this passage, rather than Diggle's transposition.)

104. Divine punishment for perjury often involved the destruction of one's children and hence of one's lineage—a theme very pertinent to this play (above, pp. 161–2).

105. Hermes is the messenger god and god of roads, lucky finds, and trickery. One of his functions is to escort the souls of the dead to the underworld.

106. The word translated here as "to be endured" is related to verbs meaning "dare," which are used both by Medea and others of her deeds (796, 816, 1325, 1328, 1339), and by Medea of Jason's (164, 583, 695). This word group can refer to mental or physical daring or endurance in either a positive or a negative way (compare also 590, where it is translated "bear"). There is thus an untranslatable verbal echo in lines 796–7: it is easier for Medea to endure the anguish of killing her children than the humiliation of being laughed at by her enemies.

107. Medea's language here recalls the Homeric warrior's desire to win a glorious reputation (*kleos*) by performing mighty exploits (above, p. 51). At 810 the Chorus will give a "feminine" response to this "masculine" assertion of values.

108. This sentence literally means either "All words between then and now are superfluous," or "all words of moderation are excessive."

109. Some editors think that Medea also exits here, in order to smear the gifts with poison (compare 789). In that case, she must reenter at the end of the choral song. On the other hand, the usual textual indicators of an exit and reentrance are absent (compare above, p. 28), and Medea does explicitly send for the gifts at 950–51. I therefore follow the majority of editors in keeping Medea onstage throughout the choral song. It seems unlikely that the audience would be disturbed by the slight incongruity with 789. Greek tragedy does not adhere to strict canons of realism, and such inconsistencies are not uncommon.

110. Erechtheus is the mythical founder of Athens, and his "children" are the Athenians. They are "children of gods" because Erechtheus was of divine origin, being a son of the goddess Earth.

Praise of Athens was, naturally, popular at Athens (above, pp. 148–9). This ode represents Athens as combining in a positive, harmonious way many things that appear elsewhere in the play in perverted or dangerous forms, including song, harmony, sexuality, and cleverness. Even the idea of moving through "bright air" (*aithēr,* 830) appears elsewhere (compare 439, 1297). There is, however, an element of fantasy or wishful thinking in the ode, as suggested by lines 832 and 838 ("they say"). And the idealization of Athens, which appears to deny any negative factors within the city, sets up the audience for a jolting change of tone and direction at 846. See further above, pp. 149–50.

111. According to Athenian myth and ideology, the Athenians had their original birth directly from the earth on which they lived (see previous note). They also gloried in the alleged fact that Athens had never been conquered. In fact it was briefly occupied by the Persians in 480 BCE, and would be occupied again by the Spartans shortly after *Medea* was produced.

112. On the translation of *sophia* as "cleverness" see above, n. 35.

113. The Cephisus was one of the two main rivers of Athens. Rivers symbolize human and agricultural fertility and the nurture of children, and are therefore considered sacred (compare 846).

114. It is standard Greek practice to represent personal deliberation as a form of interior dialogue with oneself or part of oneself (compare 1056–58, 1242–8). This can plausibly be understood as an expression of a worldview that sees the self as constituted through engagement and dialogue with others (see Gill 1996).

115. Medea speaks as if she were a mother preparing her daughter for marriage (compare 1026–7). Jason seems oblivious to this very peculiar stance, as to Medea's other ambiguities and ironies.

116. Libations are drink offerings poured to the gods at solemn ritual moments, including truces (above, pp. 11–12).

117. Medea must explain why she has cried out again, now that things are apparently going well. It seems that the mention of Jason's right hand, the symbol of the oath he has violated, prompts her to think of her revenge (which will be perpetrated with her own right hand). But her words are ambiguous. They could be understood by Jason to refer to the uncertain future lot of all human beings.

118. There is no other sign that Jason has actually done this, for example by attempting to keep them with him at Corinth.

119. The Greek word used here for "gift" suggests both a bride's dowry and the gifts or trousseau that came with her from her father's house. These included clothing and ornaments, like Medea's robe and crown, which were carried by children in a procession to the house of the newlyweds (see further above, p. 56).

120. The word for "blessed" (*makar*) has a nice ambiguity. It is used typically for the newly married and the gods (compare 825, 509), but also for the recently deceased. Similarly the word "finery" (*kosmos*), used repeatedly for Medea's gifts (787, 951, 954, 972, 981, 1156), is used commonly for bridal gifts but also for gifts to the dead (compare *Alcestis* 149, 612, 618, *Helen* 1062, 1068, 1279, and note on *Alcestis* 149). At 1065–6, when Medea imagines the princess dressing in her gifts, her words recall the dressing of a corpse for burial, which also involved a robe and crown. On marriage and death see further above, p. 418, n. 31 and pp. 56–7.

121. This refers to the reciprocal basis of Greek religion, which rested on the assumption that one could win the favor of the gods with fine temples, sacrifices and other "gifts" (above, pp. 10–11).

122. Lines 1015–16 have a double meaning, playing on verbs whose meanings include "bring home from exile" and "bring down." The Paidagogos tries to comfort Medea with the thought that her children, remaining in Corinth, will one day bring her back from exile, while she refers cryptically to the fact that she will be sending them down to the house of Hades, king of the dead (compare 1073). The play includes many such ambiguities (e.g., 758, 899–900, 1021–3, 1039).

123. There is controversy concerning the whereabouts of the children during this scene. Some scholars think that they exit at 1053 and reenter at 1069. It seems more likely, however, that despite Medea's command at 1053, the children should hesitate and remain onstage until she makes her wishes clear at 1076. The reiterated command is thus an aspect of the extraordinary fluctuations in Medea's internal debate. The fact that the children are present when she explicitly says she will kill them (1056–63) is not a problem. Dramatic conventions allow a character to speak without being heard by others onstage, and in any case the children are presented as too young to understand what is happening.

124. The ritual raising of torches at a wedding was a special function of the couple's mothers. Medea's language in this speech echoes that of funeral laments for the young, in which it was common to bewail their unfulfilled potential, and especially their lack of a marriage (see further Alexiou 1974; Holst-Warhaft 1992).

125. The Greek alludes to the activity of combing raw wool with a spiny instrument. "As an instrument of torture it was a sort of sharp-toothed harrow over which the body was dragged, lacerating the flesh and causing profuse bleeding" (Page 1938 ad loc.).

126. These lines are a grisly parody of the language used to warn off anyone whose presence at a real sacrifice might interfere with the effectiveness of the ritual. The inappropriate bystander is here told to take personal responsibility for absenting himself or herself. In this case, such bystanders include the Chorus, and in a different sense the theatrical audience.

The equation of violent human death with a perverted sacrifice is often found in tragedy (compare *Helen* 358) and literalized in the tale of *Iphigenia at Aulis* (above, p. 12). Although we are not told exactly where the children are killed, later artists sometimes showed Medea killing them at an altar (Sourvinou-Inwood 1997: 271). Human sacrifice is also associated with "barbarians" (Hall 1989: 146–8).

127. "There" refers to Medea's exile in Athens, implying that she could take the children with her if she chose to do so.

128. "Vengeful demon" translates *alastōr* (also at 1260 and 1333; *miastōr* at 1371 is similar). This is a spirit of vengeance which persecutes and punishes criminals, especially murderers. It embodies the victim's wrath, and may be personified in its own right or embodied in another human being, either the dead person or his/her avenger.

129. Medea uses a verb of reproduction more commonly used of men (like the archaic English "beget"). She also uses plural verb forms (literally "we shall kill them—we

who gave them life"). Although such "poetic plurals" are common in Greek, here they may hint that both the children's parents are responsible for their death, as Medea will declare at 1364–6 (so Gill 1996: 167 n. 259).

Medea seems to ignore the possibility considered earlier, that she could take the children away with her. Why is it now "necessary" that the children die? She could mean that the murder is "necessary" for the fulfillment of her plan, or that the Corinthians would inevitably find her children and kill them in revenge.

130. The interpretation of this whole speech, and especially these last three lines, is very controversial. The main issue is whether "my plans" (1079, echoing 372, 772, 769, 1044, 1048) refers to Medea's plans to kill the children, her plans to rescue them instead, or her rational faculty in general. Another important issue is whether there is a clear-cut opposition between "plans" and "raging heart" (*thumos*).

These questions have been of great interest to ethical philosophers. Is Medea revealing a conflict between reason and passion, or two ethical principles, or two emotions, or a "masculine" and "feminine" side, or some combination of these factors? Two recent careful studies are Rickert 1987 and Gill 1996: 216–26. My own view is that Medea is saying that her decision has been made and planned out rationally and with full awareness, but that her *thumos* drives her in the *same* direction even more powerfully.

Many critics think that parts of this speech should be excised, mostly for reasons of consistency in Medea's character, both within the speech and with the rest of the play. Staging issues are also a concern to some (compare above, p. 427, n. 123). At the extreme end of the spectrum, Diggle 1984 would excise the whole of 1056–80, but this is highly controversial. For a discussion of the issues and a defense of the speech see Michelini 1989.

131. For the theme of women, wisdom, and song, compare lines 410–30.

132. On the miseries of parenthood compare *Alcestis* 882–88.

133. On the convention of the "messenger speech" see above, p. 42. The speech in this play is exceptionally long and horrific.

134. It is quite common in Greek to refer in desperate situations to escape by land or sea. But the peculiar language here draws special attention to an important dramatic question: How will Medea succeed in escaping from Athens by herself? (compare esp. 725–30, 1296–9).

135. Despite the dark complexion of Mediterranean peoples, blond hair was a traditional feature of heroic characters, both male and female, going back to Homer, and was reproduced in tragic masks (above, pp. 36 and 153).

136. The women's quarters in an Athenian house were segregated from the men's (above, pp. 52–3), so the male messenger feels the need to explain his presence there (compare above, n. 28).

137. Compare the description of Medea herself at 30, 923, and 1006. The princess is an image of conventional femininity and an alter ego for Medea—the virginal princess that she herself once was (compare Boedeker 1997: 143–4). She receives the "proper" marriage to Jason that Medea never had, but Medea perverts this wedding too (above, p. 418, n. 32).

138. The image of a finely dressed woman with a mirror is found in Greek art, both in wedding scenes and on funeral monuments.

139. The god Pan was thought responsible for various kinds of irrational fit (including "panic" attacks). The old woman gives a ritual cry of joy in recognition of a divine visitation, but alters her response as soon as she sees her mistake. The whole speech blends imagery of marriage, death, sex, magic, warfare, athletics, and fire (which suggests the involvement of Medea's grandfather, Helios the sun-god).

140. Two hundred yards was the length of a stadium. In a race, the runners would run to the end, turn, and come back to the start. The image would convey "a short time" to the Greek audience, who did not use precise timepieces but were very familiar with athletic events (compare *IA* 185–230). It also develops the agonistic imagery of the play (1195, 1215, 1219; compare, e.g., 45, 235, 315, 366, 403, 912–3, 1077).

141. An alternate reading of this line would mean "you will find your own way to escape punishment."

142. This may allude to a different version of the story, in which the Corinthians did kill the children (above, p. 152).

143. This is a striking example both of self-address (above, p. 426, n. 114) and of Medea's heroic masculine persona (above, pp. 162–6). Her wording alludes specifically to the armor of hoplites, the heavy-armed foot-soldiers who were the mainstay of fifth-century Greek land armies.

144. Medea has been onstage, planning and controlling the action, since she first entered at line 213. Her departure at this moment therefore has strong dramatic emphasis. Contrast the repeated entrances and exits of the children. Each time they leave, we fear they may never return. The dramatist thus builds suspense concerning their eventual death.

145. The Furies are demonic underworld goddesses of revenge (compare line 1389). Note that the Chorus' prayer will ironically be answered, when Helios helps Medea to leave the house. For the idea of Medea herself as an avenging demon see 1333 with note, and compare 1059 with note. Compare also her superhuman appearance at the end of the play (above, pp. 166–8).

146. The text here is very corrupt and the meaning uncertain.

147. The Chorus conspicuously fail to run to the children's rescue, in line with the dramatic convention that the Chorus does not usually enter the house. Euripides here seems to draw attention to the convention (rather than trying to smooth over it),

especially by the unusual feature of dialogue between stage and offstage (contrast the prologue, where lyric cries are heard from offstage but no dialogue occurs). For this self-conscious use of conventions compare above, notes 21 and 87.

148. This odd expression combines imagery of entanglement (culturally coded as duplicitous or feminine) with that of the sword (coded as masculine). Compare 376–85 and above, pp. 163–4. Aeschylus uses the same combination of imagery, much more fully developed, to characterize the murder performed by the "man-woman" Klytemnestra in *Agamemnon.*

149. Ino was the wife of Athamas, King of Boeotia. According to a more familiar version of this myth, Zeus's wife Hera drove Athamas mad and he killed one of their sons. Ino fled with the other son, leapt into the sea, and drowned with him. But the Chorus here hints at a different version, unknown to us, in which Ino kills her own children. There are also tales that make her fly off the cliff to safety, and even become a goddess, which makes her an interesting parallel for Medea (compare above, pp. 166–8).

There *were* in fact other women in Greek mythology who killed their own children, most notably Prokne, a well-known Athenian heroine. Prokne killed her son Itys in order to deprive her unfaithful husband of an heir, served Itys up for dinner, and was afterward turned into a bird (compare Medea's winged chariot: below, n. 151).

Jason likewise seems to ignore the mythological parallels to Medea's behavior (1339). Both passages are rhetorically effective in emphasizing the bizarre and shocking nature of Medea's act. But this would not prevent the audience from remembering any parallels that they knew.

150. This pair of options is a conventional expression of the impossible, and as such ironically foreshadows Medea's final departure (compare *Helen* 1516).

151. The audience would expect to see the bodies brought out of the house. Medea's appearance with them above the house is thus a theatrical surprise. Its arrival and departure were probably staged with the *mēchanē*—a crane enabling characters, especially gods, to appear on high (above, p. 36). This is one of the features that marks Medea as godlike at the end of the play. Others include her prophetic ability (1386–8) and her founding of a cult (1381–3).

The dragon-chariot also answers a question that has been asked with increasing urgency throughout the play—how will Medea get away? This mode of departure underlines her magic powers, by connecting her with Helios and with flying (often viewed as a divine or magical form of locomotion).

The chariot of the sun is usually drawn not by winged snakes, but by flying horses (compare *Helen* 342). Our only evidence for dragons in *Medea* comes from an ancient commentator on the play. But snakes are appropriate to Medea, since they are associated with witchcraft, sex, fertility, and death. And after Euripides, she was shown with a dragon-chariot in the visual arts (Sourvinou-Inwood 1997: 269–75). Wiles 1997: 122 suggests that the dragons would assimilate Medea theatrically to Scylla, a monster to whom Jason likens her (see line 1343, with note).

152. This could refer to Jason laying hands on Medea in vengeance. But the same word is used twice (1403, 1412) of Jason's thwarted desire to caress his children's bodies one last time.

153. The sun is the source of light and purity, so polluted persons should conceal themselves from it (compare above, p. 417, n. 21). Jason voices a conventional reaction, apparently unaware that the sun is the source of Medea's power.

154. The verb "lead" was used when a man took a bride from her home to his own in marriage (above, p. 56).

155. This line is nicely ambigous. The surface meaning is that Medea's punishment for killing her brother has come to Jason instead. But the words also suggest that Medea herself is an avenging demon, punishing Jason for his own behavior (compare 1059, 1259–60).

156. "Hearth" hints here at the idea of sacrifice (on the hearth see above, pp. 421–22, n. 67). In other versions, Medea kills her brother either at home or on board the Argo, where she chops him up and scatters him overboard to delay their pursuers, who must collect the body for burial. See further Bremmer 1997.

157. In Greek, this is not an unusual way of referring to oneself (compare, e.g., *Alcestis* 1084, 1094). Here it seems to emphasize Jason's self-importance and evasion of responsibility for his past.

158. Scylla was a sea monster with six snaking heads, who snatched sailors to their death from passing ships. Along with another female monster called Charybdis, she guarded the dangerous Straits of Messina, the entrance to the Tyrrhenian Sea (between Italy and Sicily).

159. Note the echo of 436. The verb translated "lose" can also mean "destroy" (for the ambiguity compare *Alcestis* 892, 949).

160. This line is usually cut out, in part because Scylla lived in a cave by the sea, not on the plain (above, n. 158).

161. Or, "this removes my grief."

162. For the metaphor, compare lines 17 and 471. For the verbal echoes in this passage of stichomythia, compare above, p. 41.

163. In a sense Jason is wrong about this, since it was the violated pledge of his right hand that drove Medea to her revenge.

164. On "outrage" (*hubris*) see above, p. 19.

165. Proper burial and commemoration of the dead are extremely important in Greek culture. When Jason speaks of weeping for his children, he is referring not just to tears, but to mourning rituals that require the presence of the bodies.

166. Hera is the wife of Zeus, queen of the gods and goddess of marriage and, to a lesser extent, motherhood (for the latter see Johnston 1997: 52–5)—both significant func-

tions in connection with Medea. Akraia is a title connected with a temple at Corinth involved in various versions of the Medea myth (above, p. 152). Medea is referring to the burial of the children at this temple and the associated expiatory cult. For the establishment of a cult at the end of a play compare below, p. 93.

167. The verb "live with" (*sunoikein,* also used at 242 and 1000) often indicates marriage. In the event, Medea did live with Aigeus in Athens as his wife, with unfortunate consequences (above, p. 149).

168. The horn-like prow ornament of the Argo (compare 1335) was hung up in a temple of Hera as a dedication, but it fell down on Jason's head and killed him. The word translated "outcome" (*teleutē*) suggests ritual fulfilment (compare above, p. 418, n. 31).

169. On Furies see above, p. 429, n. 145.

170. Jason was a foreign visitor (*xenos*) when he offended Aietes, Medea's father, by stealing the Golden Fleece. But the link with oath-breaking suggests that Medea is thinking primarily of herself as his "foreign friend." On *xenia* see above, p. 21.

171. By the end of the play, Jason has been reduced to the state Medea was in at the beginning (see above, p. 166).

172. These lines occur in almost identical form at the end of several plays by Euripides (including *Alcestis* and *Helen* in this volume, also *Andromache* and *Bacchants*). This has caused some critics to doubt their authenticity. But they fit this play very well. Note especially the word "steward," which echoes 170, and is not found at the end of the other plays in question. The word "unexpected" is also well suited to Medea's remarkable appearance in her magic chariot (though it also suits other plays, including *Alcestis* and *Helen*).

Helen: Introduction

1. H. D. [Hilda Doolittle], *Helen in Egypt,* p. 36, with *variatio* pp. 47, 85. Cytheraea [Kythereia] is an epithet of Aphrodite probably derived from the island Kythera, off the southeast coast of the Peloponnesos, the first land the goddess approached after emerging from the castrated genitals of her father Ouranos, "Sky" (Hesiod, *Theogony* 192).

2. A late story relates that Eris, upset that she had not been invited to the wedding of the mortal Peleus to the goddess Thetis (the parents of Achilles), arrived unannounced and tossed an apple into the celebration inscribed "let the most beautiful take it," thus igniting the goddesses' rivalry. While it is certainly possible that this story was familiar in Euripides' day, its earliest attestation is the late first century BCE.

3. For example, Alcaeus, a male poet from the island of Lesbos roughly contemporary with Sappho (end of the seventh century BCE), frag. 42.

4. Both Suzuki 1989 and Holmberg 1995 recognize Homer's complex portrayal of Helen but suggest more restricted interpretations of its meaning.

5. The fourth-century Athenian orator, Isocrates, a contemporary of Plato's, tells the same story in his *Helen* (64), and compare also Plato's *Republic,* 586c.

6. On this theme see Winkler 1981; and specifically on Sappho and Helen, duBois 1984 and 1995; Greene 1996.

7. Generally on Helen's ritual roles see Calame 1991, 1997; Larson 1995; Lindsay 1974.

8. *Parthenos* is often translated as "maiden" or "virgin," and *partheneia* as "maidenhood." But *parthenos* does not mean a virgin in our sense of the word, which was an early Christian interpretation. It seems to refer rather to an unmarried adolescent, as a girl, especially in ancient Sparta, might be a *parthenos* and bear a child with no disfavor (Sissa 1990; Zweig 1993a).

9. In ancient Greece, marriage for procreation was expected of all, women and men (see above, p. 53). In Sparta, women had greater mobility than their Athenian counterparts; they associated primarily with other women, even after marriage, and they may have engaged freely in extramarital affairs.

10. Though the transition rites of both girls and boys ritualize their entry into their adult roles, specific rites and their meanings vary according to differentiated gender expectations (Winkler 1990a; Felson-Rubin 1994: 68–75).

11. Recently Meagher 1995: 5 states as the goal of his study "the rediscovery and exoneration of Helen."

Helen: The Play

1. Sparta is Helen's home. Menelaos rules as king by virtue of his marriage to Helen, the same reason he will enjoy the privilege of going to the Isles of the Blest after death (see Homer, *Odyssey* 4.561–9).

2. In Greece, altars were sites of sanctuary for the suppliant (compare *IA* 911). Since tombs are also sacred and the dead powerful, Helen turns the tomb of the former king into the same kind of sanctuary as an altar. See her exchange with Menelaos, lines 797–801.

3. Much is condensed into this first line of the play. The first word is the name of the river Nile. Throughout the play, here and elsewhere in Greek texts, localities, even well-known cities, are identified by the rivers that run by them: Sparta by the Eurotas, Troy by the Scamander, and Helen's location in Egypt by the Nile (see *Helen* 53, 124, 162, 252, 369, 462, 610, also *IA* 165–6, 204, 1295). All rivers are animated by spirits, some female, some male, so that swearing by a river, as Helen

does by the Eurotas 348–9, probably reflects swearing one's oath by the river deity, as by the ultimate river god by whom oaths are sworn, the Styx.

The word *kalliparthenoi,* "beautiful maidens," may be a Euripidean creation; its only other known occurrence is in Euripides' later play, *IA* 1574 (this volume). Consequently, editors are uncertain about its meaning, which may refer to the purity of Nile waters flowing from the melting snows, or to female river spirits of the Nile, further enhancing the female ritual associations evoked by the word *kalliparthenoi,* (see above, p. 228).

Note Euripides' frequent use of a form of *parthenos,* three times in the first ten lines (1, 6, and 10): *parthenōn* (gen. pl.) "of the maidens" (line 6), and *parthenon* (acc. sg.) "maiden" (line 10). I have preserved this repetition to maintain Euripides' own emphasis on this language and the progression in thought with each repetition: line 1 describing fair-maiden streams, and line 6 alluding to the Nereids, daughters of Nereus, "the maidens of the sea," so that the first reference to the *parthenos* Theonoe, line 10, identifies her intimately with water, the sea nymphs, and ritual. This repetition also evokes Helen's status as a *parthenos* (see above, pp. 227–8), suggesting her innocence, sexually and politically, of the accusations against her.

4. More literally, his name might mean renowned by, or through, a god; or inspired by a god. For another meaning of his name relevant to this play, see below, p. 436, n. 14.

5. Ancient Greek poets often created meaningful names for their characters. Theonoe's childhood name, Eido, connects to the verbal root of the words meaning "I see" and "I know," concepts linguistically connected in ancient Greek (see esp. Sophocles' *Oedipus the King*). It is also similar to a word meaning image (*eidōlon,* line 34). At *Odyssey* 4.366, Proteus' daughter, another sea nymph, is named Eidothea. Her name means her being like, or more possibly, knowing the things of the gods. These meanings come to the fore in Eido's later renaming to Theonoe, "with the mind, or thoughts of a god." Notice, too, that Theonoe receives her adult name when she reaches the age for marriage, that important stage of transition into adulthood when Theonoe's prophetic powers are known and given public confirmation. Ritual associations that we can only begin to imagine pulsate through this passage.

6. A sea god.

7. Helen's Trojan abductor is called both Paris and Alexander, in Homer's epics and in Euripides' play. Mount Ida is a mountain near Troy. Priam was king, Hecuba queen of Troy. For the story of the beauty contest among the three goddesses, see above pp. 205–6, *Trojan Women* 924–31; and *IA* 71–2.

8. Hera, known in the Olympian pantheon as queen of the gods and wife of Zeus, is associated in ritual primarily with adult, married women's lives. The island of Samos in the eastern Aegean Sea, and various sites in the northern Peloponnesus, e.g., Argos and Elis, are major ancient sites of her worship (see O'Brien 1993).

Aphrodite is called throughout this play Kypris, or Kyprian, an epithet from the major site of her worship on the island of Cyprus (Kypros), where she is said to have first stepped on land after "being born" from the sea (Hesiod, *Theogony* 199). Although worship of the goddess of passionate sexual desire seems to have been brought to Cyprus by the Mycenaean Greeks in the latter half of the second millennium BCE, the name Kypris is rare in Homer. It may be that Euripides' stress on the Cyprian association further emphasizes the foreign, "other" qualities of the play. For just as Athenians of the late fifth century considered Dionysos, whom the Mycenaean Linear B tablets confirm to be of Greek ancestry, an imported, "foreign" divinity from the East, they may have applied the same reasoning to the disturbing sexual powers of Aphrodite (see Boedeker 1974: 1–20). Patriarchal forces tried to limit her powers to the realm of married women: In Aeschylus' *Oresteia* she progresses from a goddess of wanton lust associated with the devastation caused by Helen, to a deity properly overseeing sex in marriage within a patriarchal world order. But like her counterparts in the Near East and Mesopotamia, the ritual sexuality at her temples continued, especially at Corinth.

In the Greek, Athena is also not named in this play, but designated by one of her epithets, here, as frequently, as "maiden daughter of Zeus." In light of the ritual themes of this play it is worth considering why Euripides never names Athens' patron deity directly (see further at lines 228, 245, 1468). Known as the goddess of war and wisdom, she is associated in ritual with transitions of young girls, with the female craft of weaving and the male craft of bronze-making, and with overseeing certain public affairs. Her major festival was the Panathenaia, celebrated annually, but with greater elaboration every four years (see Neils 1992). Women wove a new robe, or *peplos,* for the statue of Athena in her temple, the Parthenon, on the Acropolis. The Parthenon friezes are interpreted as depicting young women and men, *ephebes,* who are coming of age, leading the festival procession to and around her temple.

9. The Greek is literally "to have my bed," the same word, *lekhos,* is used to mean marriage at line 32 (see above pp. xii–xiii, 52).

10. The desire to lighten the earth's burden as a reason for the Trojan War is known from the *Cypria* frag. 1, one of the epic cycle of poems. Although we have no similar citation for the glorification of Achilles in those poems, it forms a major theme of the *Iliad.*

11. Compare *IA* 127–8 for a similar *logos/ergon* ("word"/"deed") dichotomy.

12. Hermes, the messenger god, relays Zeus' commands to other gods and mortals. He also guides the souls of the dead into the underworld (compare *Alcestis* 49, 95).

13. Teuker was a Greek hero, the brother of Ajax who went mad after losing the contest over the dead Achilles' armor to Odysseus, and upon returning to his senses, committed suicide; compare below lines 87–104, and Sophocles' *Ajax.* This scene with Teuker serves not only to dramatize the general Greek hatred of Helen and the local Egyptian king's hostility to Greek men, but also to establish a strong Athenian connection, since Athens controlled the nearby island of Salamis.

14. Ploutos was a god of wealth and death, the son of Persephone according to some accounts. As a god of death, Ploutos was sometimes called *Klumenos* ("famous one"), which the name Theoklymenos may be deliberately echoing. This evocation would further strengthen the associations of Egypt with death and the analogies between Helen's and Persephone's abductions to the land of death (see Wolff 1973; Robinson 1979).

15. Both Helen's question seeking Teuker's identity and his response are typical: name, father's name, and country. The Greek emphasizes patrimony; thus, *patris* ("fatherland") and words for "father" occur five times in these six lines (87–93) and are frequent throughout the play. For "fatherland," which becomes otiose in English, I at times use "homeland" or "native land," which preserve the force of the Greek without its ring of chauvinistic tedium.

16. This echo of a saying by the pre-Socratic philosopher Epicharmus—"the mind sees and the mind hears; all else is deaf and blind"—prepares for the extensive play upon the sensory basis of epistemology in the scene between Helen and Menelaos.

17. The storm was sent as punishment by the gods against the Greeks for violating the gods' sanctuaries when they conquered Troy, exemplified by Ajax' rape of Kassandra in Athena's temple in Troy (see Aeschylus, *Agamemnon* 649–67; for a different version of the storm that drove Menelaos to Egypt, see *Odyssey* 3.288–300).

18. Here referring to Kastor and Polydeukes, usually called the Dioskouroi, "sons of Zeus."

19. At the oracle of Apollo at Delphi, visitors wishing to consult an oracle typically required a local host who sponsored their request (compare Euripides, *Ion* 551, 1039).

20. Euripides also used this motif of human sacrifice as a barbarian practice in his *Iphigenia among the Taurians* and *IA.*

21. The meter now changes from the iambic trimeters of speeches and dialogue to more varied metrical patterns employed in the choral odes (see above, pp. 41–3). Dale (1967: 76 ad 167–252) describes the "peculiarly Euripidean style of iambo-trochaic" of this ode as a "smooth, light movement . . . [suggesting] . . . a 'running' or dancing rhythm; perhaps it is the smoothness of one rocking herself with grief." Helen's threnody leads into the brief and atypical choral *parodos* ("entry song"), whose verses form the antistrophes responding to Helen's strophes. (For the unusual forms taken by this play's choral odes, see above, p. 234.) The translation reflects the line divisions and numbering of Dale 1967.

As there is no Muse of dirges, Helen wonders which goddess of musical inspiration she should call upon in her lyrical wish for death. She consequently invokes the Sirens and Persephone, figures associated with death. A popular subject in art, the Sirens are represented as birds with women's heads often depicted as crowning tombs or playing musical instruments, and, after 600 BCE, in representational scenes with Odysseus. In the *Odyssey,* in order to elude the power of their song, which charms sailors into crashing on their shores, Odysseus has himself tied to a mast and puts wax in his crew's ears (*Odyssey* 12.154–200). Their song shows them to be like the Muses, possessing knowledge and the power to voice their knowledge through song. This triple association of death, knowledge, and seduction also typifies ancient Mesopotamian cultures: Compare Enkidu's acculturation by the Love Priestess of Ishtar (*The Epic of Gilgamesh,* esp. the edition by Gardner and Maier 1984) and Eve's role in the Bible's Garden of Eden story (*Genesis* 2–3); on the Sirens, see Nagler 1977 and Pucci 1979. Persephone, queen of the underworld, is also associated with female rites of transition similar to those of Helen (see the *Homeric Hymn to Demeter*).

22. The Greek says "Libyan lotus" identifying the flute by the reed of the Libyan lotus from which it was made. Moreover, "Libyan" reminds one again of the North African, that is "foreign," aspects of the play. Each of the different instruments is associated with a different quality.

23. Pan was a lusty, goat-legged god of the countryside, who played a multiple, bound set of reeds known as the panpipes and who was associated with sexuality, especially aggressive, male sexuality. Nymphs were female nature spirits, called by different names according to their association with woods, mountains, trees, or springs. Many stories tell of the pursuit and rape of nymphs by Pan or similar satyr figures, a popular subject in art.

24. The words used here are *daimōn* and *moira,* on which see above pp. 15–17.

25. This must be an important site of Athena's worship in Sparta; it is named again at line 245 and referred to at 1466–7; compare also Aristophanes' *Lysistrata.* Note that Euripides alludes to Athena through her well-known sanctuary in Sparta, but that he once again does not name the Athenian goddess. Through these scattered allusions to Athena, particularly her ritual aspects, Euripides establishes an important connection with Athenian beliefs.

26. This attempt to locate the cause of events is a common theme in Greek literature; see esp. *Medea* 1–10.

27. Hermes was the "swift-footed son of Maia." The scene of Helen's "abduction" echoes that of Persephone's in the *Homeric Hymn to Demeter.* Both girls are gathering flowers, reflecting the period of *partheneia* from which the adolescent girl is snatched into adulthood. Helen portrays herself in the ritual discourse of the unwed adolescent girl, with which her divine aspect is associated, but which appears in major contradiction to her adult, married status in the story's narrative of her abduction. There is a further irony here in that a characteristic feature of Helen's stories is maintained: Whether by Hermes or by Paris, Helen is *abducted,* here completely against her will, though Hera's intent, as goddess of marriage, is to thwart Aphrodite and preserve Helen's marriage. (On Helen, Persephone, and their abductions see Juffras 1993; on the *Hymn to Demeter,* see Foley 1994.)

28. The meter shifts to the iambic trimeters of dialogue. The Chorus often take the role of discouraging the protagonist's excessive emotion: e.g. grief, *Alcestis* 891–2, *Medea* 156; anger, Sophocles *Oedipus the King* 404–5, 617, 631–3.

29. Statues were painted in ancient Greece; cf. lines 1186–96.

30. This echoes *Odyssey* 23.109–10, 188–9, where Penelope and Odysseus recognize each other by a sign known only to the two of them, the construction of their marriage-bed. (For echoes of the *Odyssey* in this play see Eisner 1980.)

31. Suicide is a conventional way out of their problems for female characters in tragedy (e.g., Antigone and Deianeira in Sophocles' *Antigone* and *Women of Trachis,* respectively, Phaidra in Euripides' *Hippolytos*). But here, as at lines 353–7 below, Helen may be posturing.

32. Lines 299–302 are excluded by most editors as bad Greek, a tasteless sentiment interrupting the flow of thought in 298–303, and an actor's interpolation to elaborate Helen's role. However, they remain characteristically Euripidean in thought and seem apt for Helen's character.

33. The rhythm of the Greek gives this line a proverbial ring. Compare, e.g., *Medea* 259–68.

34. This song, signalled by a metrical change, is an aria by Helen rather than the choral *stasimon* we might expect: The Chorus sing only a few verses in response to Helen's lead, while she sings most of the ode.

35. The imagery reflects the semiology of women's laments (Holst-Warhaft 1992; Rehm 1994). Here, Greece is personified as a woman in deep mourning, scratching her cheeks in grief till the blood runs. At 1186–9 Theoklymenos remarks on Helen's mourning only through the signs of her changed clothing, cut hair, and tear-wet, not scratched cheeks.

36. Kallisto, a *parthenos* in Artemis' band of hunters in the isolated northern Peloponnesian region of Arcadia, was deceived by Zeus who took on Artemis' likeness in order to rape her. When her pregnancy was discovered, Artemis banished her, and she bore alone her son Arkas. Out of jealousy Hera took away her beauty by transforming her into a bear, though she still maintained her human mind. While this is the main point of Helen's reference, Kallisto's story continues: When her son was grown and was hunting in the woods, he was on the point of killing his own mother, when Zeus transposed both to the sky, creating the constellations of the Big and Little Bear, Ursa Major and Minor, now commonly called the Big and Little Dippers. Though the unmentioned part of Kallisto's story shows an ultimate celestial transcendence, Helen stresses her painful experiences as a mortal woman.

    In rituals for Artemis girls took on the aspect of a bear or deer, as is known for the sanctuary of Artemis at Brauron, on the eastern coast of Attica across from Athens (see above, p. 55; Aristophanes, *Lysistrata* 645). At *IA* 1587–8 Iphigenia is reportedly transformed into a deer. The homoerotic currents in this story have never been explored, to my knowledge. Nothing else is known about the other *parthenos* Helen cites, the daughter of Merops, who also undergoes a physical transformation.

37. For the Chorus to exit during the play is highly unusual, though not unprecedented (it occurs in Aeschylus' *Eumenides,* Sophocles' *Ajax,* and Euripides' *Alcestis*).

Reflecting Euripides' tendency to dress his aristocratic figures in rags (above, p. 71), Menelaos enters shipwrecked, dressed in tatters. This may have been Euripides' way of challenging dramatically what Socrates challenged philosophically, the common Greek assumption that nobility or moral superiority was displayed in one's appearance and clothing.

38. In his opening address to his famed grandfather Pelops, Menelaos identifies his lineage in a few lines, beginning with Pelops' establishment of his line in the Peloponnesus ("Pelops' island"). Tantalos, Pelops' father, wanting to test the gods, cut up and served his son Pelops to them at a banquet. Though the other gods refrained from this feast of human flesh, Demeter took a bite, from Pelops' shoulder, so that when he was made whole again, he needed an ivory shoulder. For his insolence Tantalos was consigned to one of the famous eternal punishments in the underworld: While he is tied in the river, the grapes hanging above his head always withdraw as he reaches toward them to eat, and the water always recedes when he bends his head to drink. (See Pindar's first Olympian ode; *IA* 504.)

Pelops later arrived at Elis in the northwestern Peloponnesus, where the local king, Oinomaos, held a test for any suitor of his daughter Hippodameia, in which they must beat him in a chariot race or die. Most died. But Pelops beat Oinomaos, in some versions by sabotaging his chariot, and killed him; he subsequently established the Olympic Games in honor of Zeus. The saga of child-murder and adultery continues in the next generation in the strife between Pelops' two sons Thyestes and Atreus, father of Menelaos and his brother Agamemnon, the commanders of the Greek expedition against Troy, "that famous pair" (line 392) known from Homer's *Iliad,* Aeschylus' *Agamemnon,* and Euripides' *Iphigeneia at Aulis.*

39. Menelaos' words thinly veil contemporary references: Athens was the acknowledged Greek naval force of the period, and as a democracy its leaders prided themselves on voluntary, willing participation in Athenian affairs, including warfare, by its (male) citizens. "The greatest naval military force against Troy" may have several references here: It is a reminder of Athenian naval greatness in repelling the Persian invaders, a justifiably proud moment in Athenian history important to recall here in order to counterbalance the more recent failures and losses of the Athenian fleet in the Peloponnesian War and in the disastrous expedition to Sicily (see above, p. 8). These losses reverberate deeply in lines 397–9, and Menelaos' words imply that young Athenian men served willingly in these fatal assaults. In this historical context, does this statement reflect support of Athenian naval military policies or is it meant with extreme irony? That these lines are spoken by Menelaos, whose mythological image as Helen's weak-willed husband and affiliation with the enemy Sparta render him a questionable character, must further complicate their impact on the contemporary Athenian audience.

40. Echoing the precedent set in the *Odyssey,* Menelaos' description of his wanderings, delayed homecoming, and shipwreck parallel Odysseus' experiences. With this parallel established, the recognition scene becomes a parody of Penelope and Odysseus' recognition and reunion in Book 23.

41. "Libya" refers generally to regions of North Africa.

42. Menelaos' boast here of having "dragged" his wife out from Troy, illustrated on some vase paintings, asserts his claim in patriarchal law to punish an adulterous wife by death. The audience may well question Menelaos' claim, however, because the literature and art show a different dynamic between the two: In *Trojan Women,* produced three years earlier, Helen's charming beauty and words thwart Menelaos' intent to kill her; an early literary source and numerous vase paintings show him dropping his sword at the sight of Helen's naked breast, the phallic symbolism evident within the narrative of the myth. The *Odyssey* eloquently shows that far from being punished, Helen remains in charge of her household.

43. This comic porter scene, reminiscent of the comic nurse in Aeschylus' *Libation Bearers,* becomes (or may already be) a conventional scene; compare Aristophanes' *Frogs,* the Roman comedy of Plautus and Terence, and the comic porter in Shakespeare's *Macbeth.*

44. Note how the stage direction comes directly from Euripides' next line.

45. The word translated as "foreigner" is *xenos,* whose meanings range from "host," or "guest," to "stranger," and which implies the obligations of *xenia,* "hospitality," that guide interactions among strangers under the protection of Zeus Xenios (above, pp. 21–22). Here Menelaos expects certain hospitable treatment according to the precepts of *xenia,* due not only to his class, but to the sudden misfortune of his circumstances as a shipwreck.

46. Euripides uses a form of the word *polemios,* referring to enemies in war, as opposed to a more general enemy, *ekhthros* (see above, pp. 20–21).

47. Giving food is one of the primary moral obligations entailed by *xenia.*

48. The immediate reference is to the swiftness of racing fillies and Bacchants as Helen rushes back to the tomb. At the same time, both images evoke women's rituals: the racing fillies are a frequent metaphor associated with rites for adolescent girls (see Alkman's *Partheneion*), while Bacchants are adult women worshipers of Dionysos. And both images reflect the dual ritual areas overseen by the goddess Helen. In her haste to return to the tomb, Helen seems to have forgotten the prophecy she just heard.

49. The same hunting imagery is used of Menelaos' pursuit of his war against Troy (50) and of Theoklymenos' pursuit of Helen for marriage (63).

50. This comment does not only reflect Helen's vanity (compare note 38 above). Notice Menelaos' concern with his clothing being touched (line 567). One can only surmise

what Helen imagined her rescuing shipwrecked husband would look like, since she is so shocked by the tatters of the man before her.

51. Although etymologists do not believe that Helen's name and the Greeks' name for themselves, "Hellenes," are from the same linguistic root, as is typical of Greek writers Euripides deliberately plays upon the similarity of these sounds, evoking such associations nevertheless (compare above, p. 227). The intellectual play as the scene progresses continues to suggest Helen's associations with language and knowledge. Line 561, missing from the manuscripts, comes from Aristophanes' parody of this scene in his *Women at the Thesmophoria* 907.

52. Hekate, associated with the underworld, night, the moon, especially the dark of the moon, and with crossroads (compare Latin *Trivia*), appropriately brings light and sends dreams out of her realm (compare *Medea* 397). As we can see from Hesiod's *Theogony,* where Hekate retains her own awesome attributes under the new reign of Zeus, and from the *Homeric Hymn to Demeter,* where Hekate is the only one to hear Persephone's cry at the beginning and joins mother and daughter as perpetual companion at the end, Menelaos' invocation of Hekate is a powerful one, which he is invoking here to ward off what he believes to be a ghostly vision.

53. On the use of *despotēs* ("master"), see note on *Medea* 232–3.

54. In addition to familiar Greek interplays between sight and knowledge, and the idea that knowledge is mental vision, revealed in a common linguistic root for the two concepts (see above, p. 433, n. 5), the following exchange also plays out contemporary intellectual debates on the nature of knowledge, how one knows what one knows, and whether the senses are a trustworthy basis for acquiring knowledge. The figure of Helen is integrally tied into these philosophical debates (see above pp. 231–3).

55. Given Euripides' characterization of Menelaos, his words here are a rejection not only of the woman before him who cannot to his mind possibly be Helen, but also of the arguments that question the basis of knowledge and that overwhelm his thinking. Instead, Menelaos finds refuge in remembering the Trojan War, where at least heroic values were assured and unambiguous. The final play in this volume, *Iphigenia at Aulis,* questions this image, however. Here, Euripides' clever interplay portrays a Menelaos so befuddled between image and reality, that in the very process of clinging to his memory of what he believes to be the reality of the recent past, he ends up creating an illusion of that very past. The human, perhaps tragic, irony, is that on some level we sympathize with Menelaos, for in the same position, we too would "hardly believe our own eyes!" Moreover, if what Helen says is true, he and the others suffered for nothing, a realization too difficult for Menelaos to accept, and perhaps difficult for many in the ancient audience to acknowledge about their own recent losses.

56. A change in meter signals Helen's and Menelaos' reunion song (compare *Iphigenia Among the Taurians* 827–99, *Ion* 1437–1509).

57. Compare the recognition scene in the *Odyssey* (23.343ff.).

58. Her hair stands on end from joy, not horror (compare Sophocles' *Ajax* 693).

59. Helen's tale is a bitter one, because while she is telling of her innocence, she must also mention the distasteful story of adultery, which haunts her even though innocent.

60. These lines distantly echo the beginning of Stesichorus' palinode: "That story is not true, / You did not mount the well-fitted ships, / You never came to the towers of Troy" (see above, p. 224).

61. Split stichomythia ("alternating lines") usually indicates a more excited, faster-paced dialogue (see above p. 41).

62. The Chorus, through their generalizing statement, return the scene to the spoken meter of dialogue.

63. Not only does Euripides often have his servant characters engage in equal dialogue with their masters, but it is not unusual for them to provide a "common sense" philosophical perspective on the issue at hand, as in this Messenger's two monologues below (compare *Medea* 1224–30).

64. On wedding customs, see above, pp. 55–6.

65. Here, and in the next lines, the servant reflects a dramatic portrayal of slaves' profession of loyalty to their masters (compare, e.g., *Medea* 53–5). He may also be reflecting contemporary debates, referred to by Aristotle almost a century later, over the concept of "natural" slavery (see above p. 10).

66. The Messenger refers to two important forms of divination, the flames during sacrifice and the flight of birds. In *IA* Agamemnon and Menelaos express similar doubts about prophecy (*IA* 520–1). Kalchas was the principal prophet for the Greek camp, who informed Agamemnon he would have to sacrifice his daughter Iphigenia (see Aeschylus, *Agamemnon* 200–4). Helenos was a Trojan prophet (though linguists resist the connection, Helenos' name could easily be a masculine form of Helen's). The old man's conventional, apparently common sense diatribe against prophets is ironic given the play's portrayal of Theonoe as a genuine seer crucial to the action of the play.

67. Nauplios lit beacon-fires to lure the Greek ships to destruction in revenge for the treacherous murder of his son Palamedes. This was the subject of a play by Euripides just three years before *Helen* (see further lines 1126–32). Perseus' lookout rock, from which he rescued Andromeda, was, according to Herodotus, 2.15, at the western end of the Nile delta.

68. The typical gesture of supplication was on one's knees, and embracing the knees or touching the chin of the person one is supplicating, a gesture that dishonors the supplicant (see above pp. 21–2; compare *Helen* 947–53; *IA* 900–1).

69. Clasping right hands marks the securing of an oath, as it still does in some contexts today. Hence, Medea's sense of Jason's betrayal of their trust (see above, p. 159; and *IA* 866).

70. Since the war was fought for Menelaos' woman, he can be held responsible or blamed for the deaths in that war; hence, his claim to be responsible for the deaths of Achilles and Ajax. Nestor, king of Pylos, the eldest of the Greek warriors at Troy, does, despite the claim here, have surviving children in *Odyssey* Book 3.

71. A typical Greek belief that the earth lies lightly on the brave and good, this view also reflects Greek attitudes to burial, where proper rites are a significant mark of honor for the dead (see, e.g., the *Iliad* and Sophocles' *Antigone* and *Ajax*).

72. The thought that a decision among the gods depends on human choice may at first appear startling, as though it attributes inordinate power to a human being. At the same time, we may see reflected in this thought the Greek idea that however the gods may set up a situation, it is ultimately human responsibility that determines the lives of mortals (see above, pp. 16–18; compare Homer's *Odyssey* and Sophocles' *Oedipus the King*). Note that in the action of the play, Theonoe's command to her attendants to tell her brother is apparently not carried out.

73. Rather than the *agōn* ("trial" or "contest") characteristic of Euripidean drama (above, pp. 41–2), in this scene Helen and Menelaos argue the same side from their differing perspectives (compare Klytemnestra's and Iphigeneia's speeches to Agamemnon, *IA* 1146–1252).

74. Grammatically problematic and illogical in context, line 905 has been bracketed by most editors.

75. Helen's mention of the injustice of theft twice in five lines (904, 908) recalls her "theft" as a possession by Paris in many versions of the story.

76. Like other ancient Mediterranean cultures, early Greek concepts of divinity appear to envision the gods as amoral (compare Homer's *Iliad* and above pp. 18–19). The Pre-Socratic philosophers of the seventh and sixth centuries seem first to have attributed moral concerns to the divine realm, an idea that finds eloquent expression in Plato. Compare Abraham's exhortations to god in *Genesis* 16 when the latter is contemplating destroying Sodom, "Far be it from you to do such a thing, to destroy the righteous with the wicked." Here, rather than the morality of the gods, it is the morality of their holy spokespeople that is in question. In both the Persian and Peloponnesian Wars, Apollo's oracle at Delphi, the most famous oracular site in ancient Greece, issued prophecies adverse to Athenian interests, which the Athenians successfully ignored, resulting in increased mistrust of prophets and oracles (compare the Messenger's words at 745–57).

77. Compare *IA* 451–2.

78. Menelaos now gives a performance within his performance, a metatheatrical play within the drama.

79. Theonoe is called *kuria,* a feminine form of the *kurios* ("authoritative, male guardian") that every Athenian woman had to have (see above, p. 49). In Athens the thought of a woman being her own guardian would seem odd. The line may reflect generally Greek knowledge of, or Euripides' imputation of, a different status for women in ancient Egypt; and it may more particularly accentuate the uniqueness and power of Theonoe's position.

80. Menelaos describes the pollution their bloody suicides on the grave will cause. For "heart" (983), the Greek has *ēpar* ("liver"), which is often regarded as the seat of life and emotions.

81. A form of the same word as "arbitrate," *brabeuein, brabeus,* referred to Helen as the "presider" over their trials in Troy (703).

82. The manuscripts have Kharis, "Grace" or "Charm" (line 1006), a name that often represents Aphrodite's sexual allure. The goddess would more appropriately be invoked under this aspect by married women, not by one professing to remain a maiden forever. Editors often accept Kypris as a likely emendation. This is the name by which Euripides calls Aphrodite throughout this play and which Theonoe uses again (line 1024). There is another irony here: Although Aphrodite represents anarchic sexuality in contrast to Hera's association with marriage, ritually, their realms are not entirely opposed (unlike Aphrodite and Artemis, e.g., in Euripides' *Hippolytos*). For part of Hera's rites entail the transformation from virgin to mature, that is sexual, woman, which involves the realm of Aphrodite (see O'Brien 1993).

83. Compare the reciprocity here, as each partner is given back to the other, with Herakles' one-sided decision to give only Alcestis back to Admetos.

84. This idea, unparalleled in ancient Greek literature, may reflect the ideas circulating among the Pre-Socratic philosophers. While it serves to emphasize the singularity of this Egyptian prophetess' theological views, it is unclear how seriously one should take it.

85. Theonoe's words revisit the earlier play between seeming and being.

86. Aigeus analogously promises to aid Medea, but leaves it up to her to find her method of escape (*Medea* 725–6).

87. Since all Menelaos' suggestions were rejected and Helen is about to suggest their successful escape plot, the effect of Helen's statement might well be ironic.

88. At 1055–6 Menelaos questions the effectiveness of this old dramatic ruse, used first, to our knowledge, in Aeschylus' *Libation Bearers,* the second play of his *Oresteia* trilogy, again in both Sophocles' and Euripides' *Elektra*'s, and at Euripides' *IT* 1029.

89. Helen claims she will satisfy typical women's gestures of mourning, but when Theoklymenos notices her at 1189, he says that her cheeks are wet with tears, not blood (see above line 374 and note).

90. Human beings often ask deities intimately associated with strong human emotions to be more moderate, especially Aphrodite and the sexual desire she inspires (compare Aeschylus' *Suppliant Women,* Euripides' *Hippolytos, Medea* 627–8, and *Bacchants,* where Dionysos is so beseeched). In many of these passages *eros,* "sexual desire," is presented as a dangerous, deadly force.

91. Two-thirds of the way into the play is extraordinarily late for the Chorus to sing their first *stasimon* (see above, pp. 41–2).

92. The story of the nightingale came to epitomize the voice of female suffering and was the subject of Sophocles' lost play *Tereus.* Tereus, husband of Prokne, raped her sister Philomela, cut out her tongue so she could not tell of her rape, and locked her away in an isolated hut. Philomela, however, depicted her experiences in a weaving, which she sent to her sister. Prokne took revenge by killing her son by Tereus, Itus, and serving him to his father. As Tereus pursued the sisters, all three were changed into birds, Tereus a hoopoe, Prokne a nightingale, and Philomela a swallow (or vice versa).

93. The real grief of the war widows may contrast with Helen's mourning masquerade.

94. On Nauplios, see note 68 above.

95. This questioning of the nature of divinity has eloquent predecessors in Greek literature (e.g., in Pindar, Aeschylus), and it reflects Euripides' strong challenges to traditional presentations of the gods (see above, pp. 76–7).

96. This is a rare expression of pacifist ideas in ancient Greek, where, however much war is deplored, the conventional choice is between fighting other Greeks or a foreign enemy, rather than considering the alternative of mediation and diplomacy instead of warfare. This sentiment may reflect the historical timing of this play; compare Menelaos' remarks, lines 393–9 above.

97. In a manner typical of the inconsistency in ancient Greek characterizations, Theoklymenos, though an Egyptian, swears by Greek gods.

98. In another metatheatrical scene, Helen is toying with the naive barbarian in her ruse (compare the scene between Iphigenia and Thoas in *Iphigenia Among the Taurians*).

99. Though it sounds odd, Euripides elsewhere also has barbarians calling themselves barbarian (compare line 1258 below and *Iphigenia Among the Taurians* 1170, 1174).

100. It is both her obligation and her privilege to carry out the funerary rites over the body; this is the principal theme of Sophocles' *Antigone* (compare 1275 below).

101. See note 69 above on supplication.

102. The expression of a deeply held religious belief in this choral song seems to provide a profound response to the Chorus' questioning of the nature of deity in their first *stasimon* (1137–50). At the same time the second *stasimon* presents many questions for interpretation. Functionally, many scholars regard it as typical of a late

Euripidean tendency to use a choral ode as an interlude in the dramatic action, without necessarily having any connection with that action. On this view this ode merely allows the momentum of the plot to advance behind the scenes during the space of the song. Other scholars believe that the ode must relate to the themes of the play, which raise in different ways questions of theodicy and belief (compare the Messenger's comments 711–5, 753–4, and those of the Chorus 1137–50; and see Austin 1994).

In fact, the song's mostly celebratory, even hymn-like qualities serve a very important purpose at this point in the play's action. As Helen's and Menelaos' plan heats up, and even though it is not yet completed, the Chorus begin to rejoice with a song with deepest spiritual associations (like the hymns in praise of God in Lee Breuer and Bob Telson's *The Gospel at Colonus*). Their song augments the mood of excitement and anticipation generated by the dramatic action, boosting the momentum with its spiritually based exuberance.

The ode reflects the syncretism of religious belief at the end of the fifth century, as the Asian Mountain Mother, Kybele, Eleusinian Demeter, and the god Dionysos were assimilated to each other through the rites of their mysteries, including many of the features named in the ode: *orgia* ("ecstatic dances"), rousing drum and cymbal rhythms, and the lion chariot (compare Euripides' *Bacchants,* and Dodds 1960).

The goddess Demeter is the principal subject of the ode, but her story differs from both the Homeric and Orphic versions more commonly known (Richardson 1974, Foley 1994). Emphasizing the Eastern connections, she is called Mountain Mother from the start, a frequent title of the Anatolian goddess Kybele; she searches for her abducted daughter to the accompaniment of the ecstatic rhythms associated with the mystery religions of the East; and she rests from her search on the snowy peaks of Mount Ida rather than at Eleusis, thereby also allying her story with Helen's. In response to Demeter's withering of all life on earth in grief for her daughter, Zeus sends not the gods to persuade her with gifts, but the Muses and Graces to charm her with their music. The last, highly problematic stanza seems to connect Helen with Demeter's rites (see further below).

103. Persephone, as queen of the dead, is a dread goddess whose name must not be spoken. The *Homeric Hymn to Demeter* also describes Persephone as being snatched from her maidens' circle dances, which included other goddesses important for the rites of *parthenoi,* such as Artemis and Athena.

104. Athena (whom once again Euripides does not name) is known by the Gorgon head on her shield or on her aegis, the mantle worn across her chest. Here, Artemis and Athena, two "maiden" goddesses, accompany Demeter in her search, fully armed and prepared to fight on behalf of another maiden, Persephone. This passage, which concludes in an affirmation of Zeus' will, may reflect another version of the story that has Zeus hurl a thunderbolt at the two armed goddesses to stop them from fighting off Persephone's attacker. (Yes, Xena has her genuine prototypes in the ancient Greek stories!)

105. Deo is another name for Demeter (compare *Hymn to Demeter* 47, 211, 492). A major function of music and dance, especially the choral music of the Muses and Graces, is to ease pain (see further next note).

106. Here Aphrodite's role is assimilated to that of Iambe in the Homeric hymn, and of Baubo in the Orphic tradition, who get Demeter to smile through raucous humor in the case of Iambe, and, in that of Baubo, by lifting her skirts and exposing her genitals (Richardson 1974; Lubell 1994). Note also the mixing of musical styles and ritual aspects in the music the different goddesses bring to assuage Demeter: the "trilling songs, hymns, and choral dances" of the Graces and the Muses, and the ecstatic, erotic *orgia* of Aphrodite. The sequence of the ode suggests that it is Aphrodite's music that elicits Demeter's laughter, a clear connection to Baubo's sexual antics in the Orphic version. Euripides' version relates directly to the play's themes: It shows Aphrodite in a new, positive perspective, not only as a goddess who wreaks havoc by imposing her divine attribute of erotic desire upon humans. Instead, her dance of erotic desire plays an important role in Demeter's story and rites, affirming the place of desire, and in particular female erotic desire, in the cycle of life. The problem, as this play and Helen's other stories portray, is the disjunction between the positive, life-affirming qualities of a power when seen in its divine aspect and the confusing, disruptive, and even destructive dimensions to that power when played out among human beings.

107. The highly corrupt state of 1353–4 and 1366–7 together with this highly unusual story have profoundly challenged interpretation of the second antistrophe. The ode's focus on the great mystery rites continues, but Helen appears to be drawn in with the Chorus' address, "my child" (1356), and by the last line's reference to a mistaken privileging of beauty. The stanza suggests some obligation that Helen appears to have improperly conducted or left unfulfilled for the Great Mother. After describing the great power of the Mother's rites for most of the stanza, in direct association with those of Dionysos, the last line reasserts Helen's focus on her beauty. The stanza discloses some tension between the areas of concern of the two deities Demeter and Helen, which, the Chorus seem to imply, Helen can rectify by her actions. Given the importance of Helen's ritual associations that underlie this play, it would be a major boon if the text were more secure. Robinson 1979 presents a different, historically based interpretation of this opposition between the two goddesses.

108. Bromios, "roarer," is an epithet of Dionysos. As Euripides' *Bacchants* so vividly portrays, the activities described in 1301–05 typify women's rites for Dionysos. Women's all-night dance rituals (1365) are common features of women's rites for different goddesses, notably Demeter and Artemis, and a fragment of Sappho's poetry shows rites taking place during the full moon: "As the full moon was shining, women stood around an altar" (Lobel and Page frag. 154). Imagery on wall paintings and gold sealing rings from the Minoan and Mycenaean periods depict women's ritual, ecstatic dancing, sometimes including men. Vase paintings, terracotta and bronze figurines throughout the Mediterranean and the Near East, dating from the

archaic period through the sixth century CE, depict women dancing. Interestingly, the earlier periods show women in groups, sometimes with men, probably reflecting choral groups, while later portrayals show a single woman dancing.

109. Despite all earlier portrayals in the play of war as an illusion that brings only death and destruction, Helen's proud assertion of Menelaos' readiness for major slaughter prepares for the apparently approving depiction of the battle of Greeks vs. Egyptians in the Second Messenger's speech (1526–1618) as the climactic dramatic action.

110. For Menelaos, as for Odysseus (*Odyssey* 23.153–162), the bathing and clothing change function as a ritual cleansing and symbolic rebirth. Both heroes then go on to arm themselves and prepare to do battle for their wives.

111. Compare similar requests to the female Choruses in *Medea* and *IA.*

112. Theoklymenos, true to his stereotypic barbarian character, denies any "living" qualities to the dead or any significance to the funerary rites for the dead. His views are portrayed in direct opposition to the notion of an aware dead held by his religiously imbued sister Theonoe (1013–6; on the contrast of Theoklymenos' portrayal with Egyptian customs, see above, pp. 230–31). Helen in the next line seems to affirm the dead's existence and the ritual and social importance of their funerary rites, at the same time that she equivocates in her responses to Theoklymenos.

113. Galaneia means "calm," hence a goddess of calm seas.

114. Perseus was considered the founder of Mycenae, Agamemnon's home, northwest of Sparta, Helen's home. The "good harbor" is apparently the harbor of Nauplion on the east coast of the Peloponnesus, which seems to serve as a landing point for both communities (compare line 1587).

115. The Chorus envision Helen's participation in rituals on her return home to Sparta: first, those for the Leukippides, "White Horse Maidens," daughters of Leukippos, whose rites are similar to the transition rituals that Helen oversees (see above, pp. 228–9). Next are the rites for Athena, identified by her epithet Pallas, which may mean "brandisher of the spear" or may refer to her virgin status. (This is the third time the play has evoked Athena's temple in Sparta.) The Hyakinthia was one of the most important festivals in Sparta, celebrating the coming into adulthood of all young people, female and male, and celebrated over several days with feasts, contests, and choral songs and dances by all members of the community. The end of the stanza recalls also the unwed status of Hermione, Helen's daughter, which was cited earlier as a reproach against Helen, and which she, in her transformed state, will now presumably be able to rectify. In the *Odyssey* (4.3ff.) and at the beginning of Euripides' *Andromache* Hermione has a childless marriage to Achilles' son Neoptolemos. In other texts she is married to Orestes, as in the latter part of Euripides' *Andromache* and in his *Orestes.*

116. Phoibos, "Shining," is a common epithet of Apollo, who is so called again at line 1511. Hyakinthos, a young man loved by Apollo, was accidentally killed by the

god's discus, after which Apollo initiated the rites of the Hyakinthia to commemorate his beloved's death.

117. Apollo was a patron deity of Troy, fighting on their side in the war. The Chorus' prayer to the Dioskouroi in this stanza is answered by the savior gods' appearance at the end in which they send favorable winds and clear their sister Helen's name. This rights their absence from the Trojan War story, where they are notable for failing to come to Helen's rescue. The last two lines of this final choral song again echo the opening lines of Stesichorus' palinode (see note 61).

118. Another unusual dramaturgical feature of this play is the presence of a second messenger delivering a second messenger speech.

119. The proper fulfillment of sacrificial rites requires the voluntary participation of the sacrifical victim, achieved in ritual by sprinkling water on the animal's head, getting it to "nod," that is, agree to its own sacrifice (see above, p. 12).

120. Despite the manuscript attribution of one part in this next exchange to the Chorus leader, some editors have questioned this because of Theoklymenos' calling his opponent "a slave" (1630). But this is suited to the thinking of barbarian despots in a form of government where everyone but the ruler is a "slave" (see line 276). The Chorus are more likely to fulfill the following role than any other late-arriving character because of their close involvement in the situation all along, proposing consultation of Theonoe, going in with Helen for this consultation, and recognized as silent collaborators in the escape plan. Dramatically, Choruses are often called upon to intervene in a dire action among the characters, though usually they are ineffectual (compare, e.g., Aeschylus *Agamemnon,* Euripides' *Medea*). This one is more daring in successfully keeping Theoklymenos away until the Dioskouroi arrive to save everyone.

121. Compare *IA* 312 for a similar sentiment.

122. For the ancient Greeks, even the gods were subject to destiny, their own activities constrained by what destiny would allow. This theme occurs frequently in the *Iliad,* where even Zeus must accept the death of his son Sarpedon, though he wants very much to save him. At the same time, the effect of these lines is ironic: The Dioskouroi acknowledge their low status in the divine pecking order as they justify their actions to human beings.

123. The Xenia, "Hospitality Festival," was a ritual feast in Sparta honoring Helen and the Dioskouroi together.

124. The island, present-day Makronisi, "Long Island," lies off the southwest coast of Attica, opposite Cape Sounion.

125. Euripides uses this same choral ending at the end of *Alcestis, Andromache, Bacchants,* and with a variation in the first line, *Medea* (see notes on the last lines of *Medea* and *Alcestis*).

Iphigenia at Aulis: Introduction

1. Makaria, daughter of Herakles, and the daughters of Erechtheus volunteer to die to assure Athens' victory in war. The death sometimes follows the war: Polyxena, daughter of Priam, is sacrificed to placate the dead Achilles after the end of the Trojan War. The victim can be male: Menoikeus dies for Thebes. Euripides wrote a play involving each of these stories; see O'Connor-Visser 1987, Wilkins 1990.
2. As Sophocles' Ajax puts it: "either living well or dying well befits the noble man" (479–80). Ajax lives up to the code by killing himself after suffering personal disgrace.
3. On changes of mind in this play see Knox 1979: 243–46 and Gibert 1995: 202–54.
4. Iphigenia's transformation into male hero resembles that of Medea; see above, pp. 162–6. See also Loraux 1987: 31–48. Foley 1985 and Rabinowitz 1993 downplay Iphigenia's assumption of masculine characteristics, emphasizing instead her love for Achilles.
5. The degree to which Klytemnestra forces herself to be a good wife to Agamemnon is accentuated by the story of his murder of her first husband and killing of their baby (1148–56).
6. For example, the anger of Achilles toward Agamemnon (928–73) recalls their quarrel which is the basis for all the events of the poem (*Iliad* 1.122–302), Agamemnon's anger at Kalkhas (520) recalls his anger at the the seer's words (*Iliad* 1. 101–120). It is possible, even probable, that the story of Iphigenia was consciously left out of the *Iliad.*
7. In his film *Iphigenia,* director Michael Cacoyannis eliminated the female chorus and added scenes showing the army as eager to get to Troy, in effect making them the chorus; director Don Taylor added a second chorus of soldiers in his video version.
8. The configuration of stars at the time of the festival was quite different from that described by the Old Man, perhaps raising questions about the validity of perception and reporting at the very beginning of the play.
9. In our 1991 production Agamemnon played his first scene in bathrobe and slippers, gradually becoming more and more militarized until in the final scene the man had disappeared under the uniform.
10. This would help explain Plato's fear of male actors being feminized by performing female roles (*Republic* 395de; see above, p. 64).
11. Taplin 1977 insists that the notion of "audience participation . . . is as alien to Greek tragedy as it is essential to Old Comedy" (130). Furthermore, "nowhere in Greek tragedy are there . . . specific references to the theatre" (132–33). Wiles 1997: 208–09 emphatically disagrees.

12. For example, *Elektra, Hippolytos, Orestes, Bacchants,* and in this volume, *Helen* 1642–79. Herakles also functions as *deus ex machina Alcestis* 1008–36, as does Medea in the sun-chariot in *Medea.*
13. For a detailed discussion of political allegory in Aristophanes' plays, see Vickers 1997.
14. Teevan 1996 translated only the "authentic" fragments.

Iphigenia at Aulis: The Play

1. Slaves are rarely referred to by name in Greek drama.
2. For the *eisodoi* in the Greek theater, see above, p. 35.
3. The meter of this opening scene as given in the manuscripts is unique among extant tragedies. Most plays start in spoken dialogue in iambic trimeter; this is often a speech providing the exposition, the necessary background to the action, usually (though not always) given by a high-ranking character. This is usually followed by a section in anapests, a meter associated with movement, for the entrance of the chorus (on meter, see above, p. 43). Here, for the first 49 lines the characters speak in anapests rather than iambic trimeter. Agamemnon's lines 49–114 are in trimeter, but anapests return at 115–62. Hence many editors have changed the order of these lines, placing Agamemnon's speech (49–114) first. But if the order given in the manuscripts is correct, Agamemnon's entrance from the scene-building leads the audience to assume he will immediately deliver the exposition. Instead he calls out the Old Man. This initial violation of theatrical and social expectations effectively sets the stage for others to come. Knox 1979: 275–94 and Foley 1985: 93–95, 102–105 agree with this ordering of the lines; Bain 1977b disagrees.
4. Agamemnon's question suggests the unlikely possibility that he doesn't recognize the brightest star in the sky, the Dog Star Sirius, which appeared in August. Calling the Old Man out and then asking him a pointless question suggests that Agamemnon doesn't want to broach what is really on his mind; he apparently realizes immediately how silly his question was, quickly changing direction in line 9. To an audience familiar with the night sky and its seasonal changes, the presence of Sirius and the Pleiades would have indicated that the season is late summer or early fall, and the time shortly before dawn. Greeks did not sail in winter, so if winter came while the expedition was stuck in Aulis it would have to wait till the next spring.
5. The ships making the Greek expedition to Troy had gathered at Aulis, on the narrow strait between the Euboean peninsula and the mainland (see map). They could not sail because of either lack of wind, as here, or contrary winds, as at 1324–30.
6. This is the first instance of a central theme in this play (and many other Athenian tragedies as well): the relative merits of high vs. common status. See also 446–450,

Medea 119–130, *Helen* 417–19. Agamemnon's antiheroic stance recalls and rejects Achilles' well-known choice of a short glorious life over a long undistinguished one; see Homer, *Iliad* 9.410–416. It also alludes to an ongoing discussion at Athens between citizens with aristocratic connections and those without; see Ober 1989: 248–92.

7. The phrase translated here as "something sent by the gods goes astray" is literally "the things of the gods, not being put right," and some have understood this as a reference to some religious duty left undone by Agamemnon. Other versions of this story refer to such events (see above, pp. 311–12) but there is no such reference in this play. A more likely interpretation involves a common metaphor: The gods shoot something into mortal lives, but not quite straight.

8. These lines exemplify the convention of Athenian drama whereby interior scenes must be "exteriorized." The Old Man reports what he has seen inside the tent, using the historical present tense for vividness. The letter referred to, a crucial prop in this scene, would have been written on a pair of flat wooden tablets coated on the inside with a thin sheet of wax. The message would have been inscribed in the wax with a stylus, the tablets tied together and sealed with a lead or wax seal; upon receipt the recipient would inspect the seal, read and scratch out the message, write a response, reseal it and send it back with the messenger.

9. Slaves often make such avowals of trustworthiness to their masters; see 312, *Medea* 54–55, *Helen* 726–33. Later (873) the Old Man will make a crucial, dangerous decision to help Klytemnestra; his prior relationship with her, revealed here, helps explain that decision. Like this Old Man, Menelaos' old servant came with Helen when she married Menelaos (*Helen* 722–25), and Medea's Nurse apparently accompanied the woman she cared for as a baby when Medea left Colchis with Jason.

10. Agamemnon now delivers the "prologue" (see above, p. 41). This speech may seem a highly artificial device for providing information to the audience, since the Old Man, as a member of the household, must be familiar with the details. Yet it also shows Agamemnon's view of the world he lives in and his place in it, especially his need to see others—Tyndareos, Helen, Paris, Menelaos, Odysseus, the Greek army, the gods—as responsible for his problems and for his limited options.

11. Tyndareos was Leda's husband and Klytemnestra's father, but there was a story that Zeus in the form of a swan copulated with Leda, begetting Helen. See *Helen* 16–21, 1143–45.

12. "What he'd been handed" translates one of the most difficult words used in ancient drama, *tukhē*—literally "what happens," so "good luck" or "bad luck"—NOT "fate." See also 351, 443, 864, and above, pp. 15–16. Tyndareos' situation was both good and bad: He had a desirable daughter, so he could make a marriage alliance with a powerful family. But the violence of Helen's suitors turned his luck bad. Competitions like this were "zero-sum contests," in which in order for someone to win all the others had to lose, leading to fierce "envy" (*phthonos* 53) towards the winner. In Homer's

Odyssey, Odysseus' wife Penelope is courted by unruly suitors during her husband's absence, creating similar dangers for her closest male relatives. For a survey of versions of the wooing of Helen in Greek texts and artifacts, see Gantz 1993: 564–67.

13. In a primarily oral culture an oath taken in the gods' name was an important sanction (above, p. 11). Compare Medea's rage at Jason's breaking his oaths to her (21, 492–95, 1392), and her demand that Aigeus swear formally that he will protect her (731–56). The ceremonies of libations (wine or other liquids poured on the ground) and animals sacrificed (then partly burned, partly cooked, and eaten) called the gods to witness and enforce the events taking place. Libations were often thought of as sinking down toward divinities under the ground, the smoke of sacrifices as rising into the air toward the Olympian gods. Such wastes of good assets signified the participants' seriousness and symbolized what would happen to those who broke their word. On libations and sacrifice, see above, pp. 11–12.

14. Taking revenge for the theft of women was imperative for males, and not only in legend; the historians Herodotus and Thucydides describe such outrages as a cause of warfare. An Athenian woman was always under the legal and economic control of a male authority (*kurios*), usually her closest male relative, who was responsible for protecting her and avoiding damage to the family's honor (above, pp. 49, 56). As *kurios* it was a father's right to choose his daughter's husband, so Tyndareos' course was unusual. Agamemnon's emphasis on Tyndareos' craftiness suggests that in hindsight he realizes that Tyndareos has managed both to avoid the immediate danger from Helen's suitors and make sure others would bear the burden of taking revenge in case of future trouble caused by his desirable daughter.

15. Agamemnon suggests that giving Helen her choice was part of her father's clever plan to protect himself. It was a common misogynistic assumption among Greeks that given the option women would behave foolishly, especially in sexual matters; hence Agamemnon describes Helen's choice as based on sexual attraction rather than practical considerations such as Menelaos' status. Agamemnon was apparently not one of the suitors, perhaps because he was already married to Klytemnestra. As given in the manuscripts line 70 can mean either "he should never have married her" or "she should never have married him." The verb is usually used with male subject and female object, so editors often change the text here, but the syntactic ambiguity emphasizes the irregularity of a marriage in which, like that of Medea and Jason, the woman chooses her mate. Menelaos went to Sparta, Helen's state, rather than bringing his wife to his own state. This may have been because Agamemnon as elder brother inherited Atreus' kingdom, but it feminizes Menelaos.

16. "He" is Paris, son of King Priam of Troy. See 1300–1308, *Helen* 23–29, and above, pp. 306–307. Doubts like this about the veracity of mythic stories occur frequently in Euripides' plays; see 794–800, *Medea* 415–30, *Helen* 21.

17. The noun translated "pansy," *khlidēma,* means both "luxury" and "effeminacy." Syntactically it agrees with "getup"; elegant dress is associated with femaleness and

duplicity (see above, p. 59). The strongly ethnocentric Greeks considered themselves tough, independent, sexually abstemious, and hypermasculine, and the "barbarian" inhabitants of the great Eastern empires (Persia, Lydia, Phrygia) soft, slavish, sexually excitable, and effeminate. In the Greek these words are antierotic, not antihomoerotic; "real" men did not betray sexual desire for partners of either gender. Agamemnon taunts Menelaos by suggesting his brother longs for his unfaithful wife 386–88. On "barbarians" see above, pp. 22–3 and 313–14.

18. Paris compounds the crime of stealing Menelaos' wife by violating *xenia,* the law which required *xenoi* ("guest"/"host"; the same word is used for both), even when from different clans or lands, to respect one another; see above, p. 18. In Aeschylus' *Agamemnon* 60–67, Zeus Xenios (Zeus Protector of *xenia*) sends the sons of Atreus to punish Paris. Paris is now characterized as uncivilized (see also 180, 574–5) though three lines earlier he was called decadent.

19. The Greek army preparing to attack Troy is not like that of a modern nation-state, with a hierarchy of members bound by regulations. It consists of a loose alliance of powerful clansmen each leading his own contingent, bound by their oath to Tyndareos and following Agamemnon, Achilles says, to "do favor" to him and Menelaos (*Iliad* 1.159). Why didn't Menelaos lead the expedition? Agamemnon is the elder, but the more probable reason is that the public disgrace of his wife's behavior diminished Menelaos' status; Agamemnon jeers at the idea of his brother leading the army (394) and Achilles refers to him as not really a man (945). The *Iliad* depicts Agamemnon's sway over this coalition as shaky; Achilles withdraws from the fighting, accusing him of greed and poor leadership. "They chose me" suggests that Agamemnon was elected leader, a suggestion reinforced by Menelaos' account of his "election campaign" (337–342). This anachronistic touch invites comparison with Athens, where each year ten *stratēgoi* (generals) were elected from the ten tribes of Attica. Athenian *stratēgoi* had political as well as military power. The overall situation—in which a leader is trying to conduct a war while mediating between the claims of the masses (the army) and his elite colleagues—certainly resembles that of Athens during the Peloponnesian War. Ober 1989 offers a portrait of Athenian democracy as an ongoing negotiation between mass and elite. On connections between this play and the Peloponnesian War, see above, pp. 317–20.

20. A problem that suggested divine displeasure needed a seer to discern what god was angry and why. The goddess Artemis, rather casually introduced as "the goddess who dwells in this land," was a very important divinity throughout Greece. See above, pp. 54–55. In Aeschylus' *Agamemnon,* Kalkhas' prophecy is quoted at length by observers 140–55. Here Agamemnon suggests that Kalkhas is acting like a politician rather than as a religious man, using the impasse to further his professional standing. Agamemnon's disdain for Kalkhas recalls his rebuke at the very beginning of the *Iliad* (1.101–120). Agamemnon, Menelaos, and Achilles express contempt for priests later in this play (520–21, 955–58); so does the Messenger in *Helen* (729–42). Gantz 1993: 582–87 describes other Greek versions of the mobilization at Aulis.

21. Greek makes a clear distinction between sacrificial killing (92) and murder (364, 396, 463, 512); Agamemnon uses the latter term here. Apart from the emotional consequences, the killing of a blood relative incurred special pollution and potential retribution. Specific procedures were required to purge a murderer of religious taboo and social stigma; see Parker 1983.

22. The word for "writing-tablet" is *deltos,* which is very close to a word for the female genitals (*delta,* "triangle"). Both items are "inscribed" by males, and both are associated with deception; see duBois 1988: 138–66 and Lewis 1996: 142–52. Rabinowitz 1993 argues that Agamemnon's letter "stands for the body of Iphigenia" (42).

23. Agamemnon, unlike Tyndareos, behaves like a customary father, consulting neither the bride nor her mother about this decision. This is a clear example of the "traffic in women" used to cement male relationships; see Rabinowitz 1993: 15–22. When she arrives Klytemnestra expresses no surprise at the suddenness with which her husband has decided to marry off Iphigenia. Yet Agamemnon's need to convince Klytemnestra of the bridegroom's rank and lineage indicates her power *within* the *oikos* ("household").

24. This fictive scenario resembles the *Iliad*'s depiction of Agamemnon's and Achilles' relationship later in the war. Agamemnon angers Achilles by taking away a female war prize (note "deprived of his wedding," 124), and the latter withdraws from the fighting. Agamemnon then tries to convince Achilles to reenter the battle by offering one of his own daughters in marriage.

25. If the Old Man knows the content of the letter he can respond to the questions Klytemnestra will ask. As a slave he is illiterate, so Agamemnon must tell him (and the audience) the contents of the letter.

26. With these words the meter changes back to anapests (indicating that the scene is coming to an end), and Agamemnon's language becomes more heightened and poetic. Many editors change the order of lines 115–118, letting the Old Man speak before Agamemnon begins to read the letter so that the Old Man doesn't interrupt the king. But a pause which prompts the Old Man to encourage his master underlines the contrast (as in the opening exchange) between Agamemnon's inability to make up his mind and the Old Man's decisiveness. The formal address (a "matronymic" based on the mother's name similar to the "patronymic" based on the father's name) and tone of this letter (much more formal than, for example, Iphigenia's letter to her brother in *Iphigenia among the Taurians* 770–786) indicates Agamemnon's respect for his wife, perhaps some fear as well. Agamemnon begins his address to Klytemnestra in Aeschylus' *Agamemnon* 914 with the same matronymic, whereas Jason never addresses Medea with anything other than *gunē* ("woman/wife").

27. Agamemnon's reply makes use of the contrast between *logos* and *ergon* ("word"/"deed," "story/fact," or "appearance"/"reality") frequent in late-fifth-century thought. Discussions by philosophers and rhetoricians focus on the need to go beyond *logos* to

discern *ergon,* and this is a central theme in *Helen.* Agamemnon treats the issue casually, saying there's no need to worry since only *logos,* not *ergon,* is involved.

28. Thetis, Achilles' mother, was the immortal daughter of Nereus, a seagod; his father Peleus was a mortal. This line contains the first of many connections (ritual, symbolic, and psychological) between marriage and death for women to be found in this play. See 461–64 below; Foley 1985: 84–92; Rehm 1994; Seaford 1987; and above, pp. 56–7, 309.

29. Literally, "speak propitious words," a religious phrase, as if Agamemnon were uttering blasphemy. The verb Agamemnon has used suggests a magical spell.

30. "Outside the gates"—of Agamemnon's city, or the Greek camp? The latter raises the stakes: Even if Iphigenia has almost reached her destination the Old Man must turn her back. She arrives so soon after this that it might be assumed that she was not far from the camp, although Athenian drama does not maintain a strictly naturalistic time frame. Agamemnon is asking a slave to take a very bold action. Slaves in Greek drama are frequently tested by masters' demands: Compare the Servant's difficulty in restraining his grief for his dead mistress as commanded by Admetos in *Alcestis* (764).

31. A reference to city walls comprised of huge stones, so large that only giants such as the one-eyed Cyclopes, who were master-builders, could have built them. The city meant seems to be Mycenae (see 265), although the city of Argos (within the territory also known as Argos) also had such walls. Argos was an ally of Athens in the Peloponnesian War.

32. Characters in Greek drama frequently utter maxims (*gnōmai*) like this. They are not necessarily expressions of "Greek beliefs" which should be accepted as true, but generalizations about a particular situation whose appropriateness to that situation varies. Here Agamemnon is avoiding taking personal responsibility for his actions by including himself among suffering mortals.

33. Like all characters in Greek drama, the Chorus must announce their identity and mission on their entrance. In this case the Chorus consist of young married women from Chalkis, a city across the straits of Euripus, who have come to see the great naval expedition encamped at Aulis. They do not continue in the anapests that Agamemnon and the Old Man have just been using, but enter singing and dancing with musical accompaniment. On the role of the Chorus in Athenian tragedy, see above, pp. 38–41; on this Chorus, see above, pp. 317–18.

34. The best-known spring called Arethusa was located in Syracuse, in Sicily, but other cities had springs with the same name. The Chorus' journey was not a major expedition (the Euripus is only about fifty yards across) but the action of these women—leaving home unescorted by their men—would have been unusual in fifth-century Athens. Respectable women, especially unmarried girls, were expected to remain within their houses. Medea has to explain her boldness in coming outside

(214), Agamemnon orders Iphigenia inside (678), and Klytemnestra's offer to bring her daughter out (992–997) is against custom. See above, pp. 51–53, 60.

35. The "beauty contest" = the Judgment of Paris. See above, pp. 306–307, and other references to the Judgment at 573–581 and 1300–1308. Such a long sentence (the whole section up to this point is a single thought expressed in a single sentence in the original) suggests the Chorus' excitement. This unusually long choral song focuses on the best-known Greek heroes and use Homeric diction and references (for example, Achilles' swift feet 206–7 recall his most frequent epithet in Homer) to express enthusiasm for the war and the warriors. Some of the details of this description almost certainly had topical resonances that are hard to gauge at this distance. For example, Athens and her allies in the Peloponnesian War, such as Argos, are more positively described than her enemies, such as Thebes. For a complex political and choreographic interpretation of this ode see Wiles 1997: 105–112. In any case the depiction of a united Greek force would have been ironic in the context of the Peloponnesian War. On traditional heroic values and fifth-century Athens, see above, pp. 45–46.

36. Many fifth-century vases were decorated with scenes of Trojan War heroes off the battlefield as well as on; one signed by Exekias, now in the Vatican Museum, shows Ajax and Achilles playing a board game. Greek athletics (from *athlon,* "contest") always involved competition between individuals rather than team sports or attempts to surpass records. Such contests kept Greek males fit and honed their war skills.

37. Chiron was a Centaur, a creature consisting of a human torso and a horse's body. Most Centaurs were fond of wine, easily aroused sexually, and violent, but Chiron, the offspring of Zeus and a daughter of Ocean, was immortal and wise. He advised Peleus to marry Thetis and undertook Achilles' education. See further 705–10, 926–7.

38. The turns were the most tricky parts of a race for a four-horse chariot. Harnessing the outside horses only to the chariot, rather than to the inside horses, allowed the driver to maneuver better but required considerable skill in handling the reins.

39. A well-known poem by Sappho (the most famous Greek female author, active in the seventh century BCE) begins, "Some people say that a line of cavalry is the most beautiful thing on the black earth; others say foot soldiers, or a line of ships; but I say it's whatever you love." This has been interpreted as a female revision of the military values of Greek epic; the women of the Chorus stick with tradition.

40. Phthia was a state in southern Thessaly, also called Pharsalia (812), which was ruled by Achilles' father Peleus. The Myrmidons, so-called because the state was founded by a man called Myrmidon, were the warriors brought by Achilles to the Trojan expedition.

41. Theseus is the major hero associated with Athens. The force from Argos is juxtaposed here with that of its ally Athens.

42. Kadmos founded the city of Thebes by killing a dragon and sowing its teeth, which grew into men.

43. Several lines are lost here.

44. Did Helen choose to go with Paris, or was she abducted? Athenian law prescribed harsher penalties for seduction than rape. Helen tells her version of events in the opening scene of *Helen* and in Euripides' *Trojan Women* (895–1059). For discussions of Helen's role in various texts see Suzuki 1989; Meagher 1995.

45. Several lines are lost here.

46. The ode ends with several reminders that what the Chorus report is a mixture of first- and second-hand information, reminding the audience that the information of eyes and of ears can contradict one another.

47. The outrage is not using physical violence (which a free man could use on another's slave, though the owner might demand reparations) but breaking the seal of the letter.

48. The staff is an emblem of authority; when an underling insults Agamemnon and urges the Greeks to leave Troy and sail home, Odysseus beats him into silence with his staff (*Iliad* 2.211–277).

49. From here to 401 the meter changes to trochaic tetrameters, a meter denoting heightened emotional excitement and tension. As usual, although three characters are onstage there is dialogue between only two of them. The Old Man says no more, and at some point during the following scene exits unnoticed into the tent. He needs to get off the stage in order to change costume and mask; he will return as the Messenger at 414.

50. The "stage directions" contained in the preceding interchange suggest that Agamemnon avoids looking at Menelaos. The phrase for looking someone else directly in the face was "a free eye" (see 994). On the "lexicon" of gestures, see above, pp. 36–7.

51. Here the use of *gnōmai* ("maxims"; see note 32) permits considerable insult without direct name-calling. The word translated "friend" is *philos,* which refers to the social relationship between family members, members of a political faction, and allies, as well as to affective ties. See above, pp. 20–21.

52. Euripidean characters often preface their monologues with this kind of rhetorical device. The verb translated "cross-examine" is a term used in law and philosophical dialogues for a point-by-point attack. It signifies the beginning of an *agōn,* or verbal battle between two characters (see above, p. 41). Such "warmups" have both practical and metatheatrical uses. They prepare the audience for a long speech, and, by demonstrating the speaker's self-awareness and the choice of stances available, remind the audience of the similarities between role-playing in drama and in life. See below 442, 977–78, 1124–26, 1540–42; and *Medea* 522–25.

53. "Public honors" = *philotimon,* a complex word that means the desire for public recognition, the means used to acquire it, and the recognition itself. See below 385, 527, and Dover 1974: 230–33, 236.

54. Menelaos here voices a basic concept of Greek popular morality: that good behavior consists in helping one's friends and hurting one's enemies. Impartiality has little place in this scheme; see Blundell 1989: ch. 2.

55. Menelaos' repetition of information previously provided has two purposes: to remind audience members of the basic plot situation, and to offer another character's perspective on these events.

56. Menelaos invokes the natural surroundings (and the gods who inhabit them) to remember the oath Agamemnon swore to sacrifice his daughter.

57. Again the mythic war situation is discussed anachronistically in terms of fifth-century Athens. The reference to "backing off" may be an allusion to the erratic conduct of Alcibiades, a dashing aristocrat, in 408–6 BCE. Recalled from exile, he was at first very humble, and succeeded in getting himself elected general. He then equipped a fleet of one hundred ships and fifteen hundred hoplites, but hesitated to use them, and after a defeat withdrew to Thrace in northern Greece.

58. The chorus normally punctuate the end of a character's monologue, especially during an *agōn,* with a short observation. Lines such as these were presumably spoken by the chorus leader.

59. Literally, "not leading my eyes up too high toward shamelessness" (*anaideia*). In Athenian legal contexts *anaideia* refers to a dispute that is incapable of reconciliation. Like Menelaos, Agamemnon prefaces his speech by outlining various options for his behavior and awareness of their consequences.

60. Characters in Greek drama frequently describe others' facial expressions. Such descriptions of course substitute for what the audience could not see because of the use of masks and the size of the theater. But this description is not necessarily accurate; Agamemnon's words are designed to bait his opponent and to win points by contrasting his own restraint and control.

61. Agamemnon insinuates that Menelaos' talk about Greek honor is a cover for his desire to get his adulterous wife back. In fifth-century Athens wives caught in adultery had to be divorced, and to be seen as erotically or emotionally dependent on a woman, or unable to control her, brought shame on a Greek man (see note 17). In *Trojan Women,* Menelaos intends to kill Helen, but soon relents and spares her. In *Odyssey* 4.78–289 they are back home in Sparta, but their pointedly different recollections of the Trojan War suggest that they are *not* living happily ever after.

62. The state of mind of a person swearing an oath (or committing an action) made no difference to the effect. In the late fifth century, however, the absolute inviolability of oaths began to be questioned. In Euripides' *Hippolytos* the title character justifies breaking an oath by arguing "My tongue swore the oath but my heart remained

unsworn" (612). Because of its shocking rejection of traditional values this became one of Euripides' most infamous lines; see Aristophanes, *Frogs* 101–2, 1471.

63. Again a question about the proper behavior of *philoi.* Agamemnon must choose between two blood kin; Menelaos insists that his conduct shows Agamemnon is not really his brother. The meter returns to iambic trimeter at 402.

64. This line indicates that Menelaos, who is about to leave to tell Odysseus, Kalkhas, and the Greek army of Agamemnon's change of plan, is interrupted by the Messenger's arrival. The Messenger has not been "announced" by any of the onstage characters, and begins his address to Agamemnon in the middle of a line, indicating that his arrival is a surprise; probably the actor has run onstage. Such surprise entrances are frequent in Euripides'plays; see above, pp. 72–3.

65. The Messenger is a slave from Agamemnon's household who has accompanied Klytemnestra to Aulis. This can explain his knowledge of Agamemnon's fondness for his children and the rather familiar tone he takes with the general. Passages like this, 431–32, and 631–685, demonstrate (*pace* Keuls 1985: 72–73, 110) that for all the high cultural value placed on male children, fathers could be very fond of their female offspring. The Messenger's perspective offers an ironic contrast to the tense scene he has interrupted, assuming as he does that his news will bring joy to Agamemnon, and describing a natural setting, relaxation, females (even the horses!), proper ritual, music, celebration.

66. Myth and literary tradition associated girls in meadows with rape and death. In the *Homeric Hymn to Demeter,* Hades, god of the underworld, abducts Persephone as she is picking flowers in a meadow.

67. The verb used by the Messenger in 433 indicates that the "ritual done before marriage" is the *proteleia* ("preliminary sacrifice"). As with the suitors' oath to Tyndareos, animal sacrifices were held before any significant undertaking. Barley (435) was sprinkled at a sacrifice; garlands of flowers (436) were worn on festive occasions (see below 1058, 1080, 1112). A sacrifice is described in detail at 1563–79. A more literal translation of 433 is "performing a preliminary sacrifice for the young girl," which allows a darker alternative meaning, "offering the young girl as a preliminary sacrifice" (to going to Troy); compare 718 below. Also in Aeschylus' *Agamemnon* (65, 227, 720) the sacrifice of Iphigenia is the *proteleia* to the expedition's departure. On ancient sacrificial practice see above, pp. 12–13; on marriage and death, see above, pp. 56–7; on sacrifice in *IA,* see above, pp. 307–309.

68. "Enough" = literally, "I praise [you]," a polite but rather cold response. Not only was Agamemnon's plan to intercept Iphigenia frustrated when Menelaos seized the letter from the Old Man, he was apparently not expecting Klytemnestra to accompany Iphigenia to the army camp. "Whatever happens" is *tukhē* again (see note 12). Agamemnon is mouthing meaningless generalities until the Messenger gets out of earshot, but the phrase "all will be well" recalls Aeschylus' *Agamemnon* (217). The Messenger needs to leave so the actor can transform himself into Iphigenia.

69. Again, a rhetorical "warmup." In this case an expression of *aporia* (uncertainty how to proceed) is used to express the speaker's indecision; at other times (for example, 1124–26) it expresses the speaker's search for the most effective form in which to frame a speech.

70. "Trap" = literally "yoke of necessity." In a society based on agriculture, the yoke on an ox's neck is a pervasive symbol of compulsion; it is used of marriage 805 below. Agamemnon's phrase explicitly recalls Aeschylus' *Agamemnon* 218.

71. Expressions of emotion, especially tears, raise issues of propriety involving both class (as here) and gender. In tragedy noble Greek men frequently refer to the need for restraint of "unmanly" tears. Menelaos carefully considers whether to weep when pleading for his life at *Helen* 947–53. "Well, then" is a "recovery" gesture, indicating that Agamemnon has given in to tears; Menelaos confirms this 477.

72. That is, "What sort of role shall I play?"—another explicitly self-conscious, metatheatrical reference.

73. A Greek mother normally took a central role in her children's weddings: see below, 716–741, *Alcestis* 317, *Medea* 1026–27. Even in this moment of frustration and rage, Agamemnon acknowledges Klytemnestra's right to come with Iphigenia. This foreshadows and deepens the later scene (695–741) when she defeats his attempts to control her.

74. A curse coming from one about to die had special force. The Athenian audience knew that Agamemnon would die together with his concubine Kassandra at Klytemnestra's hands when he returned from Troy; see Aeschylus' *Agamemnon.* Agamemnon's premonition here of Iphigenia's curse is apparently not fulfilled, however; see 1551–60.

75. In societies without archives the most important component that makes a sexual union legitimate is its public acknowledgement. Paris's and Helen's union was no secret affair, but a publicly acknowledged relationship, discussed in the *Iliad* from a variety of viewpoints: Hector calls Paris "woman-crazy" and cowardly (3.39–42), but Priam treats Helen affectionately (3.161–65) and Trojan elders agree that she is worth fighting a war for (3.156–160).

76. Agamemnon interprets Menelaos' words as a request for a gesture of submission rather than of solidarity.

77. At 406 Menelaos claimed that Agamemnon's refusal to support him demonstrated that they were not born from the same father. Now he swears in the name of both father and grandfather that he is speaking the truth, and re-emphasizes blood ties throughout this speech (492, 501). The invocations of Pelops and Atreus recall the history of violence against children in this family: Pelops was the son of Tantalos, Agamemnon, and Menelaos' great-grandfather. Tantalos tested the gods by killing, cooking, and serving Pelops to them, but the gods miraculously revived the boy and punished Tantalos in Hades by chaining him in a pool of water with fruit dangling

over his head; both food and water retreated when he reached for them. The wife of Atreus (Agamemnon and Menelaos' father) had an affair with Atreus' brother Thyestes and gave her lover a valuable possession belonging to her husband. In revenge, Atreus killed Thyestes' children and arranged for him to eat their flesh. The reference to discord between brothers (508–9) might recall Atreus' and Thyestes' feud. Menelaos' protestation, another explicit use of rhetorical technique, raises the suspicion that he is lying, that his change of heart is calculated to provoke Agamemnon's opposite reaction.

78. In addition to stressing the ethical difference between the immoral Helen and the upright Agamemnon, this comparison reflects the importance of blood relatives compared to ties created by marriage. Antigone ranks her brother above husband or children, since the latter are replaceable (Sophocles, *Antigone* 904–912).

79. This speech is full of rhetorical questions, which often raise possibilities that contradict the speaker's apparent intention. This one (repeated 1236–7) may be answered: Helen and Iphigenia are both women, and as such less important than males and male plans. Iphigenia says exactly this (1392–94). See above, pp. 315–16.

80. With these words Menelaos abjures any responsibility for the pollution Agamemnon will incur by killing Iphigenia.

81. On Tantalos see note 77.

82. Agamemnon has changed his mind again, but the reason remains obscure. He apparently feels that Iphigenia's arrival in the camp has made her sacrifice inevitable, but why this should be is never made clear. His insistence that he has no choice contrasts with the clear choice of Aeschylus' Agamemnon (*Agamemnon* 211–217). See above, p. 312.

83. "The spawn of Sisyphos" = Odysseus. At 204 he was called son of Laertes (his mother Antiklea's husband) but there was a story that Sisyphos impregnated Antiklea on the eve of her marriage. Associating Odysseus with Sisyphos, a very wily man who succeeded in tricking even the gods, casts the former's well-known intelligence in a negative light; see also 1362. Sisyphos was the mythic founder of Corinth, one of Athens' fiercest opponents in the Peloponnesian War.

84. Odysseus is said to be a better speaker than any other mortal (*Iliad* 3.221–24); he uses his power as a speaker to rectify a tactical mistake of Agamemnon's (*Iliad* 2.188–335). This picture of him haranguing the troops is also an "anachronistic" reference to contemporary Athenian debates in the popular Assembly, where demagogues tried to sway the crowd; see Ober 1989, especially chapter 3.

85. Choruses in Greek drama regularly learn secrets such as this, and protagonists regularly attempt to make them keep silent. But they usually come to question the implications of keeping the secret (*Medea* 811–19; *Alcestis* 551–67) and sometimes reveal it (*Ion* 760–807).

86. Menelaos now disappears from the play. The actor changes costume and mask to return as Klytemnestra.

87. The name of the goddess is often used to signify the sexual desire she arouses, just as "Ares" can mean "war" (764–80), "Bacchus" "wine" (1061), and so forth. Erotic desire (*erōs*) is often described in Greek texts as something to be feared and avoided, an invasion of the self by an outside force rather than an expression of the self; see *Medea* 627–44, *Hippolytos* 525–33, and *Antigone* 781–99, where the Chorus blame *erōs* for angry words between blood relatives; for a general discussion, see Thornton 1997. The overall "argument" of this song, and its connection with the dramatic action, is far from obvious. One way to construe it: The gods are responsible for dangerous, excessive erotic love, but it can be controlled by innate goodness, good upbringing, and will power. Paris and Helen are male and female examples of the personal and political consequences of losing control over *erōs,* but basic ethical principles always triumph (558–72).

88. "Excellence" (*aretē*), associated with military prowess and civic leadership, like *virtus* in Latin, is based on the word for "male." So the idea of women achieving *aretē* is by definition odd, and the Chorus go on to distinguish the *aretē* appropriate to each gender. See above, pp. 50–51.

89. Like Agamemnon, the Chorus express contempt for Paris' rustic upbringing (see 76 and note 18). Olympos was the father (or son) of Marsyas, a rustic musician and satyr who challenged Apollo to a music contest: Apollo's lyre vs. Marsyas' pipes. Upon defeating his opponent Apollo had him skinned alive. "Phrygian" is used throughout the play as a synonym for "Trojan," but here it refers to one of the modes (the most sensual) in the scheme of Greek music.

90. The word *eris* ("strife") recalls the story that the contest of the goddesses was caused by the goddess Strife, and plays on the phonic similarity between *eris* and *erōs.* See above, pp. 306–307.

91. The playing space in the Theater of Dionysos was large enough to permit a grand entrance like this, with the wagon or carriage driven by nonspeaking extras playing slaves and attendants to Klytemnestra. Characters who enter this way, however (Agamemnon and Kassandra in Aeschylus' *Agamemnon,* Andromache and Astyanax in Euripides' *Trojan Women,* Klytemnestra in Euripides' *Elektra*) are rarely headed for happiness. The Chorus switch to anapests, the "movement" meter, here.

92. Either the Chorus forget, in their excitement over the royals' arrival, about Agamemnon's plans for Iphigenia, or they are playing a role, obedient to Agamemnon's command to keep silent. The former is more consistent with their established role as naive observers (although for women from Chalkis to call Iphigenia "my mistress" [593] is odd) and increases the structural irony. As in the scene described by the Messenger, the stage is now dominated by women, and the Chorus diminish the social gulf between themselves and the aristocrats by emphasizing their mutual status as foreigners in Aulis.

93. Klytemnestra speaks of herself as *numphagōgos,* "conductor of the bride," and the procession that brings Iphigenia to Aulis resembles that which conducted a bride to her bridegroom's house. This was the most public aspect of an ancient wedding; see above, note 75, and Oakley and Sinos 1993: 26–34 and illustrations. In this case, although the wedding has not yet occurred, the public nature of the procession (complete with mention of the dowry [611–12] and the bridegroom's name [625–27]) may be interpreted to mean that a marriage has in fact taken place; Klytemnestra so interprets it (904–908) and Achilles agrees (936). Klytemnestra's guarded words (609–10) reflect women's inability to know in advance what marriage holds in store (compare *Medea* 235–40) as well as, perhaps, her own experience. But she also needs to avoid attracting divine or human *phthonos* (envy, the evil eye) which could result from drawing attention by any outstanding quality or act, positive or negative (53, 1097).

94. Presumably addressed to the attendants. Klytemnestra's commands (of the sixteen main verbs in her speech eleven are imperatives) are an example of stage directions in the text (above, p. 28) but also portray a woman used to ruling her own *oikos,* confirming what Agamemnon has said about her (99–105, 457–59) and preparing for her shock when her husband attempts to send her home before the marriage (729).

95. Klytemnestra's affection for Orestes here provides a charming domestic interlude before the storm breaks, and is part of this play's revision of Aeschylus' portrait of her in the *Oresteia,* where it is suggested that she is not a good mother to Orestes. See above, p. 317. Children appear onstage more often in the plays of Euripides than in those of any other ancient playwright; three of the four plays in this volume include children. It seems likely that these roles were taken by real children, although lines (such as the calls for help of Medea's children, 1273–78) and the lament of Alcestis' son (394–415) were presumably delivered by other actors; see Pickard-Cambridge 1988: 144. Children certainly increased the pathos of the stage event; Athenian defendants attempted to move juries by bringing their children to court. On children in Athenian culture see Golden 1990.

96. Agamemnon exited, presumably into his tent, at 542. By 630 he must be again onstage; at what point does he come back? The lack of any announcement of his return is odd, suggesting that his return is unobtrusive, overlooked in the flurry of activity, perhaps stealthy. The order of lines 631–39 is somewhat odd; some editors place 636–37 after 630. Some of these lines might have been delivered as Iphigenia ran across the stage to her father. The repetitions in Iphigenia's lines (631–35) have led editors to suppress some of them (see also 652). But they effectively convey her youth and impulsiveness and her relationship to both her parents. After her affectionate words (and no doubt an embrace, 640) she greets her father more formally (642). The very awkwardness of the scene conveys Iphigenia's love for Agamemnon, which was well established in the previous mythic and dramatic tradition; Aeschylus' Klytemnestra pictures her rushing to embrace him as he arrives in the underworld (*Agamemnon* 1555–59). But here as often Euripides "psychologizes" mythic charac-

ters. Klytemnestra's acceptance here of her daughter's preference for her father (638–39) is echoed in Euripides' *Elektra,* where she says to Elektra, "It's always been your nature to love your father. It's just that way: some children prefer their fathers, some their mothers; I understand" (1102–05).

97. In every line to his daughter Agamemnon tries to tell neither an outright lie nor the unspeakable truth. This is a classic example of "dramatic irony," since the audience knows what Agamemon knows but Klytemnestra does not. Each of the plays in this volume contains a scene in which one character struggles to maintain a role or façade: see above, pp. 71–2.

98. Again the word *philos*—literally, a "friendly" or "loving" expression; see note 52 above. Agamemnon knows his plan for Iphigenia makes him resemble an *ekhthros* ("enemy") not a *philos.*

99. Literally, "I praise you," the same formal phrase as Agamemnon used to the Messenger (440). Here it seems to indicate a recovery of composure after his cry of pain. Changes of focus such as this resemble the "asides" of later theatrical tradition, but without knowing the acting conventions of the Athenian theater we cannot specify whether Iphigenia "hears" his outcry or not. See Bain 1977a, especially 48–55.

100. The multiple ironies in lines 664–670 are made more pointed by Greek metaphors for dying as a journey to the "house" of Hades; see *Medea* 1015–16, 1021–23, and note 122. Here again is the "marriage to death" theme.

101. This "phatic" expression is a single syllable (*pheu*) which conveys grief, surprise, anger, or uncertainty (as here; Iphigenia can't understand what Agamemnon means). See other examples at 709, 977, 1124, and *Alcestis* 719, 1102.

102. In this scene Iphigenia speaks as if she has come to Aulis to visit Agamemnon, never referring directly to her marriage, although she would presumably have performed some of the rituals preceding marriage (dedicating childhood toys to Artemis, bidding farewell to her native household gods) before leaving home. Foley 1985: 71 considers this a "playful pretense of ignorance," but such ignorance on the part of a very young girl accords with Greek custom and ideology: see above, pp. 55–6.

103. In Athens respectable women were expected to stay in their own part of the house, out of the sight of males (see above, pp. 52–3). *Parthenoi* (adolescent girls) were especially well guarded; see 738.

104. Many Greek mythic figures such as Achilles, Menelaos (176), and Kassandra (758) are said to have blond or reddish hair. Most ancient Greeks, like many Mediterranean people today, were probably dark-haired and olive-skinned, but gold is metaphorically associated with nobility, youth, and beauty.

105. Agamemnon abandons the informality and emotion of his interchange with Iphigenia and addresses his wife as formally as he did in his letter (115). As in the scene with Iphigenia he must play his role carefully. Previously his affection for his daughter threatened to undermine his performance; now his wife's intelligence does.

106. The "labor" involved in rearing a daughter consisted primarily of guarding her chastity and getting her properly married off. Recent feminist scholarship has focused on the pain Greek mothers and daughters felt when the latter married; see Foley 1994. But in this play Klytemnestra expresses no explicit sorrow about losing Iphigenia to marriage (692–3 suggests that she is keeping her grief under control until the actual moment), and Agamemnon's words are convincing only if a daughter's marriage was considered a sad occasion for fathers as well as mothers.

107. Even if she has no say in the choice of a husband for Iphigenia, Klytemnestra tries to act in her daughter's interest, making sure the proposed match is socially appropriate and conducted correctly. That she professes to know little about the hero of the *Iliad* again reminds the audience that these events are taking place before Achilles attained glory at Troy, when he was just a minor prince from a minor state in northern Greece (Phthia). So far these lines may be considered part of this play's revision of the *Iliad.* Yet at 625–26 Klytemnestra knows who Achilles' mother and father are, so the real point of her questions here may be to put Agamemnon on the spot.

108. Asopos was a river-god, Aigina a goddess abducted and raped by Zeus. As he says he did in his letter (101), Agamemnon is trying to make Achilles look good by mentioning his divine ancestors.

109. There were different stories about Peleus' marriage to Thetis. Zeus (in some versions Poseidon as well) wished to marry the sea-goddess, but because of a prophecy that her son would surpass his father decided to marry her to Peleus. She resisted this marriage by transforming herself into different shapes, and in the *Iliad* frequently laments her lot as mother of a mortal son. Here Agamemnon depicts the marriage as the proper transfer of a woman from her *kurios* to her husband, not as a violation of her or her father Nereus' rights; see Foley 1985: 72 and above, pp. 56–8. This mention of women forced into marriage anticipates Klytemnestra's account of hers 1149–56; the Chorus contrast Peleus' and Thetis' wedding with Iphigenia's sacrifice 1036–97; see above, pp. 319–20.

110. The phatic expression *pheu* again (see note 101) here perhaps indicating that Klytemnestra did not know this about Achilles.

111. Agamemnon referred to Iphigenia as "my daughter" (687). Here, by reaffirming male control, he rebuffs Klytemnestra's reminder (714) that she has a stake in Iphigenia's future.

112. These lines are especially ironic, since Iphigenia herself will be the sacrifice preliminary to the army's embarking for Troy. By "the goddess" (of marriage) Klytemnestra probably means Hera, who is the principal female deity of Argos (see 738), but Agamemnon and the audience would think of Artemis, also associated with marriage.

113. The word for "hold the wedding feast" (721) is phonetically similar (though not etymologically related) to a verb that means "burn up," so Klytemnestra's words sound like "then you'll burn up the wedding?" Agamemnon is so rattled he repeats

"sacrifice" three times. In Greek the line is even more awkward, since it contains four "th-" sounds.

114. Agamemnon apparently means 723 to embellish a not very desirable location for a party with Homeric language, but after the adjective "with their beautiful sterns" he uses the word "oars" instead of "ships." (The Chorus use the same phrase 765, so this may not be a mistake. Greek ships were drawn up on the beach stern first, and the oars at the stern were large.) Klytemnestra responds sarcastically (her use of the Homeric phrase "amidst the swelling billows" [704] also sounds sarcastic) and Agamemnon flashes back at her angrily.

115. In the *Oresteia,* Agamemnon and Klytemnestra have only one other daughter, Elektra, but in the *Iliad* and Sophocles' *Elektra* there are two other daughters.

116. Another reference to the wedding procession that conducted the bride to her husband's house (see above, note 93). This procession took place at night, with participants in the wedding, especially the two mothers, carrying torches to light the way; Medea laments that she will never experience this happy moment (*Medea* 1027).

117. For a similar moment of male incomprehension of female values see *Medea* 1367–68.

118. Invoking a god's name called on the divinity to hear the words spoken, giving them the force of an oath. Men swore in the name of gods, women of goddesses; on Hera see note 112.

119. This actor's next role is Achilles.

120. The Simois river ran through the plain near Troy.

121. The plain before Troy is called "Apollo's plain" because (as the result of a failed revolt against Zeus) Apollo was condemned to serve Laomedon, king of Troy, for a year. He herded the king's flocks (compare his servitude to Admetos, *Alcestis* 1–9 and above, pp. 94–6). In the *Iliad,* Apollo is the Trojans' most important divine ally.

122. Apollo offered Kassandra the power to see the future in return for sex. She agreed, received the gift, but somehow avoided keeping her part of the bargain. Divine gifts could not be revoked even by the givers, but Apollo ensured that no one would believe Kassandra's prophecies; in Aeschylus' *Agamemnon* (1264–76) she laments the suffering this power has caused her. Laurel was sacred to Apollo; this description of inspiration by Apollo suggests the Pythia, the priestess of Apollo at Delphi who delivered the god's words in a trance. When Troy fell Kassandra was awarded to Agamemnon as a prize; on their arrival in Argos, Klytemnestra killed her together with him. As maidens caught up in Agamemnon's male politics Kassandra and Iphigenia resemble each other.

123. Ares the war god is seen as bringing war to the Trojans using the Greek army as his instrument. "He" in 774 also refers to Ares.

124. In addition to Helen and Klytemnestra, Leda bore the twins Kastor and Polydeukes (Pollux). In most versions Polydeukes was the son of Zeus, and so immortal; in order not to be separated from his brother, he arranged to share his immortality with Kastor. Together they were known as the Dioskouroi, "Zeus' boys"; see *Helen* 1643–45.

125. Lydia was a kingdom in Asia Minor. Like "Phrygian," "Lydian" is used as a synonym for "Trojan" here and elsewhere. The Chorus' attitude here is very different from Agamemnon's (73–4): The wealth of Eastern women will not keep them from pain. When a besieged city was taken, the killing of males and enslaving of women and children was standard procedure, in both myth and history. Hektor foresees this fate for the Trojans (*Iliad* 6.447–62), and in 415 the Athenian army so punished inhabitants of the island of Melos.

126. Like Helen (*Helen* 18–21) the Chorus doubt the story of Zeus mating with Leda. But no matter what the cause of the war may be—a divine or mortal woman, abducted or seduced—the suffering it brings is real. See above, pp. 317–19.

127. Achilles' entrance is unprepared by spoken dialogue, so the character must identify himself. "Here" in 801 can be interpreted as filling out "Where?," i.e., "Where around here?" But its position after "Greeks" suggests limits to Agamemnon's power: Achilles sees him as general for this specific expedition, not the natural leader of all the Greeks. Such an attitude on Achilles' part accords well with his lack of respect for Agamemnon in the *Iliad* and in the scenes to come in this play. In Homeric fashion Achilles uses a patronymic to identify himself.

128. Achilles seems to mean that warfare and domesticity are alternate life choices for males: If men are not getting on with the business of warfare, they should be at home acquiring wives and fathering children. Odysseus says any man separated from his wife for one month is unhappy (*Iliad* 2.292–3); Achilles questions the worth of warfare (*Iliad* 9. 394–429), saying he will leave Troy, go home, marry, and enjoy life.

129. Another surprise entrance. Is Klytemnestra accompanied by attendants, or alone? The latter would help explain Achilles' uncertainty about her identity and status. Unlike other members of the army he has apparently not heard about her and Iphigenia's arrival, and might even take her for a concubine of Agamemnon (although her costume would presumably indicate her royal status). The form of dialogue used in this scene, two-line stichomythia (see above, p. 37) is relatively rare.

130. "The goddess daughter of Nereus" = Thetis, Achilles' mother; instead of the patronymic Achilles uses (803) Klytemnestra addresses him with his matronymic, as at 625–27.

131. "Goddess of Propriety" = *aidōs,* a word which, like *erōs,* is sometimes personified and treated as a divinity, as here. The meaning of this very important concept differs according to rank, gender, and situation. Overall, it is fear of being seen doing something socially inappropriate, a fear which keeps people from committing such acts.

In this case, Achilles has not been expecting to see a woman outside and invokes the aid of *aidōs* to deal with this surprise appropriately. See Cairns 1993, esp. 282–84 and 309–14. Females are usually more concerned about *aidōs* than males, but throughout this scene Achilles demonstrates concern for following proper social custom, avoiding public censure, preserving honor (especially male honor) and his own good name—much more than does Klytemnestra. See also 996–1001, 1017–21, 1029–32.

132. "Self-restraint" = here *sōphronein,* elsewhere *sōphrosunē.* This difficult concept has different meanings for each gender. For males, it involves primarily curbing appetites, excess, violence; for females, maintaining sexual chastity, public modesty, and deference to males: compare 558–72 and note 88, 1159. Achilles has probably stepped back or made some courteous gesture, and Klytemnestra registers and praises his good manners. These mythic characters maintaining Athenian social conventions are "anachronistic" and potentially comic.

133. The phrase "defended by shields" is a Homeric epithet; in this context, instead of conveying the danger to the unarmed woman from male violence (as Klytemnestra states at 913), it suggests that the men are the ones who need defense.

134. Offering Achilles her right hand suggests that Klytemnestra is sealing her daughter's marriage, an action usually undertaken by a woman's male *kurios* (above, p. 50). The verb translated "arrange" that she uses at 847 is normally used only by males; Achilles uses it 841.

135. Since Achilles has been revealed as a male with no connection to her Klytemnestra is violating *aidōs* by remaining in his presence. Iphigenia similarly feels *aidōs* before Achilles 1342 once she knows he is no longer her intended bridegroom.

136. The dialogue returns to single-line interchanges in trochaic tetrameters, quickening the tempo and increasing the emotional energy.

137. "Fortune" = *tukhē* again, now personified and addressed as a divine force; the Old Man knows that what he is about to say is incredible.

138. This difficult line has been interpreted in different ways. My reading, which sticks close to the manuscripts, assumes that Achilles continues to mock the Old Man.

139. Literally, "don't wait for the right hand." The Old Man has evidently approached Klytemnestra but perhaps hesitates before speaking. She now takes command of the scene. Many take her phrase to mean "don't waste time kissing my hand," but there is no tradition of Greek slaves kissing their masters' hands. Messengers who brought bad news might be punished, so Klytemnestra's reference to her right hand means, "No matter what news you're bringing, don't wait till I formally swear that I won't hurt you to tell me your news." On the right hand as a sign of an oath, see *Medea* 21–22. The Old Man carefully presents his "credentials" in the next lines, since as he anticipated (155–57) Klytemnestra at first finds his story incredible.

140. "Evil spirits" = *alastores,* avenging spirits who exacted punishment for murder by causing new bloodshed. They embodied the victim's wrath, in some cases in a human form or by possessing a human being. In her attempt to find some motive for Agamemnon's intent Klytemnestra thinks he is driven to take revenge for some previous crime.

141. Dardanos was the ancestor of the Trojan kings.

142. Literally, "fall at your knees." Suppliants grasped the knees (literally or figuratively) of those they were imploring to keep them from moving away. Klytemnestra must overcome the shame (*aidōs*) which would normally hold her back from humbling herself publicly. Compare the scenes in which Medea supplicates Kreon and Aigeus in *Medea* and see above, pp. 21–22.

143. Klytemnestra appeals to the standards of behavior of an aristocratic male, and her actions reinforce her words by publicly staging her appeal. Since her husband, who ought to behave as her *philos,* is instead taking the role of *ekhthros* ("enemy"), her public display is calculated to place Achilles in a relationship of *philia* with her and Iphigenia, a relationship that will require him to aid them. Hence her emphasis (904–908) on the public impression that Achilles is going to marry Iphigenia: If the community believed that a relationship had been established, participants were expected to behave according to the expectations for that relationship.

144. People in danger could take refuge at or on a god's altar or other sacred spot; if pursuers pulled them away by force they incurred divine wrath (as did the Greek warrior who dragged Kassandra away from Athena's image as Troy was being sacked). The tomb of King Proteus serves as a refuge for Helen in the first scene of *Helen.*

145. Here the meter returns to iambic trimeter, presumably lowering the emotional temperature.

146. Achilles spends most of this long speech (the second longest in the play, exceeded only by the Messenger's 1540–1612) deciding in a very rational way how to conduct himself in this unusual situation. This portrayal of Achilles is very different from that in the *Iliad;* see above, p. 316.

147. The betrothal (*enguē*), a formal agreement between a woman's *kurios* and a prospective husband, was binding on both parties. Because Agamemnon has created a kind of *enguē,* Achilles seems to be taking on the role of Iphigenia's *kurios* here; compare also 964, 972, 1356, and see above, p. 56.

148. "Evil spirit" = *alastōr;* see note 141.

149. Agamemnon and Menelaos' ancestor Tantalos came from Sipylos in Lydia (in Asia Minor); see note 77.

150. Basins and barley-grains are tools used in sacrifice: basins held water to wash the participants' hands; both water and barley were sprinkled. See note 67.

151. "Shamefully abused me" = literally, "used *hubris* on me." This much misunderstood word refers to behavior that has the intent or effect of dishonoring another, includ-

ing a range of specific activities—physical and sexual violence, verbal attacks, and fraud. *Hubris* is a crucial concept in Greek social relations rather than (as it has often been treated) a character defect or a religious offense. Those who possess wealth and power are more likely to commit such offensive acts. Medea calls Jason's abandoning her and marrying the princess *hubris* (256, 603, 1365). Agamemnon's willingness to marry his daughter to Achilles might be considered a compliment, but his failure to consult Achilles is offensive. See above, p. 19.

152. Achilles' certainty that his stature impressed Klytemnestra is contradicted by 695–715, when she claimed to know little about him. Some editors delete lines 963–64 on the grounds that Achilles would not speak of Klytemnestra in the third person when she is present. I have left them in for three reasons: This speech mixes lines addressed to Klytemnestra with more abstract reflections; a long monologue such as this would not necessarily have been delivered in its entirety directly to the other actor onstage; and either his "uncomplicated character" or his narcissism might allow Achilles to speak thus even if he were standing next to Klytemnestra. Admetos' speech about how he will behave after Alcestis dies (328–367) and Medea's reflections about her children (1021–80) have a similar distance from the persons ostensibly addressed. A sacrificial victim had to be "unblemished" (see 1082). If Achilles were actually to consummate sexually his "marriage" to Iphigenia, she could not be sacrificed; see Foley 1985: 73 and above, p. 12.

153. Very similar language is used here about Klytemnestra's giving Iphigenia and Achilles' giving his name.

154. These last two lines are difficult to interpret. Is the imperative 973 a general reassurance ("Don't worry") or a particular response to something Klytemnestra does? (For example, she might flinch or step back at his threat 970–72, leading Achilles to reassure her.) Achilles' saying he will become a god may refer to his divine ancestry, or (taking the "very great god" as Zeus *Sōtēr,* Zeus "the Savior,") he may be declaring that he will indeed save the girl.

155. In most instances this exclamation (*pheu*) of grief, anger, or uncertainty occurs in the midst of speech or dialogue. Its presence at the beginning of a speech may indicate that Klytemnestra does not know how to respond to Achilles' words; compare 666, 709, and 1124, and see notes 101 and 110. She now takes quite a different tack from her previous speech, focusing her argument completely on Achilles.

156. As her opening lines suggest, Klytemnestra has to balance carefully here, both in argument (Achilles is not a *philos,* yet ought to act like one) and tone (humble appeal 985/vague threat 987–89).

157. These words may mean only "you made a thoroughly good speech," but Klytemnestra may also be hinting that she preferred Achilles' promises to help her and Iphigenia and defy Agamemnon rather than 959–67, when he spoke of being offended not by the matter of child-murder but by Agamemnon's manners toward him.

158. Klytemnestra's offer is a violation of custom; see note 103. The description of Iphigenia's expression is clearly paradoxical; frankness (literally "a free eye") involved looking another person directly in the face, while modesty (*aidōs* again) dictated looking down.

159. Literally, "it is necessary to feel *aidōs* only as much as is possible" (in an extraordinary situation like this).

160. In the *Iliad*, Achilles is forthright and straightforward; at one point, suspecting correctly that Agamemnon has lied to him he says "I hate as I hate the gates of Hades a man who hides one thing in his heart and says something else" (9.312–13). As the ancient audience knew, Achilles did not save Iphigenia (see 1568–76). And he did die in the Trojan War. These lines, that may be construed as Achilles bringing a curse on himself, are part of the revision of the *Iliad* which runs throughout this play; see above, pp. 316–20.

161. "My ally" (*philos* again) = Agamemnon. Achilles' concern for using reason and maintaining peace with Agamemnon here is very different from his quickly kindled anger and impulse to murder the king (*Iliad* 1.149–244).

162. Klytemnestra again speaks of Achilles' *sōphrosunē* (see above, line 824 and note 132) but perhaps ironically, since his concern for decorum now restrains him from taking action on her and Iphigenia's behalf .

163. Again demonstrating his concern for propriety and social niceties, Achilles speaks of Klytemnestra's embarrassing her father even though her husband is now her *kurios.* He obviously realizes that she has no concern about embarrassing her husband.

164. Since Achilles has responded to Klytemnestra's plea by putting the burden on her and warning her not to embarrass him, her calling him "a man who behaves justly," may be sarcastic, and "if not" can mean "if you don't find good fortune," "if you are not a man who behaves justly," or even "if the gods do not exist." Readers differ on whether this scene offers an ironic portrait of an unheroic Achilles: compare Conacher 1967: 259–61 and Luschnig 1988: 63–68. "Bother" = literally "why is it necessary to exert oneself?," i.e., what is the point of working at anything? why not leave everything to chance? This is one of those moments when fundamental questions—about individual morality, social organization, religious systems—are raised in tragic drama. Klytemnestra's question resembles that of the Chorus in *Oedipus the King,* who say that if evil deeds go unpunished the worship of the gods will wither away (895–910); if so, why should they continue to perform in the drama? Their doubts are presumably answered by the revelation that Oedipus is murderer of Laios. The questions raised here by Klytemnestra—whether Achilles behaves justly, whether he finds good fortune, whether the gods exist—are not answered in any obvious way.

165. The Greeks made use of only three kinds of musical instruments, pipes, stringed instruments, and percussion. The instruments mentioned here include two of the

first kind—the Libyan flute was a single hollow tube (made from a stalk of the nettle-tree) pierced by finger-holes, and the panpipe had reeds of different lengths bound together, sounded by blowing across the top. The *kithara* (from which "guitar" comes), with a wooden soundbox with sides distinct from the back and face, with seven or eight strings of gut or sinew. Choral songs in tragedy were usually accompanied by a double-reed instrument called the *aulos,* though other instruments were sometimes used, and may have been used to accompany this song.

166. A high mountain in central Thessaly. The wedding-feast described is that of Peleus and Thetis, parents of Achilles (see 701–707 and note 109). At such moments of crisis, it is common for the chorus to fantasize about some other place and time, some alternative or happy outcome to the events transpiring; compare Sophocles' *Ajax* 596–607, 1215–1222, *Helen* 1478–86, *Bacchants* 402–15. Here they imagine that the wedding of Peleus and Thetis was better than Iphigenia's awful fate. But Thetis was forced into marriage, and in the *Iliad* her mortal son causes her more pain than joy (see, for example, 1.413–18). Also, it was at this wedding feast that the contest between the goddesses began which led to the Judgment of Paris and the Trojan War; see above, pp. 306–307.

167. Ganymede was a Trojan prince who, like Paris, came to divine attention while tending herds. Zeus carried him off to Olympus, home of the gods, and made him immortal. He lived with Zeus and at feasts served as his lover's personal waiter, a position of honor. For Zeus to keep his wife and boy concubine in the same house surpasses the sexual freedom of Greek males (see *Medea* 244 and note 42 and above, pp. 59–60).

168. Thetis' sisters.

169. Bacchus = "wine;" see note 87. As their appearance (half-man, half-horse) and accoutrements (whole pine trees as spears, garlands of grass instead of flowers) suggest, the Centaurs were uncivilized, and could be trouble. At another wedding celebration (of Peirithous, prince of the Lapiths, and Hippodamia) they got drunk and tried to carry off the bride and other women. Representations of the battle between the Lapiths and Centaurs, symbolizing the conflict between civilization and barbarism, decorated the temple of Athena on the Acropolis at Athens. Here, however, the Centaurs are depicted as the sage Chiron's companions, sharing his foresight; see 705–709.

170. The warriors Achilles took to Troy; see note 40.

171. Inachos was a river-god and early king in Argos.

172. Literally, "so that no *phthonos* of the gods comes;" see note 93. Sacrificing one's own child would surely attract divine attention and punishment. In Aeschylus' *Agamemnon,* Klytemnestra argues that she is the instrument used by the gods to punish Agamemnon (1500–1504).

173. Accompanied by attendants? Iphigenia refers to female slaves (1340).

174. For a moment it seems possible that Agamemnon will tell his wife the truth, but as in the opening scene, he abruptly changes tactics (1110), perhaps because of Klytemnestra's cool reception (note that she gives him no honorific greeting).

175. A Greek woman's dress (*peplos*) was somewhere between a tunic and a mantle, with plenty of extra fabric in the upper part in which to carry a baby, or to draw over the head or before the eyes (1123).

176. The same exclamation (*pheu*) used at 666, 704, and 977. Here it seems to be a groan of disgust at Agamemnon's hypocrisy.

177. The first two goddesses invoked by Agamemnon are divine principles who rule all humans' lives; the third is a personal spirit (*daimōn*) who intervenes in an individual's life for better or worse. On these concepts see above, pp. 15–16.

178. In Aeschylus' *Agamemnon,* Klytemnestra's first words when she reappears after killing Agamemnon are "I will not be ashamed to say the opposite of the many things I said earlier to fit the occasion" (1372–3).

179. Klytemnestra's first husband is rarely mentioned elsewhere. He may be the great-grandson of the more famous Tantalos (see note 77), hence cousin of Agamemnon. These details connect Agamemnon to the curse on the house of Atreus and the murder of children, and illuminate his and Klytemnestra's relationship.

180. Literally, "you got my bed back again." The word *lekhos* ("bed") often means "marriage;" see *Medea* 18, 1367, and above, p. 58.

181. The female version of *sōphrosunē* (see note 132); here it probably includes not only sexual fidelity but making few sexual demands on her husband.

182. Lines 1180–84, 1187–90, and 1455 explicitly foreshadow Klytemnestra's murder of Agamemnon upon his return from Troy. Here she assumes that the remaining children (Elektra, Orestes, and the unnamed third daughter) would support her in taking revenge on him for Iphigenia's death. Instead, Orestes avenges Agamemnon by killing his mother, and Elektra supports him; see Aeschylus' *Libation Bearers,* Sophocles' *Elektra,* and Euripides' *Elektra.*

183. The previous two lines sound like a climax; when Agamemnon makes no response, Klytemnestra recovers her composure and tries a new tack. The phrase translated "Well, then . . ." makes a transition to the next point in the argument: "All right. Let's say you do sacrifice her . . ."

184. For the first time when speaking to an aristocrat the Chorus use an imperative and a personal name rather than a title.

185. Iphigenia's speaking here probably comes as a surprise, since Klytemnestra said she would do the talking for both of them 1121. Her boldness here prepares for her even bolder intervention later (1368).

186. Orpheus, son of Apollo and one of the Muses, sang so beautifully that he could control animals, trees, and stones. After his wife Eurydike died, he convinced the gods of the underworld to let him have her back: see *Alcestis* 357–62.

187. Suppliants (see note 142 above) sometimes announced their status by carrying olive-branches. If Iphigenia had known she would be performing this action she could have rehearsed a speech and provided herself with the appropriate props.

188. Invoking Pelops and Atreus recalls the curse on the house of Atreus—the killing of children by blood relatives; see lines 504–09 and note 77.

189. The pain and danger involved in giving birth makes women comparable to male warriors: See *Medea* 250–51 and Loraux 1995: 24–43. When Agamemnon is wounded (*Iliad* 11.267–72) his pain is compared to women's labor pains.

190. Since Agamemnon is not behaving as a *philos* Iphigenia addresses the infant Orestes as the only male relative available to help her—a strategy that creates pathos and subtly shames Agamemnon.

191. Iphigenia here rejects the masculine preference, as embodied in the choice of Achilles and other heroes, for a short glorious life rather than a long mediocre one. In Sophocles' *Ajax* the protagonist declares "either living well or dying well befits the noble man" (479–80). Agamemnon expresses doubts about this code (16–19); see also note 6. In the *Odyssey,* Achilles, now dead, has changed his mind, declaring he'd rather be a live tenant farmer than the king of all the dead (11.488–91).

192. The use of "Aphrodite" for the army's lust to destroy Troy is unusual; see note 87 and above, pp. 315, 320.

193. This speech amplifies Agamemnon's words in Aeschylus, *Agamemnon* 206–17. See above, pp. 311–12.

194. From here through 1402 there are several changes of metre. 1276–82 are in anapests, the "movement" metre; 1283–1335 are lyrics sung to musical accompaniment; 1338–1401 are in trochaic tetrameters, which convey high emotion. The unusual half-line *stichomythia* 1341–68 further increases the pace and tension.

195. In a solo aria, Iphigenia sings a lament for her own death, a song that would normally be sung by others after her death. This reversal of the conventions of death and mourning occurs frequently in tragedy: compare 1437, 1443, 1459, 1466, *Alcestis* 158–95, *Antigone* 806–882.

196. On Priam's exposure of his son Paris as an infant see above, pp. 306–307. "He" in line 1291 is Priam. Iphigenia seems to be comparing Priam's treatment of his child with Agamemnon's.

197. Growing up among the shepherds Paris earned the name "Alexander" ("Defender") by courageously defending his flocks against attacks by wild animals. When he returned to Troy he was known both by the name he was given by his parents and by the name he earned.

198. "The offspring of Sisyphos" = Odysseus; see note 83.

199. Beginning at 1365 it becomes increasingly clear that Achilles does not expect to be successful in saving Iphigenia.

200. The most surprising development in a play full of surprises. As at 1211, Iphigenia speaks up when she is not expected to; here she interrupts the fast-paced exchange to announce a change of heart. Note that the speech continues in trochaic tetrameter, suggesting that Iphigenia is not calmly reflective but excited, even exalted (see 1416). On Iphigenia's decision and its implications, see above, pp. 318–19, 322; for a comparison with other willing victims in Euripides' plays, see O'Connor-Visser 1987.

201. By calling Achilles "stranger" (*xenos*) Iphigenia reverses Klytemnestra's attempts to suggest that as Iphigenia's intended bridegroom he should behave as a *philos* (903–16).

202. "All Greece is looking at me now" = a metatheatrical reference. At this moment the whole pan-Hellenic audience is looking at the actor.

203. Editors clean up the awkward syntax of 1381–83, but I have followed the manuscripts. Such syntax suggests that Iphigenia is thinking on her feet, with her thoughts still in the process of formation (a twentieth-century actor would call this process "discovery"), so though echoing the substance of what Agamemnon said (1271–75), Iphigenia is speaking for herself.

204. This line is often cut in late-twentieth-century productions; see Bly 1996: 55–56.

205. Iphigenia here sees her self-sacrifice as achieving goals coded as masculine (fame after death) and as feminine (marriage and children); see above, pp. 50–51, 318–19, 322.

206. "Let Thetis know this" (1413) sounds like a reference to Achilles' complaint to his mother Thetis that his concubine Briseis has been taken by Agamemnon (*Iliad* 1.351–60). This makes Iphigenia the structural equivalent of Briseis; see note 24.

207. Iphigenia dismisses Achilles' appeal to weigh the consequences of her action. Yet her words here suggest that she wants to become a kind of positive Helen, dying to save Greek males rather than living to kill them. If Achilles should die for her, the fame she seeks would be compromised.

208. Black clothes and shorn hair were signs of bereavement; compare *Alcestis* 818–19.

209. For the Greeks, with their strong focus on the physical body, tombs were important sites for memorializing the dead. Greek poems commemorating fallen warriors assert that their tombs will become altars; this line reverses the convention. Throughout this section normal procedures for mourning are reversed.

210. Another indirect reference (compare 1241 and note 190) to Agamemnon's failure to fulfill the normal expectations of a male kinsman.

211. Here again is the language (e.g., "conduct") used to describe weddings; compare 609–10 and note 93.

212. The strongest revision of the conventions of death: instead of a *thrēnos* (lament) for the dead sung by others Iphigenia herself sings a hymn of praise (*paian*) for the divinity to whom she will be sacrificed (1475). All participants in a ritual were

required to maintain *euphēmia* (literally "good speech," i.e., silence) so as not to disrupt the effect of the ritual. A mother would normally lead the mourners lamenting her child's death, but Klytemnestra is forbidden to attend the sacrifice because her tears and laments would disrupt what Iphigenia wants to be a celebration.

213. The right side was associated with good fortune, the left with bad (hence "sinister" in English comes from the Latin word for "left").

214. Iphigenia calls herself *heleptolis,* "destroyer of the city" and the Chorus echo her (1511). The same epithet is applied to Helen (with a pun on her name) at *Agamemnon* 689–90.

215. Again items and actions associated with both weddings and sacrifices; compare 435–36. "Here is my hair" suggests that Iphigenia is bending her head down for the garlands to be put on, a gesture of acquiescence similar to that induced in an animal about to be sacrificed; see above, p. 12.

216. Presumably the prophecy that the fleet could not sail unless she were sacrificed.

217. People about to die far from home often bid farewell to their native land: See Sophocles' *Ajax* 859–63. Pelasgia, named for Pelasgos, a hero associated with a mythic pre-Hellenic people, is another name for the territory of Argos, which includes the citadel of Mycenae, founded by the hero Perseus and built by the Cyclopes (see 152, 265).

218. "Be a light for" = "give salvation to." Light is associated with life, safety, hope; compare *Medea* 482.

219. This prayer to Artemis can be understood as a foreshadowing of the miraculous substitution known from other versions of the story and announced by the Messenger (1581–95); see Euripides' *Iphigenia among the Taurians* 26–33 and above, p. 310.

220. At this point the play seems to be over. Many editors consider this the end and the rest of the play an interpolation. The text is certainly faulty, and there are many imperfections of language and meter, but the dramaturgy, including the false ending and the ambiguous resolution, seems utterly Euripidean; see above, pp. 73, 76–7. Other Greek dramas also employ a false ending before a surprising plot development. *Alcestis* seems over at 1005, just before the entrance of Herakles with the veiled woman; see also Taplin 1977: 180–84.

221. This messenger is often assumed to be different from the earlier one. But he is not a member of the Greek army; he addresses Klytemnestra as "dear mistress" and knows of her anger at Agamemnon. It therefore seems likely that this is the same member of Klytemnestra's household who traveled with her to the Greek camp, and who followed Iphigenia to the place of sacrifice (see 1462–63, 1543). Similarly, the messenger who tells Medea about the deaths of Kreon and his daughter 1121–1230 is a member of Jason's and Medea's household who moved to the palace when Jason married the princess.

222. Achilles now takes a central role in the sacrifice, doing what Iphigenia envisioned Agamemnon doing (1472).

223. Similarly, in Aeschylus' *Agamemnon* the Chorus say they did not see the sacrifice itself (247–48).

224. Hephaistos was the god of fire and metalworking.

225. The news that Agamemnon has sent this slave raises the possibility that the miracle is a fabrication. Klytemnestra suspects trickery (1616–18); see above, p. 324. Some translators make Iphigenia the subject of lines 1605–6, but there is no justification for this. In the Greek Agamemnon is the object of the miracle.

226. "Young calf" = Orestes. This is a fairly rare metaphor for "child"; it occurs at *Helen* 1476, but in this context suggests that Orestes is another potential sacrificial victim, like the calves at 1113–14 (where the same word is used).

227. Agamemnon's last lines remind the audience of the events that will take place ten years from now, when he returns from Troy. Klytemnestra will kill him and Kassandra, the "very splendid spoil from Troy" (1629) he brings with him, in revenge for Iphigenia's death. Orestes, now a babe in arms, will grow up and avenge his father's death by killing his mother. Cacoyannis' film of this play ends as Klytemnestra, played by Irene Papas, watches the Greek ships depart. The wind blows her black hair around her face like snakes. She is already becoming the Fury who will destroy Agamemnon. On this film see McDonald 1983: 129–91.

References

Abbreviations

AJP	*American Journal of Philology*
BICS	*Bulletin of the Institute of Classical Studies*
CA	*Classical Antiquity*
CJ	*Classical Journal*
CP	*Classical Philology*
CQ	*Classical Quarterly*
G&R	*Greece and Rome*
GRBS	*Greek, Roman and Byzantine Studies*
HSCP	*Harvard Studies in Classical Philology*
JHS	*Journal of Hellenic Studies*
TAPA	*Transactions of the American Philological Association*
TJ	*Theater Journal*
YCS	*Yale Classical Studies*

Alexiou, Margaret. 1974. *The Ritual Lament in Greek Tradition.* Cambridge: Cambridge University Press.

Allen, Paula Gunn. 1986. *The Sacred Hoop: Recovering the Feminine in American Indian Traditions.* Boston: Beacon Press.

Archer, Leonie, Susan Fischler, and Maria Wyke, eds. 1994. *Women in Ancient Societies: An Illusion of the Night.* New York: Routledge.

Arnott, P. D. 1989. *Public and Performance in the Greek Theatre.* London: Routledge.

Arrowsmith, William. 1963. "A Greek Theater of Ideas," *Arion* 2: 32–56.

———. 1975. *Euripides: Alcestis.* Oxford: Oxford University Press.

Arthur, Marylin B. 1973. "Early Greece: The Origins of the Western Attitude Towards Women," *Arethusa* 6: 7–58.

———. 1976. "Review Essay: Classics," *Signs* 2: 382–403.

Austin, J. Norman. 1975. *Archery at the Dark of the Moon.* Berkeley and Los Angeles: University of California Press.

———. 1994. *Helen and Her Shameless Phantom.* Ithaca, NY: Cornell University Press.

Bain, David. 1977a. *Actors and Audience: A Study of Asides and Related Conventions in Greek Drama.* Oxford: Oxford University Press.

———. 1977b. "The Prologues of Euripides' *Iphigenia in Aulis,*" *CQ* 27: 10–26.

Barlow, Shirley A. 1989. "Stereotype and Reversal in Euripides' *Medea,*" *G&R* 36: 158–71.

———. 1995. "Euripides' Medea: A Subversive Play?" In A. Griffiths, ed., *Stage Directions: Essays in Ancient Drama in Honour of E.W. Handley, BICS* Supp. 66: 36–45.

Barton, John, and Kenneth Cavander. 1981. *The Greeks.* London: Heinemann.

Bassi, Karen. 1993. "Helen and the Discourse of Denial in Stesichorus' Palinode," *Arethusa* 26: 51–75.

———. 1995. "Male Nudity and Disguise in the Discourse of Greek Histrionics," *Helios* 22: 3–22.

Bauman, Richard, ed. 1992. *Folklore, Cultural Performances, and Popular Entertainments.* Oxford: Oxford University Press.

Bergren, Ann. 1979. "Helen's Web: Time and Tableau in the *Iliad,*" *Helios* 7: 19–34.

———. 1981. "Helen's Good 'Drug,' Odyssey iv. 1–305," in *Contemporary Literary Hermeneutics and Interpretations of Classical Texts,* ed. Stephan Kresic. Ottawa: University of Ottawa Press.

———. 1983. "Language and the Female in Early Greek Thought," *Arethusa* 16: 69–95.

Beye, Charles. 1959. "Alcestis and Her Critics," *GRBS* 12: 109–27.

Blok, Josine. 1987. "Sexual Asymmetry: A Historiographical Essay," in *Sexual Asymmetry: Studies in Ancient Society,* ed. Josine Blok with Peter Mason, 1–57. Amsterdam: J.C. Gieben.

Blundell, Mary Whitlock. 1989. *Helping Friends and Harming Enemies: A Study in Sophocles and Greek Ethics.* Cambridge: Cambridge University Press.

———. 1990. *Sophocles' Oedipus at Colonus, Translated with Introduction, Notes and Interpretive Essay.* Boston: Focus Publishing.

———. 1993. "The Ideal of the *Polis* in *Oedipus at Colonus,*" in Sommerstein, Halliwell, Henderson, and Zimmermann 1993, 287–306.

Bly, Mark. 1996. *The Production Notebooks: Theatre in Process.* Vol. I. New York: Theatre Communications Group.

Boardman, John, and Donna Kurtz. 1971. *Greek Burial Customs.* Ithaca, NY: Cornell University Press.

Boedeker, Deborah D. 1974. *Aphrodite's Entry into Greek Epic.* Leiden: E.J. Brill.

———. 1991. "Euripides' *Medea* and the Vanity of *Logoi,*" *CP* 86: 95–112.

———. 1997. "Becoming Medea: Assimilation in Euripides," in Clauss and Johnston 1997, 127–48.

Bongie, E. 1977. "Heroic Elements in the *Medea* of Euripides," *TAPA* 107: 27–56.

Bourdieu, Pierre. 1979. *Algeria 1960,* trans. Richard Nice. Cambridge: Cambridge University Press.

Bradley, Edward. 1980. "Admetus and the Triumph of Failure in Euripides' 'Alcestis'," *Ramus* 9: 112–27.

Brecht, Bertolt. 1964. *Brecht on Theatre,* trans. John Willett. New York: Hill and Wang.

Bremmer, Jan N. 1997. "Why Did Medea Kill Her Brother Apsyrtus?" in Clauss and Johnston 1997, 83–100.

Burkert, Walter. 1966. "Greek Tragedy and Sacrificial Ritual," *GRBS* 7: 87–121.

———. 1983. *Homo Necans,* trans. Peter Bing. Berkeley and Los Angeles: University of California Press.

———. 1985. *Greek Religion,* trans. John Raffan. Cambridge, MA: Harvard University Press.

Burnett, Anne Pippin. 1960. "Euripides' *Helen:* A Comedy of Ideas," *CP* 55: 151–163.

———. 1965. "The Virtues of Admetus," *CP* 60: 240–55.

———. 1971. *Catastrophe Survived: Euripides' Plays of Mixed Reversal.* Oxford: Clarendon Press.

———. 1973. "Medea and the Tragedy of Revenge," *CP* 68: 1–24.

Butler, Judith. 1990. "Performative Acts and Gender Constitution: An Essay in Phenomenology and Feminist Criticism," in *Performing Feminisms,* ed. Sue-Ellen Case, 270–82. Baltimore: Johns Hopkins University Press.

Buttrey, T.V. 1958. "Accident and Design in Euripides' *Medea,*" *AJP* 79: 1–17.

Buxton, Richard. 1982. *Persuasion in Greek Tragedy: A Study of Peitho.* Cambridge: Cambridge University Press.

———. 1994. *Imaginary Greece: The Contexts of Mythology.* Cambridge: Cambridge University Press.

Cairns, Douglas L. 1993. *Aidos: the Psychology and Ethics of Honour and Shame in Ancient Greek Literature.* Oxford: Clarendon Press.

Calame, Claude. 1981. "Hélène: Son culte et l'initiation tribale feminine en Grèce," in *Dictionnaire des mythologies,* ed. Yves Bonnefoy. Paris: Flammarion.

———. 1997. *Choruses of Young Women in Ancient Greece: Their Morphology, Religious Role and Social Functions,* trans. Janice Orion and Derek Collins. Lanham, MD: Rowman and Littlefield.

Cameron, Averil, and Amelie Kuhrt, eds. 1983. *Images of Women in Antiquity.* Detroit: Wayne State University Press.

Case, Sue-Ellen. 1988. *Feminism and Theatre.* New York: Methuen.

Christ, C., and J. Plaskow, eds. 1979. *Woman Spirit Rising: A Feminist Reader in Religion.* New York: Harper and Row.

Clader, Linda. 1976. *Helen: The Evolution from Divine to Heroic in Greek Epic Tradition.* Leiden: E.J. Brill.

Clauss, James J., and Johnston, Sarah Iles, eds. 1997. *Medea: Essays on Medea in Myth, Literature, Philosophy, and Art.* Princeton: Princeton University Press.

Collard, C., M.J. Cropp, and K.H. Lee. 1995. *Euripides: Selected Fragmentary Plays,* Vol. I. Warminster, UK: Aris & Phillips.

Conacher, D. J. 1967. *Euripidean Drama: Myth, Theme and Structure.* Toronto: University of Toronto Press.

———, ed. and trans. 1988. *Euripides: Alcestis.* Warminster, UK: Aris and Phillips.

Csapo, Eric, and William J. Slater. 1995. *The Context of Ancient Drama.* Ann Arbor: University of Michigan Press.

Cunningham, M.P. 1954. "Medea ΑΠΟ ΜΗΧΑΝΗΣ," *CP* 49: 151–60.

Dale, A.M. 1967. *Euripides: Helen.* Oxford: Oxford University Press.

———. 1954. *Euripides: Alcestis.* Oxford: Clarendon Press.

Damen, Mark. 1989. "Actor and Character in Greek Tragedy," *TJ* 41: 316–40.

DeForest, Mary, ed. 1993. *Women's Power, Man's Game: Essays on Classical Antiquity in Honor of Joy King.* Wauconda, IL: Bolchazy-Carducci.

Demand, Nancy. 1994. *Birth, Death, and Motherhood in Classical Greece.* Baltimore: Johns Hopkins University Press.

Detienne, Marcel. 1977. *Gardens of Adonis,* trans. Janet Lloyd. Atlantic Highlands, NJ: Humanities Press.

Detienne, Marcel, and Jean-Pierre Vernant. 1989. *The Cuisine of Sacrifice Among the Greeks,* trans. Paula Wissing. Chicago: University of Chicago Press.

Diggle, J., ed. 1984. *Euripidis Fabulae* I. Oxford: Oxford University Press.

———. 1994a. *Euripidis Fabulae* III. Oxford: Oxford University Press.

———. 1994b. *Euripidea: Collected Essays.* Oxford: Clarendon Press.

Dimock, George E., Jr. 1973. "Introduction,"in *Euripides, Iphigeneia at Aulis,* trans. W.S. Merwin and George E. Dimock, Jr., 3–21. Oxford: Oxford University Press.

Dobson, Marcia W. D-S. 1992. "Ritual Death, Patriarchal Violence, and Female Relationships in The Hymns to Demeter and Inanna." *National Women's Studies Association Journal* 4: 42–58.

Doolittle, Hilda (H. D.). 1961. *Helen in Egypt.* New York: New Directions.

Douglas, Mary. 1978. *Purity and Danger: An Analysis of Concepts of Pollution and Taboo.* London: Routledge and Kegan Paul.

Dover, Kenneth. 1974. *Greek Popular Morality in the Time of Plato and Aristotle.* Oxford: Basil Blackwell.

———. 1978. *Greek Homosexuality.* New York: Random House.

———, ed. 1993. *Aristophanes: Frogs.* Oxford: Clarendon Press.

Dowden, Ken. 1989. *Death and Initiation Rites in Greek Mythology.* London and New York: Routledge.

Downing, Eric. 1990. "*Apate, Agon,* and Literary Self-Reflexivity in Euripides' *Helen:*" In *Cabinet of the Muses: Essays on Classical and Comparative Literature in Honor of Thomas G. Rosenmeyer,* ed. Mark Griffith and Donald J. Mastronarde, 1–16. Atlanta: Scholars Press.

Dubisch, Jill. 1986. *Gender and Power in Rural Greece.* Princeton: Princeton University Press.

duBois, Page. 1982. *Centaurs and Amazons.* Ann Arbor: University of Michigan Press.

———. 1984: "Sappho and Helen," in *Women in the Ancient World,* ed. John Peradotto and J.P. Sullivan. Albany, NY: State University of New York Press.

———. 1988. *Sowing the Body: Psychoanalysis and Ancient Representations of Women.* Chicago: University of Chicago Press.

———. 1994. *Sappho is Burning.* Chicago: University of Chicago Press.

Easterling, Patricia E. 1977. "The Infanticide in Euripides' *Medea,*" *YCS* 25: 177–91.

———. 1987. "Women in Tragic Space," *BICS* 34: 15–26.

Ehrenberg, Victor. 1968. *From Solon to Socrates: Greek History and Civilization During the 6th and 5th centuries BC.* London: Methuen.

Eisner, Robert. 1980. "Echoes of the *Odyssey* in Euripides' *Helen.*" *Maia* 32: 31–37.

Else, Gerald F. 1965. *The Origin and Early Form of Greek Tragedy.* Cambridge, MA: Harvard University Press.

England, E.B., ed. 1891. *The Iphigenia at Aulis of Euripides.* London: MacMillan.

van Erp Taalman Kip, A. Maria. 1990. *Reader and Spectator: Problems in the Interpretation of Greek Tragedy.* Amsterdam: Gieben.

Felson-Rubin, Nancy. 1994. *Regarding Penelope: From Character to Poetics.* Princeton: Princeton University Press.

Finnegan, Ruth. 1988. *Literacy and Orality: Studies in the Technology of Communication.* Oxford: Basil Blackwell.

Fisher, N. R. E. 1992. *Hybris: A Study in the Values of Honor and Shame in Ancient Greece.* Warminster, UK: Aris and Phillips.

Flory, Stewart. 1978. "Medea's Right Hand: Promises and Revenge," *TAPA* 108 69–74.

Foley, Helene P., ed. 1981a. *Reflections of Women in Antiquity.* New York: Gordon and Breach Science Publishers.

———. 1981b. "The Conception of Women in Athenian Drama," in Foley 1981, 127–67.

———. 1985. *Ritual Irony: Poetry and Sacrifice in Euripides.* Ithaca, NY: Cornell University Press.

———. 1988. "Women in Greece," in *Civilizations of the Ancient Mediterranean: Vol. 5. Greece and Rome,* ed. Michael Grant and Rachel Kitzinger, 1301–17. New York: Scribners.

———. 1989. "Medea's Divided Self," *CA* 8: 61–85.

———. 1992. "*Anodos* Dramas: Euripides' *Alcestis* and *Helen,*" in *Innovations of Antiquity,* ed. Ralph Hexter and D. Selden, 133–160. New York: Routledge.

———. 1993. "The Politics of Tragic Lamentation," in Sommerstein, Halliwell, Henderson, and Zimmermann 1993, 101–43.

———, ed. 1994. *The Homeric Hymn to Demeter.* Princeton University Press: Princeton.

Foucault, Michel. 1985. *The Use of Pleasure. The History of Sexuality, Vol. 2,* trans. Robert Hurley. New York: Random House.

Friedrich, Rainer. 1996. "Everything to do with Dionysos? Ritualism, the Dionysiac, and the Tragic," in Silk 1996, 257–83.

Gantz, Timothy. 1993. *Early Greek Myth: A Guide to Literary and Artistic Sources.* Johns Hopkins University Press: Baltimore and London.

Garber, Marjorie. 1992. *Vested Interests: Cross Dressing and Cultural Anxiety.* Routledge: New York.

Gardner, John, and John Maier, trans. and eds. 1984. *Gilgamesh.* New York: Vintage Books.

Garlan, Yvon. 1988. *Slavery in Ancient Greece,* trans. Janet Lloyd. Ithaca, NY: Cornell University Press.

Garner, Richard. 1990. *From Homer to Tragedy: The Art of Allusion in Greek Poetry.* New York: Routledge.

Gennep, Arnold van. 1960. *The Rites of Passage,* trans. M. Vizedom and G. Caffee. Chicago: University of Chicago Press.

Gernet, Louis. 1981. *The Anthropology of Ancient Greece,* trans. John Hamilton and Blaise Nagy. Baltimore: Johns Hopkins University Press.

Gibert, John. 1995. *Change of Mind in Greek Tragedy. Hypomnemata* Suppl. 108.

Gill, Christopher. 1996. *Personality in Greek Epic, Tragedy and Philosophy: The Self in Dialogue.* Oxford: Clarendon Press.

Girard, Rene. 1977. *Violence and the Sacred,* trans. Patrick Gregory. Baltimore: Johns Hopkins University Press.

Goff, Barbara, ed. 1995. *History, Tragedy, Theory: Dialogues on Athenian Drama.* Austin: University of Texas Press.

Goffman, Erving. 1959. *The Presentation of Self in Everyday Life.* New York: Anchor Books.

Golden, Mark. 1990. *Children and Childhood in Classical Athens.* Baltimore: Johns Hopkins University Press.

Goldhill, Simon. 1987. "The Great Dionysia and Civic Ideology," *JHS* 107: 58–76; reprinted in Winkler and Zeitlin 1990: 97–129.

———. 1993. "The Failure of Exemplarity," in *Modern Critical Theory and Classical Literature,* ed. Irene J. F. de Jong and J. P. Sullivan. Leiden: E.J. Brill.

Gomme, A. W. 1925. "The Position of Women in Athens in the Fifth and Fourth Centuries," *CP* 20: 1–25.

Gould, John. 1980. "Law, Custom, and Myth: Aspects of the Social Position of Women in Classical Athens." *JHS* 100: 38–59.

———. 1996. "Tragedy and Collective Experience," in Silk 1996: 217–43.

Gouldner, Alvin. 1965. *Enter Plato: Classical Greece and the Origins of Social Theory.* Basic Books: New York and London.

Graf, Fritz. 1997. "Medea, the Enchantress from Afar," in Clauss and Johnston 1997, 21–43.

Greene, Ellen, ed. 1996. *Reading Sappho: Contemporary Approaches.* Berkeley and Los Angeles: University of California Press.

Gregory, Justina. 1979. "Euripides' *Alcestis,*" *Hermes* 107: 259–70.

———. 1991. *Euripides and the Instruction of the Athenians.* Ann Arbor: University of Michigan Press.

Guepin, Jean-Pierre. 1968. *The Tragic Paradox: Myth and Ritual in Greek Tragedy.* Amsterdam: Hakkert.

Günther, Hans Christian, ed. 1988. *Euripides Iphigenia Aulidensis.* Leipzig: Teubner.

Hall, Edith. 1989. *Inventing the Barbarian: Greek Self-Definition through Tragedy.* Oxford: Clarendon Press.

———. 1996. "When is a Myth Not a Myth?: Bernal's 'Ancient Model'," in *Black Athena Revisited,* ed. Mary R. Lefkowitz and Guy MacLean Rogers, 333–48. Chapel Hill: University of North Carolina Press.

———. 1997. "The Sociology of Athenian Tragedy," in *The Cambridge Companion to Greek Tragedy,* ed. P. E. Easterling, 93–126. Cambridge: Cambridge University Press.

Halleran, Michael R. 1985. *Stagecraft in Euripides.* London: Croom Helm.

Halliwell, Stephen. 1997. "Between Public and Private: Tragedy and the Athenian Experience of Rhetoric," in *Greek Tragedy and the Historians,* ed. C. Pelling, 121–41. Oxford: Oxford University Press.

Halperin, David. 1990. *One Hundred Years of Homosexuality and Other Essays on Greek Love.* New York: Routledge.

Hanson, Victor Davis. 1989. *The Western Way of War: Infantry Battle in Classical Greece.* New York: Knopf.

Harris, W.V. 1989. *Ancient Literacy.* Cambridge, MA: Harvard University Press.

Harrison, A. R. W. 1968. *The Law of Athens.* Vol. I: *The Family and Property.* Oxford: Oxford University Press.

Harrison, Tony. 1985. *Medea: A Sex-War Opera,* in *Dramatic Verse 1973–1985,* 363–448. Bloodaxe Books: Newcastle upon Tyne.

Hartigan, Karelisa. 1991. *Ambiguity and Self-Deception: the Apollo and Artemis Plays of Euripides.* Frankfurt: Peter Lang.

Hatzichronoglou, Lena. 1993. "Euripides' Medea: Woman or Fiend?" in DeForest 1993, 178–93.

Havelock, Eric A. 1967. *Preface to Plato.* New York: Grosset & Dunlap.

———. 1982. *The Literate Revolution in Greece and its Cultural Consequences.* Princeton: Princeton University Press.

Henderson, Jeffrey. 1991. "Women and the Athenian Dramatic Festivals," *TAPA* 121: 133–47.

———. 1996. *Three Plays by Aristophanes: Staging Women.* Routledge: New York.

Henrichs, Albert. 1980. "Human Sacrifice in Greek Religion," in *Le Sacrifice dans l'Antiquité,* ed. Jean Rudhardt and Olivier Reverdin. *Entretiens Hardt sur l'Antiquité Classique* 27: 195–235.

Hermann, G. 1987. *Ritualized Friendship and the Greek City.* Cambridge: Cambridge University Press.

Holmberg, Ingrid E. 1995. "Euripides' Helen: Most Noble and Most Chaste," *American Journal of Philology* 116: 19–42.

Holst-Warhaft, Gail. 1992. *Dangerous Voices: Women's Laments and Greek Literature.* New York: Routledge.

Humphreys, S. C. 1978. *Anthropology and the Greeks.* London and Boston: Routledge and Kegan Paul.

———. 1993. *The Family, Women and Death: Comparative Studies.* 2nd ed. Ann Arbor: University of Michigan Press.

Jaeger, Werner. 1945. *Paideia: The Ideals of Greek Culture.* Vol. I. 2nd ed. New York: Oxford University Press.

Jameson, Fredric. 1988. "Marxism and Historicism," in Fredric Jameson, *The Ideologies of Theory,* vol. 2, 148–77. Minneapolis: University of Minnesota Press.

Jameson, Michael. 1990. "Private Space and the Greek City," in *The Greek City From Homer to Alexander,* ed. Oswyn Murray and Simon Price, 171–95. Oxford: Clarendon Press.

———. 1991. "Sacrifice Before Battle," in *Hoplites: the Classical Greek Battle Experience,* Victor Davis Hanson, ed., 197–227. New York: Routledge.

Johnston, Sarah Iles. 1997a. "Introduction," in Clauss and Johnston 1997, 3–17.

———. 1997b. "Corinthian Medea and the Cult of Hera Akraia," in Clauss and Johnston, 44–70.

Jones, D. M. 1968. "Euripides' Alcestis," in *Twentieth Century Interpretations of Euripides' Alcestis,* ed. John R. Wilson, 57–64. Englewood Cliffs, NJ: Prentice-Hall.

Jouan, Francois, ed. 1983. *Iphigénie à Aulis.* Paris: Société d'Edition Les Belles Lettres.

Juffras, Diane M. 1993. "Helen and Other Victims in Euripides' *Helen,*" *Hermes* 121: 45–57.

Kannicht, Richard. 1969. *Euripides' Helena.* 2 vols. Heidelberg: CarlWinter Universitatsverlag.

Kerferd, G.B. 1981. *The Sophistic Movement.* Cambridge: Cambridge University Press.

Keuls, Eva. 1985. *The Reign of the Phallus.* Berkeley and Los Angeles: University of California Press.

King, Helen. 1983. "Bound to Bleed: Artemis and Greek Women," in Cameron and Kuhrt 1983, 109–27.

———. 1994. "Producing Women: Hippocratic Gynaecology," in Archer, Fischler, and Wyke, 1994, 102–14.

Kitto, H.D.F. 1950.*Greek Tragedy.* Rev. ed. New York: Doubleday.

Knox, Bernard. 1977. "The *Medea* of Euripides," *YCS* 25: 193–225; reprinted in Knox 1979: 295–322.

———. 1979. *Word and Action: Essays on the Ancient Theater.* Johns Hopkins University Press: Baltimore and London.

Kovacs, David. 1993. "Zeus in Euripides' *Medea,*" *AJP* 114: 45–70.

———. 1994. *Euripidea.* Leiden: E.J. Brill.

Kraemer, Ross S. 1992. *Her Share of the Blessings: Women's Religions Among Pagans, Jews, and Christians in the Greco-Roman World.* New York and Oxford: Oxford University Press.

Krevans, Nita. 1997. "Medea as Foundation-Heroine," in Clauss and Johnston 1997, 71–82.

Lacey, W. K. 1968. *The Family in Classical Greece.* Ithaca, NY: Cornell University Press.

Larson, Jennifer. 1995. *Greek Heroine Cults.* Madison: University of Wisconsin Press.

Lattimore, Richmond, trans. 1955. *Alcestis,* in *The Complete Greek Tragedies: Euripides, Volume III.* Chicago: University of Chicago Press.

———, trans. 1969. *Four Comedies by Aristophanes.* Ann Arbor: University of Michigan Press.

Leduc, Claudine. 1992. "Marriage in Ancient Greece," in Pantel 1992, 233–95.

Lefkowitz, Mary R. 1981. *The Lives of the Greek Poets.* Baltimore: Johns Hopkins University Press.

———. 1986. *Women in Greek Myth.* London: Duckworth.

———. 1989. "'Impiety' and 'Atheism' in Euripides' Dramas," *CQ* 39: 70–82.

Lévi-Strauss, Claude. 1963. *Structural Anthropology,* trans. Claire Jacobson and Brooke Grundfest Schoepf. Garden City, NJ: Anchor Books. 1967.

Lewis, Sian. 1996. *News and Society in the Greek Polis.* Chapel Hill: University of North Carolina Press.

Lindsay, Jack. 1974. *Helen of Troy.* London: Constable.

Lloyd-Jones, Hugh. 1983. "Artemis and Iphigeneia," *JHS* 103: 87–102.

Lonsdale, Steven. 1993. *Dance and Ritual Play in Greek Religion.* Baltimore: Johns Hopkins University Press.

Loraux, Nicole. 1986. *The Invention of Athens: The Funeral Oration in the Classical City,* trans. Alan Sheridan. Cambridge, MA: Harvard University Press.

———. 1987. *Tragic Ways of Killing a Woman,* trans. Anthony Forster. Cambridge, MA: Harvard University Press.

———. 1993. *The Children of Athena: Athenian Ideas about Citizenship and the Division between the Sexes,* trans. Caroline Levine. Princeton: Princeton University Press.

———. 1995. *The Experiences of Tiresias: The Feminine and the Greek Man,* trans. Paula Wissing. Princeton: Princeton University Press.

Lovibond, Sabina. 1994. "An Ancient Theory of Gender: Plato and the Pythagorean Table," in Archer, Fischler, and Wyke 1994, 88–101.

Lubell, Winifred M. 1994. *The Metamorphosis of Baubo: Myths of Women's Sexual Energy.* Nashville: Vanderbilt University Press.

Luschnig, C. A. E. 1988. *Tragic Aporia: A Study of Euripides' Iphigenia at Aulis.* Berwick, Australia: Aureal.

Lyons, Deborah. 1997. *Gender and Immortality: Heroines in Ancient Greek Myth and Cult.* Princeton: Princeton University Press.

Martin, Richard P. 1989. *The Language of Heroes: Speech and Performance in the Iliad.* Ithaca, NY: Cornell University Press.

Mathews, Gary. 1994. "'Finding What One Wants:' Desire and Interpretation in Euripides' *Iphigeneia at Aulis.*" Unpublished manuscript.

McDermott, Emily. 1989. *Euripides' Medea: The Incarnation of Disorder.* University Park, PA: Pennsylvania State University Press.

McDonald, Marianne. 1983. *Euripides in Cinema: The Heart Made Visible,* Philadelphia: Centrum.

———. 1997. "Medea as Politician and Diva: Riding the Dragon into the Future," in Clauss and Johnston 1997, 297–323.

McGann, Jerome J. 1983. *A Critique of Modern Textual Criticism.* Chicago: University of Chicago Press.

Meagher, Robert Emmet. 1995. *Helen: Myth, Legend, and the Culture of Misogyny.* New York: Continuum.

Michelini, Ann N. 1987. *Euripides and the Tragic Tradition.* Madison: University of Wisconsin Press.

———. 1989. "Neophron and Euripides' *Medeia* 1056–80," *TAPA* 11: 115–35.

Mikalson, Jon D. 1991. *Honor Thy Gods: Popular Religion in Greek Tragedy.* Chapel Hill: University of North Carolina Press.

Mills, S. P. 1980. "The Sorrows of Medea," *CP* 75: 289–96.

Moore, Henrietta. 1988. *Feminism and Anthropology.* Minneapolis: University of Minnesota Press.

Morris, Ian. 1987. *Burial and Ancient Society.* Cambridge: Cambridge University Press.

Morrison, Toni. 1987. *Beloved.* New York: Alfred A. Knopf.

Murray, Gilbert. 1902. *Euripidis Fabulae.* Vol. I. Oxford: Clarendon Press.

Nagler, M.N. 1977. "Dread Goddess Endowed with Speech." *Archaeological News* 6: 77–85.

Nagy, Gregory. 1996. *Poetry as Performance: Homer and Beyond.* Cambridge: Cambridge University Press.

Neils, Jenifer. 1992. *Goddess and Polis: The Panathenaic Festival in Ancient Athens.* Hanover, NH: Hood Museum of Art, Dartmouth College, and Princeton: Princeton University Press.

Oakley, John H., and Rebecca H. Sinos. 1993. *The Wedding in Ancient Athens.* Madison: University of Wisconsin Press.

Ober, Josiah. 1989. *Mass and Elite in Democratic Athens: Rhetoric, Ideology, and the Power of the People.* Princeton: Princeton University Press.

O'Brien, Joan. 1993. *The Transformation of Hera.* Lanham, MD: Rowman & Littlefield.

O'Connor-Visser, E A. M. E. 1987. *Aspects of Human Sacrifice in the Tragedies of Euripides.* Amsterdam: B.R. Gruner.

O'Higgins, Dolores. 1993. "Above Rubies: Admetus' Perfect Wife," *Arethusa* 26: 77–97.

Padel, Ruth. 1992. *In and Out of the Mind: Greek Images of the Tragic Self.* Princeton: Princeton University Press.

Page, Denys L. 1934. *Actors' Interpolations in Greek Tragedy.* Oxford: Clarendon Press.

———, ed. 1938. *Euripides: Medea.* Oxford University Press: Oxford.

Palmer, Robert B. 1957. "An Apology for Jason: A Study of Euripides' Medea," *CJ* 53: 49–55.

Pantel, Pauline Schmitt, ed. 1992. *A History of Women in the West.* Vol. I. *From Ancient Goddesses to Christian Saints.* Cambridge, MA: Harvard University Press.

Parke, H.W. 1977. *Festivals of the Athenians.* Ithaca, NY: Cornell University Press.

Parker, R. 1983. *Miasma.* Oxford: Clarendon Press.

Parry, Hugh. 1992. *Thelxis: Magic and Imagination in Greek Myth and Poetry.* Lanham, MD: University Press of America.

Pelling, Christopher, ed. 1997. *Greek Tragedy and the Historian.* Oxford: Oxford University Press.

Peyser, Andrea. 1995. *Mother Love, Deadly Love: The Susan Smith Murders.* New York: HarperCollins.

Pickard-Cambridge, Arthur Wallace. 1988. *The Dramatic Festivals of Athens.* 2nd ed. Revised by John Gould and D. M. Lewis. Oxford: Oxford University Press.

Pomeroy, Sarah B. 1975. *Goddesses, Whores, Wives, and Slaves: Women in Classical Antiquity.* New York: Schocken.

———, ed. 1994. *Xenophon: Oeconomicus.* Oxford: Clarendon Press.

Powell, Anton, ed. 1990. *Euripides, Women and Sexuality.* London and New York: Routledge.

Pucci, Pietro. 1979. "The Song of the Sirens," *Arethusa* 12: 121–32.

———. 1980. *The Violence of Pity in Euripides' Medea.* Ithaca, NY: Cornell University Press.

Rabinowitz, Nancy Sorkin. 1993. *Anxiety Veiled: Euripides and the Traffic in Women.* Ithaca, NY: Cornell University Press.

———. 1998. "Embodying Tragedy: The Sex of the Actor," *Intertexts* 2.1. 3–25.

Reckford, Kenneth J. 1964. "Helen in the *Iliad,*" *GRBS* 5: 5–20.

———. 1968. "Medea's First Exit," *TAPA* 99: 329–59.

Rehm, Rush. 1989. "Medea and the Λόγος of the Heroic," *Eranos* 87: 97–115.

———. 1994. *Marriage to Death: The Conflation of Wedding and Funeral Rituals in Greek Tragedy.* Princeton: Princeton University Press.

———. 1992. *Greek Tragic Theatre.* Routledge: New York.

Richardson, N. J., ed. 1974. *The Homeric Hymn to Demeter.* Oxford: Clarendon Press.

Rickert, G. 1987. "Akrasia and Euripides' *Medea,*" *HSCP* 91: 91–117.

Robinson, D. B. 1979. "Helen and Persephone, Sparta and Demeter: The 'Demeter Ode' in Euripides' Helen," in *Arktouros,* ed. Glen W. Bowersock, Walter Burkert, and Michael J. Putnam, p. 162–72. Berlin: Walter de Gruyter.

de Romilly, Jacqueline. 1975. *Magic and Rhetoric in Ancient Greece.* Cambridge, MA: Harvard University Press.

Rosaldo, Michelle. 1974. "Woman, Culture, and Society: A Theoretical Overview," in *Women, Culture, and Society,* ed. Michelle Rosaldo and Louise Lamphere, 17–42. Stanford, CA: Stanford University Press.

———. 1980. "The Uses and Abuses of Anthropology: Reflections on Feminism and Cross-Cultural Understanding," *Signs* 5: 389–417.

Schaps, David. 1977. "The Women Least Mentioned: Etiquette and Women's Names," CQ 27: 323–30.

Schein, Seth. 1990. "*Philia* in Euripides' *Medea*," in *Cabinet of the Muses*, ed. Mark Griffith and Donald Mastaronarde, 57–73. Atlanta: Scholars Press.

Schlesinger, E. 1966. "Zu Euripides *Medea*," *Hermes* 94: 26–53. Eng. trans. in E. Segal, ed., 1968. *Euripides: A Collection of Critical Essays*. Englewood Cliffs, NJ: Prentice-Hall.

Seaford, Richard, ed. 1984. *Euripides: Cyclops*. Oxford: Clarendon Press.

———. 1987. "The Tragic Wedding," *JHS* 107: 106–30.

———. 1994. *Reciprocity and Ritual: Homer and Tragedy in the Developing City-State*. Oxford: Clarendon Press.

———, ed. 1996. *Euripides: Bacchae*. Warminster, UK: Aris and Phillips.

Segal, Charles. 1971. "The Two Worlds of Euripides' *Helen*," *TAPA* 102: 553–614.

———. 1993. *Euripides and the Poetics of Sorrow: Art, Gender, and Commemoration in Alcestis, Hippolytos, and Hecuba*. Chapel Hill, NC: Duke University Press.

———. 1996. "Euripides' *Medea:* Vengeance, Reversal and Closure," *Pallas* 45: 15–44.

Sergent, Bernard. 1986. *Homosexuality and Greek Myth*, trans. Arthur Goldhammer. Boston: Beacon Press.

Silk, M. S., ed. 1996. *Tragedy and the Tragic: Greek Theatre and Beyond*. Oxford: Clarendon Press.

Simon, Erika. 1983. *Festivals of Attica: An Archaeological Commentary*. Madison: University of Wisconsin Press.

Sissa, Giulia. 1990. *Greek Virginity*, trans. Arthur Goldhammer. Cambridge, MA: Harvard University Press.

———. 1992. "The Sexual Philosophies of Plato and Aristotle," in Pantel 1992, 46–82.

Skutsch, Otto. 1987. "Helen, Her Name and Nature," *JHS* 107: 188–93.

Slater, Philip E. 1968. *The Glory of Hera: Greek Mythology and the Greek Family*. Boston: Beacon Press.

Slatkin, Laura M. 1991. *The Power of Thetis: Allusion and Interpretation in the Iliad*. Berkeley and Los Angeles: University of California Press.

Snowden, Frank M., Jr. 1970. *Blacks in Antiquity: Ethiopians in the Greco-Roman Experience*. Cambridge MA: Harvard University Press.

Snyder, Jane McIntosh. 1989. *The Woman and the Lyre: Women Writers in Classical Greece and Rome*. Carbondale IL: Southern Illinois University Press.

Sommerstein, A. H. 1980. "The Naming of Women in Greek and Roman Comedy." *Quaderni di storia* 11: 393–419.

Sommerstein, A. H., S. Halliwell, J. Henderson, and B. Zimmermann, eds. *Tragedy, Comedy and the Polis.* Bari, Italy: Levante Editori.

Sorum, Christina Elliott. 1992. "Myth, Choice, and Meaning in Euripides' *Iphigenia at Aulis,*" *AJP* 113: 527–42.

Sourvinou-Inwood, Christiane. 1988. *Studies in Girls' Transitions.* Athens: Kardamitsa.

———. 1997. "Medea at a Shifting Distance: Images and Euripidean Tragedy," in Clauss and Johnston 1997, 253–96.

Stevens, P. T. 1956. "Euripides and the Athenians." *JHS* 76: 97–94.

Stockert, Walter. 1992. *Euripides Iphigenie in Aulis. Wiener Studien Beiheft* 16/1 & 2.

Stockton, David. 1990. *The Classical Athenian Democracy.* Oxford: Oxford University Press.

Straten, F. T. van. 1995. *Hiera Kala: Images of Animal Sacrifice in Archaic and Classical Greece.* Leiden: E. J. Brill.

Suzuki, Mihoko. 1989. *Metamorphoses of Helen: Authority, Difference, and the Epic.* Ithaca, NY: Cornell University Press.

Taplin, Oliver. 1977. *The Stagecraft of Aeschylus.* Oxford: Clarendon Press.

———. 1978. *Greek Tragedy in Action.* Berkeley and Los Angeles: University of California Press.

Teevan, Colin. 1996. "A Barbarian Activity: The Process of Translation of Euripides' *The Iphigenia at Aulis,*" in *Stages of Translation,* ed. David Johnston, 95–107. Absolute Classics: Bath.

Thomas, Rosalind. 1992. *Literacy and Orality in Ancient Greece.* Cambridge: Cambridge University Press.

Thornton, Bruce S. 1997. *Eros: The Myth of Ancient Greek Sexuality.* Boulder, CO: Westview.

Turner, Victor. 1977. *The Ritual Process.* Ithaca, NY: Cornell University Press.

Vellacott, Philip. 1975. *Ironic Drama: A Study of Euripides' Method and Meaning.* Cambridge: Cambridge University Press.

Vernant, Jean-Pierre. 1980. *Myth and Society in Ancient Greece,* trans. Janet Lloyd. Atlantic Highlands, NJ: Humanities Press.

———. 1983. *Myth and Thought among the Greeks,* trans. Janet Lloyd. London: Routledge and Kegan Paul.

———. 1991. *Mortals and Immortals: Collected Essays,* ed. Froma I. Zeitlin. Princeton: Princeton University Press.

Vernant, Jean-Pierre, and Pierre Vidal-Naquet. 1988. *Myth and Tragedy in Ancient Greece,* trans. Janet Lloyd. New York: Zone.

Vickers, Michael. 1997. *Pericles on Stage: Political Comedy in Aristophanes' Early Plays.* Austin: University of Texas Press.

Visser, Margaret. 1986. "Medea: Daughter, Sister, Wife, and Mother: Natal Family versus Conjugal Family in Greek and Roman Myths about Women," in M. Cropp, E. Fantham, and S.E. Scully, eds., *Greek Tragedy and its Legacy,* 149–65. Calgary: University of Calgary Press.

Walker, Susan. 1983. "Women and Housing in Ancient Greece," in Cameron and Kuhrt 1983, 81–91.

Walton, J. Michael. 1980. *Greek Theatre Practice.* Westport and London: Greenwood Press.

Warner, Marina. 1994. *Managing Monsters: Six Myths of our Time.* London: Vintage. Published in the U.S. in 1995 as *Six Myths of our Time.* New York: Vintage.

Warner, Rex. 1955. *Medea,* in *Euripides I,* ed. David Grene and Richmond Lattimore. Chicago: University of Chicago Press.

Webster, T. B. L. 1967. *The Tragedies of Euripides.* London: Methuen.

Wiles, David. 1997. *Tragedy in Athens: Performance Space and Theatrical Meaning.* Cambridge: Cambridge University Press.

Wilkins, John. 1990. "The State and the Individual: Euripides' Plays of Voluntary Self-Sacrifice," in Powell 1990, 177–94.

Williamson, Margaret. 1990. "A Woman's Place in Euripides' *Medea,*" in Powell 1990, 16–31.

Wilson, Lyn Hatherly. 1996. *Sappho's Sweetbitter Songs: Configurations of Female and Male in Ancient Greek Lyric.* London and New York: Routledge.

Winkler, John J. 1981. "Gardens of Nymphs: Public and Private in Sappho's Lyrics." in Foley 1981, 63–89.

———. 1990a. *The Constraints of Desire: The Anthropology of Sex and Gender in Ancient Greece.* New York and London: Routledge.

———. 1990b. "The Ephebes' Song: *Tragōidia* and *Polis,*" in Winkler and Zeitlin 1990, 20–62.

Winkler, John J., and Froma I. Zeitlin, eds. 1990. *Nothing to Do with Dionysos? Athenian Drama in its Social Context.* Princeton University Press: Princeton.

Wolff, C. 1973. "On Euripides' *Helen,*" *HSCP* 77: 61–84.

Zaidman, Louise Bruit, and Pauline Schmitt Pantel. 1992. *Religion in the Ancient Greek City,* trans. Paul Cartledge. Cambridge: Cambridge University Press.

Zeitlin, Froma I. 1978. "The Dynamics of Misogyny: Myth and Mythmaking in the Oresteia." *Arethusa* 11: 164–93.

———. 1981. "Travesties of Gender and Genre in Aristophanes' *Thesmophoriazusae,*" in Foley 1981, 169–217; reprinted in Zeitlin 1995, 375–416.

———. 1982. "Cultic Models of the Female: Rites of Dionysus and Demeter," *Arethusa* 15: 129–57.

———. 1985. "Playing the Other: Theater, Theatricality, and the Feminine in Greek Drama," *Representations* 11: 63–94; reprinted in Winkler and Zeitlin 1990: 63–96, and in Zeitlin 1996: 341–74.

———. 1986. "Configurations of Rape in Greek Myth," in *Rape,* ed. Sylvana Tomaselli and Roy Porter, 122–51. Oxford: Blackwell.

———. 1990. "Thebes: Theater of Self and Society in Athenian Drama," in Winkler and Zeitlin 1990, 130–67.

———. 1994. "The Artful Eye: Vision, Ecphrasis and Spectacle in Euripidean Theatre," in Simon Goldhill and Robin Osborne, eds., *Art and Text in Ancient Greek Culture,* 139–96. Cambridge: Cambridge University Press.

———. 1996. *Playing the Other: Gender and Society in Classical Greek Literature.* Chicago: University of Chicago Press.

Zweig, Bella. 1981a. "Drawing from Mythology in Women's Quests for Selfhood," in *The Politics of Women's Spirituality,* ed. C. Spretnak, 138–151. New York: Doubleday.

———. 1981b. "Paean to Helen," *Woman/Spirit* 28: 23–25.

———. 1992. "The Mute, Nude Female Characters in Aristophanes' Plays," in *Pornography and Representation in Greece and Rome,* ed. Amy Richlin, 73–89. New York and Oxford: Oxford University Press.

———. 1993a. "The Only Women Who Give Birth to Men: A Gynocentric, Cross-Cultural View of Women in Ancient Sparta," in DeForest 1993, 32–53.

———. 1993b. "The Primal Mind: Using Native American Models to Approach the Study of Women in Ancient Greece," in *Feminist Theory and the Classics,* ed. Nancy Sorkin Rabinowitz and Amy Richlin, 145–180. New York: Routledge.